THE MAMMALS OF TEXAS

W9-ABZ-613

Number Fifty-nine
THE CORRIE HERRING HOOKS SERIES

THE MAMMALS

BY DAVID J. SCHMIDLY

OF TEXAS

Revised Edition

 UNIVERSITY OF TEXAS PRESS, AUSTIN

Publication of this book has been made possible in part by subsidies from the Texas Parks and Wildlife Department, Wildlife Division, and by the Harvey Weil Sportsman Conservationist Award Trust.

Library of Congress Cataloging-in-Publication Data

Schmidly, David J., 1943–
    The mammals of Texas / David J. Schmidly.— Rev. ed.
        p.   cm. — (The Corrie Herring Hooks series ; no. 59)
Rev. ed. of: Mammals of Texas / William B. Davis. Rev. 1974.
    ISBN 0-292-70241-8 (pbk. : alk. paper)
    1. Mammals—Texas.   I. Davis, William B., 1902– Mammals of Texas.   II. Title.   III. Series.
QL719.T4S345   2004
599'.09764—dc22   2003026430

TABLE OF CONTENTS

PREFACE

This book is devoted to mammals, which are the class of vertebrate animals possessing hair, with the females having milk-secreting glands. One group of mammals, the cetaceans (whales and dolphins), have a layer of blubber instead of hair. Mammals, having among their representative genera certain species that fly, others that glide, swim, climb, burrow, leap, or run, are perhaps the most versatile and adaptable of the vertebrate animal groups in Texas.

Texas, with its variety of soils, climate, vegetation, and topography, as well as extensive coastline and offshore ocean, is the home of at least 184 free-ranging species of mammals. The locomotive versatility of the various members of the class is responsible in part for the occurrence of mammals in our deserts, forests, mountains, prairies, high plains, inland and coastal waters, and oceans.

This book represents the sixth account detailing the kinds of mammals that occur in Texas with information about their lives and economic importance. The Texas Parks and Wildlife Department and its predecessor, the Texas Game and Fish Commission, published the previous five editions. Dr. W. P. Taylor and Dr. W. B. Davis collaborated in 1947 to prepare *The Mammals of Texas* as Bulletin No. 27 of the former Texas Game and Fish Commission. Recognizing the growing interest in Texas mammals and the expanding knowledge about the many kinds of mammals in the state, Dr. Davis in 1960 wrote an entirely new bulletin, designated as Bulletin No. 41 of the Texas Parks and Wildlife Department, which served as an identification key to Texas mammals and also provided information on their distribution and life histories. Dr. Davis revised Bulletin No. 41 in 1966 and again in 1974. The bulletin was revised for a fifth time in 1994, with myself (DJS) as coauthor, and distributed by the University of Texas Press. Dr. Davis died in 1995, and by agreement with him this version is authored solely by DJS. The University of Texas Press has agreed to publish this latest revision in cooperation with Texas Parks and Wildlife.

This latest edition incorporates updated and needed revisions in the species distribution maps, taxonomic names, and other portions of the bulletin. Most of the changes were made to update the identification keys and geographic ranges of mammals in Texas and its adjacent waters. The natural history descriptions include some of the same information detailed by Dr. Davis and DJS in the 1994 edition, as well as pertinent new material.

Simplicity is the basic goal in organizing this book. Accounts for each species are arranged so that they contain in sequence: (1) a brief description of the mammal, with special emphasis given to distinguishing features, accompanied in most cases by a photograph; (2) a description of the geographic distribution of the species in Texas, with reference to a map; (3) a list of the subspecies recognized for each species (not provided for introduced, nonnative species); (4) a discussion of some of the basic life history of the mammal, including habitat preferences, reproduction, behavior, and food habits; and (5) a brief discussion of the conservation status of the species in Texas. The information for the life history discussions has been taken from observations recorded by other researchers and reported in the scientific literature, as well as the personal experience of DJS based on nearly 40 years of studying mammals in Texas. On the distribution maps, counties where specimens of mammals have been reported, either in the literature or represented by a scientific specimen located in a museum collection, are indicated by black dots; the probable range for most species is shaded in.

This is the first edition of this guide to include subspecies of mammals in the state. Subspecies are geographically defined aggregates of local populations that differ taxonomically (usually morphologically) from other such subdivisions of the species. Where the boundaries of subspecies abut, they interbreed with one another, creating zones of intergradation, whereas different species in areas of abutment or overlap are reproductively isolated and maintain their distinctness. The subspecies designations have been adapted from "Annotated Checklist of Recent Land Mammals of Texas," by Richard Manning and Clyde Jones (*Occasional Papers* 182, The Museum, Texas Tech University, 1998). Subspecies are not depicted on the distribution maps because detailed studies of geographic variation have not been performed on all Texas mammals, making it difficult to map subspecies boundaries accurately.

Another new feature of this guide is information about the conservation status of each species. This information is adapted from my book, *Texas Natural History: A Century of Change,* for land mammals, and from *The Marine Mammals of the Gulf of Mexico,* by Bernd Würsig, Thomas Jefferson, and DJS, for marine mammals. Other useful references about the conservation status of Texas' mammal fauna have been included in Appendix 3. Species considered to be in trouble are those with legal status as endangered or threatened as determined by the U.S. Fish and Wildlife Service and the Texas Parks and Wildlife Department. The late J. Knox Jones, Jr., of Texas Tech University, wrote a paper in the *Texas Journal of Science* on the concept of threatened and endangered species as applied to Texas mammals. The Texas Organization for Endangered Species and the Texas Natural Heritage Program database, administered by the Nature Conservancy of Texas, maintain lists of rare or watch-list species that may be in trouble. Many rare species have highly localized distributions and others are only migrants in the state. Others were formerly widely distributed and in recent decades have suffered from a variety of circumstances that caused local extinctions in substantial parts of their range in the state. Finally, several native mammals in Texas are now extinct, primarily as a result of overharvesting in the latter part of the nineteenth and early part of the twentieth centuries.

Those readers interested in more detail about the natural history of Texas mammals are referred to the *Mammalian Species* series, published by the American

Society of Mammalogists. The series provides detailed references and information for individual species of mammals. To date, *Mammalian Species* accounts are available for 137 of the 184 species of Texas mammals. Appendix 5 provides a list of the accounts available for Texas mammals. *Mammalian Species* may be found in many university libraries or can be ordered from the Web site at http://www.science.smith.edu/departments/Biology/VHAYSSEN/msi/. Many of the accounts can be downloaded free from that site. In addition, the Web site of the American Society of Mammalogists, www.mammalsociety.org, is an excellent resource for information about mammals and the science of mammalogy.

ACKNOWLEDGMENTS

Since this is the first edition of *The Mammals of Texas* to be authored solely by me, I want to express my gratitude to the late William B. Davis for providing the scientific framework for the continued updating, revision, and publication of this book. The science of mammalogy in Texas owes much to the leadership of Doc Davis, a legend in the wildlife field.

A project of this scope is greatly facilitated by colleagues. In that regard, I am fortunate to have had a faculty appointment at an institution, Texas Tech University, with a long legacy of excellence in mammalogy. (I am now retired from the faculty of Texas Tech, with the title of Professor Emeritus.) To that end, I am deeply indebted to my colleagues who gave generously of their time to edit, review, and provide suggestions about various topics and chapters in the book. They include Robert J. Baker, Robert Bradley, Clyde Jones, and Nick Parker. Several graduate students at Texas Tech University also assisted. They are Chris Hice, Joel Brant, Jana Higginbotham, and Robert DeBaca. Generous financial and other support was provided by the Natural Science Research Laboratory of the Museum at Texas Tech University, by a special line item funded by the Texas Legislature for Texas Tech to create a biological database, and by the Office of the Vice President of Research at the university. The Texas Parks and Wildlife Department (TPWD), the state agency responsible for stewardship of wildlife resources in Texas, generously provided the resources to publish this as well as earlier versions of the book. I thank the previous TPWD director, Andrew Sansom, and the current director, Robert Cook, for their commitment to the current project. Many TPWD employees provided valuable assistance, including Jerry Cooke, Larry Hodge, Doug Humphreys, Karen Leslie, Pat Morton, David Riskind, Paul Robertson, and Butch Young.

Other valuable assistance with individual species accounts was provided by Marcia Revelez and Bob Dowler, Angelo State University; Ron Van Den Bussche, Oklahoma State University; and Jerry Dragoo, University of New Mexico. Jenny Litz of the National Oceanic and Atmospheric Administration provided updated cetacean stranding data from the SEUS Marine Mammal Stranding Database. The Texas Department of Health Rabies Lab, and particularly Bonny Mayes, provided information on county records of bats.

One of the challenges in producing a field guide is to locate good photographs and illustrations that adequately capture the mammals. In that regard, many individuals were generous in allowing me to use their photographs, and they have been acknowledged throughout the book. Special thanks are due to my friend and photographer John Tveten, and to Merlin Tuttle of Bat Conservation International.

Artists Pieter Folkens and Larry Foster graciously provided illustrations of marine mammals.

The Texas Cooperative Fish and Wildlife Research Unit, a division of the U.S. Geological Survey Biological Resources, located at Texas Tech University, through its GAP Laboratory, graciously provided the technical assistance to produce the distribution maps electronically. Nick Parker, who directs that program, and Sheri Haskell deserve thanks for their efforts in this regard.

Finally, and most important, a project like this requires someone who can shepherd it to a successful endpoint. This was especially important given my busy administrative role as the president of Texas Tech. This project could never have been completed without the hard work and dedication of my able assistant, Lisa Bradley. Lisa's commitment, diligence, thoroughness, and accuracy were essential to my achieving a fruitful outcome. For that reason, it is with great pleasure that I dedicate this book to her.

Of course, as with any endeavor of this nature, the final product—that which is correct and that which is not—remains my sole responsibility. With that said, it is my sincere hope that the citizens of Texas who have an interest in wildlife resources and conservation find much useful information and enjoyment from this new version of *The Mammals of Texas*.

THE MAMMALS OF TEXAS

TEXAS MAMMALS

The importance of Texas in relation to geography and wildlife is no accident. Within the state is such a wide variation of soils, climate, and topography that the resultant vegetation and animal life are unusually rich. This diverse environment supports a resident fauna of 143 species of native terrestrial mammals, a number exceeded in the United States only by California and New Mexico. In addition to the native species that occur in the area naturally, there are also 12 exotics or nonnative species that have been introduced accidentally (house mouse, roof rat, Norway rat) or intentionally (nutria, red fox, feral pig, axis deer, fallow deer, sika deer, nilgai, barbary sheep, and blackbuck) by humans and have become established as a part of the free-living fauna. An asterisk (*) beside the common name in species lists and species accounts indicates a nonnative species.

Terrestrial mammals in Texas belong to the orders Didelphimorphia (opossums), Xenarthra (armadillos), Insectivora (shrews and moles), Chiroptera (bats), Carnivora (carnivores), Artiodactyla (even-toed ungulates), Rodentia (rodents), and Lagomorpha (hares and rabbits). In addition, Texas is bounded by the waters of the Gulf of Mexico, and 29 marine mammals of the orders Cetacea (whales and dolphins), Carnivora (suborder Pinnipedia, seals), and Sirenia (manatees) enter the coastal waters and have either been sighted in the bays and ocean or stranded on the beaches of the state. The number of genera and species of Texas mammals in each of these groups is given in Table 1. The total of 184 mammals does not include several large, exotic ungulates that recently have been brought into the state and are kept for the most part under high fence and two domesticated species (dog and cat) that have taken up life in the wild state in many places and have significant effects on other mammals living in those areas.

Texas is a keystone in understanding the distributional patterns of Recent mammals in the United States. Several species reach distributional limits within the state. The mammalian fauna includes many species that occur throughout the central United States, especially those associated with the central grasslands, others with the southeastern deciduous forests, many characteristic of the desert regions of the Mexican Plateau and the southwestern United States, and a few associated with the mountain regions of the western United States and the tropical regions of northeastern Mexico.

Other important features of the terrestrial mammalian fauna of Texas are the number of endemic species and the variability within species as reflected by the number of described subspecies. Seven species are virtually confined in their distribution to Texas. There are currently 223 described subspecies of native terrestrial mammals in the state, and 58 species are represented by more than one subspecies.

Table 1. The number of genera and species of mammals in Texas[1]

Order	Genera	Species
Didelphimorphia (Opossums)	1	1
Xenarthra (Armadillos)	1	1
Insectivora (Shrews and Moles)	4	5
Chiroptera (Bats)	16	33
Carnivora (Carnivores)	19	28
Cetacea (Whales and Dolphins)	17	27
Sirenia (Manatees)	1	1
Artiodactyla (Even-toed Ungulates)	10	14
Rodentia (Rodents)	28	69
Lagomorpha (Hares and Rabbits)	2	5
Totals	99	184

[1]*Includes 12 introduced species for which accounts are provided in this book (4 rodents, 1 carnivore, 7 ungulates).*

DIVERSITY OF LAND MAMMALS

There is considerable change in the diversity of Texas mammals with geography. This is not surprising given the large size and configuration of the state, which results in pronounced gradients in temperature, precipitation, and other environmental conditions. Texas sits at the crossroads of four major North American biomes (Eastern Deciduous Forests, Great Plains, Rocky Mountains, and Southwest Deserts), each of which comprises many different ecological regions and habitats (Fig. 1).

Mammalian species distributions appear to differentiate along two major gradients: a dominant east-to-west gradient of decreasing precipitation and productivity and a south-to-north gradient of decreasing mean annual temperature, increasing winter cold, and increasing seasonal variation of temperature (Figs. 1 and 2). Species richness of mammals increases consistently in the state from east to west. Major shifts in the diversity pattern are evident on either side of the Balcones Escarpment and between the western portion of the Edwards Plateau and the Mountains and Basins of the Trans-Pecos region. The pattern is much more irregular, without any general trend, along the north-south transect. Diversity is highest in the Escarpment Breaks of the High Plains, the Balcones Canyonlands of the Edwards Plateau, and the subtropical brushlands of the South Texas Plains but lowest in the coastal sands of the South Texas Plains.

Overall there are more species of mammals in the western, southern, and northwestern regions of Texas than elsewhere. There are fewer species in the eastern, coastal, and central parts of the state. The highest diversity of mammals exists

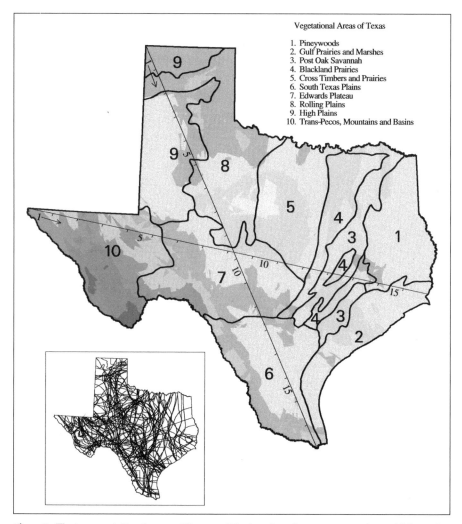

Figure 1. The ten vegetational areas of Texas and the location of two transects along which species diversity was analyzed. Gray shading indicates mammal diversity, with species richness increasing from light to dark. Inset represents the composite range extent for all Texas mammals. Sources: Vegetational regions from F. W. Gould, *Texas Plants: A Checklist and Ecological Summary* (Texas Agricultural Experiment Station, MP-585, 1962). Mammal diversity and inset map from E. A. Holt, K. E. Allen, N. C. Parker, and R. J. Baker, "Ecotourism and conservation: Richness of terrestrial vertebrates across Texas," Occasional Papers, The Museum, Texas Tech University 201 (2000): 1–16.

in the Basin and Range, or Big Bend region, in the western reaches of the Trans-Pecos, and the lowest is in the eastern Gulf Prairies and Marshes along the coast and the central Texas woodlands. Other areas with high mammal diversity include the northern Panhandle and the Stockton Plateau, the eastern edge of the High Plains, and the Rio Grande Plains. Mammal species richness also is positively related to the number of vegetation types, the range of elevation, and the types and textures of soils.

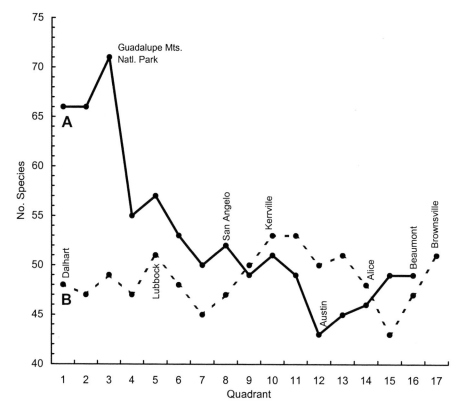

Figure 2. Species diversity plots for the quadrants along the two transects illustrated in Figure 1. Solid line (A), east-west transect. Dashed line (B), north-south transect.

Two important generalizations are evident about the diversity of Texas mammals. First, there is no strong correlation between land area of the vegetation regions and species diversity (Fig. 3). For example, the High Plains region is slightly larger in area than the Trans-Pecos region, yet it supports only half as many species of mammals. Second, those natural regions of Texas where vegetative and topographic heterogeneity are the greatest provide a broader spectrum of potential mammalian habitats and thus support a greater number of mammalian species.

Overall, an analysis of mammalian species ranges indicates constantly changing spatial configurations of species numbers and degree of sympatry. James Owen, a former doctoral student of mine, has authored a series of papers about the spatial distribution patterns of Texas mammals. His analyses suggest that changes in mammalian community structure in Texas are the result of species-specific responses to environmental conditions, rather than broad-scale community responses. Moreover, Owen found that species turnover patterns are relatively even in both north-south and east-west directions.

Owen's data also reveal some interesting patterns of species richness among different taxonomic groups of mammals. For example, variation in elevation is a strong positive predictor for species richness of all mammals, rodents, and bats, but a weaker predictor for carnivores. This can be attributed to an increase in the number of habitats present in areas with high levels of topographic relief. Surprisingly, productivity is negatively correlated with species richness for all groups except carnivores, which show a positive relationship. Texas carnivores show an initial increase with increased productivity, a peak at intermediate levels of productivity, and a decline at higher levels of productivity. Carnivores also displayed two other patterns not observed in other taxa. High levels of species richness are distributed over a greater area for carnivores, and carnivore communities are generally richer in species than those of other taxa. Both patterns can be explained by the larger geographic ranges of carnivores.

Those natural patterns of mammalian diversity could be altered drastically in the twenty-first century if scenarios of climate change come true. Under general climate circulation models, which predict changes in global climate due to

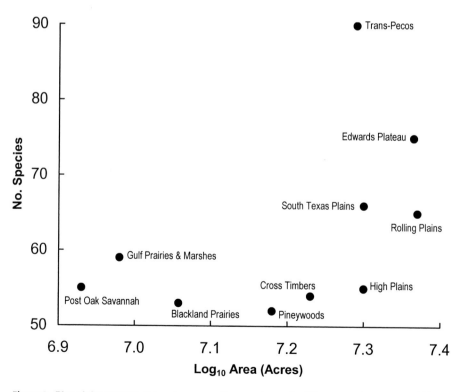

Figure 3. Plot of the number of species versus the area for each of the vegetative regions of Texas shown in Figure 1.

increased levels of atmospheric carbon dioxide, environmental variables in Texas could change rapidly and, in turn, change the distribution and diversity of mammals. Changes in temperature and rainfall patterns will cause changes in the distribution of plant communities, which in turn would affect the distribution of mammals throughout the landscape.

Guy Cameron, formerly of the University of Houston, and his students used models of climate-vegetation association to predict mammalian distributions under current conditions and under two future climates that would occur if carbon dioxide levels double, as has been predicted. Both future climates were warmer, but one was wetter and the other drier than current conditions. Under both future climatic conditions, all temperate vegetation in Texas would be lost. Under drier conditions, steppe and scrub habitats would appear in the state; under wetter conditions, subtropical habitats would appear.

In general, rodents are predicted to be the most adaptable group of mammals to global climate change. Cameron's analysis predicts extinction for only two rodent species, the Mexican vole (*Microtus mexicanus*) and Coues's rice rat (*Oryzomys couesi*), both of which have restricted ranges in the state. Four rodents are predicted to show large increases in geographic distributions, including the gray-footed chipmunk (*Tamias canipes*), the brush mouse (*Peromyscus boylii*), and the Mexican woodrat (*Neotoma mexicanus*) under the drier climate and those plus the northern rock mouse (*Peromyscus nasutus*) under the wetter climate. Half of rodent species ranges are predicted to decrease under drier climates and 63 percent are predicted to decrease under wetter climates. For both insectivores and lagomorphs, no species are predicted to go extinct in the state, but species ranges are predicted to contract under both drier and wetter conditions and species diversity is predicted to decrease in the southern part of the state. Ranges of bats dependent on fixed roosts such as caves and rock crevices are predicted to decrease substantially under wetter climatic conditions, but a few are predicted to expand under the drier model. Conversely, tree-roosting and generalist bat ranges are predicted to increase under both climatic scenarios. Under both future climates, species richness is predicted to decrease in west Texas because of the loss of cavity-roosting bats but to increase in southern and central Texas with the expansion of tree-roosting bats. Again, no species are predicted to go extinct under new climatic conditions.

Analyses of mammal communities as a whole in Texas reveal that individual species are predicted to respond differently to climate change. This suggests that mammal communities do not shift together as a whole, but each species shifts independently of other species, which will result in new associations of mammals and different mammal community structure as climatic conditions change. This also may be true of plant species. If so, vegetation communities may not shift as a unit, and the result will be new kinds of plant communities. These observations are consistent with the observations made about the influence of environmental variables on the current distribution of mammals.

GEOGRAPHIC DISTRIBUTION OF LAND MAMMALS

Texas may be conveniently arranged into four regions based on the ecological distribution of mammals. The regions are the Trans-Pecos, the Plains Country, East Texas, and the Rio Grande Plains (Fig. 4). The Trans-Pecos region includes the mountain and basin country west of the Pecos River. The Plains Country includes the High Plains, Rolling Plains, Cross Timbers area, and the Edwards Plateau. Included within the East Texas region are the Pineywoods, Post Oak Savannah, Blackland Prairies, and Gulf Prairies and Marshes. The Rio Grande Plains encompasses the south Texas brushlands. The Balcones Escarpment serves as the major physiographic barrier separating the Plains Country from East Texas and the Rio Grande Plains. The boundary between East Texas and the Rio Grande Plains is positioned between the Guadalupe and San Antonio rivers where pedocal and pedalfer soils meet.

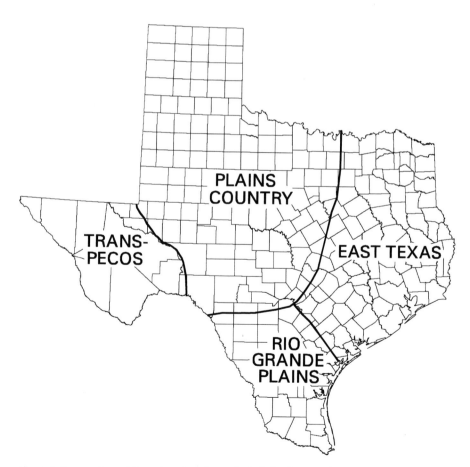

Figure 4. Four regions of Texas based on the ecological distribution of mammals.

The distributional patterns of land mammals in Texas conform to five general patterns: (1) ubiquitous species that range throughout most, or all, of the state (included in this group are several species that are now extinct or whose distributions have shrunk markedly in the past 150 years, as well as two species, the pygmy mouse and the armadillo, whose ranges have expanded in the last 100 years, and an introduced species, the red fox, which has spread over most of the state); (2) species that are distributed primarily in one of the four divisions of the state; (3) western species distributed in the Trans-Pecos and Plains Country; (4) western species distributed in the Trans-Pecos and Plains Country but that also occur on the Rio Grande Plains; and (5) eastern species distributed principally east of the 100th meridian. Mammals assigned to each of these categories are listed below. It should be noted that certain species occur slightly outside the boundaries of the category to which they have been assigned, as indicated by the comments in the various species lists.

The greatest number of unique elements in the mammal fauna of Texas occurs in the Trans-Pecos region. Approximately one-third, or 30, of the mammals that occur in the Trans-Pecos are primarily restricted in distribution to that region. Most of them are species characteristic of the arid Mexican Plateau and southwestern United States or the montane woodlands of the western United States. The fewest number of unique elements (9) is found in the Plains Country, and with the exception of the black-footed ferret all of these species are rodents. The 14 mammals unique to East Texas are species characteristic of the deciduous forests and coastal prairies of the southeastern United States, which reach their western distributional limits in Texas. The Rio Grande Plains region supports 11 unique elements, most of which are characteristic of the tropical lowlands of northeastern Mexico and reach their northern distributional limits in south Texas.

MAMMALS GENERALLY DISTRIBUTED THROUGHOUT THE STATE

Virginia Opossum	*Didelphis virginiana* (absent from driest portions of the Trans-Pecos)
Nine-banded Armadillo	*Dasypus novemcinctus* (absent from far west Texas)
Eastern Red Bat	*Lasiurus borealis*
Hoary Bat	*Lasiurus cinereus*
Silver-haired Bat	*Lasionycteris noctivagans*
Big Brown Bat	*Eptesicus fuscus* (absent from a belt extending throughout the center of the state)
Brazilian Free-tailed Bat	*Tadarida brasiliensis*
Coyote	*Canis latrans*
*Red Fox	*Vulpes vulpes* (absent from far western and southern Texas)
Common Gray Fox	*Urocyon cinereoargenteus*

American Black Bear	*Ursus americanus* (now extinct except for remnant populations in the Trans-Pecos)
Ringtail	*Bassariscus astutus*
Northern Raccoon	*Procyon lotor*
Long-tailed Weasel	*Mustela frenata* (absent from northern Panhandle)
American Badger	*Taxidea taxus* (absent from extreme eastern Texas)
Striped Skunk	*Mephitis mephitis*
Mountain Lion	*Puma concolor* (now gone from much of the range except south Texas and the Trans-Pecos)
Bobcat	*Lynx rufus*
Jaguar	*Panthera onca* (now extinct in Texas)
White-tailed Deer	*Odocoileus virginianus*
American Bison	*Bos bison* (now extinct in Texas)
Hispid Pocket Mouse	*Chaetodipus hispidus* (not in the Big Thicket of East Texas)
American Beaver	*Castor canadensis* (absent from the High Plains and the Trans-Pecos except along the Rio Grande)
Fulvous Harvest Mouse	*Reithrodontomys fulvescens* (absent from the High Plains and Concho Valley)
White-footed Mouse	*Peromyscus leucopus*
Deer Mouse	*Peromyscus maniculatus*
Northern Pygmy Mouse	*Baiomys taylori* (absent from extreme northeastern Texas and the Trans-Pecos)
Hispid Cotton Rat	*Sigmodon hispidus*
Eastern Cottontail	*Sylvilagus floridanus*
Black-tailed Jackrabbit	*Lepus californicus* (not in the Big Thicket of East Texas)

MAMMALS OCCURRING PRINCIPALLY IN THE TRANS-PECOS

Mexican Long-nosed Bat	*Leptonycteris nivalis*
California Myotis	*Myotis californicus* (disjunct record from Rolling Plains)
Fringed Myotis	*Myotis thysanodes* (disjunct record from Rolling Plains)
Long-legged Myotis	*Myotis volans* (disjunct record from Rolling Plains)
Yuma Myotis	*Myotis yumanensis* (disjunct record from Rio Grande Plains)

Western Red Bat	*Lasiurus blossevillii*
Western Yellow Bat	*Lasiurus xanthinus*
Spotted Bat	*Euderma maculatum*
Pocketed Free-tailed Bat	*Nyctinomops femorosaccus*
Western Mastiff Bat	*Eumops perotis*
Elk	*Cervus elaphus* (native population extinct; reintroduced into Guadalupe Mountains)
Bighorn Sheep	*Ovis canadensis* (native population extinct; reintroduced into several mountain ranges)
Gray-footed Chipmunk	*Tamias canipes*
Texas Antelope Squirrel	*Ammospermophilus interpres* (range extends into the broken country just east of the Pecos River and there is a record from Gaines County on the edge of the Llano Estacado)
Desert Pocket Gopher	*Geomys arenarius*
Chihuahuan Desert Pocket Mouse	*Chaetodipus eremicus* (a few records east of the Pecos River)
Rock Pocket Mouse	*Chaetodipus intermedius* (one record north of the Pecos River)
Nelson's Pocket Mouse	*Chaetodipus nelsoni* (one record from Webb County in south Texas)
Merriam's Kangaroo Rat	*Dipodomys merriami* (a few records east of the Pecos River and one record from DeWitt County in south Texas)
Banner-tailed Kangaroo Rat	*Dipodomys spectabilis* (also in southern part of High Plains)
Brush Mouse	*Peromyscus boylii*
Cactus Mouse	*Peromyscus eremicus* (also in extreme western part of Rio Grande Plains)
Northern Rock Mouse	*Peromyscus nasutus*
Mearns's Grasshopper Mouse	*Onychomys arenicola* (a few records just east of the Pecos River)
Tawny-bellied Cotton Rat	*Sigmodon fulviventer*
Yellow-nosed Cotton Rat	*Sigmodon ochrognathus*
Mexican Woodrat	*Neotoma mexicana*
Mexican Vole	*Microtus mexicanus*
Hooded Skunk	*Mephitis macroura*
Davis Mountains Cottontail	*Sylvilagus robustus*

MAMMALS OCCURRING PRINCIPALLY IN THE PLAINS COUNTRY

Black-footed Ferret	*Mustela nigripes* (now extinct in Texas)
Thirteen-lined Ground Squirrel	*Spermophilus tridecemlineatus* (also in a narrow strip through central Texas from the Red River and Dallas region south to Corpus Christi and east to Atascosa County in south Texas)
Plains Pocket Gopher	*Geomys bursarius*
Jones's Pocket Gopher	*Geomys knoxjonesi*
Llano Pocket Gopher	*Geomys texensis*
Plains Pocket Mouse	*Perognathus flavescens* (also in El Paso County)
Texas Kangaroo Rat	*Dipodomys elator*
Texas Mouse	*Peromyscus attwateri*
Prairie Vole	*Microtus ochrogaster* (subspecies *haydeni*)

MAMMALS OCCURRING PRINCIPALLY IN THE RIO GRANDE PLAINS

Mexican Long-tongued Bat	*Choeronycteris mexicana*
Southern Yellow Bat	*Lasiurus ega*
White-nosed Coati	*Nasua narica* (also in Big Bend region of the Trans-Pecos)
Ocelot	*Leopardus pardalis* (formerly more widely distributed)
Margay	*Leopardus wiedii* (now extinct in Texas)
Jaguarundi	*Herpailurus yaguarondi*
Texas Pocket Gopher	*Geomys personatus*
Strecker's Pocket Gopher	*Geomys streckeri*
Gulf Coast Kangaroo Rat	*Dipodomys compactus*
Mexican Spiny Pocket Mouse	*Liomys irroratus*
Coues's Rice Rat	*Oryzomys couesi*

MAMMALS OCCURRING PRINCIPALLY IN EAST TEXAS

Southern Short-tailed Shrew	*Blarina carolinensis*
Southeastern Myotis	*Myotis austroriparius* (disjunct record from central Texas)
Seminole Bat	*Lasiurus seminolus* (disjunct record from Val Verde County)
Rafinesque's Big-eared Bat	*Corynorhinus rafinesquii*
Eastern Gray Squirrel	*Sciurus carolinensis* (introduced population in Lubbock County on the High Plains)

Southern Flying Squirrel	*Glaucomys volans* (barely enters the Cross Timbers area of the Plains Country)
Attwater's Pocket Gopher	*Geomys attwateri* (barely extends into the northern part of the Rio Grande Plains)
Baird's Pocket Gopher	*Geomys breviceps*
Marsh Rice Rat	*Oryzomys palustris* (also in coastal region of Rio Grande Plains)
Eastern Harvest Mouse	*Reithrodontomys humulis*
Cotton Mouse	*Peromyscus gossypinus*
Golden Mouse	*Ochrotomys nuttalli*
Prairie Vole	*Microtus ochrogaster* (subspecies *ludovicianus,* now extinct in Texas)
Swamp Rabbit	*Sylvilagus aquaticus* (a few records from the Edwards Plateau)

MAMMALS OCCURRING PRINCIPALLY IN WEST TEXAS (PLAINS REGION AND TRANS-PECOS)

Western Small-footed Myotis	*Myotis ciliolabrum*
Western Pipistrelle	*Pipistrellus hesperus*
Townsend's Big-eared Bat	*Corynorhinus townsendii*
Pallid Bat	*Antrozous pallidus* (disjunct record from lower Rio Grande Valley)
Swift or Kit Fox	*Vulpes velox*
Grizzly or Brown Bear	*Ursus arctos* (now extinct in Texas)
Mule Deer	*Odocoileus hemionus*
Rock Squirrel	*Spermophilus variegatus*
Black-tailed Prairie Dog	*Cynomys ludovicianus*
Botta's Pocket Gopher	*Thomomys bottae*
Yellow-faced Pocket Gopher	*Cratogeomys castanops* (disjunct record from Cameron County in lower Rio Grande Valley)
Silky Pocket Mouse	*Perognathus flavus*
Western Harvest Mouse	*Reithrodontomys megalotis*
Plains Harvest Mouse	*Reithrodontomys montanus* (also in the Blackland Prairies of East Texas)
White-ankled Mouse	*Peromyscus pectoralis* (a record from Webb County in south Texas)
Pinyon Mouse	*Peromyscus truei* (known only from the Guadalupe Mountains in the Trans-Pecos and Palo Duro Canyon in the Panhandle)
Eastern White-throated Woodrat	*Neotoma leucodon*

MAMMALS OCCURRING PRINCIPALLY IN WESTERN TEXAS (TRANS-PECOS OR PLAINS REGION) AND RIO GRANDE PLAINS

Desert Shrew	*Notiosorex crawfordi*
Ghost-faced Bat	*Mormoops megalophylla*
Cave Myotis	*Myotis velifer*
Big Free-tailed Bat	*Nyctinomops macrotis* (two records from East Texas)
Gray Wolf	*Canis lupus* (now extinct in Texas)
Western Spotted Skunk	*Spilogale gracilis*
Hog-nosed Skunk	*Conepatus leuconotus* (Big Thicket population now extinct)
Collared Peccary	*Pecari tajacu*
Pronghorn	*Antilocapra americana* (now extinct in Rio Grande Plains)
Mexican Ground Squirrel	*Spermophilus mexicanus*
Spotted Ground Squirrel	*Spermophilus spilosoma*
Merriam's Pocket Mouse	*Perognathus merriami*
Ord's Kangaroo Rat	*Dipodomys ordii*
Northern Grasshopper Mouse	*Onychomys leucogaster*
Southern Plains Woodrat	*Neotoma micropus*
North American Porcupine	*Erethizon dorsatum*
Desert Cottontail	*Sylvilagus audubonii*

MAMMALS OCCURRING PRINCIPALLY EAST OF THE 100TH MERIDIAN

Elliot's Short-tailed Shrew	*Blarina hylophaga*
Least Shrew	*Cryptotis parva* (also occurs in the Plains Country)
Eastern Mole	*Scalopus aquaticus* (also occurs in the northern Plains Country, and there is an old record from Presidio County)
Northern Yellow Bat	*Lasiurus intermedius*
Eastern Pipistrelle	*Pipistrellus subflavus* (a few records from the Plains Country and a recent record from the Trans-Pecos)
Evening Bat	*Nycticeius humeralis* (disjunct records from Midland and Presidio counties)
Red Wolf	*Canis rufus* (now extinct in Texas)
American Mink	*Mustela vison* (one record from the northern Panhandle)
Eastern Spotted Skunk	*Spilogale putorius* (records from northern High Plains and Panhandle)

Northern River Otter	*Lontra canadensis* (one record from the Panhandle)
Eastern Fox Squirrel	*Sciurus niger* (extends westward into the Plains Country)
Eastern Woodrat	*Neotoma floridana*
Woodland Vole	*Microtus pinetorum*
Muskrat	*Ondatra zibethicus* (also in Canadian, Pecos, and Rio Grande drainages)
*Nutria	*Myocastor coypus* (still spreading westward)

Six species of mammals are unique to Texas in the sense that most or all of their known geographic range is confined to the mainland and barrier islands of the state. They are:

Texas kangaroo rat (*Dipodomys elator*)—known from ten counties in the mesquite plains of north-central Texas and one county in Oklahoma;

Gulf Coast kangaroo rat (*Dipodomys compactus*)—known from the barrier islands of Texas and Tamaulipas, Mexico, and the South Texas Plains;

Attwater's pocket gopher (*Geomys attwateri*)—known from East Texas (between the Brazos and San Antonio rivers);

Texas pocket gopher (*Geomys personatus*)—known from the barrier islands of Texas and Tamaulipas, Mexico, and the Rio Grande Plains;

Strecker's pocket gopher (*Geomys streckeri*)—known from Zavala and Dimmit counties in south Texas; and

Llano pocket gopher (*Geomys texensis*)—known from eleven counties in the Texas Hill Country.

There are three species of mammals (hairy-legged vampire bat, *Diphylla ecaudata;* southwestern little brown bat, *Myotis occultus;* northern long-eared myotis, *Myotis septentrionalis*) whose occurrence in Texas is most likely accidental. Resident breeding populations of these species have never been discovered within the state. The Texas records for all three are far outside their main range, and only a single record exists for each in the state. Furthermore, all three are bats, which are well known for their wandering movements.

MAMMALS OF THE BARRIER ISLANDS OF TEXAS

More than two-thirds of the 367 miles of Texas Gulf shoreline is composed of six major barrier islands, including, from north to south, Galveston, Matagorda, San Jose, Mustang, Padre, and South Padre islands (Fig. 5). The islands can be divided into three geographic groups based on the physical characteristics of the coastline. The first group includes Galveston Island, which is separated from the next island group by approximately 90 miles. The second group includes Matagorda and San Jose islands, which are occasionally joined at very low tide. They are separated from the third group by Aransas Pass, one of the most durable passes along the Texas coast. The third group includes Mustang, Padre, and South Padre islands. Padre and South Padre were one island until 1957 when Mansfield Channel was dredged, and Mustang Island has enjoyed frequent connections with Padre Island during its history.

From the Gulf to the bay side, the habitat types of each barrier island grade from open, sandy beach to the dune ridges, then to coastal prairie dotted with freshwater to brackish ponds and marshes, and finally to salt marsh. The plant species within these habitats are similar from island to island, which is not surprising because the plants must be adapted to a lack of freshwater and have a tolerance of highly saline conditions.

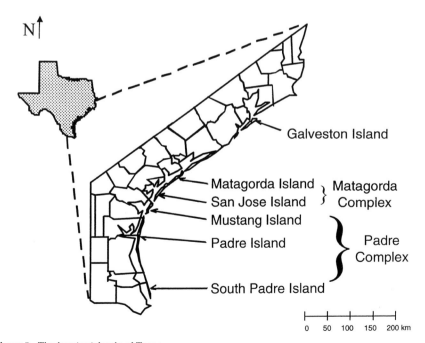

Figure 5. The barrier islands of Texas.

The barrier islands of Texas have a depauperate mammal fauna compared with that of the mainland Texas coast. One of my graduate students, Chris Hice, and I have studied the mammal fauna of the barrier islands in comparison to the adjacent mainland areas. In total, 28 species have been sighted on one or more of the islands. On Galveston Island, only 8 of 42 (19%) potential species have colonized the island; in the Matagorda complex, the number is 10 of 46 (22%) on Matagorda Island and 9 of 46 (20%) on San Jose Island; and for the Padre complex it ranges from 22 (49%) on Mustang Island to 23 (51%) of 45 potential mainland species on Padre and South Padre islands. Only four species of mammals (eastern cottontail, *Sylvilagus floridanus;* marsh rice rat, *Oryzomys palustris;* hispid cotton rat, *Sigmodon hispidus;* and the raccoon, *Procyon lotor*) occur on each of the barrier islands. Three other species (fulvous harvest mouse, *Reithrodontomys fulvescens;* black-tailed jackrabbit, *Lepus californicus;* and coyote, *Canis latrans*) have invaded all of the islands except Galveston Island. The opossum (*Didelphis virginiana*) is present on all of the islands except the Matagorda complex. Most of the discrepancy between the numbers of species that occur on each island complex results from the absence of ground squirrels, heteromyid rodents, and pocket gophers on the northern two complexes of islands.

A number of factors have influenced the faunal composition of the barrier islands, including hurricane events, the mainland species pool for the island to draw on, and the degree of isolation of the island from the mainland. Differences in species richness and composition among island complexes can be attributed to the diversity of the adjacent mainland area, and the island area. Thus, it appears that the dearth of mammal species on the islands has not resulted from a lack of colonization events but rather from their inability to survive in the harsher island environments.

DIVERSITY OF MAMMALS IN THE COASTAL WATERS AND GULF OF MEXICO

The Gulf of Mexico is a small oceanic basin covering about half a million square miles of the Atlantic Ocean bounded by the United States, Mexico, and Cuba. Texas forms the northwestern land boundary of the Gulf and includes 367 miles of coastline. The Gulf has only two openings: the Yucatan Channel, toward the Caribbean Sea, and the Straits of Florida, toward the southwestern North Atlantic. The Gulf is characterized by a wide, smooth, and gently sloping continental shelf that makes up about 35 percent of its surface. Another 40 percent is composed of deep canyons along the continental slope, and the remaining 25 percent is the deep ocean. Two major features dominate the Gulf of Mexico: the Loop Current of the western Gulf, and the Mississippi River, which deposits nutrients and sediment loads in a plume from the river mouth covering several thousand square miles. There is extensive human activity in the Gulf, including offshore drilling and shipping; pollution from agricultural, municipal, and industrial runoff; and commercial fishing. Over 72 percent of the oil and 97 percent of the natural gas produced in the United States come from the Gulf, with as many as 15,000 wells in operation.

Gordon Gunter wrote the first account of marine mammals in the Gulf in 1954, documenting 12 known species based on a historical accumulation of incidental sightings and strandings. Knowledge grew dramatically over the next decades. Researchers such as David and Melba Caldwell, Jim Layne, and Joe Moore in Florida; George Lowery in Louisiana; and Gordon Gunter in Texas and later Mississippi made many contributions. In 1981 I attempted the first comprehensive account of marine mammals in the Gulf. Subsequently, two recent reports have provided more recent and accurate updates. In 1997 Tom Jefferson and Amy Schiro updated and verified my maps and corrected the information about species identification. A recent book, *The Marine Mammals of the Gulf of Mexico,* by Bernd Würsig, Tom Jefferson, and me, provides a comprehensive treatise about the marine mammals from the waters of the Gulf. Today, a number of marine mammalogists have located in the Gulf, and the region is now one of the leading centers for marine mammal research and education in the world.

Thirty-one species (28 cetaceans, 2 pinnipeds, and 1 manatee) of marine mammals are known from the entire Gulf of Mexico. Of the 28 cetacean species, 27 have either stranded along the Texas or Louisiana coast or been observed in the waters of the continental shelf or deeper waters in the central Gulf and therefore could move into Texas waters. Accounts for these 27 species have been provided in this edition of *The Mammals of Texas.* Of the two pinnipeds, one (the West Indian monk seal, *Monachus tropicalis*) is now extinct. The second pinniped, the California sea lion (*Zalophus californianus*), was introduced and occurred only in the feral condition during the past, and an account for this species is not included in this edition. The West Indian manatee (*Trichechus manatus*) is the only sirenian in the Gulf, and although a manatee was recently sighted on our coast, there is no evidence that breeding populations of this endangered species ever existed along the Texas coast.

The cetacean fauna of the Gulf includes 7 mysticete or baleen whales and 21 ondontocete or toothed whales representing four families. The Gulf cetacean fauna is clearly not depauperate. Half of the genera and more than a third of the cetacean species in the world have been recorded from the Gulf. From a biogeographic perspective, representatives from four geographic assemblages of species occur in the Gulf, including cosmopolitan, eurythermic species; endemics to the Atlantic Ocean; pantropical, warm-stenothermal species; and antitropical, cold-stenothermal species.

Of the 27 cetacean species recognized for the Texas waters of the Gulf, 9 are cosmopolitan species that occur in most major oceans and for the most part are eurythermic with a broad range of temperature tolerances. They are the minke whale, *Balaenoptera acutorostrata;* sperm whale, *Physeter macrocephalus;* pygmy sperm whale, *Kogia breviceps;* dwarf sperm whale, *Kogia sima;* Cuvier's beaked whale, *Ziphius cavirostris;* Blainville's beaked whale, *Mesoplodon densirostris;* killer whale, *Orcinus orca;* Risso's dolphin, *Grampus griseus;* and bottlenose dolphin, *Tursiops truncatus.*

Three species (Gervais's beaked whale, *Mesoplodon europaeus;* Atlantic spotted dolphin, *Stenella frontalis;* and Clymene dolphin, *Stenella clymene*) have a distribution confined to the Atlantic Ocean. All have stranded on Texas beaches or been sighted near our beaches at one time or another.

Ten cetaceans have distributions peculiar to tropical, warm waters of both hemispheres and may be considered warm-stenothermal forms. They include Bryde's whale, *Balaenoptera edeni;* short-finned pilot whale, *Globicephala macrorhynchus;* false killer whale, *Pseudorca crassidens;* pygmy killer whale, *Feresa attenuata;* melon-headed whale, *Peponocephala electra;* rough-toothed dolphin, *Stena bredanensis;* pantropical spotted dolphin, *Stenella attenuata;* spinner dolphin, *Stenella longirostris;* striped dolphin, *Stenella coeruleoalba;* and Fraser's dolphin, *Lagenodelphis hosei.* All but Bryde's whale have stranded on Texas beaches.

Five species (northern right whale, *Eubalaena glacialis;* blue whale, *Balaenoptera musculus;* fin whale, *Balaenoptera physalus;* sei whale, *Balaenoptera borealis;* and humpback whale, *Megaptera novaeangliae*) have disjunct bipolar (antitropical) distributions and are regarded as cold-stenothermal forms based on where they feed. The humpback whale, however, enters tropical waters to breed. All of these species, except for the sei whale, also have stranded on Texas beaches.

At least 7 of the Texas cetacean species are migratory, including several species of rorquals (the blue, fin, sei, and minke whales), the humpback, and the northern right whales. These species generally travel between a breeding zone in which they do not eat and a feeding zone of high productivity in cooler waters. The sperm whale is known to be migratory in other parts of the world, but female groups appear to be year-round residents in the Gulf of Mexico.

Several generalizations are evident about the cetacean fauna of the Gulf. The most common species is the bottlenose dolphin, *Tursiops truncatus.* Bottlenose dolphins are frequently seen in bays, ship channels, and even estuaries. They occur in depths of less than 1,000 meters and are absent from the deeper central parts of the Gulf.

Several cetaceans are rare or extralimital in the Gulf, including all of the baleen whales, with one possible exception, and all of the beaked whales. Only Bryde's whale (*Balaenoptera edeni*), a baleen whale that is a year-round inhabitant of tropical and subtropical waters, occurs with any regularity. Records are scattered throughout the year, suggesting it is likely that the Gulf represents at least a portion of the range of a dispersed, resident population of Bryde's whales. Most of the sightings have been from the northeastern Gulf along the shelf edge near De Soto Canyon.

With the exception of the Atlantic spotted dolphin (*Stenella frontalis*), there are more records of sperm whales (*Physeter macrocephalus*) in the Gulf than any other species of offshore cetaceans. The Gulf was even a significant sperm whaling ground for nineteenth-century Yankee whalers. Sperm whales have stranded or been sighted in all months and seasons of the year. Most sightings are from deep waters beyond the edge of the continental shelf, although there are a few records from over the shelf, such as the Mississippi River delta.

All of the world's species of *Stenella* occur in the Gulf and many of them in fairly large numbers. The pantropical spotted dolphin (*Stenella attenuata*) is the most common and abundant delphinid in oceanic waters deeper than 200 m. The Atlantic spotted dolphin (*Stenella frontalis*) is a common offshore dolphin in waters from 20 to 200 m deep, with scattered records out to 1,000 m. There are more Gulf records of these dolphins than for any other species of offshore cetacean, and it is the only species, other than the bottlenose dolphin, that commonly occurs over the continental shelf. There are fewer records of the spinner dolphin (*Stenella longirostris*), which has a pantropical distribution, than for any other species of *Stenella* in the Gulf. The Clymene dolphin (*Stenella clymene*) is an endemic of Atlantic tropical and subtropical waters that ranges primarily between the 100 m and 2,000 m depth contours. The striped dolphin (*Stenella coeruleoalba*) is a deepwater species and occurs worldwide in tropical and warm temperate waters.

Other delphinids thought to be rare based on stranding records actually appear to be common in deeper oceanic waters. Rough-toothed dolphins (*Steno bredanensis*) rarely strand, but they have been sighted on many occasions throughout all seasons in the Gulf. Melon-headed whales (*Peponocephala electra*) were first recorded on the basis of strandings in the past decade, but now they have been sighted numerous times in waters 200 to 2,000 m deep. The Gulf has produced more sightings of Fraser's dolphin (*Lagenodelphis hosei*) than anywhere else in the Atlantic Ocean. Sightings have been made in the northern Gulf in waters around 1,000 m deep. There are numerous sightings of Risso's dolphin (*Grampus griseus*), which previously was thought to be rare in the Gulf, along the upper continental slope off Alabama, Mississippi, and eastern Louisiana.

Previous editions of *The Mammals of Texas* included an account for the common dolphin, *Delphinus delphis*. Common dolphins were recently split into two species, a short-beaked form (*D. delphis*) and a long-beaked form (*D. capensis*). This edition, however, does not include an account for either species. Although both stranding and sighting records exist for the Gulf, it now appears that earlier workers consistently misidentified some other species, mainly Clymene dolphins (*Stenella clymene*), as common dolphins. All museum skulls previously noted as *Delphinus* have been reidentified as either *Stenella clymene* or the pantropical spotted dolphin, *Stenella attenuata*. Thus, there is no definitive evidence that common dolphins occur in the Gulf of Mexico. Because of their known distribution in similar latitudes in other places in the world, both common dolphin species may eventually be found in the Gulf, most likely in the southern waters that have not been surveyed adequately.

Some of the larger whales that occur in the Gulf have been placed on the Endangered Species List of the U.S. Fish and Wildlife Service Register. These include the northern right whale, sei whale, blue whale, fin whale, and humpback whale (see Table 2). The sperm whale also is listed as endangered, but recent information suggests that it is the most common large whale in the Gulf of Mexico.

No dolphins or other odontocetes in the Gulf are considered endangered at the species level, but Texas Parks and Wildlife lists as threatened the pygmy sperm whale, dwarf sperm whale, Gervais's beaked whale, Cuvier's beaked whale, killer whale, false killer whale, pygmy killer whale, short-finned pilot whale, rough-toothed dolphin, and Atlantic spotted dolphin (see Table 2). There is really no basis for these listings other than rarity in the stranding record.

There are environmental problems in the Gulf of Mexico that could threaten marine mammals. Agricultural pesticide runoff is particularly heavy from the Mississippi River and other river systems that run into the Gulf, and about 30 percent of all petrochemical refining and fully 50 percent of hydrocarbon product production (paints and plastics) in the United States occurs around the shores of Galveston Bay. Pollution problems are more prevalent in shallow waters near shore and could be especially deleterious to the bottlenose dolphin (*Tursiops truncatus*). Recently, bottlenose dolphins suffered major die-off epidemics along the Texas shore, with 201 animals stranding in 1990, 245 in 1992, and 286 in 1994 (the average since 1987 in the nonpeak years is only 128 stranded dolphins). The 1994 die-offs involved a strain of morbillivirus that was found in a number of animals. Almost all of the stranded dolphins exhibited abnormally high amounts of nontoxic lesions, growths, and other abnormalities in their body parts. Dan Cowan, a well-known pathologist at the University of Texas Medical Branch in Galveston, documented previously unknown abnormalities in these animals. It is not known if high levels of artificial toxins caused some of the deaths, but there is reason to be suspicious, since high levels of heavy metals and polychlorinated products were found in body tissues. The dolphins and whales of deep water simply have not been studied enough to form reasonable conclusions on the health of individuals.

Offshore oil and gas exploration is another source of negative interaction between humans and marine mammals. This has gone on in the Gulf for more than 50 years, although the effects on marine mammals of these waters have been largely unstudied. Disastrous oil spills, like the huge 1989 *Exxon Valdez* spill in southern Alaska, represent another area of concern. Oil spills are drastically harmful to marine mammals that use fur to thermoregulate, such as sea otters, seals, and sea lions, but toothed dolphins and whales use a shiny surfaced and oil-repellent skin over a thick blubber layer to thermoregulate, and they can move to avoid oil on the surface while feeding on fishes and squid well below the surface. An oil spill in 1990 (the *Mega Borg* spill) off Galveston, Texas, however, showed that bottlenose

Table 2. Critical Texas mammals as defined by Texas Parks and Wildlife Department and U.S. Fish and Wildlife Service[1]

Scientific Name, Common Name	TPWD	USFWS
Leptonycteris nivalis, Mexican Long-nosed Bat	E	E
Lasiurus ega, Southern Yellow Bat	T	
Euderma maculatum, Spotted Bat	T	
Corynorhinus rafinesquii, Rafinesque's Big-eared Bat	T	
Canis lupus,[2] Gray Wolf	E	E
Canis rufus,[2] Red Wolf	E	E
Ursus americanus, Black Bear	T	T/SA
Ursus arctos,[2] Grizzly Bear		T
Nasua narica, White-nosed Coati	T	
Mustela nigripes,[2] Black-footed Ferret	E	E
Leopardus pardalis, Ocelot	E	E
Leopardus wiedii,[2] Margay	T	E
Herpailurus yaguarondi, Jaguarundi	E	E
Panthera onca,[2] Jaguar	E	E
Monachus tropicalis,[2] West Indian Monk Seal		E
Eubalaena glacialis, Northern Right Whale	E	E
Balaenoptera musculus, Blue Whale	E	E
Balaenoptera physalus, Fin Whale	E	E
Balaenoptera borealis, Sei Whale		E
Megaptera novaeangliae, Humpback Whale		E
Physeter macrocephalus, Sperm Whale	E	E
Kogia breviceps, Pygmy Sperm Whale	T	
Kogia sima, Dwarf Sperm Whale	T	
Mesoplodon europaeus, Gervais's Beaked Whale	T	
Ziphius cavirostris, Cuvier's Beaked Whale	T	
Orcinus orca, Killer Whale	T	
Pseudorca crassidens, False Killer Whale	T	
Feresa attenuata, Pygmy Killer Whale	T	
Globicephala macrorhynchus, Short-finned Pilot Whale	T	
Steno bredanensis, Rough-toothed Dolphin	T	
Stenella frontalis, Atlantic Spotted Dolphin	T	
Trichechus manatus, West Indian Manatee	E	E
Dipodomys elator, Texas Kangaroo Rat	T	
Oryzomys couesi, Coues's Rice Rat	T	

[1] *As of July 2002. T, Threatened; E, Endangered; T/SA, Similarity of Appearance to a Threatened Taxon.*

[2] *Species considered by the author to be now extinct in Texas.*

dolphins do not know how to avoid extensive oil-covered areas. Observations revealed that the dolphins repeatedly surfaced in even the very volatile fresh areas of a spill, areas in which humans become sick to their stomach in minutes and lung tissue becomes rapidly coated in oil volatiles. Under such conditions, their breathing apparatus would become clogged and the animals would suffocate. Since offshore currents did not bring carcasses close to shore, it is not known how many dolphins succumbed to the *Mega Borg* spill, but it can be surmised that fatalities occurred.

HISTORICAL CHANGES IN THE TEXAS MAMMAL FAUNA

Texas is fortunate to have a good historical perspective about its mammal fauna. From 1889 to 1905 a team of federal scientists from the United States Bureau of Biological Survey (forerunner of today's U.S. Fish and Wildlife Service) surveyed the flora and fauna of the state, emphasizing mammals as the target group. Vernon Bailey, chief naturalist of the Survey and director of field efforts in Texas, was one of the leading mammalogists of his era, and he summarized the results of the Texas survey in a 222-page 1905 publication titled the *Biological Survey of Texas.* This publication constitutes the primary comprehensive study of Texas mammals at the end of the nineteenth century. By comparing the mammal fauna during Bailey's time with the fauna today, it is possible to make some general statements about past conditions and the extent of biological change in the twentieth century.

I have written a separate book, titled *Texas Natural History: A Century of Change,* describing the history of the biological survey and chronicling the magnitude of twentieth-century changes in the Texas mammal fauna. On a macroscale the diversity of mammals changed substantially during the twentieth century. There has been a substantial turnover in species composition, involving both a loss and gain in species, since 1900. A significant number of mammals are now extinct, and a growing number of species are regarded as endangered and threatened. Almost 35 percent of the mammal species (50 out of 144 native, terrestrial species) either have become extinct or had subspecies or metapopulations become extinct, or they are rare and appear to face some sort of problem that potentially threatens their existence.

Among the most significant trends during the twentieth century, six are particularly important and worthy of discussion. These are briefly described below, but a more extensive explanation is provided in *Texas Natural History: A Century of Change.*

Proliferation of Extinctions

Species extinctions increased dramatically during the twentieth century. When Bailey published his work in 1905, the only extirpated mammals were the bison, elk, and West Indian monk seal. During the course of that century, the grizzly bear, gray wolf, red wolf, black-footed ferret, jaguar, margay, bighorn sheep, and mana-tee all joined the list of extirpated species.

A variety of factors can cause extinction, but in the case of these species, exploitation and habitat alteration by humans probably had more to do with their disappearance than any other single factor. Overhunting definitely seems to have caused the disappearance of the grizzly, elk, and bison. Predator control activities probably had much to do with the extirpation of the gray wolf and the jaguar. The red wolf disappeared as a result of predator control efforts and the genetic effect of interbreeding with coyotes. The black-footed ferret disappeared primarily as a result of destruction of prairie dog towns, which removed most of the ferret's nat-ural food supply. The big factors in the decline of the bighorn sheep were compe-tition with domestic sheep and the use of net wire fences that prevented the sheep from wandering about from one mountain range to another. The margay was prob-ably only marginal in Texas and never represented by an established breeding population.

West Indian monk seals were the only seal native to the Gulf of Mexico. They were distributed tropically and limited to the Gulf of Mexico coast, the Yucatan Peninsula, western Caribbean Sea, the Greater and Lesser Antilles, the Bahamas, and the Florida Keys. Their remains have been excavated from archeological sites in coastal Texas, supporting their possible occurrence in the western Gulf. As explained in the account of the West Indian monk seal, some mammalogists have questioned the validity of the Texas records, bringing into question whether this species ever occurred in the state.

Declines in Geographic Distribution and Population Abundance

A notable number of Texas mammals, including species of all sizes and life history traits, have undergone drastic range reductions and today occupy a mere scant portion of their former range. Examples of species that are now severely reduced in distribution or abundance include the pronghorn (*Antilocapra americana*), black-tailed prairie dog (*Cynomys ludovicianus*), muskrat (*Ondatra zibethicus*), and mountain lion (*Puma concolor*).

The pronghorn once occurred over the western two-thirds of Texas, but the great herds that once roamed the Trans-Pecos and Panhandle regions were reduced to a mere handful by the early twentieth century. The decline was associ-ated with overgrazing of grasslands by domestic livestock, uncontrolled hunting, and extensive cultivation of prairie habitat. The pronghorn is now restricted to isolated patches of suitable habitat from the Panhandle to the Trans-Pecos.

No Texas mammal has suffered more from population decline this century than has the black-tailed prairie dog. It has been estimated that in the early 1900s, prairie dog colonies covered 100 million to 250 million acres throughout North

America. Such concentrations were a heavy drain on range vegetation, and ranchers enlisted the federal government to combat them. Using mainly strychnine-treated grain, the ranchers, along with government rodent control specialists, poisoned millions of prairie dogs. By 1960 the once overwhelming populations had been reduced to scattered, small colonies. More recently, sylvatic plague has devastated many of the remaining small colonies and has contributed significantly to the decline of black-tailed prairie dog populations across much of their range. Today, it is estimated that 98 percent of the population has been lost, and that only 300,000 prairie dogs remain in Texas. Records indicate that prairie dog habitat declined 61 percent just in the last two decades of the twentieth century. At this rate of population decline and habitat fragmentation, prairie dog extinction could occur during this century.

Another interesting case is that of the muskrat. In some regions of the state, such as the Panhandle and the Trans-Pecos, muskrat populations appear to have declined or even disappeared, whereas in other regions, particularly the upper Texas coast, they have invaded and increased in abundance. Their decline in the Panhandle and the Trans-Pecos was apparently a result of the reduction in the availability of natural surface water.

Historically, mountain lions occurred virtually throughout the state. Years of predator control efforts by livestock producers, however, forced the remaining mountain lions into the more remote, thinly populated areas. Today, the largest mountain lion populations are in the desert mountain ranges of the Trans-Pecos, especially in the Big Bend region, and the dense brushlands of the Rio Grande Plains. Predator control efforts have slowed since about 1970, and lion populations appear to be stabilizing.

Range Expansions and Regional Faunal Changes

Since the beginning of the twentieth century, a number of mammals have expanded their ranges in Texas. Notable examples include the armadillo (*Dasypus novemcinctus*), the northern pygmy mouse (*Baiomys taylori*), and the porcupine (*Erethizon dorsatum*). At the time that Bailey and the federal agents roamed the state, all of these species had restricted distributions, whereas today they are much more wide-ranging and common.

Documentation of range expansions has been very prevalent for bats in recent decades. Three species, the eastern pipistrelle (*Pipistrellus subflavus*), the evening bat (*Nycticeius humeralis*), and the Seminole bat (*Lasiurus seminolus*), previously thought to be confined to the eastern half of the state, have now been collected in far western Texas. These examples suggest the Rio Grande may be serving as a dispersal corridor, allowing eastern species of mammals to expand their ranges gradually westward during the last decade.

Unfortunately, not much is known about microscale changes in diversity, such as reductions or expansions of geographic ranges, changes in species abundance and community structure, and extinctions of local populations and subspecies. From the evidence at hand, however, it seems obvious that the faunal composition in several areas of the state changed during the twentieth century.

Documentation of Additional Faunal Elements and Discovery of Cryptic Species

Even though Bailey and the federal agents did a thorough job of documenting the mammal fauna of Texas at the turn of the nineteenth century, mammalogists working in the state throughout the twentieth century continued to document additional species and subspecies, and they have altered the taxonomy of mammals based on new information about the status of populations, subspecies, and species. Such taxonomic changes undoubtedly will continue as more is learned about the genetic relationships of mammalian populations.

Twenty-four additional species of mammals have been documented since the publication of Bailey's *Biological Survey of Texas.* Of these 24 species, almost two-thirds are bats. The primary reason for the addition of numerous bat species to the fauna is improvements in bat-collecting techniques during the last century, especially since the 1954 development of the use of mist nets for capturing bats. More recently, the western yellow bat (*Lasiurus xanthinus*) was documented from four different localities in western Texas and represents a species that is clearly expanding its distribution northward from Mexico.

Probably the most remarkable discovery of a new species of mammal during the last century was the documentation by Fred Stangl of Midwestern University of a third species of cotton rat (*Sigmodon fulviventer,* the tawny-bellied cotton rat) from an isolated population near Fort Davis in Jeff Davis County. The species was previously known only from southeastern Arizona and southwestern New Mexico. At this time, the extent of the tawny-bellied cotton rat's range and relative abundance in Texas remain unknown.

The twentieth century also saw a dramatic shift in the philosophy for classifying mammals for the purpose of taxonomic designation. With the advent of modern techniques of genetics and molecular biology in the latter three decades of the century, new tools have become available to measure genetic (and evolutionary) relatedness among populations. These techniques allow scientists to study chromosomes (called karyology) and the sequence of genes in animals. Likewise, new sophisticated techniques of statistics have allowed for more refined assessments of morphology (called morphometrics) among populations of mammals.

Using these new techniques, we have learned of many situations where populations have diverged substantially in their chromosomes and genes but have undergone little, if any, morphological change. These populations are referred to as cryptic species, meaning they cannot easily be differentiated on the basis of observed morphological characteristics, although they are genetically distinct and reproductively isolated, thus meeting the basic requirement for biological species distinctness. To the contrary, other cases have been described where populations very different from one another morphologically (different enough to be called separate species) are in fact almost identical genetically and thus are fully capable of interbreeding and producing viable offspring. Modern taxonomists typically arrange such populations as different subspecies of the same species.

The best example of cryptic species is represented by the pocket gophers of the genus *Geomys*. Recent studies by specialists trained in cytological and molecular taxonomy have revealed the existence of five species of pocket gophers ranging over what was formerly considered the range of *G. bursarius*. These species (plains pocket gopher, *G. bursarius;* Attwater's pocket gopher, *G. attwateri;* Baird's pocket gopher, *G. breviceps;* Jones's pocket gopher, *G. knoxjonesi;* and Llano pocket gopher, *G. texensis*) are considered cryptic species, meaning they cannot be easily differentiated on the basis of observed morphological characteristics although they are genetically distinct and reproductively isolated. Although all of the species appear to be allopatric in range, karyotypic, electrophoretic, and mitochondrial DNA data are required to distinguish questionable specimens with confidence.

Similar instances of such cryptic species have now been discovered in several other groups of rodents, including deer mice, grasshopper mice, pocket mice, kangaroo rats, shrews of the genus *Blarina,* and dolphins of the genus *Stenella.* These types of discoveries, resulting from taxonomic revisions, account for much of the change in the taxonomy and classification of mammals during the twentieth century.

One of the best examples of the opposite situation (where new taxonomic approaches have resulted in a combining of species formerly considered to be distinct and separate) is the case of the arid-land foxes of the genus *Vulpes.* For most of the last century, arid-land foxes were regarded as comprising two similar but separate species, the swift fox (*Vulpes velox*) and the kit fox (*Vulpes macrotis*), and that was the arrangement used by Bailey. A recent taxonomic study of these foxes using advanced morphometric and protein-electrophoretic methods concluded, however, that the taxa are not sufficiently distinct to warrant separate species status. Thus, the two foxes are now grouped into a single species, *Vulpes velox,* comprising two subspecies, *V. v. velox* from the Panhandle and adjacent areas and *V. v. macrotis* from the Trans-Pecos.

Similarly, Jerry Dragoo of the University of New Mexico, Rodney Honeycutt of Texas A&M University, and I recently examined the taxonomic status of the hog-nosed skunks (genus *Conepatus*). Two species of hog-nosed skunks have been recognized in Texas, *C. mesoleucus* in western Texas and the Hill Country and *C. leuconotus* along the Texas coast. Using external and cranial morphology as well as mitochondrial DNA sequences, we have concluded that hog-nosed skunks are represented by only a single species, for which the taxonomic name *Conepatus leuconotus* has priority. The former designation of *Conepatus mesoleucus* for the hog-nosed skunks of western and central Texas is no longer valid.

Finally, our understanding of higher taxa (above the species level) of mammals is being challenged by molecular genetics. Studies of gene sequences, subjected to phylogenetic analysis, are revealing different genera and even families of mammals. A classic example in Texas is represented by the big-eared bats of the genus *Plecotus*. In the earliest editions of *The Mammals of Texas* these bats were arranged in the genus *Corynorhinus*, reflecting a division of the New World big-eared bats from the Old World big-eared bats of the genus *Plecotus*. Then, for reasons of morphological similarity, Charles Handley of the National Museum of Natural History lumped the two genera together and placed all species in the genus *Plecotus*. For the next several editions of *The Mammals of Texas*, the two Texas species were arranged in that genus. In 1992, however, a phylogenetic analysis of 25 morphological and 11 karyological characters suggested that *Corynorhinus* should be afforded generic distinction from *Plecotus*, and more recently, a sequence analysis of mitochondrial genes has provided additional support for that taxonomic interpretation. Thus, in this edition of *The Mammals of Texas* the Texas species are once again placed in the genus *Corynorhinus*. We can expect more of these kinds of classification revisions as our knowledge of mammalian gene sequences increases.

Growth in the Number of Threatened, Endangered, and Rare Species

Several land mammals are viewed as having some sort of biological problem that threatens or potentially threatens their existence. These are species that, in the opinion of biologists and conservation groups, currently face or likely will face serious conservation problems in the future.

Many of the species in jeopardy share life history attributes that make them especially vulnerable to local extinction events. Some species, such as bats, have low reproductive rates, which means they are slow to recover from population declines caused either by catastrophic events or by habitat destruction. Others, such as many of the carnivores and larger herbivores, are large in body size and have an extensive home range, which coupled with low population densities and their trophic level makes them highly vulnerable to human disturbance. Many have a confined geographic range, limited to a handful of places, which makes them highly vulnerable to local extinction events. Another category of vulnerability includes those species dependent on some highly specialized but scarce resource. The organism may be a masterpiece of adaptation, but it is vulnerable because of one requirement within its habitat that must be met.

State and federal agencies as well as private organizations have developed lists of rare and endangered mammals. The U.S. Fish and Wildlife Service (USFWS) publishes a list of endangered and threatened species that includes mammals listed in these categories in the Federal Register, and the Texas Parks and Wildlife Department (TPWD) has a list of protected nongame wildlife. They are the official lists governed by federal and state law, statutes, and regulations.

The legal protection of plants and animals considered to be endangered or threatened was not an issue during the time of Bailey and the federal agents. The concept of federal and state laws to protect wildlife was just taking root at the beginning of the twentieth century. It was only in the latter half of the century that federal and state laws were developed to protect nongame animal species, including invertebrates, and also plants. The first federal legislation in this area was the Endangered Species Preservation Act of 1966, replaced soon thereafter by the Endangered Species Act of 1969 and culminating in congressional passage of the Endangered Species Act of 1973, which was subsequently reauthorized in 1988 and amended in 1992 and 1996.

According to the USFWS, Texas ranks sixth in the nation in terms of the number of endangered species living within its borders. Forty-five animals and 27 plants protected under the Endangered Species Act have been recorded from Texas, a number that reflects the state's large size, diverse array of habitats, and growing development pressures. According to a 1994 report, 39 percent of the endangered plant and animal species found in Texas are still declining, only 24 percent are judged to be improving or stable, and for the remaining 37 percent the USFWS lacks the resources to determine how they are faring.

In 1973 the Texas Legislature authorized the Texas Parks and Wildlife Department to establish a list of endangered and threatened animals in the state. Currently, TPWD lists 32 terrestrial Texas vertebrates as endangered and 70 as threatened.

Mammals included in the federal and state lists are distributed throughout the state as well as our coastal and offshore waters (see Table 2). There is no obvious geographic pattern or concentration of occurrence of these species, suggesting that the conservation pressures on our rare and endangered resources are statewide and not just regional or local in nature. Rare mammals occur in 54 of the 91 plant communities in Texas. Thirteen plant communities contain state or federal endangered mammals. These results demonstrate that no single habitat can be targeted for conservation of rare mammals in Texas.

Seven land mammals currently are listed as endangered in Texas by both the USFWS and TPWD. Three of them (the Mexican long-nosed bat, the ocelot, and the jaguarundi) still have extant populations in the state. The other four species (red wolf, gray wolf, black-footed ferret, and jaguar) listed as endangered by both agencies are now extinct in Texas.

Eight species of mammals are regarded as threatened by the TPWD: southern yellow bat, spotted bat, Rafinesque's big-eared bat, Texas kangaroo rat, Coues's rice rat, black bear, white-nosed coati, and margay. The margay is now extinct in Texas. The grizzly bear is listed as threatened by the USFWS, but it also is now extinct in Texas.

Three extant taxa of Texas mammals have been considered candidates for listing as endangered or threatened on the federal list. They are the Davis Mountains cottontail, the eastern hog-nosed skunk (now considered to be conspecific with the western hog-nosed skunk), and the swift fox. Table 2 in the 1994 edition of this book listed six mammals (Mexican long-tongued bat, *Choeronycteris mexicana;* southeastern myotis, *Myotis austroriparius;* southwestern little brown bat, *Myotis occultus;* northern long-eared myotis, *Myotis septentrionalis;* western mastiff bat, *Eumops perotis;* and the yellow-nosed cotton rat, *Sigmodon ochrognathus*) as Category 2 species in the USFWS list, meaning that the information at hand indicated it was possibly appropriate to list the species as endangered or threatened but that substantial biological data were not available to support a proposed ruling. The 1996 Endangered Species Act, as amended, dissolved Category 2 and moved these taxa to the Candidate Species list, which is why they have not been included in Table 2 of the new edition.

There are several species of terrestrial mammals, or populations thereof, in Texas that may well warrant protection in the future. Certainly their situation bears watching; in some cases, considerable additional data are needed to establish the facts necessary to arrive at a meaningful and biologically defensible position as to their status. Species and subspecies of concern include Elliot's short-tailed shrew, *Blarina hylophaga;* southeastern myotis, *Myotis austroriparius;* western red bat, *Lasiurus blossevillii;* western yellow bat, *Lasiurus xanthinus;* western mastiff bat, *Eumops perotis;* pocketed free-tailed bat, *Nyctinomops femorosaccus;* big free-tailed bat, *Nyctinomops macrotis;* gray-footed chipmunk, *Tamias canipes;* Attwater's pocket gopher, *Geomys attwateri;* Strecker's pocket gopher, *Geomys streckeri;* a subspecies of Texas pocket gopher, *Geomys personatus maritimus;* two subspecies of Botta's pocket gopher, *Thomomys bottae limpiae* and *T. b. texensis;* the Pecos River muskrat, *Ondatra zibethicus ripensis;* northern rock mouse, *Peromyscus nasutus;* river otter, *Lontra canadensis;* hooded skunk, *Mephitis macroura;* western spotted skunk, *Spilogale gracilis;* and eastern spotted skunk, *Spilogale putorius.* A more thorough discussion of the status of these mammals is provided in my book *Texas Natural History: A Century of Change.*

Introductions of Nonindigenous Species

Throughout this century a number of species have been introduced into the state, including exotic mammals (rodents and ungulates), birds, fish, and insects. The character and composition of the fauna have changed substantially as a result of these biological invaders.

Early explorers and settlers brought Old World rats (genus *Rattus*) and mice (genus *Mus*) to the United States. The red fox was introduced for sporting purposes into eastern and central Texas during the 1890s. Since 1900, however, the number of mammals introduced has increased at a staggering rate. These introduced mammals include the nutria (*Myocastor coypus*), feral hog (*Sus scrofa*), and numerous species of ungulates native to Asia and Africa. During the 1990s, a colony of feral Japanese snow monkeys (*Macaca fuscata*) even became established in south Texas.

Texas has the most widespread and abundant populations of nonindigenous ungulates within the United States. The number of species and their populations has proliferated since their first known introduction on the King Ranch in southern Texas in the late 1920s. Landowner and hunter interest in stocking exotic game has grown rapidly in recent years in response to the potential economic return to landowners, the aesthetic value of the animals, and the demand for recreational harvest opportunities for these species.

From 1963 to 1988, the exotic population in Texas grew from about 14,000 animals of 13 species to more than 164,000 animals and 67 species. In 1994 Texas was home to about 195,000 exotic animals and 71 species. The estimated population of free-ranging exotics in 1994 was about 77,000 (39 percent of total) with 50 percent in the Edwards Plateau and 42 percent in the South Texas Plains, respectively.

Among the numerous exotic ungulates, six species have such large populations in a free-living condition that they must now be considered permanent additions to our mammal fauna, and accounts for these species are provided in this book.

Ranching of exotics has become a significant source of revenue for landowners, but there is considerable concern among game biologists and mammalogists about the long-term effects of these introduced animals on native wildlife. This controversy pits the private sector, eager to diversify its agricultural base, against traditional sportsmen and government agencies, worried about how such activities may threaten indigenous free-ranging wildlife, particularly ungulates and their habitat.

Some of the issues that concern conservationists and wildlife professionals about wildlife ranching and farming include disease-related interactions between commercial livestock and native animals, competitive interactions between native and exotic big game, and potential consequences of interbreeding between native and exotic big game, which could alter the genetic makeup of affected populations. There are also indications that high densities of exotic ungulates, combined with overgrazing by native deer and livestock, may severely damage rare native plants. Certainly, exotics are here to stay, but their presence challenges Texas wildlife managers to minimize habitat degradation, disease, competition, and possibly hybridization with native wildlife while at the same time retaining the economic and aesthetic attraction of such introductions. These issues emerged in the latter half of the twentieth century, but they loom even larger for the twenty-first century.

The only example of a nonindigenous marine mammal is the California sea lion (*Zalophus californicus*), which was introduced to the Gulf by humans, but no verified sightings have been reported since 1972.

HISTORY OF MAMMALOGY IN TEXAS

During the time that Bailey and the federal agents worked in Texas there were no professionally trained mammalogists living in the state. A number of private citizens called themselves amateur naturalists, and they collaborated with the federal agents. The person who came the closest to being an expert was probably H. P. Attwater from San Antonio. Mr. Attwater made extensive collections in the regions about San Antonio and Aransas Pass and discovered a number of new forms (including Attwater's prairie chicken) that were described by Dr. J. A. Allen in various bulletins of the American Museum of Natural History.

Vernon Bailey's 1905 publication was the first comprehensive study of mammals in the state and set the stage for further studies of their distribution, taxonomy, and natural history. An updated checklist was published in 1926 by John K. Strecker, curator of the museum at Baylor University, but the progress of mammalogy in Texas was slow for the first three decades of the twentieth century. It was not until the decade of the Great Depression that the science started in earnest again. During the latter half of the twentieth century, the science of mammalogy exploded in Texas as a major field of research and education. A detailed account of this history, including the major events and the many individuals who made significant contributions to it, is beyond the scope of this book, but highlights of the subject can be found in several of the sources listed in Appendix 3.

Among the most significant developments, the following are especially noteworthy:

- The establishment of the Cooperative Wildlife Research Unit at Texas A&M in 1935, under the leadership of Walter P. Taylor, which was the first organized research unit to study wildlife management in the state.
- The establishment of the Department of Fish and Game (now the Department of Wildlife and Fisheries Sciences) at Texas A&M in 1937, which began, under the direction of William B. Davis, to train graduate and undergraduate students in mammalogy and started the Texas Cooperative Wildlife Collections, the first major collection of mammals in the state.
- The publication of *The Mammals of Texas* in 1947 by Walter Taylor and William B. Davis, the first comprehensive survey of Texas mammals since Bailey's 1905 publication. The publication was revised three times by William B. Davis (1960, 1966, and 1974), once by Davis and Schmidly (1994), and again in this current account.
- The establishment of the Museum and the Natural Science Research Laboratory at Texas Tech University in 1971. Texas Tech has now become the leading center for the study of mammals in the state, and it houses the state's largest scientific collection of mammals. The *Occasional Papers* and the *Special Publications of the Museum,* both produced at Texas Tech, have become the leading publication outlets for mammalian natural history studies. As of 2001, more than 215 scientific papers on mammalogy have

been published in these two outlets. The leaders in the establishment of this program were Robert L. Packard, Robert J. Baker, J. Knox Jones, Jr., Clyde Jones, and Dilford Carter.

- In 1990 the Texas Cooperative Fish and Wildlife Research Unit was reopened at Texas Tech University, and in 1993 this lab affiliated with the nationwide Gap Analysis Program (GAP). Gap Analysis was begun by the USFWS in 1989 as a protocol to identify geographic areas with important wildlife and habitat attributes in need of protection. Using geographic information system technology, a statewide database has been developed that represents vegetation communities, terrestrial vertebrate distributions, and boundaries of federal and state conservation areas. GAP is intended to provide resource managers with the most advanced and comprehensive tools to prioritize land use and conservation decisions.

- The establishment of the marine mammal stranding network and the research and graduate education program at Texas A&M University at Galveston. This is the largest academic research program in the world devoted to the study of whales, dolphins, and manatees. The Stranding Network, established in 1974, has collected information on more than 1,000 marine mammals that have washed ashore on Texas beaches during the last three decades of the century. The key people who helped establish the marine mammal program in Galveston were myself, William Merrill, Bernd Würsig, Bill Evans, Randy Davis, and Graham Worthy.

With the explosion of trained scientific talent in mammalogy, including both terrestrial and marine forms, academic institutions all across the state began to hire mammalogists and make the subject an important area of research and education. Almost every university in Texas, both public and private, has at one time or another employed a mammalogist and offered an academic course on the subject. More recently, mammalogists have been employed by state and federal governmental agencies responsible for natural resource management in the state (e.g., the Texas Parks and Wildlife Department, the U.S. Fish and Wildlife Service, and the National Park Service) as well as many nongovernmental organizations (e.g., the Nature Conservancy of Texas and Bat Conservation International).

The literature about mammalogy in Texas grew exponentially throughout the last century. Students and professionals working in the state published several thousand scientific papers about Texas mammals. A comprehensive list of these papers was compiled in 1962, and the list has been updated every subsequent decade.

The twentieth century also witnessed the growth of collections of mammals in Texas. The major collections, with more than 70,000 specimens, are located at

Texas Tech and Texas A&M. The collection at Texas Tech recently reached 100,000 specimens, including 30,000 specimens with frozen tissues available for genetic study. Collections of more than 10,000 specimens are housed at Midwestern State University and Angelo State University.

The crowning achievement in the growth of mammalogy in Texas was the establishment of a separate scientific society, the Texas Society of Mammalogists, in 1981. The late Robert L. Packard of Texas Tech University was the lead organizer of the society. Texas is the only state in the United States with a state scientific society devoted to mammalogy, and there are more professional mammalogists living in Texas than in any other state in the United States.

The mission of the Texas Society of Mammalogists, as stated in its constitution, is to "promote the study of mammals, living and fossil" in Texas. Beginning in 1983, the society has met in February of every year at the site of Texas Tech's Junction Campus in Kimble County. Mammalogists and students from throughout the state convene and present papers and hold discussions about the biology and conservation of Texas mammals. The membership of the Texas Society of Mammalogists now numbers approximately 240.

Clearly, Bailey and the federal agents planted a seed that would grow into a major scientific field of study. They probably had no idea this would happen, but it is almost certain they would be pleased with the outcome. The scope of the science of mammalogy and the scientific talent available in the state will be crucial to our ability to manage and conserve mammalian species and communities wisely in the twenty-first century.

CONSERVATION STRATEGIES

The twentieth century proved as significant for changes made by humans in the landscape—its soils, waters, atmosphere, climate, habitats, and wildlife—as for its technological advancements. The risks as we progress through the twenty-first century are not just the extinction or restriction of wildlife; there are serious economic ramifications associated with the continued loss of biological diversity. As species disappear, the human capacity to maintain and enhance agricultural, forest, and rangeland productivity decreases, and with the degradation of ecosystems, the valuable services that natural and seminatural systems provide will be lost.

It seems inevitable that the twenty-first century will be as different from the twentieth century as the twentieth century was from the nineteenth, perhaps more so given the accelerating pace of change in lifestyle and technology. The next hundred years is likely to decide the future of wildlife in Texas and other states. Decisions will be made, directly or indirectly, as to how much and what kind of nature survives. Conservation pressures in the next century will come from a variety of sources. Habitat loss, fragmentation, and degradation are the most important causes of wildlife decline, but overharvesting and poaching, trade in wild animal products, introduction of exotic species, pollution from pesticides and her-bicides, and other causes also take a significant toll. Global warming or climate change could exacerbate the loss and degradation of biodiversity by increasing the rate of species extinction, changing population sizes and species distributions, modifying the composition of habitats and ecosystems, and altering their geo-graphic extent.

Essentially the problem centers on proliferating human populations and asso-ciated land conversion, which is powerfully changing the form and shape of the landscape. People now constitute a pressure on the global environment that is evident everywhere. There are no longer any unoccupied frontiers; every square centimeter of the earth's surface is affected by the activities of human beings. This results in insufficient habitat for many species or situations in which habitats are isolated in separate pieces too small or too unstable to sustain viable popula-tions of species and thus biological diversity. The theory of biogeography reveals that species richness is a function of land area. All environmental variables being equal, the greater area, the more species it supports. Thus, as habitats are fragmented and isolated into small islands, they lose the capacity to support wildlife diversity.

A recent study conducted by scientists associated with the United Nations Environment Program (UNEP) has estimated that almost a quarter of the world's mammals, approximately 1,130 species, could face extinction within 30 years. The loss of habitats by human encroachment is largely responsible for the predicament faced by 83 percent of the threatened mammals listed in the report. The report concludes that all the factors that have led to the extinction of species in recent decades continue to operate with "ever-increasing" intensity.

Texas has a great treasure in its mammalian fauna, which provides our citizens with important recreational, commercial, aesthetic, and scientific values. The state is home to more than 20 percent of the nation's total deer population, over three-quarters of the carnivore species, and all but ten species of bats that occur in the United States. The question is whether these resources can be sustained in the future. For that to happen, we must employ several conservation strategies. It has become clear in most cases that single approaches will not work successfully to conserve wildlife diversity. We must build long-range thinking and planning into conservation, and we must find ways for diverse groups, including state and fed-eral agencies, academic institutions, private landowners and organizations, and public groups to network and explore new collaborative ventures that bring sepa-rate approaches together in a complementary way. The challenge is daunting. We face a monumental task, far beyond our existing abilities, but now is the time to look ahead, coordinate and plan, before our options are further narrowed.

There are hundreds of resource-based natural areas in Texas that potentially could serve as biological reserves for the protection of species and the supporting environment. They include national parks, forests, preserves, and recreation areas; national wildlife refuges; state wildlife management areas; state parks, natural areas, and historic sites; and local parks (including cities, counties, and river authorities). More than four million acres of land are contained in these units, which are distributed throughout the state and provide habitat for most Texas mammals. In addition, several private conservation organizations, most notably the Nature Conservancy of Texas, have land acquisition programs for conservation. Over a ten-year period, Nature Conservancy holdings grew from about 20,000 acres to almost 250,000 acres.

Although protected areas play a key role in the preservation of natural diversity, their ability to preserve our mammalian fauna is limited and sometimes overestimated. Their capacity for preservation is restricted by a number of internal and external factors. First, the parks and preserves of Texas are scattered throughout the state, but the geographical distribution is far from proportional. Thus, many of the natural areas in Texas, such as native grasslands and prairies, are poorly represented. Second, most protected areas are too small and widely scattered to preserve biological diversity effectively. A 1987 publication in the scientific journal *Nature* concluded that the fourteen largest national parks in western North America were too small to retain an intact mammalian fauna. No protected area in Texas is as large as the smallest of the fourteen parks used in that study. Thus, a major goal of conservation must be to expand the number of protected areas to include a cross-section of all major ecosystems in the state and to link them via conservation corridors so they are more effective.

Protected areas alone, however, will not be sufficient to conserve mammalian diversity in Texas. To be effective in the long term, conservation strategies must consider the needs of local residents to maintain or enhance their quality of life. For that reason, conservation-based rural development is indispensable to any successful conservation strategy in Texas. With about 94 percent of the state in private land, it will not be possible to conserve mammalian diversity in Texas without the support and participation of landowners. In order to retain the stability and diversity of this habitat, it must be managed and utilized by landowners in an economically and ecologically viable manner. A system of responsible wildlife management, sportsmanship, and land ethics must be developed. Aldo Leopold, the father of American conservation, recognized this more than 50 years ago when he wrote about the need to recognize the landowner as the custodian of public game on all private lands and to compensate landowners for putting land in productive condition by making game management a partnership enterprise so that the landowner, the sportsman, and the public each contribute appropriate services as well as deriving appropriate rewards.

A basic weakness in a conservation system based wholly on economic motives is that most species of a land community have no economic value. Without a land ethic and a stewardship concern for the diversity and integrity of the land, landowners will favor those management practices that make the most money without a consideration of the whole biotic system. Landowner rights and wildlife management, including the protection of endangered species, can and must be integrated to achieve effective conservation of mammals in Texas. We must learn to manage the landscape for sustained local diversity, maintenance of ecosystem function, and renewable yields of natural resources for economic development.

Texas has one of the most aggressive landowner assistance programs in the nation. Several state and federal agencies, as well as private organizations, offer incentive programs that provide technical or cost-share assistance to private landowners for voluntarily enrolling environmentally sensitive land or wildlife habitat in conservation programs to protect or enhance natural resources. Such programs might include anything from advice about cross-fencing to habitat restoration for endangered species. Texas Parks and Wildlife has been particularly aggressive in fostering landowner assistance programs, with almost 15 million acres of private land being managed under individually tailored wildlife management plans designed and shepherded by state employees. Other tools that are gaining popularity among landowners as we enter the twenty-first century include land trusts and conservation easements. Collectively these various programs provide some sort of wildlife management to almost 16 million acres of land in Texas. Given that agriculture is the prevalent land use on approximately 136 million acres of Texas lands, representing about 81 percent of the state's total land area, almost 12 percent of the state's available acreage is under some form of wildlife management. As we look to the future, there is a need for even more programs designed to encourage private landowners to practice conservation.

We also must improve our biological knowledge about mammals. We know precious little of the life history of most mammals in Texas. In fact, for many species, our knowledge is insufficient even to assess their status accurately. Decisions as to whether a species is threatened, rare, or endangered are often based entirely on biological guesswork without proper knowledge of the population dynamics, reproduction, food habits, or behavior of the species considered. Future research efforts, whether they involve biologists working for state and federal agencies or scientists associated with academic institutions, should focus on correcting those omissions.

Conserving wildlife, which recognizes neither ownership nor boundaries, calls for good science, first-rate technology, excellent management, and a broad constituency willing to make some concessions to save it. Whether we act, and how, will depend on factors such as politics, education, socioeconomics, recreation interests, and planning capabilities. Broad-based conservation education programs, designed to diffuse conservation information to the public, must become an important priority. Without an understanding of the need for action, and without a commitment to that action, citizens will not contribute to the effort, nor will they cooperate with those so engaged. People must be educated to understand what the continuation—or destruction—of wildlife means to their future and that of their descendants, and they must be persuaded to act on their resulting concern in ways respectful to the diversity of wildlife and to their own cultural values.

KEY TO THE MAJOR GROUPS (ORDERS) OF MAMMALS IN TEXAS

1. Body covered dorsally, and tail completely, by bands of bony plates; snout tapering and lacking teeth anteriorly; eight peglike teeth on each side of upper and lower jaws. Order Xenarthra, armadillos, sloths, and allies, p. 43.

   Not as above 2

2. Body torpedo-shaped; hind legs absent; front limbs developed into paddles; hairless or nearly so; live in ocean or coastal waters 3

   Not as above 4

3. Body ending in a broad, horizontally flattened, rounded fluke; no dorsal fin; muzzle squarish, covered with stout bristles; short bristle-like hairs scattered sparingly over rest of body; nostrils terminal; length 2.5 to 4.5 m. Order Sirenia, manatees and allies, p. 254.

   Body ending in horizontal, expanded (not rounded) flukes; blowhole (nostrils) on top of head; most Texas forms with dorsal fin; length 2.5 to 30 m. Order Cetacea, whales, porpoises, and dolphins, p. 211.

4. Hand and arm developed into leathery wing. Order Chiroptera, bats, p. 62.

   Hand and arm normal, not developed into a wing 5

5. Hoofed mammals; two, three, or four toes on each foot. Order Artiodactyla, even-toed ungulates, p. 256.

   Toes usually armed with claws, not hooves 6

6. Total of 10 upper incisors; big toe of hind foot without claw; tail prehensile. Order Didelphimorphia, opossums, p. 38.

   Total of six or fewer upper incisors; all toes armed with claws; tail not prehensile 7

7. Snout highly flexible and protruding conspicuously beyond mouth; eyes very small or hidden; length of head and body usually less than 150 mm. Order Insectivora, shrews and moles, p. 49.

   Snout normal, or if protruding conspicuously then length of head and body much more than 150 mm; eyes normal 8

8. Total of two incisors in lower jaw, one on each side 9

   Total of four or more incisors in lower jaw (two or three on each side). Order Carnivora, carnivores, p. 137.

9. Total of two incisors in the upper jaw, one on each side so that incisor formula is 1/1. Order Rodentia, rodents, p. 295.

   Total of four incisors in the upper jaw, two on each side, one in front of the other in tandem; incisor formula 2/1. Order Lagomorpha, hares and rabbits, p. 458.

ORDER DIDELPHIMORPHIA
Opossums and Allies

T he order Didelphimorphia is the only representative of the subclass Marsupialia in North America. Opossums, as a group, are among the oldest, most primitive mammals of the New World. Some scientists call them living fossils because they have survived relatively unchanged for at least 50 million years. They are intermediate in many respects between the most primitive of all mammals, the egg-laying monotremes of Australia, and the higher placental mammals. Their chief character is the marsupium, or pouch, that develops on the abdomen of females.

FAMILY DIDELPHIDAE (OPOSSUMS)

The family Didelphidae is a distinctive component of the New World fauna and the only family in the order Didelphimorphia. The family is represented by 16 genera and 67 species. Most members of the family, however, occur in the tropical and sub-tropical regions of Central and South America. The Virginia opossum is a unique exception—it is the only marsupial to occur in North America north of Mexico.

Virginia Opossum (*Didelphis virginiana*). Photo by John and Gloria Tveten.

Virginia Opossum, black color phase. Photo by John and Gloria Tveten.

All species of this family are small to medium in size, and most, including the Virginia opossum, are characterized by the external pouch, or marsupium, in which they carry their young during early postnatal development. Most species are nocturnal or crepuscular, solitary, and omnivorous.

Virginia Opossum
Didelphis virginiana Kerr

Description.   A mammal about the size of a terrier dog, with long, scaly, prehensile tail; short, black, leathery ears; long, slender snout; five toes on each foot, the big toe on hind foot lacking a claw, thumblike and opposable; soles naked; pouch for young developed during breeding season on abdomen of female; pelage of long guard hairs and short soft underfur; two color phases, grayish and blackish; basal fourth or more of tail black, terminal section whitish; legs and feet blackish; toes often white or whitish. Dental formula: I 5/4, C 1/1, Pm 3/3, M 4/4 x 2 = 50. External measurements of males average: total length, 782 mm; tail, 324 mm; hind foot, 66 mm; of females, 710-320-63. Weight, 1.8–4.5 kg; males are usually larger and heavier than females.

Distribution.   Occurs statewide except for the most xeric areas of the Trans-Pecos.
Subspecies.   *D. v. virginiana* in northern and central Texas and *D. v. pigra* in the
south and southeast.
Habits.   Opossums are primarily inhabitants of deciduous woodlands but are
often found in prairies, marshes, and farmlands. In the western part of their native
range they generally keep to the woody vegetation along streams and rivers, a
habit that permits them to penetrate the otherwise treeless grasslands and deserts
of west Texas.

Hollow trees and logs are preferred sites, but opossums will den in woodpiles,
rock piles, crevices in cliffs, under buildings, in attics, and in underground burrows. Since they are not adept at digging burrows for themselves they make use of
those excavated by other mammals.

Movements of opossums monitored in East Texas showed that these animals
typically frequent a home range approximately 4.6 ha in size, although the mini-
mum size of home ranges may vary from 0.12 ha to 23.4 ha. Home ranges tend to

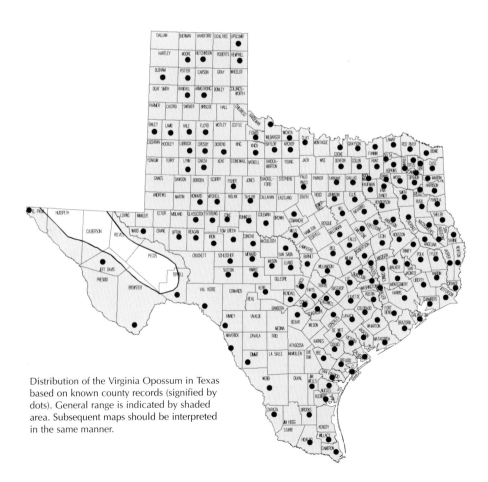

Distribution of the Virginia Opossum in Texas
based on known county records (signified by
dots). General range is indicated by shaded
area. Subsequent maps should be interpreted
in the same manner.

Newborn opossums. Photo by John Wood, courtesy Texas Parks and Wildlife Department.

overlap considerably. In East Texas woodland habitat the density of opossums is about one opossum every 1.6 ha, but in sandy, coastal parts of the state the density is about one opossum every 6 ha.

The opossum is more or less solitary and strictly nocturnal, venturing forth to feed shortly after dark. It feeds on a variety of foods, including rats, mice, young rabbits, birds, insects, crustaceans, frogs, fruits, and vegetables. Analyses of six stomachs from winter-trapped opossums in Texas revealed that the following foods (expressed in percentages) had been eaten: insects (grasshoppers, crickets, beetles, bugs, ants), 62.8; mammals (cottontails), 19.5; birds (sparrow family), 15.5; reptiles (lizards and snakes), 1.0; mollusks (snails), 1.0; crustacea (crayfish), 0.2. In June the food for four opossums was about the same except that fruits and berries were added and birds were lacking.

Their mating season extends from January or February to June or July. Females, which are in heat for about 30 days, breed the first season following birth. The mating period is not longer than 36 hours and terminates with copulation, which is done in a manner similar to dogs. Young opossums have been observed as early as 24 January and as late as 15 August. Usually two litters are produced, one in February and one in June. The young, 5 to 21 in number, are born after a gestation of 11–12 days and each weighs about 3 grains (one-fifth of a gram, or one-2,380th of a pound!). Blind, nearly helpless, hardly larger than honeybees, and embryonic in appearance, they crawl unaided into the abdominal pouch of the mother, each attaching itself to a nipple. Shortly after a young one begins to nurse, the nipple swells and completely fills its mouth, thereby firmly attaching it to its mother. It remains attached until it is about 7 weeks of age, at which time it has grown large enough to detach itself. This peculiar adaptation compensates in part for the brief period of uterine development and assumes part of the function performed by the placenta in higher mammals. Since the number of teats is seldom more than 13, young born in excess of that number are doomed to die.

Mortality is high during the first year of life, and population turnover is relatively rapid. Known predators include foxes, coyotes, horned owls, and barred owls. Opossums are commonly seen killed on highways. The normal life span may be as short as 2 years.

The opossum is the third most commonly harvested fur-bearing animal in Texas, but the value of its pelt is low. During the 1999–2000 season, the average value of an opossum pelt was only 50 cents. Many trappers do not consider opossums worth skinning out. Their fur is used primarily for trim on less expensive coats and hats.

Conservation Status.   The opossum appears to be in good shape in Texas. By dispersing along streams and rivers, it expanded its range throughout the twentieth century, and it adapts well to most human conditions.

ORDER XENARTHRA
Armadillos, Sloths, and Allies

Thurs order seems to have developed in South America and only recently invaded North America. Its members are bizarre creatures and highly specialized in structure and habits. The toothless anteaters are provided with heavy claws to tear apart termite nests and a long, slender, protrusible, sticky tongue to capture the insects. The slow-moving, plant-eating sloths are tree dwellers, with a rudimentary tail and only two or three toes on each foot. In the large group of armadillos, the presence of a bony carapace is unique among mammals.

FAMILY DASYPODIDAE (ARMADILLOS)

The Dasypodidae comprises 8 genera and 20 species, and most are restricted to tropical regions of Central and South America. Only one species, the nine-banded armadillo, ranges north to the United States, and because of its uniqueness has been designated the official state small mammal of Texas. Armadillos are characterized by their bony carapace, which is a series of plates interspersed with more flexible skin, thus allowing the animals to move about in normal mammalian fashion. The species of this family range in size from 125 mm to almost a meter. Most armadillos have small ears and relatively long snouts, with small peglike teeth and a protrusible tongue. All members of this family are terrestrial and usually solitary in nature. They feed primarily on insects, invertebrates, and some plant material.

Nine-banded Armadillo (*Dasypus novemcinctus*). Photo by John and Gloria Tveten.

Nine-banded Armadillo

Dasypus novemcinctus Linnaeus

Description.   About the size of a terrier dog, upperparts encased in a bony cara-pace with large shields on shoulders and rump and nine bands in between; front feet with four toes, middle two longest; hind foot five-toed, the middle three longest, all provided with large, strong claws; tail long, tapering, and completely covered by bony rings; color brownish, the scattered hairs yellowish white. There are 30 or 32 peglike teeth. External measurements average: total length, 760 mm; tail, 345 mm; hind foot, 85 mm. Weight of adult males, 5–8 kg; females, 4–6 kg.

Distribution.   Occurs over most of the state, except for the western Trans-Pecos.

Subspecies.   *D. n. mexicanus.*

Habits.   Soil texture exerts a definite influence on the number of armadillos pres-ent in a given area. Those soils that are more easily dug, other factors being equal, will support a greater population density. In the sandy soils of Walker County, a

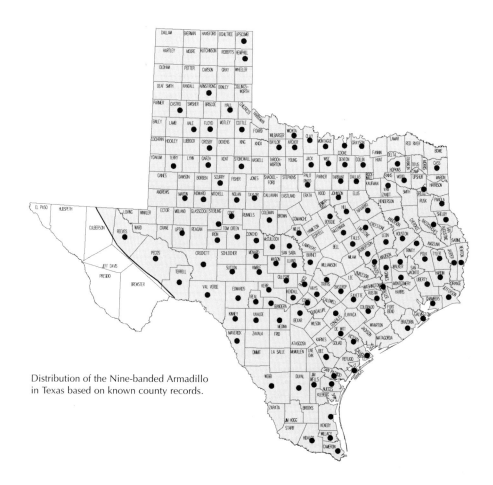

Distribution of the Nine-banded Armadillo in Texas based on known county records.

population density of about one armadillo to 1 ha is common; in Brazos County, where the soils are more heavily impregnated with clay and become packed during the dry seasons, density averages one armadillo to 4 ha; in the rocky terrain of the Edwards Plateau, the animals tend to concentrate in the alluvial stream bottoms and den in the cracks and crevices of the numerous limestone outcroppings in that area. In the blackland section of Texas, where the soils are heavy clays, the animals are extremely rare and restricted to the vicinity of streams where they can burrow into the banks and probe for food in the relatively soft soils near water. Perhaps the most important factor contributing to the distribution of armadillos is the hardness of the soil during the dry season, because the food of the animal is obtained largely by probing for insects and other forms of animal life in the ground.

Armadillos are fond of water; where climatic conditions tend to be arid, the animals concentrate in the vicinity of streams and water holes. Tracks in the mud around small ponds give evidence that the armadillos visit them not only for purposes of drinking and feeding but also to take mud baths. Excess water, however, has a limiting effect on them because they avoid marshy areas.

Few animals of comparable size have so many dens per individual as the armadillo. The length, depth, and frequency of occurrence of their burrows depend somewhat on soil conditions. In sandy areas the animals are extremely active diggers; in addition to numerous occupied burrows, one finds many that have been abandoned or are used only occasionally as shelters. In central Texas, the majority of their dens are along creek banks, whereas in the sandy soils of eastern Texas they are found almost everywhere. On the coastal prairies the sandy knolls are especially sought as den sites, more for protection from floods than for ease of digging. In the Edwards Plateau natural caves, cracks, and crevices among the limestone outcroppings afford abundant shelter; excavated burrows are few in number and usually shallow.

Dens vary from 1 to 5 m in length and from a few centimeters below the surface to a depth of 1.3 m. Averaging between 17 and 20 cm in diameter, their plan is usually simple, with few turns except those caused by obstacles such as roots, rocks, and so forth. Many of the shallow burrows serve as food traps, where insects and other invertebrates take refuge and where the armadillo visits on his foraging excursions. Burrows that are used for breeding purposes usually have a large nest chamber 45 cm or more in diameter and contain a rather loosely constructed nest of dried leaves, grasses, and other plant items. These materials are merely stuffed into the chamber, and the animal pushes its way in and out each time the nest is used. Usually, each occupied burrow is inhabited by only one adult armadillo.

Because of their almost complete lack of hairy covering, armadillos are easily affected by climatic conditions. In the summer season they are more active in the cool of the evening and at night, but in midwinter their daily activities are reversed and the animals become active during the warmest part of the day, usually in mid-afternoon. They do not hibernate, nor are they equipped to wait out long periods of inclement weather. Long periods of freezing weather effectively eliminate armadillos from an area.

Of special interest is the behavior of this animal in the water. Its specific gravity is high, and the animal normally rides low in the water when swimming. Apparently, it tires easily when forced to swim for any distance. If the stream to be crossed is not wide, the armadillo may enter on one side, walk across the bottom, and emerge on the other side. If the expanse of water to be traversed is of considerable extent, the animals ingest air, inflate themselves, and thus increase their buoyancy. The physiological mechanism by which the armadillo can ingest air and retain it in its digestive tract to increase buoyancy is not known, but it appears to be under voluntary control.

Many legends have arisen concerning the food habits of armadillos. Among the rural folks in the South they are commonly called gravediggers and are thought to dig into human graves and dine on the contents. Also, they have quite a reputation as a depredator of quail, chicken, and turkey eggs. Observations by field workers strongly indicate that the armadillo, which usually leaves conspicuous signs of its presence, often is accused of the destruction of quail and chicken nests when the culprit is actually some other animal. A study of their food habits by examination of more than 800 stomachs revealed that no fewer than 488 different food items are eaten. Ninety-three percent (by volume) of their food is animal matter, chiefly insects and other invertebrates. Among the insects, nearly 28% were larval and adult scarab beetles, forms that are highly destructive to crops and pastures; termites and ants composed about 14%; caterpillars nearly 8%; earthworms, millipedes, centipedes, and crayfish appeared conspicuously in their diet at times. Reptiles and amphibians constituted only a small part of their diet, usually captured during periods of cold weather.

Slightly less than 7% of the diet was vegetable matter, and more than two-thirds of that was material ingested with other food items and represented nothing of economic importance. Berries and fungi made up 2.1% of the entire diet. Reports indicate that at times the armadillo may feed on such fruits as tomatoes and melons, but the amount of damage done to those crops is relatively small. Carrion is readily eaten when available, and dead carcasses of animals frequently are visited not only for the carrion but also for the maggots and pupae of flies found on or near them.

Reproduction in the nine-banded armadillo is marked by two distinct and apparently unrelated phenomena: the long period of arrested development of the blastocyst prior to implantation (delayed implantation), and specific polyembryony, which results in the normal formation of identical quadruplets. In normal years about half of the females become pregnant by the end of July, which is the beginning of the breeding season. At 5–7 days the ovum forms a blastocyst and passes into the uterus. At that point development ceases, and the vesicle remains free in the uterus. Here it is constantly bathed in fluids secreted by the glandular lining of the uterus, which supplies enough nutrition and oxygen for survival. Implantation does not occur until November, about 14 weeks after fertilization. During this process, the blastocyst divides into growth centers, each of which very shortly redivides to produce four embryonic growth centers attached by a common placenta to the uterus. Development of each of the embryos then proceeds normally, and the four young are born approximately 4 months later in March, although some females have been noted with new litters as early as February and as late as the latter part of May. Young are born fully formed and with eyes open. Within a few hours they are walking, and they begin to accompany the mother on foraging expeditions within a few weeks. The nursing period is probably less than 2 months, but the young may remain with the mother even after weaning until they are several months old. Normally the young born in one year mature during the winter and mate for the first time in the early summer of the following year.

Delayed implantation may account, in part, for the successful invasion of the armadillo into temperate regions. Without this characteristic of the reproductive cycle, the young would be born at the beginning of winter, when their chance of survival would be greatly reduced. Apparently, the reproductive cycle is easily affected by adverse environmental conditions, particularly drought conditions, probably because of the shortage of ground insects or the difficulty of obtaining them in sandy or hard dried soils.

Armadillos are believed to pair for each breeding season, and a male and a female may share a burrow during the season. Because of the bony carapace and ventral position of the genitalia, copulation occurs with the female lying on her back.

Armadillos are frequently utilized as food in parts of Texas and Mexico. The meat is light colored and when properly cooked is considered by some the equal of pork in flavor and texture.

The common occurrence of this species in eastern Texas is a phenomenon that has developed largely since 1900. When Vernon Bailey published his *Biological Survey of Texas* in 1905, he mapped the distributional limits of the armadillo as between the Colorado and Guadalupe rivers with extralimital records from Colorado, Grimes, and Houston counties. By 1914 the armadillo had crossed the Brazos River and moved to the Trinity River, and along the coast had already reached the Louisiana line in Orange County. The northward and eastward range expansions continued over the next 40 years, and by 1954 the armadillo was known from everywhere in eastern Texas except Red River and Lamar counties. By 1958 it was known from those two counties as well and today is abundant everywhere in the region.

Apparently pioneering was most successful in riparian habitat, and invasion was especially rapid parallel to rivers, which served as dispersal conduits. Average invasion rates have been calculated at 4–10 km per year in the absence of obvious physical or climatic barriers. Possible reasons for the armadillo's northward expansion since the nineteenth century include progressive climatic changes, encroaching human civilization, overgrazing, and decimation of large carnivores.

Conservation Status. There is reason to be concerned about the status of this unique mammal in Texas. In 1999 Rollin Baker, a retired mammalogist living in Eagle Lake, undertook a survey of professional mammalogists in Texas and found that almost all agreed that armadillos are rare at best when compared with populations a few years ago. Baker concluded that armadillo numbers along the Texas coast are truly down, and he suggested the decline might correlate with a dramatic upsurge in the past decade of feral hogs, which may feed on newborn armadillos. Also, it has become popular for people to make jewelry and other trinkets from armadillo shells, which has likely increased the commercial harvest of the species. For those reasons, our official state small mammal deserves careful monitoring in the future.

ORDER INSECTIVORA
Shrews and Moles

The name "Insectivora," meaning "insect eater," has reference to the food habits of the group as a whole. Although moles and shrews are not all strictly insectivorous, insects and other small animal life constitute the chief dietary items of most members of the group. Some kinds, the otter shrews of Africa and the star-nosed mole of North America, for example, feed also on fish. The Townsend mole of the Pacific Northwest often is a nuisance to bulb growers because of its fondness for the bulbs of many kinds of plants.

Moles, as a group, are subterranean in habit and spend most of their lives in the darkness of underground tunnels that they usually excavate for themselves. Correlated with this fossorial habit, the eyes of all moles are very small; in some species the eyes actually do not open to the outside and are of little value to the animal. On the other hand, the senses of touch and smell are highly developed in moles.

Most North American shrews live on the surface of the ground and occupy burrows only for sleeping or resting. Most of them have a decided preference for damp or boggy habitats where rank vegetation, surface litter, rocks, or rotting logs afford adequate protection. Some species, notably the desert shrew, are adapted to the arid regions of our western deserts. At the opposite extreme are the water shrew and the marsh shrew, neither of which occurs in Texas.

Shrews and moles are active throughout the year; the former often tunnel through snow or walk on top of it in search of food. Some species, notably the short-tailed shrew, store food for winter use, but this habit is not common. Surprisingly little is known regarding the habits of many species. The exact gestation period is not known for most species, and practically nothing is known about the growth and development of the young except that they grow rapidly and reach adult proportions in about six weeks. The length of life of shrews is thought to be less than two years, but specific information is lacking.

Texas is not blessed with a rich insectivore fauna. Of the 39 species of shrews and moles in North America, only 5 (about 13%) occur in Texas—1 species of mole and 4 species of shrews.

KEY TO THE INSECTIVORES OF TEXAS

1. Front feet broad and paddle-shaped; eyes nonfunctional. *Scalopus aquaticus* (eastern mole), p. 58.

   Front feet normal, not paddle-shaped; eyes small, but functional...2

2. Total number of teeth 30 or 32 (unicuspids 4 or 5); ears nearly hidden in the fur; tail short, less than twice as long as hind foot....3

Total number of teeth 28 (unicuspids 3); ears rather conspicuous; tail more than twice as long as hind foot; total length about 80 mm. *Notiosorex crawfordi* (desert shrew), p. 56.

3. Total number of teeth 30; 4 upper unicuspids, with only 3 readily visible in lateral view; color of dorsum brownish or brownish gray. *Cryptotis parva* (least shrew), p. 54.

   Total number of teeth 32; 5 upper unicuspids, with 4 readily visible in lateral view; color of dorsum dark slate to sooty black or tinged with brown 4

4. Restricted to the pine-oak forest and pine forest regions in the eastern one-third of the state; pelage dark gray often tinged with brown; cranial breadth usually less than 10.5 mm. *Blarina carolinensis* (southern short-tailed shrew), p. 50.

   Known only from three counties in the central and coastal regions of the state; pelage not tinged with brown; cranial breadth usually greater than 10.5 mm. *Blarina hylophaga* (Elliot's short-tailed shrew), p. 53.

FAMILY SORICIDAE (SHREWS)

Shrews are characterized by their small body size and high metabolic rate. These traits force them to spend much of their time actively foraging. They are primarily insectivorous, but they are able and willing to take down whatever small prey they encounter. Some species have poisonous salivary secretions that help to subdue prey.

Shrews are nocturnal creatures, and they are usually solitary except during breeding seasons. Most shrews are terrestrial, although a few species are aquatic, and they are typically found in moist habitats.

Southern Short-tailed Shrew

Blarina carolinensis (Bachman)

Description. A rather robust, short-legged, short-tailed shrew with long, pointed, protruding snout; external ears short and nearly concealed by the soft, dense fur; tail less than half the length of head and body, usually less than twice as long as hind foot; upperparts dark slate to sooty black, often tinged with brown; underparts paler; tail black above, paler below. Dental formula: I 4/2, C 1/0, Pm 2/1, M 3/3 × 2 = 32. External measurements average: total length, 88 mm; tail, 17 mm; hind foot, 11 mm. Weight, 18–28 g.

Distribution. Eastern one-fourth of the state, with a disjunct record from Bastrop State Park (Bastrop County).

Subspecies. *B. c. carolinensis* in the northern part of the range in Texas (south at least to Nacogdoches County) and *B. c. minima* in the south.

Habits. Short-tailed shrews occur in forested areas and their associated meadows and openings. Adequate cover and food appear to be more important in determining their presence than type of soil or vegetation.

Southern Short-tailed Shrew (*Blarina carolinensis*). Photo by John and Gloria Tveten.

Their burrows usually occupy two zones, one several centimeters below the surface or directly on it and the other at a deep level, often 40–60 cm below the surface. These two levels are joined at irregular intervals. Frequently, their runs follow just beneath a log, sometimes penetrating and honeycombing the log if it is rotten and easily worked.

These creatures are short-legged and slow of gait, but they always seem to be in a hurry, running along with their tails elevated at an angle. A slow-walking person can easily overtake them. They are well adapted for digging; the front feet are wide, strong, and slightly larger than the hind feet. Burrowing is accomplished by the combined use of forefeet, head, and nose. Timed individuals were capable of burrowing at the rate of about 30 cm a minute in soft soil.

Like the least shrew (*Cryptotis*), *Blarina* seem to be more sociable than long-tailed shrews. Several individuals seem to use a common burrow system, and seldom do they fight when two or more are placed in a cage. It appears certain that the male and female remain together during the prebreeding season.

The food habits of these shrews are strangely unshrewlike in that they consume relatively large quantities of vegetable matter (nuts, berries, and so forth). Analyses of more than 400 stomachs from East Texas revealed the following items (expressed in percentages of occurrence): insects 77.6; annelids, 41.8; vegetable matter, 17.1; centipedes, 7.4; arachnids, 6.1; mollusks (mostly snails), 5.4; vertebrates (mice and salamanders), 5.2; crustacea (mostly sow bugs), 3.7; undetermined matter, 2.4. There is considerable evidence that *Blarina* stores snails for winter use.

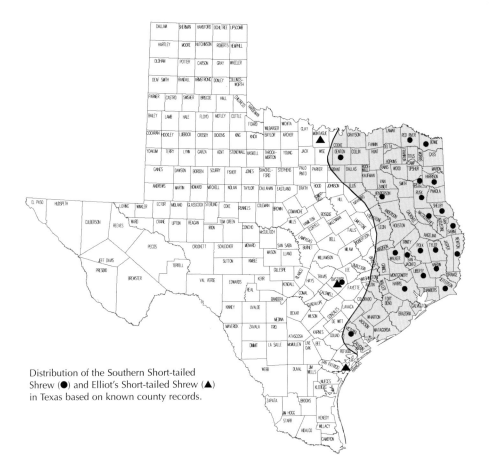

Distribution of the Southern Short-tailed Shrew (●) and Elliot's Short-tailed Shrew (▲) in Texas based on known county records.

An interesting feature of this shrew is the poison produced by the submaxillary glands, which is present in the saliva and may be introduced into wounds made by the teeth. Injections of 6 mg of an extract prepared from the submaxillary gland are strong enough to kill mice, but there is little likelihood of the venom having any serious effect on humans.

The breeding season of *Blarina* extends from February through November. There appear to be two and possibly three litters of two to six young produced in this period. The gestation period is probably between 21 and 30 days. The young are pink, blind, and helpless at birth, and they weigh slightly more than 1 g. They are relatively slow in developing; the eyes of young born in captivity were still closed on the twenty-second day. The young are born in a special nest of grasses and other dry vegetation under a rotten log or stump or under the ground; in each instance, entrance to the nest is gained by way of an underground tunnel. These nests are much larger than the more commonly found resting nests. Records indicate that very few of these shrews attain an age of 2 years.

Since the reproductive potential is high in this shrew, one can assume that its natural enemies are many. Known predators include the milk snake, black snake, red-tailed hawk, red-shouldered hawk, American kestrel, broad-winged hawk, barn owl, short-eared owl, barred owl, great horned owl, long-eared owl, screech owl, fox, weasel, and skunk. Doubtless, others could be added to the list.

Conservation Status.   This shrew is still common in the Big Thicket of southeastern Texas and appears to be in good shape there. It is rare in Bastrop County, and that population bears watching in the future.

Elliot's Short-tailed Shrew
Blarina hylophaga Elliot

Description.   Elliot's short-tailed shrew is nearly identical in appearance to the southern short-tailed shrew, *B. carolinensis;* both being tiny, slate-gray to brownish colored shrews with short tails and no external ears. *B. hylophaga* differs in having slightly larger cranial measurements and a noticeably larger fourth premolar. Also, *B. hylophaga* tends to be grayish in coloration, whereas *B. carolinensis* is often tinged with brown. Dental formula and external measurements as in *B. carolinensis.*

Distribution.   Known in Texas only from Montague, Bastrop, and Aransas counties. Pleistocene fossils of this shrew are known from cave sites throughout the Hill Country. See distribution map in the account for *Blarina carolinensis.*

Subspecies.   *B. h. hylophaga* from Montague and Bastrop counties and *B. h. plumbea* from Aransas County.

Habits.   In Aransas County, these shrews inhabit mottes of live oak trees on sandy soils, where they excavate their diminutive burrows. In Bastrop County, they have been collected in pitfall traps placed in grassy vegetation with an overstory of loblolly pine. Specimens from Montague County were obtained in a pitfall trap set in grassy vegetation several meters from some post oak trees. As with *B. carolinensis,* they may burrow extensively under leaf litter and logs and deeply into the soil, but ground cover is not required. At Aransas Wildlife Refuge their burrows may be in areas with little or no ground cover, but they are always where soft, damp soils afford easy burrowing.

As with the southern short-tailed shrew, this shrew is slightly venomous and may occasionally prey on animals larger than itself, such as mice. More frequently consumed food items are insects, arthropods, and earthworms.

Females produce one or two litters of six to seven young (on average) each year. Breeding season and reproductive habits are probably similar to *B. carolinensis.* Young are weaned and leave the nest at one month of age. *B. hylophaga* has an average life span of only 8 months.

Conservation Status.   The only place where this shrew has been taken in any numbers is in the oak mottes of the Aransas National Wildlife Refuge in Aransas County along the lower Texas coast. A number of land management practices have been instituted in that habitat, including burning, land clearing, and grazing. The potential effects of such procedures on the shrew are unknown. Given its rare status, this is a species that should be carefully monitored in the future.

Remarks. The best way to distinguish this species from its cryptic relative, *B. carolinensis,* is to study the karyotype (number and morphology of chromosomes). *B. hylophaga* has a diploid number of 52 and a fundamental number of 60, 61, or 62; *B. carolinensis* has a diploid number of 37–46 and a fundamental number of 44.

Least Shrew
Cryptotis parva (Say)

Description. One of the smallest mammals; snout long and pointed; ears small and concealed in the short fur; eyes small; tail never more than twice as long as hind foot; fur dense; upperparts grizzled olive brown, paler below. Dental formula: I 3/2, C 1/0, Pm 2/1, M 3/3 x 2 = 30. External measurements average: total length, 79 mm; tail 18 mm; hind foot, 10.5 mm. Weight, 4–7.5 g.

Distribution. Occurs in eastern, southern, and northwestern portions of the state; absent from the Trans-Pecos and adjacent areas and from much of the Edwards Plateau.

Subspecies. *C. p. parva* throughout most of the distribution in Texas and *C. p. berlandieri* on the Rio Grande Plains.

Least Shrew (*Cryptotis parva*). Photo by John and Gloria Tveten.

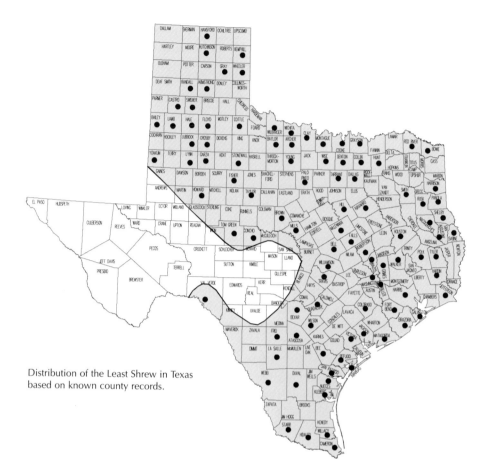

Distribution of the Least Shrew in Texas
based on known county records.

Habits. The least shrew is an inhabitant of grasslands where it utilizes the surface runways of cotton rats (*Sigmodon*) and other grassland rodents. It seldom occurs in forests but occasional individuals have been found under logs and leaf litter in moist, forested areas.

Most of its foraging seems to be done on the surface of the ground, but the behavior of captive individuals suggests that occasionally they may tunnel through leaf litter and loose, damp soil, much as do moles, in search of food. The home proper is a small underground burrow or a series of shallow runways under flat stones or fallen logs. Burrows excavated in east-central Texas were about 2.5 cm in diameter, from 25 cm to 1.5 m long, and seldom more than 20 cm below the surface at the deepest point. Each burrow had an enlarged chamber at the end or in a side branch for the nest, which was composed of dry, shredded blades of grass. These nests were used for rearing young or as resting places for groups of adult and half-grown shrews.

In contrast to most species of shrews, *Cryptotis* is sociable, and several individuals may be kept together in captivity without serious conflict. They sleep together and cooperate to some extent in digging tunnels and capturing food. One nest examined in December in Texas contained a dozen shrews that seemed to be established there for the winter; another examined near Nacogdoches was occupied by at least 31 individuals.

These tiny shrews are active at all hours of the day, but the peak activity comes at night. Also, they are difficult to trap except in winter when the supply of natural food is low; then they respond more readily to bait. In Texas, they tend to concentrate in favorable areas in winter and to disperse over wider areas when conditions are more favorable. That they are abundant at times in favorable areas is attested by the large numbers that barn owls capture and consume. Least shrews made up 41% of the food items of a pair of barn owls as revealed by examination of owl pellets from Colorado County. In Jefferson County, 73% of the animals represented in barn owl pellets were *Cryptotis.*

The food of these tiny creatures is entirely animal matter—snails, insects, sow bugs, and other small animals. They occasionally set up housekeeping in beehives and feed on the bees. Shrews kept in captivity preferred black crickets, then grasshoppers, sow bugs, and hard-shelled beetles in the order named. Those captive shrews stored excess food in one corner of the cage, suggesting that they may behave likewise in the wild.

The breeding season extends from early March to late November. No winter-taken specimens from Texas have been in breeding condition. Females produce two or more litters each season. The young, three to six in number, are hairless, blind, and helpless, and they weigh about 0.3 g each at birth. They grow rapidly and attain adult proportions in about 1 month.

Conservation Status. This shrew appears to be common throughout its range in Texas and in no serious danger of population depletion.

Desert Shrew

Notiosorex crawfordi (Coues)

Description. A small shrew with conspicuous ears and long tail (more than twice as long as hind foot); upperparts lead gray; underparts paler. Dental formula: I 3/2, C 1/0, Pm 1/1, M 3/3 x 2 = 28. External measurements average: total length, 81 mm; tail, 27 mm; hind foot, 10 mm. Weight, 2.9–6.3 g.

Distribution. Western two-thirds of state, including portions of north-central Texas and southern Texas.

Subspecies. *N. c. crawfordi.*

Habits. Desert shrews are found in the more arid, western and southern parts of the state but do not appear to be restricted to any particular habitat. Specimens have been taken in cattail marshes, in beehives, under piles of cornstalks, among yuccas, in woodrat nests, and beneath piles of brush and refuse. In such places they construct their tiny nests of grasses and other dried vegetation. Unlike other

Desert Shrew (*Notiosorex crawfordi*). Photo by John and Gloria Tveten.

shrews from Texas, desert shrews do not appear to construct or make use of underground burrows.

This shrew is thought to feed largely on both larval and adult insects; captive specimens have eaten a wide variety of food, including mealworms, cutworms, crickets, cockroaches, houseflies, grasshoppers, moths, beetles, earwigs, centipedes, the carcasses of skinned small mammals and birds, and dead lizards. Conversely, captives refused live rodents, salamanders, scorpions, and earthworms. In captivity, desert shrews eat about 75% of their body weight each day and can subsist without drinking water.

Little is known about the breeding habits of this shrew. The breeding season lasts from spring into the fall months, perhaps occasionally as late as November. Litter size averages three to five young, but it is not known if more than one litter is produced each season.

The life span is not known. Predators include great horned owls and barn owls.

Conservation Status.   Given the amount of literature that exists, this appears to be a species that is more common than realized and is not threatened. Rollin Baker, however, identified it as one of the species potentially at risk in the Chihuahuan Desert biome, mainly because of its apparent scarcity and poorly known habits. No specific threats have been identified.

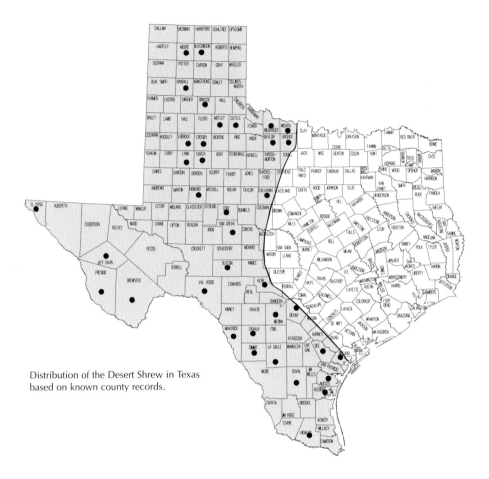

Distribution of the Desert Shrew in Texas
based on known county records.

FAMILY TALPIDAE (MOLES)

Five genera and seven species of moles are known from North America. Small creatures with long, tubular bodies, they are well adapted for their burrowing lifestyle. They lack external ears, have very small eyes, and their limbs are modified for digging.

All moles are insectivorous. Their habit of burrowing in lawns and gardens, which has garnered them a reputation as a pest, is probably more often beneficial than harmful, as they aerate and loosen the soil and consume harmful soil insects and grubs.

Eastern Mole

Scalopus aquaticus (Linnaeus)

Description.   A relatively small, robust, burrowing mammal with broadened, shovel-like front feet webbed to base of claws; no visible eyes or ears; sharp-pointed nose;

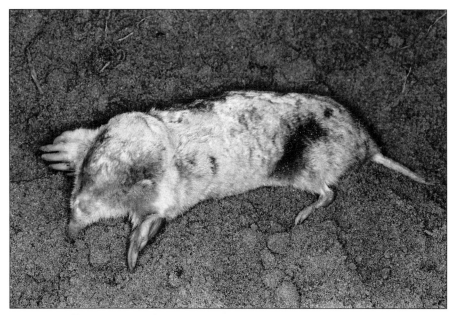

Eastern Mole (*Scalopus aquaticus*). Photo by John and Gloria Tveten.

plushlike fur; short, sparsely haired tail. Dental formula: I 3/2, C 1/0, Pm 3/3, M 3/3 x 2 = 36; middle upper incisors enlarged; canines small and undifferentiated; molars with W-shaped outline when viewed from biting surface. Color brown, often with silvery sheen; suffusion of orange on nose and wrists; underparts silvery gray, faintly washed with orange. External measurements average: total length, 165 mm; tail, 29 mm; hind foot, 22 mm. Weight, 60–90 g.

Distribution. Eastern two-thirds of the state, including eastern portions of south Texas. In northern Panhandle extends to New Mexico line along Canadian River drainage. Isolated record from Presidio County.

Subspecies. Five known in Texas: *S. a. aureus* in the extreme east and also the Panhandle region, *S. a. alleni* in south-central Texas, *S. a. cryptus* in the east-central part of the state, *S. a. inflatus* on the southern part of the Rio Grande Plains, and *S. a. texanus* in Presidio County.

Habits. Moles spend most of their life in underground burrows they excavate for themselves or usurp from other mammals, particularly pocket gophers (genus *Geomys*). Because of this, they are restricted in their distribution by the nature of the soil. In Texas, they occur largely in moist (not wet), sandy soils. Deep, dry sands and heavy clays are avoided.

Two types of underground burrows are used: (1) the shallow surface run, which is associated with food-getting activities, and (2) the deep burrow for protection and rearing of the young. The deep burrow is marked by conical mounds of earth the occupant has pushed to the surface, whereas the shallow burrow is

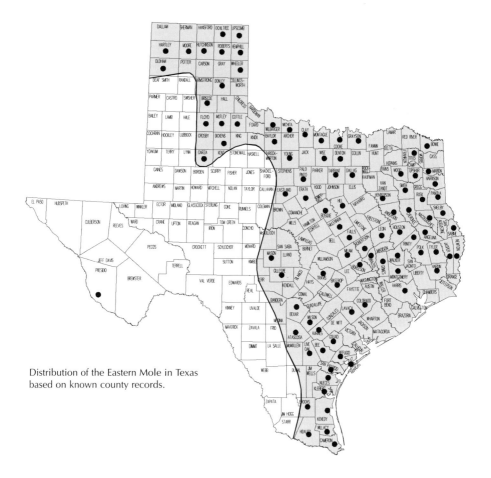

Distribution of the Eastern Mole in Texas
based on known county records.

marked by a meandering ridge of earth pushed up by the mole as it tunnels
through the loose topsoil. Moist, well-drained fencerows, terraces, lawns, and
knolls rich in organic matter are favored areas for surface burrows because food is
more abundant there. Certain of the surface burrows are used frequently as highways; others, especially intricate side branches, are used but once in the food-
getting process and are then allowed to collapse.

Moles cannot see and spend almost all of their time underground. They may
be found active at any hour of the day but generally are more active by day than
by night in response to the movement of earthworms in and out of the soil. Also,
they are active throughout the year.

The mole excavates its burrow by backward strokes and lateral thrusts of the
front feet. Loose earth is moved and pushed to the surface by thrusts of the front
feet. In excavating shallow runs, the mole merely pushes up the earth to form a
ridge, again by lateral thrusts of the front feet while the mole is turned partly on
its side.

The home range of individual moles consists of several hunting grounds galleried with surface burrows on knolls, terraces, or along fencerows, all of them connected by a single long burrow. One burrow along a fencerow in Van Zandt County was 360 m long. Such systems may be in continual use for as long as 5 years, either by one mole or by successive occupants. At times, moles travel overland in search of new locations or, perhaps, of mates. This is evidenced by the occasional appearance of dead moles on the highways.

Throughout most of the year moles are solitary, but in late winter and early spring males seek out females. In south-central Texas, the breeding season begins in February, as evidenced by the large testes of males and the swollen uteri of females. Although the breeding period may last 3–4 months, peak activity occurs in a short period of 3–4 weeks. A single litter of two to five young is produced each year. The gestation period is about 4–6 weeks. The young are born hairless but otherwise are miniature adults. Females reach sexual maturity in 1 year.

Moles feed largely on earthworms and grubs, although beetles, spiders, centipedes, insect larvae and pupae, and vegetable matter may also be eaten. In captivity, they have consumed mice, small birds, and ground beef.

The average daily food consumption is about 32% of the body weight of the animal, although a mole can consume more than 66% of its body weight in 18 hours. Active prey is killed by crushing it against the sides of the burrow with the front feet or by piling loose earth on the victim and biting it while thus held. Captive moles kill earthworms by biting them rapidly in several places, often nearly cutting the worm in two.

Moles do damage by their burrowing activities, especially on the greens of golf courses, in lawns, and in situations where accelerated soil erosion may result. Also, they may destroy row crops by burrowing along a row and killing the plants. It must be kept in mind, however, that the mole usually is searching out animal food and that often the larval insects taken do far more actual damage to the vegetation than does the mole. Larval June beetles, for example, feed on the roots of grasses and may, if present in large numbers, completely destroy the sod in an area. The burrowing activities of the mole also tend to aerate the soil, with beneficial results to plants.

Conservation Status.   Moles remain common in Texas wherever suitable soils exist. The subspecies *S. a. texanus,* however, from Presidio County, has not been documented since its discovery in 1887. In 1951 Rollin Baker also documented a mole from the Sierra del Carmens in northern Coahuila, Mexico, just across the border from the Big Bend of Texas. A concerted effort is needed to determine if moles still occur in those regions and to monitor their status.

ORDER CHIROPTERA
Bats

"Chiroptera," meaning "hand wing," alludes to the great elongation of the fingers that support the flying membrane. Among mammals, bats are unique in that they have true powers of flight; other mammals, such as flying squirrels, can only volplane, or glide, always from a higher to a lower elevation.

Bats as a group are crepuscular or nocturnal; their eyes are small and inefficient, although their ears are usually well developed. Bats use high-frequency, ultrasonic sounds (generally above 20 kilohertz) outside our hearing range to navigate and avoid obstacles and capture prey in the dark. The ability to produce ultrasonic pulses and to interpret the echoes rebounding from objects in their path is called echolocation.

In the temperate regions, the young are born in late spring; in the tropics there appears to be no definite breeding season—young bats may be found in every month of the year. Most bats feed on insects, but some kinds feed regularly on fruits, nectar, or fish, and some, the vampire bats, are peculiarly adapted to feed on blood.

Bats live nearly everywhere on the earth with the exception of the polar regions, highest mountains, and some remote islands. Their diversity and abundance, however, are greatest in tropical regions, declining steadily north and south of the equator. Bats are common in the United States and can be found easily in most regions, although they are most abundant in the Southwest. Thirty-three of the 43 species of bats in the United States occur in Texas, the richest variety of bat species found in any state in the country.

Bats occur in all the major ecological regions of Texas, but the Big Bend region of the Trans-Pecos, with its topographic pattern of high mountains and desert lowlands, supports more kinds of bats (18 species) than any other part of Texas. Several extremely rare or unusual bats occur in this region, and they are more abundant here than anywhere else in the country. The Edwards Plateau also maintains a high diversity of bats, primarily cavern-dwelling species that inhabit the numerous caves of the region, often in staggering numbers. Caves are excellent roosting and hibernation sites for bats, and they play a prominent role in the distribution of many bats in our state. Bat species diversity and numbers are lower in the northern, eastern, and southern portions of the state, where topographic heterogeneity is low and caves are uncommon.

In many parts of North America, bats either migrate or hibernate in winter. If they migrate, their distributions in winter and summer are often very different. In parts of Texas where the climate is mild, bats may not migrate or hibernate if weather conditions are such that a sufficient and suitable food supply is available year round. In general, however, there is a tendency for most species of bats in our state either to move from one region to another or to move out of the state altogether during the months of November through March.

In 1991 I published a book, *The Bats of Texas,* that provides great detail about the natural history, distribution, and taxonomy of Texas bats. The interested reader should refer to it for more information. Since the publication of that book, another species new to the state, the western yellow bat (*Lasiurus xanthinus*), has been recorded in the Big Bend region, and several unusual occurrences of Texas bats have been recorded.

KEY TO THE BATS OF TEXAS

1. Distinct, upwardly and freely projecting, triangular nose leaf at end of elongated snout 2

   Nose leaf absent, indistinct, or modified as lateral ridges or low moundlike structure; snout normal 3

2. Tail evident, projecting about 10 mm from dorsal side of interfemoral membrane; distance from eye to nose about twice distance from eye to ear; forearm less than 48 mm. *Choeronycteris mexicana* (Mexican long-tongued bat), p. 69.

   Tail not evident; eye about midway between nose and ear; forearm more than 48 mm. *Leptonycteris nivalis* (Mexican long-nosed bat), p. 71.

3. Thumb longer than 10 mm; hair straight, lying smoothly, glossy tipped. *Diphylla ecaudata* (hairy-legged vampire bat), p. 73.

   Thumb less than 10 mm; hair slightly woolly, pelage lax, not usually lying smoothly, not glossy tipped 4

4. Prominent grooves and flaps on chin; tail protruding from dorsal surface of interfemoral membrane. *Mormoops megalophylla* (ghost-faced bat), p. 66.

   No notable grooves or flaps on chin; lumps above nose or wrinkled lips possible, most faces lacking even these characteristics; tail extending to or beyond the edge of the interfemoral membrane 5

5. Tail extending conspicuously beyond free edge of interfemoral membrane 6

   Tail extending to free edge of interfemoral membrane 9

6. Forearm more than 70 mm; upper lips without deep vertical grooves. *Eumops perotis* (western mastiff bat), p. 133.

   Forearm less than 70 mm; upper lips with deep vertical grooves 7

7. Forearm less than 52 mm 8

   Forearm more than 52 mm (58–64). *Nyctinomops macrotis* (big free-tailed bat), p. 130.

8. Ears not united at base; second phalanx of fourth finger more than 5 mm. *Tadarida brasiliensis* (Brazilian free-tailed bat), p. 123.

Ears joined at base; second phalanx of fourth finger less than 5 mm. *Nyctinomops femorosaccus* (pocketed free-tailed bat), p. 129.

9. Ears disproportionately large, more than 25 mm from notch to tip 10

   Ears of normal size, less than 25 mm from notch to tip 13

10. Color black with three large white spots on back, one just behind each shoulder, the other at the base of the tail. *Euderma maculatum* (spotted bat), p. 114.

    Color variable, but not black; no white spots on back 11

11. Dorsal color pale yellow; no distinctive glands evident on each side of the nose. *Antrozous pallidus* (pallid bat), p. 120.

    Dorsal color light brown to gray; distinctive glands (large bumps) evident on each side of the nose 12

12. Hairs on belly with white tips; strong contrast in color between the basal portions and tips of hairs on both back and belly; presence of long hairs projecting beyond the toes; known from eastern one-third of state. *Corynorhinus rafinesquii* (Rafinesque's big-eared bat), p. 117.

    Hairs on belly with pinkish buff tips; little contrast in color between basal portions and tips of hairs on both back and belly; absence of long hairs projecting beyond the toes; known from western half of state. *Corynorhinus townsendii* (Townsend's big-eared bat), p. 119.

13. At least the anterior half of the dorsal surface of the interfemoral membrane well furred 14

    Dorsal surface of interfemoral membrane naked, scantily haired, or at most lightly furred on the anterior third 21

14. Color of hair black, with many of the hairs distinctly silver-tipped. *Lasionycteris noctivagans* (silver-haired bat), p. 105.

    Color various, but never uniformly black 15

15. Color yellowish 16

    Color reddish, brownish, or grayish (not yellowish) 18

16. Total length more than 120 mm. *Lasiurus intermedius* (northern yellow bat), p. 99.

    Total length less than 120 mm 17

17. Hairs of dorsal uropatagium bright yellow with little darkness. *Lasiurus xanthinus* (western yellow bat), p. 102.

    Hairs of dorsal uropatagium lacking bright yellow sheen and having a distinct smoky appearance. *Lasiurus ega* (southern yellow bat), p. 97.

18. Forearm more than 45 mm; color wood brown heavily frosted with white. *Lasiurus cinereus* (hoary bat), p. 95.

    Forearm less than 45 mm; upper parts reddish or mahogany 19

19. Upper parts brick red to rusty red, frequently washed with white 20

    Upper parts mahogany washed with white. *Lasiurus seminolus* (Seminole bat), p. 101.

20. Color reddish with frosted appearance resulting from white-tipped hairs; interfemoral membrane fully haired. *Lasiurus borealis* (eastern red bat), p. 93.

    Color rusty red to brownish without frosted appearance; posterior one-third of interfemoral membrane bare or only scantily haired. *Lasiurus blossevillii* (western red bat), p. 92.

21. Tragus (projection within ear) short, blunt, and curved 22

    Tragus long, pointed, and straight 24

22. Forearm more than 40 mm. *Eptesicus fuscus* (big brown bat), p. 110.

    Forearm less than 40 mm 23

23. Forearm more than 32 mm; interfemoral membrane naked; color brown. *Nycticeius humeralis* (evening bat), p. 112.

    Forearm less than 32 mm; interfemoral membrane lightly furred on anterior third of dorsal surface; color drab to smoke gray. *Pipistrellus hesperus* (western pipistrelle), p. 106.

24. Dorsal fur tricolored when parted (black at base, wide band of light yellowish brown in middle, tipped with slightly darker contrasting color); leading edge of wing membrane noticeably paler than rest of membrane. *Pipistrellus subflavus* (eastern pipistrelle), p. 108.

    Dorsal fur bicolored or unicolored with no light band in the middle; leading edge of wing same color as other parts of membrane...... 25

25. Calcar with well-marked keel 26

    Calcar without well-marked keel 28

26. Forearm more than 36 mm; foot more than 8 mm long; underside of wing furred to elbow; pelage dark brown. *Myotis volans* (long-legged myotis), p. 88.

    Forearm less than 36 mm; foot less than 8 mm long; underside of wing not furred to elbow; pelage light brown to buff brown 27

27. Hairs on back with dull reddish brown tips; black mask not noticeable; thumb less than 4 mm long; naked part of snout about as long as width of nostrils when viewed from above. *Myotis californicus* (California myotis), p. 77.

    Fur on back with long, glossy, brownish tips; black mask usually noticeable; thumb greater than 4 mm long; naked part of snout approximately 1.5 times the width of the nostrils. *Myotis ciliolabrum* (western small-footed myotis), p. 79.

28. Forearm more than 40 mm 29

    Forearm usually less than 40 mm 30

29. Conspicuous fringe of stiff hairs on free edge of interfemoral membrane. *Myotis thysanodes* (fringed myotis), p. 84.

    No conspicuous fringe of stiff hairs on free edge of interfemoral membrane. *Myotis velifer* (cave myotis), p. 86.

30. In Texas occurring generally west of 100th meridian 31

    In Texas occurring generally east of 100th meridian 32

31. Dorsal fur usually with a slight sheen; forearm more than 36 mm; total length more than 80 mm. *Myotis occultus* (southwestern little brown bat), p. 81.

    Dorsal fur usually lacking a sheen; forearm less than 36 mm; total length less than 80 mm. *Myotis yumanensis* (yuma myotis), p. 90.

32. Ear more than 16 mm, extending more than 2 mm beyond nose when laid forward; tragus long (9–10 mm), thin, and somewhat sickle-shaped. *Myotis septentrionalis* (northern long-eared myotis), p. 83.

    Ear less than 16 mm, not extending more than 2 mm beyond nose when laid forward; tragus shorter and straight. *Myotis austroriparius* (southeastern myotis), p. 75.

FAMILY MORMOOPIDAE (MORMOOPID BATS)

Eight species of New World bats make up the family Mormoopidae, which includes the mustached, naked-backed, and ghost-faced bats that are variously distributed from the southern United States through Mexico, Central America, and South America to southern Brazil. Characterized by fleshy appendages on the snout and chin and a short tail protruding dorsally from the interfemoral membrane, these bats are abundant in the tropics as well as semiarid and subtropical environments. The only species of this family to occur in the United States is the ghost-faced bat, *Mormoops megalophylla,* which has been recorded in Texas and Arizona.

Ghost-faced Bat

Mormoops megalophylla Peters

Description.   A medium-sized, reddish brown or dark brown bat with conspicuous, leaflike appendages on chin; ears short, rounded, united across forehead; lower part of ear forming a copious pocket below eye; tail projecting dorsally from near middle of interfemoral membrane; crown of head highly arched; skull markedly shortened, cranium high and abruptly arched. Dental formula: I 2/2, C 1/1, Pm 2/3, M 3/3 x 2 = 34. External measurements average: total length, 90 mm; tail, 26 mm; foot, 10 mm; length of forearm, 54 mm. Weight, 15–16 g.

Distribution.   In Texas this bat is known from the Trans-Pecos, southern edge of the Edwards Plateau, and South Texas Plains. It is typically found in lowland areas, especially desert scrub and riverine habitats, as at Big Bend Ranch, but it also has been captured in the mountainous country of the Apache, Davis, Chinati, and Chisos mountains and in the Sierra Vieja range. It is a common winter (November to 15 March) resident of caves along the extreme southern edge of the Edwards Plateau, although its occurrence at specific localities is highly variable and unpredictable. *Mormoops* has been collected at Frio Cave (Uvalde County), Webb Cave (Kinney County), Haby Cave (Bexar County), and Valdina Farms Sinkhole (Medina County) in December, January, February, March, May, September, and November,

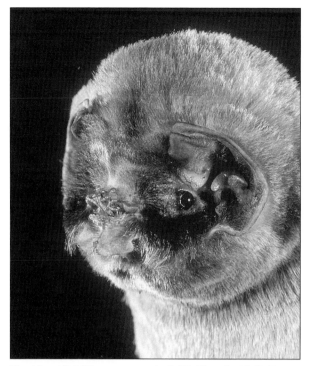

Ghost-faced Bat (*Mormoops megalophylla*). Photo by Merlin D. Tuttle, Bat Conservation International.

suggesting that it uses the Edwards Plateau caves as a winter retreat. Many apparently suitable caves near those listed above are not used, although they are occupied by bats often associated with *Mormoops*. In contrast to the winter records from the Edwards Plateau, those from the Trans-Pecos tend to be from the warmer months of the year (March to October). This is suggestive of seasonal migration between the two regions, although such movements have yet to be substantiated.

Subspecies.   *M. m. megalophylla.*

Habits.   Ghost-faced bats typically roost in caves, tunnels, and mine shafts, but they also have been found in old buildings. In addition to the caves listed above, these bats have been taken in a railroad tunnel near Comstock in Val Verde County. Specimens also were captured in January and February in the junior high school at Edinburg. Students found them hanging from the rough plaster ceiling in one of the halls.

Once out of the roost, individuals fly quickly to foraging sites along arroyos and canyons. These bats are relatively strong, fast fliers, and they travel at high altitudes to foraging areas. Foraging may occur over standing water, and these bats often are collected using mist nets positioned over ponds of water along arroyos and canyons. Clyde Jones and his graduate students at Texas Tech captured many

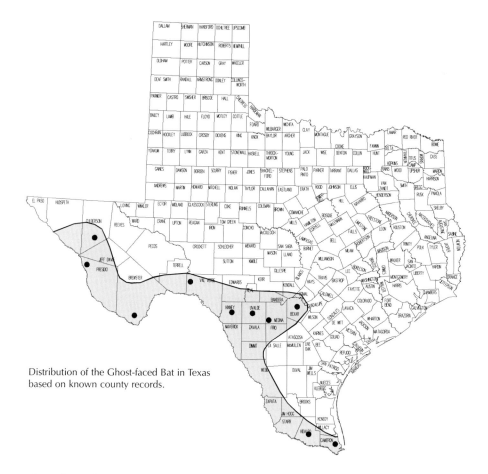

Distribution of the Ghost-faced Bat in Texas based on known county records.

ghost-faced bats under such conditions in Big Bend Ranch State Park (Presidio County) and along Limpia Creek in the Davis Mountains (Jeff Davis County).

Although they may congregate in large numbers at a roosting site (as many as 500,000 individuals), these bats do not form the compact clusters typical of many other species; rather, they tend to space themselves approximately 15 cm apart across the roost ceiling. Therefore, larger sites are required to house great numbers of these bats. Other species that often cohabit roosting sites with *Mormoops,* and that generally greatly outnumber them, include the cave myotis (*Myotis velifer*) and the Brazilian free-tailed bat (*Tadarida brasiliensis*).

Few data on the breeding habits of *Mormoops* in Texas are available. In Big Bend National Park 2 pregnant females, each containing a single embryo, were captured in mid-June. At Big Bend Ranch State Park, 30 pregnant females were taken from 29 April to 9 June, and each contained only a single embryo. Lactating females have been captured there from mid-June to early August. In Coahuila and Nuevo Leon, two Mexican states bordering Texas, gravid females have been captured in March, April, and May. Each gravid female contained a single embryo.

Based on data collected in Central America and Mexico, it seems that in this species mating begins in late December. Sexually mature females taken between January and June are likely to be gravid or lactating; no gravid females have been reported from late June through January. Thus, it appears that the period of reproduction is confined to late winter and early spring, even in the tropics, and that each reproductively active female gives birth to only one offspring each year.

Their food appears to consist entirely of insects that are captured in flight. The stomachs of two individuals from Big Bend National Park were entirely filled with moths. At Big Bend Ranch State Park, the stomachs of 45 individuals included lepidopterans (100% occurrence), coleopterans (4.4%), homopterans (2.2%), hemipterans (2.2%), and neuropterans (2.2%). The bats begin returning to their caves and roosting sites, on average, about seven hours after they first leave them. **Conservation Status.** This species is probably not as rare within its geographic range as previously thought. At Big Bend Ranch State Park in Presidio County, it was one of the most common bats collected. All cave-dwelling bats are vulnerable because large segments of a regional population often roost at a single site where they are susceptible to disruption, disturbance, and extirpation.

FAMILY PHYLLOSTOMIDAE (LEAF-NOSED BATS)

The Phyllostomidae are a large family of New World bats primarily limited to tropical and subtropical areas, although a few species reach northward to subtemperate areas in the United States. The 141 species included in this family are characterized by a fleshy appendage, or nose leaf, projecting from the rostrum. Most of these bats feed on fruit or nectar, but the family also contains a few insectivores, carnivores, and the true vampire bats. Three species of phyllostomid bats have been recorded in Texas, including one vampire, but none is widely distributed or very common.

Mexican Long-tongued Bat
Choeronycteris mexicana Tschudi

Description. A medium-sized bat with a long, slender muzzle and prominent nasal leaf. A minute tail is present and extends less than halfway to the edge of the interfemoral membrane. Color is sooty gray to brownish. Dental formula: I 2/0, C 1/1, Pm 2/3, M 3/3 x 2 = 30. External measurements average: total length, 85 mm; tail, 10 mm; foot, 14 mm; ear, 16 mm; forearm, 44 mm. Weight, 25 g.
Distribution. A Mexican species that enters the United States in extreme southern Texas, New Mexico, and Arizona. Before the year 2000, this species had been known in Texas only from photographs of a single individual and observations of others from Santa Ana National Wildlife Refuge in Hidalgo County. Recently, a specimen was obtained from Laguna Atascosa National Wildlife Refuge in Cameron

Mexican Long-tongued Bat (*Choeronycteris mexicana*). Photo by Merlin D. Tuttle, Bat Conservation International.

County, and the Texas Department of Health has a specimen from Midland County. Thus, the distribution of this bat in Texas is enigmatic. It could be another southern species that is gradually making its way into Texas.

Subspecies. Monotypic species.

Habits. These bats inhabit deep canyons where they use caves and mine tunnels as day roosts. They also have been found in buildings and often are associated with big-eared bats (*Corynorhinus*).

Choeronycteris mexicana feeds on fruit, pollen, nectar, and probably insects. Because of its longer tongue, this bat may be able to recover nectar from a greater variety of night-blooming plants than the other nectar-feeding bat in Texas, *Leptonycteris nivalis.*

Parturition occurs from June to early July in Arizona and New Mexico, with young reported as early as mid-April in Sonora, Mexico. A single young is born per female. A pregnant *C. mexicana,* collected in May, gave birth shortly after capture in the San Carlos Mountains of northern Tamaulipas, Mexico, which is no more than 241 km south of Santa Ana Wildlife Refuge. Pregnant and lactating females have been recorded in March and June in Coahuila, Mexico, to the south of the Texas border.

It is not possible to determine if the few records of this species in Texas are accidental occurrences or if there is a tenuous, seasonal population of this bat in southernmost Texas.

Conservation Status. For a long time this species was known in Texas on the basis of a single individual captured in Hidalgo County, leading to speculation that it was only of accidental occurrence in Texas. Recent documentation, however, of a

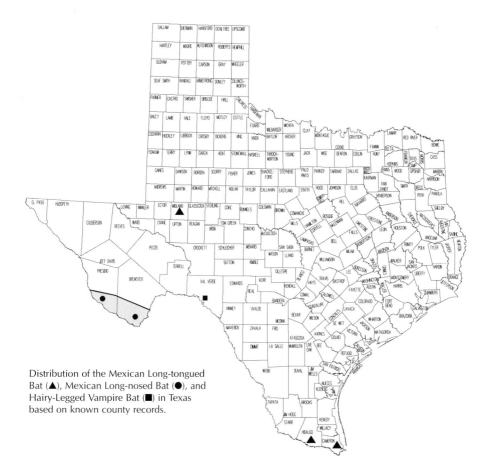

Distribution of the Mexican Long-tongued Bat (▲), Mexican Long-nosed Bat (●), and Hairy-Legged Vampire Bat (■) in Texas based on known county records.

specimen in Cameron County and another in Midland County in the western part of the state suggests there is a need to look for the species elsewhere in Texas. This species is listed as endangered by the Mexican government, and it should proba-bly be afforded the same status in Texas.

Mexican Long-nosed Bat
Leptonycteris nivalis (Saussure)

Description. A medium-sized bat with short ears, no tail, and a distinct nasal leaf; forearm furred above at elbow; upperparts drab brown, the hairs white basally; underparts pale drab, tips of hairs silvery. Dental formula: I 2/2, C 1/1, Pm 2/3, M 2/2 x 2 = 30. External measurements average: total length, 83 mm; foot, 17 mm; ear, 15 mm; forearm, 58 mm. Weight, 24 g.

Distribution. A Mexican species that enters Texas in the Big Bend region. Known in Texas from southern Brewster and Presidio counties. See distribution map in the account for *Choeronycteris mexicana.*

Mexican Long-nosed Bat (*Leptonycteris nivalis*). Photo by Merlin D. Tuttle, Bat Conservation International.

Subspecies. Monotypic species.

Habits. This is a colonial, cave-dwelling bat that usually inhabits deep caverns. The only known records of these bats in the United States are from a large cave on Mount Emory in Big Bend National Park and from the Chinati Mountains in Presidio County.

At the Emory Peak cave, *L. nivalis* forms a large cluster with half-grown young and adults intermingled. Adult males and females may be present. They share the cave with a large colony of big-eared bats (*Corynorhinus*); each colony roosts in a different part of the cave, but not more than 6 m apart. The air in this cave is considerably cooler in summer than that outside, and a distinct breeze blows through it at all times. The cave is not used in winter; the inhabitants migrate to Mexico. This bat has a strong, musky odor similar to that of the Brazilian free-tailed bat.

Leptonycteris nivalis feeds on the nectar and pollen of flowers, especially those of the century plant (*Agave* spp.). The seasonal occurrence of *L. nivalis* in Texas is probably related to food availability, as their presence seems to coincide with the blooming of century plants in June. The plants open their flowers at night and attract bats with copious amounts of nectar. As the bats feed, their fur gets coated with pollen grains. When they fly to another plant in search of more food, they transfer the pollen to a new flower, assisting in cross-fertilization of the plants. This mutual relationship is so strong that both the bats and the century plants cannot survive without the other. As the flower stalks of the agaves die by late summer, the bats disappear, as there is nothing left for them to eat.

The breeding season is restricted to April, May, and June. Females give birth to one young annually. The young are born in Mexico, prior to the bats' arrival in Texas, and are weaned in July to August, which is the peak of the rainy season and the peak of flower abundance.

Conservation Status. This bat is listed as endangered throughout its range by both the U.S. Fish and Wildlife Service and the Texas Parks and Wildlife Department. It acquired this status primarily because it is known in the United States only in the Big Bend region. Although the species occurs throughout much of Mexico, there are indications of substantial population decline both in the United States and Mexico. The population at the only known roosting site in the United States, a cave in Big Bend National Park, fluctuates widely in numbers from one year to the next, although there appears to be a downward trend in the numbers of bats at this colony. The reasons for the population decline are not entirely understood but are thought to be associated with loss of roosting sites and food sources.

Hairy-legged Vampire Bat
Diphylla ecaudata Spix

Description. A relatively large, sooty-brown bat with no tail; a narrow, hairy inter-femoral membrane; short, rounded ears; and a short, pug-nosed snout. The dentition is highly modified, with the middle upper incisors larger than the canines; the outer incisors very small and set so close to the canines that they are easily over-looked; the crowns of the outer lower incisors seven-lobed, fan-shaped, and more than twice as wide as the inner lower incisors; premolars and molars very small and probably nonfunctional. Dental formula: I 2/2, C 1/1, Pm 1/2, M 2/2 x 2 = 26. External measurements average: total length, 85 mm; foot, 13 mm; forearm, 53 mm. Weight, 30–40 g.

Distribution. From southern Texas southward to eastern Peru and Brazil. Known from Texas on the basis of one female taken 24 May 1967 from an abandoned rail-road tunnel 19 km west of Comstock, Val Verde County. See distribution map in the account for *Choeronycteris mexicana.*

Subspecies. Monotypic species.

Habits. This bat is primarily an inhabitant of tropical and subtropical forestlands. Its daytime retreat is normally a cave, which it may share with other species of bats, but it has also been found roosting in mine tunnels and hollow trees. In the Mexican state of San Luis Potosi, Walter Dalquest found that these vampire bats were more solitary than the common vampire bat (*Desmodus*), and they did not gather in groups, even when several individuals inhabited a cave. Consequently, pools of digested blood do not form, and there is only a slight odor of ammonia in the caves they inhabit. He found about 35 individuals, mostly females with young, in one cave, but usually only 1, 2, or 3 were present in a given cave. These bats are shy, quick of movement, and readily take flight when molested.

The food of *Diphylla* is the blood of warm-blooded vertebrates, mainly birds, including domestic chickens. Ernest Walker reported that *Diphylla* attacks the legs and cloacal region of chickens. One bat was "observed alighting on the tail of a chicken, hanging by its hind legs and biting the exposed skin in the cloacal region, and then lapping up the blood while in an upright position."

Hairy-legged Vampire Bat (*Diphylla ecaudata*). Photo by Merlin D. Tuttle, Bat Conservation International.

This species seems to be reproductively active throughout the year. Pregnant females have been reported from Mexico and Central America in March, July, August, October, and November. The number of embryos per female is normally one, but one female captured on 8 July in Chiapas, Mexico, contained two nearly full-term (crown–rump length 34 mm) embryos. The reproductive condition of the female captured in Texas was not recorded.

Although only one specimen of the hairy-legged vampire bat is known from Texas, it is possible that a thorough search of the caves in the Hill Country and along the Rio Grande will reveal additional records of this species or the common vampire (*Desmodus rotundus*), which have been taken in northern Mexico no more than 200 km from the Texas border. Since *Diphylla* is a possible reservoir of bovine paralytic rabies, it is of economic importance to the cattlemen and sportsmen of Texas.

Conservation Status. This vampire bat does not appear to be threatened at this time. In addition, it is probably of accidental occurrence in Texas. There is no reason to place it on any list of rare and threatened species at the present time.

FAMILY VESPERTILIONIDAE (VESPERTILIONID BATS)

Chiefly insectivorous bats, the Vespertilionidae constitute the largest family of bats (more than 300 species) and are distributed worldwide with the exception of arctic regions. Consequently, these bats are found in nearly every conceivable habitat from tropical forests to desert and temperate regions. Many are highly migratory and traverse great distances between summer and winter ranges. Others, however, do not migrate and, instead, hibernate on summer ranges.

Vespertilionids lack the facial adornments found in other families of bats and are often referred to as plain-faced bats. Several species have extremely large and complex ears, but most have small, simple ears. These bats typically have small eyes and a long tail completely enclosed by a well-developed interfemoral membrane.

More than 30 species of vespertilionid bats range across the United States; of these, 25 are known from Texas.

Southeastern Myotis
Myotis austroriparius (Rhoads)

Description. A small bat with dense, dull, woolly fur; upperparts brownish to sooty; fur of underparts with white tips and black bases, the general white appearance contrasting sharply with the upperparts; cranium globose and normally with a low sagittal crest. Dental formula as in *M. californicus*. External measurements average: total length, 88 mm; tail, 36 mm; foot, 9 mm; forearm, 38 mm. Weight, 5–7 g.

Southeastern Myotis (*Myotis austroriparius*). Photo by Merlin D. Tuttle, Bat Conservation International.

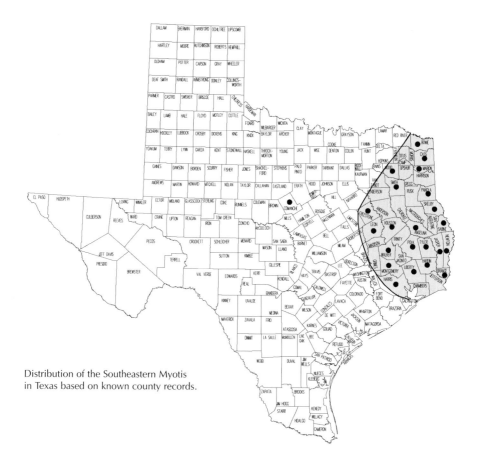

Distribution of the Southeastern Myotis
in Texas based on known county records.

Distribution.   Southeastern United States, westward into eastern Texas. Known
previously only from the Pineywoods region; in 1996 three county records extended the range of this species westward to Leon, Freestone, and Walker counties. A
specimen collected in Comanche County in 1995 extended the known range of the
species approximately 240 km west in the state.

Subspecies.   *M. a. austroriparius.*

Habits.   *M. austroriparius* is predominantly a cave bat in that part of its range
where suitable caves occur. In Texas, however, these bats roost primarily in live,
hollow, bottomland hardwood trees close to slow-moving rivers and in man-made
structures such as abandoned houses and culverts. When they leave their diurnal
roosts late in the evening (usually about dark), they fly to nearby ponds and
streams where they drink and forage. They fly low over the water, usually within 60
cm of the surface, capturing insects. Specific foods are not known, but small
moths, midges, mosquitoes, and flies are probably of importance.

Where suitable caves are available, both males and females congregate in large
numbers in late March and April to bear their young. In caveless areas, old buildings may serve as nursery sites. Parturition occurs in late April to late May, and the

young are large enough to fly 5 or 6 weeks later. The southeastern myotis is unusual among bats of its genus as it usually gives birth to twin offspring (other *Myotis* usually bear only one young per year). At birth, the young bats weigh slightly more than 1 g each. They grow rapidly, and sexual maturity is reached in both sexes before the bats are a year old.

Their most important predators appear to be rat snakes, corn snakes, opossums, and certain species of owls. Large cockroaches may prey on newborn young that fall to the ground.

Conservation Status.   This bat has been listed as a watch-list species by the Texas Organization for Endangered Species. Low population density has been the main concern, but recent information suggests it is not as rare as previously thought and probably should not be included on any species list of special concern. There has been speculation that this species could be threatened by logging of bottomland hardwoods and by destruction of major cave roosting sites.

California Myotis
Myotis californicus (Audubon and Bachman)

Description.   A small *Myotis* with small foot, short forearm, and relatively long tail; ears disproportionately large, extending slightly beyond snout when laid forward; ratio of foot to tibia 37 to 46, usually 43 to 46; ratio of tail to head and body 91 to 98; pelage full, long, and dull; profile of skull rises sharply to the forehead and decidedly flat-topped cranium; upperparts ochraceous tawny. Most easily confused with *M. ciliolabrum* but differs in smaller thumb (thumb and wrist together

California Myotis (*Myotis californicus*). Photo by J. Scott Altenbach.

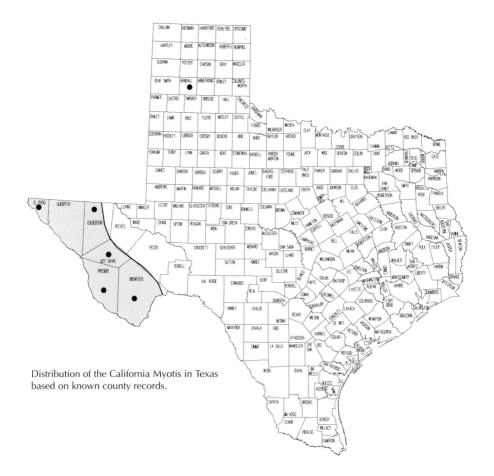

Distribution of the California Myotis in Texas based on known county records.

6–7.5 mm instead of 8–8.5 mm); smaller teeth; profile of skull rising abruptly, rather than gradually, to forehead; braincase broader. Dental formula: I 2/3, C 1/1, Pm 3/3, M 3/3 x 2 = 38. External measurements average: total length, 78 mm; tail, 37 mm; foot, 5.5 mm; ear, 13 mm; forearm, 32 mm. Weight, 3–5 g.

Distribution. A western species known in Texas from the Trans-Pecos region and one disjunct record from the Panhandle (Randall County). This is one of the few species that winters in the Trans-Pecos, where it is found in desert, grassland, and wooded habitats.

Subspecies. *M. c. californicus.*

Habits. These small bats are inhabitants of wooded canyons, open deciduous and coniferous forests, and brushy hillsides. Their daytime roosts are in crevices in the tops or sides of shallow caves, in cliffs and cavities, and in houses. They do not form the compact clusters typical of many other *Myotis* but roost in small colonies of 1–25 individuals. These bats seem to use buildings more frequently than other *Myotis*. They appear on the wing much later in the evening than most species of *Myotis*.

Specific food items are unknown, but this bat appears to feed primarily on small moths and beetles that occur between, within, or below the vegetative canopy. Their flight is relatively slow, fluttery, and highly erratic.

They winter in at least part of their summer range, where they hibernate in houses or caves. They are fairly active in winter, and winter records are relatively abundant from the southwestern United States. In summer, these bats seem quite transient and will use any suitable and immediately available site for shelter.

The single young is probably born in May, June, or July. Pregnancy records vary from 29 April to 6 July.

Conservation Status. This is one of the most common bats in the western part of Texas and does not appear to be in conservation trouble.

Western Small-footed Myotis

Myotis ciliolabrum (Merriam)

Description. A small *Myotis* with small feet, short ears, and relatively long tail; ratio of tail to head and body about 95; ratio of foot to tibia 40–45; upperparts light buff to warm buff, with slight tricolor effect; individual hairs blackish basally, succeeded by pale intermediate section and flaxen tips; underparts pale buff to nearly white; muzzle, chin, ears, and tragus blackish; sides of face from muzzle to ears blackish brown. Most easily confused with the small-footed *M. californicus* (see same for differences). Dental formula as in *M. californicus*. External measurements average: total length, 79 mm; tail, 37 mm; foot, 7 mm; ear, 13 mm; forearm, 33 mm. Weight, 4–5 g.

Western Small-footed Myotis (*Myotis ciliolabrum*). Photo by Merlin D. Tuttle, Bat Conservation International.

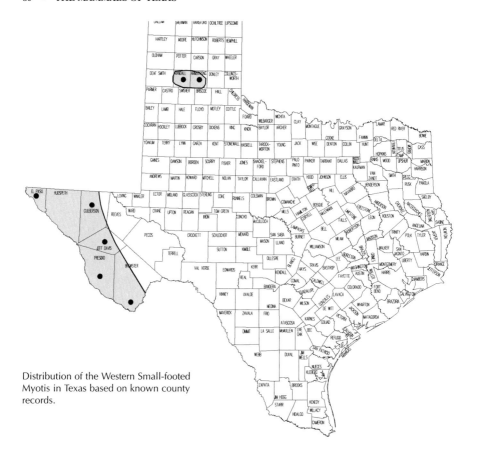

Distribution of the Western Small-footed
Myotis in Texas based on known county
records.

Distribution.   Restricted in Texas primarily to the Trans-Pecos region, although
two records are known from the High Plains of the Panhandle (Armstrong and
Randall counties). A small, resident population may occur in this area in the vicinity of Palo Duro Canyon.

Subspecies.   *M. c. ciliolabrum.*

Habits.   In the western United States, these bats are inhabitants of the deserts,
semideserts, and desert mountains. Their daytime roosts may be in crevices and
cracks in canyon walls, caves, mine tunnels, behind loose tree bark, or in abandoned houses. These bats hibernate in suitable caves or mine tunnels within the
range occupied in summer. Bats observed in winter are often found wedged deeply
into narrow cracks and crevices in the rock ceilings of old mines. When probed
from these crevices they are able to fly, which indicates they do not go into a deep
winter sleep.

Western small-footed myotises eat moths, flies, beetles, bugs, and ants, and
where the species occurs with the California myotis, it tends to forage in different
areas, often over rocky arroyos, and on different species of prey. They may feed
over water and close to the ground over desert chaparral vegetation. This bat is
strong enough to take off from the surface of water.

This bat follows a typical pattern of mating in the fall, sperm storage in the winter, and fertilization following ovulation in the spring. Records indicate that the single young born annually appears in late May to early July and begins to fly about one month later.

Conservation Status. This is a relatively rare bat in the western part of Texas, but there is not enough information available to determine its status accurately. For that reason, it is a species that should be monitored in the future.

Remarks. Scientists have had a difficult time determining the correct name of this species, as explained in the following account taken from *The Smithsonian Book of North American Mammals.* "It was known for years as *Myotis keenii* and was believed to occur throughout much of the United States and Canada. Later, it was called *M. subulatus,* and was divided into three races: *leibii, subulatus,* and *melanorhinus.* Subsequently, van Zyll de Jong showed that there were two species of small-footed bats: *Myotis leibii* in eastern North America and *M. ciliolabrum* in the west. *M. ciliolabrum* is divided into two subspecies: *ciliolabrum* and *melanorhinus.* Because of this confusion, one must be careful to determine whether a given author is discussing eastern or western small-footed myotis." Previous editions of *The Mammals of Texas* referred to these bats as either *M. subulatus* or *M. leibii.*

Southwestern Little Brown Bat
Myotis occultus (Holister)

Description. A small bat; hairs of back with long, glossy tips that produce a conspicuous sheen; pelage long and full, longest hairs about 10 mm; upperparts ranging from bronzy brown to olive brown; underparts grayish with rich, buffy suffusion; interfemoral membrane sparsely haired above, about to line joining knees; foot relatively large, a little more than half the length of tibia; ratio of tail to head and body less than 80; dorsal profile of skull gradually rising from relatively short rostrum. Dental formula as in *M. californicus.* External measurements average: total length, 85 mm; tail, 35 mm; foot, 9 mm; ear, 13 mm; forearm, 39.5 mm. Weight, 7–9 g.

Distribution. Only a single specimen of this bat has been collected in Texas. This specimen, consisting of a skin and skull only (U.S. Nat. Mus., 21083/36121), was collected in the early 1900s at a locality near Fort Hancock in Hudspeth County in the Trans-Pecos. *M. occultus* is relatively uncommon in the southwestern United States and northern Mexico. In New Mexico, *M. occultus* is known from low-elevation riparian areas in the Rio Grande Valley and montane highlands, and its occurrence near Fort Hancock would be consistent with this interpretation.

Subspecies. Monotypic species.

Habits. This bat spends the daytime in crevices in canyon walls, caves, attics, or other places of concealment and emerges shortly before dark. Its flight is erratic and relatively slow.

In the northeastern United States, these bats may migrate up to 320 km between winter and summer ranges, but in the west they are believed to hibernate

Southwestern Little Brown Bat (*Myotis occultus*). Photo by
Merlin D. Tuttle, Bat Conservation International.

near their summer range. As cold weather approaches the bats move to suitable
caves, mine tunnels, or other quarters where they hibernate and sleep through the
winter. During the period of preparation for winter, males and females are found
together and breeding takes place, but the ova are not fertilized at that time. This
habit of breeding in the fall has led some students to estimate the gestation period
of this species to be 300 days; however, the period of gestation is actually 50–60
days. The sperm from the fall mating are retained in the reproductive tract of the
female and fertilization of the ova does not take place until the following spring,
shortly before the bats leave their winter quarters. This ability is known as delayed
fertilization. A short breeding period may also occur in the spring. The single
young is born in June or July.

Food consists of insects captured in flight. Remains of small, night-flying beetles, bugs, and flies have been identified in their stomachs. These bats forage primarily over or near water.

Conservation Status.   This is one of the rarest species of bats in Texas. Populations
have declined sharply in much of its historical range in California as a result of pesticides, control measures in nursery colonies, and disturbance at hibernation sites.
It needs to be looked for elsewhere in the Trans-Pecos of Texas before its status
can be determined.

Remarks.   There has been a lengthy debate among taxonomists about whether *M.
occultus* is a distinct species or a subspecies of the more wide-ranging *M. lucifugus*.
Indeed, previous editions of *The Mammals of Texas* treated it as the latter, a subspecies of *lucifugus*. But recent molecular genetic studies published in the *Journal
of Mammalogy* by Mike Bogan and associates suggest that *occultus* is separated

from *lucifugus* by sufficient genetic distance to be considered a separate species. Those authors regard *M. occultus* as an uncommon but relatively widespread southwestern endemic bat that could be in jeopardy because of major population declines.

Northern Long-eared Myotis
Myotis septentrionalis (Trouessart)

Description. This is a small bat with dull, gray-brown pelage. Compared to other *Myotis* from Texas, *M. septentrionalis* has relatively long ears and an unkeeled calcar. As with all *Myotis,* this bat also has a narrow and sharp-pointed tragus. Dental formula as in *M. californicus.* External measurements average: total length, 78 mm; tail, 26 mm; foot, 9 mm; ear, 13 mm; forearm, 35 mm. Weight, 6–9 g.

Distribution. Widely distributed over eastern and northern North America, this bat is known in Texas on the basis of only one specimen collected in 1942 from Winterhaven, Dimmit County, in south Texas.

Subspecies. Monotypic species.

Habits. This bat hibernates in caves and mine tunnels in eastern Canada and in the United States from Vermont to Nebraska southward to Louisiana and Mississippi. It is more solitary in its habits than other *Myotis,* generally found singly or in small groups of up to 100 individuals. In summer, this bat may occasionally be found in hollow trees, rock crevices, behind tree bark, and in buildings.

Northern Long-eared Myotis (*Myotis septentrionalis*). Photo by Merlin D. Tuttle, Bat Conservation International.

M. septentrionalis commonly forages along forest edges, over forest clearings, and occasionally over ponds, but specific food habits remain unknown. These bats typically take their prey from the ground, branches, or foliage rather than catching them in flight. They usually carry their catches to perches to feed.

Little is known of the reproductive habits of this bat. Small nursery colonies seem the rule, and twinning may occasionally occur.

Conservation Status. This species is known in Texas on the basis of a single specimen collected in south Texas more than 50 years ago. Until recently, this was thought to represent a vagrant or wandering individual; however, the recent discovery of a population in western Louisiana, just across the border from Texas, raises the possibility of a permanent resident population in our state. Obviously, there is a need for more fieldwork in eastern Texas to determine the status of this species.

Remarks. Although it was previously considered a subspecies of *Myotis keenii* (*M. k. septentrionalis*), van Zyll de Jong elevated *M. septentrionalis* to full species status based on cranial, dental, and external characters. This taxonomic rearrangement created two monotypic species, *M. keenii* of the northwestern United States and Canada and the paler *M. septentrionalis* of eastern North America.

Fringed Myotis
Myotis thysanodes Miller

Description. A relatively large *Myotis* with large ears and a distinct fringe of short, stiff hairs on free edge of the membrane between hind legs; tail from 75 to 81% of length of head and body; foot from 50 to 75% of length of tibia; ears projecting about

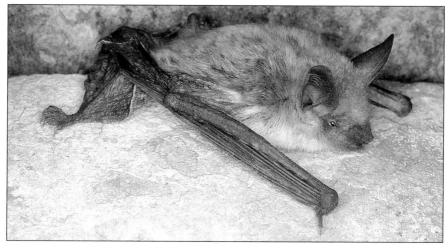

Fringed Myotis (*Myotis thysanodes*). Photo by John and Gloria Tveten.

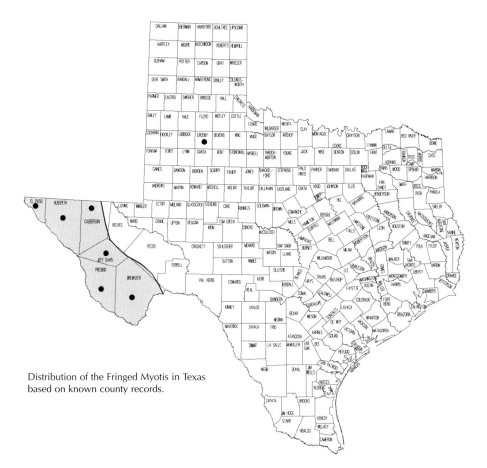

Distribution of the Fringed Myotis in Texas based on known county records.

5 mm beyond snout when laid forward; pelage full and about 9 mm long on the back; upperparts uniform warm buff, tips of hairs shiny, bases fuscous black; underparts dull whitish. Dental formula as in *M. californicus.* External measurements average: total length, 86 mm; tail, 35 mm; foot, 9 mm; ear, 16.5 mm; forearm, 43 mm.

Distribution.   A western bat known from Texas in the Trans-Pecos region in summer. Two specimens have been captured from northwest Texas (Crosby County), but they were probably seasonal migrants. The fringed myotis has been captured in habitats ranging from mountainous pine, oak, and pinyon-juniper to desert scrub but seems to prefer grassland areas at intermediate elevations.

Subspecies.   *M. t. thysanodes.*

Habits.   These bats roost in caves, mine tunnels, rock crevices, and old buildings in colonies that may number several hundred. This is a highly migratory bat that arrives in Trans-Pecos Texas by May, at which time it forms nursery colonies. The colonies begin to disperse in October, and the winter locales and habits of this bat remain a mystery.

This species appears late in the evening to forage. They fly slowly and are highly maneuverable, allowing the bats to forage close to the vegetative canopy or about the face of small cliffs. No data are available on their specific food habits in Texas, but specimens from New Mexico contained mostly small beetles.

The single young is born in late June or early July after a gestation period of 50–60 days. Gravid females captured on 28 June each contained a single fetus nearly ready for birth. Immature individuals have been found in July and August in colonies of adult females. The young are able to fly at 16–17 days of age. As with other species of *Myotis,* adult males and females do not associate with each other in summer.

Conservation Status. This is one of the most common bats in the Trans-Pecos region of Texas, and there are no known threats to its existence at this time.

Cave Myotis
Myotis velifer (J. A. Allen)

Description. Largest of the *Myotis* in Texas; hind foot large, more than half as long as tibia; ear short, reaching to or slightly beyond nostril when laid forward; upperparts uniform dull sepia; underparts much paler, tips of hairs pale cream buff. Dental formula as in *M. californicus.* External measurements average: total length, 90 mm; tail, 40 mm; foot, 9 mm; forearm, 42 mm. Weight, 12–15 g.

Distribution. Occurs over most of the Trans-Pecos, south Texas, eastern portions of the Panhandle, north-central Texas, and the Edwards Plateau.

Cave Myotis (*Myotis velifer*). Photo by Merlin D. Tuttle, Bat Conservation International.

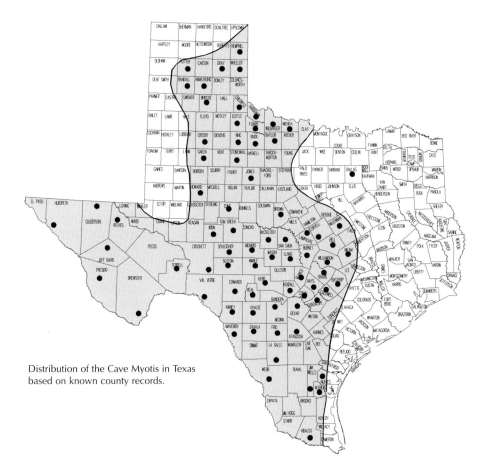

Distribution of the Cave Myotis in Texas based on known county records.

Subspecies. *M. v. incautus* in the south and *M. v. magnamolaris* northwestwardly.
Habits. This species is a colonial, cave-dwelling bat. They may also roost in rock crevices, old buildings, carports, under bridges, and even in abandoned cliff swallow nests. The cave myotis is second in abundance only to *Tadarida brasiliensis* on the Edwards Plateau, and it hibernates in central Texas caves in winter. It also hibernates in the gypsum caves of the Panhandle region. The bats usually roost in clusters that may number into the thousands. Other species occasionally found with the cave myotis include big-eared bats (*Corynorhinus*), free-tailed bats (*Tadarida*), big brown bats (*Eptesicus*), yuma myotis (*Myotis yumanensis*), and ghost-faced bats (*Mormoops*). Although those bats may roost at the same site as the cave myotis, the different species usually segregate, with different bats inhabiting separate areas or rooms of the roosting site.

These bats appear shortly after sunset and again just before sunrise to forage. They have been observed on several occasions coming into pools of water and open tanks in the late evening to drink. Their flight is stronger and less erratic than that of other species of *Myotis*.

Cave myotises are opportunistic insectivores that feed on a wide variety of insects, depending on what is most available on a given night. Small moths make up the largest portion of the diet, although small beetles, weevils, and ant lions are also taken. Because of their larger size and stronger flight, the cave myotis may be able to forage farther abroad than other species of *Myotis.*

In Texas, females have been found with embryos as early as mid-April. On the Edwards Plateau, lactating females are frequently captured in May, suggesting that birth of the single young occurs in early May.

Conservation Status. This species still appears to be common throughout its range in Texas, especially in areas where caves are common. Disruption of roost sites and pesticides have been implicated as threats in other parts of its range, though very little is known about such problems in Texas. At this time, there does not appear to be any reason to be concerned about the long-term status of this bat in Texas.

Long-legged Myotis
Myotis volans (H. Allen)

Description. A rather large *Myotis,* with relatively long tail, short ears and moderately large foot; underside of wing membrane well furred out as far as line joining elbow and knee; ratio of tail to head and body averaging 90–94; tibia relatively long, ratio of foot to tibia near 40; pelage full and about 7 mm long on back; profile of

Long-legged Myotis (*Myotis volans*). Photo by Merlin D. Tuttle, Bat Conservation International.

braincase rises abruptly from rostrum, giving a pug-nosed effect; ears short and rounded at tip. Dental formula as in *M. californicus*. External measurements average: total length, 93 mm; tail, 45 mm; foot, 7 mm; ear, 13 mm; forearm, 39 mm. Weight, 5–9 g.

Distribution. A western bat that occurs in Texas primarily in the central range of the Trans-Pecos, but it has also been recorded from the Rolling Plains (Knox County). It is doubtful that resident populations inhabit the Rolling Plains.

Subspecies. *M. v. interior.*

Habits. Over much of their range, long-legged bats are forest inhabitants, and they prefer high, open woods and mountainous terrain. Nursery colonies, which may contain several hundred individuals, form in summer in places such as buildings, cliff crevices, and hollow trees. These bats apparently do not use caves as day roosts, although they may use such sites at night. In winter, they hibernate in caves and mine tunnels.

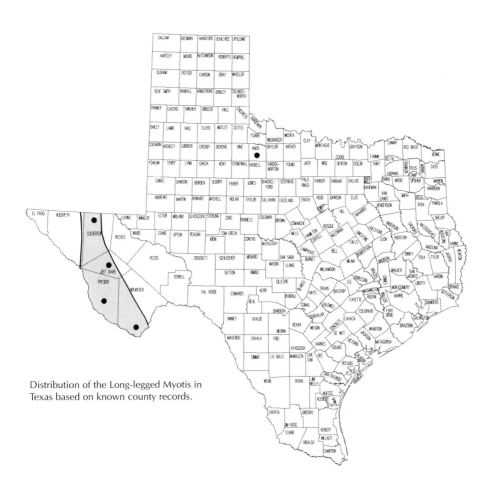

Distribution of the Long-legged Myotis in Texas based on known county records.

These bats emerge shortly before dark to forage around cliffs, trees, and over water. They are strong, direct fliers, and certain flyways seem to be used regularly. They feed mainly on moths but have been known to eat a variety of other soft-bodied insects.

Copulation occurs in late summer, but females store the sperm in their reproductive tracts during hibernation. Ovulation occurs in the spring, and a single young is born usually in June or July.

Conservation Status. Based on collecting records, this species is relatively rare in Texas, making it virtually impossible to determine its status. There is a need for more fieldwork to determine its population abundance so that potential threats can be assessed.

Yuma Myotis

Myotis yumanensis (H. Allen)

Description. A small bat similar to *M. occultus;* feet relatively large, more than half as long as tibia; ratio of tail to head and body more than 80; coloration dull, pale pinkish, or cream buff; immature individuals darker, nearly cinnamon buff; membranes pale brownish; underparts pale buff, nearly white; pelage short as compared with *M. occultus;* viewed from the side, the skull rises more abruptly from the rostrum than in *M. occultus;* dental formula as in *M. californicus.* External measurements average: total length, 78 mm; tail, 34 mm; foot, 8 mm; forearm, 34 mm. Weight, 4–8 g.

Distribution. Restricted in Texas to the southern Trans-Pecos eastward to Val Verde County, with a disjunct record from Starr County.

Subspecies. *M. y. yumanensis.*

Habits. This species, primarily an inhabitant of desert regions, is most commonly encountered in lowland habitats near open water, where it prefers to forage. It

Yuma Myotis (*Myotis yumanensis*). Photo by Merlin D. Tuttle, Bat Conservation International.

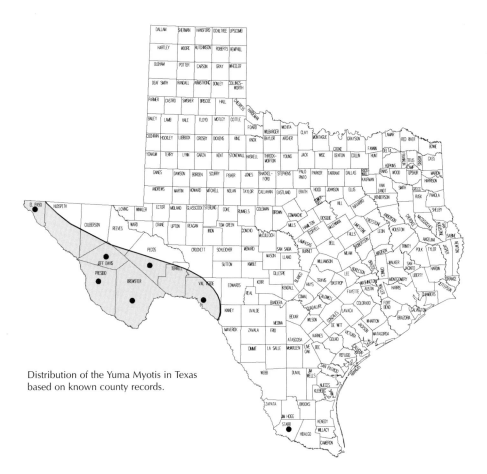

Distribution of the Yuma Myotis in Texas
based on known county records.

roosts in caves, abandoned mine tunnels, and buildings. In the Big Bend region of
Texas, it is common in summer along the Rio Grande, where it comes to drink just
after sundown. Specimens have been taken in riparian areas associated with cottonwood and willow trees and above open waters along the Rio Grande. The
species is known to occur in the Trans-Pecos from April through November, and
there is speculation it may hibernate in the area over the winter.

The stomachs of bats captured in Big Bend National Park contained moths,
froghoppers and leafhoppers, June beetles, ground beetles, midges, muscid flies,
caddisflies, and craneflies.

Females give birth from May to early July, and usually only one young is born
to each female.

Conservation Status. This bat appears to be relatively common in the desert
lowland habitats near the Rio Grande. At the present time, it does not appear to
be in bad shape, although there is a need for more information on population
abundance.

Western Red Bat (*Lasiurus blossevillii*). Photo by Merlin D. Tuttle, Bat Conservation International.

Western Red Bat

Lasiurus blossevillii Lesson and Garnot

Description.   A medium-sized bat similar in appearance to the eastern red bat (*Lasiurus borealis*). Pelage coloration is rusty red to brownish and lacks the white-tipped hairs that give the frosted appearance so characteristic of *L. borealis.* The posterior one-third of the interfemoral membrane is bare or only sparsely haired. *L. blossevillii* is slightly smaller than *L. borealis,* and most cranial measurements (greatest length of skull, zygomatic breadth, mastoid breadth, and length of maxillary tooth row) are significantly smaller. Dental formula: I 1/3, C 1/1, Pm 2/2, M 3/3 x 2 = 32. External measurements average: total length, 103 mm; tail, 49 mm; foot, 10 mm; ear from notch, 13 mm; forearm, 40 mm. Weight, 7–15 g.

Distribution.   Across the southwestern and far western areas of the United States south into Mexico and Central America. Known in Texas from only one specimen, from the Sierra Vieja in Presidio County of the Trans-Pecos.

Subspecies.   *L. b. teliotis.*

Habits.   Western red bats appear to prefer riparian areas, where they roost in tree foliage. In New Mexico and Arizona this bat is occasionally captured in riparian habitats dominated by cottonwoods, oaks, sycamores, and walnuts and is rarely found in desert habitats. In Mexico, this bat has been captured in riparian, xeric thorn scrub and pine-oak forests of the San Carlos Mountains, only 160 km south of the Texas border. The Texas specimen was captured over permanent water in desert scrub habitat.

This bat appears to be migratory in the southwestern United States. Specimens from Arizona, New Mexico, and Texas are all from summer. A winter withdrawal from this region to Mexico is likely.

The food habits and reproductive biology of this bat are poorly known. Females pregnant with three fetuses have been captured, and pregnant bats from New Mexico have been caught from mid-May to late June. *L. blossevillii* may raise as many as three young annually, with parturition occurring in mid-May through late June.

Conservation Status. There is but one record of this species in western Texas and little is known of its status. There is a real need to look for it in other areas of the Trans-Pecos. In Arizona, it is relatively common in riparian forest canopies associated with streams in desert mountain ranges.

Eastern Red Bat
Lasiurus borealis (Müller)

Description. A medium-sized, distinctly reddish bat with ears short, broad, rounded, and partly furred; membrane between hind legs densely furred above. Not easily confused with any other bat except *L. seminolus* and *L. blossevillii.* Upperparts reddish, the tips of the hairs white, producing a frosted appearance;

Eastern Red Bat (*Lasiurus borealis*). Photo by Merlin D. Tuttle, Bat Conservation International.

males usually lack the white-tipped hairs and are much redder. Dental formula as in *L. blossevillii.* External measurements average: total length, 108 mm; tail, 48 mm; foot, 9 mm; ear, 12 mm; forearm, 40 mm. Weight, 10–15 g.

Distribution.   Statewide, but rare in the Trans-Pecos.

Subspecies.   Monotypic species.

Habits.   Eastern red bats are forest-dwelling, solitary bats and are one of the few North American species that roost in the open in trees. They do not use caves, mine tunnels, or similar sites often frequented by other species. Roosting sites are common in tree foliage or Spanish moss, where the bats are concealed as they resemble dead leaves.

This bat is migratory and moves northward in spring and southward in fall. It is considered a year-round resident of eastern Texas but may only be a summer migrant in the western part of the state. These bats winter in the southern United States, Mexico, Bermuda, the Antilles, and perhaps even farther south.

They appear on the wing early in the evening to forage, and they typically follow a specific territory while feeding. They often hunt around street lamps in

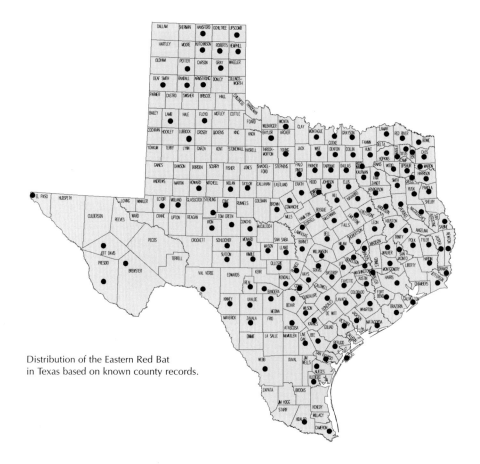

Distribution of the Eastern Red Bat
in Texas based on known county records.

towns and occasionally alight to capture insects. Twilight-flying insects such as moths, scarab beetles, planthoppers, flying ants, leafhoppers, ground beetles, and assassin beetles are among their favorite prey items.

The breeding range in the western United States appears to coincide with the bat's known distribution. Young bats are born in localities as far south as southern Texas and as far north as southern Canada. The young, two to four in number (usually three), are born in May, June, or July. This is one of the few bats that has more than two teats. The young ones remain with their mother for some time after they have learned to fly, and the family group roosts together.

Conservation Status.   The red bat occurs statewide, but it is much more common in the eastern part of the state, where it is a year-round resident, than in the Trans-Pecos, where it occurs only in the summer. At this time, there is no reason to be concerned about its status.

Hoary Bat

Lasiurus cinereus (Palisot de Beauvois)

Description.   A large bat; ears short, rounded, and with black rims; dorsal surface of membrane between hind legs and feet densely furred; upperparts grayish or brownish, heavily frosted with white; membranes brownish black except along forearm, where they are yellowish. Not easily confused with any other North

Hoary Bat (*Lasiurus cinereus*). Photo by Merlin D. Tuttle, Bat Conservation International.

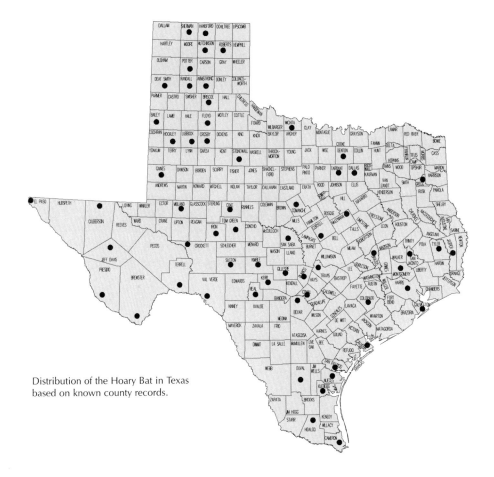

Distribution of the Hoary Bat in Texas
based on known county records.

American bat. Dental formula as in *L. blossevillii.* External measurements average: total length, 136 mm; tail, 57 mm; foot, 12 mm; ear, 18 mm; forearm, 52 mm. Weight, 20–35 g.

Distribution. Statewide migratory species.

Subspecies. *L. c. cinereus.*

Habits. This bat is migratory and moves northward in spring and southward in winter. Like its relative the red bat, with which it frequently associates, the hoary bat is more or less solitary and frequents wooded areas, where it roosts in the open by hanging from a branch or twig. It is a strong flier, and in association with other bats it is readily recognized by its large size and swift, erratic flight. This bat usually emerges rather late in the evening, but during migration it frequently is observed in daylight hours.

The chief food is moths, although they are also known to eat beetles, flies, grasshoppers, termites, dragonflies, and wasps. Apparently, the hoary bat feeds by approaching a flying moth from the rear, engulfing the abdomen-thorax, and then biting down, allowing the sheared head and wings to drop to the ground. Mating occurs during autumn migration, but implantation is delayed until spring. The usual number of young is two but ranges from one to four. In Texas, parturition occurs in mid-May into early July.

Conservation Status. This is a spring-fall migratory bat that is locally abundant at many places in the state. At this time, there appear to be no concerns about its status.

Southern Yellow Bat
Lasiurus ega (Gervais)

Description. A yellowish brown bat similar to *Lasiurus intermedius* but smaller. Dental formula: I 1/3, C 1/1, Pm 1/2, M 3/3 x 2 = 30. External measurements average: total length, 118 mm; tail, 51 mm; foot, 9 mm; forearm, 47 mm. One of the best characters to distinguish *L. ega* from *L. intermedius* is the length of the maxillary tooth row: in *ega* it is less than 6 mm, in *intermedius* more than 6 mm. Weight, 10–15 g.

Distribution. This is a Neotropical species that reaches the United States in southern California, southern Arizona, and southern Texas, where it has been recorded from Cameron, Hidalgo, Kleberg, Nueces, San Patricio, and Aransas counties. Its range extends southward east of the Andes to Uruguay and northeastern Argentina.

Subspecies. *L. e. panamensis.*

Habits. Like other members of the genus *Lasiurus,* southern yellow bats are associated with trees that can provide them with daytime roosting sites. In the vicinity of Brownsville, numbers of them inhabit a natural grove of palm trees (*Sabal*

Southern Yellow Bat (*Lasiurus ega*). Photo by Merlin D. Tuttle, Bat Conservation International.

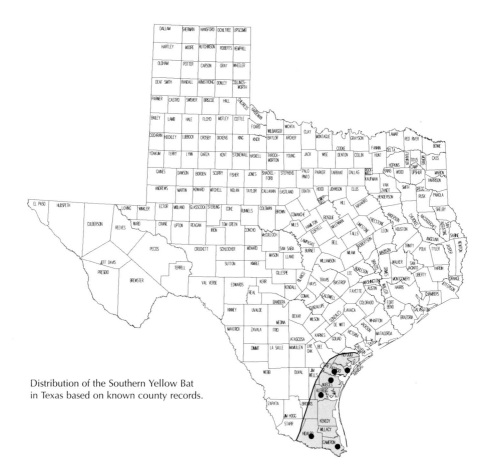

Distribution of the Southern Yellow Bat in Texas based on known county records.

texana). L. ega may be a permanent resident in that area; they have been captured there in six different months of the year, including December. These bats may be increasing their range in Texas as the use of ornamental palm trees in landscaping increases.

These bats feed on insects that they probably capture in flight. Bats observed in the Mexican state of San Luis Potosi started foraging about dusk. Nets stretched over ponds where bats came to drink did not catch any *L. ega* until about 2 hours after darkness. Stomachs of those captured at that time were crammed with insect remains.

The breeding season is in late winter in the south Texas area. Six females captured in late April all carried embryos; one had two very small embryos (3 mm crown–rump length), and the other five had three embryos each, with crown–rump lengths ranging from 11 to 14 mm. Of 11 females captured on 8 June, only one was pregnant. She contained four embryos, whose average crown–rump length was 25 mm. Nine of the other 10 females were lactating. Three females captured in June in the neighboring Mexican state of Tamaulipas were also lactating.

Conservation Status. Texas Parks and Wildlife has listed this bat as threatened only because of its limited distribution in the southern part of the state. It is common around Brownsville and in other parts of the Rio Grande Valley, northward to Corpus Christi. Tall palms are necessary roost sites, and this species would be really threatened only if such habitats were destroyed or in danger of destruction.

Northern Yellow Bat
Lasiurus intermedius H. Allen

Description. A large, yellowish brown bat with short ears and long, silky fur; membranes brownish; membrane between hind legs well haired on basal third or half, the terminal half and underside are nearly naked. Dental formula as in *L. ega.* External measurements average: total length, 140 mm; tail, 51 mm; foot, 11 mm; forearm, 58 mm. Weight, 14–31 g.

Distribution. Eastern and southern parts of state from Lamar County southward to Cameron County and westward to Bexar County.

Subspecies. *L. i. intermedius* from Victoria County southward and *L. i. floridanus* from Bexar and Travis counties eastward and north to Lamar County.

Habits. The distribution of this bat in the United States closely coincides with that of Spanish moss, which is its preferred roosting site. In south Texas, however,

Northern Yellow Bat (*Lasiurus intermedius*). Photo by Merlin D. Tuttle, Bat Conservation International.

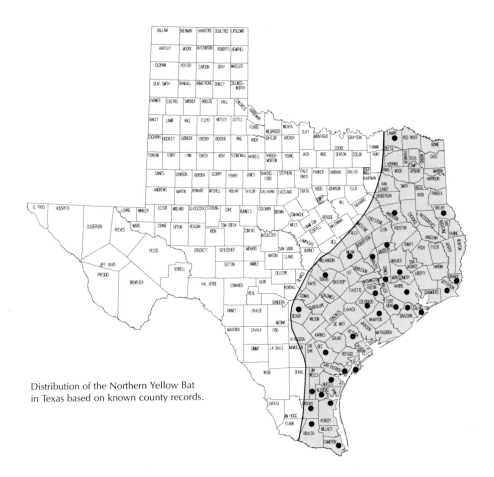

Distribution of the Northern Yellow Bat in Texas based on known county records.

these bats roost in palm trees, where they are well concealed beneath the large, drooping fronds. A single roosting site may contain several bats, and such groups are often quite noisy, especially when young are present; their bickering gives them away from below. Migration and winter habits are poorly known.

Northern yellow bats forage over open, grassy areas such as pastures, lake edges, and golf courses and along forest edges. In Florida they often form groups while feeding. Such foraging groups are segregated by sex; males are rarely found in such groups, and they seem to be more solitary in their habits than are females. Specific prey items include leafhoppers, dragonflies, flies, diving beetles, ants, and mosquitoes.

Females carry three to four embryos in spring, and litter size is believed usually to be two or three. Parturition probably occurs in late May or June in Texas.

Conservation Status.   This species occurs primarily along the Gulf Coast and the South Texas Plains, but it does not appear to be common anywhere in its range. Little is known of its status in Texas.

Seminole Bat (*Lasiurus seminolus*). Photo by Merlin D. Tuttle, Bat Conservation International.

Seminole Bat

Lasiurus seminolus (Rhoades)

Description. Similar to *Lasiurus borealis* but rich mahogany brown, slightly frosted with whitish. Dental formula as in *L. blossevillii.* External measurements average: total length, 103 mm; tail, 44 mm; hind foot, 10 mm; ear, 11 mm; forearm, 39 mm. Weight, 9–14 g.

Distribution. From the southeastern United States (Florida and the Carolinas) westward to Texas. In Texas the species is known primarily from the oak-hickory, pine-oak, and longleaf pine forest regions, with recent records extending the range westward to Hunt, Dallas, Coryell, and Williamson counties. Even more recently, a single specimen was collected in Val Verde County, approximately 275 km west of the known range for the species.

Subspecies. Monotypic species.

Habits. The distribution of Seminole bats seems to be closely associated with the distribution of Spanish moss, the clumps of which provide roosting sites. The adult bats are solitary, and roosts are usually occupied by a single individual or a female with young. Bat-inhabited moss clumps are usually shaded from the sun and often on the west and southwest exposures of oak trees. Bats have been observed roosting in such clumps from 1 to 5 m above the ground.

The bats emerge from their daytime roosts early in the evening and forage among or above the crowns of the trees, over watercourses, and around clearings. They may occasionally alight on vegetation to capture prey. Their food consists of true bugs, flies, beetles, and even ground-dwelling crickets.

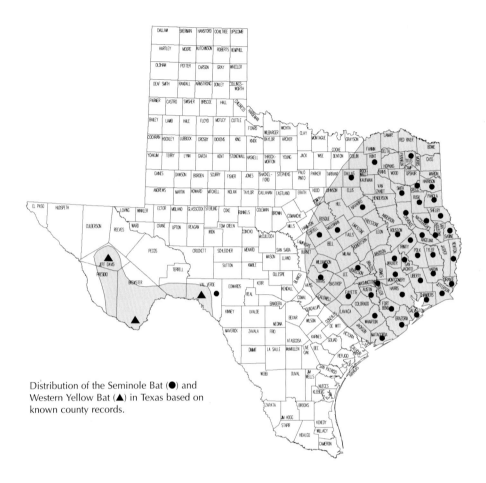

Distribution of the Seminole Bat (●) and Western Yellow Bat (▲) in Texas based on known county records.

The two to four (normally two) young are born in late May or June. The young bats grow rapidly and are thought to be capable of flight at the age of 3 or 4 weeks.

Seminole bats are thought to be resident within their range in the Deep South. They do not hibernate in the true sense but rather are active throughout the winter when weather conditions permit. Observations indicate that on days when the ambient temperature is below 20°C the bats do not leave their daytime roosts, but whenever temperatures in the evening exceed 20°C they emerge and take wing.

Conservation Status. This nonmigratory species is locally abundant throughout the forested regions of eastern Texas and does not appear to have declined substantially during the twentieth century.

Western Yellow Bat

Lasiurus xanthinus (Thomas 1897)

Description. Very similar in appearance to *Lasiurus ega*. Dorsal coloration is a pale yellow; brighter yellow hairs of the interfemoral membrane contrast with

Western Yellow Bat (*Lasiurus xanthinus*). Photo by Robert D. Bradley.

dorsal coloration. Lacks a dark face mask. Maxillary tooth row length in females, 5.7–5.9 mm. External measurements average: total length, 105 mm; hind foot, 10 mm; ear, 13.5 mm; forearm, 45 mm. Weight, 12–19 g.

Distribution. Ecologically, *L. xanthinus* seems to be associated with the dry, thorny vegetation of the Mexican Plateau, coastal western Mexico including parts of Baja California, and the deserts of the southwestern United States. Its occurrence in Texas is very recent (1990s), having been recorded from both Big Bend National Park and Black Gap Wildlife Management Area in Brewster County; from the Davis Mountains, Jeff Davis County; and from Del Rio, Val Verde County. See distribution map in the account for *Lasiurus seminolus*.

Subspecies. Monotypic species.

Habits. This species represents a recent addition to the fauna of Texas. All evidence suggests that this addition is a result of an expansion of the range of the species rather than the absence of previous collecting success. The reasons for a range expansion by this species are not well understood, but the most probable explanation is the warmer temperatures recently associated with west Texas. Vegetational changes in the region also may have facilitated the northward range expansion of the species. Cottonwood trees and other riparian vegetation in the Trans-Pecos region were almost exterminated early in the twentieth century, but the establishment of Big Bend National Park and other protected areas in the region have allowed the recovery of natural vegetation. This woody, riparian growth provides suitable roosting habitat for *L. xanthinus*.

Although only eight specimens have been reported from west Texas, the Black Gap and Davis Mountains specimens were captured during the summer and the Davis Mountains specimen was a lactating female, suggesting that a breeding population of this species occurs in the region.

Little is known of the diet of *L. xanthinus*. A fecal sample from one specimen collected during the fall in Big Bend National Park contained the remains of true bugs, flies, ants, moths, beetles, and grasshoppers.

Conservation Status.   This is an excellent example of a species that has recently invaded Texas in the Trans-Pecos region of the state. Its complete distribution and population abundance must be studied before its conservation status can be accurately determined. Collecting records suggest it is rare, although not as rare as *L. blossevillii, Myotis occultus,* or *M. septentrionalis.*

Remarks.   Until very recently the western yellow bat was considered to be conspecific with the southern yellow bat, *Lasiurus ega.* Recent karyotypical and electrophoretic studies by Robert J. Baker and his students at Texas Tech University, however, have shown that not only are *ega* and *xanthinus* specifically distinct but that *xanthinus* is more closely related in an evolutionary sense to *L. intermedius* than it is to *ega.*

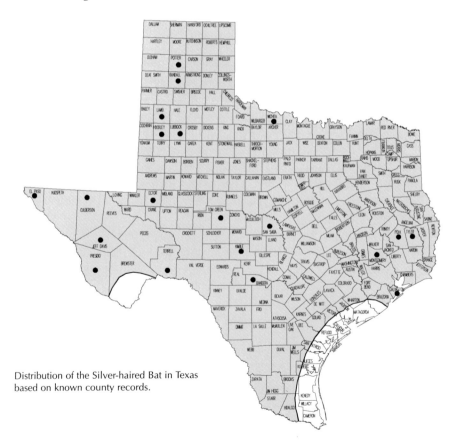

Distribution of the Silver-haired Bat in Texas based on known county records.

Silver-haired Bat (*Lasionycteris noctivagans*). Photo by
Merlin D. Tuttle, Bat Conservation International.

Silver-haired Bat

Lasionycteris noctivagans (Le Conte)

Description. A medium-sized, nearly black bat with dorsal surface of interfemoral membrane densely furred at least on the basal half and usually to near margins; upper and lower parts sooty brown or black with white tips of hairs producing a frosted appearance; membranes and ears sooty brown or black. Dental formula: I 2/3, C 1/1, Pm 2/3, M 3/3 x 2 = 36 (upper incisors and first lower premolar very small and easily overlooked). External measurements average: total length, 100 mm; tail, 40 mm; hind foot, 8 mm; ear, 16 mm; forearm, 41 mm. Weight, 8–12 g.

Distribution. Broadly but erratically distributed across northern North America; recorded from 20 widely distributed counties in six physiographic regions of Texas (Pineywoods, Gulf Prairies and Marshes, Edwards Plateau, Rolling Plains, High Plains, and Trans-Pecos). The species is apparently a fall-spring migrant. These bats are denizens of forested areas and seldom are observed in xeric areas except in migration. Except for the Guadalupe Mountains in the Trans-Pecos, midsummer records do not exist for Texas.

Subspecies. Monotypic species.

Habits. Cavities in trees and spaces under loose bark are favorite daytime retreats, but these bats may also use buildings. This species is migratory, at least in part. It spends the summer in northern latitudes and winters toward the south, even crossing several hundred kilometers of ocean to reach Bermuda. Surprisingly few winter records are available; thus, the mystery of just where these bats spend the winter is still not completely solved. It is likely that many of them winter on their breeding grounds because occasional individuals have been found hibernating as far north as New York and British Columbia. Interestingly, most summer records of this bat across the Southwest are of males, suggesting that geographical segregation of the sexes may occur during the warmer months. Females appear to move north in spring and summer to bear young, whereas the males remain behind at more southern locales.

This bat typically forages in or near coniferous or mixed deciduous forests adjacent to ponds or other sources of water. It is a relatively late flier that often appears after other bats have begun feeding. As with most other insectivorous bats, *Lasionycteris* is opportunistic in its feeding habits and takes a wide variety of small to medium-sized insects. The diet consists mostly of moths, with beetles, leafhoppers, true bugs, midges, flying ants and termites, and small flies also taken.

Mating presumably occurs during autumn, when the bats are migrating, and females presumably store sperm in their reproductive tracts over the winter. Following a gestation period of 50 to 60 days, twins are born in June or July. Small maternity colonies may form in hollow trees and abandoned bird nests. The young are black and wrinkled at birth and are able to fly when about 3 weeks old.

Conservation Status. This species is widely distributed in Texas, but it is not common. There do not appear to be any immediate threats to its status.

Western Pipistrelle

Pipistrellus hesperus (H. Allen)

Description. A small drab-gray or smoke-gray bat with distinct black, leathery facial mask and black membranes; tragus short, blunt, and slightly curved; underparts pale smoke-gray. Dental formula: I 2/3, C 1/1, Pm 2/2, M 3/3 x 2 = 34. External measurements of males average: total length, 66 mm; tail, 27 mm; foot, 5 mm; forearm, 28 mm; of females, 73-30-5-28. Weight, 3–6 g.

Distribution. Western Texas east to Uvalde, Knox, and Haskell counties.

Subspecies. *P. h. maximus.*

Habits. This bat is associated chiefly with rocky situations along watercourses. Its daytime retreat is in the cracks and crevices of canyon walls or cliffs, under loose rocks, or in caves.

These are among the most diurnal of bats, beginning their foraging flights very early in the evening and often remaining active throughout the early morning hours. Pipistrelles are slow bats and may be distinguished on the wing by their

Western Pipistrelle (*Pipistrellus hesperus*). Photo by Merlin D. Tuttle, Bat Conservation International.

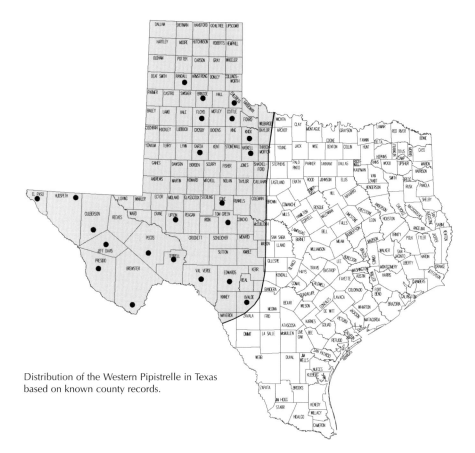

Distribution of the Western Pipistrelle in Texas based on known county records.

slow, fluttery flight, which is restricted to small foraging circuits. Occasionally, individual bats have been observed on the wing during midday, during which time they water to alleviate stress caused by the arid environment they inhabit.

Western pipistrelles forage from 2 to 15 m above ground on small, swarming insects and consume about 20% of their body weight in insects per feeding. Specific prey items include caddisflies, stone flies, moths, small beetles, leaf and stilt bugs, leafhoppers, flies, mosquitoes, ants, and wasps. Stomach contents of individual bats often contain only a single species of insect, or if more than one species is present the remains are clumped together within the stomach, suggesting that they take advantage of swarming insects and feed intensively within such swarms.

The young, numbering one or two (usually two), are born in June and July after a gestation period of approximately 40 days. Maternity colonies may be established in buildings or rock crevices. The newborn bats weigh slightly less than 1 g at birth but grow rapidly. By August they can fly and are difficult to distinguish from adults.

Conservation Status.   The western pipistrelle is one of the most common bats of the desert Southwest and does not appear to be in any conservation trouble.

Eastern Pipistrelle
Pipistrellus subflavus (F. Cuvier)

Description.   A small bat with leading edge of wing and the edges of the membrane between the hind legs much paler than rest of membranes; tragus long and slender; upperparts pale yellowish brown, with grizzled effect; the individual hairs

Eastern Pipistrelle (*Pipistrellus subflavus*). Photo by Merlin D. Tuttle, Bat Conservation International.

tricolored, dark basally, grayish yellow medially, and tipped with dusky. Dental formula: I 2/3, C 1/1, Pm 2/2, M 3/3 x 2 = 34. External measurements average: total length, 85 mm; tail, 41 mm; foot, 8 mm; ear, 14 mm; forearm, 35 mm. Weight, 4–6 g.

Distribution.   Eastern half of state including the Rolling Plains west to Armstrong County and central Texas as far west as Irion and Val Verde counties. Recent records from Lubbock and Presidio counties suggest the species may be expanding its range westward.

Subspecies.   *P. s. subflavus* over much of the range of the species in the state and *P. s. clarus* in the extreme southwest.

Habits.   These small bats are some of the earliest to emerge in the evening from their daytime retreats in caves, crevices in cliffs, buildings, and other man-made structures offering concealment. They are relatively slow and erratic in flight and often flutter and flit along watercourses or over pastures and woodlands like large moths. They appear to favor watercourses as foraging grounds. They are much more closely associated with woodlands than is the western pipistrelle.

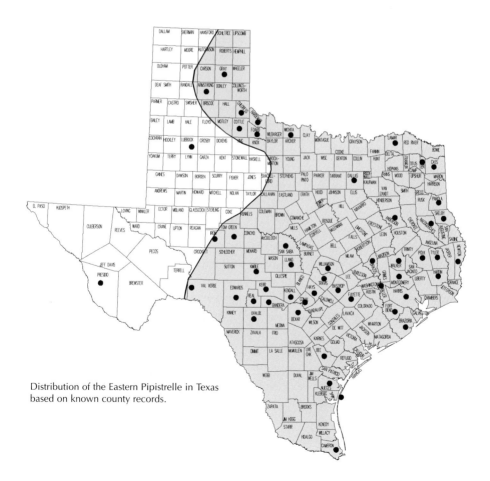

Distribution of the Eastern Pipistrelle in Texas based on known county records.

This species is known to spend the winter hibernating in suitable caves within its summer range. Its hibernation is more complete than that of most other American bats, and they generally roost singly or in small groups. Individuals may hang in one spot for weeks on end, and their torpor is so deep that they are not easily disturbed. They emerge from hibernation early in the spring and remain active well into the fall.

Little is known of their food habits in Texas. In Indiana they are known to eat small leafhoppers, ground beetles, flies, moths, and ants. Insects are caught in considerable quantities in a short period, and within 20 minutes the bats are gorged. They probably feed at intervals throughout the night and hang up to digest their meals between feeding times.

Mating takes place in the fall. They have been observed copulating as late as November, but males and females have been observed roosting together as early as August. During the period from March to August adult males and females usually occupy separate roosts. Data suggest that the sperm may remain viable in the vaginal tract of the female until spring, when ovulation occurs (in March or April) and fertilization of the ova takes place; however, copulation in the spring also has been observed.

Following a gestation period of about 60 days, twin pups are born, usually during June. The young grow rapidly and are able to fly at 2–3 weeks of age. They are weaned at about 4 weeks.

Conservation Status.   The eastern pipistrelle is one of the most common bats in the eastern part of Texas and appears to be expanding its range westward. At the present time, there are no reasons for concern about its status.

Big Brown Bat

Eptesicus fuscus (Palisot de Beauvois)

Description.   A medium-sized bat with upperparts rich chestnut brown; ears relatively small, thick, leathery, and black; membranes blackish; underparts paler than back; ears and membranes devoid of hair, or nearly so; wing short and broad, length of fifth metacarpal almost equal to that of third. Dental formula: I 2/3, C 1/1, Pm 1/2, M 3/3 x 2 = 32. External measurements average: total length, 114 mm; tail, 46 mm; foot, 11 mm; forearm, 47 mm. Weight, 13–20 g, rarely to 30 g.

Distribution.   Widely distributed over most of the eastern and western parts of Texas, but not yet recorded in the central part of the state. The eastern and western forms are regarded as different subspecies and may differ in reproductive habits as discussed below.

Subspecies.   *E. f. fuscus* in the east and *E. f. pallidus* in the west.

Habits.   This species is normally a forest dweller, but it does not hesitate to utilize attics and crevices in buildings, caves, and crevices in rocks for daytime retreats. Favorite roosts are under the loose bark of dead trees and in cavities of trees.

Big Brown Bat (*Eptesicus fuscus*). Photo by Merlin D.
Tuttle, Bat Conservation International.

Distribution of the Big Brown Bat in Texas
based on known county records.

These bats emerge rather early in the evening and feed among the trees, often following a regular route from one treetop to another and back again. In contrast to red bats (*Lasiurus borealis*), big brown bats prefer to forage among the crowns of the trees rather than under the forest canopy. Their flight is relatively slow and direct.

Big brown bats are relatively ferocious when captured. They usually squeal when handled and produce a rapid ratchetlike sound; they continually try to bite and usually draw blood when they succeed in doing so. They cannot produce a serious wound, however. In the water they swim well, but they cannot take off from the surface as can some of the smaller bats (*Myotis* and *Pipistrellus*). In winter they migrate or seek hibernation quarters in caves or buildings.

Their food is entirely insects, which they capture in flight. Fecal pellets of these bats have shown that they feed on beetles, bees and their allies, flies, stone flies, mayflies, true bugs, nerve-wings, scorpion flies, caddisflies, and cockroaches. Peculiarly, moths are seldom found. Food items vary, of course, from one region to another.

These bats mate in the fall, and the one or two young are born from May to August. Four embryos have been found in a female, but it is unlikely that they all would have survived because the mother has only two teats. Big brown bats in the eastern part of the United States usually produce two young per litter, whereas in the Rocky Mountains and westward only one young is produced. Since Texas spans both of these ranges, it is probable that bats in the High Plains, Rollings Plains, and Trans-Pecos have one young, whereas those of the Pineywoods typically produce twins. No fetal counts are available for East Texas specimens, but bats captured in the Trans-Pecos have contained only one fetus.

At birth, the young bats weigh about 3 g and grow quickly, gaining as much as 0.5 g per day. Maternity colonies are often located in buildings and may contain from 20 to 300 individuals. Adult males usually are not present in maternity colonies until the young mature, when they may begin using maternity colonies more frequently. At 4 weeks of age the young bats begin foraging for themselves and reach adult size approximately 2 months after birth.

Their known enemies include barn owls, great horned owls, and black snakes. **Conservation Status.** This species is a year-round resident and is common over most of its range in Texas. There are no known threats to its status.

Evening Bat

Nycticeius humeralis (Rafinesque)

Description. A small, nearly black or blackish brown bat; ears small, blackish, thick and leathery; underparts paler. Immature individuals are darker than adults. Dental formula: I 1/3, C 1/1, Pm 1/2, M 3/3 x 2 = 30. External measurements average: total length, 93 mm; tail, 39 mm; foot, 8.5 mm; forearm, 36 mm. Weight, 5–7 g.

Evening Bat (*Nycticeius humeralis*). Photo by Merlin
D. Tuttle, Bat Conservation International.

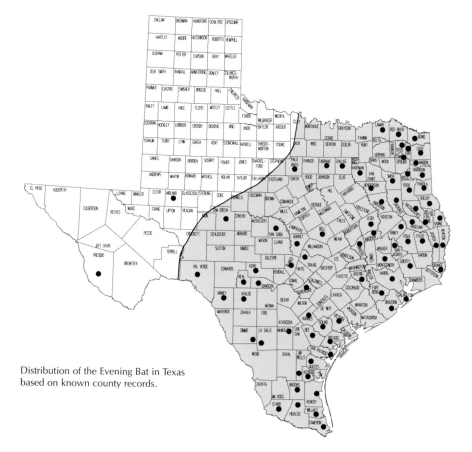

Distribution of the Evening Bat in Texas
based on known county records.

Distribution. Eastern one-third of state west to about Clay County in the north and Val Verde County in the south. The Tom Green and Val Verde county records are recent. Even more recent records from Midland and Presidio counties suggest a westward expansion of the range of this species.

Subspecies. *N. h. humeralis.*

Habits. These bats frequent forested areas and watercourses and utilize hollow trees as roosting sites and nurseries. They use the attics of houses and other man-made structures as roosts when natural sites are not available. They have been captured in all months of the year in Texas, indicating that they are year-round residents of the state. Their winter habits are not known. In summer the adult males and females do not use the same roosts.

Evening bats seem to have two preferred times of foraging, one in the early evening hours and then again just before dawn. Specific prey items include small night-flying insects such as bugs, flying ants, spittle bugs, June beetles, pomace flies, Japanese beetles, and moths.

Copulation takes place in the fall, but it is not known where this occurs. Two young are born to the female in late May to early June. Nursery colonies may contain several hundred individuals, and at this time the colonies are usually segregated by sex, with adult males rarely encountered in the nursery colonies. The young ones, at least on occasion, accompany their mother, attached to her breast. The young bats are volant at approximately 20 days of age and are nearly adult size by 1 month of age.

Conservation Status. The evening bat is common east of the 100th meridian in Texas, and apparently has begun a gradual expansion west of that line. It is a year-round resident, roosting in hollow trees and in attics of buildings, and has probably been served well by human development.

Spotted Bat

Euderma maculatum (J. A. Allen)

Description. A moderately large bat with extremely large ears and a conspicuous dorsal color pattern of three large white spots, one on each shoulder and one on the rump, on a black background; a small white patch at the base of each ear; hairs on the underparts with white tips and blackish bases. Ears and membrane in living individuals pinkish; pale brownish in preserved specimens. Dental formula: I 2/3, C 1/1, Pm 2/2, M 3/3 x 2 = 34. External measurements average: total length, 124 mm; tail, 51 mm; ear, 42 mm; forearm, 51 mm; foot, 12 mm. Weight, 16–20 g.

Distribution. The semiarid regions of the western United States and northern Mexico from southwestern Idaho and south-central Montana southward to the Mexican states of Durango and Queretaro. Known in Texas only from specimens captured in Big Bend National Park, Brewster County.

Subspecies. Monotypic species.

Spotted Bat (*Euderma maculatum*). Photo by Merlin D. Tuttle, Bat Conservation International.

Habits. Although unmistakable in appearance, the spotted bat is one of the least understood of American bats, primarily because of its relative scarcity, at least in collections. There have been scattered records of this bat throughout the western United States dating back to 1891, but it has been taken with any regularity only in California, Arizona, New Mexico, southern Utah, and southern Colorado. It was first found in Texas by David Easterla, who captured two adult females in early August 1967 in mist nets set above a pool in a shallow, barren, hot, dry canyon in Big Bend National Park.

The infrequency of capture of this bat has caused much confusion and speculation regarding its habitat. Several authors have reported captures in pine forests at high elevations (2,400 m); others from a pinyon pine–juniper association, and still others from open scrub associations in desert areas. One worker has suggested that females give birth to their young in forested situations and later move to the lower elevations; another suggests that the bat is a cliff dweller and roosts in cracks and crevices of canyon walls. A large number of the known specimens were captured in mist nets set over permanent streams or water holes adjacent to steep cliffs in open scrub desert country.

Little is known of the behavior of the spotted bat except that it appears to be most active well after dark. Most individuals caught in mist nets set over water, where bats come to drink, have been captured after midnight. Easterla speculated that its swoop over a water hole is made at relatively high speeds because several of the bats he has captured have been injured when they struck the nets. While in flight the bat emits a series of strident tics similar to, but higher pitched than, those of the Mexican big-eared bat, *Idionycteris phyllotis*. Several authors have commented on the docile disposition of captive spotted bats, but occasional individuals are ill tempered. Available data indicate that moths are highly important in their diet. In fact, these bats may feed almost exclusively on moths.

Data on reproduction are sparse. A gravid female captured by Easterla on 11 June, in Big Bend National Park, gave birth a few hours later to a single male baby that weighed 4 g (one fourth of his mother's weight!). One of two females Easterla captured in the park in early August was lactating; the other was in a postlactating condition. Two females captured 30 June and 1 July in Catron County, New Mexico, were in postpartus condition and lactating, as were three females collected in Garfield County, Utah, in mid-August. Thus, it appears that a single offspring is born to each sexually active female in June or July. The young are altricial and do not show the characteristic spotted color pattern of the adults.

Conservation Status. This beautiful bat has a wide distribution in western North America, from southern Canada to central Mexico, but is not known to be common anywhere within its range. In Texas, it is known only from Big Bend National Park but probably will be found elsewhere in the Trans-Pecos region. The restricted range in Texas accounts for its listing by Texas Parks and Wildlife as a threatened species. The U.S. Fish and Wildlife Service has taken the position that much more knowledge is needed before any type of endangered or threatened listing should be considered.

Rafinesque's Big-eared Bat (*Corynorhinus rafinesquii*). Photo by Merlin D. Tuttle, Bat Conservation International.

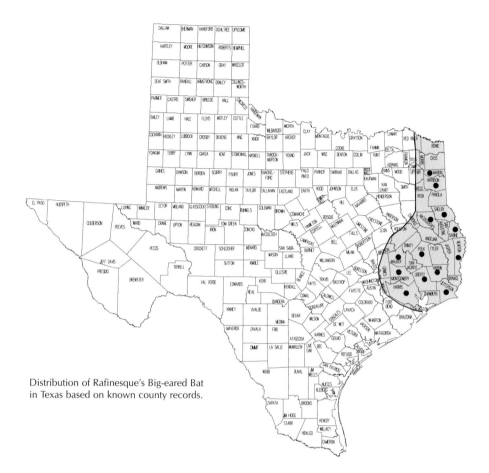

Distribution of Rafinesque's Big-eared Bat in Texas based on known county records.

Rafinesque's Big-eared Bat

Corynorhinus rafinesquii (Lesson)

Description.   Similar to Townsend's big-eared bat, but hairs of the underparts have white tips that contrast sharply with the dark bases; long hairs on foot project noticeably beyond the ends of the toes; middle upper incisors with a secondary cusp; median postpalatal process triangular in shape with a broad base. Dental formula as in *C. townsendii*. External measurements average: total length, 100 mm; tail, 46 mm; foot, 12 mm; forearm, 43 mm. Weight, 7–13 g.

Distribution.   A bat of the southeastern United States, Rafinesque's big-eared bat reaches the westernmost portion of its range in the pine forests of East Texas.

Subspecies.   *C. r. macrotis.*

Habits.   Unlike the closely related *C. townsendii*, Rafinesque's big-eared bat occurs in forested regions largely devoid of natural caves. Its natural roosting places are in hollow trees, crevices behind bark, and under dry leaves. It has been observed most frequently in buildings, both occupied and abandoned. Texas specimens have been captured in barns and abandoned wells. *C. rafinesquii* appears to be a solitary bat, although colonies of 2–100 may be encountered in summer. Winter aggregations, usually of both sexes, are more numerous, but even then solitary individuals are frequently found. The bats probably do not hibernate in East Texas, but in the northern part of their range they tend to seek out underground retreats and hibernate through the winter.

Corynorhinus rafinesquii emerges from its daytime roost well after dark to forage. Specific food items have not been recorded, but small, night-flying insects, especially moths, are probably important.

The single young is born in late May or early June; they shed their milk dentition by mid-July and reach adult size and appearance in August or September.

Conservation Status.   One of the rarest bats in the state, this species has been listed by Texas Parks and Wildlife as threatened. It bears special watching because of its scarcity, lack of knowledge concerning population levels, and the considerable potential that exists for degradation of roosting and feeding sites by commercial logging practices in preferred habitat. There is a real need to determine the effects of modern timber management practices on this species.

Remarks.   In previous editions of *The Mammals of Texas,* the New World big-eared bats were arranged in the genus *Plecotus.* In 1992, however, Darrel Frost and Robert Timm reported the results of an analysis of 25 morphological and 11 karyological characters that support separate generic status for *Corynorhinus.* More recently, this interpretation has been strongly supported by genetic sequence analyses conducted by Steven Hoofer and Ronald Van Den Bussche of Oklahoma State University.

Townsend's Big-eared Bat (*Corynorhinus townsendii*). Photo by Merlin D. Tuttle, Bat Conservation International.

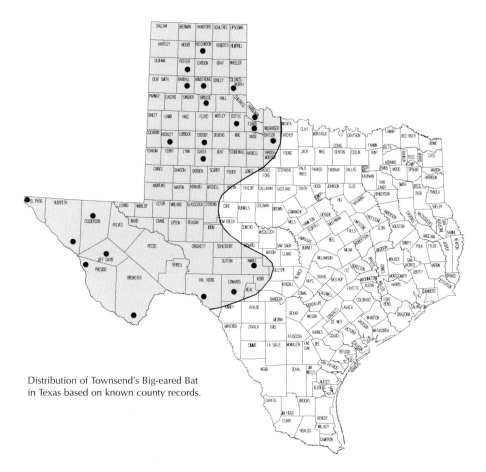

Distribution of Townsend's Big-eared Bat in Texas based on known county records.

Townsend's Big-eared Bat

Corynorhinus townsendii (Cooper)

Description. A medium-sized bat with extremely long ears and a small glandular outgrowth on each side of the snout. Upperparts near clove-brown on back, wood-brown on sides, underparts slightly paler; membrane between hind legs full, wide, and hairless. The combination of large flexible ears, nearly uniform color, and the lumps on the snout identifies this bat. Dental formula: I 2/3, C 1/1, Pm 2/3, M 3/3 x 2 = 36. External measurements average: total length, 100 mm; tail, 46 mm; foot, 11 mm; ear, 35 mm; forearm, 44 mm. Weight, 7–12 g.

Distribution. Suitable habitat in western half of state.

Subspecies. *C. t. pallescens.*

Habits. The distribution of this bat is correlated largely with rocky situations where caves or abandoned mine tunnels are available. They do not seem to utilize crevices in such sites and may occasionally inhabit old buildings. In the Trans-Pecos, this is probably the most characteristic bat of caves and mines.

Townsend's big-eared bats hibernate throughout their range during winter months when temperatures are between 0°C and 11.5°C. The bats hibernate in tight clusters, which may help stabilize body temperature against external changes in temperature. While torpid, the large ears are rolled up and laid back against the animal's neck. Males may select warmer hibernacula than do females and are more easily aroused and active in winter than are females. Their winter sleep is interrupted by frequent periods of wakefulness during which they move about in the caves or from one cave to another. They become very fat before hibernation. This fat provides them with sufficient food to maintain their lowered metabolism during the winter months when they do not eat. Males and females occupy separate roosting sites during summer. During this season, males appear to lead a solitary lifestyle, while females and young form maternity colonies that may number 12–200, although in the eastern United States colonies of 1,000 or more are known.

These bats emerge late in the evening to forage and are swift, highly maneuverable fliers. Prey items include small moths, flies, lacewings, dung beetles, and sawflies.

The single young is born in late May to early June, at least in Texas. The baby bat weighs approximately 2.4 g at birth and is pink, naked, and completely helpless. At 4 days of age the newborn bat begins to display hair growth and by 1 month of age is volant and nearly adult size. At 2 months of age the juveniles are weaned and the nursery colonies begin to disperse.

Conservation Status.   This species occurs in suitable habitat (preferring caves and mine tunnels) in the western half of the state. It is among the rarest bats in Texas, and the recent practice of blasting old mine tunnels to shut them off permanently could destroy significant numbers of these bats. This is definitely a species that bears watching in the future.

Pallid Bat

Antrozous pallidus (Le Conte)

Description.   A rather large, pale, yellowish brown bat. Ears about 2.5 cm long, broad, naked, and crossed by 9 or 11 transverse lines; bases of hairs light (nearly white), tips dusky; large light spot between shoulders; underparts paler and lacking dusky-tipped hairs; membranes nearly naked and brownish; nostrils surrounded by a glandular ridge producing a blunt snout; feet relatively large and strong. Dental formula: I 1/2, C 1/1, Pm 1/2, M 3/3 x 2 = 28. External measurements average: total length, 113 mm; tail, 46 mm; foot, 12 mm; ear, 28 mm; forearm, 48 mm. Weight, 12–17 g.

Distribution.   A common resident of the western half of Texas.

Subspecies.   *A. p. pallidus* over most of the range in the state; *A. p. bunkeri* in the vicinity of the Red River and in the Panhandle.

Habits.   Pallid bats inhabit rocky outcrop areas where they commonly roost in rock crevices, caves, and mine tunnels, but they also roost in the attics of houses,

Pallid Bat (*Antrozous pallidus*). Photo by Merlin D. Tuttle, Bat
Conservation International.

Distribution of the Pallid Bat in Texas
based on known county records.

under the eaves of barns, behind signs, in hollow trees, and in abandoned adobe buildings. Colonies are usually small and may contain 12–100 bats. Pallid bats usually appear on the wing relatively late at night, well after dark. Although occasional individuals have been reported from the United States in winter, their winter habits are poorly known. The species appears to migrate on a limited basis, and the bats are thought to move locally to deep recesses of mine shafts or caves to avoid cold winter weather.

Their feeding habits are unlike those of most American bats. For years naturalists have noted the kitchen middens of discarded wings and other hard parts of insects under their feeding roosts. Among them were remains of Jerusalem crickets, scorpions, and other flightless arthropods, although their diet also includes flying insects. To some extent though, pallid bats are terrestrial foragers. They have been observed flying, apparently at random, over an area at levels of 15–90 cm above the ground. When prey is located, often by passive sound (in addition to echolocation), the bat abruptly drops to the ground, searches briefly, grabs its victim in its mouth, and takes off. Captured prey is taken to a feeding station where it is consumed. A. E. Borell described how one of these bats consumed a grasshopper. While eating, the bat hung from a perch head upward, supported by the thumbs, with the wings partly spread. The legs held the posterior part of the body well out from the timber and with the tail curved forward against it; the interfemoral membrane formed a pouch to catch parts of the large insect as they dropped.

Other than the items mentioned above, pallid bats also eat moths, froghoppers and leafhoppers, June beetles, and grasshoppers. In fact, 54 different types of prey have been documented for the pallid bat. Large night-flying insects and ground-dwelling arthropods are most prevalent in the diet, however.

Mating occurs in fall, with parturition in early summer. Females may carry one to four embryos, but the birth of twins is usual. The length of gestation is 53–71 days. In Texas, the baby bats are born in early May to mid-June. Newborn bats weigh approximately 3 g and seem to develop more slowly than other species. The eyes open at 8–10 days of age, hair is evident at 10 days, and the young are volant by 6 weeks of age. Young bats have been found to contain both milk and insect remains in their stomachs, indicating that the young continue to nurse after becoming volant.

Conservation Status. Pallid bats are among the most abundant bats in the western sector of Texas. At this time, there is no need to worry about the conservation status of this species.

FAMILY MOLOSSIDAE (FREE-TAILED BATS)

Nearly 90 species of the family Molossidae, or free-tailed bats, are found worldwide, primarily in tropical and subtropical regions of the Old World and Mexico south through South America. These bats are medium to large-sized, insectivorous, and characterized by a tail that extends beyond the free edge of the uropatagium.

Molossids are swift, strong fliers and often fly great distances between roosting and feeding sites. Many species also make extensive migrations between winter and summer ranges. Because of their narrow wings, free-tailed bats have difficulty taking off from the ground and often roost high in buildings, cliffs, and caves. They require a free-fall for takeoff to enable them to achieve sufficient momentum to sustain level flight.

In North America free-tailed bats occur from Canada to Mexico, but they are most common in the southern and southwestern regions of the United States. Of the 6 species that occur in North America, 4 are known from Texas.

Brazilian Free-tailed Bat
Tadarida brasiliensis (I. Geof. St.-Hilaire)

Description. A medium-sized bat with broad ears, large feet, and terminal half of tail free; ears broad, extending to tip of snout when laid forward, apparently, but not actually, united across forehead, with a series of wartlike structures on anterior rim; tragus small and blunt; second joint of fourth finger 6–9 mm long; feet with distinct white bristles on sides of outer and inner toes; ratio of foot to tibia about 75; pelage short (3–4 mm) and velvety; upperparts varying from reddish to black;

Brazilian Free-tailed Bat (*Tadarida brasiliensis*). Photo by John and Gloria Tveten.

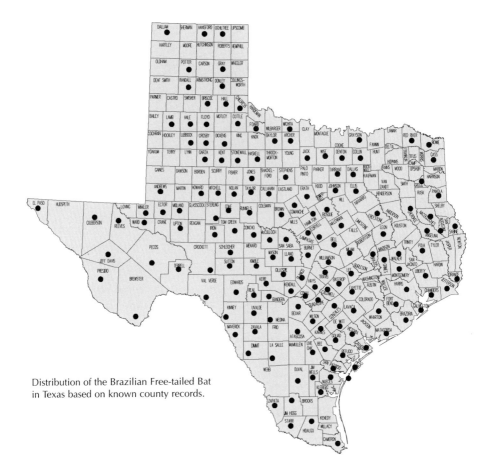

Distribution of the Brazilian Free-tailed Bat in Texas based on known county records.

underparts slightly paler; membranes and ears blackish. Dental formula: I 1/2 or 1/3, C 1/1, Pm 2/2, M 3/3 x 2 = 30 or 32. The total number of lower incisors is variable, usually six, sometimes four, occasionally five. External measurements average: total length, 95 mm; tail, 38 mm; foot, 10 mm; ear, 19 mm; forearm, 42 mm. Weight, 11–14 g.

Distribution. Statewide in summer; western subspecies migrates to Mexico in autumn; eastern subspecies a year-round resident.

Subspecies. *T. b. cynocephala* in the eastern fourth of the state and *T. b. mexicana* elsewhere.

Habits. These bats utilize caves, mine tunnels, old wells, hollow trees, human habitations, bridges, and other buildings as daytime retreats. The prime necessity for a roost seems to be some relatively dark, dry retreat where from several dozen to several million individuals can hang up in close association and have an unobstructed space below into which they can drop when taking wing. Hollows under the roofs, spaces between downtown buildings, attics, narrow spaces between signs and buildings, and spaces in the walls of buildings all offer suitable refuge sites for these bats. Because of their frequent occurrence about and in buildings, they frequently are termed house bats.

Brazilian free-tailed bats appear every year in Texas in multimillion numbers to inhabit a few select caves (known as guano caves) located in the Balcones Escarpment and the adjacent Edwards Plateau. The total population of these bats that inhabit Texas caves during the summer has been estimated at 95 million–104 million. These same caves have been the summer homes of this animal for at least the past 100 years. Few, if any, house bats ever overwinter in the Texas guano caves. They spend the depth of winter, from early December to late February, at lower latitudes, probably in Mexico, Central America, or even South America. In East Texas, where these bats are common inhabitants of old buildings and similar structures, they are nonmigratory and are year-round residents of that part of the state.

Bracken Cave, near New Braunfels along the southeastern edge of the Hill Country, is the world's largest bat colony, serving as a nursery colony for adult female free-tailed bats and their young and housing perhaps as many as 20 million to 40 million bats during the summer. Likewise, the largest urban colony of bats in North America is at the Congress Avenue Bridge in Austin. This colony, which numbers about 2.5 million free-tailed bats in the summer, has become one of the major tourist attractions in that city. So common and well known are these bats in Texas that they have been designated as the official state flying mammal of Texas.

Brazilian free-tailed bats appear on the wing several minutes before dark. The famous bat flights at Carlsbad Caverns are made up almost entirely of this species. William B. Davis watched these bats emerge from the attic of a house one evening. They fell from the exit, dropped nearly to the ground, then zoomed upward and, flying high, disappeared from view, each bat following the general direction of the one in front of it. In foraging, the bats fly rather high (15 m or more as a rule), except when sweeping over some body of water to drink. Their flight is rapid and aggressive, reminding one of swifts, and the long, angular, narrow wings, plus relatively large size, make them easy to identify.

Samples of their droppings collected at San Antonio contained remains of the following insects: moths (nearly 90% of the total number of insects eaten), ground beetles, leaf chafers, weevils, leaf beetles, flying ants, water boatmen, green blowflies, and leafhoppers. A separate food habits study showed these bats take small prey 2–10 mm in length and listed the following food items and proportions: moths (34%), flying ants (26.2%), June beetles and leaf beetles (16.8%), leafhoppers (15%), and true bugs (6.4%). *Tadarida brasiliensis* often feeds on swarms of insects. The huge summer colonies of these bats clearly would have a great impact on nearby insect populations; they are estimated to destroy from 6,000 to 18,000 metric tons of insects annually in Texas.

This bat has received considerable attention because it is a known carrier of rabies. Specimens of the Brazilian free-tailed bat are submitted to the Texas

Department of Health (TDH) more often than any other species, and the species typically has the highest incidence of rabies of those submitted. Of 1,455 specimens submitted to the TDH from 1994 to 1998, 258 (18%) tested positive for the rabies virus. Although the total number of confirmed rabies cases is minuscule when compared to the population of bats as a whole, caution should be exercised when one of these bats is encountered, or any species of bat for that matter.

The major event in the life of the house bats summering in Texas is the birth and development of their young. Well over 90% of the returning females produce young each year. Most mating in the Texas population is accomplished each spring before the bats arrive at the Texas caves. Male house bats predominate at the caves for a brief period in early spring, but they are quickly outnumbered by females as populations build steadily with the approach of parturition. By mid-June, adult females outnumber adult males more than three to one.

More than 70% of the young are born within a brief span of about 10 days. More than 90% of all births occur within 15 days of the mid-June mean birth date. The newborn young are deposited together, naked and flightless, on specific areas of the ceiling in continuous colonies and are not carried by their mothers during the nocturnal feeding flights.

The almost simultaneous arrival of the babies creates marked crowding in the cave colony clusters. In the past it was thought that adult females made no attempt to locate their own young within these masses, but nursed the first two young encountered on their nightly return to the roost. Studies have shown that females do indeed recognize their own young, which is a remarkable feat given the confusion with such huge swarms of bats. The mothers locate their pups using a combination of locational, vocal, and olfactory information. The babies grow rapidly in the incubator-like climate of the caves. Within a month after birth the majority of babies are furred, of body length almost equal to that of the adults, and capable of flying out to feed on their own.

The sudden increase in numbers of flying bats resulting from the mass achievement of fledgling status among the babies creates additional congestion in the caves. The congestion is relieved by the rapid disappearance of the adults as the fledglings appear. These adults presumably move rapidly south out of Texas; the missing adults have not been found elsewhere in Texas at this time. After late July, fledglings predominate in the diurnal feeding flights from the caves, and they tend to reside at the cave of their birth until the onset of cool weather in October and November drives them south out of Texas.

In Texas, the Brazilian free-tailed bat seems to be primarily a cave dweller, and its use of buildings as roosts is likely a relatively recent, possibly expanding practice. Only a small fraction of the numbers of bats found in caves is ever found in the total of all roosts in buildings. Every town in the Brazilian free-tailed bat's range in Texas is likely to have at least 15 roosts per 5,000 human population, but the occupation of buildings is especially common in eastern Texas. Most roosts in buildings house fewer than 100 bats at a time, but a few buildings traditionally house many hundreds each year. Overwintering in buildings occurs infrequently in the southern Gulf Coast prairies of Texas.

No particular style, size, age, state of repair, or use by humans exempts a building from use by Brazilian free-tailed bats. The critical feature is whether the building has any accessible small cracks or niches that permit bats to retreat into semidarkness during the day. Such openings usually are to be found even in the most modern, compact types of structure. One architectural type common in south Texas, the Spanish-style building with clay tile roof, is among the most vulnerable to invasion by Brazilian free-tailed bats. The bats roost under the tiles, and seldom can they be driven out permanently either by killing those present or by chemical treatment of the surface of the roost. The simplest, most effective method is to close the entrance to the roost. With clay tile roofs this is almost impossible, unless the tile is replaced by some other kind of roofing material.

The abundance of Brazilian free-tailed bats roosting in Texas buildings follows an annual pattern of one peak in spring and another in fall, with general midsummer and midwinter lows or periods of complete absence. This pattern complements that of bat abundance in the guano caves. Brazilian free-tailed bats in Texas buildings during spring and fall usually are itinerant between tropical latitudes and the midlatitude guano caves of Texas, Oklahoma, Kansas, and New Mexico. Sufficient interchange of banded Brazilian free-tailed bats has occurred among the guano caves of Texas and between those in Texas and the ones in neighboring states to demonstrate that individual bats are not compelled to return each year to the cave of their birth. Rather, Brazilian free-tailed bats exhibit the ability to range over great distances and find the widely separated, often well hidden, entrances to the few traditional guano caves and roosts in buildings.

The flight of Brazilian free-tailed bats on leaving and returning to a roost uniformly is accomplished in groups. It is presumed, therefore, that group flight is the norm in this animal. Yet, in the roosting clusters, where grouping is also the norm, there is strong evidence that each bat has an affinity not to a specific, stable group of acquaintances but to any convenient group of its kind.

The gestation period of Brazilian free-tailed bats appears to be slightly in excess of 90 days. No more than one young is born per year by each adult female. Females in Texas are almost all pregnant the summer following birth. The left horn of the uterus does not carry an embryo. Lactation begins after delivery of the young, and two long mammae are located laterally, each with one functional pectoral teat. A vaginal plug still exists in some females arriving at the Texas caves in early spring.

Adult male Brazilian free-tailed bats arriving in Texas in spring are still sexually active, but sperm production is waning. Their sex glands decrease steadily in size in spring and reach a resting-stage size by early May. The small proportion of the male population that shows no sexual activity is composed principally of the youngest age class. In these males, the testes, prostate, and hedonic glands are smaller than the resting-stage sizes of the same glands in adult males. In late fall, the few adult males remaining in Texas again show some increase in size of testes and prostates, but sperm are absent. Peak production of sperm, thus, must occur during winter while the males are in lower latitudes. Since the highly dispropor-tionate ratio of male to female Brazilian free-tailed bats in Texas cannot be explained easily as resulting from higher mortality among males, it must be that most males do not summer in Texas.

Another colonial bat (*Myotis velifer*) is a common associate of the Brazilian free-tailed bat in the guano caves. This bat also gives birth to its young in the guano caves, but at a time about 2 weeks in advance of the Brazilian free-tailed bats. Although the two kinds of bats tend to roost in separate clusters, some mix-ing may occur.

A number of species of snakes, birds, and mammals prey on house bats at the caves, but this loss of bats represents a very small proportion of the total bat population.

The annual movement of this animal between Texas and Mexico may be accomplished by most individuals in a few direct, long-distance flights between guano caves. Most adult male Brazilian free-tailed bats apparently do not leave the tropical and subtropical portion of the range and play no part in the sociology of bearing and rearing the young.

The accumulation, under crowded conditions, of millions of Brazilian free-tailed bats per guano cave each summer in Texas for the purpose of giving birth and rearing young may be an outgrowth of overpopulation, but it probably is func-tional in creating favorable conditions for survival of the young. Mortality among prenatal and prefledgling babies, as well as among adults, appears to be low. Longevity of adults probably is great, with an average of more than 11 years.

Conservation Status. The Brazilian free-tailed bat is probably the most common species of bat in Texas. The major threat to this species would be destruction and disturbance of cave sites, either in the United States or Mexico, where the bats roost in great concentrations.

Several roosting sites of these bats (e.g., Bracken Cave, James River Bat Cave in Mason County, and the Fredericksburg Railroad Tunnel in Gillespie County) are protected by private conservation organizations or Texas Parks and Wildlife. The other cave sites are on private property. In Mexico, cave destruction has been on the increase under the mistaken belief that it is a way to control vampire bats. So, although this species appears to be in reasonably good shape in Texas, it is vulnerable while it overwinters in Mexico.

Remarks. The taxonomy of *T. brasiliensis* and its various subspecies has been one of confusion for many years. Two subspecies are known from Texas, according to the latest taxonomic revision of the species in the state. *T. b. cynocephala* is a non-migratory resident of the eastern one-fourth of the state, and *T. b. mexicana* is the highly migratory subspecies found throughout the remainder of Texas.

Morphologically, these two subspecies are distinguished by differences in several skull characteristics (i.e., greatest length of skull, zygomatic breadth, and breadth of cranium), all of which are larger in *T. b. cynocephala.*

Most populations of the migratory subspecies, *mexicana,* have normally completed their move into Mexico before the onset of breeding, whereas *cynocephala* remains in the United States during the breeding season. This movement pattern would indicate that the two races are reproductively isolated and possibly separate species. Overwintering populations of *mexicana,* however, have been discovered in an area of contact between the two in southeastern Texas. A colony of *mexicana* was known to overwinter at the old Animal Pavilion on the Texas A&M University campus in College Station (Brazos County), which is only 160 km from colonies of *cynocephala* in extreme eastern Texas. A morphological analysis of cranial measurements from free-tailed bats captured near Navasota (Grimes County) found these bats to be intermediate between *cynocephala* and *mexicana.* Thus, it appears the two subspecies are not reproductively isolated and that they likely interbreed in this part of Texas.

These morphological data dictate that *cynocephala* and *mexicana* be regarded only as subspecies rather than as separate species, which has been the tendency in the past. Recent biochemical genetic studies of these bats have pointed strongly to specific status for each, however. Additional study will be required to settle the taxonomy of this most interesting bat.

Pocketed Free-tailed Bat

Nyctinomops femorosaccus (Merriam)

Description.   Similar to the Brazilian free-tailed bat, *Tadarida brasiliensis,* but the bases of the ears are joined at the midline; second phalanx of the fourth digit less (not more) than 5 mm; anterior part of hard palate narrowly, rather than broadly, excised; upper incisors placed close together, their longitudinal axes nearly parallel, not convergent, distally. A fold of skin stretching from the inner (medial) side of the femur to the middle of the tibia produces a shallow pocket on the underside

Pocketed Free-tailed Bat (*Nyctinomops femorosaccus*). Photo by Merlin D. Tuttle, Bat Conservation International.

of the interfemoral membrane in the vicinity of the knee, a structure to which the common name alludes. Dental formula: I 1/2, C 1/1, Pm 2/2, M 3/3 x 2 = 30. External measurements average: total length, 112 mm; tail, 46 mm; foot, 10 mm; ear, 23 mm; forearm, 46 mm. Weight, 10–14 g.

Distribution. Southwestern United States and northwestern Mexico; records from southern California, southern Arizona, southeastern New Mexico, western Texas; southward in Mexico to the state of Michoacan. Known in Texas only from Big Bend National Park, Brewster County.

Subspecies. Monotypic species.

Habits. This species is an inhabitant of semiarid desertlands. It has been found using day roosts in caves, crevices in cliffs, and under the roof tiles of buildings. Nothing is known about the winter habits of these bats; apparently, they are absent from Texas during this time.

These bats leave their day roost late in the evening to forage, exhibiting swift, powerful flight. Philip Krutzsch recorded the following observations made at a colony of 50–60 of these bats he found at a daytime roost in a crevice in the face of a cliff in San Diego County, California, on 17 March. The first bats left the colony at 6:15 P.M.; others followed in twos and threes for another half-hour. The bats dropped from 1 to 1.5 m before taking wing. Their flight appeared to be a rapid, complete wing beat. When first taking flight, they uttered a shrill, sharp, high-pitched, chattering call, which was repeated while the bats were in full flight. They also squeaked a great deal while in the roost. He described the odor of this bat as similar to that of the house bat, but not quite so strong.

This rapid-flying bat pursues insects on the wing. The stomachs of 13 bats captured in Big Bend National Park were found to contain moths, crickets, flying ants, stinkbugs, froghoppers and leafhoppers, lacewings, and unidentified insects.

Data on reproduction in this species are scarce, but they apparently give birth to a single young each year, usually in July. Fifteen females captured at Big Bend National Park between 10 June and 12 July each contained a single embryo. Lactating females have been caught in this area from 7 July to 8 August. The young are flying by mid- to late August.

Conservation Status. The pocketed free-tailed bat is rare throughout its range in both the United States and Mexico. As in the case of the spotted bat, the animal has not been studied enough to determine whether its rarity is due to a normal biological process of species evolution and extinction, human interference, or simple inability on the part of biologists to study the animals in their normal habitats. At any rate, no threats have been identified.

Big Free-tailed Bat

Nyctinomops macrotis (Gray)

Description. Similar to the Brazilian free-tailed bat, *Tadarida brasiliensis,* but much larger; ratio of foot to tibia about 53; second joint of fourth finger 2.5 mm in

Big Free-tailed Bat (*Nyctinomops macrotis*). Photo by Merlin D. Tuttle, Bat Conservation International.

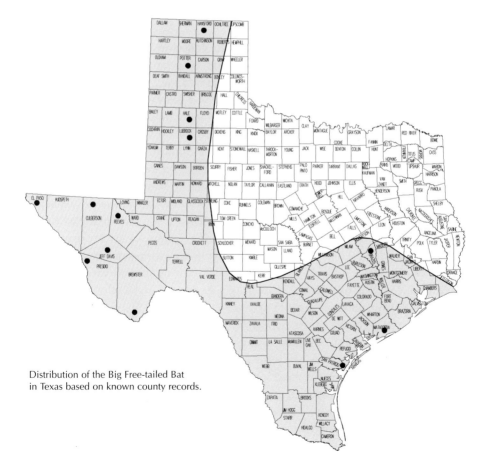

Distribution of the Big Free-tailed Bat in Texas based on known county records.

length; ears large and joined at their bases for a short distance over forehead; upperparts ranging from light reddish brown to rich dark brown; underparts similarly colored but paler. Dental formula as in *Tadarida brasiliensis*. External measurements average: total length, 134 mm; tail, 51 mm; foot, 9 mm; ear, 25 mm; forearm, 61 mm. Weight of nonpregnant females in June, 22 g; of fat, October-taken, nongravid females, 24–30 g.

Distribution. Widely, but seemingly sparingly, distributed from Iowa and southwestern British Columbia in the north, southward through Mexico and the West Indies as far as Uruguay in South America. Known in Texas from scattered localities in the Trans-Pecos, Panhandle, and southeastern portion of the state.

Subspecies. Monotypic species.

Habits. This bat is rare in collections and little is known of its habits. In Texas these bats have been recorded primarily from the Trans-Pecos, where they seem to be seasonal inhabitants of rugged, rocky country in both lowland and highland habitats. With the exception of a single specimen from San Patricio County, which was found hanging on a screen door at the Welder Wildlife Refuge in December 1959, no winter records of this species have been recorded for Texas. In summer, a segregation of sexes apparently occurs, as evidenced by the small number of males taken in the Trans-Pecos.

Preferred roosting sites are crevices and cracks in high canyon walls, but these bats have also been captured in buildings. A specimen from Brazos County was obtained when it flew down a chimney and into the owner's house. The only known nursery colony of these bats in the United States was discovered in the Chisos Mountains of Brewster County in Big Bend National Park by A. E. Borell on 7 May 1937. His attention was attracted to a horizontal crevice in a cliff near the head of Pine Canyon by the squeaking of bats. He estimated the number of adults using the site to be about 150, and all those he collected were adult females, most of which were pregnant. He revisited the colony on 19 October 1938 and collected 4 more specimens, all females. On 27 October 1958, some 20 years later, William B. Davis visited the colony with Richard D. Porter. Their notes, written the next day, follow: "We hiked up Pine Canyon as far as the falls (a trickle of water over a cliff about 100 feet [30 m] high). The canyon is narrow and steep-sided and has a few large yellow pines, but most of them are dead. To the right of the falls the cliff is overhanging, and it has several more-or-less horizontal crevices paralleling the top. One of them, about 50 feet [15 m] above the talus and some 100 feet [30 m] north of the falls, contained the colony. We could clearly hear the bats chattering, much like the muted coo of doves." A considerable quantity of guano on the talus at the base of the cliff marked the place above which the bats were roosting. None of the bats voluntarily left the roost while they were there.

Borell found that the bats left the roost on 7 May at 8:20 P.M. (MST), when it was almost dark, and nearly an hour after the first western pipistrelle was observed. The bats left in small groups during a period of 15 minutes. The swish of their wings was plainly audible, and their flight was rapid. It was so dark when they emerged that he could not determine whether they flew up or down the canyon. Possibly their habit of leaving their daytime roosts so late is the reason they seldom are seen and rarely collected.

Another maternity colony is thought to be in McKittrick Canyon in Guadalupe Mountains National Park. In June 1968 and August 1970, Richard LaVal netted 14 *N. macrotis* at a pool 8 km inside the canyon, where steep walls rise nearly 540 m above the narrow canyon floor. In this section of the canyon the bats were heard vocalizing from far above the floor. All individuals captured were females. Eight of the 12 taken in June contained a single large embryo each. One of the 2 females captured in August was lactating.

The winter habits of this bat are unknown, although they may possibly hibernate in the Trans-Pecos. Richard LaVal found that individuals kept in a refrigerator at 5°C for 24 hours entered a deep torpor, from which they emerged within 15 minutes after their removal. Another bit of evidence suggesting hibernation is that adult, October-taken females were very fat and weighed about 20% more than nonpregnant, June-taken females. Because they are strong fliers and prone to wander somewhat in fall, these bats often turn up far from their normal range during this season. Records from the Panhandle and southeastern Texas may represent juveniles dispersing from breeding populations in the Trans-Pecos.

David Easterla and John Whitaker, Jr., examined the stomach contents of 49 *N. macrotis* and reported that by far the most important food items found were the bodies of large moths. The only other items regularly found were the remains of crickets and longhorn grasshoppers. Other items the bats had consumed were flying ants, stinkbugs, beetles, and leafhoppers. In the stomachs that contained crickets and longhorn grasshoppers, they usually made up less than 25% of the contents, but in a few they comprised as much as 50%. One stomach contained only small flying ants, and one contained only large ants. These workers speculated that while in flight the bats captured the ground-dwelling insects (crickets, longhorn grasshoppers, and large ants) by picking them from the walls of the cliffs.

Little is known about reproduction and development of the young in this bat. Seemingly, each gravid female gives birth to a single offspring in late June to early July. Development is rather rapid, because by October the young of the year are nearly full-grown and difficult to distinguish from adults. The females gather in nursery colonies, from which adult males are excluded, to rear their young.

Conservation Status.   This is another rare and poorly known species whose situation bears watching. Considerable additional data are needed to establish the facts necessary to arrive at a meaningful and biologically defensible position as to its status.

Western Mastiff Bat
Eumops perotis (Schinz)

Description.   A large free-tailed bat, similar to *Tadarida* and *Nyctinomops* in general appearance but nearly twice as large; foot large, ratio of foot to tibia about 60;

Western Mastiff Bat (*Eumops perotis*). Photo by Merlin D. Tuttle, Bat Conservation International.

ears large, united across the forehead and projecting about 10 mm beyond the snout; second joint of fourth finger about 6 mm; pelage short and velvety; upperparts brown or grayish brown, bases of hairs whitish; underparts paler. Males have a peculiar glandular pouch on the throat. Dental formula: I 1/2, C 1/1, Pm 2/2, M 3/3 x 2 = 30. External measurements average: total length, 167 mm; tail, 57 mm; foot, 17 mm; ear, 40 mm; forearm, 76 mm. Weight, 60–70 g.

Distribution. From southwestern United States (western Texas to California) southward to northern Argentina and southern Brazil, but not yet reported from Central America. In Texas, it has been taken at localities near the Rio Grande in Val Verde, Brewster, and Presidio counties.

Subspecies. *E. p. californicus.*

Habits. Away from human habitations, this bat generally seeks diurnal refuge in crevices in rocks that form vertical or nearly vertical cliffs. The roost entrances typically are horizontally oriented, have moderately large openings, and face downward so they can be entered from below. In Capote Canyon in Presidio County, these bats were found utilizing a crevice formed by exfoliation of the nearly vertical rim rock. There are openings on both the lower and upper edges of the slab. At this site the canyon wall is about 38 m high, and the rather steep slope below the cliff has no tall vegetation that might obstruct the takeoff and landing of the bats. Most authors agree that the bats choose a roost with an unobstructed drop of several meters so that the emerging bats can drop and gain sufficient

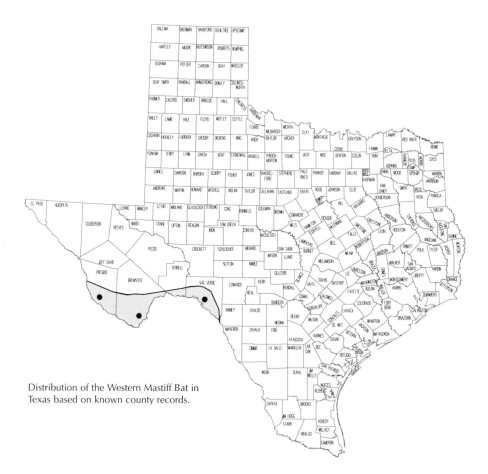

Distribution of the Western Mastiff Bat in Texas based on known county records.

momentum to become airborne. Captive bats are unable to take off from the ground or from flat surfaces and also are unable to maintain flight after launching themselves from the tops of tables. Bats tossed 4.5 m high in the air, however, are able to become airborne, but those thrown half that distance cannot.

Colony size varies from two or three individuals to several dozen. Twenty individuals is a large colony of these bats, although colonies of up to 70 are known. Harry Ohlendorf counted 71 individuals as they left the Capote Canyon roost about sunset on 30 January. The first bats emerged about 6:45 P.M. (MST), and within 10 minutes 30 of them had taken wing. During the next 15 minutes 19 more emerged, 12 more took off during the next 10 minutes, 4 more in the next 15 minutes, and 2 more in the last 10 minutes. Thus, the exodus of the 71 bats was strung out over a period of 50 minutes. Just before launching themselves into flight, and during flight, the bats utter a series of loud, shrill, chattering calls that can be heard for a considerable distance.

These bats leave their day roosts late in the evening to forage. The stomachs of 18 bats collected in Big Bend National Park contained moths (79.9%), crickets, (16.5%), grasshoppers (2.8%), and unidentified insects (0.7%). Bees, dragonflies, leafbugs, beetles, and cicadas have also been reported in their diet. These bats are not believed to use night roosts, but instead soar at great altitudes (up to 600 m) all night long so that they can feed over wide areas (up to 24 km from the roost). Insects carried aloft by thermal currents probably furnish an important portion of their diet. The presence of flightless insects, such as crickets, in their diet is interesting as these bats are unable to take off from the ground and therefore cannot alight to capture such prey. These prey items could be picked from canyon walls as the bats forage.

Observations indicate that males and females of this species remain together throughout the year, even during the period when young are produced. As a nonmigrating, nonhibernating mammal, reproductive activity occurs in the spring, with ovulation occurring soon after copulation. The gestation period is approximately 80–90 days. Normally only one young is produced per pregnancy, but occasionally a female may give birth to twins. The period of parturition is most commonly from June to early July, although young have been born as early as April and as late as August. A nursery colony may contain young ranging from newborn individuals to ones that are several weeks old. At birth the young are dull black in color.

Conservation Status.   This is another rare and poorly known species whose situation bears watching. Considerable additional data are needed to establish the facts necessary to arrive at a meaningful and biologically defensible position as to its status. The lack of information on the animal and its apparent decline in other parts of its range (e.g., California) indicate a need to study its basic biology and population dynamics in Texas.

ORDER CARNIVORA
Carnivores

To this group belong some of our most common and best-known wild mammals: dogs, cats, bears, weasels, skunks, raccoons, and so forth. Carnivores are split into two suborders, Fissipedia (terrestrial forms) and Pinnipedia (marine forms). One pinniped, the West Indian monk seal, supposedly occurred in Texas waters, but it is now extinct throughout its range. Dale Rice, a noted marine mammalogist, has questioned the veracity of the Texas record, but given that the species is now extinct, that becomes a moot point.

The carnivores are nearly worldwide in distribution and occur in the native wild state on all the continents. They are absent, except for introduced domesticated kinds, from all the oceanic islands and are represented in Australia only by the dingo, a wild dog.

The habits of the group are diverse. Coyotes and wolves are terrestrial and adapted for running; martens, fishers, and cats are expert at climbing trees; the badger is adept at digging in the ground; otters are expert swimmers and spend much of their time in the water. Most forms subsist on flesh either as carrion or freshly killed. Bears, raccoons, ringtails, coyotes, and foxes, however, feed on a variety of foods, including insects, fruits, nuts, grain, and other plant materials, as well as flesh.

Texas has a varied carnivore fauna, including 27 native species and 1 introduced species (red fox) in seven families. At least 7 of those species, however, are now extinct in the state, and several others are in danger of the same fate.

Many carnivores, namely the badger, fox, weasel, mink, otter, raccoon, ringtailed cat, skunk, and civet cat (spotted skunk), are legally defined as fur-bearing animals; no one may take such an animal or its pelt in this state without a trapper's license. Although not legally considered furbearers, bobcats, mountain lions, and coyotes are harvested for sale and should be included in this category. Bobcat pelts taken in Texas must be permanently tagged prior to purchase, sale, or transport outside the state. Laws pertaining to fur-bearing animals are enacted by the Texas Legislature.

KEY TO THE CARNIVORES OF TEXAS

1. Catlike; total number of teeth 30 or less; claws retractile 2

   Not catlike; total number of teeth 34 to 42; claws usually not retractile 7

2. Tail 10 to 15 cm, shorter than hind foot; total number of teeth 28; upperparts reddish or grayish brown streaked with black. *Lynx rufus* (bobcat), p. 204.

    Tail 30 to 100 cm, much longer than hind foot; total number of teeth, 30..3

3. Upperparts uniformly colored in adults, not spotted 4

    Upperparts spotted with black rosettes with light centers at all ages 5

4. Total length of adults up to 3 m; tail about 1 m; weight usually more than 45 kg; color tawny. *Puma concolor* (mountain lion), p. 197.

    Total length of adults up to 1 m; tail about 45 cm; weight up to 7 kg; upperparts reddish or grayish. *Herpailurus yaguarondi* (jaguarundi), p. 203.

5. Total length of adults 2 m or more; weight more than 45 kg. *Panthera onca* (jaguar), p. 207.

    Total length usually less than 1.2 m; weight usually less than 18 kg 6

6. Length of hind feet more than 120 mm; length of head and body alone about 75 cm; weight 7 to 16 kg. *Leopardus pardalis* (ocelot), p. 199.

    Length of hind foot less than 120 mm; length of head and body about 50 to 55 cm; weight 2 to 3 kg. *Leopardus wiedii* (margay), p. 202.

7. Doglike; total number of teeth, 42 8

    Not doglike; total number of teeth less than 42 (except in bears) 13

8. Hind foot usually less than 170 mm; weight less than 9 kg (foxes) 9

    Hind foot usually more than 170 mm; weight more than 9 kg (coyotes, wolves)..11

9. Tip of tail white; upperparts yellowish or reddish; feet and lower part of legs black; hind foot near 160 mm. *Vulpes vulpes* (red fox), p. 152.

    Tip of tail black; hind foot usually less than 150 mm........................10

10. General color of body grizzled grayish; legs reddish brown; tail with black stripe on upperside and black tip; hind foot usually more than 140 mm. *Urocyon cinereoargenteus* (common gray fox), p. 155.

    General color of body grayish tan; hind foot usually less than 140 mm. *Vulpes velox* (swift or kit fox), p. 149.

11. Hind foot less than 200 mm; nose pad less than 25 mm in width; weight usually less than 18 kg. *Canis latrans* (coyote), p. 141.

    Hind foot more than 200 mm; nose pad more than 25 mm in width; weight usually more than 18 kg 12

12. Hind foot more than 250 mm; general color grayish. *Canis lupus* (gray wolf), p. 143.

    Hind foot less than 250 mm; general color tawny or reddish mixed with black. *Canis rufus* (red wolf), p. 145.

13. Tail considerably shorter than hind foot; total number of teeth, 42; weight of adults usually more than 100 kg; color black or brown (bears)..14

    Not as above..15

14. Claws of front feet 7 to 12 cm long; face distinctly dished in; ruff or mane present between shoulders; last upper molar nearly twice as large as the one in front of it. *Ursus arctos* (grizzly or brown bear), p. 160.

Claws on front feet seldom as long as 7.5 cm; face slightly arched or nearly straight in profile; no ruff or mane; last upper molar about 1.5 times as large as the one in front of it. *Ursus americanus* (American black bear), p. 158.

15. Total number of teeth, 40; tail usually with indications of alternating dark and light rings 16

Total number of teeth, 32 to 36; tail lacking dark and light rings ...18

16. Tail as long as or longer than head and body, with 14 to 16 alternating black and white rings and a black tip; hind foot less than 80 mm; weight 1 to 2 kg. *Bassariscus astutus* (ringtail), p. 161.

Tail shorter than head and body and with 6 to 7 alternating dark and light rings or rings inconspicuous; hind foot of adults 85 mm or more..17

17. Snout extending conspicuously beyond mouth and highly flexible; tail about 5 times as long as hind foot; alternating rings obscured in adults. *Nasua narica* (white-nosed coati), p. 167.

Snout not extending conspicuously beyond mouth; tail 2 to 3 times as long as hind foot, rings conspicuous at all ages. *Procyon lotor* (northern raccoon), p. 164.

18. Upperparts black with longitudinal white stripe or stripes (skunks). 19

Upperparts not black and white striped 23

19. Total number of teeth, 32; back with single, broad white stripe from head to tail; nose pad large and flexible. *Conepatus leuconotus* (hog-nosed skunk), p. 193.

Total number of teeth, 34; back normally with two or more white stripes; nose pad normal 20

20. Six distinct broken or continuous white stripes on anterior part of body; white spot in center of forehead; hind foot seldom more than 50 mm 21

Not as above..22

21. Black and white stripes on back nearly equal in width; white spot on forehead large, covering more than half of the area between the eyes; white stripes beginning between the ears or just behind them. *Spilogale gracilis* (western spotted skunk), p. 183.

Black stripes on back wider than the white ones; white spot on forehead small, seldom more than 15 mm in diameter; white stripes on back begin about 25 mm behind the ears. *Spilogale putorius* (eastern spotted skunk), p. 185.

22. Dorsal white stripe bifurcate; sides black. *Mephitis mephitis* (striped skunk), p. 190.

Dorsal stripe white or black but never bifurcate; sides usually with narrow white stripe beginning at ear. *Mephitis macroura* (hooded skunk), p. 188.

23. Total number of teeth, 36; feet webbed; tail long, heavy, tapering; ears short; color chocolate brown; total length 1 m or more. *Lontra canadensis* (northern river otter), p. 179.

    Total number of teeth, 34; feet not webbed; total length less than 1 m 24

24. Tail about as long as hind foot; claws on front feet about 25 mm in length and much longer than those on hind foot; body thickset, heavy; fur lax and long. *Taxidea taxus* (American badger), p. 177.

    Tail noticeably longer than hind foot; body long and slender; fur relatively short..25

25. Color chocolate brown to black; midline of belly white. *Mustela vison* (American mink), p. 174.

    Color yellowish brown; head usually with black and white markings; tip of tail black and contrasting markedly with rest of tail 26

26. Feet brown or tan; hind foot 50 mm or less; weight 500 g or less. *Mustela frenata* (long-tailed weasel), p. 169.

    Feet black; hind foot more than 50 mm; weight 500 to 1,500 g. *Mustela nigripes* (black-footed ferret), p. 172.

FAMILY CANIDAE (CANIDS)

Members of this family, which are easily recognized by their doglike features, are adapted to swift running on relatively open terrain. Seven species of this family are known from Texas, but two (the red wolf and the gray or timber wolf) are now extinct.

There is often considerable confusion concerning the identification of coyotes, gray wolves, red wolves, and domestic dogs, and it is documented that these species can successfully interbreed and produce fertile hybrids. A few reports are received each year concerning the occurrence of red and gray wolves in Texas;

Coyote (*Canis latrans*). Photo by John and Gloria Tveten.

however, in those instances where it has been possible to study the specimen, all
have proven to be unusually large coyotes.

Coyote
Canis latrans Say

Description. A medium-sized, slender, doglike carnivore, similar in appearance to
the red wolf but usually smaller, more slender, with smaller feet, narrower muzzle,
and relatively longer tail; colors usually paler, less rufous, rarely blackish; differs
from gray wolves in much smaller size, smaller feet and skull; upperparts grizzled
buffy and grayish overlaid with black; muzzle, ears, and outersides of legs yellowish buff; tail with black tip, and with upperpart colored like back. Dental formula: I
3/3, C 1/1, Pm 4/4, M usually 2/2, occasionally 3/3, 3/2, or 2/3 x 2 = 40, 42, or 44.
External measurements average: total length, 1,219 mm; tail, 394 mm; hind foot, 179
mm. Weight, 14–20 kg.
Distribution. Statewide.
Subspecies. *C. l. latrans* in the Panhandle, *C. l. texensis* in the western half of the
state south of the Panhandle, and *C. l. frustror* in the eastern half of the state.
Habits. Coyotes eat a wide variety of food items, and this dietary versatility is
undoubtedly important to their success. The stomach contents of 168 coyotes collected in Arkansas contained the following items (listed as percent occurrence):
poultry, 34; persimmons, 23; insects, 11; rodents, 9; songbirds, 8; cattle, 7; rabbits,
7; deer, 5; woodchucks, 4; goats, 4; and watermelons, 4. Considerable seasonal variation is evident, with carrion of large game animals such as deer being important
in winter and various rodents and fruits increasing in importance in the spring,
summer, and fall.

The basic social unit of coyotes is the family, which has its inception in midwinter when a female comes into heat (estrus) and attracts a sexually active male.
The female and her selected mate spend much of the last few days of her estrous
period copulating. The pair then establishes a territory and prepares a den for
their family. Coyote mates maintain a close social bond throughout the year. They
hunt and sleep together, but late in the pregnancy the male frequently hunts alone
and brings food to his mate.

Nonfamily coyotes include bachelor males, nonreproductive females, and
near-mature young. They may live alone or form a loose association with one
another for social contact or killing prey so that they can survive until the next
breeding season. Two to six such animals may band together loosely to form coyote packs. One animal in this group is usually dominant, but the interaction among
pack members is only temporary.

The percentage of females that breed during a given year varies with local conditions. Normal litter size is 2–12, averaging about 6. The gestation period is
approximately 63 days. The female is monestrous, showing one heat period per
year, usually between January and March.

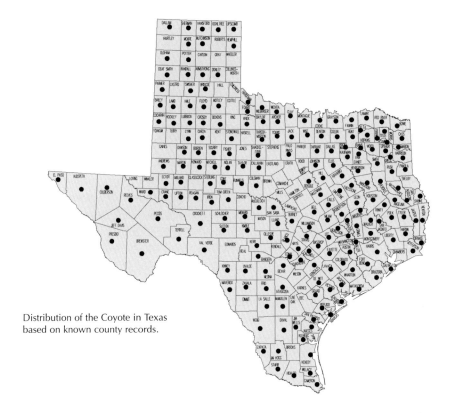

Distribution of the Coyote in Texas based on known county records.

Newborn coyotes weigh 200 to 250 g, depending on the litter size. They are born blind and helpless, usually in an excavated den located along brush-covered slopes, steep banks, thickets, hollow logs, or rock ledges. The pups are nourished by milk for the first 10 days. Their eyes open on the tenth day, at which time they can move about somewhat. Their incisors appear on the twelfth day, and the canines at the sixteenth day. They can walk by 20 days, and they can run by 6 weeks of age. At 12–15 days of age, adults start to supplement the pups' diet with regurgitated foods. Pups begin to eat solid food, such as mice, at 4–6 weeks when their milk teeth are functional. Lactation is progressively reduced after 2 months.

The months of May, June, and July are the basic training period for pups. They learn to accept regurgitated food from their parents, to climb in and out of the den, to catch insects, and finally to hunt and catch larger prey. The den is abandoned by late June or early July, at which time the family begins to wander. November and December are the primary months when the young disperse.

Coyotes may be active throughout the day, but they tend to be more active during the early morning and around sunset. Their movements include travel within a territory or home range, dispersal from the den, and long migrations. The home-range size of coyotes seems to vary geographically, seasonally, and individually within populations.

Few coyotes live more than 6–8 years in the wild. Losses are due mainly to predation, parasites and disease, and humans. Mortality is particularly high for pups, who are vulnerable to hawks, owls, eagles, mountain lions, and even other coyotes. Hunting and trapping account for many adult deaths.

Although dogs and coyotes are mortal enemies for 10 months of the year, there is virtual compatibility between sexes of the two species during the breeding season. Coyote-dog hybrids, called coy-dogs, occur occasionally throughout the range of the coyote, and many of them retain coyote behavioral patterns. The breeding season of hybrids is random, however, and most of them are unable to breed back into the coyote population.

Coyotes communicate with one another by calling and scent-marking. Among the most vocal of all North American wild mammals, they emit three distinct calls (squeaks, howl calls, and distress calls). The wavering calls of coyotes on clear nights serve primarily to announce the position and hunting success of the caller. These coyote songs are more frequent during the breeding season than at other times of the year. A visiting coyote will often urinate or defecate on a scent post, which may be a fence post, stump, bush, rock, dried cow dung, or a bare spot. A coyote may go many meters upwind to investigate a scent post and leave his mark. Whether his actions represent a territorial claim, a warning device to other coyotes, or simply indicate the presence of an individual is not known.

In recent years, the coyote has declined in economic importance as a fur-bearing animal in the state. In 1998 the coyote was ranked third in terms of economic importance, behind the raccoon and the bobcat. In 1999, however, few fur buyers were active, and they were not purchasing the pelts of coyotes and many other common furbearers.

Conservation Status. Coyotes are common throughout all of Texas and remain in good shape. They have adapted well to man and his habits and show no signs of decline. Intensive efforts by trappers to control their numbers fail more often than they succeed. This is a species that will likely continue to flourish as humans exert more and more influence over the natural landscape.

Gray Wolf
Canis lupus Linnaeus

Description. A large, doglike carnivore with heavy, broad skull and muzzle; height at shoulder slightly greater than at rump, imparting a suggestion that the animal is partly crouched; legs relatively long (as compared with a coyote); tail relatively short; upperparts grayish, usually heavily washed with blackish, occasionally predominantly blackish; head more or less tinged with cinnamon; underparts whitish or buffy; tail black-tipped. Dental formula as in the coyote. External measurements of a male: total length, 1,626 mm; tail, 419 mm; hind foot, 267 mm; of a female, 1,473-360-269. Weight of males, 30–80 kg; of females, 20–60 kg.

Gray Wolf (*Canis lupus*). Photo courtesy U.S. Fish and Wildlife Service.

Distribution. The gray wolf formerly ranged over the western two-thirds of the state, but native populations are now extirpated over all of the west, including Texas. The last authenticated reports of gray wolves in Texas are of two males, the skulls of which were donated to Sul Ross State University. According to James Scudday, one wolf was shot 5 December 1970, on the Cathedral Mountain Ranch, 27 km south of Alpine, Brewster County. The other was trapped several days before 28 December 1970, on the Joe Neal Brown Ranch, at about the point where Brewster, Pecos, and Terrell counties meet.

Subspecies. *C. l. nubulis* in the Panhandle and eastward to Montague County, *C. l. monstrabilis* throughout west-central and southern Texas, and *C. l. baileyi* in extreme western Texas, west of the Big Bend.

Habits. The gray wolf inhabits forests, brushlands, or grasslands, preferring broken, open country in which suitable cover and denning sites are available. Formerly, wolves occurred commonly in the grassland plains with the buffalo, which they relied on for their chief food supply.

Wolves have marvelous stamina and endurance and can travel for hours without apparent fatigue. They usually travel and hunt in packs, occasionally in pairs or singly, relying on their own endurance or numbers to wear down the intended large prey. The family group constitutes the nucleus of the pack, to which bachelor friends or members of another family may be added. The usual pack consists of 6 to 10 individuals, but packs twice that size are not uncommon. Packs of as many as 50 individuals are rare.

Under natural conditions, the food of wolves consists of the larger herbivores (deer and pronghorns). When such game is scarce they turn their attention to mice, ground squirrels, and rabbits. The young pups normally spend considerable time in stalking and capturing small mice. Where natural foods are scarce and domesticated livestock available, wolves soon learn that such items are satisfactory substitutes.

The extirpation of the wolf over most of its former range released predator pressure on such big game as deer, which in part created a serious problem of overpopulation of this game animal in several localities in Texas.

Wolves mate for life. The young, usually four to six in number, are whelped in late winter or early spring in a den dug into a hillside or cut bank, or in a crevice in a rocky bluff. The breeding season begins in late December and continues through February; the gestation period is about 63 days. At first the young are blind, naked, and helpless, but they grow rapidly. At about 9 days of age their eyes open, at which time they are covered by woolly, juvenile fur. By October they are nearly full-grown. Females are sexually mature when 2 years old; males mature about a year later.

Conservation Status. Gray wolves are extinct in Texas and not likely ever to return. There have been some discussions of reintroducing them to Big Bend National Park, but any action on that proposal is years away and is likely to be strongly questioned by representatives of the livestock industry. Wolves have been successfully reintroduced in southwestern New Mexico and across the border in Arizona.

Both Texas Parks and Wildlife and U.S. Fish and Wildlife list the gray wolf as endangered, with the exception of the reintroduced populations that are designated as experimental and nonessential.

Red Wolf

Canis rufus Audubon and Bachman

Description. A rather small, slender, long-legged wolf resembling the coyote in color but often blackish; typically larger, with wider nose pad, larger feet and coarser pelage; smaller and more tawny than the gray wolf. Dental formula as in the coyote. External measurements of an adult male: total length, 1,473 mm; tail, 362 mm; hind foot, 235 mm; of a female, 1,448-355-216 mm. Weight of large males, 30–40 kg; of large females, 20–30 kg.

Distribution. Formerly, red wolves ranged throughout the eastern half of Texas, but their numbers and range quickly declined under pressure of intensive land use in the region. Also, early lumbering and farming practices allowed the coyote to expand its range into East Texas; hybrid offspring of interbreeding red wolves and coyotes more closely resembled coyotes, and the genetic identity of the red wolf was gradually suppressed.

Red Wolf (*Canis rufus*). Photo by Curtis J. Carley, courtesy Texas Parks and Wildlife Department.

The last pure group of the eastern subspecies of red wolf, found along the Gulf Coast south of Houston, seems to have been genetically swamped by 1970. The central Texas subspecies of red wolf survived for a few more years in extreme southeast Texas and southern Louisiana, but it subsequently disappeared in the wild.

I still get inquiries from Texas citizens who claim to be in possession of or to have seen a red wolf. The comparisons in Table 3, derived mainly from a review of the status and knowledge of the red wolf prepared by G. A. Riley and R. T. McBride, are useful in distinguishing coyotes from red wolves. To date, none of the reports or specimens I have seen has proved to be a red wolf.

Subspecies. *C. r. gregoryi* along the eastern border of the state and *C. r. rufus* in the remainder of the range in Texas.

Habits. Red wolves inhabited brushy and forested areas, as well as the coastal prairies. They are more sociable than coyotes. Three or more may maintain a group structure throughout the year. Riley and McBride, on the basis of systematic tracking, estimated that the home range is approximately 40–80 km^2, averaging 56 km^2.

They are known to feed on cottontails and other rabbits, deer, native rats and mice, prairie chickens, fish and crabs (along the Gulf Coast), as well as on domestic livestock, especially free-ranging pigs. Riley and McBride list nutria (which they consider an important buffer between red wolves and domestic livestock), swamp rabbit, cottontail, rice rat, cotton rat, and muskrat as specific food items.

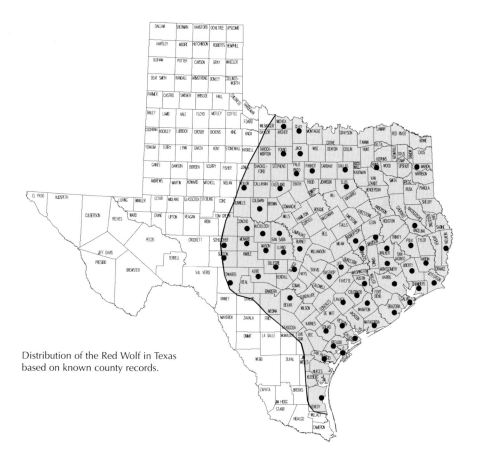

Distribution of the Red Wolf in Texas
based on known county records.

Breeding occurs in January and February, and the three or four pups are born in March and April. The nursery den normally is dug in the slope or crest of a low, sandy mound or hill, or in the bank of an irrigation or drainage ditch. Man-made culverts and drainpipes occasionally are utilized. The dens average about 2.4 m in length and normally are no deeper than 1 m. Den entrances vary from 60 to 75 cm in diameter and normally are well concealed. Both sexes take part in rearing the young. Frequently, young of the previous year occur in the vicinity of a nursery den, but they do not appear to participate in guarding, feeding, or training of the pups of the year. When about 6 weeks old the pups may forsake the nursery den.

Conservation Status. Red wolves are extinct in the wild in Texas. Before the complete spread of the hybridization process, however, a few dozen pure red wolves were brought into captivity. Using the progeny of that captive stock, translocations back into native range in North Carolina began in 1987, when red wolves were released onto Alligator River National Wildlife Refuge. Red wolves have also been released in the Great Smoky Mountains and on Pocosin Lakes National Wildlife Refuge. The current free-ranging red wolf population consists of approximately 100 wolves roaming over approximately one million acres. It was understood from the

Table 3. Comparison of red wolf and coyote traits

	Red Wolf	Coyote
Mean weight (kg) (extremes in parentheses)	22.7 (17.3–34.5) Male 20.0 (16.3–24.5) Female	15.0 (10.0–16.0) Male 13.1 (9.5–15.9) Female
Total length (m)	1.42 (1.32–1.60) Male 1.34 (1.22–1.42) Female	1.27 (1.21–1.35) Male 1.20 (1.12–1.30) Female
Hind foot (cm)	23.1 (21.0–24.9) Male 22.1 (20.3–24.1) Female	20.5 (19.0–21.3) Male 19.8 (17.8–21.6) Female
Ear length (cm)	12.7 (11.4–14.0) Male 12.2 (11.4–12.7) Female	11.6 (10.7–12.2) Male 10.9 (8.6–12.2) Female
Width of nose pad (mm)	More than 25	Less than 25
Length of skull (mm)	More than 215; usually more than 220	Less than 215; usually less than 210
Tracks (mm, from back of heel pad to end of longest claw)	102.0 (89.0–127.0)	66.0 (57.2–72.4)
Stride (cm)	65.8 (55.8–76.2)	41.4 (32.4–48.3)
Muzzle and head	Normally broad	Normally narrow
Muzzle coloration	White area around lips may extend well up on sides of muzzle	White area around lips thin and sharply demarcated
Threat behavior (when trapped or cornered)	Tail held upright; snarl exposes only the canines and a few front teeth; ruff on neck and back raised	Tail held between legs; mouth opened wide and all teeth exposed; back arched and ruff may or may not be raised

Red Wolf, showing longer ears, wider nose pad and muzzle, and facial markings that distinguish the Red Wolf from the Coyote. Photo by Curtis J. Carley, courtesy Texas Parks and Wildlife Department.

beginning of the project that one of the key issues that would determine the success of the introductions would be limiting hybridization with coyotes. Indeed, recent studies in North Carolina are finding hybrid individuals, and it is predicted that at current hybridization rates, the genetic integrity of the species could be lost in as few as three to six generations. An intensive effort is currently under way to reduce red wolf–coyote hybridization on the Alligator River Refuge and in the surrounding areas.

Both Texas Parks and Wildlife and U.S. Fish and Wildlife list the red wolf as endangered. Because of the density of the human population on the upper Texas coast, it is doubtful that reintroductions of red wolves could ever be successful in our state.

Swift or Kit Fox
Vulpes velox (Say)

Description. Smallest of the American foxes; upperparts pale buffy yellow, frosted with white and lightly washed with blackish; back of ears yellowish brown; tail buffy gray with black tip and black spot at base on upperside; underparts whitish. Dental formula as in the red fox. External measurements average: total length, 840 mm; tail, 330 mm; hind foot, 135 mm; ear, 75 mm. Weight, 1–3 kg.

Swift or Kit Fox (*Vulpes velox*). Photo by John and Gloria Tveten.

Distribution. Known from western one-third of state east to Menard County.

Subspecies. *V. v. velox* in the Panhandle and Llano Estacado regions and *V. v. macrotis* in the Trans-Pecos and southwestern Edwards Plateau.

Habits. These small foxes, not much larger than a good-sized house cat, generally live in the open desert or grasslands, where they often have dens and hunt mesa country along the borders of valleys, sparsely vegetated habitats on sloping plains, hilltops, and other well-drained areas. Also, they have adapted to pasture, plowed fields, and fencerows. They rely on speed and nearness to their dens for safety.

Swift or kit foxes are primarily nocturnal, although they may occasionally be seen in the daylight hours. Usually, they emerge from their dens shortly after sunset for hunting, which occurs sporadically throughout the night. Foxes may cover several kilometers while systematically hunting for prey but seldom venture more than 3 km from their dens. Home ranges may overlap broadly, and foxes from different family groups hunt the same areas, although not at the same time.

The diet of swift foxes consists largely of small mammals, particularly rodents, but also includes insects, small passerine birds, lizards, amphibians, and fish. Known food items are kangaroo rats, jackrabbits, cottontails, small birds, grasshoppers, Jerusalem crickets, and other insects. W. L. Cutter examined 12 stomachs and 250 scats (droppings), collected mainly in late spring, summer, and early fall, to determine the food habits of these foxes. Rabbit remains, both cottontails and jackrabbits, were found almost as frequently (60 times) as all other vertebrates combined (68 times). Small rodents occurred 26 times; passerine birds, 33 times; lizards, 4 times; and fish, 3 times.

No remains of gallinaceous birds, either game birds or poultry, were found, although two of the dens were no more than 170 m from a farmyard where poultry was raised. Insect remains (11 families represented) composed approximately 29% of the bulk of the stomach contents and 55% of the bulk of the scats. Short-horned grasshoppers occurred most frequently, followed by beetles of 3 families. Grass was found in 43 scats and 10 stomachs. Thus, it appears that the swift or kit fox is not in conflict with human interests insofar as its feeding habits are concerned.

Male and female foxes establish pair bonds during October and November, during which time large family dens are used. These foxes are monogamous for a breeding season, but the pairs are not necessarily the same from year to year. Breeding occurs from December to February, and most litters are born in March or early April. Litter size varies from three to six and the swift fox is monestrous. W. L. Cutter observed that in the Texas Panhandle (Hansford County) these foxes usually den in open, overgrazed pastures. Of 25 occupied dens that he observed, 19 were so located; 2 were in plowed fields and 4 were along north-south fencerows. The den is a simple structure with one or more openings. One that Cutter excavated had a circular entrance 20 cm in diameter and a total of 378 cm of open, underground

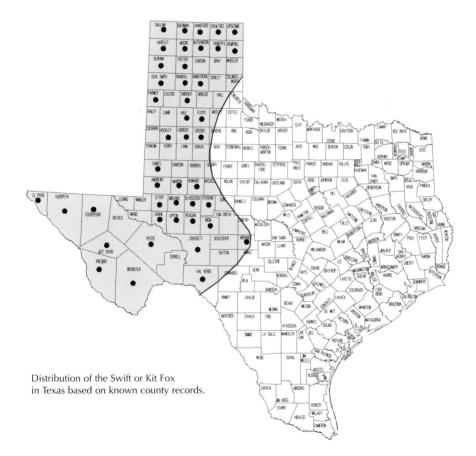

Distribution of the Swift or Kit Fox
in Texas based on known county records.

tunnel. The main chamber was 30 cm wide, 22 cm high, and 80 cm below the surface of the ground. Three dens were as close as 85 m to human habitation. These foxes spend most of the daytime in their dens; when they do come out in daylight, they remain close to the den, into which they retreat when molested.

Swift or kit foxes are relatively unafraid of humans and are far less cunning than most other foxes. They are so unsuspicious that they are easily trapped and even more easily poisoned. Consequently, wherever trappers are active, and especially wherever control campaigns involving the use of poison have been carried out against predatory animals on areas inhabited by these foxes, the foxes have been greatly reduced in number or entirely eliminated.

Conservation Status. Concern has been expressed from time to time about the swift and kit foxes. They occur throughout much of the western part of Texas and were driven close to extinction by indiscriminate poisoning campaigns directed at wolves and later coyotes. With curtailment of this practice, the populations appear to have rebounded, but there is still a need to monitor this species carefully. U.S. Fish and Wildlife lists *V. velox* as a candidate species, and it is on the watch list of the Texas Organization for Endangered Species.

Remarks. For most of the last century, the arid-land foxes were regarded as comprising two similar but separate species, the swift fox (*Vulpes velox*) and the kit fox (*Vulpes macrotis*). In a taxonomic study of these foxes using advanced morphometric and protein-electrophoretic methods, however, Jerry Dragoo and his colleagues concluded that they are not sufficiently distinct to warrant separate species status. Thus, the two foxes are now grouped into a single species, *Vulpes velox,* comprising two subspecies, *V. v. velox* from the Panhandle and adjacent areas and *V. v. macrotis* from the Trans-Pecos.

Red Fox*

Vulpes vulpes (Linnaeus)

Description. Similar in size to the gray fox but conspicuously different in color and in cranial characters. Considerably larger and more reddish than the swift or kit fox. Tail a thick bush, circular in cross section, and white-tipped; face rusty fulvous, grizzled with white; upperparts bright golden yellow, darkest along middle of back; chin, throat, and midline of belly white; forefeet and legs to elbow black; black of hind feet extends as a narrow band along outer side of leg to thigh; backs of ears black. Several color phases: cross, black, silver, Sampson, and the normal red. Young duller in color than adults. Dental formula: I 3/3, C 1/1 Pm 4/4, M 2/3 x 2 = 42. External measurements average: total length, 972 mm; tail, 371 mm; hind foot, 163 mm; females average slightly smaller than males. Weight, 3–5 kg.

Distribution. Red foxes are not native to Texas, having been introduced for purposes of sport around 1895 in the eastern and central parts of the state. Today, they occur over most of the state except for the far western and southern regions.

Subspecies. *V. v. fulva.*

Habits. Their favored habitat is mixed wooded uplands interspersed with farms and pastures. Vegetative types containing brush and a ground cover of grasses and sedges also are heavily used. Thus, they seem to select diverse areas that support a mixture of vegetative components and avoid large homogeneous tracts of any single type.

Red foxes are social. The family unit is composed of the male and female (called the vixen) plus their young of the year. Adult foxes are thought to remain in the same area for life. The size of their home range varies with terrain, complexity of the habitat, and food supply.

Red foxes are most active at night, with a tendency toward crepuscular activity. Activity peaks typically correspond with peaks in prey activity. They often travel the same routes, which may become worn into trails.

The major food items of foxes are small rodents, rabbits, wild fruits and berries, and insects. They are opportunistic feeders and take any acceptable food in proportion to its availability. While hunting for mice, the fox stands motionless with tail arched stiffly to the rear, ears erect, listening and watching intently. The capture or attempted capture is executed by a leap in which the stiffened forelegs are brought down sharply. There may be frantic striking with the feet and searching with the nose as the intended victim attempts to escape.

Female red foxes have a single estrous period each year and reputedly remain mated for life. Males and females pair off and mate from late December to January

Red Fox (*Vulpes vulpes*). Photo by John and Gloria Tveten.

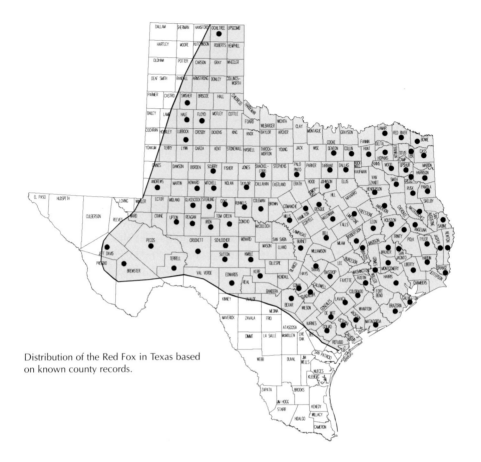

Distribution of the Red Fox in Texas based
on known county records.

or February. Females have a very short period of heat that lasts only 2–4 days. The
young, which may number anywhere from 1 to 10 (average 4–6) are born in March
or April following a gestation period of about 53 days.

The female establishes the den site for the young in late winter, but both parents live together while raising the young. Foxes either dig their own dens or utilize those of other burrowing animals. Sometimes two litters may occupy one den.

Pups first open their eyes at 9 days of age, appear outside the den at about 1
month, and are weaned at 8–10 weeks. Both parents may bring solid food to the
den for the pups. The family unit remains together until early fall, when the young
are full-grown and dispersal occurs. After dispersal, foxes remain more or less solitary until they pair and travel together during the mating season.

The life expectancy of a pup in the wild is less than 1 year, and few foxes live
beyond the age or 3 or 4 years, particularly in areas where they are hunted and
trapped heavily. Humans and domestic dogs are their major predators, although
pups may be lost to great horned owls and other predators. Red foxes are susceptible to a variety of diseases, including rabies, distemper, and infectious canine
hepatitis.

The red fox ranks low among furbearers in numbers of individuals harvested. The most important ecological regions for harvesting red foxes are the Pineywoods, Cross Timbers and Prairies, Edwards Plateau, and Rolling Plains.

Conservation Status. This introduced fox has done remarkably well in Texas, having expanded to cover most of the state except for the far western and southern regions, although they do not seem to be abundant anywhere.

Common Gray Fox

Urocyon cinereoargenteus (Schreber)

Description. A medium-sized fox with grayish upperparts, reddish brown legs, tawny sides, and whitish throat, cheeks, and midline of belly; sides of muzzle and lower jaw with distinct blackish patch; tail with distinct blackish stripe on upperside and black tip (no white on end of tail as in the red fox); tail roughly triangular, not round, in cross section; skull with distinct lyrate temporal ridges, which meet only at hind part of skull. Dental formula as in the red fox. External measurements average: total length, 970 mm; tail, 347 mm; hind foot, 143 mm. Weight, ordinarily 3–5 kg, occasionally as much as 9 kg.

Distribution. Statewide.

Subspecies. *U. c. floridanus* east of the Balcones Fault Zone and *U. c. scottii* in the western two-thirds of the state.

Common Gray Fox (*Urocyon cinereoargenteus*). Photo by John and Gloria Tveten.

Distribution of the Common Gray Fox
in Texas based on known county records.

Habits. Gray foxes are especially common in the Post Oak Savannah, Cross Timbers and Prairies, and Edwards Plateau regions, where they occupy both upland and bottomland communities. They apparently benefit from habitat edges created by humans. They seem to prefer the borders of woodlands that result from the common practice of clearing small, irregular areas for croplands or pastures. They also do well around human habitations, being almost equally at home on the outskirts of cities as in less disturbed habitats.

Gray foxes are social animals, with the primary unit being the family consisting of an adult male and female plus a number of juveniles. These foxes are thought to be monogamous, with the pair bond remaining intact throughout the year. The breeding season probably extends over several months from December to early March, with peaks from late January to early February. There is only one litter per year, and the range in litter size is about two to six, averaging four. The gestation period is about 53 days.

Gray foxes are most active at night, although they occasionally move about during the early morning and late afternoon. While traveling from one location to another, they frequently follow old roads or open trails. Otherwise, they forage erratically through thickets of dense underbrush.

These foxes use a variety of places for denning sites, such as scrap or brush piles, space under old houses, holes in rocky outcroppings, cavities in hollow trees, and occasionally underground burrows dug by other animals or the foxes themselves. Dens in hollow trees may be as high as 9 m above ground. Den sites are commonly located in dense cover and not very far from water.

Gray foxes are adept climbers, which is unusual for canids. They climb trees to escape predators, feed on birds, or to rest and sun. They use their rounded claws to ascend the tree trunk in a fashion like that of bears, and they are capable of leaping from branch to branch like a cat.

Their diet varies seasonally, but the most important items (in order of decreasing importance) are small mammals, birds, plants, and insects. They eat a variety of small mammals, including white-footed mice, woodrats, cotton rats, pocket mice, harvest mice, and cottontail rabbits, with the latter being the most important item in their diet. They also eat a variety of passerine birds, but they seem particularly fond of robins, towhees, and mourning doves as well. Persimmons are their most important plant food, although they also eat yaupon and deciduous holly berries, acorns, and grasses. Insects are relatively unimportant in the diet.

Gray foxes are thought to live 6–10 years in the wild. Major factors causing mortality include predation, parasites, diseases, and humans. Large hawks occasionally take pups, and adults may be eaten by golden eagles, coyotes, and bobcats. Rabies and mange also appear to serve as a control mechanism in fox populations when density is great.

The gray fox is among the six more important fur-bearing animals in Texas. The most important ecological regions for harvesting gray foxes are the Cross Timbers and Prairies and the Edwards Plateau.

Conservation Status. The gray fox is widely distributed throughout most of the state. It remains common throughout its range, although more so in the eastern part than elsewhere. Potential threats to this species could include overharvesting by trappers and predator control practices.

FAMILY URSIDAE (BEARS)

Bears are large, highly variable animals, which has led to considerable taxonomic uncertainty, especially regarding subspecies recognition. Currently, nine species are recognized worldwide, and three of those species occur in North America (black bear, grizzly or brown bear, and polar bear). In Texas, the black bear is an extant species, but the grizzly bear has been extirpated from the state since very early in the twentieth century. Both species are strongly herbivorous, although they will take fish and occasionally scavenge on other available animal food.

American Black Bear
Ursus americanus Pallas

Description. A medium-sized bear, black or brown in color; snout brownish in the black color phase; front claws slightly longer than the hind claws, curved, adapted for climbing; profile of face nearly straight, not dished in (concave) as in the grizzly; fur long and rather coarse. Dental formula: I 3/3, C 1/1, Pm 4/4, M 2/3 x 2 = 42. External measurements average: total length, 1,500 mm; tail, 125 mm; hind foot, 175 mm; height at shoulder about 625 mm. Weight, 100–150 kg; occasionally as much as 225 kg.

Distribution. Formerly widespread throughout the state. Now primarily restricted to remnant populations in mountainous areas of the Trans-Pecos region, but numbers and distribution within the state appear to be growing.

Subspecies. *U. a. amblyceps* in the Trans-Pecos area and northward along the New Mexican border, *U. a. americanus* in the central part of the state, and *U. a. luteolus* in the east adjacent to Louisiana.

Habits. Largely creatures of woodland and forested areas, black bears are more at home on the ground than they are in the trees. They are expert climbers, however, and, especially when young, often seek refuge in trees. Ordinarily they are shy and retiring and seldom are seen. They appear to use definite travelways or runs, a habit that is frequently taken advantage of by hunters.

American Black Bear (*Ursus americanus*). Photo by John and Gloria Tveten.

In the colder parts of their range, black bears hole up in a windfall, at the base of a tree, under a shelving rock, or in some other suitable site, and are inactive for a part of the winter. They do not exhibit the characteristics of true hibernation; their temperature does not drop markedly, nor are the heartbeat and respiratory rate materially reduced. Often the bears are nearly fully exposed to the winter weather during their prolonged sleep. They may awaken and become active during a warm spell in midwinter and return to the nest to sleep again when the temperature drops.

Their food is extremely varied, as reflected by the crushing type of molar teeth. They are known to feed on nest contents of wild bees, carpenter ants and other insects, manzanita berries, coffee berries, wild cherry, poison oak, apples, pine nuts, acorns, clover, grass, roots, fish, carrion, and garbage about camps. Occasional animals become killers of livestock and young deer.

The breeding season is in June or July, but implantation of the fertilized eggs does not occur until November. The one to four young (usually two) are born in January or February, while the mother is denning. At birth the young are blind, covered with a sparse growth of fine hair, and almost helpless. They weigh less than 500 g and are about 15 cm long. They grow rather slowly at first; their eyes open in about 6 weeks. By the time the mother is ready to leave her winter den they are strong enough to follow. The cubs remain with her until the fall of their second year, when they venture forth on their own. By that time, the female is preparing for her next family. Normally, old females mate every other year, and young females do not mate until 2 years or more of age.

Bears have few enemies other than humans. Their chief economic value is as a game animal. Their pelts have little value on the fur market, but they are prized as trophies.

Conservation Status. Until recently, the black bear was considered to be extinct in Texas, although bears were occasionally sighted in the Chisos Mountains of Big Bend National Park. The last decade of the twentieth century, however, witnessed the natural restoration of black bear populations in Texas as a result of a coalescing of biogeographic, ecological, and sociological factors. The presence of bears in adjacent but geographically isolated mountain ranges in northern Mexico facilitated the colonization of populations. In Coahuila, Mexico, just across the border from Texas, black bear populations have increased from previously endangered levels to one of the highest densities in North America because of landowner initiatives and encouragement from the Mexican government. Bear populations are now spilling over into the Big Bend region and other areas of west and southwest Texas. This case is worth noting because natural recolonization of historical range by large carnivores is uncommon in today's world of habitat fragmentation, disturbance, and destruction. Bear sightings especially increased in the Chisos Mountains area during the last decade. There have even been recent sightings of stray New Mexico bears that have wandered into the Panhandle of Texas near Friona and Dalhart. These sightings suggest that the core of a breeding population now exists in the Chisos and Guadalupe mountains and, coupled with other recent sightings in the Davis and Glass mountains, as well as the far reaches of the Edwards Plateau around Comstock in Val Verde County, may signal the return of permanent black bear populations to west Texas.

Black bears are sighted very rarely in the wooded areas of eastern Texas, primarily the result of individuals that have wandered into the state from release sites in Louisiana. There has been some discussion of reintroducing black bears into the Big Thicket of southeastern Texas, where they flourished until the early part of the twentieth century.

The Texas Parks and Wildlife Department currently lists the black bear as threatened in Texas. The U.S. Fish and Wildlife Service lists the Louisiana subspecies (*U. a. luteolus*) as threatened and designates the entire species as "threatened, by similarity of appearance to a threatened taxon."

Grizzly or Brown Bear

Ursus arctos Linnaeus

Description. Largest of the carnivores in western United States; head large with face distinctly dished in, or concave; body robust; legs strong, massive, and relatively short; tail much shorter than hind foot; last upper molar about as large as the two teeth in front of it combined; front claws 7–12 cm in length; upperparts brownish or yellowish brown, often with intermixture of white-tipped hairs; underparts similar to upperparts but lacking white-tipped hairs. Dental formula as in the black bear. External measurements of adult male: total length, 1,982 mm; length of tail, 76 mm; hind foot, 280 mm; height at shoulder, 1,017 mm. Females smaller. Weight of males, 180–360 kg, seldom as much as 500 kg; of females, 130–180 kg, seldom as much as 360 kg.

Distribution. The grizzly or brown bear probably occurred sparingly in western Texas from the Panhandle to the Trans-Pecos up until the days of early exploration of the region.

Only two specimens of grizzly bears are available from Texas. According to Vernon Bailey, who wrote of this bear in his *Biological Survey of Texas,* a large and very old male grizzly was killed in the Davis Mountains in October 1890 by C. O. Finley and John Z. Means. Measurements of the skull are: greatest length, 370 mm; basal length, 310 mm; zygomatic breadth, 220 mm; mastoid breadth, 157 mm; interorbital breadth, 71 mm; postorbital breadth, 69 mm. Finley reported that the claws on the front feet were about 3.5 inches (9 cm) long, and the color of the bear was brown with gray tips to the hairs. Its weight was estimated at 1,100 pounds (500 kg) "if it had been fat." Finley found that the bear had killed a cow and eaten most of it in a gulch near the head of Limpia Creek, where the dogs took the trail. Out of a pack of 52 hounds, only a few would follow the trail, although most of them were used to hunting black bear. Those few followed rather reluctantly, and after a run of about 8 km over rough country stopped the bear, which killed one of them before it was quieted by the rifles of Finley and Means. It took four men to put the skin, with head and feet attached, on a horse for the return to camp.

Walter Dalquest reported examining the partial skull of a grizzly bear that had washed out on the banks of the Red River (Montague County) about 1950. That specimen has since been lost.

Subspecies. *U. a. horribilis.*

Habits. The grizzly is essentially an inhabitant of rough, mountainous country today, but considerable evidence makes it clear that 100 years ago it was also very much at home in the plains of the West. The pressures of contact with the white man have forced the grizzly to make its last stand in rough wilderness terrain.

Like the black bear, the grizzly holes up and sleeps through the severe part of the winter, subsisting on fat stored in the body. It does not hibernate in the true sense of the word. The young are born while the mother is in her winter den.

The natural food of grizzlies is extremely varied. Results of a study made in Montana revealed these diets: in early spring, winter-killed animals, green grasses, and weeds; in middle and late spring, bulbs and roots, increasing use of grasses and sedges, few rodents, occasional young elk calves; in summer, continued use of green vegetation, ants, beetles, and other insects, fruits and berries, few rodents; in fall, largely pine nuts, few rodents. In certain sections they feed extensively on salmon during the spring run; occasional individuals turn renegade and become killers of livestock.

The breeding season is in June and July, but implantation of the fertilized eggs is delayed until November or December. One to four cubs (usually two) are born between January and March. The young cubs weigh about 750 g at birth, are about 20 cm long, and their eyes and ears are closed. Their eyes open in 8 or 9 days, in contrast to 6 weeks in the black bear.

Conservation Status. The grizzly is extinct in Texas and almost certain never to return. The USFWS lists the grizzly as a threatened species throughout its range.

FAMILY PROCYONIDAE (PROCYONIDS)

Procyonids occupy much of the temperate and tropical parts of the New World from southern Canada through much of South America. Three species of this family (coati, raccoon, and ringtail) occur in Texas, and the latter two are among our most important furbearers.

Ringtail

Bassariscus astutus (Lichtenstein)

Description. A cat-sized carnivore resembling a small fox with a long raccoonlike tail; tail flattened, about as long as head and body, banded with 14 to 16 alternating black and white rings (black rings incomplete on underside), and with a black tip; five toes on each foot, armed with sharp, curved, nonretractile claws;

Ringtail (*Bassariscus astutus*). Photo by John and Gloria Tveten.

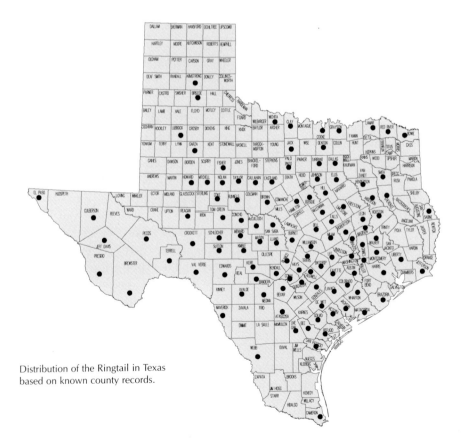

Distribution of the Ringtail in Texas
based on known county records.

upperparts fulvous, heavily overcast with blackish; face sooty gray with large, distinct, whitish area above and below each eye, and one at anterior base of each ear; eye ring black; back of ears whitish toward tip, grayish basally; underparts whitish, tinged with buff; underfur all over plumbeous. Dental formula as in raccoons. External measurements of males average: total length, 802 mm; tail, 410 mm; hind foot, 78 mm; of a female, 714-350-65 mm. Weight, 1–1.5 kg.

Distribution. Statewide. Ringtails are common in the Trans-Pecos, Edwards Plateau, and Cross Timbers regions of western and central Texas. They are less common in the woodland areas of eastern Texas. In the Edwards Plateau and Trans-Pecos regions, ringtails are denizens of rocky, brushy country. To the east they live in wooded areas, usually close to water, and they den in hollow trees and logs.

Subspecies. *B. a. flavus.*

Habits. Ringtails are strictly nocturnal and are active mainly during the middle of the night. They are as much at home in a tree as a gray squirrel and are notably quick in running, jumping, and climbing. Their hind feet can be rotated outward at least 180 degrees, permitting them to run rapidly down a tree trunk or steep rock headfirst instead of having to back down, the way a domestic cat does.

Ringtails normally den alone, although members of a family group (a female and her kittens) may den close together. Favored den situations include rock caves, hollow trees and logs, and brush piles. Females seem to prefer rock dens, whereas males tend to select dens in hollow trees and brush piles.

Ringtails have rather sizeable home ranges. Those of females average about 20 ha and males about 43 ha. Home ranges of females do not overlap, although they are overlapped by those of one or more males. Home ranges of males do not overlap. The overlap of a female's home range by one or more males enhances the female's chances of breeding.

Breeding occurs from mid-March to mid-April. The young, which number from two to four, are born from mid-May to mid-June. Newborn young are small, pink, fuzzy, helpless creatures with closed eyes and no teeth. The eyes open 31–34 days after birth, by which time the young are fully furred. The kits will eat meat when 7 weeks old, and they are weaned in August at about 8 weeks of age, at which time they begin to forage with their parents. They begin to den independently about the end of September but associate with their mother until at least the onset of winter. They exhibit the first signs of sexual activity when only 13 weeks of age, and by 19 weeks they are of adult appearance and behavior.

Ringtails emit barking and mating calls. The barking sound is made by both sexes whenever they become frightened or agitated. The sound intensifies nearly to a growl when a ringtail is further disturbed. When females come into heat, they emit a series of loud chirping calls that may serve as a signal to the male that the female is ready to copulate.

Ringtails eat a wide range of both plant and animal food. Small mammals form the largest part of the diet (62% of the volume), and fruits represent 28%. Small birds are third in importance (7%), with the remainder consisting, in descending order of importance, of insects, invertebrates other than insects, and cold-blooded vertebrates.

Next to the raccoon, the ringtail is the most important fur-bearing animal on the Edwards Plateau, but its importance is considerably less in other regions of the state. **Conservation Status.** Ringtails remain common in the rocky habitats of the western and central parts of the state. They are less abundant in eastern and southern Texas. There do not appear to be any serious threats to them, although continued habitat fragmentation in the Hill Country would certainly be a long-term issue.

Northern Raccoon
Procyon lotor (Linnaeus)

Description. A robust, medium-sized carnivore with distinctive, blackish facial mask outlined with white, and with alternating black and buff (or whitish) rings on the bushy tail; tip of tail black; general color of upperparts grayish, suffused with orange and heavily sprinkled with blackish buff; top of head mixed gray and brownish black, giving a grizzled effect; throat patch brownish black; rest of underparts brownish, thinly overlaid with light orange buff; limbs similar to underparts, but becoming whitish on feet except for dusky marking near heels; the complete hind foot touches the ground when the animal walks; five toes on each foot, claws non-retractile; soles naked; pelage coarse, long, and full. Young like adults, but fur woolly. Molar teeth flat-crowned and adapted for crushing, not for cutting as in dogs

Northern Raccoon (*Procyon lotor*). Photo by John and Gloria Tveten.

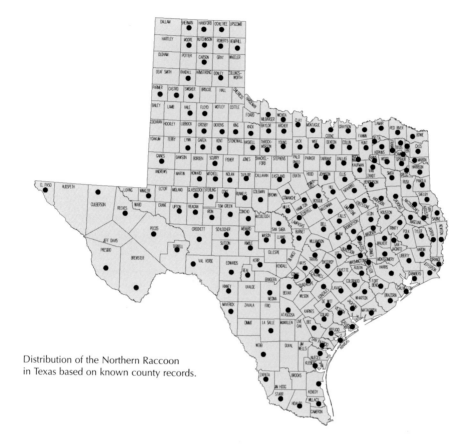

Distribution of the Northern Raccoon
in Texas based on known county records.

and cats. Dental formula: I 3/3, C 1/1, Pm 4/4, M 2/2 x 2 = 40. External measurements
of adult male: total length, 880 mm; tail, 265 mm; hind foot, 125 mm; of female, 834-
243-123 mm. Weight, 4–13 kg.

Distribution. Raccoons are widely distributed across southern Canada, most of the
United States (except parts of the Rocky Mountains and the arid Southwest) and
southward through Mexico. They occur statewide in Texas.

Subspecies. *P. l. hirtus* in the Panhandle north of the Canadian River, *P. l. mexicanus*
in the western part of the Trans-Pecos, and *P. l. fuscipes* throughout the remainder
of the state.

Habits. Raccoons occur statewide in all vegetative regions of Texas, but they are
seldom found far from water, which has an important influence on their distribution. They prefer hardwood-timbered habitats and are especially abundant in the
eastern half of the state along the larger streams where wide floodplains and adjacent sloping uplands support mature stands of hardwood timber. They occupy a
variety of other habitats, including bottomland swamps, marshes, around lakes or
ponds surrounded by narrow stands of trees, farmlands (especially those with
corn or maize fields), and heavily wooded residential areas in cities. They are
abundant in western Texas, where they occur along permanent streams as well as

in the driest desert places where humans have brought water by windmills, pumps, or surface tanks. Raccoons also inhabit the montane regions of the Trans-Pecos where sources of water are associated with wooded areas.

Raccoons live in dens located primarily in trees or rock ledges. The absence, however, of suitable natural den sites does not seem to limit them, as they commonly use barns, attics, and other available buildings. Raccoons are also known to share the same ground dens used by striped skunks and opossums, although not necessarily at the same time.

Raccoons are nocturnal and typically spend the day in their dens. Activity begins around sunset and ceases around sunrise, lasting about 9 hours. Raccoons do not hibernate, but during cold winter periods they may remain in the den for several days and live off their body-fat reserves. Raccoon movement patterns vary seasonally and with a variety of conditions, such as habitat type, population density, and reproductive condition.

Adults are seemingly solitary, although they often associate in groups of two or more individuals. Associations of adult males and females are largely restricted to the breeding season.

Raccoons eat a wide range of both plant and animal food. They are selective when food is abundant but eat whatever is available when it is scarce. Plant food, particularly acorns and fruits, makes up over 50% of the annual diet. Insects, especially grasshoppers, are second in importance, followed in descending order by mammals (cottontails and small rodents), invertebrates other than insects (crayfish and crabs), cold-blooded vertebrates (snakes and frogs), and birds (cardinals, blackbirds, sparrows, and meadowlarks).

The mating season begins in February and continues through August. A higher percentage of females mate in March than in any other month, and most of the young are born in April or May. The gestation period is about 63 days. The number of young per litter varies from 2 to 4, with an average of 2.8.

Young raccoons are well haired at birth, have dark skin with no rings on the tail, and the eyes and ears are closed. The eyes open between the eighteenth and twenty-third day. Females have the prominent or sole role in caring for the young. Weaning of the young occurs between the ages of 7 and 12 weeks. Families den together during the winter, and most young do not disperse from their natal area until the year after their birth.

Most raccoons in the wild live less than 5 years (the average is somewhere between 1.8 and 3.1 years). Their major predator is humans, particularly hunters and trappers. Predators that occasionally eat them include bobcats, foxes, coyotes, and owls. Other factors causing mortality include food shortages, disease, parasitism, and physiological stress arising from high population densities.

Raccoons carry a variety of diseases that can be communicated to humans, including leptospirosis, rabies, Chagas' disease, and tularemia. In the southern United States, both leptospirosis and tularemia have their largest reservoirs in raccoon populations, and the pathogens causing these diseases are transmissible through direct contact with raccoons or by means of water contaminated with raccoon urine or feces.

Raccoons are the most economically important furbearer in Texas. Most of the catch is in the eastern half of the state. Despite declining demand and prices for furs, the raccoon remains the most valuable fur-bearing species in the state because the total harvest far exceeds that of any other species.

Conservation Status. This is one of the most common carnivores in Texas. It has adapted well to human conditions and appears to be in good shape.

White-nosed Coati
Nasua narica (Linnaeus)

Description. A raccoonlike carnivore, but more slender and with longer tail; snout long, slender, and projecting well beyond lower lip; five toes on each foot; tail with six or seven indistinct light bands; ears short; general color of upperparts grizzled yellowish brown, fulvous on top of head; snout and areas around eyes white, as is inside of ears; dark brown facial band across snout between eyes and whiskers, interrupted on top of snout by extensions of white from stripe above eye; lower legs and tops of feet blackish brown; underparts pale buff, lightest (nearly white) on chin. Young like adults, but bands on tail more conspicuous. Molars adapted for crushing, not shearing as in most carnivores; upper canines flattened laterally, broad basally, shaped like a spear point; lower canines with a deep groove on inner face. Dental formula as in the raccoon. External measurements of adult male: total length, 1,130 mm; tail, 500 mm; hind foot, 91 mm; ear, 30 mm. Weight, 4–5 kg.

White-nosed Coati (*Nasua narica*). Photo by Alfred M. Bailey, courtesy Texas Parks and Wildlife Department.

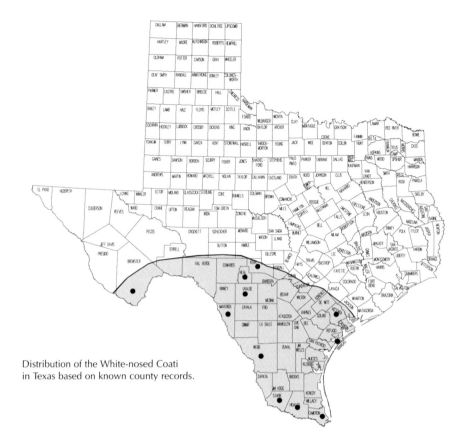

Distribution of the White-nosed Coati
in Texas based on known county records.

Distribution. Coatis inhabit woodland areas of the warmer parts of Central America, Mexico, and the extreme southern United States including southern Texas. In Texas, they are only known from the southern part of the state, from Brownsville northwest to the Big Bend region of the Trans-Pecos and east to Kerr and Victoria counties.

Subspecies. *N. n. molaris.*

Habits. Coatis spend considerable time on the ground, but they climb trees as easily as a squirrel. When in trees, their long tail seems to function, as does that of a squirrel, largely in maintaining balance. They also occur in some of the rocky canyons that enter the mountains from the lowlands.

Coatis are sociable creatures, and adult females travel in bands that may include subadult and younger coatis of both sexes. Band sizes vary, with bands of up to 40 individuals reported. Adult males are usually solitary.

Unlike their relatives the raccoons and ringtails, coatis are largely active by day, particularly in the early morning and late afternoon. They are omnivorous and consume a wide variety of available food, including insects and other ground-dwelling arthropods, lizards, snakes, carrion, rodents, nuts and fruits of native trees, and prickly pear. Captives have eaten bananas, milk, and bread.

Their breeding habits are not well known in the United States. Studies of coatis in tropical forests suggest that during the breeding season (spring) an adult male may temporarily join a band, but that male may not sire all of the litters from that band. The gestation period is 10–11 weeks. Before parturition, a pregnant female selects a nesting site in a tree, where she gives birth to a litter of one to six altricial young. The mother cares for the young in the nest for 4–5 weeks, at which time the mothers in a band bring their young out of the nests, and the social band is reformed.

Mortality rates are high for young coatis, particularly during the first few weeks after leaving the nest. Predation by large cats, white-faced monkeys, boa constrictors, and even adult male coatis has been reported in tropical forest populations.

Conservation Status. Because of the coati's erratic distribution and destruction of much of its habitat, Texas Parks and Wildlife lists the coati as threatened, and it is on the watch list of the Texas Organization for Endangered Species. The U.S. Fish and Wildlife Service has not listed it as threatened or endangered, evidently because of the relatively good populations extant in southeastern Arizona. It is widespread in Mexico and Middle America. Little is known about the life history or abundance of the coati, and it definitely is in need of serious study. Most of the Texas sightings have been from the southernmost portion of the state along the Rio Grande. The most recent sightings occurred in Victoria County in 1994 and 1995. Coatis could be seriously affected by the degradation and loss of much of the riparian woodland habitat in south and west Texas. These animals require a sizeable area of habitat to maintain a viable population.

FAMILY MUSTELIDAE (MUSTELIDS)

Mustelids are typically small to medium-sized, long-bodied carnivores with short limbs and pushed-in faces. They are more strictly carnivorous than dogs and have short, powerful jaws adapted to delivering an accurately placed death bite. They are worldwide in distribution but are more commonly found in north temperate regions. Anal glands (musk glands) are present. In Texas, the family is represented by three genera and five species. Of these, the mink and river otter are considered important fur-bearing animals in other regions of the United States, but they are of little economic importance in the Texas fur market.

Long-tailed Weasel

Mustela frenata Lichtenstein

Description. A slender, long-bodied carnivore with small head, long neck, short legs, and relatively long, slender tail; upperparts yellowish brown; head blackish; spot between eyes, broad band (confluent with color of underparts) on each side of head between ear and eye, chin and upper lip white; tip of tail black, remainder colored

Long-tailed Weasel (*Mustela frenata*). Photo by Robert J. Baker.

like back; underparts, except for chin, orange buff, which color extends down back of front legs over forefeet and on inside of hind legs to foot and sometimes onto toes. Dental formula: I 3/3, C 1/1, Pm 3/3, M 1/2 x 2 = 34. External measurements of males average: total length, 488 mm; tail, 192 mm; hind foot, 51 mm; of females, 438-187-42 mm. Weight of adult males, about 300–500 g; females slightly less.

Distribution. These weasels are widely distributed in Texas, except for the northern part of the state. They occupy a variety of habitats, including brushlands, fencerows, upland woods and bottomland hardwoods, forest edges, and rocky, desert situations. They usually live close to water and occasionally under a house or barn in proximity to people. It has been suggested that the absence of water to drink may be a factor limiting distribution of long-tailed weasels.

Subspecies. *M. f. neomexicana* mostly west of the 100th meridian, *M. f. texensis* in the central part of the state, *M. f. primulina* in the extreme northeastern part of the state, *M. f. arthuri* east of the Balcones Fault Zone in east-central and southeastern areas, and *M. f. frenata* in the southern part of the state along the Gulf Coast and adjacent to Mexico.

Habits. Long-tailed weasels typically nest in a rotten log, hollow stump, under tree roots, or in a hole in the ground. Their nest is made of grass and leaves and is lined with rodent and rabbit fur. Depending on the condition of their habitat, they may have one or several homes. Weasels are active both in the daytime and at night, but more so after dark. They are active year round and show no tendency to hole up or hibernate during winter. They range over a fairly large hunting circuit, which may take them several days to cover. Their nightly forays usually cover only a portion of their home range. When running, weasels arch their back up in a fashion reminiscent of a measuring worm.

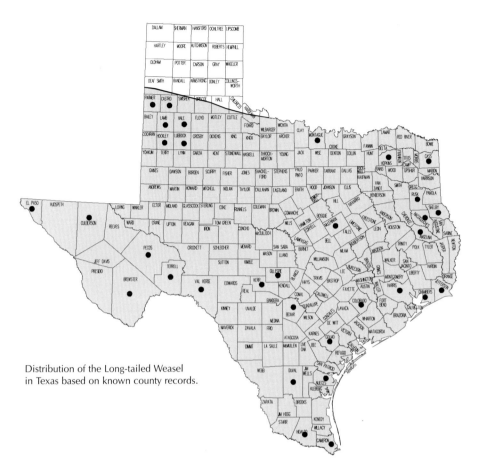

Distribution of the Long-tailed Weasel
in Texas based on known county records.

The bulk of their diet is composed of small mammals, including moles, shrews, ground squirrels, tree squirrels, flying squirrels, pocket gophers, woodrats, cotton rats, deer mice, harvest mice, and small cottontails. Occasionally, they will eat small birds, reptiles, amphibians, and insects. Most of their prey is killed by a bite on the back of the neck, with the body and legs of the weasel hugging the back of the victim. Weasels often kill more than they need, in which case the surplus is stored for future use.

Weasels are polygamous and breed mainly in July or August. Implantation is delayed for several months, and the embryos resulting from the mating do not become active until early spring, when they develop to full term in less than 27 days after becoming implanted. The single litter, which may number up to nine young (average four to five), is produced in April or May. The gestation period, including implantation delay, varies from 205 to 337 days (average 279 days).

Newborns are blind, nearly helpless, and covered with fine white hair. The eyes open at 36 days, at which time they are already weaned and feeding on solid food. There is some indication that the male may aid in rearing the young. The young remain with the female until they are fully grown. The scent glands begin to function at 6 weeks of age. Sexual maturity and adult size is reached in females at about 3 months, but not in males until 12 months.

Known predators include rattlesnakes, cottonmouths, foxes, bobcats, house cats, and dogs. While it lasts, the scent of this species is almost as powerful as that of a skunk and no doubt serves the animal as an excellent defensive weapon.

Although they are listed as a fur-bearing animal by state law, long-tailed weasels are of little economic importance because of their small body size and limited market demand.

Conservation Status. There is a real concern about the long-term status of weasels in Texas because of the loss of natural surface water, which is a preferred part of their habitat. This species should be carefully monitored in the future.

Black-footed Ferret

Mustela nigripes (Audubon and Bachman)

Description. A large edition of the common long-tailed weasel; upperparts pale buffy yellow, overcast with brown hairs on head and back; underparts buffy or cream colored; feet and tip of tail blackish; broad black mask across face and eyes. External measurements of males average: total length, 570 mm; tail, 133 mm; hind foot, 60 mm; of females, 500-120-55 mm. Weight, probably 850–1,400 g in males, 450–850 g in females.

Black-footed Ferret (*Mustela nigripes*). Photo courtesy U.S. Fish and Wildlife Service.

Distribution. Originally the same as that of the black-tailed prairie dog, roughly the northwestern third of Texas including the Panhandle, much of the Trans-Pecos, and a considerable part of the Rolling Plains east and southeast of those areas. Now extirpated from Texas. The last Texas records were from Dallam County (1953) and Bailey County (1963).

Subspecies. Monotypic species.

Habits. Black-footed ferrets are associated primarily with prairie dogs and prairie dog towns. Although individuals have been seen under haystacks, in alfalfa fields, and in buildings, most of these sightings were made during the fall dispersal of the young. Historically, the range of the ferret has coincided closely with that of the various species of prairie dogs, which are the main source of the ferret's food. In addition, prairie dog burrows provide the ferrets with shelter and nursery sites for rearing their young.

Both the young and the adults are primarily nocturnal. Young ferrets rarely appear above ground during daylight hours until about mid-August. Adults, however, occasionally leave their burrows during the day to sunbathe or to forage. When a ferret is active in daylight, the prairie dogs stay above ground, keep the intruder under surveillance, and appear to be highly nervous and agitated. That behavior of the prairie dogs is a reliable clue that a ferret is present in the dog town. A better clue, however, is the presence of a peculiar, shallow trench leading from a prairie dog burrow. When a ferret alters a prairie dog burrow or digs one of its own, it backs out with the dirt held against its chest and drags the dirt farther from the burrow entrance each time. The result is a trench 8–12 cm wide and up to 3.5 m long. These trenches are formed mostly at night and, if fresh, are a sure sign of the presence of a ferret. No other species of animal living in a dog town leaves this type of structure.

As mentioned above, the mainstay of black-footed ferrets is prairie dogs, which the ferrets capture and kill in their burrows at night. Analyses of 56 scats revealed that remains of prairie dogs occurred in 51 of them and comprised 82% of the identifiable animal material. Mouse remains occurred in 19 scats and made up the remaining 18%. Ferrets have also been seen chasing birds and catching moths. Determining their food habits by scat analyses can become quite a chore because the ferrets deposit most of their feces in the burrows they occupy. Only a few scats have ever been found above ground by investigators diligently searching for them.

Mating is believed to occur in April or May. One female killed on 16 May appeared to be in heat; a female trapped on 3 May was pregnant; a nursing female was captured on 20 June. The female alone cares for her litter of four or five young, even though the male may stay in the same dog town. As soon as the young are able to travel, the female coaxes them out of the nest burrow and leads them as she carefully checks several other burrows, finally selecting one for her litter and a separate one for herself. As they grow older, the young readily follow their mother; from June to mid-July they may be seen regularly at night as the family extends its activities. By mid-July the young are half-grown and readily eat prey that the female kills. By early August the young ferrets are usually occupying separate burrows in the dog town, and by mid-August they are often out during the early morning, playing, and following their mother. By early September the young are nearly full-grown and begin to disperse from their birthplace. It is during the period of dispersal that the young are exposed to the greatest danger. More than 40% of the dead ferrets found outside prairie dog towns were recorded from mid-August to mid-October. Ferrets do not hibernate, and during late fall, winter, and spring they are usually found singly.

Conservation Status. The black-footed ferret was driven to extinction in Texas with the drastic decline of prairie dog populations. By 1979 the species was thought to be extinct in the wild throughout its range. In 1984, however, one surviving colony, numbering about 130 individuals, was discovered at Meteetsee, Wyoming. That colony subsequently suffered an epidemic of canine distemper. In 1986 the remaining 18 ferrets known to have survived at the Meteetsee site were captured and put into a captive breeding program, with the hope that successful matings would one day allow for the return of this species to its natural habitat. In the fall of 1991, the first group of captive-born ferrets was released in the Shirley Basin area of Wyoming. An additional 83 captive-born ferrets were released in Shirley Basin during the fall of 1992. Those initial attempts at reintroduction were disappointing, but in the last decade much has been learned about the successful breeding of ferrets as well as their ecology, and reintroduction efforts are meeting with more success. In 1999 there were an estimated 200 ferrets in the wild at sites in Wyoming, South Dakota, Arizona, and Montana. The South Dakota site has documented a positive wild population growth, with survival rates of young born in the wild approaching 90% in 1998. Although captive breeding and reintroduction capabilities continue to improve, habitat availability remains a limiting factor in the effort to restore this species to the North American landscape. A recent USFWS evaluation indicated that only ten sites exist in all of North America that have prairie dog complexes of sufficient size and density to support viable ferret populations. The most formidable challenge now facing ferret recovery is the conservation of prairie dog habitats, which are vital to black-footed ferrets.

Texas Parks and Wildlife and U.S. Fish and Wildlife list the black-footed ferret as endangered.

American Mink
Mustela vison Schreber

Description. A weasel-like carnivore about the size of a house cat and semiaquatic in habit; general color dark chocolate brown, darkest on back, and nearly black on feet and end of tail; underparts paler than back, with considerable white on midline from chin to vent; neck long, head hardly larger around than neck; tail long and moderately bushy; eyes and ears small; legs short; pelage soft and dense, overlaid with longer, blackish guard hairs. Dental formula as in the long-tailed weasel.

American Mink (*Mustela vison*). Photo by Donald F. Hoffmeister.

External measurements of an adult male: total length, 560 mm; tail, 190 mm; hind foot, 67 mm; of a female, 540-180-60 mm. Weight of males, 680–1,300 g; of females, 450–700 g.

Distribution. Known from eastern half of state and the northern Panhandle in habitats near permanent water.

Subspecies. *M. v. mink.*

Habits. Mink are decidedly semiaquatic mammals. Their thick underfur prevents water from penetrating to the skin, and the toes of the hind feet are slightly webbed. They swim well enough to catch fish, and they can remain submerged for considerable periods of time.

Mink live in dens located near water in such places as natural rock crevices or cavities among rocks, at the bases of bridges or dams, under roots of trees, in holes in the banks of streams, in debris piled along streams, or in muskrat homes.

Mink are active all year and do not hibernate. They are chiefly nocturnal but often come out at dawn and dusk and less frequently during the day. They are not social animals and live alone except when the young are being raised. The territories of males overlap, and several males may use various dens in succession. Females usually occupy only one homesite during the year.

Mink produce one litter each year in the spring. Males are polygamous, but they generally stay with the last female bred to assist in rearing the young. Mating occurs from January to March. Delayed implantation is exhibited, with birth occurring about 30 days after implantation. The total gestation period ranges from 40 to 75 days (average 51 days). A typical litter contains 3–4 kits, but litters of more than 10 have been recorded.

Kits are about 100 mm long at birth and weigh about 6 g. They are born blind, helpless, and covered with a coat of fine, short, silvery white hair. The coat color changes to reddish brown in about 14 days, and the eyes open at 37 days. The young leave the nest for the first time at 7 weeks and are weaned at 8–9 weeks. The family stays together until the end of August.

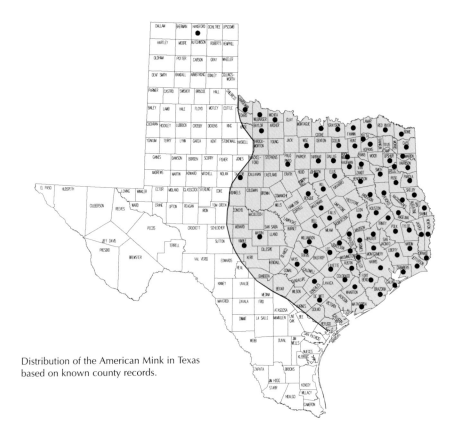

Distribution of the American Mink in Texas
based on known county records.

Their diet varies seasonally; crayfish and some mammals and frogs make up most of the summer diet, and small mammals are the major food item in winter. Mammals eaten by mink include shrews, moles, bats, rats and mice, squirrels, and young muskrats.

Mink seldom live more than 1.5–2 years in the wild. They have few enemies other than humans, but young animals may fall victim to bobcats, coyotes, dogs, foxes, owls, and alligators in coastal marshes.

The mink is one of the principal fur-bearing animals in the eastern United States and is one of the few animals that can be reared economically on fur farms. In Texas, mink ranked only thirteenth both in numbers of individuals harvested and in economic value to trappers during the 1998–1999 trapping season, as determined in a survey conducted by the Texas Parks and Wildlife Department. During the 1999–2000 season, however, mink were one of the only seven species being purchased by fur buyers in Texas, and their individual pelts ranked second in value only to the beaver.

Conservation Status. The mink is another species that appears to be suffering as a result of the reduction of natural surface water in the state. It has declined in abundance since the early twentieth century and does not appear to be common anywhere in the state. It should be carefully monitored in the future.

American Badger
Taxidea taxus (Schreber)

Description. A rather large, robust, short-legged version of a weasel; body broad and squat; tail short, thick and bushy, usually shorter than the outstretched hind legs; pelage long and shaggy, especially on back and sides; upperparts grizzled grayish yellow in color; a distinct white stripe from near tip of nose back over top of head to shoulder area, also a white crescent on each side of face just back of eye and another at anterior base of ear, enclosing or outlining a large blackish area; snout and rest of head grayish or blackish; underparts yellowish white; feet blackish; five toes on each foot; front feet large, with claws 25 mm or more in length; hind feet smaller, claws much shorter; skin loose on the body; eyes and ears small; neck short. Dental formula: I 3/3, C 1/1, Pm 3/3, M 1/2 x 2 = 34. Young similar to adults in color and color pattern. External measurements of adult male: total length, 788 mm; tail, 133 mm; hind foot, 120 mm; of female, 730-150-114 mm. Weight of adults, 4–10 kg, averaging about 7 kg.

Distribution. Now distributed throughout much of the state except for the extreme eastern part; may be extending its range eastward as a result of land-clearing operations.

American Badger (*Taxidea taxus*). Photo by R. D. Porter, courtesy Texas Parks and Wildlife Department.

Distribution of the American Badger
in Texas based on known county records.

Subspecies. *T. t. berlandieri.*

Habits. Badgers occupy a variety of habitats. They are most common in the prairie and desert sections of the West, but limited numbers venture into the mountains, where individuals have been seen or captured at elevations well above 3,000 m. In general, they occupy the entire range inhabited by ground squirrels and prairie dogs, which they rely on in large measure for food. In Texas, they range from sea level, as on Padre Island, to at least 1,500 m in the Davis Mountains.

As suggested by the disproportionately long front claws, badgers are expert diggers, and their short, powerful front legs can move earth with amazing speed. A badger was encountered on Padre Island as it sought refuge in a shallow burrow in a sandbank. Three people, working frantically with shovels for more than an hour, were so outdistanced in their race to capture the animal that they gave up.

It is a common belief that badgers hibernate in winter, but such is not the case. They may sleep through several days of inclement weather, as do skunks and bears, subsisting on fat stored in the body, but they do not experience the physiological changes characteristic of true hibernation (namely, considerably reduced rate of respiration and heart beat, lowered body temperature, and insensibility). They are frequently encountered in winter, particularly on mild days, and in the southern parts of their range they are active throughout the entire year.

As indicated above, the chief food of badgers is ground squirrels. In addition, pocket gophers, kangaroo rats, other burrowing rodents, and cottontails are dug out, caught, and eaten. They also eat lizards, birds, eggs, insects, and occasionally carrion.

Badgers are ordinarily solitary except during the mating season. They breed in summer and early autumn. Males are probably polygamous and mate with more than one female. Implantation is delayed until between December and February, and the young are not born until March or April. Litter size ranges from one to five, averaging about three. The young are born in an underground nest and are lightly furred and blind at birth. The eyes open at 4 weeks, and weaning occurs at about 8 weeks of age, when the young are half-grown. The young remain with their mother until late fall, when the family scatters.

Badgers have few natural enemies other than humans. They are ferocious fighters and are usually more than a match for any dog. In one recorded instance a badger successfully defended itself in a fight with two coyotes.

The fur of the badger ordinarily does not command a high price, which is why relatively few are trapped. In 1999 fur buyers were not purchasing badger pelts. Data indicate that the population is now increasing except in those parts of the animal's range where poison is used, ostensibly to reduce the population of coyotes. The badger's chief value lies in helping to keep down excessive populations of rodents.

Conservation Status. Badgers are still locally abundant at many places in the state and not in bad shape overall. They have been expanding their range and seem to be reasonably adaptable to human conditions, although land clearing and conversion and habitat fragmentation represent potential threats where development is accelerating. Careful monitoring would be prudent in the future.

Northern River Otter
Lontra canadensis (Schreber)

Description. Looks like a large, dark brown weasel with long, slender body; long, thick, tapering tail; webbed feet; head broad and flat; neck very short; body streamlined; legs short, adapted for life in the water; five toes on each foot, soles more or less hairy; pelage short and dense; upperparts rich, glossy, dark brown, grayish on lips and cheeks; underparts paler, tinged with grayish. Dental formula: I 3/3, C 1/1, Pm 4/3, M 1/2 x 2 = 36. External measurements average: total length, 1,168 mm; tail, 457 mm; hind foot, 124 mm. Weight, 6–7 kg, occasionally as much as 10 kg.

Distribution. Historically, otters ranged throughout eastern Texas and along the Red River drainage into the Panhandle as well as along the Brazos and Colorado river watersheds into central Texas. Today their range is limited to the eastern

Northern River Otter (*Lontra canadensis*). Photo by John and Gloria Tveten.

quarter of the state in the Pineywoods, Post Oak Savannah, and Gulf Prairies and Marshes ecological regions. Otters occupy a variety of aquatic situations because they are very mobile and capable of changing habitats at any time. Ideal habitat is a deepwater swamp, which supplies both food and shelter, adjacent to a large, log-filled, fish-producing lake, which furnishes additional food and abundant water for swimming or play. Otters seemingly prefer clear rather than muddy waters.

Subspecies. *L. c. lataxina.*

Habits. Most otters locate their dens in excavations close to water under tree roots, rock piles, logs, or thickets. The hollow bases of cypress trees and tupelo gums are especially popular. Occasionally, they will take over beaver lodges or muskrat dens for their own use after killing the occupants. A typical den consists of a hole leading into a bank, with the entrance below water level. Otters may occupy two dens, one as a temporary resting den and the other as a permanent nesting den.

Otters are sociable and friendly mammals. They are very playful even as adults. Play is usually focused along water and seems to accompany almost every activity they engage in. They take particular delight in sliding down mud banks into the water.

Otters have been studied in the coastal marshes of the J. D. Murphree Wildlife Management Area in Jefferson County. Eleven otters were captured there, and radio transmitters were surgically implanted so their movements could be monitored. Otter activity was greatest during the winter season and during the morning crepuscular period, and increased substantially with decreasing temperature. Male

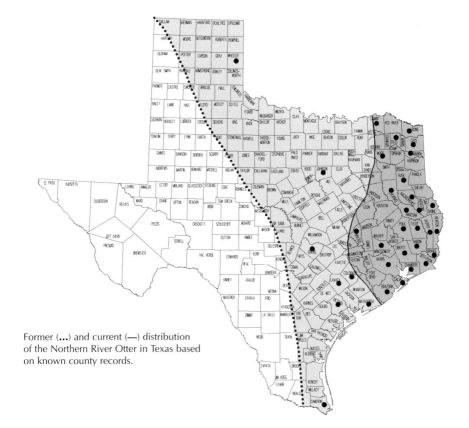

Former (...) and current (—) distribution of the Northern River Otter in Texas based on known county records.

otters exhibited higher overall activity levels than females. Otter home ranges averaged 337 ha, but activity centers averaged only 86 ha. These values are lower than those reported from other studies and probably reflect the plentiful and constant food supply in the coastal marsh. Otters did not make extensive long-distance movements away from the Murphree Area. The average 24-hour movement was only 3.5 km, and the maximum movement recorded was 7.3 km. Otters did not show strong preference for individual habitat components within their home range. Borrow ditches and sloughs were most preferred, and bayous were least preferred. Most wetland habitat components were used in proportion to availability.

Otters are not specific in their food habits. Their main diet consists of fish, crustaceans, mollusks, amphibians, reptiles, invertebrates, birds, and mammals. One of the otter's choicest morsels is crayfish, and where they are abundant, an otter will consume a tremendous number annually. The fish otters eat are primarily rough fish. They will also eat aquatic plants such as pond weeds and roots. Otters typically search for food by swimming along the bottom, poking their nose and front paws into cracks beneath rocks, rooting around submerged logs, and digging in the mud.

Virtually nothing is known about their reproduction in Texas. They probably breed in the fall, but males generally do not mate until they are 4 years of age, and females rarely breed before 2 years. Males typically engage in fierce combat during the mating season, and they are believed to be solitary except when accompanying estrous females. Estrus lasts 40 to 45 days, and the female is receptive to the male at about 6-day intervals. Mating usually occurs in the water. Delayed implantation extends the gestation period to as much as 270 days. Litter size varies from one to five, with two about average. Females may mate again as soon as 20 days following birth, which means that otters may remain continuously pregnant once they reach sexual maturity.

Newborns are about 275 mm in total length and weigh about 130 g. They are fully furred, but the eyes are closed and none of the teeth are erupted. Their eyes open at 22 to 35 days, and they are weaned at 18 weeks. The adult waterproof pelage appears after about 3 months.

Otters are long-lived animals capable of living 15–20 years in captivity. Other than humans, they have few natural enemies. There are unverified reports of coyotes killing young otters and speculation that other carnivores and large birds of prey, as well as alligators, may kill them.

Even though their pelts command a high price, otters are not a major fur-bearing animal in Texas because so few pelts are harvested. Otters are harvested in the Pineywoods, Gulf Prairies and Marshes, and Post Oak Savannah areas.

Conservation Status. In the last few decades, concern has been voiced about the disappearance of otters in many portions of their range as a result of habitat loss, heavy trapping pressure, and drowning in fish traps. In response, the Texas Parks and Wildlife Department prepares reports on the status of the otter in Texas, which suggest that otters are increasing in abundance in much of their remaining suitable habitat. The highest density of inland otter was documented in the Sabine and Angelina-Neches river drainage of the Pineywoods region. Apparently, the reestablishment and abundance of beaver and the improved habitat diversity and productivity associated with beaver activity have benefited the otter. Human-induced changes in habitat, such as impoundments, canals, levees, and so forth, are also providing improved conditions.

Remarks. In previous editions, this species was referred to as *Lutra canadensis.*

FAMILY MEPHITIDAE (MEPHITIDS)

Long considered a subfamily of Mustelidae, the skunks were raised to the familial level based on molecular systematic studies by Jerry Dragoo and Rodney Honeycutt. Nine species and three genera of mephitids occur in the New World. Five species belonging to three genera are known from Texas.

The North American skunks are familiar animals, particularly known for their anal scent glands, an effective antipredator device. All skunks have also developed a striking black-and-white color pattern. The susceptibility of skunks to the rabies virus serves to keep populations under control and occasionally poses a health risk to humans.

Western Spotted Skunk
Spilogale gracilis Merriam

Description. Color pattern resembles that of the eastern spotted skunk, *Spilogale putorius,* but white marking is more extensive, the black and white stripes on upper back nearly equal in width (in *putorius* the black areas are much more extensive than the white); dorsal pair of white stripes begin between the ears or just posterior to them (on back of head in *putorius*); white area on face large, extending nearly from nose pad to a line back of eyes and covering more than half of area between eyes; underside of tail white for nearly half its length, the tip extensively white (Fig. 6). Dental formula: I 3/3, C 1/1, Pm 3/3, M 1/2 x 2 = 34. External measurements of males average: total length, 423 mm; tail, 134 mm; hind foot, 43 mm; of females, 360-129-40 mm. Weight of males, 565 g; of females, 368 g.

Distribution. Recorded from southwestern part of state as far north as Garza and Howard counties and eastward to Bexar and Duval counties.

Subspecies. *S. g. leucoparia.*

Habits. This skunk occupies a variety of habitats and often occurs in close association with humans. In Texas most records of capture indicate that it is most often associated with rocky bluffs, cliffs, and brush-bordered canyon streams or streambeds. In the Edwards Plateau, rock fences seem to be especially attractive, possibly because they also provide denning sites and serve as refuges for many kinds of animals on which the spotted skunks feed. They also have been reported denning in hollow logs and, since they are adept at climbing, in the attics of houses.

Western Spotted Skunk (*Spilogale gracilis*). Photo by R. D. Porter, courtesy Texas Parks and Wildlife Department.

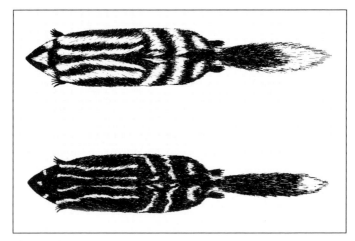

Figure 6. Color pattern of the western spotted skunk (top) and the eastern spotted skunk (bottom). See text for an explanation of differences.

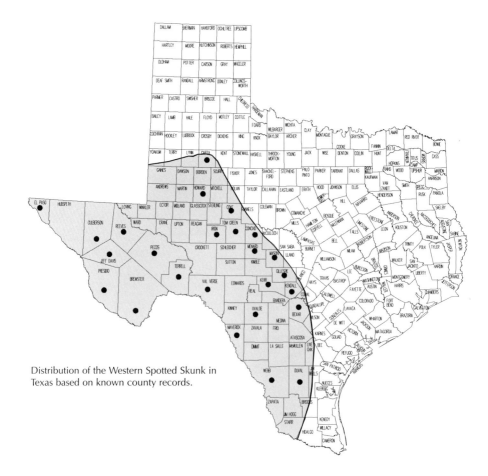

Distribution of the Western Spotted Skunk in Texas based on known county records.

Their natural foods are not well documented, but they are known to feed on turkey eggs, young rabbits, mice, and such arthropods as grasshoppers and scorpions.

Sexually mature females come into heat in September, and most of them are bred by the first week in October. The blastula stage of the embryo spends 180–200 days floating free in the uterus of the female before it becomes implanted. The two to five (average four) young are born in late April and May after a total gestation period of 210–230 days. Young females become sexually mature when only 4 or 5 months of age. Testes of both adult and young males begin to enlarge in March, are producing quantities of sperm by May, and reach their largest size during the height of the breeding season in September. In October, the testes begin to regress in size and the formation of sperm is halted. Thus, the males are incapable of fertilizing the females during the period from November through March. Even though the males are capable of breeding several months before the females come into heat, no breeding takes place until the females are receptive.

Conservation Status. Populations of this species appear to be declining, apparently in response to the degradation of prairie habitat in the state. This is a species that requires careful monitoring in the future.

Remarks. In his 1959 revision of the genus *Spilogale*, Richard Van Gelder suggested that the only differences between the eastern (*S. putorius*) and the western (*S. gracilis*) forms were size and color patterns. He therefore relegated *S. gracilis* to a subspecies of *S. putorius*. Thus, spotted skunks in Texas were treated as a single, wide-ranging species with four subspecies (designated *gracilis, leucoparia, interrupta,* and *putorius*). Using reproductive data, however, Rodney Mead found that the eastern and western spotted skunks in the United States were behaving as separate species. The western form exhibited an extended period of delayed implantation that was absent or short (2 weeks) in the eastern form, which meant their breeding seasons were separate and they were reproductively isolated. A recent molecular study of the spotted skunks by Jerry Dragoo and associates has corroborated those differences. So, in Texas today, there are two species of spotted skunks, *Spilogale gracilis leucoparia* in the western part of the state and *Spilogale putorius interrupta* in the eastern part.

Eastern Spotted Skunk
Spilogale putorius (Linnaeus)

Description. A small, relatively slender skunk with small white spot on forehead and another in front of each ear, the latter often confluent with dorsolateral white stripe; six distinct white stripes on anterior part of body, the ventrolateral pair beginning on back of foreleg, the lateral pair at back of ears, the narrow dorsolateral pair on back of head; posterior part of body with two interrupted white bands; one white spot on each side of rump and two more at base of tail; tail black except for a small terminal tuft of white; rest of body black (Fig. 6). Ears short and low on

Eastern Spotted Skunk (*Spilogale putorius*). Photo by John and Gloria Tveten.

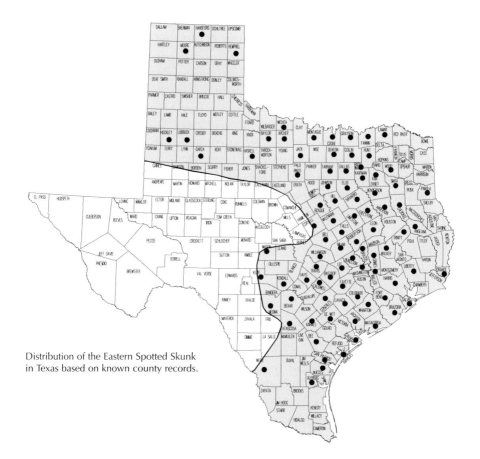

Distribution of the Eastern Spotted Skunk
in Texas based on known county records.

side of head; five toes on each foot, the front claws more than twice as long as hind claws, sharp and recurved. Dental formula as in *S. gracilis.* External measurements of males average: total length, 515 mm; tail, 210 mm; hind foot, 49 mm; of females, 473-170-43 mm. Weight of males, about 680 g; of females, about 450 g.

Distribution. Occurs in eastern half of state, westward onto the eastern Edwards Plateau and through north-central Texas to the Panhandle as far south as Garza County.

Subspecies. *S. p. interrupta.*

Habits. Spotted skunks are much more active and alert than any of the other skunks. They occur largely in wooded areas and tall-grass prairies, preferring rocky canyons and outcrops when such sites are available. They are less common in the short-grass plains. In areas where common, they have a tendency to live around farmyards and often den under or in buildings.

Their den sites are varied. In rocky areas they prefer cracks and crevices in the rocks or a burrow under a large rock. Since they are expert climbers, they occasionally den in hollow trees or in the attics of buildings. In settled communities they frequently live under buildings, in underground tile drains and in underground burrows. They are almost entirely nocturnal and seldom are seen in the daytime.

Their food habits are largely beneficial to the agriculturist, although they can do considerable damage to poultry if they develop a taste for such food. Their seasonal natural foods consist of: in winter, cottontails and corn; in spring, native field mice and insects; in summer, predominantly insects, with smaller amounts of small mammals, fruits, birds, and birds' eggs; in fall, predominantly insects, with small amounts of mice, fruits, and birds. They are excellent rat-catchers and can soon rid a barn of the pests.

Mating occurs in March and April. Some females possibly mate again in July and August and produce a second litter. The gestation period is estimated to be 50–65 days, with only a 2-week period of delayed implantation. The number of young in a litter may range from two to nine, but the usual litter consists of four or five young.

At birth the young are blind, helpless, and weigh about 9 g each; the body is covered with fine hair. The black and white markings are distinct. Their eyes open at the age of 30–32 days; they can walk and play when 36 days old, can emit musk when 46 days old, and are weaned when about 54 days old. When 3 months old they are almost as large as adults. Sexual maturity is reached at the age of 9–10 months in both sexes.

Their enemies, other than humans, include dogs, coyotes, foxes, cats, bobcats, and owls. Their defensive behavior consists of a rapid series of handstands, which serve as a warning to aggressors. If approached too closely, they drop to all fours in a horseshoe-shaped stance, lift their tail, and direct their anus and head toward the potential aggressor. The foul-smelling musk can be accurately discharged for a distance of 4–5 m.

Conservation Status. Once relatively common, this species is now rare in some areas, and its current status in the state is unknown. Because these small skunks consume many insects, there is a concern that some of the population decline can be attributed to widespread use of chlorinated hydrocarbon insecticides, with the deadly effect passed (and concentrated) up the food chain. This is a species that requires careful monitoring in the future. *S. p. interrupta* was listed as Category 2 by the USFWS prior to 1996.

Hooded Skunk

Mephitis macroura Lichtenstein

Description. Superficially similar to the striped skunk, *Mephitis mephitis,* but differs in having longer, softer fur and a distinct ruff of longer hair on the upper neck. Three color patterns: a white-backed phase with upperparts chiefly white, frequently with two narrow, short white stripes on each side behind shoulder, and underparts black or mottled with white; a black-backed phase with upperparts black, except for two narrow lateral white stripes, and underside of tail frequently white (occasionally tail wholly black, but bases of hairs always white); and a combination phase that is intermediate between the white-backed and black-backed forms (Fig. 7). In the white-backed phase, a broad white band begins between the eyes and covers most of the back and upper surface of the tail; the white stripe never bifurcates as in the striped skunk. Differs from the hog-nosed skunk in much finer fur, small snout, smaller size, and much longer tail. Dental formula as in the

Hooded Skunk (*Mephitis macroura*). Photo by Richard B. Forbes and Jerry W. Dragoo.

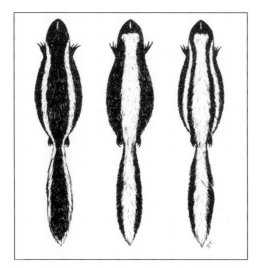

Figure 7. Three color phases in hooded skunks: left, black-backed phase; middle, white-backed phase; right, combination black-and-white-backed phase.

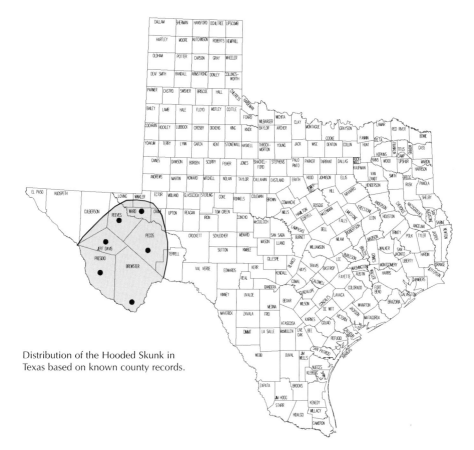

Distribution of the Hooded Skunk in Texas based on known county records.

western spotted skunk. External measurements of an adult male: total length, 700 mm; tail, 377 mm; hind foot, 69 mm; of adult female, 650-370-60 mm. Weight of males, 800–900 g; of females, 400–700 g.

Distribution. Primarily a Mexican species. Occurs in Texas in the central Trans-Pecos region. Recorded definitely only from Brewster, Jeff Davis, Pecos, Presidio, Reeves, and Ward counties.

Subspecies. *M. m. milleri.*

Habits. These slender, white-sided skunks occur along stream courses where they resort to rocky ledges or tangles of streamside vegetation for safety. Occasionally they resort to burrows in the banks of washes. One captured in Brewster County was trapped in a heavy stand of willows along the sandy banks of Tornillo Creek. It had been feeding in that vicinity in company with hog-nosed skunks.

Little is known of the natural history of hooded skunks, which are the rarest of the skunks in Trans-Pecos Texas. Males and females are in breeding condition from the middle of February to the last of March. Two litters, each consisting of three individuals, have been recorded. Hooded skunks are primarily insectivorous, although they also eat some vertebrates (shrews and rodents) as well as plant materials (prickly pear fruit).

The fur of this animal is much longer and softer than that of any other skunk, but it does not command a high price on the fur market.

Conservation Status. Hooded skunks have not been sighted in almost two decades in west Texas. The reasons for this decline are unclear, but the species should be carefully monitored in the future and probably warrants some type of protection status.

Striped Skunk
Mephitis mephitis (Schreber)

Description. A medium-sized, stout-bodied skunk with two white stripes on sides of back that join each other in the neck region and extend onto the head anteriorly and onto each side of the tail posteriorly; stripe pattern varies (Fig. 8); tip of tail black; two large scent glands, one on each side of the anus, produce the characteristic skunk musk; ears short, rounded; eyes small; five toes on each foot, front ones armed with long claws; hind feet with heel almost in contact with ground; tail long and bushy; pelage long, coarse, and oily. Dental formula as in the western spotted skunk. Sexes colored alike, but males usually larger than females. External measurements of males average: total length, 680 mm; tail, 250 mm; hind foot, 90 mm; of females, 610-225-65 mm. Weight, 1.4–6.6 kg, depending on age and amount of fat.

Distribution. Statewide.

Subspecies. *M. m. varians* in the western part of the state and *M. m. mesomelas* east of the 100th meridian.

Habits. Striped skunks are largely nocturnal, normally venturing forth late in the day and retiring to their dens early in the morning. Under ordinary circumstances

Striped Skunk (*Mephitis mephitis*). Photo by John and Gloria Tveten.

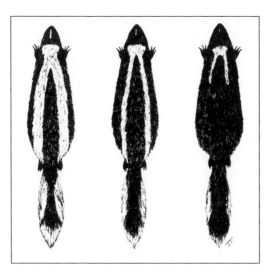

Figure 8. Three stripe patterns in striped skunks: left, broad-striped; middle, narrow-striped; right, short-striped.

they remain within 1.6 to 3.2 km of the den during their nightly foraging. Although not true hibernators, skunks store quantities of body fat in winter, and with the advent of cold weather they may become dormant in underground dens for short periods of time.

Striped skunks construct their homes wherever a convenient place is found. Rocky crevices and outcrops are favorite denning sites, as are natural cavities

Distribution of the Striped Skunk in Texas
based on known county records.

along the edge of a stream. When natural denning sites are absent, they may utilize the burrows of armadillos, badgers, foxes, and other animals or establish themselves under deserted houses or barns.

Striped skunks are gregarious, living in families from the time the young are old enough to walk until they are able to fend for themselves. The mother, occasionally accompanied by the male, may often be seen feeding with her brood. The members of the family separate in the fall, but winter aggregations of as many as 7–10 individuals, either adults or a mixture of adults and young, have been reported in well-situated dens.

Female striped skunks are in estrus from late February though March. Occasionally they may breed as late as the middle of June, but this is an exception and probably occurs only when the female has lost an earlier litter. Males are in prime breeding condition throughout February and March. Most young are born during the first part of May following a gestation period of 62 to 75 days. Litter size ranges from three to nine and averages about five.

Young striped skunks are born with short hair, a distinct stripe pattern, closed eyes, and closed ear canals. Their mean weight is about 21 g. The eyes and ears open after about 30 days, at which time they are also able to musk. They are weaned at 8 to 10 weeks; once babies are able to leave their dens, they follow their mother about as she forages for food. Dispersal of family units takes place during late summer and autumn.

Striped skunks are omnivorous. Their favorite foods are insects, especially grasshoppers, beetles, and crickets, followed by birds, mammals, and plants. Depending on the season, insects may constitute anywhere from 52 to 96% of their diet. They are also fond of nestling birds and eggs. Field mice, young rabbits, and small reptiles are other sources of food. Freshwater clams are often dug for in the loose sands along the banks of a stream, and once it acquires the habit, a skunk can become a persistent visitor to chicken houses and apiaries, causing considerable damage.

Striped skunks have few natural enemies. Owls, hawks, coyotes, bobcats, foxes, and dogs may occasionally take one, but most predators are repulsed by the odor of their musk. Striped skunks are highly susceptible to being struck by vehicles, and road-killed animals are frequently seen along highways throughout Texas. Individuals seldom live more than 2 years in the wild.

When disturbed or startled, skunks utter a peculiar purring sound and often growl when attacked by humans. They typically express their anger by rising on their hind feet, lurching forward, stamping both front feet, and at the same time clicking their teeth. The expelling of musk generally follows this behavior.

Striped skunks are commonly obtained by trappers, but because of the low value of their pelt, they are not an important fur producer in Texas.

Conservation Status. This is the most common skunk throughout Texas, and it appears to be in good shape. It has adapted well to human conditions and is doing better than any other species of skunk.

Hog-nosed Skunk

Conepatus leuconotus (Lichtenstein)

Description. Largest of the North American skunks; a single, broad white stripe from top of head to base of tail; long, bushy tail white all over with a few scattered black hairs beneath; rest of body blackish brown or black; white stripe on head truncate or wedge-shaped; snout relatively long, the naked pad about 20 mm broad and 25 mm long; nostrils ventral in position, opening downward; ears and eyes small; five toes on each foot; claws of forefeet much larger than on rear feet, strong and adapted for digging; pelage relatively long and coarse; underfur thin. Young colored like adults; sexes alike in coloration. Dental formula: I 3/3, C 1/1, Pm 2/3, M 1/2 x 2 = 32. External measurements of males average: total length, 577 mm; tail, 248 mm; hind foot, 65 mm; of females, 542-202-68 mm. Weight, 1.1–2.7 kg, rarely to 4.5 kg. Females are smaller than males.

Distribution. Ranges across southern and central Texas, north at least to Collin and Lubbock counties. A former isolated population in the Big Thicket region of eastern Texas has been extirpated.

Hog-nosed Skunk (*Conepatus leuconotus*). Photo courtesy
Texas Parks and Wildlife Department.

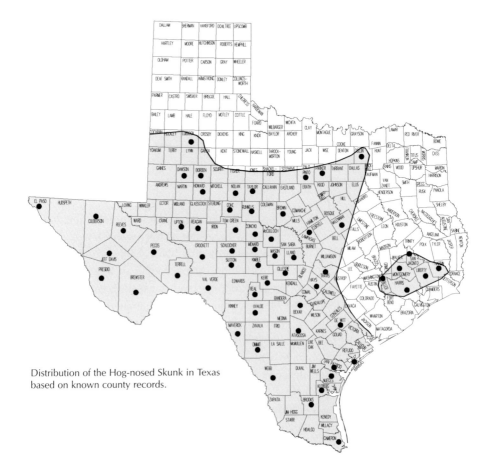

Distribution of the Hog-nosed Skunk in Texas
based on known county records.

Subspecies. *C. l. leuconotus* throughout most of the range in the state and *C. l. tel-malestes* (now extinct) from the Big Thicket region.

Habits. These white-backed skunks inhabit mainly the foothills and partly tim-bered or brushy sections of their general range. They usually avoid hot desert areas and heavy stands of timber. The largest populations occur in rocky, sparsely timbered areas such as the Edwards Plateau of central Texas and the Chisos, Davis, and Guadalupe mountains of Trans-Pecos Texas. In south Texas they have been collected or observed in several habitat types, including live oak brush, mesquite brushland, and improved pasture within semiopen native grassland. Their pres-ence in an area usually can be detected by the characteristically plowed-looking patches of ground where the skunks have rooted and overturned rocks and bits of debris in their search for food. Their hoglike habit of rooting has led to the adop-tion of the term "rooter skunk." Most Texans know the skunk by that name.

Although largely nocturnal, they are not strictly so. In midwinter in central Texas, many of them prefer to feed during the heat of the day. In this respect they remind one of the habits of the armadillo at that season. They seldom are as abundant in any part of their range as the striped skunk, *Mephitis mephitis.* Like other skunks, they are relatively unafraid of man or beast and do not hesitate to defend themselves with their powerful musk if unduly molested. In the Guadalupe Mountains of western Texas, William B. Davis watched one at close range at night with the aid of a flashlight for nearly 30 minutes as it rooted about in search of food. When approached too closely, fair warning was given as the skunk elevated its tail and maneuvered to place the observer in the line of fire.

As mentioned previously, these skunks prefer rocky situations when available because the numerous cracks and hollows can serve as den sites. Not only do they winter in such dens, but they also use them as nurseries. Unlike the striped skunk, this species is more or less unsocial. Usually only one individual lives in a den, but a trapper in central Texas reported that he once found a winter den occupied by two of them.

Their food habits make them valuable assets in most areas. Based on analysis of stomachs and other viscera of 83 rooters from central Texas, their seasonal food (expressed in percentages) consists of: in fall, insects (52), arachnids (4), vegeta-tion (38), reptiles (6); in winter, insects (76), arachnids (12), small mammals (9), vegetation (3), with reptiles and mollusks making up the balance; in spring, insects (82), arachnids (12), reptiles (6); in summer, insects (50), arachnids (9), small mammals (3), vegetation (31), snails (5), reptiles (2).

The breeding season begins in February, and most females of breeding age are with young in March. The female has only 6 teats (as opposed to 12–14 in the striped skunk), suggesting small litters of young. Robert Patton found that females generally produce two litters, each consisting of three individuals. J. D. Bankston of Mason, Texas, reported that he had never seen more than four young with a female. The young are born in late April or early May. The gestation period is approxi-mately 2 months. Nothing has been recorded on the growth and development of

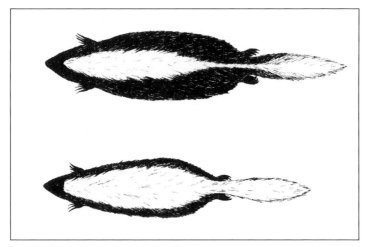

Figure 9. Color patterns of the Gulf Coast (top) and western (bottom) forms of the hog-nosed skunk. See text for an explanation of differences.

the young, but we do know that they can crawl about in the nest before their eyes are open and that at that tender age they can emit a drop or two of musk. By the middle of June they are about the size of kittens and weigh about 450 g. By August most of them are weaned and are rooting for their living.

Conservation Status. Hog-nosed skunks have disappeared from the Big Thicket and appear to have met the same fate in the South Texas Plains region. Although they are still considered common in the central part of the state, especially in the Hill Country, there is a growing consensus among professional mammalogists that the overall population level of hog-nosed skunks in Texas has declined drastically during the past few decades. Relatively little is known about the ecology and behavior of these animals, and the reasons for their decline are unknown at this time. Several possible explanations that have been proposed include the conversion of brushy habitats to row-crop agriculture, competition with feral hogs, and the use of pesticides that may limit the insect food source for the skunks. This is another species of skunk that will require careful monitoring in the future.

Remarks. The hog-nosed skunks of Texas were formerly treated as two species, *Conepatus leuconotus* and *C. mesoleucus*. Recently, Jerry Dragoo, Rodney Honeycutt, and I combined the two as one species based on morphological and genetic analyses. There are, however, differences in the color pattern of the two forms (Fig. 9). The western form (formerly *C. mesoleucus*) has one broad stripe running from the top of the head to the base of the tail. The tail is long, bushy, and white all over except for a few scattered hairs underneath. The Gulf Coast form (formerly *C. leuconotus*) resembles the western form, but it is larger and the white stripe on the back is much narrower, wedge-shaped rather than truncate on the head, and reduced in width or entirely absent on the rump. The upper side of the tail is white, but the underside is black toward the basal half and white toward the tip.

FAMILY FELIDAE (CATS)

This cosmopolitan, highly predatory family includes 18 genera and 36 species worldwide. In North America, there are 5 genera and 7 species. Of those 7 species, 6 presently occur or have occurred historically in Texas. Today, the margay and jaguar are extirpated from Texas, and the jaguarundi and ocelot are highly endangered. Both the mountain lion and the bobcat range widely in the state.

Mountain Lion
Puma concolor (Linnaeus)

Description. A large, long-tailed, unspotted cat; body long and lithe; tail more than half the length of head and body, rounded in cross section, and black-tipped; claws long, sharp, and curved; soles haired, but pads naked; ears small, rounded, without tufts; upperparts and sides dull tawny, darkest on middle of back and tail; face from nose to eyes grayish brown; a pale patch above each eye; back of ear blackish; chin, lips, throat, and underparts whitish; underside of tail grayish white. Dental formula: I 3/3, C 1/1, Pm 3/2, M 1/1 x 2 = 30; upper molar very small, sometimes absent. External measurements of a large adult male: total length, 2.6 m; tail, 927 mm; hind foot, 259 mm. Total length of three males averaged 2.3 m; of females, 2 m. Weight of three males, 160–227 kg; of six females, 105–133 kg.

Distribution. Once statewide; now known with certainty, except for occasional occurrences northward, only in desert mountain ranges of the Trans-Pecos region, especially in Big Bend National Park, on parts of the Edwards Plateau, and in the dense brushlands of the Rio Grande Plains.

Mountain Lion (*Puma concolor*). Photo by John and Gloria Tveten.

Distribution of the Mountain Lion in
Texas based on known county records.

Subspecies. *P. c. stanleyana.*

Habits. These cats spend most of their time on the ground, but they are adept at climbing trees and often do so when pursued by dogs. Their chief range preferences are rocky, precipitous canyons, escarpments, rimrocks, or, in the absence of these, dense brush. Heavily timbered areas usually are avoided. Retiring and shy by nature and nocturnal by habit, they are seldom seen in their native haunts. The presence of a mountain lion in an area can usually be detected by looking for scrapes, the signpost of the male; he scrapes together small piles of leaves, grasses, and so forth and urinates on them. They are best found on the cats' travel routes along the ridges and rimrocks.

Contrary to popular opinion, mountain lions seldom use caves as dens. An area under an overhanging ledge, a crevice in a cliff, a dry cavity in a jumbled pile of rocks, an enlarged badger burrow, a cavity under the roots of a tree, or a dense thicket seem to be more desirable.

Their food is almost entirely animal matter, but as with domestic cats, grasses may be eaten occasionally. The chief item of the diet is deer. Analyses of stomachs revealed that in the Southwest, the mule deer accounted for 54% of the total food (by frequency of occurrence); white-tailed deer, 28%; porcupines, 5.8%; cottontails,

3.9%; jackrabbits, 2%; domestic cows, 1.6%; miscellaneous (including sheep, goats, skunks, foxes, coyotes, beavers, prairie dogs, and grasses), 4.7%. In certain areas they are known to kill and feed on horses, particularly colts. In general, the mountain lion's food habits are of neutral or beneficial character. The high percentage of predation on deer probably is beneficial from a game management view in most instances because the mountain lion tends to prevent overpopulation of deer, which is the bane of the game manager in many areas where this cat has been exterminated.

Mountain lions are solitary except for a short breeding period of up to 2 weeks duration, when the female is in estrus. The gestation period is about 3 months. The number of young ranges from two to five, averaging three. At birth, the kittens are woolly and spotted, have short tails, and weigh about 450 g each. They develop teeth when about a month old, are weaned when about 2 or 3 months old, and may remain with their mother until more than 1 year old. Adult females usually breed for the first time between 2 and 3 years of age and breed once every 2 or 3 years afterwards.

Conservation Status. Historically, mountain lions occurred virtually throughout the state. Years of predator control efforts by livestock producers, however, forced the remaining mountain lions into the more remote, thinly populated areas. Today, the largest mountain lion populations are in the desert mountain ranges of the Trans-Pecos, especially in the Big Bend region, and in the dense brushlands of the Rio Grande Plains. Also, reports of these large cats are still common in parts of the Edwards Plateau and even in the Big Thicket. Predator control efforts have slowed since about 1970, and mountain lion populations appear to be stabilizing.

Texas is the only state with a resident mountain lion population that does not regulate taking of the species. Current management practices are controversial and relate to whether the species should be listed as nongame in an effort to regulate harvest within the state. Presently, Texas Parks and Wildlife classifies the species as a predator, thus allowing unregulated trapping, killing, and transporting of mountain lions. Although still regarded by many as unwanted predators, mountain lions have begun in recent years to receive some recognition for their ecological, aesthetic, and sporting value. Efforts by concerned private citizens and environmental groups may someday result in their being recognized as a game animal, hunted in season and under license.

Remarks. In previous editions the scientific name for the mountain lion was given as *Felis concolor*.

Ocelot

Leopardus pardalis (Linnaeus)

Description. A medium-sized, spotted and blotched cat with a moderately long tail; about the size of a bobcat but spots much larger, tail much longer, and pelage shorter; differs from the jaguar in much smaller size and in presence of parallel

Ocelot (*Leopardus pardalis*). Photo by John and Gloria Tveten.

black stripes on nape and oblique stripes near shoulder; upperparts grayish or buffy, heavily marked with blackish spots, small rings, blotches, and short bars; underparts white, spotted with black; tail spotted, and ringed with black; both sexes colored alike. Dental formula as in the mountain lion. External measurements of males average: total length, 1,135 mm; tail, 355 mm; hind foot, 157 mm; of females, 930-285-135 mm. Weight, 10–15 kg.

Distribution. Once ranged over southern Texas with occasional records from north and central Texas; now restricted to several isolated patches of suitable habitat in three or four counties of the Rio Grande Plains.

Subspecies. *L. p. albescens.*

Habits. The ocelot is a Neotropical felid that once inhabited the dense, almost impenetrable chaparral thickets of south Texas, the Gulf Coast, and the Big Thicket of eastern Texas. In Kerr County, where ocelots occurred as late as 1902, Howard Lacey reported that he found them in the roughest, rockiest part of the dense cedar brakes. He was of the opinion that they travel in pairs and that they often rest in trees and so escape the dogs.

Ocelots feed on a variety of small mammals and birds, as well as some reptiles, amphibians, and fish. Lacey reported that they are fond of young pigs, kids, and lambs; E. W. Nelson says that birds, including domestic poultry, are captured on their roosts, and rabbits, woodrats, and mice of many kinds, as well as snakes and other reptiles, are important items in their diet.

The den is a cave in a rocky bluff, a hollow tree, or the densest part of a thorny thicket. The two young are born in September, October, or November. Like other

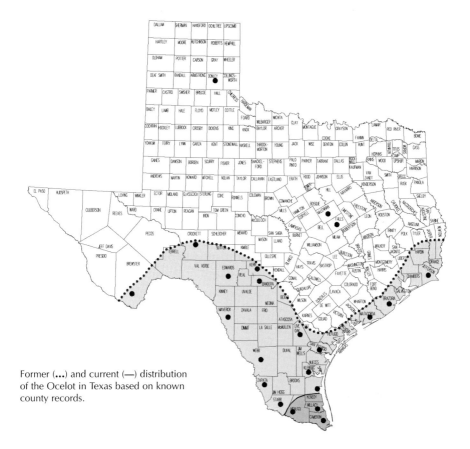

Former (•••) and current (—) distribution of the Ocelot in Texas based on known county records.

young of the cat family, they are covered with a scanty growth of hair, and the eyes are closed at birth. Gestation has been estimated to last 70–80 days, and captive kittens opened their eyes 15–18 days after birth.

Conservation Status. Predator control and habitat destruction have greatly reduced the range and numbers of the ocelot in Texas, and consequently it is listed as endangered on both the TPWD and federal lists and under the Convention on the International Trade in Endangered Species. Although still abundant in parts of Mexico, Central America, and South America, within the United States the current ocelot population consists of 80–120 individuals confined to two isolated populations restricted to several small patches of suitable habitat in three or four counties in the lower Rio Grande Valley. Modifications of the landscape during the twentieth century, as a result of mechanical farming and brush eradication, have fragmented its range, reduced its numbers, and presumably established barriers to dispersal between south Texas populations and the larger, more continuously distributed populations in northern Mexico. The ocelot is considered endangered throughout its range, and habitat restoration will be important in enhancing its recovery.

Remarks. In previous editions the scientific name for the ocelot was given as *Felis pardalis.*

Margay
Leopardus wiedii (Schinz)

Description. A small, spotted cat similar to the ocelot in color and color pattern but smaller, more slender, and usually with longer tail; skull seldom exceeding 110 mm in greatest length. Dental formula as in the mountain lion. External measurements: total length, 862 mm; tail, 331 mm; hind foot, 112 mm. Weight, 2–3 kg.

Distribution. The margay is a Neotropical felid that ranges from northeastern Mexico to northern Argentina. It is recorded from Texas on the basis of a specimen taken near Eagle Pass, Maverick County, before 1852. Remains of this cat have been found in Pleistocene deposits along the Sabine River in Orange County, so a few thousand years ago it ranged over a considerable part of southern Texas.

Subspecies. *L. w. cooperi.*

Habits. The margay inhabits the forested areas of tropical America. It is not a common animal and its habits are not well known. It is expert at climbing trees, in which it is likely to be found resting during the day. The margay spends some of its time foraging in trees catching birds and small mammals, but also captures prey on the ground. Its reported prey include monkeys, tamarins, sloths, squirrels, opossums, birds, rats and smaller mammals, various reptiles and amphibians, and domestic chickens.

Little is known about the reproductive habits of margays. They appear to be sexually mature at 6 to 12 months of age. Females normally give birth to a litter of just one or two kittens after a gestation period of 9 to 12 weeks.

Conservation Status. This species is extinct in Texas, having been known on the basis of a single specimen taken near Eagle Pass sometime before 1852. It presently is known from tropical eastern and western Mexico southward to Paraguay and northern Argentina. One of the smallest of American spotted cats, it is regarded as endangered throughout its range.

Remarks. The genus name for this species has been changed from *Felis* to *Leopardus.*

Margay (*Leopardus wiedii*). Photo by John and Gloria Tveten.

Jaguarundi

Herpailurus yaguarondi (Lacépède)

Description. Small, slender-bodied, long-tailed, unspotted, weasel-like cat; size somewhat larger than the ordinary alley cat; legs short for a cat; two color phases. Grayish phase: upperparts grizzled, salt-and-pepper gray; underparts slightly paler; more black in winter pelage. Red phase: upperparts reddish, intermixed with blackish; head and legs more brownish; lips and throat usually whitish. Dental formula as in the mountain lion. External measurements of an adult male: total length, 1,070 mm; tail, 572 mm; hind foot, 137 mm; females usually smaller. Weight, 4–8 kg.

Distribution. Brush country of extreme southern Texas in Cameron, Hidalgo, Starr, and Willacy counties.

Subspecies. *H. y. cacomitli.*

Habits. Jaguarundis are denizens of the dense, thorny thickets of southern Texas where cacti, mesquite, catclaw, granjeno, and other spine-studded vegetation abound. They spend most of their time on the ground, but they are expert climbers and garner part of their food in the trees and bushes. They are largely active at night but move about a good deal in the daytime, often going to water to drink at midday.

Their food consists of rats, mice, birds, and rabbits. They also are reputed to make inroads on poultry. Robert Snow has stated that their chief food is birds and that the young in the dens are fed a similar diet. He reported seeing one old cat

Jaguarundi (*Herpailurus yaguarondi*). Photo by John and Gloria Tveten.

spring about 1.5 m into the air and knock feathers out of a low-flying dove. An analysis of stomach contents from 13 Venezuelan jaguarundis revealed the remains of lizards, rodents, small birds, cottontail rabbits, and grass.

Their breeding habits are not well known. F. B. Armstrong was of the opinion that they have no regular breeding season. He found young in both summer and winter, born probably in March and August. This suggested two litters of two young each year. Snow found their dens under fallen trees grown over with grass and shrubs and in thickets. They were merely forms in this protective cover. He found young in the den only in March, the number always being three. The young of a litter may all be slate blue, all chocolate brown, or some of them may be blue and the others brown. He reported finding several litters in the vicinity of Raymondville, Willacy County. No information is available on their home life, growth, and development.

Conservation Status. The rarest of all the native cats, jaguarundis are now thought to be represented in the lower Rio Grande Valley by no more than 15 individuals. With numbers so low, it is doubtful it will survive. As with the jaguar and ocelot, predator control and habitat destruction took their toll on this species. The clearing of brushlands in the Rio Grande Valley destroyed its habitat, and only habitat restoration and reintroductions can save this species from extinction in Texas. The USFWS, TPWD, and the Nature Conservancy of Texas have been working for several years in a cooperative effort to restore habitat in the Rio Grande Valley.

Both TPWD and USFWS list the species as endangered throughout its range.

Remarks. The genus name for this species has been changed from *Felis* to *Herpailurus.*

Bobcat

Lynx rufus (Schreber)

Description. A medium-sized, short-tailed, reddish brown or grayish cat about the size of a chow dog; upperparts reddish brown, streaked with black; underparts whitish, spotted with black; back of ears black-rimmed, with white in center; ears usually slightly tufted; hair on sides of head long, producing a ruff; pelage elsewhere rather short; tail usually shorter than hind foot; the tip black above and white below, with three or four blackish bars above just in front of tip; legs relatively long; feet large, with five toes in front, four behind. Dental formula: I 3/3, C 1/1, Pm 2/2, M 1/1 x 2 = 28. External measurements of males average: total length, 870 mm; tail, 146 mm; hind foot, 171 mm; of females, 772-144-158 mm. Weight of adults, 5–9 kg, occasionally as much as 16 kg in old animals.

Distribution. The bobcat is widely distributed over most of the United States and occurs throughout Texas. It mainly inhabits wooded and broken country but sometimes occurs on the plains far from forests or hills. It is well known in the Pineywoods of eastern Texas, showing a preference for heavily wooded uplands and bottomland forests, especially second-growth timber. It also occurs in the

Bobcat (*Lynx rufus*). Photo by John and Gloria Tveten.

Distribution of the Bobcat in Texas based on known county records.

rocky limestone region of the Edwards Plateau and is common in parts of south Texas where brush has spread over the former plains. The bobcat is fairly common throughout the Trans-Pecos, where it shows a decided preference for rocky canyons, gulches, and cliffs when such are available.

Subspecies. *L. r. texensis.*

Habits. Little has been learned about bobcats in Texas because of their stealth, nocturnal habits, and remote habitat. They are mainly active at night but may begin hunting long before sundown. During the day, they stay in a rest shelter located in a thicket, a standing or fallen hollow tree, or in a rocky cliff crevice. They are active year round and do not hibernate.

Bobcats may travel 3.2–8 km each night in their hunting forays, but the exact size of their home range depends on prey availability and season of the year. Bobcats frequently hunt from roads and railroad tracks. They depend on their keen sense of eyesight, smell, and hearing to detect prey, and hunting skill is strongly related to experience. Their usual method of procuring prey is to sneak up and pounce on it, but sometimes they lie in wait on the edge of a game trail until something comes along.

Bobcats are primarily carnivorous in their diet, although they occasionally eat grass. Rabbits are by far their most important food, followed by squirrels and rats and mice. Minor items in their diet include opossums, raccoons, skunks, birds, and snakes. Deer, mostly carrion, is sometimes consumed in autumn and winter following deer hunting season, and domestic animals are sometimes killed or eaten as carrion.

Breeding activity reaches a peak in February and March, but some breeding may occur as early as November and as late as July. The major months of birth are April and May, and young may be born as early as January or as late as September. The litter, which ranges in size from 1 to 5 (average 2.7), is born following a gestation period of about 62 days. Nutrition plays an important role in the reproductive process of bobcats. At times of nutritional stress, reproductive activities may be reduced and abortion or embryo resorption may occur.

The young are born well furred and spotted, but with their eyes closed, in a denning nest constructed of dead leaves, grass, and moss. They are weaned at about 2 months of age and generally are able to fend for themselves by 6 months. Family ties are not generally broken until the female mates and becomes pregnant again. Females do not breed during their first year, but they may mate successfully between their first and second years and continue doing so until they are at least 8 or 9 years of age.

Bobcats are fairly long-lived animals. Individuals 12 to 13 years of age have been reported in the wild, and a significant portion of the population may be older than 6 years. Mortality is high among juveniles, then decreases to a low level at 5 years, and then gradually increases again. Humans and dogs are their most important predators, but foxes, coyotes, and great horned owls probably feed on the young.

Bobcats were the second most valuable fur-bearing species in the state during the 1998–1999 season, and they were one of the few species in demand by fur buyers during the 1999–2000 season.

Conservation Status. Unlike the other wild cats of Texas, the bobcat is highly adaptable and in most areas has coped well with the inroads of human settlement. A concern did develop in the 1970s because of high harvest levels by fur trappers. It was concluded that populations might have been overharvested in some local areas and that the illegal transport of pelts from Mexico to Texas might have contributed to high harvest densities in some border counties. The most serious threats to this species are predator control and habitat destruction and fragmentation.

Jaguar

Panthera onca (Linnaeus)

Description. Largest of the spotted American cats; form robust; tail relatively short and tapering; ears small, short, and rounded, without tufts; pelage short and rather bristly; upperparts spotted at all ages; ground color buffy to tan, spots blackish, often with light-colored centers; underparts and inner surfaces of legs white, heavily spotted with black; tail with irregular black markings. Dental formula as in the mountain lion, but canines relatively smaller. External measurements of an adult male: total length, 1,933 mm; tail, 533 mm; of a female, 1,574-432 mm; height at shoulder of a large male, 712 mm. Weight, up to 90 kg; one male from Texas weighed 63.6 kg, another, 42 kg.

Distribution. The jaguar inhabits the dense chaparral and timbered sections of the New World tropics and seldom ventures into the high, cooler inland areas. Apparently, it was once fairly common over southern Texas and nearly the whole of the eastern part of the state to Louisiana and north to the Red River, but this beautiful cat is now extirpated from the state.

Subspecies. *P. o. veraecrucis.*

Habits. Jaguars are the third largest cat of the world, ranking behind the tiger and African lion. In spite of their large size and powerful build, however, jaguars are shy and retiring. They seldom, if ever, attack humans unless cornered or at bay. They are thought to roam over a large territory, much as does the mountain lion, and nowhere are they abundant.

Their food habits are not well known. In Mexico, they are known to prey on peccaries. They probably prey also on deer and large ground-dwelling birds. Jaguars are reputed to be so destructive of cattle and horses that the larger Mexican ranches retain persons known as tiger hunters to kill them or at least to drive them away. Jaguars are also fond of sea turtle eggs, and they roam the beaches on spring nights to dig up and eat the eggs that are buried in the sand.

The den is a rocky cave or the security of a dense, thorny thicket. The mating season is in December and January, and the two to four young are born in April or May after a gestation period varying from 93 to 110 days. The kittens are covered

Jaguar (*Panthera onca*). Photo by Lowell Nash, courtesy Texas
Parks and Wildlife Department.

with woolly fur, are heavily spotted at birth, and have their eyes closed. When
about 6 weeks old they are as large as house cats and begin to follow their parents
about. The parents mate at least for the season of parenthood, and both cooperate
in rearing the young, although most of the burden falls on the mother. The family
unit is maintained until the kittens are nearly a year old, at which time they begin
to fend for themselves.

Conservation Status. The jaguar is extinct in Texas today. There are many records
and sightings that date from the late 1800s and early 1900s, and this large cat actually was regarded as common in some areas. The most recent documented record
from the state was in the early 1950s. This species is regarded as endangered
throughout its relatively broad range in Central and South America.

Suborder Pinnipedia
Seals, Walruses, and Allies

The suborder Pinnipedia (the name means "fin foot") has at times been recognized
as an order but is most commonly recognized as a suborder of the Carnivora.
Swimming is accomplished by means of the front (sea lions, walruses) or hind

(seals) limbs. The hands and feet are elongated, and the digits are bound together by webs of skin. The tail is rudimentary. Its function as a steering apparatus is taken over by the backward-directed hind feet and the flipperlike front feet. The dentition is of simple, peglike teeth, except for the crabeater seal.

The entire group is adapted to feeding on fish, mollusks, and other aquatic animal life. The suborder is worldwide in distribution, restricted largely, of course, to the oceans and their borders.

FAMILY PHOCIDAE (EARLESS SEALS)

Earless seals are currently represented by nine species and five genera in North America. Only one species, however, was ever known from the waters of the Texas Gulf Coast, and that species is now extinct.

West Indian Monk Seal
Monachus tropicalis (Gray)

Description. The West Indian monk seal was a relatively small seal, the upperparts nearly uniform brown, tinged with gray; sides paler; underparts pale yellow or yellowish white; soles and palms naked; pelage very short and stiff; nails on anterior digits well developed, on posterior digits rudimentary. Dental formula: I 2/2, C 1/1, Pm 4/4, M 1/1 x 2 = 32. Total length of males about 2.25 m; females slightly smaller. Weight, 70–140 kg.

Distribution. Now extinct, the West Indian monk seal was the only seal native to the Gulf of Mexico. The species was tropically distributed but limited to the Gulf of Mexico coast, Yucatan Peninsula, western Caribbean Sea, the Greater and Lesser Antilles, the Bahamas, and the Florida Keys. Records from Texas include one sighting in 1932 and several instances of remains recovered from coastal archaeological sites. *M. tropicalis* probably became extinct by the mid-1950s.

Subspecies. The Texas population was never assigned to a subspecies.

Habits. Although this seal has been known from the time of Columbus, no specimens reached museums until the middle of the nineteenth century, when its numbers were already so depleted that it had become rather rare. Likewise, very little life history information is at hand.

West Indian Monk Seal (*Monachus tropicalis*). Illustration by Pieter A. Folkens.

These seals preferred sandy beaches for hauling-out grounds, such as the low, sandy islets making up the Triangle Keys west of Yucatan. While on land they were sluggish and had no fear of humans, a trait that permitted their slaughter to the point of extinction. In former years they were used extensively as a source of oil.

Virtually nothing was learned about the life history of the West Indian monk seal before its extinction. Apparently, the young were born in early December, because several females killed in the Triangle Keys during that time had well-developed fetuses. No information is available on their food habits, but they probably ate fish and mollusks.

Conservation Status. This seal rarely occurred in Texas waters but once was common in the Gulf of Mexico to the south and east. It now is totally extinct throughout its range.

Remarks. Dale Rice asserts that none of the alleged sight records from Texas are credible, and Gerald Raun suggested that specimens from archeological sites in Texas were probably traded from elsewhere.

ORDER CETACEA
Whales, Porpoises, and Dolphins

S mall to extremely large, hairless, fish-shaped mammals that are adapted strictly to an aquatic habitat; front limbs modified as flippers or fins, hind limbs absent, except for vestigial internal remnants; eyes and ears small, the latter valvular and lacking external parts; skull telescoped so that nostrils open on top of head through a single or double blowhole; no vocal apparatus, the so-called roar being produced by expelled air; soft palate and epiglottis so modified that nasal cavities connect directly with lungs and not with mouth; tail lengthened and dermal elements expanded into broad, flattened flukes; mammary glands situated on either side of vaginal opening, the single teat lodged in a slitlike recess; penis and testes contained within the body integument; skin glands, except for conjunctival and mammary, lacking; teeth present or absent.

This group contains the largest of all known mammals, living or extinct. The blue whale sometimes reaches a length of 33 m and may weigh up to 135 metric tons. As a group whales are slow breeders—one young every two years is generally the rule. The teat in a 15 m whale is no larger than a man's thumb, and the mouth of the young calf is so constructed that it cannot suck. Perhaps the milk is forced into the mouth of the baby by contraction of muscles over the udder or by the butting of the young one. In a freshly killed, lactating female palpation of the udder may force out jets of cream-colored milk.

Cetaceans have no voice but many produce distinct sounds used in mating rituals, communication, and echolocation. Such sounds are specific in character, and many are audible for distances of a kilometer or more. Bats and cetaceans are the only mammals known to echolocate; they use sound emissions and echoes to form mental images of their surroundings.

Many of the whales have retained teeth in both jaws. Some have retained them in the lower jaw only, whereas others have lost them completely and have developed instead peculiar structures termed baleen or whalebone. These are elongated, flattened, leaflike modifications of the ridges in the roof of the mouth. Two series of plates, one on each side, hang from the roof of the mouth, and the long, fibrous, hairlike structures on the inner edge of one plate overlap with those of its neighbor in such a way that an efficient sieve is produced. All whales with such structures feed on small organisms strained from the water. Toothed whales feed on larger animal life, such as fish, seals, or even other whales.

The spout is characteristic of many species. It is produced by expelling moisture-laden air from the lungs into the air. As the air escapes it cools, condenses, and becomes visible if the temperature of the outside air permits and then quickly dissipates. When not in use, the blowholes are closed by external flaps that prevent water from entering the lungs. All whales must come to the surface to breathe; if they are forced to remain submerged, they drown.

Many whales and porpoises live near the coast, frequenting shallow water, but a large number of them are pelagic and roam the open seas. Many of the pelagic species perform regular migrations. In winter they inhabit temperate or tropical waters where they mate and give birth to their young a year later; in summer they move to the Arctic or Antarctic seas among the ice floes. Most of the food in the ocean is produced where cold and warm streams meet, and it is there that whales flock in great numbers.

Twenty-eight species of cetaceans have been documented within the Gulf of Mexico, and all but two of them have been documented from the waters of Texas. Three other species may occur in the Gulf of Mexico but have not yet been documented. This assemblage includes approximately 40 percent of the genera and 35 percent of the cetacean species in the world.

The terms "whale," "dolphin," and "porpoise" need explanation. As here used, "whale" is all-inclusive and may be applied to any cetacean. "Dolphin" applies to those small whales that have a distinct snout or beak and numerous conical teeth that are roughly circular in cross section. "Porpoise" applies to those small, blunt-nosed whales that have flat, spade-shaped teeth. Based on those definitions, all the small, beaked whales in Texas waters with numerous conical teeth are dolphins. No porpoises are known to occur in Texas waters.

One of the more interesting biological aspects of marine mammals, especially cetaceans, is their propensity to strand—to ground or beach themselves out of water and be unable to return under their own power. Generally, there are two types of strandings: those of a single individual, which are by far the most prevalent; and multiple or mass strandings of two or more animals, excluding parent-offspring combinations. Marine mammal stranding is a subject of considerable interest to scientists and the general public, and stranding studies have proven to be an undeniably good source of information about aquatic mammals.

The Texas Marine Mammal Stranding Network was organized in 1980, as a means of discovering, gathering, and reporting information of marine mammals stranded along the Texas coast. It also assists live stranded animals, administering first aid and transporting them to facilities where they can be treated. The network consists of scientists, students, federal and state agencies, marine veterinarians, and other interested individuals.

From 1987 through 2001, a total of 2,300 strandings was documented for the Texas Gulf Coast. Of those, 93 percent were represented by bottlenose dolphins, the most common inshore species. Thirty-three percent of strandings occurred in Galveston County. Live strandings accounted for only 3 percent of all strandings. Most live strandings occur near Port Aransas, where deeper waters are closer to shore. Years of particularly high die-offs have been correlated with various causes, including freezing temperatures, pesticide runoff, and viruses.

Although there has been much speculation and theorizing, scientists do not completely understand why cetaceans beach themselves. Oftentimes when live strandings are observed, attempts to return the animals to sea fail. Many, when released, simply turn and head for shore once more. Undoubtedly, many factors may account for this suicidal form of behavior. Among the possible causes suggested for strandings are parasites, disease, and illness; choking on ingested objects; wounds from gunshots and boat and ship encounters; difficulties in the birth process; starvation; bad or rough weather; seaquakes, tremors, and underwater explosions; pollution; net entanglements associated with commercial fishing; fouled sonar systems; and panic caused by the pursuit of other animals (predators). Social facilitation (or, as it is more commonly known, the "follow the leader" theory) is widely given as a reason for mass strandings. Social facilitation involves a cohesive group behavior that causes an entire group to follow suit when a dominant individual suddenly beaches itself.

KEY TO THE WHALES AND DOLPHINS OF THE TEXAS COAST

1. No teeth present; baleen plates in upper jaw; twin blowholes; skull symmetrical; no mandibular symphysis (baleen whales) 2

    Teeth present (although sometimes not erupted); no baleen plates; single blowhole; skull slightly to moderately asymmetrical; mandibular symphysis present (toothed whales) 8

2. Dorsal fin and ventral throat grooves present; no growths on top of head; upper jaw relatively flat when viewed from the side and broad from the top.. 3

    No dorsal fin or ventral throat grooves; crusty growths (callosites) present on head; upper jaw arched when viewed from the side and relatively narrow from the top. *Eubalaena glacialis* (northern right whale), p. 217.

3. Throat grooves end well before navel 4

    Throat grooves extend to or beyond navel 5

4. 50–70 ventral grooves, longest ending between flippers; 231–285 white or yellowish white baleen plates per side, less than 21 cm long; conspicuous white bands on flippers; maximum body length 9 m. *Balaenoptera acutorostrata* (Minke whale), p. 219.

    32–60 ventral grooves, longest ending well short of navel; 219–402 pairs of black baleen plates, less than 80 cm long; flippers totally dark; maximum body length 16 m. *Balaenoptera borealis* (sei whale), p. 220.

5. Flippers more than 25% of body length, heavily scalloped on the leading edge, and marked on the underside with a variable pattern of white. *Megaptera novaeangliae* (humpback whale), p. 225.

    Flippers less than 25% of body length, smooth on the leading edge, and without a distinct pattern of white on the underside. 6

6. Head with only one prominent ridge from blowhole to snout; 55–100 ventral grooves; maximum body length more than 20 m 7

   Head with series of three parallel ridges from blowhole to snout; 40–50 ventral grooves; maximum body length less than 15 m. *Balaenoptera edeni* (Bryde's whale), p. 221.

7. Head broad and almost U-shaped from above; dorsal fin very small (< 33 cm) and set in the last one-third of back; 270–295 black baleen plates per side; coloration of head symmetrical; body mottled gray; maximum body length 30 m. *Balaenoptera musculus* (blue whale), p. 222.

   Head V-shaped and pointed at tip as viewed from above; dorsal fin up to 61 cm tall and set more than one-third forward from fluke notch; 260–480 white to gray baleen plates per side; head coloration asymmetrical (left side gray, much of right side white); back dark, with light streaks; maximum body length 24 m. *Balaenoptera physalus* (fin whale), p. 224.

8. Upper jaw extending well past lower jaw; lower jaw very narrow ... 9

   Upper jaw not extending much or at all past lower jaw; lower and upper jaw about the same width 11

9. Body length 4–18 m; head squarish and large, up to one-third of body length; blowhole at left side of front of head; low roundish dorsal hump present, followed by a series of bumps; 18–25 teeth in each side of lower jaw, fitting into sockets in upper jaw. *Physeter macrocephalus* (sperm whale), p. 227.

   Body length less than 4 m; head much less than one-third of body length; blowhole set back from front of head; prominent dorsal fin present; 8–16 teeth in each side of lower jaw 10

10. Throat creases generally absent; dorsal fin small and located in last one-third of body; distance from tip of snout to blowhole greater than 10.3% of total length; 12–16 (rarely 10–11) teeth in each half of lower jaw. *Kogia breviceps* (pygmy sperm whale), p. 229.

    Two small creases present on throat; dorsal fin generally tall and located near midpoint of back; distance from tip of snout to blow-hole less than 10.2% of total length; 8–11 (rarely up to 13) teeth in each side of lower jaw. *Kogia simus* (dwarf sperm whale), p. 231.

11. Two conspicuous grooves on throat; notch between flukes absent or indistinct; enlarged teeth numbering no more than two pairs in lower jaw (beaked whales) 12

    No conspicuous grooves present on throat; prominent median notch in flukes; teeth present in both upper and lower jaws (dolphins and toothed whales) 14

12. One or two pairs of teeth at or near tip of lower jaw, erupted only in some adults; beak indistinct; head small relative to body size; body to at least 7 m long. *Ziphius cavirostris* (Cuvier's beaked whale), p. 232.

    One pair of teeth well behind tip of lower jaw, erupted only in adult males; moderate beak, not sharply demarcated from forehead; body to 4–5 m long 13

13. Tooth positioned approximately 7.5–10 cm from tip of mandible (one-third the length of mandible). *Mesoplodon europaeus* (Gervais's beaked whale), p. 234.

    Tooth positioned at midpoint of mandible on bony prominences near corners of mouth. *Mesoplodon densirostris* (Blainville's beaked whale), p. 233.

14. Beak not sharply delineated from head by a distinct crease 15

    Beak sharply delineated from head by a distinct crease 21

15. Head blunt, with no prominent beak 16

    Head long and conical, but beak runs smoothly into forehead, with no crease; body dark gray to black above and white below with narrow cape on back. *Steno bredanensis* (rough-toothed dolphin), p. 242.

16. Head divided medially by a heavy vertical crease; coloration gray with heavy scarring in the form of numerous scratches; no teeth in upper jaw (1–2 rarely present), 0–7 teeth present in each side of lower jaw. *Grampus griseus* (Risso's dolphin), p. 243.

    Head not divided by a vertical, median crease; body coloration predominantly black with some white markings; teeth (7 or more pairs) in both upper and lower jaws 17

17. Striking black and white coloration, with white postocular patches, white lower jaw, and light gray saddle behind dorsal fin; dorsal fin tall and erect (up to 0.9 m in females and 1.8 m in males); flippers large and paddle-shaped; 10–12 large oval teeth (2.5 cm in diameter) in each tooth row; body to at least 9 m long. *Orcinus orca* (killer whale), p. 235.

    Coloration predominantly black with little, if any, gray or white markings; dorsal fin less than 0.5 m in height; flippers long and pointed to slightly rounded at tips; body never more than 7 m long and often considerably less 18

18. Low, broad-based dorsal fin located on forward third of back; head bulbous; body black, with light anchor-shaped patch on belly and often light gray saddle-shaped flippers, one-fifth to one-sixth of body length; 7–9 pairs of teeth in front half of each tooth row; body about 6–7 m long. *Globicephala macrorhynchus* (short-finned pilot whale), p. 236.

    Dorsal fin located near midpoint of back; body typically less than 6 m long 19

19. Flippers with distinct hump on leading edge giving S-shaped appearance; body predominantly black; 7–12 large teeth in each half of both jaws; body up to 6 m long. *Pseudorca crassidens* (false killer whale), p. 238.

    Flippers lack hump on leading edge and not S-shaped; body predominantly black but with some white markings on belly and chin or lips; 8–25 teeth in each half of the jaws; body considerably less than 5 m long 20

20. Fewer than 15 teeth in each half of both jaws; flippers rounded at tip; body mostly black with white belly patch which may extend onto sides in area of anus; head rounded from above; body to almost 3 m long. *Feresa attenuata* (pygmy killer whale), p. 239.

More than 15 teeth per side of each jaw; flippers sharply pointed at tip; body black to brownish black on back, light gray on sides, light gray to white on belly, lips often white; head triangular from above; body to at least 2.7 m long. *Peponocephala electra* (melon-headed whale), p. 240.

21. Flippers, flukes, and dorsal fin relatively small; broad dark stripe from eye to anus area; dorsal fin only slightly recurved; body stocky; extremely short but well-defined beak. *Lagenodelphis hosei* (Fraser's dolphin), p. 251.

    Beak moderate to long (> 3% of body length); appendages of normal dolphin proportions 22

22. Body coloration dark gray on back, lighter gray on sides, with white to pink belly; no stripes or spots; beak relatively short and thick; 20 to 26 teeth present in each side of upper jaw and 18 to 24 teeth present in each side of lower jaw. *Tursiops truncatus* (bottlenose dolphin), p. 244.

    Body coloration includes numerous spots, mottling, or stripes; beak relatively long and slender; up to 200 total teeth present in mouth 23

23. Body coloration heavily mottled with light or dark spots.............. 24

    Body coloration without spots but traversed by one or more longitudinal stripes 25

24. Coloration characterized by spinal blaze sweeping up and back below the dorsal fin; peduncle not divided into upper dark and lower light halves; no black stripes connecting eyes and flipper with jaws; background of dark ventral spots is white; total number of vertebrae, 67–72. *Stenella frontalis* (Atlantic spotted dolphin), p. 249.

    Coloration not characterized by a spinal blaze; peduncle divided into upper dark and lower light halves; dark stripe from flipper to lower jaw; background of dark ventral spots is gray; total number of vertebrae, 74–84. *Stenella attenuata* (pantropical spotted dolphin), p. 246.

25. Black stripes extending from eye to anus, eye to flipper, and from above flipper toward belly; 43–50 teeth present in each side of both jaws. *Stenella coeruleoalba* (striped dolphin), p. 248.

    Black side stripes absent.. 26

26. Dark-colored rostrum with gray or white mustache area; chin white to cream-colored; tip of upper jaw to apex of melon less than 12 cm; seldom more than 46 teeth in each side of the jaw. *Stenella clymene* (Clymene dolphin), p. 247.

    Dark rostrum without mustache; tip of upper jaw to apex of melon more than 12 cm; chin gray to black; usually more than 46 teeth in each side of the jaw. *Stenella longirostris* (spinner dolphin), p. 250.

FAMILY BALAENIDAE (RIGHT WHALES)

This family, which includes three species, has the most extravagant baleen apparatus of all baleen whales. The head is correspondingly enormous, in some species up to almost 40% of the body length; there are no throat and chest grooves, as in the Balaenopteridae, and no dorsal fin. The baleen plates are the longest in the Cetacea. A single species of this family is known from the Gulf of Mexico, and it is of extralimital distribution in the region.

Northern Right Whale
Eubalaena glacialis Müller

Description. A large, blackish whale with the following features: no dorsal fin; head huge, about one-fourth of total length; baleen (whalebone) about 2 m long, 30 cm wide, and between 200 and 250 in number on each side of mouth; closure of mouth highly arched; no furrows on the throat; prominent, large, wartlike areas (called bonnets), the one near tip of snout largest. Total length of adults, 14–17 m; weight, 20–30 metric tons.

Distribution. Worldwide in distribution but extremely rare. Only 3,000–4,000 remain in the world's oceans, with about 300 constituting the North Atlantic population. Known in Texas from a single individual that beached in February 1972, at Surfside Beach near Freeport, Brazoria County.

Subspecies. *E. g. glacialis.*

Habits. Right whales were so named by early whalers because they were the right whale to kill; they are slow swimmers and were thus easily caught, floated when dead, and produced large quantities of oil and baleen. Consequently, right whales were decimated early by the world's whaling industries and have yet to recover.

Right whales spend spring, summer, and autumn at high-latitude feeding grounds and migrate to more southerly, warmer waters in winter for mating and calving. Northern and southern populations do not interbreed because the seasons of the two hemispheres are asynchronous.

Right whales produce a variety of vocal sounds as well as percussive sounds of breaching, flipper slapping, and tail slapping. A distinctive clacking sound has been described for these whales as they feed at the surface. Termed the baleen rattle, this sound is produced by small wavelets rattling the baleen plates when they are held partially out of water. Right whale sounds appear to differ with changing behavior and, thus, may be important in communication. Right and other baleen whales probably do not echolocate.

Right whales feed by skimming through concentrations of krill. They have been seen feeding at depths ranging from the surface down to 10 m, although they may also feed at deeper levels. Location of krill concentrations in the water column probably determines feeding depth.

Northern Right Whale (*Eubalaena glacialis*). Illustration by Pieter A. Folkens.

After a one-year gestation period, females give birth to a single calf in winter. Calves are 5–6 m in length at birth but grow rapidly during the subsequent period of lactation, which lasts about 13 months. Calves remain with their mothers for 2–3 years following weaning and probably reach sexual maturity at about 10 years of age. Females give birth at 2- to 7-year intervals.

Conservation Status. Northern right whales occur only accidentally in the Gulf of Mexico, and this is certainly one of the rarest of cetaceans in these waters. The central Gulf may have been a whaling ground for right whales in the 1880s, but nothing is known of that reputed whaling effort. There has been only one stranding of a right whale along the Texas coast. U.S. Fish and Wildlife and the International Union for Conservation of Nature and Natural Resources (IUCN) list this species as endangered.

FAMILY BALAENOPTERIDAE (RORQUALS OR BALEEN WHALES)

This family comprises two genera and six species that occur in all oceans and adjoining seas of the world, with all six species having been recorded from the Gulf of Mexico. The term "rorqual" is derived from the Norwegian words "ror," for tube or groove, and "qual," for whale. These whales vary enormously in size, with head and body length of sexually mature adults 6.7–31 m and weight up to 160,000 kg. In each species, the females are larger than the males of the same age. All of these whales are characterized by longitudinal folds or pleats on the throat, chest, and, in some species, the belly. The furrows allow the throat to expand enormously and thus greatly increase the amount of material that the whale can take in when feeding. The Balaenopteridae are distinguished from the Balaenidae by the presence of throat and chest furrows, a more elongate and streamlined body form with relatively smaller head and more tapering pectoral fin, a softer and less massive tongue, and shorter and less flexible baleen. They also have a small dorsal fin.

Minke Whale

Balaenoptera acutorostrata Lacépède

Description. Smallest of the baleen whales in the Gulf of Mexico, adult minkes may reach only 10 m in length and 9 metric tons in weight. As with all baleen whales, females are slightly larger than males of comparable age. Minke whales have a very narrow and pointed rostrum and a broad white band on the dorsal surface of the flippers. Coloration is dark gray to black above and white below. The baleen plates are yellowish white or cream-colored. The dorsal fin, on the posterior third of the back, is tall and falcate, and the throat grooves end just beyond the flippers.

Distribution. Worldwide in distribution, minke whales are the most numerous of baleen whales. Known in Texas on the basis of a single stranding from Matagorda Peninsula on 29 March 1988.

Subspecies. *B. a. acutorostrata.*

Habits. As with most other baleen whales, minke whales tend to be highly migratory and move to cold temperate and polar waters in spring and then return to warmer waters in autumn. The movements of minke whales in the North Atlantic are heavily influenced by spawning concentrations of capelin, on which they feed. Also, seasonal segregation by sex and age is pronounced in these whales. Mature males tend to migrate farther north in spring and summer than do females and immatures.

Minke whales feed on krill, fish (including sand lance, sand eel, salmon, capelin, mackerel, cod, coalfish, whiting, sprat, wolffish, dogfish, pollack, haddock, and herring), and squid. Capelin are the dominant food item of North Atlantic minkes.

Although baleen whales are generally thought incapable of echolocation, minke whales are known to produce a variety of sounds that include narrow-band pulses suitable for echolocation. Such sounds are described as a series of clicks and may aid in locating food concentrations. Other sounds of these whales are described as grunts, pings, zips, ratchets, and clicks.

Minke Whale (*Balaenoptera acutorostrata*). Illustration by Pieter A. Folkens.

In the North Atlantic, mating occurs from October to March. Females give birth to a single calf annually in early winter. The gestation period is about 10 months. Newborn minke whales are 2.4–2.7 m in length, and the lactation period is 4–5 months. Age at sexual maturity is approximately 6 years for males and 7 years for females.

Conservation Status. Most reports of minke whales from the Gulf of Mexico have come from the Florida Keys, although strandings in western and northern Florida, Louisiana, and Texas have been reported. Because of the winter-spring nature of the strandings, these animals may represent a northward migration of whales from the open ocean or the Caribbean Sea. Minkes are not listed by the USFWS as either endangered or threatened.

Remarks. The minke whale that stranded on the Texas coast was an immature female that was alive when first observed. It not only was the first of its kind known for Texas, but its physical features were also particularly interesting in that the white bands usually present on the dorsal surface of the flippers were absent, and the baleen plates were partially black and numbered only approximately 240 per side. Typically, minke whales have about 300 baleen plates on each side of the mouth, and they are cream-white in color. These features initially caused confusion in the identification of the whale; however, measurements of the tympanic bullae confirmed that it was, indeed, a minke whale.

Sei Whale
Balaenoptera borealis Lesson

Description. A medium-sized baleen whale, typically reaching lengths of 15–16 m. Females are usually slightly larger than males of comparable age and may attain maximum lengths of 20 m. Average weight is 13,000–15,000 kg. Coloration is dark bluish-gray with a white patch in the area of the ventral pleats. Flanks and belly are mottled with light gray to whitish marks. Dorsal fin is tall, up to 61 cm in height, strongly curved or hooked, and situated farther forward on the body than in blue or fin whales. These whales are similar in color and size to Bryde's whale, and the two are difficult to distinguish at a distance; close inspection of the head reveals that sei whales generally have a single head ridge, whereas Bryde's whales have three head ridges.

Distribution. In the western North Atlantic, sei whales are found mainly in offshore waters from the Gulf of Mexico and Caribbean Sea northward to Nova Scotia and Newfoundland. This species has not yet been documented from the Gulf shores of Texas. Strandings have been documented in the Gulf of Mexico in eastern Louisiana and the Florida panhandle areas.

Subspecies. *B. b. borealis.*

Habits. Like other baleen whales, sei whales are highly migratory. Calving and mating occur during the winter in tropical and subtropical waters. In spring and

Sei Whale (*Balaenoptera borealis*). Illustration by Pieter A. Folkens.

summer, they move to high-latitude feeding grounds but rarely penetrate far into polar regions.

Sei whales are usually encountered in small groups of 2–5 animals but may be found in larger congregations in summer feeding grounds. Unlike most other balaenopterids, which feed by engulfing huge amounts of water at one time, sei whales often skim their food from the water surface. This behavior has been observed as the whale fed on plankton near the surface. They also feed on fish, however, including anchovies, mackerel, cod, and others.

Adult females give birth to a single calf at 2- to 3-year intervals following a gestation period of 11–12 months. Newborns suckle for approximately 6 months and are sexually mature at 8 years.

Conservation Status. This whale has stranded in Louisiana and Florida but never in Texas. Population estimates and natural history information on the species in the Gulf are lacking, but it is obviously rare in the waters adjacent to Texas. The USFWS lists the sei whale as endangered.

Bryde's Whale
Balaenoptera edeni Anderson

Description. Bryde's whale is the second smallest of the rorquals, averaging only 12.2–13.1 m in length and 12 metric tons in weight. As with all rorquals, females tend to be a little larger than males. Maximum length is about 15.5 m. Bryde's whales are unique in having three head ridges extending from the blowholes to the end of the rostrum. This is the only baleen whale with this feature, although several have one such ridge, and the presence of three head ridges will always distinguish *B. edeni*. Coloration is a dark bluish gray overall but somewhat lighter in the throat area. The dorsal fin is only about 46 cm in height and rises abruptly from the back. Bryde's whales have ventral pleats extending to, or slightly beyond, the navel.

Distribution. Bryde's whales are not yet known from Texas but have stranded on nearby beaches in Louisiana. It is probable that one of these whales will one day strand along the Texas coast.

Bryde's Whale (*Balaenoptera edeni*). Illustration by Pieter A. Folkens.

Subspecies. The taxonomic status of *Balaenoptera edeni* is unresolved, but at this time the species is regarded as monotypic.

Habits. Bryde's whales appear to be near-shore, year-round residents of tropical and subtropical waters. Although most commonly seen in groups of 5–6, large groups of 30–40 have been observed in areas of food concentrations. This whale frequently feeds on pelagic fish such as pilchard, mackerel, herring, mullet, and anchovies; however, cephalopods and pelagic crustaceans (krill) are also eaten.

Bryde's whales are believed to breed year round, and their gestation period is estimated to be 12 months. Calves are about 4 m long at birth and weigh 1 metric ton. Sexual maturity is reached at 8–10 years, when the animals are about 12 m long.

Conservation Status. Bryde's whale is the most frequently observed baleen whale in the Gulf of Mexico. These whales have stranded on Gulf beaches in winter, spring, and summer, indicating they are year-round residents of these waters. Estimated abundance in the northern Gulf of Mexico is presently about 50 whales, and that number may rise with further studies. The USFWS does not list this whale as either endangered or threatened.

Blue Whale

Balaenoptera musculus (Linnaeus)

Description. Largest of the whales; upperparts slate gray with bluish cast, darker on head, lips, and throat; paler on sides; underparts often yellowish, sometimes spotted with white; dorsal fin small, located posterior to vent; pectoral fin small, about one-tenth of total length; commissure of mouth nearly straight, except for downward curve near corner; grooves on underparts numerous and extending posteriorly past navel; whalebone black, broad basally, short (60–80 cm), and averaging 370 to each side; snout broad and U-shaped. Blue whales commonly reach lengths of 24–26 m and weigh approximately 100 metric tons. Exceptional individuals may attain 30 m and weigh 150 metric tons.

Distribution.   Blue whales occur in all oceans of the world. There are only two records from the Gulf of Mexico; one stranded near Sabine Pass, Louisiana, in 1924 and one stranded on the Texas coast between Freeport and San Luis Pass in 1940. Both identifications have been questioned, however, and the occurrence of the blue whale in the Gulf of Mexico is problematical. The current worldwide population is only 11,000–12,000, with the current North Atlantic population numbering in the low hundreds.

Subspecies. *B. m. musculus.*

Habits. Spring and summer find northern hemisphere blue whales migrating northward to arctic feeding grounds. In fall and winter the whales move back to temperate waters where mating and parturition take place. The same trend is exhibited by southern hemisphere blue whales, although feeding grounds are in the Antarctic. As the seasons are reversed in the two hemispheres, northern and southern blue whales do not interbreed in temperate and equatorial waters.

Feeding occurs mainly in higher latitudes but is also common during migration. In the North Pacific, for example, blue whales stop to feed off California every fall of the year, on their way toward northern waters. Small, shrimplike crustaceans known as krill predominate in the diet, and tremendous amounts of them are required to sustain a single whale. An adult blue whale must consume about 3,000–5,000 kg of krill daily to meet its energy requirements.

Female blue whales give birth to a single calf in temperate or equatorial waters during the winter months. Gestation is about 11 months, and females bear young every other year. The birth of a blue whale has never been observed, but records from past whaling activities indicate that a newborn blue whale is about 8 m in length and weighs 2–3 metric tons. The baby whale nurses for about 8 months, and during that time it gains 90 kg per day, or 3.75 kg per *hour.* Sexual maturity is reached at 5–6 years, and the life span is unknown.

Conservation Status.   Blue whales probably occur only accidentally in the Gulf of Mexico, and they remain one of the rarest cetaceans known from these waters. The only known stranding in Texas occurred in 1940. Despite their protected status, blue whale stocks have yet to show an increase in numbers over the past decade, and the USFWS and the IUCN list them as endangered.

Blue Whale (*Balaenoptera musculus*). Illustration by Pieter A. Folkens.

Fin Whale
Balaenoptera physalus (Linnaeus)

Description. A large, slender whale similar to the blue whale, but head V-shaped in dorsal view rather than U-shaped; dorsal fin high and placed even with or posterior to anus, on posterior one-fourth of body; pectoral fin about one-ninth of total length; head flattened, with right side more whitish than left; right lower jaw white, left grayish to black; upperparts gray, underparts pure white; grooves on throat numerous and extending beyond navel; whalebone lead color with whitish or yellowish fringes, 45–90 cm long, and more than 400 blades on each side. External measurements of an immature animal: total length, 18 m; tip of snout to corner of mouth, 3.6 m; expansion of flukes, 4.3 m. Old individuals attain a length of 25 m or more; females average slightly larger than males. Weight of a 21 m female, 59.4 metric tons.

Distribution. Cosmomarine, but rare in Texas waters. One young individual, 5.5 m long, was stranded on the beach at Gilchrist, Chambers County, on 21 February 1951. It is the only known Texas record.

Subspecies. *B. p. physalus.*

Habits. Fin whales are highly migratory. The whales move to high-latitude feeding grounds during spring and summer and return to southerly, temperate waters for mating and calving during autumn and winter. Because of asynchronous seasons, northern and southern hemisphere populations do not interbreed.

Fin whales feed mainly on krill but also eat schooling fish, including herring, cod, mackerel, pollack, sardine, and capelin. Fish are eaten more often in winter.

The reproductive habits of these whales remain largely unknown; however, females are thought to give birth only at 3-year intervals. Mating and calving occur from November to March in temperate waters. The gestation period is

Fin Whale (*Balaenoptera physalus*). Note the asymmetry of the color pattern on the left and right sides of the head. Illustration by Pieter A. Folkens.

approximately 11 months, and newborn fin whales are about 6.4 m in length and weigh 1.8 metric tons. The period of lactation lasts 6–7 months, and after weaning, the young whales are approximately 12.2 m long. Sexual maturity is reached at 6–12 years of age.

Conservation Status. Sightings and stranding records have been made of the fin whale throughout the year in the Gulf, and it is the second most frequently reported baleen whale from the Gulf, after Bryde's whale. Adequate data do not exist for reliable population estimates, however, and it is likely that fin whales are simply accidentals from outside the Gulf. The USFWS lists these whales as endangered.

Humpback Whale
Megaptera novaeangliae (Borowski)

Description. Humpback whales typically reach lengths of 14.6–15.2 m and weights of 31–41 metric tons. Females are usually slightly larger than males, and an exceptional individual may be up to 18.9 m in length and weigh 48 metric tons. For their length, humpbacks tend to be greater in girth than the other balaenopterid whales. Coloration is black overall, with irregular white markings on the throat, sides, and abdomen. In some individuals the belly may be entirely white, or there may be white patterns dorsally. The flippers are very long (up to 4.6 m) but are narrow. The flippers typically are white below but range from black to patterns of black and white dorsally, or even entirely white. The tail flukes are broad, serrated on the free edge, and black above with black and white coloration ventrally. Distinctive tail flukes may serve to identify individual humpback whales in many cases.

As with other balaenopterid whales, humpbacks have a dorsal fin, which may be up to 31 cm in height and is falcate to rounded in profile. Although the humpback does have throat pleats, they are fewer and spaced wider apart than is typical for balaenopterids. Humpbacks, therefore, are not usually classed as rorquals. Other differences of the humpback whale include lack of a median head ridge,

Humpback Whale (*Megaptera novaeangliae*). Illustration by Pieter A. Folkens.

enormous flippers, and the presence of numerous knobby structures, or dermal tubercles, about the dorsal surface of the snout, chin, and mandible. The number and location of the head tubercles vary between individuals. Each tubercle contains a sensory hair.

Humpbacks typically submerge for 6–7 minutes at a time, with occasional dives of 15–30 minutes. The blow may be up to 3 m high and is not a slender plume but rather bushy. When diving, humpbacks arch the back steeply, thus the common name. The flukes rarely show in shallow dives, but when a deep dive is accomplished the flukes may be lifted well above the water's surface.

Distribution. Humpback whales occur in all oceans of the world. In the western North Atlantic these whales are distributed from north of Iceland, Disko Bay and west of Greenland, south to Venezuela and around the tropical islands of the West Indies. Population estimates indicate that the worldwide prewhaling population of humpbacks was approximately 100,000. The present stock numbers 9,500–10,000, with about 5,800 occurring in the western North Atlantic.

In the Gulf of Mexico humpback whales have been captured in the Florida Keys and northern Cuba. Sightings have occurred off the west coast of Florida and Alabama. The only known occurrence along the Texas coast is of a young, immature animal observed by Victor Cockraft and David Weller at the inshore side of Bolivar Jetty near Galveston on 19 February 1992. No population estimates are available for Gulf humpbacks.

Humpbacks are highly migratory. In the western North Atlantic these whales occupy high-latitude feeding grounds from Cape Cod to Iceland during spring, summer, and fall. In late autumn and winter the whales then move into Caribbean waters for mating and calving.

Subspecies. Monotypic species.

Habits. Humpbacks often congregate in groups of 20–30 to perhaps 100–200. These are among the most acrobatic and visible of whales; they breach completely out of water in spectacular displays of strength. Humpbacks commonly slap their tail flukes or flippers on the water's surface and occasionally lift their huge heads above water to peer about, a behavior known as spyhopping. Tail slapping, breaching, and other such behaviors may serve in communication between the whales, possibly as warnings or a means of indicating location.

Humpbacks also produce a number of unusual sounds described variously as moans, groans, cries, squeals, chirps, and clicks. Sounds may be arranged into complex and predictable patterns known as songs. Humpback songs may be repeated for long periods of time and have been most often recorded on low-latitude breeding grounds. Although yet to be proven, songs are thought to be broadcast by sexually mature, lone males and may have some purpose in mating rituals.

Humpback whales eat krill, mackerel, sand lance, capelin, herring, pollack, smelt, cod, sardines, salmon, and anchovies. These whales are lunge feeders but use several different techniques to concentrate their food before lunging. An especially interesting technique is known as bubble netting, in which one or more humpbacks exhale while circling below a food source. The resulting bubble column effectively forms a net to concentrate food items; the whale then lunges through the concentrated food with open mouth.

Females give birth to a single calf in tropical or subtropical waters in winter. The gestation period is approximately 11 months. Newborn humpbacks are 4.6 m in length and weigh about 1.3 metric tons. The period of lactation lasts approximately 5 months. Sexual maturity is reached at 2–5 years, when the young whales measure about 12 m in length. Physical maturity occurs at 12–15 years of age. Females breed every other year.

Conservation Status. In the Gulf of Mexico, humpback whales occasionally were hunted near the Florida Keys, but they are uncommon in the Gulf proper. Sightings have been made off the west coast of Florida and near Alabama in the eastern Gulf, and off the jetties in Galveston, Texas. A resident population of these whales apparently does not occur in the Gulf of Mexico, and it is likely that humpbacks in the Gulf are accidentals from the Caribbean. The USFWS and the IUCN list humpbacks as endangered.

FAMILY PHYSETERIDAE (SPERM WHALE)

This family includes a single species, the sperm whale, which occurs in all oceans and adjoining seas of the world, except in polar ice fields. This is the largest toothed mammal in the world and the most sexually dimorphic of all cetaceans. The most striking morphological feature is the huge spermaceti organ in the head, filled with up to 1,900 liters of waxy oil. The sperm whale is by far the most common large whale in the Gulf of Mexico.

Sperm Whale
Physeter macrocephalus Linnaeus

Description. A large, blackish brown whale with huge head and truncate snout; lower jaw small, long, and slender, the symphysis extending half the length of the ramus; the single blowhole on anterior left edge of snout; no dorsal fin, but conspicuous hump; eye very small, low, and near angle of mouth; pectoral fin short and relatively broad; upper jaw lacking functional teeth; lower jaw with 22–24 large, sharp teeth on each side. Total length of males, up to 20 m; females much smaller. Weight of a male 13 m long, 39 metric tons.

Distribution. Sperm whales are worldwide in distribution and occur in all oceans, including Arctic and Antarctic waters, but are primarily found in temperate and tropical waters of the Atlantic and Pacific oceans. Sperm whales are the most numerous of the great whales in the Gulf of Mexico, and sightings near the Texas coast are relatively common. There are an estimated 300–400 sperm whales in the northwestern Gulf.

Subspecies. Monotypic species.

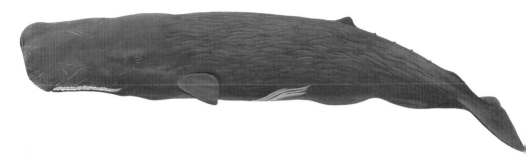

Sperm Whale (*Physeter macrocephalus*). Illustration by Pieter A. Folkens.

Habits. Sperm whales are highly migratory, especially the males. Adult males move into high-latitude temperate waters during summer, leading a solitary lifestyle, while females remain grouped in tropical or subtropical waters. In winter, the bulls return to lower latitudes for mating.

These whales regularly dive to depths of 1,000 m but are known to reach depths of more than 2,100 m and may be capable of dives to 3,000 m. At such depths these remarkable animals hunt their primary prey, squid. Much speculation has arisen concerning the feeding method of sperm whales, as no light penetrates to those depths, and squid are highly elusive swimmers. The whales may feed by ambushing prey as they lie relatively motionless near the ocean floor, attracting squid with a bioluminescent glow emanating from the whale's mouth, or perhaps by stunning prey with ultrasonic sounds. Because of the great depths at which these animals feed, the exact method of the sperm whale's feeding habits has yet to be determined. These whales are known to produce a variety of click sounds occurring in sequence and termed codas. Such sounds are probably used in echolocation and may play an important role in locating prey while feeding.

Up to 1 metric ton of squid per day is required to sustain a single sperm whale. Besides squid, these whales occasionally consume other deepwater prey including octopus, lobsters, crabs, jellyfish, sponges, and several varieties of fish.

Breeding behavior in sperm whales is similar to harem formation; a single, dominant male accompanies a group of females and defends the group against competing males. During this time, smaller males are driven off to form their own bachelor groups, and battles between rival males for control of the harem may occur. A harem may comprise 20–30 females, but many of them may already be pregnant or tending young. The gestation period is approximately 15 months, the period of lactation is 1–2 years, and there is a resting period of up to 10 months following weaning before the females will mate again. The breeding cycle, therefore, may take as long as 5–7 years.

Newborn sperm whales are about 4 m in length and weigh approximately 1 metric ton. Although twin calves are known, a single calf per female is believed the rule. Sexual maturity is reached at about 10 years of age.

Sperm whales were once the mainstay of the pelagic whaling industry. Before the advent of cannon harpoons, diesel-powered catcher boats, and massive factory ships, the hunting of sperm whales was a dangerous occupation. Sperm whales are known to have effectively fought back on occasion; one even sank an American whaler, the *Essex,* in 1820. In spite of the danger, sperm whales were hunted the world over for the array of valuable products they contained: whale oil for lamps and lubricants; spermaceti (oil from the forehead) for high-quality, smokeless candles; and ambergris, a waxy by-product of digestion, which was used in the manufacture of fragrances. By the early twentieth century, whaling had become an efficient, wide-open business that threatened not only the sperm whale but all of the other great whales with extinction. Finally, in the 1970s, whaling was banned worldwide.

Conservation Status. Sperm whales are by far the most numerous large whale in the Gulf of Mexico and at one time were hunted in these waters. Aerial and shipboard sightings have been made off the Texas coast year round. Strandings or sightings have been made in every month of the year, suggesting there is a stock of sperm whales unique to the Gulf, but that remains to be substantiated. The USFWS lists the sperm whale as endangered.

FAMILY KOGIIDAE (PYGMY AND DWARF SPERM WHALES)

This family includes two species of the genus *Kogia,* both of which occur commonly in the Gulf of Mexico. The facial part of the skull in these whales is among the shortest in cetaceans. These whales resemble the sperm whale (*Physeter*) by having a spermaceti organ in the head and functional teeth confined to the lower jaw. That is why the pygmy and dwarf sperm whales were typically combined into a single family with *Physeter.* Both species of *Kogia,* however, have blowholes situated on top of the head, instead of at the end of the snout, and a distinct, curved dorsal fin; *Physeter* has no true dorsal fin. Thus, the pygmy and dwarf sperm whales are now regarded as members of the family Kogiidae.

Pygmy Sperm Whale
Kogia breviceps (Blainville)

Description. A small, toothed whale; upperparts, top of pectoral fins, and flukes blackish; underparts and upper lip, white; dorsal fin small, situated posteriorly to the midpoint on back, the tip pointing backward; pectoral fin short and spear-shaped; blowhole an oblique crescent left of midline; mouth small and subterminal; snout blunt; skull short, broad, spongy, and markedly asymmetrical; left naris large, right one degenerate, as in the sperm whale; front part of skull deeply bowl-shaped; teeth small, slender, and widely spaced, 12–16 in each lower jaw; total length 2–4 m. Measurements of one whale: total length, 3.2 m; snout to anterior edge of dorsal fin, 1.7 m; height of dorsal fin, 76 mm; length of pectoral fin, 495 mm. Weight of adults, more than 300 kg.

Distribution.   These whales are found in warm waters worldwide. In the western North Atlantic they occur from Nova Scotia to Cuba and as far westward as the Texas coast, where strandings occur relatively frequently. They were once thought to be quite rare, but stranding records indicate they may be more common than originally believed.

Subspecies.   Monotypic species.

Habits.   This is a deepwater, pelagic species about which very little is known. They occur in small groups of 3–6 individuals and appear slow and deliberate in their actions. Low frequency, low intensity, pulsed sounds have been recorded from these whales, suggesting that they may be capable of echolocation.

Their food habits are not well known. Stomachs that have been examined contained carapaces and appendages of green crabs, shrimp, and beaks of squid.

Information available suggests that mating takes place in late summer and the young are born the following spring after a gestation period of some 9 months. The young calf stays with its mother during its first year, as judged from records of capture of pregnant females accompanied by offspring of the previous year. Newborns are about 1.2 m long and weigh 54 kg. Strandings of these whales may often be related to calving, as females with newborn young often strand, as well as females whose reproductive tract shows evidence of parturition just prior to stranding.

Conservation Status.   Pygmy sperm whales frequently strand on the coastline of the Gulf of Mexico. These whales are most likely a common element in the nearshore Gulf fauna, but their habits prevent them from being readily observed. Estimate of abundance from shipboard and aerial sightings in all seasons was about 1,000 individuals in the northern Gulf.

Pygmy Sperm Whale (*Kogia breviceps*). Illustration by Pieter A. Folkens.

Dwarf Sperm Whale (*Kogia sima*). Illustration by Pieter A. Folkens.

Dwarf Sperm Whale
Kogia sima (Owen)

Description. Similar to *Kogia breviceps* but smaller (rarely reaching 3 m in length); dorsal fin higher (relatively and actually) and located near center of back; number of teeth in the lower jaw normally 8–11, rarely as many as 13; usually 3 rudimentary teeth in each upper jaw. Total length of adults usually less than 2.5 m, rarely to 2.7 m. Weight, less than 300 kg.

Distribution. Like *Kogia breviceps,* the dwarf sperm whale is probably cosmomarine and is found in warm-water oceans. In the western North Atlantic, these whales are known from Virginia to the Lesser Antilles and the Gulf of Mexico. They strand fairly frequently but not so often as *K. breviceps.*

Subspecies. Monotypic species.

Habits. Until the mid 1960s, dwarf sperm whales were routinely grouped with *K. breviceps* in stranding and sighting reports. As a result, few data are available on the natural history of these whales.

Dwarf sperm whales make deep and prolonged dives in quest of food. Squid and fish are known to occur in the diet.

The reproductive habits of *K. sima* are almost completely unknown. At birth, calves are estimated to be about 1 m in length and 45 kg in weight. The young reach maturity when they are about 2 m in length.

Conservation Status. Stranding records of dwarf sperm whales from the Gulf of Mexico are more abundant than would be expected for a truly rare animal. This whale occurs about half as frequently as *K. breviceps,* with strandings throughout the year.

FAMILY ZIPHIIDAE (BEAKED WHALES)

This family comprises 5 genera and 19 species, which occur in all the oceans and adjoining seas of the world. The vernacular name is derived from the long, narrow beak that forms a continuous smooth profile with the head in all forms known from the Gulf of Mexico. In most ziphiids, the teeth show strong sexual dimorphism, with males having one pair of unusually large teeth in the lower jaw; in females, the teeth are absent or vestigial. The cetacean fauna of the Gulf includes 2 genera and 4 species of beaked whales that are among the least known of cetaceans in these waters. They usually remain well out to sea, avoid ships, and dive to great depths to secure cephalopods and fish. The taxonomy of beaked whales is presently being revised; with analysis of newly discovered skull fragments and newly acquired genetic samples, it is likely that several new species will be described in the next several years.

Cuvier's Beaked Whale

Ziphius cavirostris G. Cuvier

Description. A moderately small-beaked whale with upperparts ranging in color from dark brown to lead gray or blackish; underparts paler but not whitish; occasionally head and upper back whitish; beak moderately prominent and the forehead rising rather sharply; lower jaw longer than upper; pectoral fin relatively small and the dorsal fin placed on posterior third of body; prominent keel extends from dorsal fin to tail; length of rostrum less than twice its breadth at notch; lower jaw of males with one large tooth (about 7 cm in length and 4 cm in diameter) at the tip; in females the teeth are small and seldom break through the gums, so the animal appears to be toothless; two converging grooves on throat. Total length of adults, 5–7 m. Weight, 2.5–4.5 metric tons.

Distribution. Sparsely distributed throughout tropical and subtropical waters of the world. In the western North Atlantic, these whales are found from Massachusetts to Florida and the Gulf of Mexico. This is the most commonly stranded beaked whale from the Gulf of Mexico.

Subspecies. Monotypic species.

Habits. Little is known of this whale beyond information revealed by stranded specimens. They are often observed in groups of 10–25. These whales are deep divers and may remain below water for 30 minutes or longer. They are known to eat squid, fish, crabs, and starfish.

The reproductive habits are almost unknown. There does not seem to be a distinct breeding season, as calves are born year round. Calves are about 2.1 m long at birth. The length of gestation is unknown.

Cuvier's Beaked Whale (*Ziphius cavirostris*). Illustration by Pieter A. Folkens.

Conservation Status. Life history information on this whale is extremely sparse, and there are no estimates of abundance in the Gulf. Stranding records of this off-shore species are rare along the Texas coast, and it is difficult to determine its status accurately.

Blainville's Beaked Whale

Mesoplodon densirostris (Blainville)

Description. A medium-sized whale that reaches lengths of 4.6–4.9 m and weighs about 1 metric ton. Slender in form; flippers short and set low on body; dorsal fin present. Rostrum slender and pointed. Coloration dark gray to black dorsally and somewhat lighter ventrally. Typically mottled with grayish scars left by parasites, squid sucker marks, and scratches incurred in intraspecific fighting. Males have a single large tooth at the midpoint of each side of the mandible. This tooth may be up to 20 cm in total length and is embedded in a large hump of supporting bone that gives a high, arching contour to the lower jaw. Females do not have so prominent a tooth and crested jaw.

Distribution. These whales are uncommon residents of warm waters worldwide. In the western North Atlantic they are rare but occur from Nova Scotia to Florida and the Gulf of Mexico. Known in Texas on the basis of a single individual stranded on Padre Island on 29 February 1980.

Subspecies. Monotypic species.

Habits. Little natural history information is available for these rare and secretive whales. They are normally observed in small groups of 3–6 and are known to feed on squid.

Sounds recorded from a young male stranded in Florida were described as chirps and whistles. Sound spectrograms showed that at least some of the sounds were pulsed, indicating that echolocation by these whales may occur.

The reproductive habits of these whales are completely unknown.

Conservation Status. Although thought to be rare, no substantial population data exist for this unusual whale, and seasonal movements remain undocumented. Thus, it is difficult to determine its status in the Gulf of Mexico. It is not listed on any sort of endangered or threatened list.

Blainville's Beaked Whale (*Mesoplodon densirostris*). Illustration by Pieter A. Folkens.

Gervais's Beaked Whale
Mesoplodon europaeus (Gervais)

Description. A rather small whale with a prominent beak and only one large tooth in each lower jaw, placed about 15 cm back from the tip and beside the posterior end of the symphysis of the lower jaws. In males this tooth is large, protrudes from the closed mouth, and fits into a groove in the skin of the upper lip; in females the tooth usually does not project above the gums, so the animal appears to be toothless. No teeth in upper jaw. Upperparts of body described as dark slate black; lowerparts lighter; no special or distinctive markings. External measurements of an adult male reported by J. C. Moore: total length, 4.3 m; circumference immediately in front of flipper, 1.85 m; width across flukes, 91.5 cm; height of dorsal fin, 18.7 cm; distance from corner of eye to corner of mouth, 20 cm. Maximum known length, 5.45 m. Skulls of females are larger than those of males, so the assumption is that females are also larger in body size than males.

Distribution. Gervais's beaked whales are known primarily from the western North Atlantic, but they are stranded in the Gulf of Mexico fairly commonly. Several strandings have been reported on Texas beaches. Although there are no population estimates for these whales, they are thought to be rare.

Subspecies. Monotypic species.

Habits. Almost nothing is known about the life history of these whales. They are believed to inhabit deep waters close to shore, but little information is available on movements. They are known to feed on squid and fish.

Strandings of these whales are believed to be associated with calving, which probably takes place in shallow waters. A 4-meter female with a 2-meter calf stranded in Jamaica, and a pregnant female with a near-term fetus stranded along the Texas coast.

Specific data on the reproductive habits are not available.

Conservation Status. This is one of the most frequently stranded beaked whales in the waters of the Gulf of Mexico, and it is probably the most widely distributed ziphiid in the Gulf, although this is not certain. It is virtually impossible to determine its status accurately, given the paucity of information.

Gervais's Beaked Whale (*Mesoplodon europaeus*). Illustration by Pieter A. Folkens.

FAMILY DELPHINIDAE
(TOOTHED WHALES AND DOLPHINS)

This is the most diverse family of cetaceans in the world, with a total of 17 genera and 33 species. It includes all of the classic dolphins, those smaller cetaceans with beaklike snouts and slender, streamlined bodies. Head and body length of delphinids in the Gulf of Mexico ranges from as little as 1.8 m in species of *Stenella* to as much as 9.8 m in *Orcinus;* weight in fully grown individuals ranges from about 50 to 10,000 kg. The blowhole is located well back from the tip of the beak or the front of the head. The pectoral and dorsal fins are falcate, triangular, or broadly rounded, and the dorsal fin is near the middle of the back. The Delphinidae include the most agile and some of the speediest cetaceans. They commonly surface several times a minute and frequently leap clear of the water.

Killer Whale
Orcinus orca (Linnaeus)

Description. Killer whales are the largest of the dolphin family. Adult males reach up to 9.8 m in length, although 8.2 m is average. Females typically reach 7 m in length, with the maximum about 8.5 m. Maximum weight is about 7.5 metric tons for females and 10 metric tons for males. Body form is stocky, the snout is blunt, and the flippers are large and paddle-shaped. In males the dorsal fin may be up to 1.8 m tall, but it is considerably shorter in females. Coloration is black dorsally and white ventrally from the chin to slightly behind the anus. An area of white extends up the side posterior to the dorsal fin, and a white oval is located just above and behind the eye. Each side of both jaws has 10–12 slightly curved teeth that are about 13 cm in length and interlock when the mouth is closed. The teeth are oval in cross section.

Killer Whale (*Orcinus orca*). Illustration by Pieter A. Folkens.

Distribution. Killer whales are distributed worldwide, including polar seas. They are rare in the Gulf of Mexico, although sightings have increased in recent years. Known in Texas on the basis of one stranding on South Padre Island and one sighting in waters off Port Aransas.

Subspecies. Monotypic species.

Habits. Killer whales are most often observed as gentle giants of marine aquariums, but they are, in fact, the supreme carnivore of the world's oceans. At sea they are usually seen in pods of 5–20, although up to 150 have been seen together at one time. Large groups probably consist of several pods that have temporarily aggregated. Pods themselves appear stable for many years, with little emigration or immigration. They are highly cooperative, and the group functions as a unit when hunting, making these delphinids extremely efficient predators. Groups usually contain adults of both sexes, but sometimes females with young will form their own groups.

Food items include squid, fish, skates, rays, sharks, sea turtles, sea birds, seals, sea lions, walrus, dolphins, porpoises, and large whales such as fin whales, humpback whales, right whales, minke whales, and gray whales. They are even known to attack the sperm whale and blue whale. On the Atlantic coast of South America, as well as on islands of the Indian Ocean, killer whales have been observed lunging through the surf—and coming right onto the beach—in pursuit of elephant seals and sea lions. After such an attack the whales have to wriggle and slide back into depths adequate for swimming. In captivity, killer whales eat about 45 kg of food per day, but free-ranging animals probably require much more. Although they are obviously proficient and voracious hunters, killer whales are not known to have ever attacked a human in the wild.

The reproductive habits of these whales are poorly known. The males may mate with more than one female, and mating may occur throughout the year, although most calves seem to appear in autumn or winter in shallow waters. Their period of gestation is about 12 months. Calves are approximately 2.4 m long at birth and reach sexual maturity when 4.9–6.1 m in length.

Conservation Status. Stranding records from the Gulf of Mexico are few and poorly documented for this unique whale, but sightings, including a few off South Padre Island, have occurred in recent years. It is not known whether these animals stay within the confines of the Gulf or range more widely. From all appearances they are extremely rare in the Gulf and may not be year-round residents.

Short-finned Pilot Whale
Globicephala macrorhynchus Gray

Description. A rather large, black delphinid with globose head, no beak, and a bulbous swelling on the forehead in adults; dorsal fin far forward on body, beginning about on plane with back of pectoral fins; pectoral fins long and narrow, about one-fifth of body length; mouth oblique; teeth large, about 10 mm in diameter, 20 mm

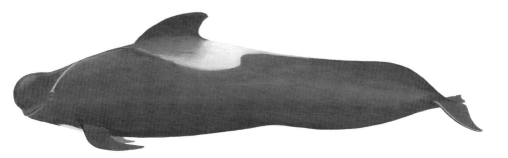

Short-finned Pilot Whale (*Globicephala macrorhynchus*). Illustration by Pieter A. Folkens.

high, conical, incurved, placed only in anterior part of jaw, and numbering 8–10 in each tooth row. External measurements: total length of male, 4.72 m; tip of snout to dorsal fin, 1.37 m; tip of snout to pectoral fin, 838 mm; length of pectoral fin, 864 mm; breadth of flukes, 1.07 m.

Distribution. Common inhabitants of offshore tropical, subtropical, and warm temperate waters of the world. They are common in the Gulf of Mexico and numerous stranding and sighting records are available from Texas.

Subspecies. Currently regarded as monotypic, although the taxonomic status of the species is unsettled and requires further research.

Habits. Short-finned pilot whales may congregate in large numbers offshore; schools of several hundred have been observed, but group size usually ranges from 10 to 60. They are seen inshore at infrequent intervals and occasionally become stranded by severe storms. In fact, they are among the most frequently stranded of cetaceans and often mass strand. These dolphins have mass stranded 15 times in the Gulf of Mexico, although none of the events occurred in Texas. Pilot whales are highly communicative and make a variety of sounds, including noises described as "squealing, whistling, loud smacking, whining, and snores." They probably are excellent echolocators.

The food habits of pilot whales are not well known. In the wild they feed on squid and fish; a captive whale consumed 20 kg of squid per day. This particular whale showed no interest in the fish fed to dolphins in the same tank.

Breeding and calving take place in winter. Gestation lasts about 12 months. Calves are about 1.4 m long at birth and weigh approximately 59 kg. Females are believed to give birth only once every 3 years.

Conservation Status. Although short-finned pilot whales generally are considered common offshore residents of the Gulf of Mexico, stranding records have declined dramatically over the past decade. Pilot whale reports account for 7.1% of all cetacean strandings in the historic record (before 1978) and only 4.1% of the modern record (after 1978). Given the increased awareness of cetaceans in the past two decades, coupled with the appearance of stranding networks specifically organized to document reports of cetaceans, the modern record should show an increase in sighting and stranding reports if population levels remained stable. Although certainly not conclusive, the available evidence points to the possibility of declining populations of these whales in the Gulf of Mexico.

False Killer Whale
Pseudorca crassidens Owen

Description. A small, entirely black delphinid; no beak, the head slopes gradually from tip of snout to the blowhole; dorsal fin small, narrow, placed slightly forward of midpoint of the back and directed backward; pectoral fins small, about one-eighth of total length and tapering; teeth large, conical, elliptical in cross section, 15–25 mm in diameter, the largest ones projecting 30 mm or so above the gums (40 mm above jawbone), and 8–11 in each tooth row. Adult males reach a length of 5.7 m; females, 4.9 m. Superficially resembles the short-finned pilot whale (*Globicephala*) but lacks the bulbous forehead, and the teeth are nearly twice as large.

Distribution. Found throughout deep tropical, subtropical, and warm temperate waters of the world. Known in Texas on the basis of two strandings from the upper Texas coast.

Subspecies. Monotypic species.

Habits. Groups of these whales may number from two to several hundred, with both sexes and all age groups represented. These delphinids are known to emit whistling sounds audible to humans and probably are good echolocators. They eat squid and fish.

For unknown reasons false killer whales often strand, sometimes en masse. There are three known mass strandings of these whales in the Gulf of Mexico, but the best-known such stranding occurred on the Atlantic coast of southern Florida. On 11 January 1970, 150–175 false killer whales beached themselves and refused to return seaward, despite the best efforts of volunteers. All of the whales subsequently died, and the cause of this mysterious event was never determined.

False Killer Whale (*Pseudorca crassidens*). Illustration by Larry Foster.

Their reproductive habits are poorly known. Breeding probably occurs year round, and the gestation period lasts approximately 15 months. Newborn false killer whales are about 1.5 m in length and weigh 80 kg.

Conservation Status. This whale has stranded several times in the Gulf, including on the Texas coast. Virtually nothing is known about its population abundance and status.

Pygmy Killer Whale

Feresa attenuata Gray

Description. A small, blunt-nosed, toothed cetacean similar to the false killer whale (*Pseudorca*), but dorsal fin larger and teeth considerably smaller; body color black with white patches around mouth and on chest and abdomen; dorsal fin about 220 mm high, 375 mm long at base, and located near midpoint of back; teeth about 8 mm in diameter at alveolus, less than 30 mm in length, and with 9–13 in each tooth row; 68–71 vertebrae (50 in *Pseudorca*). Total length about 2.5 m.

Distribution. Deep tropical, subtropical, and warm temperate waters of the world. Known in Texas on the basis of three strandings and one sighting of 20–25 animals about 130 km off the south Texas coast in November 1980.

Subspecies. Monotypic species.

Habits. One of the best accounts of this whale to date is that by Taylor Pryor, Karen Pryor, and Kenneth Norris that appeared in the *Journal of Mammalogy* in 1965. The following account is adapted from their report.

On 6 July 1963 a school of about 50 pygmy killer whales of several sizes (lengths varying from 1 to 2.5 m or so) was sighted from a boat off the island of Hawaii in waters about 600 fathoms deep. The school was resting quietly at the surface in a roughly circular group. The whales were aware of the approach of the boat, but they did not flee; instead, they circled and dived in the same general area. When the crew of the boat netted an adult animal, the others made no attempt to assist the struggling captive, although they remained within 30 or so meters of it.

Pygmy Killer Whale (*Feresa attenuata*). Illustration by Pieter A. Folkens.

The captive animal was unusually aggressive, as compared with other cetaceans its size, when it was being handled. It snapped at its captors and emitted a blatting or growling noise by forcing air through its blowhole. When released in the training tank at Sea Life Park, it made almost no attempt to avoid an observer but instead acted as if it expected the observer to move. The day after capture, the animal was once observed to swim quickly with its mouth open toward the arm and hand of a man who was reaching into the tank to check a water input. The man withdrew his arm when the whale was about 2 m away, whereupon the animal closed its mouth and swam past. Ten days after capture the animal was moved to a tank containing an adult and an immature pilot whale (*Globicephala*). The pygmy killer became much more active than usual and swam ceaselessly. It was attracted to the small pilot whale and frequently chased it. One morning the small blackfish was found dead. Autopsy revealed that it had been killed by a single powerful blow, possibly a lethal butt from the pygmy killer whale, to the temporal region of the cranium. The animal also exhibited aggressive behavior toward spotted dolphins (*Stenella*).

While in captivity, the pygmy killer whale learned to feed readily on mackerel, and it consumed as much as 5 kg of such food a day. It also accepted squid.

Nothing seems to be known regarding reproduction and development in this species.

Conservation Status. The first stranding of this small whale occurred on 21 January 1969, near Brazos Santiago Pass, South Padre Island. Now 13 other strandings have taken place, from southern Florida to south Texas, with an apparent peak of strandings in winter. It is virtually impossible to determine the conservation status of this species.

Melon-headed Whale

Peponocephala electra Gray

Description. Melon-headed whales are about the same size as pygmy killer whales (*Feresa attenuata*), with adult males up to 2.7 m and adult females up to 2.6 m in length. Maximum weight is about 275 kg. The profile of the melon-headed whale may appear similar to that of the pygmy killer whale; however, whereas the pygmy killer whale's head is totally rounded and bulbous, that of the melon-headed whale is rounded in profile and on the top, flat below, and, seen from bottom or top, forms a distinct triangle between the eyes and the tip of the snout. The dorsal fin is distinct and falcate and located at the middle of the back. The flippers are long and, unlike those of the pygmy killer whale, pointed at the tips. Each upper jaw has 20–25 sharp-pointed teeth, and there are 22–24 teeth in each lower jaw, about twice the number found in the pygmy killer whale and the false killer whale (*Pseudorca crassidens*). The number of teeth is a firm identification mark for even decomposed animals.

Melon-headed Whale (*Peponocephala electra*). Illustration by Pieter A. Folkens.

Coloration is black except on the belly and around the mouth, with the white lips resembling those of pygmy killer whales. Although the belly may be very white, it is usually a light gray and not as distinct as the white belly patch of the pygmy killer whale.

Distribution. Found worldwide in tropical and subtropical waters, they are most numerous in the Philippine Sea. They appear to favor warm, pelagic waters and rarely stray over the continental shelf. This species was first known in Texas on the basis of one animal that stranded alive on Matagorda Peninsula in June 1990. Previously, the nearest record of occurrence was from the island of St. Vincent in the Caribbean. More recently, in 1998, a young male stranded alive south of Corpus Christi.

Subspecies. Monotypic species.

Habits. Melon-headed whales travel in groups of 100–1,000, although even larger groups have been reported. In the tropical Atlantic, Pacific, and Indian Ocean they have been reported traveling with Fraser's dolphin (*Lagenodelphis hosei*) and with spinner and spotted dolphins (*Stenella* spp.).

Little is known about their reproductive habits. Calving appears to peak in early spring in the low latitudes of both hemispheres. The length of gestation is not known but is probably about 12 months. These whales are not known to migrate, and strandings occur year round in tropical and subtropical waters. Melon-headed whales feed mainly on squid and fish.

Conservation Status. The first record of this whale in the Gulf was an individual that stranded alive on west Matagorda Peninsula, Matagorda County. This is a deep-water species that rarely strays into the relatively shallow depths over the continental shelf, which accounts for the rarity of strandings. Large groups of this small whale have been sighted in the northern Gulf of Mexico, and there is no reason to believe that it is in any kind of conservation trouble.

Rough-toothed Dolphin
Steno bredanensis (Lesson)

Description. A small, grayish black dolphin with the forehead rising gradually from the beak; 20–27 fairly large teeth in each tooth row, the crowns of which have many fine, vertical wrinkles (thus the name "rough-toothed"); length of rostrum about three times its width. Total length, 2–2.7 m; weight, 100–135 kg.

Distribution. Tropical and warm temperate waters of the world. In the western North Atlantic they are sparsely distributed from Virginia to the northeastern coast of South America. Known in Texas on the basis of two strandings near Galveston.

Subspecies. Monotypic species.

Habits. Little is known about the life history of these dolphins. They occasionally travel in groups of 50 or more, but smaller groups are normal. They are probably good echolocators and are easily trained.

A mass stranding of these dolphins occurred on the upper Gulf coast of Florida in May 1961. Sixteen of them ran aground in a shallow, marshy area, but the cause was never determined.

Food habits are almost unknown. They are known to eat octopus, squid, and fish. Nothing is known about their reproductive habits; in captivity, they have mated with bottlenose dolphins and produced hybrid offspring.

Conservation Status. There are many recorded strandings of this dolphin on the beaches of the Gulf of Mexico, including Texas, where it was first observed in late June 1969. These are generally offshore, deepwater dolphins, and there are no reliable population estimates, which makes it difficult to predict its overall status accurately.

Rough-toothed Dolphin (*Steno bredanensis*). Illustration by Pieter A. Folkens.

Risso's Dolphin
Grampus griseus (Cuvier)

Description. This is a medium-sized dolphin that averages 3 m in length and 300 kg in weight. Maximum size is about 4.3 m in length and 680 kg in weight. Body form is stocky from the dorsal fin forward, but the tailstock is slender. The head is blunt, beakless, and divided medially by a heavy crease. Coloration is dark gray with lighter gray patches ventrally. In older individuals the face and area just forward of the dorsal fin is also light gray. They are often heavily scarred by parasites and by wounds inflicted by other Risso's dolphins. The blunt, creased head and extensive scarring are noticeable as the animals ride boat bow waves, or spyhop, and are probably the best field characters for distinguishing these dolphins. Stranded specimens are distinguished by the unique head shape and crease and by the teeth. There are up to 7 teeth in each side of the lower jaw and none in the upper jaw.

Distribution. Found worldwide in warm temperate and tropical waters, they are uncommon in the Gulf of Mexico and are most frequently observed in the eastern part of these waters. There is only one stranding from Texas; a group of nine Risso's dolphins was seen in the Gulf waters off the south Texas coast in November 1980.

Subspecies. Monotypic species.

Habits. Risso's dolphins have been observed in large groups of several hundred, but smaller groups of 3–30 are more common. They eat squid and fish.

Their reproductive habits are poorly known. There appears to be a summer calving peak in the North Atlantic. Newborns are about 1.4 m long at birth, and these dolphins may live as long as 24 years. A well-known Risso's dolphin called Pelorus Jack was sighted in a New Zealand harbor for over 20 years.

Pelagic sightings of Risso's dolphins in the Gulf of Mexico show that these dolphins appear to prefer deep offshore waters; they have been sighted at ocean depths of 200–1,530 m. They are probably rare near the northern Gulf Coast where the continental shelf is broad and the nearshore waters are relatively shallow. In

Risso's Dolphin (*Grampus griseus*). Illustration by Pieter A. Folkens.

deep, offshore waters of the Gulf these dolphins may be more common than previously thought; however, additional data are needed to assess their status in the Gulf effectively.

Conservation Status.   This is another offshore, deepwater species that rarely strands. Thus, it is not common near the Texas coast. Aerial sightings are common in the deeper waters of the Gulf. Its status cannot be determined with the information at hand.

Bottlenose Dolphin
Tursiops truncatus (Montague)

Description.   A rather stout, short-beaked (seldom more than 75 mm long) dolphin with sloping forehead and projecting lower jaw; dorsal fin high, falcate, and situated about midway from snout to flukes; pectoral fin broad at base, obtusely rounded at tip; upperparts plumbeous gray, more or less tinged with purplish, becoming black soon after death; sides pale gray, belly white; teeth 23/23, large, nearly round in cross section in adults, and conical, height above jawbone 12–17 mm, diameter 5–9 mm. Total length of adults may reach 3.5 m. A subadult male measured: total length, 2.9 m; length of mouth, 319 mm; tip of snout to dorsal fin, 1,275 mm; length of pectoral fin, 395 mm; vertical height of dorsal fin, 229 mm; breadth of flukes, 612 mm.

Distribution.   Bottlenose dolphins are distributed worldwide in tropical and temperate waters. In the western North Atlantic these dolphins occur as far north as Nova Scotia but are most common in coastal waters from New England to Florida, the Gulf of Mexico, the Caribbean, and south to Venezuela. This is the most common cetacean of the Gulf of Mexico and along the Texas coast.

Subspecies.   The taxonomic status of *Tursiops truncatus* is in question, and further research is required to determine if subspecies assignments are justified.

Habits.   Bottlenose dolphins may be seen in groups numbering up to several hundred, but smaller social units of 2–15 are more common. Group size is affected by

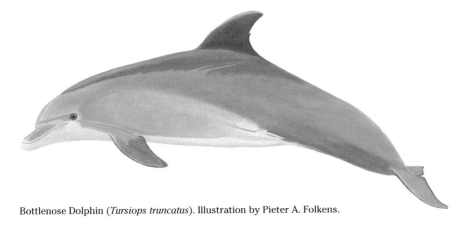

Bottlenose Dolphin (*Tursiops truncatus*). Illustration by Pieter A. Folkens.

habitat structure and tends to increase with water depth. Group members interact closely and are highly cooperative in feeding, protective, and nursery activities. These dolphins make numerous sounds and are probably both good echolocators and highly communicative.

Bottlenose dolphins eat a wide variety of food items, depending on what is available and abundant at a given time. In Texas waters they eat sharks and fish, including tarpon, sailfish, speckled trout, pike, rays, mullet, and catfish. They are also known to eat anchovies, menhaden, minnows, shrimp, and eel. They eat about 18–36 kg of fish each day. Commonly observed feeding behaviors include foraging around shrimp boats, either working or not, to feed on fish attracted to the boats. The dolphins also eat bycatch dumped from working trawlers. Groups of these dolphins have been observed cooperating in prey capture, with several dolphins herding fish into tight schools that are more easily exploited. Bottlenoses are also known to chase prey into very shallow water and may lunge onto mud banks and shoals in pursuit of panicked fish.

Of 15 females captured in Texas waters, 6 that were pregnant were taken between 17 December and 19 March. On the first date the fetus was 78 cm long and weighed 5 kg; on the last date fetuses were almost as large as some of the small calves. Nursing females were all taken between 20 April and 11 September. Those data suggest that breeding occurs in the summer and that the young are born the following March to May. At birth the calf, usually about 1 m in length, is more than one-third as long as its mother. Females give birth to a single calf every 2–3 years. Males mature at 10–13 years of age and females at 5–12 years, when about 2.4 m in length. That the family group may remain intact for nearly a year is suggested by the capture on 24 February of a pregnant female and a young male approximately 1.5 m in length. The two animals were traveling together and were presumably mother and son.

Bottlenose dolphins are the most widespread and common cetacean of the coastal Gulf of Mexico and are commonly seen in bays, estuaries, and ship channels. Two distinct forms may occur in the Gulf: inshore animals that inhabit shallow lagoons, bays, and inlets; and oceanic or offshore populations that remain in deeper, offshore waters. Interaction between the two populations is thought to be minimal. Populations of these dolphins in the southern and central portions of the Texas coast appear to increase dramatically in fall and winter. Either offshore dolphins move into nearshore waters during these seasons, or dolphins from adjacent bay systems move into the coastal sections. There is some evidence of a winter decline in dolphin numbers off Galveston.

This is the only cetacean for which census techniques have yielded useful population estimates in the Gulf of Mexico. There are an estimated 78,000 bottlenose dolphins in the northern Gulf of Mexico, about 5,000 of them in bays, 18,000 along the coast, and 55,000 in deeper continental slope waters.

All cetaceans, including bottlenose dolphins, are protected from hunting by strict laws but are affected by other human activities. In the Gulf these include petroleum resource development, heavy boating traffic, and the pollution of Gulf waters, but the cumulative effects of those factors on dolphins are difficult to determine. Bottlenoses have been observed swimming through heavy oil spills and superficially show no ill effects. Bottlenoses may be able to adapt to human activities, but they probably are readily affected by pollution and would make a good indicator species signaling the overuse and excessive pollution of Gulf waters.

Conservation Status. Bottlenose dolphins are the most widespread and common cetacean of the coastal Gulf of Mexico, frequently seen in bays, ship channels, and even estuaries. There is no suggestion that populations are declining along the Texas coast. Potential long-term threats include petroleum resource development, heavy boating traffic, and the pollution of Gulf waters.

Pantropical Spotted Dolphin

Stenella attenuata Gray

Description.   A small dolphin with a relatively short, black beak, blackish back, grayish sides, and white underparts; eyes usually encircled with black rings joined by a black stripe across base of rostrum; dorsal fin, flipper, and flukes black; the pale sides and abdomen often covered with small blackish spots; posterior to the dorsal fin the blackish upperparts and the flippers often covered with grayish white dots. Teeth small (diameter at alveolus 2.5–3 mm), 38–42 in each tooth row. Total length, 1.6–2.5 m. Similar to *S. frontalis* but upperparts blackish, general size smaller, beak narrower, and the teeth smaller and more numerous.

Distribution.   Occurs in the tropical and subtropical oceans of the world. Known in Texas from three individuals that were beached near Yarborough Pass on Padre Island during Hurricane Fern in September 1971, and two separate individual strandings near Port Aransas in 1989 and 1990.

Subspecies.   Subspecies designations have not been assigned for this species in most of its range.

Pantropical Spotted Dolphin (*Stenella attenuata*). Illustration by Pieter A. Folkens.

Habits. These dolphins are usually seen in groups of 5–30, although large herds of 1,000 or more are occasionally observed. Unlike many other dolphins, groups of pantropical spotted dolphins do not appear to be segregated by sex and age. These dolphins feed at or near the surface on fish (including mackerel and flying fish), squid, and shrimp.

In the eastern tropical Pacific, the following reproductive data are known. The gestation period lasts 11.5 months and lactation lasts about 11 months. At birth the calves average 80 cm in length and at 1 year are 1.4 m long. Males attain sexual maturity at about 6 years of age; females reach maturity at 5 years. The calving interval is 26 months. No data on reproductive habits are available for the Gulf of Mexico.

In the Pacific, these dolphins are killed incidentally in the course of seining for tuna. In 1970 about 400,000 were killed by U.S. vessels alone, but that figure was reduced to 15,000–20,000 by 1978. Currently, incidental catch is limited by U.S. law to 20,500 per year but is usually lower than that because of declining tuna-seining efforts and the recent adoption of a porpoise mortality reduction program; this international agreement among all major tuna-seining countries had a goal of reducing total incidental catch to less than 5,000 dolphins per year by 1999. In the Atlantic and Gulf of Mexico, the problem of incidental catch is limited and was never as great as in the Pacific.

Conservation Status. This is the most common cetacean in deep Gulf waters. It occasionally strands on the Texas coast, but populations appear to be in good shape overall.

Clymene Dolphin
Stenella clymene (Gray)

Description. This is a small dolphin that averages about 1.8 m in length and 75 kg in weight. It can be distinguished by its moderately short beak; tripartite color

Clymene Dolphin (*Stenella clymene*). Illustration by Pieter A. Folkens.

pattern of white belly, light gray sides, dark cape that dips in two points (above the eye and below the dorsal fin); and distinctive facial markings including black eye ring, dark lips and snout tip, and dark line on top of snout, sometimes incorporating a mustache near the apex of the melon. The cape is sometimes obscured by blotchy patches on the sides, and occasionally a faint spinal blaze may be present. The dorsal fin is gray but bordered with dark margins. Average total number of teeth is 200.

Distribution.   Found only in the tropical and subtropical waters of the Atlantic Ocean. Known in Texas from four strandings, including three recent strandings along Padre and Mustang islands.

Subspecies.   Monotypic species.

Habits.   This dolphin was not described as a distinct species until 1981 and is rarely observed alive. Consequently, it is one of the most poorly known dolphins of the world.

It has been observed at sea only in deep water. These dolphins eat small fish and squid and appear to feed at night or in midwater depths. Squid remains found in their stomachs are of species that characteristically live at intermediate depths and surface at night.

These dolphins may leap and spin out of water, but their movements are not so high or complex as those of the spinner dolphin, *S. longirostris.* Stranding records from the Gulf of Mexico indicate that they are probably year-round residents of this region.

The Clymene dolphin is not found outside Atlantic waters, an unusual distribution for a tropically distributed cetacean. This dolphin may possibly have evolved in the Atlantic.

Conservation Status.   This is another offshore, deepwater dolphin that occasionally strands along the Texas coast. There is no reason to suspect any conservation problems, although accurate population estimates and trends are not available.

Striped Dolphin

Stenella coeruleoalba (Meyen)

Description.   A slender dolphin that reaches lengths of about 2.4 m and averages 100 kg in weight. Maximum size approximately 3 m in length and 129 kg in weight. Strikingly colored in shades of gray or brown; dark dorsally fading to lighter sides and white ventrally with black stripes extending from the eye to the anus and from the eye to the flipper. Dorsal fin tall, beak relatively short and uniformly dark. There are 43–50 teeth in each side of both jaws, average total 200. Only *Stenella longirostris* has more average total teeth (224).

Distribution.   Worldwide in tropical and temperate waters. Although they are occasionally seen in the western Gulf of Mexico near Texas, these dolphins are better known from waters around Florida.

Subspecies.   Monotypic species.

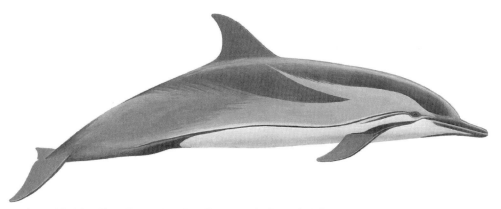

Striped Dolphin (*Stenella coeruleoalba*). Illustration by Pieter A. Folkens.

Habits. Striped dolphins may be observed in herds of several hundred to several thousand, with such groups usually segregated by sex and age. In the Gulf of Mexico group size ranges from 1 to 130 and averages 16 dolphins per group. They are usually found in deep, offshore waters where they feed on small pelagic fish, squid, and shrimp.

Adult females bear young once every 3 years, and the gestation period is 12 months. Calves are approximately a meter long at birth. In the Gulf of Mexico, calves have been seen in June, August, October, and February, indicating that the breeding season is not sharply defined. Males reach maturity at about 9 years of age and females at 7 years.

Conservation Status. This deepwater species is regularly sighted in the eastern Gulf of Mexico and around southern Florida but is seldom seen in the western Gulf. One stranding was reported from Jefferson County, Texas, in 1994. It is doubtful that the species occurs regularly in our waters.

Atlantic Spotted Dolphin
Stenella frontalis (Cuvier)

Description. A rather small, long-snouted, spotted dolphin; ground color purplish gray, appearing blackish at a distance, usually with numerous small white or gray spots on sides and back; sides paler, belly whitish; young grayish, unspotted; dorsal fin high and strongly recurved, strongly concave at rear; beak deeper than wide and about 6% of total length of animal; teeth small and slightly incurved, especially toward tip of snout in upper jaw, varying in number from 31/31 to 37/34; height of teeth above jawbones seldom over 10 mm; total length, 2.2 m; girth in front of dorsal fin, 1.2 m; length of anterior edge of dorsal fin, 431 mm; width of flukes, 661 mm. Weight, 125 kg.

Distribution. A common offshore resident of tropical and warm temperate waters of the Atlantic Ocean. Not known outside the Atlantic. In the Gulf of Mexico, this dolphin is second in abundance only to the bottlenose dolphin, *Tursiops truncatus*.

Atlantic Spotted Dolphin (*Stenella frontalis*). Illustration by Pieter A. Folkens.

Subspecies. The taxonomic status of *Stenella frontalis* is unresolved and further research is required to determine if subspecies assignments are justified.

Habits. Atlantic spotted dolphins may be seen in groups of up to 50 animals, but smaller groups of 6–10 are more common. They eat small fish including herring, anchovies, and flounder, as well as squid.

These dolphins make a variety of sounds used in echolocation and communication. Sounds are described as "loud whistles, chirps, low-intensity click trains, squawks, barks, growls, and cracks."

These dolphins mate and calve in summer. Sexual behavior has been observed in the Gulf of Mexico in mid-May. The gestation period lasts 12 months, and calves are born in offshore waters.

Although this dolphin is a common offshore resident of the Gulf of Mexico, it may move into nearshore waters in late spring and summer in Florida. That movement may be related to the movements of certain prey species for the dolphins; such migrations are not known for Texas waters.

Conservation Status. This is a common offshore dolphin of the Gulf of Mexico. Only rarely do individuals strand along the Texas coast, but there is no reason to suspect a population decline.

Spinner Dolphin
Stenella longirostris (Gray)

Description. A small dolphin that averages less than 1.8 m in length and 75 kg in weight. Maximum size about 2.1 m and 95 kg. Very slender, with a long, slender beak that is black above and white below. Coloration dark gray dorsally fading to lighter gray on the sides; belly white; a dark stripe extends from the flipper to the eye. Average total teeth, 224, more than any other Texas cetacean.

Distribution. Worldwide in tropical and warm temperate waters. Known in Texas from strandings along Padre Island National Seashore.

Subspecies. The subspecies in the Gulf is thought to be *S. l. centroamericana.*

Spinner Dolphin (*Stenella longirostris*). Illustration by Pieter A. Folkens.

Habits. Spinner dolphins derive their name from a habit of leaping from the water and warping their bodies into graceful curves, or spinning lengthwise before splashing back. The motives for this behavior are not known, but such actions are often in themselves enough to distinguish this species.

They usually occur in groups of 30 to several hundred but may number into the thousands. Spinner dolphins feed on mesopelagic fish, squid, and shrimp.

Adult females give birth to a single calf at 2-year intervals. Parturition usually occurs in early summer but can occur in any season. Gestation is 11 months, and calves are about 75 cm long at birth.

Two mass strandings of spinner dolphins have been reported in the Gulf of Mexico. One stranding of 36 animals occurred on Dog Island, Florida, in 1961, and the other was near Sarasota, Florida, in 1976, involving 50–150 spinners that beached themselves at several points during an extremely low tide. The dolphins came ashore with much "squealing and crying," but the noise later subsided and the animals were quite passive on the beach. Several of the animals were returned, apparently successfully, to the sea; however, others merely stranded again, and at least 10 died.

In the eastern tropical Pacific this species is often caught and drowned in large numbers by the tuna fishing industry. Over the last 20 years the total population in those waters has declined about 80%, from 2 million to 400,000, because of incidental catch. Gulf of Mexico populations do not receive this pressure. At least 15,000 spinner dolphins are believed to occur in the northern Gulf, generally in waters much deeper than 100 m, but almost all sightings have been east and southeast of the Mississippi Delta.

Conservation Status. This is another offshore, deepwater dolphin that has only occasionally stranded or been sighted near the Texas coast. It is relatively abundant, and there is no reason to question its conservation status.

Fraser's Dolphin
Lagenodelphis hosei Fraser

Description. Robust dolphin with a very short beak (3–6 cm), small dorsal fin (maximum 22 cm high), and small flippers and flukes. Adult males reach 2.7 m in

Fraser's Dolphin (*Lagenodelphis hosei*). Note the variation in color patterns of an adult (top), juvenile (center), and calf (bottom). Illustration by Pieter A. Folkens.

length and weigh at least 210 kg; females somewhat smaller. At birth, 105–110 cm in length. Adults develop a complex color pattern characterized by a dark cape, light gray or brownish sides, and a white belly sometimes with a pinkish hue; appendages all dark; a dark line on upper beak, a dark chin-to-flipper stripe, and a delphinid bridle with a dark line from the melon apex surrounding the eye; a gray stripe of variable intensity and width runs from the facial area to the anus. Variability in the side stripe appears to be geographic as well as age-related. There are 34–44 small, sharp teeth in each tooth row; skull has deep grooves along the palate. Only common dolphins (*Delphinus* spp.) have palatal grooves as deep as Fraser's dolphins.

Distribution. Tropical and subtropical animals, occurring in deep waters beyond the continental shelf edge. The first record for this species in the Gulf of Mexico was a 1981 mass stranding in the Florida Keys. No other reports of the species were recorded until 1992, when the first sightings of live animals occurred. Several sightings and at least three strandings (in Florida and Texas) have occurred since 1992 in the northern Gulf.

Subspecies. Monotypic species.

Habits. These are very active animals, often seen traveling quickly, making splashy leaps, and turning the water's surface into a froth. Bow riding is rare in some areas but is a common behavior in the Gulf. They occur in large groups of several dozen to hundreds (or even thousands) of individuals. Fraser's dolphins often school with melon-headed whales. They feed primarily on small midwater fish and squids.

The reproductive biology is not well known. Gestation is a little over a year, and calves are born year round, possibly with seasonal peaks in some areas. Males off Japan become sexually mature at about 7–10 years of age, females at 5–8 years. The lactation period is not known.

Conservation Status. They appear to be more common in the Gulf of Mexico than anywhere else within their range. A few sightings have occurred on the Texas coast, and apparently there are no reasons for concern about this dolphin's status.

ORDER SIRENIA
Manatees and Allies

The Sirenia are large, plump, torpedo-shaped mammals adapted to an aquatic habitat; they live in bays and coastal waters in tropical regions of the world. The front limbs are developed into paddles, the hind limbs are absent externally, and the tail is expanded into a rounded, horizontal fluke. Having evolved from ungulates, the Sirenians are the only marine mammals that feed exclusively on plants.

FAMILY TRICHECHIDAE (MANATEES)

This family includes three species, one of which, the West Indian Manatee, occupies the coastal waters and some connecting rivers from Virginia around the Gulf of Mexico and the Caribbean Sea to eastern Brazil, the Orinoco basin, and the Greater and Lesser Antilles. This species inhabits shallow coastal waters such as bays, estuaries, lagoons, and rivers, utilizing both salt water and fresh water, although it may prefer fresh water.

West Indian Manatee
Trichechus manatus Linnaeus

Description. A large, grayish, nearly hairless, aquatic mammal without hind limbs; tail broadened into a horizontal, rounded paddle; front limbs paddlelike. Dental formula: I 2/2 (nonfunctional), C 0/0, Pm 0/0, M 6/6 (variable and continuously being replaced) x 2 = 32. Total length of adults, 2.5–4.6 m; weight typically 200–600 kg, up to a record of 1,650 kg.

Distribution. West Indian manatees are found in rivers, estuaries, and coastal areas of the tropical and subtropical New World from the southeastern coast of the United States along Central America and the West Indies to the northern coastline of South America. Manatees are extremely rare in Texas, although near the turn of the century they apparently were sighted in the Laguna Madre. Texas records also include specimens from Cow Bayou, near Sabine Lake, Copano Bay, San Jose Island, the Bolivar Peninsula, and the mouth of the Rio Grande.

Subspecies. *T. m. manatus.*

Habits. These animals occur chiefly in the larger rivers and brackish bays. They are able to live in salt waters of the sea, however, and travel from one island to another or from place to place along the coast. They are extremely sensitive to cold and may be killed by a sudden drop in the temperature of the water to as low as 8°C. This intolerance doubtless limits their northward distribution in North

West Indian Manatee (*Trichechus manatus*). Illustration by Pieter A. Folkens.

America. Their irregular occurrence along the Texas coast suggests that they do considerable wandering. Specimens from Texas probably represent migrants from coastal Mexico.

Sluggish and easily captured, West Indian manatees were once extensively exploited as a food source. Although now protected, manatees still face occasional losses from poaching and from collisions with speedboats. Additionally, habitat loss to land development and channelization continues to pose problems for them. Conversely, in Florida the construction of power plants and industrial parks has apparently been beneficial in creating new warm-water habitat that may be preferred by manatees in winter.

Manatees are opportunistic, aquatic herbivores that feed exclusively on aquatic vegetation, although captive animals have eaten lawn grass, dandelions, palmetto, and garden vegetables. Wild manatees seem to prefer submergent vegetation, followed by floating and emergent species. Manatees consume 30–50 kg of food per day. In saline waters, they feed on sea grasses.

Manatees occur in loosely knit groups but are not gregarious by nature. Breeding and calving occurs year round, with the gestation period lasting 12–13 months. Newborn manatees are about a meter long at birth and weigh 18–27 kg. One young is born.

Conservation Status. The West Indian manatee is listed as an endangered species. Excluding the Florida coast, manatees are rare in the Gulf of Mexico. They were often observed in the Laguna Madre of south Texas around the first decade of the twentieth century, but they were never common along the Texas coast, and those reports may have been from strays in Mexican waters farther to the south. Populations have been maintained along the Florida coast, but it is unlikely they will ever become reestablished in Texas.

Remarks. Stephanie Fernandez and Sherman Jones reported a stranding of a manatee on the Texas coast in February 1986. A local fisherman found the carcass of a male manatee, in an advanced state of decomposition, rolling in the surf about 1.5 km west of Caplen, Bolivar Peninsula. It was the first manatee stranding recorded by the Texas Marine Mammal Stranding Network since its inception in 1980.

ORDER ARTIODACTYLA
Even-toed Ungulates

T his order is characterized by either two or four (usually) hoofed toes on
each foot, with the exception of the peccary, which has four toes on each
forefoot but only three on the hind. The American forms of the order are
readily divisible into two groups on the basis of structure of the teeth, presence or
absence of horns, and structure of the stomach and feet. The pig group has crushing cheek teeth, upper incisors, a simple stomach, no horns, four hoofed toes, and
includes the peccaries. The cow group has rasping cheek teeth, no upper incisors,
two or four hoofed toes on each foot, complex stomach, and horns or antlers in
most species. The order includes the deer, elk, and allies; cows and allies; and the
pronghorn.

Seven species of artiodactyls are native to Texas, although three of them (the
bighorn sheep, bison, and elk) have been extirpated. Recent reintroductions of
these big-game animals account for their current presence in the state. In addition,
at least 123 species of ungulates not native to Texas have been imported into the
state since 1930. For the most part, these exotic animals have been confined on private ranches; however, seven species have escaped, reproduced, and now exist in
parts of Texas as free-ranging, feral populations that constitute a part of the local
fauna. As the possibility of sighting or finding the remains of these unusual animals
mounts yearly in Texas, accounts for the most common exotics have been included in this revision. Accounts of exotics are adapted from the book *Exotics on the
Open Range,* by Elizabeth Cary Mungall and William J. Sheffield (Texas A&M
University Press, College Station, 1994).

KEY TO THE EVEN-TOED UNGULATES OF TEXAS

1. Medium size; body form stocky and barrel-like; head long and point-
    ed with very short neck; legs short; snout with terminal nasal disk
    (piglike); upper incisors present 2

    Large size; body form slender or cowlike; head with well-developed
    neck; legs long; snout never piglike; upper incisors absent..............3

2. Sparsely covered with coarse bristly hair; some individuals with a
    scantily haired dorsal mane; tail approximately 300 mm in length;
    each foot with four toes (the middle two are flattened and have
    hooves, while the lateral toes are higher up on the limb and do not
    normally touch the ground); adult weight up to 350 kg. *Sus scrofa*
    (feral pig), p. 258.

Pelage thick and bristly; well-developed dorsal mane of long, stiff hairs extending along back from crown to rump; tail length 15–55 mm; front feet with four toes, hind feet with three toes; adult weight 14–30 kg. *Pecari tajacu* (collared peccary), p. 260.

3. Two toes on each foot; males with prominent, forked horns; horn sheaths shed annually; females usually with smaller horns that do not shed annually. *Antilocapra americana* (pronghorn), p. 279.

   Four toes on each foot; horns or antlers present 4

4. Males (rarely females) with branching antlers that are shed annually. Family Cervidae...5

   Males and females (except in nilgai) with backward curving, unbranched horns, no part of which is shed 10

5. Adults with reddish, brown, or dark brown pelage generally heavily speckled with white spots...6

   Adults with unspotted pelage (juveniles often spotted)...................8

6. Antlers flattened, palmate, and with numerous points. *Cervus dama* (fallow deer), p. 265.

   Antlers not palmate 7

7. Antlers 75–100 cm in length along outer curve; normally with only 3 tines; brow tines project outward to form a nearly 90-degree angle with main beam. *Cervus axis* (axis deer), p. 263.

   Antlers 28–48 cm in length; normally with 3 or 4 tines branching from main beam. *Cervus nippon* (sika deer), p. 270.

8. Large size (cow size); conspicuous white or cream-colored rump patch; upper canine teeth normally present. *Cervus elaphus* (elk), p. 267.

   Medium size; white rump patch reduced; upper canine teeth absent 9

9. Antlers usually equally branched (dichotomous) and normally with 5 or more tines per side, including brow tine; metatarsal gland on hind leg narrow and elongate, 75–125 mm long, and situated above midpoint of shank; tail narrow at base. *Odocoileus hemionus* (mule deer), p. 272.

   Antlers with all tines branching off the main beam in a nearly vertical position; metatarsal gland on hind leg nearly circular and about 25 mm or less in diameter; tail broad at base, when alarmed held erect to show conspicuous white flag. *Odocoileus virginianus* (white-tailed deer), p. 276.

10. Large size; body form stocky and compact (cowlike); conspicuous hump dorsally over shoulder. *Bos bison* (American bison), p. 285.

    Medium size; body form slender and deerlike; dorsal hump absent 11

11. Horns short and smooth; or tall, marked with strong transverse wrinkles, and twisted in a corkscrew pattern; but in all cases rising straight above head in a V-shaped pattern.....................................12

Horns massive (in males), curving out and back from head and then inward to form a curl at side of head; females with smaller horns that do not curl; horns in both sexes marked with strong transverse wrinkles 13

12. Large size; height at shoulder greater than height at rump, giving a backward-sloping appearance to profile; males with short, straight horns, seldom exceeding 18 cm in length; coloration uniform light brown to iron gray. *Boselaphus tragocamelus* (nilgai), p. 283.

Medium size; height at shoulder equal to height at rump, no backward slope to profile; males with long, twisted horns up to 79 cm in length; coloration tan to black dorsally with striking white eye rings, chin, chest, belly, and inner legs. *Antilope cervicapra* (blackbuck), p. 293.

13. Conspicuous ventral mane of long hairs hanging from throat and chest; coloration light rufous brown; whitish rump patch small and inconspicuous. *Ammotragus lervia* (Barbary sheep), p. 290.

Ventral mane absent; coloration light brown to gray; white rump patch large and prominent. *Ovis canadensis* (bighorn sheep), p. 288.

FAMILY SUIDAE (PIGS)

The family Suidae includes five genera and nine species worldwide. The species *Sus scrofa* is assigned to both the European wild hog and the domestic pig; it is the species that has established itself in feral populations in parts of North America.

*Feral Pig**

Sus scrofa Linnaeus

Description. Feral pigs in Texas are descended from introductions of European wild hogs for sporting purposes and from escaped domestic swine that have established feral populations. European wild hogs have several distinguishing characteristics that set them apart from domestic or feral hogs, including brown to blackish brown color, with grizzled guard hairs, a mane of hair (8–16 cm long) running dorsally from the neck to the rump, a straight heavily tufted tail, and ears covered with hair. Characteristics of feral hogs are varied, depending on the breed of the ancestral stock. European wild hogs and feral hogs interbreed readily, with traits of European wild hogs apparently being dominant.

Distribution. Feral pigs have established sizeable, free-ranging populations in various places across the state.

Habits. Good feral pig habitat in timbered areas consists of diverse forests with some openings. The presence of a good litter layer to support soil invertebrates or the presence of ground vegetation affording green forage, roots, and tubers is desirable. Pigs are also fond of marsh and grass-sedge flats in coastal areas, particularly if wild grapes are common. During hot summer months, wallows or depressions dug in the mud by feral pigs are much in evidence near marshes or standing water, such as along roadside ditches.

Feral Pigs (*Sus scrofa*). Photo by Wendell G. Swank.

On the Texas coast, feral pigs eat a variety of items, including fruits, roots, mushrooms, and invertebrates, depending on the season. The major foods in spring are herbage, roots, invertebrates, and vertebrates. Fruit, invertebrates, and herbage are most common in fall and winter diets. Herbage eaten by feral pigs includes water hyssop, pennywort, frog fruit, spadeleaf, onion, and various grasses. Important roots used for food include bulrush, cattail, flatsedges, and spikesedges. Fruits and seeds such as grapes, acorns, and cultivated sorghum are important, and animal matter ingested by feral pigs includes earthworms, marsh fly larvae, leopard frogs, snakes, baby armadillos, and rodents.

Feral pigs can have detectable influences on wildlife and plant communities as well as domestic crops and livestock. Extensive disturbance of vegetation and soil occurs as a result of their rooting habits. The disturbed area may cause a shift in plant succession on the immediate site. Feral pigs also compete, to some degree, with several species of wildlife for certain foods, particularly mast.

Feral pigs generally breed year round; litters range from one to seven, averaging two per sow. An average of one to three suckling pigs usually accompanies brood sows. The heat period is only about 48 hours in duration, and the average gestation period is 115 days.

Conservation Status. Feral pigs constitute one of the most serious conservation threats in Texas. They have now spread to 200 of the 254 counties, and it is estimated that more than 1 million individuals are now living in Texas. Because of their prolific reproductive potential and adaptability, feral pigs pose a danger to other mammals. For example, where the range of the feral pig overlaps that of the collared peccary, there is some indication the two species may compete to the detriment of the native species. Likewise, along the Texas coast they have been implicated in the decline of the armadillo, and they could be responsible for the demise of the hog-nosed skunk. Wild swine alter their diet during drought or seasonal challenges, and in many cases, their food choices overlap with those of native species. Feral pigs disturb (root up) the ground and vegetation when feeding on plant roots and soil invertebrates, and pig rooting reduces the number of plant species in an area. Besides their growing population, wild pigs pose another serious problem—disease spread. They play a major role in the transmission of such diseases as brucellosis, pseudorabies, and swine fever. Slowing the population explosion of these animals can be achieved only through hunting, dying through natural causes, or trapping and removal of the pigs. One of the major conservation challenges we face in Texas is to find ways to control the spread and population explosion of feral pigs.

FAMILY TAYASSUIDAE (PECCARIES)

This family comprises three genera, each with only a single species. All are found in South America; only the collared peccary ranges northward to the United States. The peccaries have a piglike body form, but the legs are long and slim and the hooves are small. They inhabit grasslands, desert scrub communities, and arid woodlands. These are highly social and territorial animals. They are omnivorous but feed primarily on fruits, seeds, roots, tubers, and cacti.

Collared Peccary
Pecari tajacu (Linnaeus)

Description.   These piglike creatures are characterized by the presence of four hoofed toes on the front feet but only three on the hind feet (outer dewclaw absent); short, piglike snout; crushing molars; nearly straight and daggerlike canines (tusks); harsh pelage with distinct mane from crown to rump; distinct musk gland on rump; two pairs of mammae, inguinal in position; distinct whitish collar across shoulder in adults, rest of upperparts grizzled black and grayish, with dark dorsal stripe; young reddish to yellowish brown, with black stripe down back. External measurements average: total length, 870–1,016 mm; tail, 12 mm; hind foot, 210 mm; height at shoulder, 816 mm. Dental formula: I 2/3, C 1/1, Pm 3/3, M 3/3 x 2 = 38. Weight, 13–25 kg.

Distribution.   Formerly north to the Red River and east at least to the Brazos River Valley. Now restricted to western Texas and the brush country south of San Antonio. An introduced population occurs in several counties of north-central Texas.

Collared Peccary (*Pecari tajacu*). Photo by John and Gloria Tveten.

Subspecies. *P. t. angulatus.*

Habits. In Texas, collared peccaries (often called javelinas) occupy the brushy semidesert where prickly pear is a conspicuous part of the flora. They are commonly found in dense thickets of prickly pear, chaparral, scrub oak, or guajillo; also in rocky canyons where caverns and hollows afford protection and in barren wastelands. Peccaries are active mainly in early morning and late afternoon and often bed down in dense brush or prickly pear thickets during the heat of midday.

They travel in bands ranging from a few animals to several dozen and have a rather limited home range. In the brush country of south Texas, for example, marked individuals moved within home ranges varying in size from 73 to 225 ha. Home ranges of adjacent peccary herds may overlap slightly, but usually only one herd at a time is found in this border. The boundaries of the home range are marked by scent emitted from the conspicuous musk gland on the animal's rump, which also serves the individual in keeping contact within the herd.

Legendary tales of the peccary have caused inexperienced hunters to kill them through fear rather than for either sport or food. Through exaggerated tales of the peccary's ferociousness, it has been charged that peccaries will kill or injure dogs and that they are a menace to deer hunters in the dense brush. It is true that encounters between peccaries and untrained dogs usually end with dead or crippled dogs, but it is also true that in these battles the dog is always the aggressor, and any animal will defend its life to the best of its ability when attacked. The peccary is absolutely harmless to the range, to livestock, and to people.

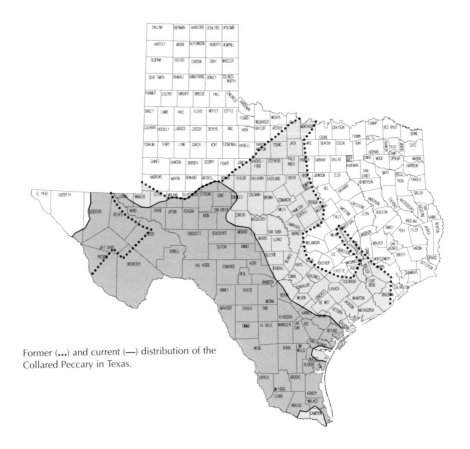

Former (...) and current (—) distribution of the Collared Peccary in Texas.

Peccaries are chiefly herbivorous and feed on various cacti, especially prickly pear, mesquite beans, sotol, lechuguilla, and other succulent vegetation. In areas where prickly pear is abundant, peccaries seldom frequent water holes because the plants provide both food and water. Contrary to the habits of the common pig, peccaries rarely root in the ground but rather push around on the surface, even where the soil is very sandy and loose, turning up chunks of wood and cactus. Mast, fruits, and terrestrial insects also are eaten.

The collared peccary is the only wild ungulate of the western hemisphere with a year-round breeding season. The number of young is usually two, but litters range in size from one to five. The gestation period is 142–149 days (5 months). At birth the young are reddish or yellowish in color and weigh about 500 g. They are able to follow the mother within a few days, at which time the family joins the rest of the herd. Young females attain sexual maturity in 33–34 weeks, young males in 46–47 weeks.

In Texas the peccary was hunted commercially for its hide until 1939, when it was given the status of a game animal. Perhaps a far greater value is in its relationship to range vegetation, as peccaries are able to control (by eating) certain undesirable cacti present on overstocked rangeland.

Conservation Status. Although statewide population estimates for the peccary are not available, observations by Texas Parks and Wildlife personnel, while censusing deer and pronghorn, provide estimates of relative population density in the various ecological regions they occupy. Apparently, they are most numerous in the Trans-Pecos and South Texas Plains ecoregions. The 1999 Big Game Harvest Survey indicated that 17,730 peccary were harvested that year. Overall, populations are declining in many areas where habitat destruction and fragmentation have occurred and where large populations of feral pigs are known. This is a mammal that should be carefully monitored in the future.

Remarks. In previous editions the scientific name of the collared peccary was given as *Tayassu tajacu.*

FAMILY CERVIDAE (CERVIDS)

The family Cervidae comprises 43 species and 16 genera worldwide. Three species are native to Texas. Several species native to Europe, Asia, and Africa have been introduced as game animals, however, and at least 3 species are free-ranging and populous enough to be considered a permanent component of the state's fauna.

*Axis Deer**
Cervus axis (Erxleben)

Description. A moderately large, spotted deer with three tines on each antler; the brow tine forms a nearly right angle with the beam, and the front (or outer) tine of the terminal fork is much longer than the hind (or inner) tine; a gland-bearing cleft is present on the front of the pastern of the hind foot; upperparts yellowish brown to rufous brown, profusely dappled with white spots; abdomen, rump, throat, insides of legs and ears, and underside of tail white; dark stripe from nape to near tip of tail. Dental formula as in *Cervus elaphus,* but upper canines (the so-called elk teeth) usually lacking. External measurements of males average: total length, 1.7 m; tail, 200 mm; height at shoulder, 90 cm; females smaller and usually without antlers. Weight of males, 30–75 kg; of females 25–45 kg.

Distribution. Native to India, where it is known as the chital, the axis deer was introduced into Texas about 1932 and now occurs in a number of counties in the central and southern part of the state, with more than 15,000 free-living individuals. Axis deer are among the most abundant exotic ungulates in Texas.

Habits. Axis deer are inhabitants of secondary forest lands broken here and there by glades (with an understory of grasses, forbs, and tender shoots) that supply adequate drinking water and shade. They tend to avoid rugged terrain. Their food consists largely of grasses in all seasons, augmented with browse. Green grasses less than 10 cm high seem to be preferred. In Texas, they graze on grasses such as paspalum, switchgrass, and little bluestem. Sedges are favorite spring foods. Browse species include live oak, hackberry, and sumac.

Axis Deer (*Cervus axis*). Photo by Martin T. Fulfer, courtesy Texas Parks and Wildlife Department.

These animals are gregarious and usually are found in herds ranging from a few animals to 100 or more. In each herd the leader is usually an old, experienced doe. Unlike our native deer, adult male axis deer normally are found living with herds of young and old animals of both sexes. Anatomically, axis deer are more closely allied to the North American elk than to our native deer. Like our elk, rutting male axis deer emit buglelike bellows, and both sexes have alarm calls or barks.

The reproductive pattern in axis deer is similar to that in domestic cattle. In the wild, bucks with hardened antlers and in rutting condition may be found throughout the year. Each buck seems to have a reproductive cycle of its own, which may not be synchronized with that of other bucks in the herd. Consequently, when some bucks are coming into rut, others are going out or are in a nonbreeding condition, with no antlers and with their testes quiescent. Likewise, females experience estrous cycles throughout the year, with each cycle lasting about 3 weeks. Gravid females may be found throughout the year, but the major breeding season lasts from mid-May through August with a June–July peak in activity. The bucks make no attempt to collect or retain harems of does, but instead they seek out and service the does in each herd as they become receptive.

Normally, only one fawn is produced per pregnancy after a gestation period of 210–238 days. Reflecting the summer peak in rutting activity, nearly 80% of Texas fawns are born in early January to mid-April, although fawns may arrive in all seasons. Following parturition, females again mate during the subsequent breeding period, so adult females tend to produce one fawn each year. Twins are rare.

Fawns begin eating green forage by 5.5 weeks of age, but weaning is delayed until 4–6 months. Permanent dentition is acquired when 2.5–3 years of age, and adult size is reached at 6 years for females and 4–5 years for males. Possibly, does may breed in the breeding season following birth, but most do not breed until the following season, when 14–17 months of age. Life span is 9–13 years, although zoo animals may reach 18–22 years of age.

Conservation Status. This exotic is mostly found on managed ranches, many under high fence, but with several free-living individuals now established. Its effect on the native fauna and flora has not been fully determined and should be monitored so that action can be taken, as necessary, to protect our native wildlife.

Fallow Deer*
Cervus dama Linnaeus

Description. A medium-sized, rangy deer; adult males with large palmate antlers. Bucks develop spike antlers beginning in their first year and, until 3–4 years old, grow and cast only antlers composed of beams and simple points. At 3–4 years of age males may develop antlers with broad, palmate areas that measure 8–25 cm in width; total length of antlers is up to 39 cm.

Coloration is highly variable, but four color forms predominate:

1. Common—rust color with white rump patch and belly, white spots on back and sides merging into a white line along the lower side and near the rump on the haunches; a black line runs down the back and often connects with the black upper surface of the tail; in winter, spots become indistinct.
2. Menil—contrasts with common color form in that ground coloration is tan rather than rust and dorsal lines are brown rather than black; white spotting remains distinct in winter coat.
3. White—coloration is white, with dark eyes; not true albinism.
4. Black—very dark, but not truly black; spotting barely visible; in winter appears as dull brown.

In Texas, black, white, and menil color forms predominate.

Fallow deer stand 91–97 cm at the shoulder and appear thin. Males weigh 79–102 kg but may lose 9–23 kg during rut. Females weigh 36–41 kg.

Distribution. Native to the Mediterranean region of Europe and Asia Minor, fallow deer are the most widely kept of the world's deer and have been introduced to all inhabited continents. Texas now has more than 10,000 individuals, about one-third outside confinement, mostly on the Edwards Plateau and adjacent areas.

Fallow Deer (*Cervus dama*). Photo by John and Gloria Tveten.

Habits. Fallow deer do much of their feeding in open, grassy areas but require tree cover and undergrowth for shelter and winter food. Deciduous or mixed wood-lands on gently rolling terrain are best, but conifer forests may be suitable in some places. The Edwards Plateau region, with its mosaic of oak mottes, juniper brush-land, and grassy areas, is well suited for fallow deer.

Food availability appears to determine whether fallow deer in an area are pre-dominantly grazers or browsers. On the Kerr Wildlife Management Area (Kerr County), fallow deer ate 54% browse, 30% grass, 12% forbs, and 5% other, although those figures varied as the degree of competition with domestic livestock and white-tailed deer varied. Live oak, shin oak, hackberry, and Spanish oak were the dominant browse species taken; Texas wintergrass, fall witchgrass, and common curlymesquite were the predominant grasses eaten. Increased competition for browse with white-tailed deer caused fallow deer to increase their dependence on grasses, and increased livestock competition for grasses led fallow deer to increase their use of browse.

Rutting may begin in mid-September and continue into November but peak breeding activity takes place in October. During rut, bucks mark off and defend a small area, known as a stand, from which other rutting males are excluded; females and young remain within the male territories, and as each doe comes into heat, she is followed until mating is accomplished. After the rut, males gradually cease defending their territories and form bachelor groups, while females and young remain segregated from males in their own groups.

The gestation period is approximately 7.5 months, with most fawning occurring from late May through June. Generally, only a single fawn is born, although twins are not uncommon.

Females reach sexual maturity at 16 months and can bear their first fawn by 2 years of age. Bucks mature sexually at 14 months but rarely compete successfully in rutting until several years later. Bucks attain physical maturity at 6 years of age. Life span is about 11–15 years, with a maximum record of 25 years.

Conservation Status. This exotic is mostly found on managed ranches, many under high fence. Its effect on the native fauna and flora has not been accurately determined but should be monitored so that action can be taken, as necessary, to protect our native wildlife.

Elk

Cervus elaphus Erxleben

Description. Large, deerlike; males with large, usually six-pointed antlers that are shed annually; hair on neck long and shaggy; upperparts buffy fawn, the head, neck, legs, and belly dull rusty brown to blackish; large rump patch creamy buff to whitish; metatarsal gland oval, about 75 mm long, the center white; tail a mere rudiment. Dental formula: I 0/3, C 1/1, Pm 3/3, M 3/3 x 2 = 34. External measurements of males average: total length, about 2 m; tail, 160 mm; hind foot, 670 mm. Weight, up to 300 kg, averaging about 275 kg. Females are smaller and usually without antlers.

Distribution. Native to the Guadalupe Mountains (Culberson County) but extirpated by 1900. Reintroduced to the Guadalupe Mountains in 1928 and later to other mountains of the Trans-Pecos. Presently, free-ranging elk exist in Texas in five small herds in the Guadalupe Mountains, Glass Mountains (Brewster County), Wylie Mountains (Culberson County), Davis Mountains (Jeff Davis County), and Eagle Mountains (Hudspeth County). The total population of free-ranging elk in the Trans-Pecos was estimated in 1995 at 330 individuals. Others are kept in deer-proof pastures on scattered ranches across the state.

Subspecies. The native subspecies was *C. e. merriami* (now extinct); the reintroduced animals are *C. e. nelsoni.*

Habits. Elk formerly inhabited the plains region of the western United States in winter and open, forested areas in summer. They migrated from one to the other seasonally. Now they are forced by land-use practices into yearlong use of the

Elk (*Cervus elaphus*). Photo by John and Gloria Tveten.

mountainous regions. Lack of adequate winter range is one of the big obstacles to the increase or even maintenance of elk on much of their former range.

Elk are gregarious at all seasons, but in spring and summer the old bulls usually are solitary or in bachelor herds. Except during the period of rut, the herd invariably is under the charge of a cow, and it is she who leads them to water, to the feeding grounds, and so forth. When the herd is bedded for the night, for the noonday siesta, or when feeding, a sentinel is posted (again a cow) to stand guard and give the alarm if danger threatens. On sensing danger the sentinel or any other cow gives warning by an explosive bark that instantly alerts the entire herd. When elk are traveling or feeding, the rear stragglers are usually immature animals.

The normal gait of elk is a saunter, but they can trot or gallop, depending on the mood of the individual. After a really bad scare, the animals may gallop at top speed for a kilometer or so, then stop and reconnoiter; if the alarm has proven serious, the herd may resume flight at a dogtrot, often in single file, a pace that can be maintained for several hours. In spite of their large size, elk are rather agile and can readily jump over fences and corrals as high as 2 m.

Although their senses of sight and hearing are well developed, it seems that elk depend largely on the sense of smell to detect danger. One can easily stalk them upwind as long as the animals do not scent the stalker. Elk are known to use three kinds of calls: (1) the bark of the cow, usually a danger signal, (2) the bugling of the bull during the period of rut, and (3) the bleating of calves and yearlings.

The antlers usually are shed between 15 February and 15 April, and new growth starts soon after the old scars are healed. Between the time of shedding and the latter part of August or early September, the adult bull grows a new set of antlers weighing as much as 15–20 kg. During this period, W. B. Sheppard found that animals kept in confinement consumed seven times the ration customarily eaten during other times of the year. The normal number of points per antler in old males is six, very often five, and rarely as many as nine.

Elk are both grazers and browsers. Palatability studies in northern Idaho revealed that the key forage species on the summer range are willow, maple, broom grass, ryegrass, and elk sedge. Serviceberry, mountain ash, and bitter cherry also were heavily utilized browse species. There is limited information about their food habits in Texas. In the Guadalupe Mountains, they feed on mountain mahogany, agaves, and several species of grasses.

Bugling, which marks the onset of the breeding season, usually starts in the latter part of August, shortly after the velvet has been shed from the antlers. Breeding activities increase until mid-September and close by November. Not all cows come into heat at the same time. Shortly after bugling starts, the herds break up and bulls collect their harems of 5–15 adult females. Sheppard maintains that the bulls do not actively seek out the cows, but rather the cows gravitate toward the larger, more virile bulls. Usually the younger, unattached bulls remain near a harem, and although the leader tries to keep them at a distance, he finds it difficult to do so. Adult bulls start into the rut excessively fat, but they usually emerge in poor physical condition. The larger bulls become emaciated because for the 6-week rutting season they are constantly on the alert to ward off the younger bulls and have little time to eat or even sleep. Old bulls do not ordinarily stay with the same harem throughout the breeding period but move from one herd to another. It frequently happens that the larger bulls become so exhausted that they retire from the herd for a time to recuperate. Toward the close of the rutting season the larger bulls desert the cows for good and seek seclusion.

The average gestation period of elk is about 8.5 months (249–262 days). The main calving period extends from about the middle of May to the middle of June; the number of young is almost invariably one. At birth the calf is long-legged and reddish brown in color, with interspersed white spots on the back and sides. The rump patch is poorly defined. For the first few days the calves are rather helpless and, except for the feeding periods, remain hidden beside logs, under bushes, or in other places. When about 2 weeks old they are able to follow the females; soon after that the mother and her young one rejoin the main herd. At the age of 1 month, elk calves eat grass and other vegetation, and when 2 or 3 months old they graze regularly with the adults. Weaning evidently does not take place until October or even after the rutting season. Sexual maturity in females ordinarily is not reached until the second year. Bulls do not enter actively into the rut until they are about 3 years old.

Conservation Status. This well-known species once ranged over parts of northern and western Texas, but there seem to be no actual specimens to document its modern occurrence there. In any event, it was hunted to extinction within the borders of the state before the beginning of the twentieth century. In 1928 Judge J. C. Hunter and his associates imported 44 elk from the Black Hills of North Dakota and released them at McKittrick Canyon in the Guadalupe Mountains. They multiplied rapidly and expanded their range to nearly all parts of the mountains. The estimated population size in 1938 was 400. In 1959 elk were added to the list of game that could be hunted, and the population was estimated to number about 300. The most recent estimates place the Guadalupe Mountain herd size at no more than 40 individuals. In 1992, introduced herds in the Eagle, Davis, and Wylie mountains each were estimated to number 15–40 individuals, while the Glass Mountain herd numbered 150–180 elk.

Sika Deer*
Cervus nippon Temminck

Description. A small to medium-sized deer that has hybridized extensively in Texas and, as a result, is highly variable in size and coloration. In general, sika are all compact in form; appear dainty-legged; and have a short, trim, wedge-shaped head. Males carry antlers that average 28–48 cm in length, although exceptional racks may be up to 74 cm in length. Sika antlers have three or four points branching from a main beam; there is no palmate growth as in the fallow deer. Females have a pair of black bumps on the forehead, their placement corresponding to that of the male's antlers.

Coloration is drab brown to a deep mahogany brown mottled with numerous white spots. The degree of spotting is highly variable, however, and in some individuals spotting may be absent. The head, as well as the hair tuft over each metatarsal gland, tends to be lighter than the body. A distinctive, white rump patch is evident, especially when the animal is alerted.

Texas sika range in size from the smaller Japanese and Formosan varieties of 76–89 cm shoulder height and 45–80 kg, to the larger Dybowski's variety of 89–109 cm shoulder height and 68–109 kg. Female Dybowski's sika stand about 81 cm in height and weigh 45–50 kg.

Distribution. Formerly, sika were native from southern Siberia and the adjacent Japanese island of Hokkaido south, along both the mainland and islands, to southeastern China and Formosa. Sika have rapidly disappeared from much of their natural range following habitat loss. Sika have been introduced in 77 counties of central and southern Texas, with free-ranging populations known from 12 of these counties. In 1994 the total statewide population was estimated to be more than 5,500 individuals, about half of which were free-ranging.

Habits. Sika are woodland deer characteristic of broad-leaved and mixed forests where snowfall does not exceed 10–20 cm and snow-free sites are also available.

Sika Deer (*Cervus nippon*). Photo by John and Gloria Tveten.

Large forest tracts with dense understory and occasional clearings are ideal; the patchwork of brush cover and open grassland found in the Edwards Plateau and South Texas Plains regions are well suited to these deer.

Sika feed on grasses, leaves, twigs, and tender shoots of woody plants, depending on seasonal availability. In Texas, the spring preference is for grasses, although browse may also be consumed regularly, and browse use increases after the flush of spring growth has passed. The most important food for sika in Texas is live oak, with hackberry, wild plum, mustang grape, Texas sotol, and greenbrier also serving as important browse species. Favored grasses include Texas winter-grass, fall witchgrass, and meadow dropseed. Forb use generally increases in summer, and is lowest in winter.

Sika males are territorial and keep harems of females during the rut, which peaks from early September through October but may last well into the winter months. Territory size varies with type of habitat and size of the buck; strong, prime bucks may hold up to 2 ha. Territories are marked with a series of shallow pits, called scrapes, into which the males urinate and from which emanates a strong, musky odor. Fights between rival males are sometimes fierce, long, and may even be fatal.

The time of fawning is primarily May through August. After a 7.5–8 month gestation period, a single fawn is born; twins are rare. Zoo longevity records typically range from 15 to 18 years, although an exceptionally long life span of 25 years 5 months is known for one animal.

Conservation Status. This exotic is mostly found on managed ranches, many under high fence. Its effect on the native flora and fauna has not been determined, but there is a need to assess its interactions if conservation actions are required in the future.

Mule Deer
Odocoileus hemionus (Rafinesque)

Description. A moderately large deer with large ears; antlers typically dichotomously branched and restricted almost entirely to males; metatarsal gland 8–12 cm long, narrow, and situated above midpoint of shank; upperparts in winter cinnamon buff suffused with blackish, more reddish in summer; brow patch whitish; ear grayish on outside, whitish on inside; tail usually with black tip and white basal portion; underparts white. Dental formula: I 0/3, C 0/1, Pm 3/3, M 3/3 x 2 = 32. External measurements of males average: total length, 1,755 mm; tail, 152 mm; hind foot, 555 mm; of females, 1,453-175-475 mm. Weight, 57–102 kg.

Distribution. Occurs over most of the Trans-Pecos and Panhandle regions of Texas and in some areas immediately east of there, partly as a result of introductions. The population size in Texas ranges from about 150,000 during dry conditions to about 250,000 during wetter periods. Approximately 80–85% of the herd inhabits the Trans-Pecos region; the remainder is found in the Panhandle and western Edwards Plateau regions. The range of the mule deer steadily declined during the past 150 years because of habitat loss and fragmentation. Their range has expanded in the Panhandle since 1986, however, and they now occur in almost 90% of the counties there. Deer biologists believe this expansion is related to the adequate cover provided by crop fields enrolled in the Conservation Reserve Program.

Subspecies. *O. h. crooki.*

Habits. Mule deer occupy to some extent almost all types of habitat within their range but, in general, seem to prefer the more arid, open situations in which sagebrush, juniper, pinyon pine, yellow pine, bitter brush, mountain mahogany, and such plants predominate. In western Texas, rocky hillsides covered with lechuguilla, sotol, juniper, and pinyon pine provide the essentials.

The mule deer is noted for its peculiar, high-bouncing gait. Estimates of their speed vary, but Donald McLean was able to force one to a speed of 58 km an hour on a dry lake flat in California. After the first short burst of speed, the animal dropped to about 35 km an hour and was badly winded after a chase of less than 1.5 km. When allowed to choose their own gait, they are able to travel at about 30 km an hour for a considerable period of time. In rough, broken country they are at their best. There, the long, high bounds send them over the rocks and brush much faster than the average running animal can go through or around the obstructions. The longest bounds are generally made when the animals are going downhill or leaping across gullies. McLean measured two flat jumps, one of 5.9 m and the other

Mule Deer (*Odocoileus hemionus*). Photo by John and Gloria Tveten.

7.1 m. A downhill bound on a 7% slope measured 8.7 m. They can easily clear a fence 2 m high.

Although equipped with acute senses of sight and hearing, these deer rely largely on the sense of smell in detecting danger. Stationary objects are easily over-looked by them, but they readily detect any that are in motion.

Mule deer of both sexes normally do most of their feeding in early morning before sunrise or in late afternoon and evening after sundown. They spend the mid-dle of the day bedded down in cool, secluded places. In summer, the bucks retire as soon as the sun shines where they are feeding and go to the dense shade of some grove to bed down for the day. In general, mature bucks prefer rocky ridges for bedding grounds because there they seem to feel more secure from the approach of danger. Does and fawns are more likely to bed down in the open. In winter, however, they often seek out sunny places well screened on at least three sides by vegetation. At night, they usually bed down in the open away from trees and bushes.

The food of the mule deer is quite varied. In the Trans-Pecos, the flowering stalks of lechuguilla, the basal parts of sotol, mesquite, juniper, and a number of forbs contribute to their diet. Feeding time varies with the weather, the phase of the moon, the time of the year, and type of country. During cold, snowy, winter months when food is difficult to obtain and a considerable amount is required to maintain body heat and energy, deer feed at all times of day and night. During the

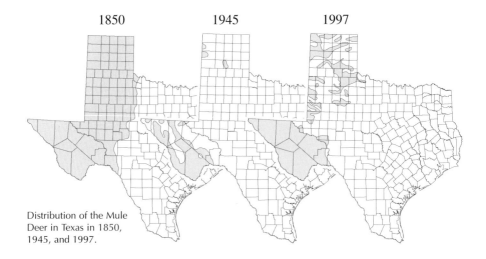

Distribution of the Mule Deer in Texas in 1850, 1945, and 1997.

rutting season, feeding is often erratic, especially with bucks. During the hunting season, when many hunters are on the range, bucks do the major part of their feeding at night. Deer are more prone to feed on dark nights and are relatively quiet and bedded down when the moonlight is intense. In spring and summer, mule deer tend to feed to a greater extent on green leaves, green herbs, weeds, and grasses than they do on browse species; the reverse is true in fall and winter.

The rut begins in the fall, usually in November or December, but varies with locality and climatic conditions and continues until the latter part of January or even into February. During this period, the bucks have terrific battles in which the antlers are used almost exclusively. Bucks that are evenly matched in size and strength may fight until almost exhausted before one or the other is the victor. The animals are polygamous. The stronger, more virile bucks attract females to them and attempt to defend them against the attentions of the younger bucks. Small, persistent bucks can cause a large buck to lead a miserable life, leaving him little time to take care of family duties or even to eat, because of his continued attempts to drive them away. In this period the necks of bucks become swollen, a development that is closely associated with reproduction.

The gestation period is approximately 210 days, and the fawning period extends over several weeks in June, July, and August. The female sequesters herself and drops her fawn in a protected locality, where it remains for a period of a week or 10 days before it is strong enough to follow her. At birth fawns are spotted and weigh approximately 2.5 kg. They are nursed at regular intervals by the female, 10 minutes of nursing usually sufficing for a full meal. The young ones are weaned at about the age of 60 or 75 days, at which time they begin to lose their spots. The weaning time is a critical one because if green forage is not available, the fawns seldom make their transfer from milk to a diet of vegetation. If the fawn is not weaned, both mother and fawn are likely to experience difficulty in surviving a severe winter. Sexual maturity is attained at the age of about 18 months in does, but ordinarily young bucks are not allowed to participate actively in the rut until they are 3 or 4 years old.

Antlers are shed after the breeding season, from mid-January to about mid-April. Most mature bucks in good condition have lost theirs by the end of February; immature bucks generally lose them a little later. New antler growth begins immediately following the shedding of the old. Growth is extremely rapid, and massive antlers develop fully in about 150 days. While the antlers are growing, the bucks remain on the open slopes and benches where the brush is short or scattered to avoid injuring the soft, new growth. Mature bucks normally have four main points on each antler, but beyond the third year there is little or no correlation between the number of points and the age of the deer. Beyond the prime of life, the so-called Pacific buck type may develop, which consists of only two points, or a spike, on each side of a large set of antlers.

The age of mule deer can be determined fairly accurately up to about 24 months. At birth the fawn is equipped with upper premolars, the third and fourth lower premolars, the lower canines, and the entire lower incisor series. The second lower premolar may erupt shortly after birth or within the first 60 days. By the age of 3.5 months, the first upper molar is functional. At the age of approximately 1 year, the middle lower incisor is shed and replaced by a permanent one. Each permanent incisor is wider than its predecessor. At the age of 15–18 months, the molars erupt and take their place in the series, and at the age of 24–25 months, the premolars are replaced by the permanent dentition.

There is some competition between mule deer and livestock on the range, particularly in spring and early summer. Furthermore, such maladies as hoof-and-mouth disease can be transmitted from deer to livestock, and vice versa, so that once the disease is established in wild animals drastic measures must be taken to curb it. Anthrax is also said to be propagated and spread by deer, and these animals are also capable of harboring the causative agents of tularemia or rabbit fever.

Conservation Status. Mule deer are of considerable economic importance as a big game animal, but their populations are considerably lower and thus of more concern than those of white-tailed deer (*Odocoileus virginianus*). There are some indications that hybridization with or replacement by white-tailed deer, or both, is occurring in some regions. In several studies, sympatric populations of mule deer and white-tailed deer in western Texas have been found to interbreed and produce hybrid offspring. Genetic analyses indicate that these hybrids are more characteristic of white-tailed deer than of mule deer; thus, it appears that hybridization may be one factor contributing to the displacement of mule deer by white-tailed deer in this region.

Long-term drought conditions in the Trans-Pecos region also appear to be pushing mule deer populations downward. The Panhandle population, however, has been increasing in both numbers and distribution.

This is a species that bears special monitoring in the twenty-first century.

White-tailed Deer
Odocoileus virginianus (Boddaert)

Description. A relatively small deer with relatively short ears; all major points of the antlers come off the main beam; tail relatively long, broad basally, and white underneath; metatarsal gland small and circular; females usually antlerless; upperparts reddish brown in summer, bright grayish fawn sprinkled with black in winter; face and tail usually lack blackish markings; underparts white. Dental formula as in the mule deer. External measurements of males average: total length, 1,800 mm; tail, 300 mm; hind foot, 450 mm; females slightly smaller. Weight of males, 30–70 kg.
Distribution. Suitable brushy or wooded country throughout the state.
Subspecies. Originally included *O. v. carminis,* known only from the Big Bend area, *O. v. macroura* in the extreme northeastern corner of the state, *O. v. mcilhennyi* along the Gulf Coast, and *O. v. texana* throughout the central part of the state. Native animals of the subspecies *O. v. mcilhennyi* and *O. v. macroura* were eliminated in eastern Texas, and the area was restocked with individuals of *O. v. texana.*
Habits. White-tailed deer occur almost entirely in the hardwood areas within their general range, except for the southeastern section of Texas where the principal vegetation is a mixture of pines and hardwoods or nearly pure stands of pines. In the Chisos Mountains of Texas they occur in the mountains, whereas the mule deer occupies the lower foothills and broken deserts; in most other places this habitat

White-tailed Deer (*Odocoileus virginianus*). Photo by Larry Williamson, courtesy Texas Parks and Wildlife Department.

relationship is reversed. For example, in the Guadalupe Mountains the whitetail occurs almost entirely in the foothills; the mule deer, in the higher mountains.

White-tailed deer have a relatively small home range and cruising radius. Normally, when food conditions are adequate, the deer tend to stay in one locality for long periods. For example, in the Edwards Plateau region, where deer were belled in an experimental study, many of the marked deer remained on an area of 259 ha for at least 3 years. A few of them were found as far away as 8 km.

Deer are most active just before sunset and again shortly after sunrise. It has been found in experimental trials that they are most easily observed in the hour just before dark. During the middle part of the day they are generally bedded down in some thicket or on some promontory where they are more or less protected. Under cover of darkness it is not uncommon for them to feed well into the night, but there is usually a period of resting and cud chewing during the middle part of the night. In regions heavily populated with deer, their trails and beds (usually scraped-out places under the protection of overhanging boughs or at the bases of trees) are readily seen and give some clue to the density of the population.

As with most other mammals, the feeding habits of whitetails vary from place to place and from season to season. E. L. Atwood listed more than 500 different plants utilized by whitetails in the United States. Availability determines in large measure what the animals will eat, but if adequate food is available, the deer are dainty eaters and exercise considerable choice in the items taken. In the Chisos Mountains of Trans-Pecos Texas, whitetails feed extensively on mountain mahogany and other low shrubs. In the Edwards Plateau region the deer graze twice as much as they browse. There, 67% of their total feeding time was spent in grazing on forbs and grasses, 26% in eating fruits and mast, and only 7% in browsing. In southern Texas, however, browse species make up the bulk of the diet.

The 10 most favored foods as observed in the Edwards Plateau of Texas are grasses and weeds, Mexican persimmon, live oak acorns, live oak leaves, mesquite beans, oats or other grain, Spanish oak acorns, spike rush, *Foresteria* or elbow bush, and turkey pear. On the basis of food consumed, seven deer will eat about as much as one medium-sized cow.

White-tailed deer are polygamous. The rut begins in early fall and continues through early winter. The onset of breeding varies considerably from one section of the country to another. In coastal Texas, for example, breeding sometimes begins as early as September. In the Edwards Plateau, not more than 300 km distant, the peak of the breeding season is in November, whereas in the southern brush country of Texas the peak is in late November and December.

The fawns, usually one or two in number, are dropped after a gestation period of approximately 7 months and hidden by the female for 10 days to 2 weeks. She goes several times daily to nurse them, but as soon as they are strong enough to follow her about they do so. The spots are retained until the fawns molt in early fall, by which time they are usually weaned. Normally, females do not reach sexual maturity until the second year, but occasionally, when food conditions are excellent, female fawns mate the first fall and produce offspring the following spring, when they themselves are only 1 year old. That appears to be unusual throughout most of their range, however.

There is a relationship between testicular activity and the growth and shedding of antlers. The antlers begin their annual growth when the testes and accessory organs are inactive, harden and lose their velvet when the glands are enlarging, and are shed when they begin to decline. Castration following loss of the velvet results in shedding within 30 days. New growth, which occurs at the normal time, is abnormal in shape, and the velvet is not lost. Growth ceases at the usual time, and part of the growth, being somewhat fragile, may be lost by accident. Renewed growth activity follows in the spring. Eventually, an aggravated burr is produced. These events have been interpreted as indicating that antler growth is under the influence of a nontesticular hormone, possibly from the anterior pituitary, and antler hardening and subsequent loss of the antler is due to the action of a testicular hormone.

One can estimate the age of whitetails by examination of the teeth. At 9 months of age the fawn will be acquiring the middle pair of permanent incisors while the remainder of the incisors as well as the premolars will be milk teeth. At this age one molar on either side of each jaw is well developed while the second is barely breaking through the gum. At the age of 1.5 years, all milk incisors have been replaced by permanent teeth. At least two molars are fully developed while the third may be in any condition, from barely emerging from the mandible to fully emerged. At the age of 2 years, the full set of permanent teeth is acquired. Beyond 2 years, age determination is somewhat uncertain but can be roughly estimated by the wear evident on the teeth. Wear of the teeth is gradual until, at 5 years, the ridges of enamel are no longer sharp but rise slightly and gradually above the dentine. At still later ages the crowns of the premolars and molars rise only a short distance above the gums, and the grinding surfaces are worn practically smooth.

Contrary to popular opinion, it is almost impossible to determine the age of deer accurately from the number of points on the antlers. For example, the shed antlers collected from one buck in Texas over a period of 5 years had each year either four or five points on each side. There is some correlation between age and diameter of the beam of the antler, however. The older bucks tend to have heavier antlers, but antler development is also so closely associated with nutrition that it is hazardous to make generalizations concerning age and diameter of the beam. Also, a certain amount of geographic variation is seen in antler development.

On some ranges there is considerable competition for forage between whitetailed deer and domestic livestock. This is particularly true between deer and domestic goats. Competition between deer and cattle is not so severe. Where abundant in farming areas, deer often become pests and destroy such crops as peas, peanuts, wheat, oats, and other small grains.

Conservation Status. This is the most economically important big game animal in Texas. It is estimated that our 1999 white-tailed deer population numbered more than 3.72 million, and 420,187 were harvested by hunters in that year. The population seems to be stable and healthy and steadily increasing in some regions of the state. Improved habitat management efforts and protection by private landowners offer a serious opportunity to increase deer numbers. The problem in Texas is that we do not harvest enough deer across the state; consequently, deer numbers are expanding and beginning to affect native animals and plants.

FAMILY ANTILOCAPRIDAE (PRONGHORN)

The pronghorn is the only member of this family. It is endemic to North America and represents the only surviving member of a group of about a dozen species that occurred during the Pleistocene of North America. Pronghorns are adapted to open country, where they use their speed and endurance to escape predators.

Pronghorn
Antilocapra americana (Ord)

Description. A small, deerlike mammal with black, pronged horns that reach beyond the tip of the ears in males; in females they are shorter and seldom pronged; only two toes on each foot (no dewclaws); rump patch, sides, breast, belly, side of jaw, crown, and band across throat white; chin and markings on neck black or dark brown; black patch at angle of jaw in males (absent in females). Dental formula: I 0/3, C 0/1, Pm 3/3, M 3/3 x 2 = 32. External measurements of males average: total length, 1,470 mm; tail, 135 mm; hind foot, 425 mm; females, 1,250-135-400 mm. Weight of males, 40–60 kg; females somewhat smaller, averaging about 40 kg.

Distribution. Formerly distributed over the western two-thirds of Texas, as far eastward as Robertson County in the north and Kenedy County in south Texas. Now restricted to isolated areas from the Panhandle to the Trans-Pecos.

Subspecies. *A. a. americana* in the Panhandle and *A. a. mexicana* in western and central Texas, although reintroductions may have altered the subspecies distribution in the state.

Habits. The fleet-footed, large-eyed pronghorn is an animal of the plains. Adapted for speed and for seeing long distances, it inhabits areas where both its sight and its running will be unimpaired by woodland vegetation. Water in the immediate vicinity is not a requisite because the pronghorn is so adapted physiologically that it can go for long periods without drinking. Apparently, it has the ability to conserve body water and to produce metabolic water.

Among North American mammals, pronghorns are the most fleet-footed. The top speed at which they can run probably does not exceed 70 km an hour, and certainly it varies with individuals. An interesting trait of pronghorns is their highly developed sense of curiosity. They insist on examining at close range any unrecognized object, particularly one that is in motion. Because of this, it is possible for a person to lure the animals within close range by hiding behind a bush and

Pronghorn (*Antilocapra americana*). Photo courtesy Texas Parks and Wildlife Department.

waving a handkerchief or other object slowly back and forth. Indians, and some-times our present-day hunters, have utilized this ruse in bagging them. Another peculiar trait is their disinclination to jump over fences or other objects. A low brush fence no more than a meter high will ordinarily turn the animals, and small bands have been reduced almost to the point of starvation within a fenced enclo-sure while plenty of food was available on the outside. They can jump over mod-erately high obstructions, however, when hard pressed. Ordinarily, they crawl under or between the wires of barbed-wire fences.

Their pattern of daily activity varies considerably with the season, daily weather, and interruptions from enemies or human activities. Usually, the animals rise shortly after daybreak and begin a period of intensive feeding lasting 1–3 hours, followed by a period of lying down to rest. Resting for about 1 hour is followed by a long period of feeding through most of the morning. Near midday, another extended period of lying down occurs, succeeded by one or two feeding periods during the afternoon. When the heat of the day is intense in spring and summer, little activity takes place. After about 5 P.M., pronghorns feed steadily until nightfall, at which time they recline for a long period of rest. The alternation of feeding and resting is repeated at night, with longer periods of lying down than during the day.

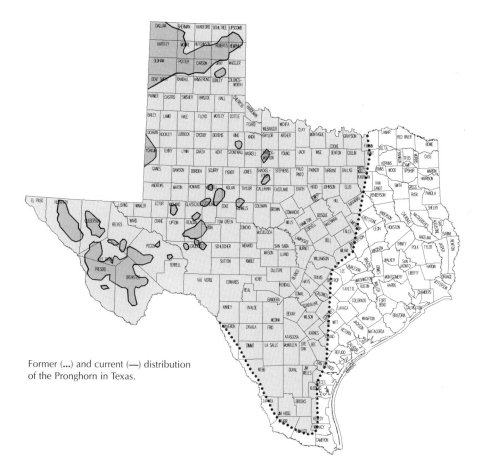

Former (...) and current (—) distribution of the Pronghorn in Texas.

Pronghorns feed entirely on vegetation, chiefly shrubs and forbs. Helmut Buechner found that their summer forage consists of about 62% forbs, 23% browse, and 15% grasses. All parts of the plants were consumed, including leaves, stems, flowers, and fruits.

Pronghorns have a particular fondness for flowers and fruits. The flowers of cutleaf daisy, white daisy, stickleaf, paper flower, and woolly senecio are consumed in large amounts. Although paper flower is poisonous to sheep and woolly senecio is poisonous to cattle, pronghorns apparently suffer no ill effects from either and consume large quantities of both. They do suffer from locoweed (*Astragalus mollissimus*), although few eat enough of it to die from its poisonous effects.

Autumn forage consists of about 59% forbs, 34% browse, and 7% grasses. More browsing is done in fall than in summer. Winter forage is the same as that in late autumn, with some variation when snow covers the ground, during which time pronghorns consume larger quantities of green woolly senecio; the dried stems and old flower parts of broomweed, stickleaf, and groundswell; old heads of grama grasses; dried leaves of goatweed; and browse species such as javelina bush, Mexican tea, and sacahuiste. Little attempt is made to paw away the snow to get the plants. Cedar is used throughout the winter where available in large quantities. Four of the most important winter foods are cutleaf daisy, paper flower, fleabane, and wild buckwheat. In late February, early annuals become available. Early spring flowers, which appear about the middle of March, are eagerly sought. More grass is taken when new green growth appears in spring.

The breeding season of the pronghorn extends from the last week in August to the first week in October. The most vigorous bucks gather small harems of 2–14 does. Young bucks frequently linger at the outskirts of the harem herd and at times attempt to steal a doe or even to interfere with a mature buck in his mating activities. The master of the harem has an endless task in keeping his does together and warding off intruding bucks. The gestation period is 7–7.5 months. The young (usually two) weigh 2–4 kg each and appear in May or June. The female hides her young ones, and at first the fawns are active only a small part of the day. The female goes to them three or more times a day so they can nurse. When about a week old, they are able to walk and run well and begin nipping at vegetation. When a month old, they graze readily on green vegetation. When the fawns are a month to 6 weeks old, does and fawns gather together in small herds that are maintained well into and sometimes throughout the winter season. Nursing continues until the fawns are about 4 months old, so that most of them are weaned about the time of the onset of mating activities.

Sexual maturity is reached at the age of about 1 year in both sexes. There is some indication, however, that young does may breed late in the year in which they are born, as is the case in white-tailed deer. The covering of the horns is shed shortly after the breeding season, beginning about the middle of October and ending in early November. New horn growth is rapid, but the prong is not evident until about the first week in December.

An apparently satisfactory method of judging the age of pronghorns is one also used for domestic sheep. Fawns are born with only two lower incisors and develop four teeth (three incisors and a canine) on each side of the lower jaw by fall. At the age of about 15 months the first middle incisors are being replaced by permanent teeth, at 2.5 years the second incisors are replaced, at 3.5 years the third incisors are replaced, and at about 4 years the pronghorn has a full set of permanent front teeth. After 4 years, age must be judged on the spread of the two middle incisors and the amount of wear on all of the teeth. The life span under natural conditions may be as much as 12–14 years, but the average age attained is probably considerably less.

It is commonly believed that these animals compete seriously with livestock for available forage on the range. According to Buechner, the total amount of competition between cattle and pronghorns is approximately 25%. Competition with sheep is much more severe, reaching at least 40%, as determined by studies in Trans-Pecos Texas. Pronghorns are far more dependent on weeds than are sheep, and where sheep have eliminated those plants on heavily stocked ranges, pronghorns cannot successfully maintain themselves.

Conservation Status. Pronghorn populations have steadily declined in association with overgrazing of grasslands by domestic livestock, uncontrolled hunting, and extensive cultivation of prairie habitat. It is a desirable game species, but despite extensive management efforts, including restocking programs begun in the 1940s and continuing even today, pronghorn numbers appear to be declining. Their decline now appears to be associated with drought and predation as well as the hand of man in the form of fencing and land use. The statewide population estimate in 1999 was 11,507, with approximately 60% of the population in the Trans-Pecos and 40% in the High Plains and Rolling Plains. The harvest in 1999 was 603 bucks. This is a species that will require serious monitoring and management in the future.

FAMILY BOVIDAE (BOVIDS)

The bovids are the largest group of artiodactyls, with 137 species worldwide. Five species occur in North America, only 2 of which are native to Texas. Several exotic species, however, have been introduced to the state from Europe, Asia, and Africa. Accounts are provided for 3 species that are free-ranging and common in parts of the state.

*Nilgai**
Boselaphus tragocamelus (Pallas)

Description. A large antelope with short, smooth horns in males. Horns average only 18 cm in length, with lengths of only 23–30 cm the maximum. Females usually do not grow horns but may occasionally. Nilgai stand 119–150 cm at the shoulder, with prominent withers giving them a backline that slopes to the rump. In bulls, powerful shoulders and a thick neck tend to accentuate this sloping profile. Overall coloration is gray to brownish gray in males; females and young are brown to orangish brown. Patches of white on the face and below the chin, extending into a broad white bib on the throat, break up the ground coloration. A narrow white band along the brisket area broadens over the abdomen and spreads between the hind legs to form a narrow rump patch that is edged with darker hair. Below the white bib hangs a tuft of hair, or beard, which may be as long as 13 cm in males. Bulls weigh 109–288 kg, with the maximum about 306 kg. Females weigh 109–213 kg.

Distribution. Nilgai are native to India and Pakistan, where they are the largest species of antelope. Nilgai were imported into Texas as game animals and have readily reproduced and established free-ranging populations. They are among the most abundant free-ranging exotic ungulate in Texas, with an estimated population of 15,000 individuals now living in south-central and southern Texas. The majority of Texas nilgai are found in free-ranging populations on several large ranches in Kenedy and Willacy counties.

Nilgai (*Boselaphus tragocamelus*). Photo courtesy Texas Parks and Wildlife Department.

Habits. Avoiding densely wooded areas, nilgai inhabit relatively dry areas of flat to rolling country with a moderate cover of thin forest or scrub. The south Texas brush country is ideally suited to these animals.

Forage preference is based primarily on availability. Nilgai both graze and browse, with grasses constituting the bulk of the diet. In Texas, mesquite, oak, partridge pea, croton, nightshade, and a variety of grasses are eaten.

Nilgai typically herd in small groups of about 10 animals, although larger groups of 20–70 are occasionally seen. Males and females remain segregated for most of the year, with bulls joining the cow-calf groups only for breeding. In Texas most mating activity occurs from December through March; however, breeding can occur throughout the year. The period of gestation is 240–258 days, and nilgai commonly bear twins. In favorable conditions females only 18 months of age can conceive, but few females mate before 3 years of age. Males become sexually mature by 2.5 years of age but usually cannot compete successfully with other males until about 4 years old.

In south Texas the life expectancy of nilgai is about 10 years, providing they survive the most vulnerable period, from birth to about 3 years of age, when adult proportions are attained. In Texas, coyotes are the primary predator of nilgai calves but are not of sufficient size to take full-grown animals. In addition to people and coyotes, cold weather can cause significant mortality among nilgai in south Texas. Nilgai have a thin coat and store only a meager winter fat reserve. Although rare in south Texas, prolonged periods of cold temperatures will dramatically reduce nilgai populations. During the severe winter of 1972–1973, 1,400 of 3,300 nilgai were killed by the weather in south Texas. This die-off was exacerbated by previous brush clearing, which resulted in forage loss and increased competition with livestock and other wildlife.

Conservation Status. This exotic is mostly found on open range, where it appears to coexist nicely with native ungulates. It has occurred in Texas longer than any other exotic ungulate and does not appear to harm native species.

American Bison
Bos bison (Linnaeus)

Description. A large, cowlike mammal with distinct hump in the shoulder region; head, neck, shoulders, and forelegs with long, shaggy hair; hind part of body with short hair; head heavy with short, curved, black horns; tail short and ending in tuft of hair; color brownish black anteriorly, brownish posteriorly. Dental formula: I 0/3, C 0/1, Pm 3/3, M 3/3 x 2 = 32. External measurements of males approach: total length, 3,400 mm; tail, 610 mm; hind foot, 610 mm; height at shoulders, 1,800 mm; females somewhat smaller. Weight of bulls, 700–1,000 kg; females, 300–400 kg.

Distribution. Before extirpation from the state, bison were widespread in the western two-thirds of Texas. Bison are now present in Texas only in private herds on some ranches, and a captive herd was recently established at Caprock Canyons State Park in the Panhandle.

Subspecies. *B. b. bison.*

American Bison (*Bos bison*). Photo by John and Gloria Tveten.

Habits. In early days the bison was found in great numbers over a vast range in North America. With the westward expansion of the white settlers, it became an object of exploitation on a tremendous scale, which resulted in its total disappearance from the East and its almost complete extermination over much of its western range. By 1825 it had become practically extinct east of the Mississippi River. The building of the transcontinental railways after 1830 hastened the slaughter of the vast herds west of the river. In the 1870s hundreds of thousands were recklessly killed for their hides and tongues. In 1877–1878 the last great slaughter of the southern herd took place south of the main transcontinental railroads. In the north their numbers likewise rapidly decreased.

When protection of the buffalo was under consideration by the Texas Legislature, Gen. Phil Sheridan opposed it, pointing out that the sooner the buffalo was eliminated the sooner the Native Americans would be starved into submission. Sure enough, before 1900 the bison passed into oblivion and the few remaining American Indians were relocated.

During the big slaughter of 1877–1878 there were reported to be 1,500 hunting outfits working out of Fort Griffin (Shackelford County) alone. More than 100,000 hides were taken in the months of December and January of that winter. From 1881 to about 1891 there were shipments of buffalo bones from Texas totaling $3 million in value.

In the late 1880s it was realized that the bison was approaching extinction. By then, there were left in the United States only a few privately owned herds and a herd in Yellowstone National Park. It was not until May 1894 that an effective law for the preservation of the bison was passed by the United States Congress, and subsequently, the various herds were built up in the United States and Canada. By 1933 the total population of bison in North America was estimated at 21,000, of which the greater part (17,000) were in Canada on the Buffalo National Park near Wainwright, Alberta.

The bison of the western United States is normally a dweller of open prairies. The subspecies *B. b. athabascae* of Canada and the Old World relative (*Bos bonasus*), however, are forest animals. Our plains bison also lacks the keen eyesight of most plains dwellers but has a keen sense of smell, suggesting that at some remote time in the past the plains bison, too, lived in woodland areas.

Bison are gregarious creatures that live together in herds, except for the old bulls, which lead a more or less solitary existence, especially in spring and early summer. During the period of rut in July and August, and again in winter, the old bulls tend to be more tolerant of the herd. Normally, bison are unobtrusive, but when angered or when called on to protect their calves they are vicious and dangerous. As with domestic cattle, old bulls are surly and may attack with slight provocation, as will cows with calves.

The daily activity of bison is much like that of domestic cattle. The chief feeding periods are early morning and late afternoon, with midday given over to cud chewing, siesta, and wallowing. Normally, nighttime is a period of rest. Formerly, the plains bison migrated seasonally, going south as far as Florida and Texas in winter and northward again in summer. Their normal gait is a plodding walk, which may break into a swinging trot or, when frightened or angered, a stiff-legged gallop.

Plains bison are predominantly grazers, feeding chiefly on grasses and secondarily on forbs. Browse species contribute slightly to their menu. Because of their similar diets, competition between bison and domestic cattle for range forage is so great that we cannot afford, for economic reasons, the return of the bison to anything like its former numbers.

The period of rut is July and August. The animals are promiscuous in mating habits, but usually only the large, mature bulls do the breeding. Young and undersized bulls are driven from the herd to linger on the outskirts and await with anticipation the opportunity to participate whenever the herd bull is off guard. As with range cattle, a scale of social dominance is established, with each bull dominating those below him on the scale.

The period of gestation is 8.5–9 months, and the calves arrive in April, May, or early June. One calf at a time is the rule; twins are rare. The young one normally is weaned in late fall, but occasionally it continues to nurse until the arrival of the next calf. Sometimes cows breed only in alternate years. Sexual maturity is reached in the third year. According to V. H. Cahalane, cows have remained productive for 40 years, indicating a life span of at least 45 years.

Conservation Status. This magnificent creature, once numbering in the millions and ranging over most of the state, was hunted to extinction in the wild in Texas. The last verified report of wild bison was from the northwestern part of the Panhandle in Dallam County in 1889.

In 1996 a visionary plan was set in motion to rebuild a herd of southern plains bison and reestablish them in the wild. This plan was made possible more than 100 years ago by the foresight of legendary rancher Charles Goodnight, owner of the JA Ranch in the Palo Duro Canyon area. Goodnight witnessed firsthand the great slaughter of the plains bison in Texas during the 1870s. Fearing that the end was near for the southern plains buffalo, Goodnight captured a small herd of the animals and relocated them to his ranch. There, for more than a century, the animals and their offspring ranged freely over the JA and surrounding ranches of west Texas. They are the last genetically pure examples of the original stock of the southern plains bison and are unique from all other bison in the world today.

By 1994, Texas Parks and Wildlife was concerned about the future of the herd, as its size had declined to fewer than 30 individuals. In 1996 it was determined by genetic testing that the animals were indeed unique, and efforts were initiated to preserve the herd. Later that year, the owners of the JA Ranch donated the bison to Texas Parks and Wildlife. The animals were transferred to breeding facilities at Caprock Canyons State Park in the winter of 1997–1998, and the Texas State Bison Herd was established. The short-term goal of Texas Parks and Wildlife is to preserve these invaluable specimens and allow the population to grow. The long-range goal is to restore the southern plains bison on a 100,000-acre refuge within its historic Panhandle range as part of a native prairie ecosystem. It is hoped that in the near future these magnificent and unique creatures will once again roam the open plains of Texas.

Bighorn Sheep
Ovis canadensis Shaw

Description. A large, dark brown sheep with heavy, tapering, curled brown horns in males (horns much smaller and less curled in females) and conspicuous white rump patch; pelage hairy, not woolly; four black hooves on each foot; tail short; mammae two. Dental formula: I 0/3, C 0/1, Pm 3/3, M 3/3 x 2 = 32 (lower canine is shaped like an incisor). External measurements of males average: total length, 1,763 mm; tail, 107 mm; hind foot, 439 mm; of females, 1,431-107-407 mm. Weight of rams, 75–150 kg; of females, 45–65 kg.

Distribution. Formerly ranged throughout the isolated mountain ranges of the Trans-Pecos; however, native populations are now extirpated. The last native sheep were seen in the Sierra Diablo in 1959, when the total population was estimated at 14. Recent introductions of bighorn sheep in the Sierra Diablo–Baylor–Beach mountains complex, the Van Horn Mountains, Elephant Mountain Wildlife Management Area, and Black Gap Wildlife Management Area have resulted in small, wild populations in those areas.

Subspecies. The native subspecies was *O. c. mexicana,* but other subspecies have been introduced.

Bighorn Sheep (*Ovis canadensis*). Photo by John and Gloria Tveten.

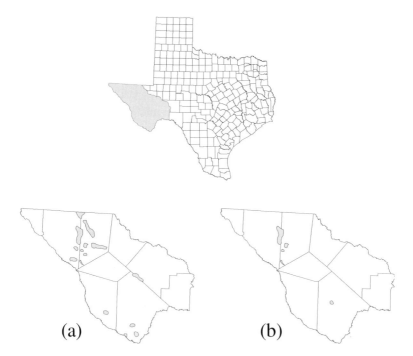

Former (a) and current (b) distribution of the Bighorn Sheep in Texas. Native populations of bighorn are now extinct.

Habits. In general, bighorn sheep are inhabitants of rough, rocky, mountainous terrain. They are not forest dwellers but prefer bluffs and steep slopes where the vegetation is sparse and the view unobstructed.

Beds are conspicuous indicators of the presence of sheep. Two distinct types are utilized. The day bed, used during midday siestas, is a temporary affair constructed when and where the individual sheep decides to rest. Usually, each adult animal, particularly among the rams, excavates a shallow depression by executing three or four pawing scratches with each forefoot before lying down. Lambs and yearlings usually omit the pawing activity. The night beds are more elaborate structures. They are usually situated on steep, rocky slopes, on top of rocky rims, or on a slope between two bluffs. In such places the sheep receive adequate protection, for they have an unobstructed view in all directions except uphill, from which direction the approach of a predator would be signaled by rolling stones. The animals tend to bunch together at night. Individual beds are ovoid in shape with the long axis on the contour of the slope. Beds are typically 7–10 cm in depth, about 75 cm in length, and 60 cm in width. No bedding of any sort is utilized; the animals lie on the bare earth. Beds in constant use are rimmed with piles of feces and strong with the odor of urine.

The food of bighorn sheep depends on availability and season. In western Texas, deer brush, sotol, and ocotillo were utilized extensively by bighorns. Vernon

Bailey reported them as feeding on mountain mahogany, Mexican tea, trumpet flower, mock orange, prickly pear, wild onions, and penstemon. The fruits of datil (*Yucca*) and prickly pear are especially choice foods in the desert areas. Bighorns rarely need water. Apparently, they derive sufficient water from the green and succulent vegetation on which they feed.

The breeding season begins in November and continues for a period of approximately 6 weeks. The rams do considerable fighting in this period, and usually the larger and stronger ones prevent the weaker ones from mating. The bighorn ram does not assemble and guard a harem but moves from flock to flock seeking ewes that are ready to mate. Ewes become sexually mature in 2.5 years and give birth to their first lambs at 3 years of age. Rams under 3 years of age appear to take little, if any, active part in breeding activities. The gestation period is approximately 180 days. The first lambs are born in mid-May, with others appearing until about mid-June. Usually, only one lamb is produced, but twins are fairly frequent. The lambs are weak and helpless at first, but they develop rapidly and by the age of 1 week are able to follow the ewes about with ease.

Age in bighorn sheep can be estimated by examination of the teeth. The formula at birth is I 0/3, C 0/1, Pm 2/2, M 0/0 (milk dentition); at 8 months, I 0/3, C 0/1, Pm 3/3, M 1/1 (molars permanent); at 15–18 months, I 0/3, C 0/1, Pm 3/3, M 2/2 (molars permanent); 24 months, first (middle) incisor is shed and replaced by permanent tooth; 36 months, first two premolars are shed and replaced by permanent teeth; 42 months, third molars are fully erupted, second milk incisor replaced, last premolars shed and replaced; 48 months, full set of permanent teeth.

Conservation Status. At one time bighorn sheep were widespread in Trans-Pecos Texas, but the advance of civilization and the inroads of domestic sheep on the range of the wild animals led to a steady decline of the bighorn population. In spite of laws affording full protection to the sheep, they continued to decline in numbers. Today the native population is extinct. The Texas Parks and Wildlife Department has established wild-trapped sheep from other states in several Trans-Pecos mountain ranges. The 2000 bighorn sheep census indicated a total of 381 individuals in the Trans-Pecos.

*Barbary Sheep or Aoudad**
Ammotragus lervia (Pallas)

Description. A relatively large sheep with horns curving outward, backward, and then inward and marked with strong transverse wrinkles; horns of females similar but somewhat smaller; tail relatively long, reaching nearly to hocks and with long hairs on terminal half; a conspicuous growth of long hair on throat, chest, and upperparts of front legs; no beard as is found in goats; upperparts and outer surface of legs uniform rufous or grayish brown; blackish middorsal line from head to middle of back; flanks, inner surface of legs and belly whitish, but the chest

Barbary Sheep or Aoudad (*Ammotragus lervia*). Photo courtesy Texas Parks and Wildlife Department.

colored like the sides; horns yellowish brown, darkening with age, set close together (nearly touching at the bases), and attaining a length of 50–80 cm. External measurements of a moderately large adult male: total length, 1,650 mm; tail, 141 mm; hind foot (tip of hoof to hock), 363 mm; ear, 116 mm; height at shoulder, 950 mm. Weight of males up to 145 kg; females to 65 kg. Dental formula: I 0/3, C 0/0, Pm 3/3, M 3/3 x 2 = 30.

Distribution. Native to the dry mountainous areas of northern Africa; introduced into the Palo Duro Canyon area of Texas in 1957–1958, where it has become firmly established. Also present in the Edwards Plateau, Trans-Pecos, South Texas Plains, Rolling Plains, and Post Oak Savannah regions as a result of private introductions.

Habits. This sheep is adapted to a dry, rough, barren, and waterless habitat, much as is the native bighorn sheep of our southwestern deserts. Consequently, it is quite likely that the two species could not survive together in the same area because of competition between them.

These sheep live in small groups comprising old and young animals of both sexes. They are expert climbers and can ascend and descend slopes so precipitous that humans can negotiate them only with great difficulty. Consequently, they are difficult to hunt.

Their food consists of a wide variety of vegetation including grasses, forbs, and shrubs. Apparently, they are capable of producing metabolic water and can survive for long periods without access to fresh water. When water is available, however, they utilize it for both drinking and bathing.

In studies conducted in New Mexico, Herman Ogren found that 79 species of plants were included in the diet of these sheep; of those, 13 were grasses, 20 were shrubs, and the remainder forbs. Mountain mahogany (*Cercocarpus breviflorus*) was the most sought-after single plant. Throughout the year, this species constituted nearly 22% of the items found in rumens of the sheep. Ogren found some seasonal variation in the diet. In winter, grasses were 86% of the rumen contents; browse, 11%; forbs, 3%. In spring, summer, and fall the browse species, mainly oaks and mountain mahogany, made up about 60% of the diet; grasses, about 26%; and forbs (various species of weeds), the balance. Over a year, browse species composed 49% of the diet; grasses, 42%; forbs, 9%.

The breeding season appears to be rather extended, but most of the breeding is concentrated in the 2 months from mid-September to mid-November. The gestation period is about 160 days. Consequently, most of the lambs are born between late February and late April, but some lambs are born as late as November.

According to Ogren, females may become sexually mature at the age of 8 months, but normally they are older. All females 19 months of age or older that were collected in the fall and winter season were gravid, lactating, or ovulating.

Conservation Status. These sheep were first brought to the United States in about 1900 and have been reared in zoos and on private preserves for a number of years. They were first released in the wild in New Mexico in 1950 and in Texas in 1957, when 31 were released southwest of Claude in Armstrong County. Thirteen more were released near Quitaque. Today they exist along much of the eastern edge of the Llano Estacado, in the rough country of the Trans-Pecos, and on parts of the Edwards Plateau, with a total population thought to exceed 5,000.

Whether this animal will eventually become a pest, as have most of the successful introduced animals, remains to be seen. There is some evidence that they compete directly with mule deer for food. They also have been observed feeding on winter wheat crops growing adjacent to Palo Duro Canyon. In the Trans-Pecos, Barbary sheep may have a deleterious effect on bighorn sheep reintroduction efforts.

The full effect of aoudads on Texas wildlife and rangelands has not been determined but should be carefully monitored in the future. It should be a priority to keep this species away from areas where efforts are ongoing to introduce native sheep.

Blackbuck*

Antilope cervicapra (Linnaeus)

Description. A medium-sized antelope with ringed, unbranched, corkscrew horns that rise above the head of males in a tall, V-shaped pattern. Measured from base to tip, horns reach up to 79 cm in length, although Texas blackbuck rarely have horns exceeding 58 cm. Normally, females are hornless. Coloration in mature males is black dorsally; females and young males are tan. All blackbuck have white eye rings, chin patch, chest, belly, and inner legs. In the nonbreeding season, after the spring molt, adult males may lighten considerably and retain their darkest coloration only on the face and legs. In Texas, adult males average 38 kg in weight, with a range of 20–57 kg. Females weigh 20–33 kg, averaging 27 kg.

Distribution. Native to India and Pakistan, blackbuck were originally released in Texas in the Edwards Plateau (Kerr County) in 1932. Now there are approximately 20,000 individuals living in the wild, but relatively few are found outside controlled areas.

Habits. In India and Pakistan, blackbuck were once widespread in plains and open woodlands; wet coastal areas, western deserts, and northern mountains limited their distribution. Today, extensive hunting and habitat destruction have restricted blackbuck to only small, isolated populations in their former native habitat.

Blackbuck (*Antilope cervicapra*). Photo by John and Gloria Tveten.

More than 80% of the blackbuck in Texas inhabit the Edwards Plateau region, where the patchwork of open grassland and brush provides both excellent forage and cover. Their range is restricted to the north and west by cold winters, to the south by coyote predation, and to the east by parasitism.

Blackbuck prefer to graze on short to midlength grasses but also browse on common brush species. Forage selection is primarily determined by availability, with sedges, fall witchgrass, mesquite, and live oak commonly eaten. Forb use by blackbuck is low.

Adult males are highly territorial and defend areas ranging from 1.2 to 12 ha in size against trespass by other males. Female groups may graze through male territories, and breeding activity may take place at such times, but other males are excluded. Young males and bucks without territories form their own all-male groups. At physical maturity (2–2.5 years of age) young bucks may split from the all-male group to establish or win their own territory.

Breeding may take place at any time of the year; however, bucks are more active in spring and fall. Fawns are born at all seasons, but the fewest births occur in winter. The length of gestation is about 5 months, and within a month of parturition the female may breed again. A single fawn is the rule.

Females reach sexual maturity by 8 months of age but usually do not breed until nearly 2 years of age. Physical maturity is reached at 1 year. Males mature later than females and are able to breed at 18 months of age. The life span is up to 15 years.

Conservation Status. This exotic is mostly found on managed ranches, many under high fence, but with several free-living individuals now established. Its effect on the native flora and fauna has not been fully determined and should be carefully monitored so that action can be taken, as necessary, to protect our native wildlife.

ORDER RODENTIA
Rodents

T he name "Rodentia" is derived from the Latin verb "rodere" (to gnaw), an allusion to the gnawing habits of the group. Among North American mammals, rodents are unique in that the incisors are reduced in number to one on each side above and below, in the absence of canines, and in the presence of never more than two premolars in each jaw above and one below. The dental formula varies from I 1/1, C 0/0, Pm 0/0, M 3/3 x 2 = 16 to I 1/1, C 0/0, Pm 2/1, M 3/3 x 2 = 22. Most animals assigned to the order are small in size; some, for example the beaver, may exceed 25 kg in weight. Rodents constitute more than one-third of the known kinds of mammals, and individually they are the most abundant mammal in many sections of the world. Sixty-five species of native rodents occupy Texas, making this the most diverse group of mammals in our state.

In habits, members of this order are diverse. Most of them are nocturnal or crepuscular; ground squirrels and tree squirrels are strictly diurnal; others may be active either by day or by night. Considerable adaptive radiation occurs in the group. Some species (pocket gophers) are fossorial; others are aquatic (beaver), arboreal (tree squirrel), volant (flying squirrels), or terrestrial (cotton rats). Most rodents feed on vegetation, but a few species, notably the grasshopper mouse, feed extensively on animal matter. Most rodents are active throughout the year, but others, notably ground squirrels, may hibernate for several months.

KEY TO THE RODENTS OF TEXAS

1. Presence of external, fur-lined cheek pouches 2

   Absence of external, fur-lined cheek pouches 16

2. Front feet much larger than hind feet; ear (pinna) short and inconspicuous; tail about half the length of head and body (pocket gophers) 3

   Front feet much smaller than hind feet; ear (pinna) conspicuous; tail as long as (or longer than) head and body (pocket mice and kangaroo rats) 5

3. Upper incisors not grooved on outer face; claws of front feet relatively small and slender. *Thomomys bottae* (Botta's pocket gopher), p. 327.

   Upper incisors distinctly grooved on outer surface; claws of front feet large and long (longest ones about 15 mm) 4

4. Upper incisors with one deep groove; feet blackish. *Cratogeomys castanops* (yellow-faced pocket gopher), p. 346.

Upper incisor with two distinct grooves; feet whitish (species of the genus *Geomys*):

> Eight species of the genus *Geomys* occur in Texas. These are cryptic species, identifiable primarily on the basis of geographic distribution and characters of the karyotype and genes. Only specialists working with prepared study specimens can identify them using morphological features.
>
> (1) *Geomys arenarius* (desert pocket gopher) occurs in El Paso County in far western Texas, p. 330.
>
> (2) *Geomys attwateri* (Attwater's pocket gopher) occurs in the south-central part of eastern Texas, p. 332.
>
> (3) *Geomys breviceps* (Baird's pocket gopher) occurs in eastern and northeastern Texas, p. 334.
>
> (4) *Geomys bursarius* (plains pocket gopher) occurs in northwestern and north-central Texas, p. 336.
>
> (5) *Geomys knoxjonesi* (Jones's pocket gopher) occurs on the southwestern plains of Texas, p. 339.
>
> (6) *Geomys personatus* (Texas pocket gopher) occurs along the southern coastal plain and inland areas of south Texas, p. 341.
>
> (7) *Geomys streckeri* (Strecker's pocket gopher) occurs in parts of two south Texas counties (Dimmit and Zavala) in the vicinity of Carrizo Springs and Crystal City, p. 343.
>
> (8) *Geomys texensis* (Llano pocket gopher) occurs in the Llano Basin region of the Hill Country in central Texas and in an isolated area on the northern border of the South Texas Plains, p. 344.

5. Hind legs more than twice as long as front legs; tail long and bushy at end; head broad, 25 mm or more in width (kangaroo rats)..........6

   Hind legs less than twice as long as front legs; head about 15 mm in width (pocket mice) 10

6. Large size, total length of adults 300 mm or more; tip of tail with conspicuous white banner..7

   Smaller, total length of adults usually less than 250 mm; tip of tail usually dusky, not white 8

7. Hind foot (from tip of longest claw to heel) 50 mm or more in length; length of tail about 200 mm. *Dipodomys spectabilis* (banner-tailed kangaroo rat), p. 372.

   Hind foot less than 50 mm; tail normally less than 200 mm. *Dipodomys elator* (Texas kangaroo rat), p. 366.

8. Hind foot with five toes (one is very small and difficult to detect)...9

   Hind foot with only four toes. *Dipodomys merriami* (Merriam's kangaroo rat), p. 368.

9. Pelage long and silky, brownish; mastoid bullae greatly inflated, giving skull a triangular appearance; interparietal narrow and triangular in shape. *Dipodomys ordii* (Ord's kangaroo rat), p. 370.

Pelage short and coarse, with orangish cast; mastoid bullae less inflated; interparietal broad and rectangular to roundish in shape. *Dipodomys compactus* (Gulf Coast kangaroo rat), p. 364.

10. Size small, total length 100 to 130 mm; weight 6 to 8 grams; pelage silky and soft 11

   Size larger, total length 150 mm or more; pelage harsh, often bristly, never silky...12

11. Length of tail usually 60 mm or more; total length usually 120 mm or more; length of skull usually more than 21 mm; postauricular patch inconspicuous. *Perognathus flavescens* (plains pocket mouse), p. 349.

   Length of tail usually less than 60 mm; total length usually less than 120 mm; length of skull usually less than 21 mm; postauricular patch conspicuous. Silky pocket mice:

   > Two species of silky pocket mice occur in Texas, but only specialists working with prepared study specimens can identify them.
   > (1) *Perognathus flavus* (silky pocket mouse) occurs in the Panhandle and Trans-Pecos portions of Texas, p. 350.
   > (2) *Perognathus merriami* (Merriam's pocket mouse) occurs in the Great Plains, central, and southern regions of Texas, p. 352.

12. Upper incisors plain, not grooved, on outer face; pelage spiny to touch. *Liomys irroratus* (Mexican spiny pocket mouse), p. 375.

   Upper incisors distinctly grooved on outer face...............................13

13. Length of tail less than length of head and body (tail laid forward over back does not reach snout), and without terminal tuft; weight 30 to 47 grams. *Chaetodipus hispidus* (hispid pocket mouse), p. 357.

   Length of tail greater than length of head and body (tip of tail extends beyond snout when laid forward), and with terminal tuft....14

14. Rump with strongly developed and conspicuous black-tipped spines projecting beyond normal guard hairs; small white patch present at base of ear. *Chaetodipus nelsoni* (Nelson's pocket mouse), p. 362.

   Rump spines absent or, if present, fewer and less conspicuous and not black-tipped; small white patches at base of ear absent 15

15. Rump spines absent; interparietal separated from mastoid bulla by thin projections of the parietal and supraoccipital. *Chaetodipus eremicus* (Chihuahuan desert pocket mouse), p. 355.

   Weak rump spines present; interparietal in contact with mastoid bulla, or nearly so. *Chaetodipus intermedius* (rock pocket mouse), p. 360.

16. Tail paddle-shaped, naked, scaly; hind feet webbed; size large. *Castor canadensis* (American beaver), p. 377.

   Tail not paddle-shaped..17

17. Pelage with intermixed sharp quills; adults large, 5–11 kg. *Erethizon dorsatum* (North American porcupine), p. 451.

    Pelage without quills 18

18. Lower jaw with four cheek teeth on each side 19

    Lower jaw with only three cheek teeth on each side 29

19. Hind feet fully webbed; adults weigh up to 12 kg; tail long, naked, and nearly circular in cross section. *Myocastor coypus* (nutria), p. 454.

    Hind feet not fully webbed 20

20. Flying membrane between front leg and hind leg on each side; color wood brown above, white below. *Glaucomys volans* (southern flying squirrel), p. 325.

    Legs normal, no flying membrane 21

21. Upperparts striped or distinctly spotted or both 22

    Upperparts not striped or distinctly spotted 26

22. Upperparts striped 23

    Upperparts spotted 25

23. One white stripe on each side; underside of tail grayish white (held over back while animal is running); upperparts grizzled grayish. *Ammospermophilus interpres* (Texas antelope squirrel), p. 304.

    Three or more white or light stripes on upperparts 24

24. Six continuous, whitish stripes alternating with seven rows of whitish spots; ground color brown. *Spermophilus tridecemlineatus* (thirteen-lined ground squirrel), p. 311.

    Four whitish stripes alternating with five dark brown stripes; sides of face striped. *Tamias canipes* (gray-footed chipmunk), p. 303.

25. Spots in 10 or more distinct rows; tail narrowly bushy and about three times as long as hind foot. *Spermophilus mexicanus* (Mexican ground squirrel), p. 306.

    Spots scattered, never in distinct rows; tail about twice as long as hind foot. *Spermophilus spilosoma* (spotted ground squirrel), p. 309.

26. General color yellowish brown; tail very short (1.5 times length of hind foot) and black-tipped. *Cynomys ludovicianus* (black-tailed prairie dog), p. 316.

    General color gray, brown, or blackish; tail long and bushy 27

27. Belly reddish or rusty in color; upperparts grayish; hind foot 70 mm or more. *Sciurus niger* (eastern fox squirrel), p. 322.

    Belly whitish or grayish; not reddish; hind foot 70 mm or less 28

28. Belly white; upperparts gray, unspotted. *Sciurus carolinensis* (eastern gray squirrel), p. 319.

Belly grayish, back grayish with faint light spots, or shoulders and head black and rump grayish or brownish. *Spermophilus variegatus* (rock squirrel), p. 314.

29. Tail flattened laterally, sparsely haired and scaly; hind toes fringed with stiff hairs; length of adults about 45 cm. *Ondatra zibethicus* (muskrat), p. 449.

    Tail round, sparingly haired or bushy 30

30. Enamel pattern of molar teeth with transverse or oblique folds or triangles..31

    Enamel pattern of molar teeth with two or three rows of cusps (unworn condition) or roughly circular with slight lateral indentations (worn condition) 40

31. Mouse size, total length usually less than 150 mm; tail less than 50 mm; ears nearly hidden in the fur..32

    Rat size, total length of adults 225 mm or more; tail 100 mm or more; ears conspicuous or partly hidden in the dense fur 34

32. Tail less than 25 mm in length; hind food usually less than 18 mm; color glossy, reddish brown. *Microtus pinetorum* (woodland vole), p. 446.

    Tail more than 25 mm in length; hind foot usually more than 18 mm; color brownish gray or blackish..33

33. Enamel pattern of third upper molar with no more than two closed triangles, often with no closed triangles, hence with three loops; never more than two inner reentrant angles. *Microtus ochrogaster* (prairie vole), p. 444.

    Enamel pattern of third upper molar with three closed triangles or, if with only two closed triangles, then with three inner reentrant angles. *Microtus mexicanus* (Mexican vole), p. 443.

34. Ears conspicuous; tail in adults usually 150 mm or longer; eyes large, black, and bulging in life; fur rather soft; whiskers long, usually more than 50 mm (woodrats) 35

    Ears partly hidden in dense pelage; tail 100–125 mm long; pelage rather harsh; whiskers 25–35 mm long (cotton rats) 38

35. First upper molar tooth with a relatively well-developed and deep antero-internal fold extending halfway across the crown; tail not sharply bicolored; dorsal color olivaceous, lateral sides buffy in color..36

    Antero-internal reentrant angle of first upper molar poorly developed, shallow, and not across the crown; tail distinctly bicolored; dorsal color steel gray or buffy brown; lateral sides gray or brown in color 37

36. Total length of adults more than 375 mm. *Neotoma floridana* (eastern woodrat), p. 429.

    Total length of adults less than 375 mm. *Neotoma mexicana* (Mexican woodrat), p. 435.

37. Upper parts typically steel gray; gular hairs dark at base. *Neotoma micropus* (southern plains woodrat), p. 436.

Upper parts not steel gray, washed with buffy hairs; gular hairs white at base. *Neotoma leucodon* (eastern white-throated woodrat), p. 432

38. Underparts buffy to ochraceous; tail entirely black; top surface of feet buffy. *Sigmodon fulviventer* (tawny-bellied cotton rat), p. 423.

Underparts whitish and not buffy or ochraceous; tail bicolor, dark above and light below; top surface of feet whitish...........................39

39. Snout and eye rings yellowish or orangish and conspicuously different from color of back and sides; hind foot usually less than 30 mm; total length usually less than 260 mm. *Sigmodon ochrognathus* (yellow-nosed cotton rat), p. 427.

Snout and eye rings not conspicuous and same color as sides and back; hind foot usually more than 30 mm; total length usually more than 260 mm. *Sigmodon hispidus* (hispid cotton rat), p. 424.

40. Rat size, total length 230 mm or more...41

Mouse size, total length usually less than 200 mm..........................43

41. Cusps on upper molars in two rows; hind foot narrow and slender (rice rats):

> There are two species of rice rats in Texas that only a specialist can identify with certainty.
>
> (1) *Oryzomys palustris* (marsh rice rat), a grayish brown form characteristic of marshy areas along the coast from Brownsville northward into deep East Texas, p. 381.
>
> (2) *Oryzomys couesi* (Coues's rice rat), a tawny form that occurs in marshy areas in extreme south Texas (Hidalgo and Cameron counties), p. 380.

Cusps on upper molars in three rows (introduced rats).................42

42. Tail slender and as long as or longer than head and body (tail reaches to or beyond nose when laid forward); color brownish or black; weight to 225 g. *Rattus rattus* (roof rat), p. 440.

Tail chunkier and shorter than head and body; color brownish; weight to 450 g. *Rattus norvegicus* (Norway rat), p. 438.

43. Outer face of each upper incisor with deep groove (harvest mice) 44

Outer face of upper incisors not grooved...47

44. Tail much longer than head and body (projects beyond nose when laid forward along back); last lower molar with dentine in the form of an S. *Reithrodontomys fulvescens* (fulvous harvest mouse), p. 383.

Tail shorter than or about as long as head and body; last lower molar with dentine in the form of a C...45

45. Color rich brown to blackish brown; a distinct labial shelf or ridge, often with distinct cusplets on first and second lower molars. *Reithrodontomys humulis* (eastern harvest mouse), p. 386.

   Color mainly grayish brown or light buff; no distinct labial shelf or ridge on first and second molars...46

46. Tail shorter than head and body; dark dorsal strip on tail narrow, approximately one-fourth diameter of tail; breadth of braincase not exceeding 9.5 mm. *Reithrodontomys montanus* (plains harvest mouse), p. 390.

   Tail length about equal to, or slightly longer than, head and body; dark dorsal stripe on tail broader and indistinct, approximately half diameter of tail; breadth of braincase of adults usually over 9.5 mm. *Reithrodontomys megalotis* (western harvest mouse), p. 388.

47. Upper incisors with distinct notch at tip when viewed from the side; distinctly musky odor. *Mus musculus* (house mouse), p. 441.

   Upper incisors lacking distinct notch at tip 48

48. Total length of adults 100 mm or less; tail short, 35 mm, about three times length of hind foot; color blackish or sooty. *Baiomys taylori* (northern pygmy mouse), p. 416.

   Total length of adults 125 mm or more; color not blackish or sooty 49

49. Tail less than 60% of head and body; coronoid process of mandible extends high above level of condyloid process; soles of feet furred (grasshopper mice) 50

   Tail more than 60% of head and body; coronoid process of mandible does not ascend above tip of condyloid process; soles of feet only slightly furred (deer mice and relatives)..51

50. Tail less than half length of head and body; crown length of maxillary tooth row 4 mm or more. *Onychomys leucogaster* (northern grasshopper mouse), p. 421.

   Tail more than half length of head and body; crown length of maxillary tooth row 3.9 mm or less. *Onychomys arenicola* (Mearns's grasshopper mouse), p. 419.

51. General color golden yellow. *Ochrotomys nuttalli* (golden mouse), p. 414.

   General color brown, buff, or gray (white-footed mice) 52

52. Tail much shorter than head and body...53

   Tail as long as or longer than head and body 55

53. Hind foot (of adults) greater than 23 mm. *Peromyscus gossypinus* (cotton mouse), p. 400.

   Hind foot (of adults) less than 23 mm 54

54. Tail with narrow and distinct dorsal stripe; total length of adults usually less than 170 mm; length of tail usually less than 75 mm; greatest length of skull usually less than 26 mm. *Peromyscus maniculatus* (deer mouse), p. 404.

    Tail with broad dorsal stripe and not sharply bicolored; total length of adults usually more than 170 mm; length of tail usually more than 75 mm; greatest length of skull usually more than 26 mm. *Peromyscus leucopus* (white-footed mouse), p. 402.

55. Nasals decidedly exceeded by premaxillae; two principal outer angles of first and second upper molars simple, without (or at most with rudimentary) accessory cusps or enamel lophs; sole of hind foot naked to end of ankle; no pectoral mammae; inguinal mammae, 2-2. *Peromyscus eremicus* (cactus mouse), p. 397.

    Nasals slightly or not at all exceeded by premaxillae; two principal outer angles of first and second upper molars with well-developed accessory tubercles or enamel lophs; sole of hind foot hairy on proximal fourth to ankle; pectoral mammae, 1-1, inguinal mammae, 2-2 56

56. Ear longer than hind foot; tail about as long as head and body (except in *P. t. comanche,* in which it is longer); bullae unusually inflated. *Peromyscus truei* (pinyon mouse), p. 412.

    Ear equal to or shorter than hind foot; tail usually longer than head and body; bullae moderately or less inflated 57

57. Hind foot length of adults more than 24 mm. *Peromyscus attwateri* (Texas mouse), p. 392.

    Hind foot length of adults less than 24 mm 58

58. Tarsal joints of ankles white like upper side of hind foot; baculum with long cartilaginous spine at its terminal end. *Peromyscus pectoralis* (white-ankled mouse), p. 410.

    Dusky color of hind leg extending to end more or less over tarsal joint; baculum with a short cartilaginous spine at its terminal end 59

59. Dorsal coloration grayish black, and often like immature pelage; top of head and flanks of adults predominantly grayish; first two lower molars usually with one or more accessory lophids or stylids. *Peromyscus nasutus* (northern rock mouse), p. 407.

    Dorsal coloration with considerable yellow or buff; top of head same color as back; flanks of adults predominantly bright yellowish brown; first of two lower molars usually without any accessory lophids or stylids. *Peromyscus boylii* (brush mouse), p. 395.

FAMILY SCIURIDAE (SQUIRRELS AND ALLIES)

This family includes chipmunks, marmots, ground squirrels, prairie dogs, flying squirrels, and tree squirrels. Most squirrels are diurnal, and they are among the more visible of rodents. All are strongly vegetarian, feeding on a variety of nuts, fruits, barks, buds, and leaves. Texas is home to six genera and ten species of squirrels.

Gray-footed Chipmunk
Tamias canipes V. Bailey

Description. A small, grayish squirrel, the upperparts marked with four whitish and three to five brownish stripes; the nape and shoulders usually with a distinct wash of smoke gray; dark dorsal stripes black or brownish black; inner pair of light stripes smoke gray, outer pair grayish white. Dental formula: I 1/1, C 0/0, Pm 2/1, M 3/3 x 2 = 22. External measurements average: total length, 225 mm; tail, 102 mm; hind foot, 35 mm.

Distribution. These are forest-dwelling chipmunks that occur in Texas only in the higher elevations (1,800–2,500 m) of the Sierra Diablo and Guadalupe Mountains in the Trans-Pecos region (Culberson County).

Subspecies. *T. c. canipes.*

Habits. Favorite haunts of the gray-footed chipmunk are down logs at the edge of clearings. They occur also in dense stands of mixed timber (oaks, pines, firs) and on brushy hillsides, particularly where crevices in rocks offer retreats. When alarmed, they usually seek seclusion in crevices or underground burrows; occasionally they take to the trees.

Gray-footed Chipmunk (*Tamias canipes*). Photo courtesy U.S. Fish and Wildlife Service.

Their food consists of a variety of items such as acorns, seeds of Douglas fir, currants, gooseberries, mushrooms, green vegetation, and insects.

Little is known of their breeding habits. The young are about half-grown in midsummer and almost full-grown in September and October, but one female taken in August in the Guadalupe Mountains contained four embryos. One litter a year is normal.

These chipmunks are most numerous in coniferous forests where fallen logs, in which they often build their nests, are common. In addition to the two populations in Culberson County, Texas, they have been recorded from three areas in New Mexico. Hugh Genoways and associates in 1979 obtained nine specimens near the Bowl and in Upper Dog Canyon at the higher elevations of Guadalupe Mountains National Park.

Conservation Status. The status of this species appears to be good within the protected confines of Guadalupe Mountains National Park. Clearly, however, in Texas it could be vulnerable to local catastrophic events such as a massive fire within the national park.

Texas Antelope Squirrel

Ammospermophilus interpres (Merriam)

Description. A small ground squirrel with one narrow white line on each side of back from shoulder to rump, and underside of tail grayish white, the lateral tail hairs with three black bands; upperparts vinaceous buff in summer and drab gray

Texas Antelope Squirrel (*Ammospermophilus interpres*). Photo by John and Gloria Tveten.

in winter; ears short, hardly more than a rim; tail held over back in life. Dental formula: I 1/1, C 0/0, Pm 2/1, M 3/3 x 2 = 22. External measurements average: total length, 226 mm; tail, 74 mm; hind foot, 38 mm. Weight of males, 104 (94–121) g; of females, 104 (84–115) g.

Distribution. Known throughout the Trans-Pecos region (and not just adjacent to the drainages of the Rio Grande and the Pecos River), extending eastward to the extreme western portion of the Edwards Plateau, where specimens have been reported from Crane, Crockett, Reagan, Upton, and Val Verde counties, and northward to the southern edge of the High Plains in Gaines County.

Subspecies. Monotypic species.

Habits. These squirrels are characteristic of desert regions in the Southwest, where they live chiefly around the edges of the lower valleys and in the low hills. They seem to prefer hard-surfaced, gravelly washes or rocky hill slopes and are less common or entirely absent on level, sandy terrain. On the Edwards Plateau, they seem to be limited to rocky, broken terrain, with little ground cover. In this area, they are often associated with creosote and juniper vegetation.

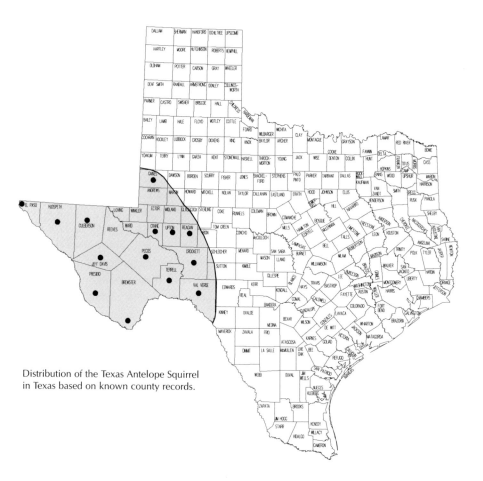

Distribution of the Texas Antelope Squirrel in Texas based on known county records.

They usually live in burrows, but crevices in and among rocks may serve as den sites. They also make use of abandoned burrows of other rodents. Their burrows are usually situated at the side of a clump of bushes, a boulder, or in a cut bank. There is usually no mound of earth to mark the entrance. One burrow found in a cut bank was excavated in friable soil under a bed of hardpan about 1 m below the top of the ground and 50 cm above the roadbed. The main tunnel was 8.7 cm in diameter, 3 m long, and lay parallel to and about 30 cm back from the face of the cut. Access was by three openings. Midway in the tunnel was the nest chamber, which measured 12.5 cm in width, 17.5 cm in length, and 10 cm in height. An accessory loop back of the nest and two blind pockets at one end of the main tunnel completed the system. The nest was composed of rabbit fur, shredded bark, feathers, dried grasses, and bits of cotton.

Ammos are fidgety, nervous creatures and seldom are still for long. They are nimble-footed and can run with surprising speed, and they are well adapted for climbing. Their peculiar habit of carrying the tail arched forward over the back, exposing to view the contrastingly colored undersurface, is a readily usable field characteristic. The nervous flicking of the tail when the animals are excited and the mellow, rolling, trill-like calls further help to identify them. They spend most of the time on the ground, but they may be seen in the tops of low bushes, yuccas, and prickly pears, where they also forage. Available evidence indicates that at lower elevations these ground squirrels do not hibernate.

Antelope ground squirrels are one of the few mammals that may remain active during the hottest parts of west Texas summer days. By occasionally retreating to a shady spot where they lie outstretched, with their limbs spread-eagled and their belly in contact with the cooler terrain, the squirrels can lose excess heat accumulated during their activities and maintain a safe body temperature. After such rests the squirrels once again venture into the summer sun to conduct their business. Their food is largely a wide variety of plant materials, including the fruits, seeds, and stems of yucca, juniper, salt grass, prickly pear and cholla cactus, mesquite, sotol, and creosote bush, but insects may be consumed as well.

Breeding begins in February. One litter of 5–14 young, based on embryo counts, is reared each year, but there is evidence that some females may rear a second brood. The young ones remain in the nest until they are about one-fourth grown, at which time they venture above ground and begin eating solid foods. Information on other phases of reproduction appears to be lacking.

Conservation Status. This species is widely distributed in western Texas, and there does not appear to be any immediate threat to its status.

Mexican Ground Squirrel

Spermophilus mexicanus (Erxleben)

Description. A rather small ground squirrel with usually nine rows of squarish white spots on back; tail about two-fifths of total length, moderately bushy; ears

Mexican Ground Squirrel (*Spermophilus mexicanus*). Photo by John and Gloria Tveten.

short and rounded; upperparts wood brown or buffy brown with rows of conspicuous white spots; sides and underparts whitish or pinkish buff. Dental formula: I 1/1, C 0/0, Pm 2/1, M 3/3 x 2 = 22. External measurements average: total length, 301 mm; tail, 118 mm; hind foot, 41 mm. Weight of males, 227–330 g; of females, 137–198 g.

Distribution. Occurs throughout much of southern and western Texas (west to Culberson, Jeff Davis, and Presidio counties and possibly into Hudspeth and El Paso counties in the Trans-Pecos), north almost to the Red River just east of the Panhandle. This is the most common ground squirrel residing on the Edwards Plateau.

Subspecies. *S. m. parvidens.*

Habits. Mexican ground squirrels inhabit brushy or grassy areas. In southern Texas, they are frequently associated with mesquite and cactus flats. In Kerr County, they are most common in pastures and along the highways. In the Trans-Pecos, they are frequently found in areas dominated by creosote bush (*Larrea*). On the Llano Estacado, they are associated with mesquite pastures and various other brush and cacti but also occur on golf courses, in cemeteries and city parks, and along highway rights-of-way. On the Edwards Plateau, they favor areas mowed and maintained by humans and seem to thrive in overgrazed pasturelands.

They live in burrows, the openings to which are usually unmarked by a mound of earth. Sandy or gravelly soils are preferred, but the squirrels are by no means restricted to them. One squirrel may utilize several burrows, one of which is the homesite; the others are temporary refuges. The burrows are typically 6–8 cm in diameter, enter the ground at a 30–50-degree angle, and range from 30 to 125 cm

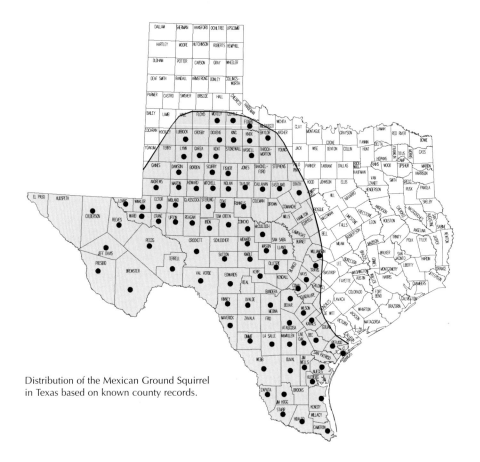

Distribution of the Mexican Ground Squirrel
in Texas based on known county records.

below the surface. The brood chamber is usually at the deepest part in a side tunnel. There are often two openings to the burrow system, possibly to facilitate escape. They also utilize burrows of pocket gophers. Although somewhat colonial, they are rather unsocial and drive away other squirrels that intrude on their privacy. Their home range is about 45 m in radius.

Near Midland, most of the squirrels are in hibernation by 20 November, although there is some activity throughout the winter. Likewise, in the Trans-Pecos they are occasionally seen in winter, but in south Texas they remain active throughout the year.

Their food in early spring is chiefly green vegetation. They are known to feed on mesquite leaves and beans, agarita leaves and berries, Shasta lily, Johnsongrass, pin clover, and cultivated grains. Insects are also important in their diet. In early summer about half of their diet is insects. They are fond of meat and frequently can be seen feeding on small animals killed on the highways. In captivity they exhibit a cannibalistic tendency and kill and eat their cage mates, particularly if a strange squirrel is placed with them. Occasionally they climb into low bushes to forage, but most of their food is gathered on the ground.

Breeding begins in late March or early April and lasts for a week or two. The gestation period is probably not more than 30 days. Females captured in the month of May from the Edwards Plateau carried 2–10 embryos, with the most common number being 6. The young are born blind and almost naked and weigh 3–5 g.

Conservation Status. This species remains in good shape throughout its range in Texas.

Spotted Ground Squirrel
Spermophilus spilosoma Bennett

Description. A small ground squirrel with scattered, more or less squarish, light spots on back (spots not in rows as in *S. mexicana* and *S. tridecemlineatus*); ears inconspicuous; tail about one-third of total length, pinkish buff or cinnamon buff beneath; upperparts smoke gray, light drab or fawn color, the white spots small and obsolete, especially on shoulder; underparts white. Dental formula: I 1/1, C 0/0, Pm 2/1, M 3/3 x 2 = 22. External measurements average: total length, 214 mm; tail, 65 mm; hind foot, 32 mm. Weight, 100–125 g.

Distribution. Known from western half of state and southward on Rio Grande Plains. It is uncommon and restricted to the western edge of the Edwards Plateau in Crane, Glasscock, Howard, Reagan, and Val Verde counties.

Subspecies. *S. s. annectens* in the southern part of the state, *S. s. canescens* in the western Trans-Pecos, and *S. s. marginatus* in the remainder of the range.

Spotted Ground Squirrel (*Spermophilus spilosoma*). Photo by R. D. Porter, courtesy Texas Parks and Wildlife Department.

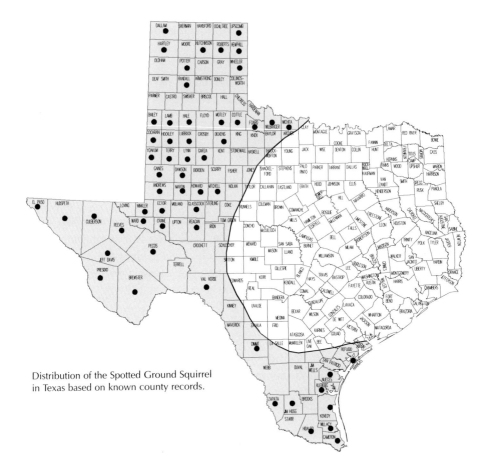

Distribution of the Spotted Ground Squirrel
in Texas based on known county records.

Habits. Spotted ground squirrels seem to prefer dry, sandy areas, but they are also found in grassy parks, open pine forests, scattered brush, and occasionally on rocky mesas. Disturbed areas along highways and roads also are utilized, as well as areas along the sides of arroyos and overgrazed pastureland. On Mustang Island, off the coast of Texas, they live in the sand dunes and share their runways through the sparse vegetation with kangaroo rats, grasshopper mice, and other small rodents. Near Van Horn they are rather common in the sandhills covered with yuccas and other desert shrubs, and in the southern part of the Big Bend they occur in small numbers on rather hard ground covered with creosote bushes. The opening to their burrows is usually under bushes or overhanging rocks. One excavated burrow had three openings, was about 4 m long, descended no more than 50 cm, and terminated in a nest chamber. A burrow in the Big Bend had an opening about 5 cm in diameter and was marked by a slight mound. On the Llano Estacado, burrows often are placed near the base of brushy vegetation such as mesquite, shinnery oak, or sand sage, and individuals occasionally inhabit developed areas such as golf courses.

These squirrels are extremely shy. One can work in an area several days without seeing them. They are most active in early morning and late afternoon to avoid the midday heat. They seldom go far from their burrows and retreat to them at the slightest sign of danger. Their movements are rapid and interrupted by abrupt stops, reminding one of a lizard. In running, the body and tail are held close to the ground.

Hibernation probably is not complete in these squirrels, especially in the southern part of their range, but their activity is severely curtailed during cold weather. Specimens have been taken in November, December, January, and February in Texas. *S. spilosoma* also may estivate during hot, dry periods.

Their food is largely green vegetation and seeds. Specific items are cactus pulp, mesquite beans, saltbush seeds, sandbur, sunflower, gourd, iris, grasshoppers, and beetles. Insects are included in the diet during times of abundance, and these ground squirrels have even been observed feeding on lizards and kangaroo rats.

Their breeding habits are not well known. Females captured in mid-June, at which time half-grown young were common, contained five to seven embryos. This indicates that two litters may be reared yearly. Young, presumably about a month old, have been observed above ground as early as 28 April and as late as 17 September, which would suggest that mating begins in February and continues into mid-July. The gestation period is not known but is probably about 30 days. Six young spotted ground squirrels reared in captivity were found to weigh an average of 17 g at 34 days of age, their eyes opened at 27–28 days, and they were weaned at about 48 days.

Conservation Status. This species remains in good shape throughout its range in Texas.

Thirteen-lined Ground Squirrel
Spermophilus tridecemlineatus (Mitchill)

Description. A small ground squirrel with usually 13 alternating dark and light stripes, the dark ones containing a series of squarish or buffy spots, the light stripes occasionally broken into spots; dark dorsal stripes dark brown or black in color, the light stripes usually continuous and buffy white; underside of tail russet at base, shading to orange buff toward tip; lower sides cinnamon buff; belly pinkish buff; chin white; ears small. Dental formula: I 1/1, C 0/0, Pm 2/1, M 3/3 x 2 = 22. External measurements average: total length, 285 mm; tail, 105 mm; hind foot, 40 mm. Weight of males averages 154 g (up to 212 g); females, 160 g (to 220 g).

Distribution. Known from northern Texas and in a corridor extending from Tarrant and Dallas counties in north-central Texas south to Atascosa, Bee, and Calhoun counties along the Gulf Coast.

Subspecies. *S. t. arenicola* in the Panhandle and adjacent areas to the south and *S. t. texensis* elsewhere within the distribution in the state.

Thirteen-lined Ground Squirrel (*Spermophilus tridecemlineatus*). Photo by John and Gloria Tveten.

Habits. These squirrels are typically inhabitants of short-grass prairies, but they have invaded the tall-grass areas in Texas, where they live principally in pastures and along fencerows. They live in burrows in the ground from which radiate well-marked paths to the feeding grounds. In tall grass the paths may become tunnels. In cultivated areas they seem to prefer fencerows and excavate their burrows near fence posts. Occasionally, they usurp abandoned burrows of pocket gophers or even those of prairie dogs. Their own burrows are about 5 cm in diameter, have two or three openings, descend to a depth of 10–115 cm, and may be 7 m or more in length.

These squirrels are strictly diurnal, but their annual cycle of activity includes a very long period of hibernation. In Texas, studies conducted by Howard McCarley revealed that the period of hibernation lasts about 240 days. Adults enter hibernation in July and young of the year in August or September. They emerge from the middle of February to the first of March in the Texas Panhandle. In southern Texas they have been observed above ground as late as 27 October and as early as January.

Their food is chiefly green grasses and herbs in early spring, but seeds, flower heads, and insects become important to their diet as the season advances. Grasshoppers are often conspicuous items in their stomach contents, and often more than half of the stomach contents consists of insects, including grasshoppers, crickets, caterpillars, beetles, ants, and insect eggs. They also eat mice and have been reported capturing and eating small chickens. Quantities of dry seeds stored in underground caches probably serve to carry the squirrels through the period of scarcity shortly after they emerge in the spring.

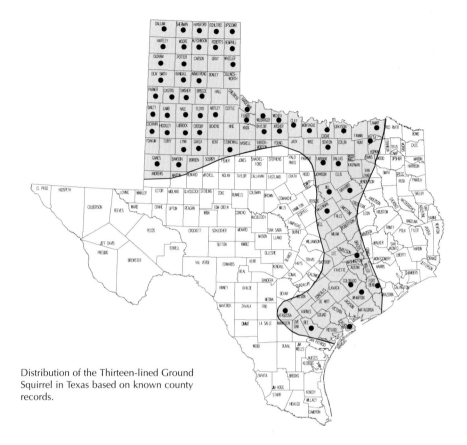

Distribution of the Thirteen-lined Ground
Squirrel in Texas based on known county
records.

Mating activities begin about 2 weeks after squirrels emerge from hibernation. The males are sexually active for only 2–3 months, which of necessity restricts the length of the breeding season. Normally only one litter is produced annually, but one study found about 25% of the females observed in a marked population produced two litters. The gestation period is 27–28 days. The young vary in number from 2 to 13; the yearling females produce the smallest litters. The young are blind, hairless, and toothless at birth and weigh 3–4 g each. By the eighth day they are dark dorsally; on the twelfth the stripes begin to appear and hair sparsely covers the back; on the twenty-sixth their eyes begin to open. The female then begins to wean them, and at the age of 6 weeks they are entirely dependent on their own resources. They mature sexually at about 9 or 10 months of age.

Where concentrated in pastures and farming areas these squirrels may cause serious loss of forage and crops, but their fondness for insects partly offsets any damage they may do. On rangelands they usually do no serious damage.

Conservation Status. This is a widely occurring and common ground squirrel throughout the Texas Panhandle, but the populations from the central part of the state have declined dramatically as a result of the degradation of grassland habitat. The central populations need to be monitored carefully.

Remarks. The thirteen-lined ground squirrel is reputed to hybridize with the closely related Mexican ground squirrel at Hobbs, New Mexico, and at Andrews and Big Spring in Texas. It reaches the limit of its geographic distribution in broad contact with the Mexican ground squirrel on the southern Llano Estacado. *S. tridecemlineatus* is a species of the Great Plains, whereas *S. mexicanus* is a species of desert grasslands, but competitive interaction between them has not been documented other than in the supposed areas of hybridization.

Rock Squirrel
Spermophilus variegatus (Erxleben)

Description. A large, moderately bushy-tailed ground squirrel; upperparts mottled grayish brown, the hind back and rump more brownish (head or head and upper back blackish in some parts of the state); tail mixed buff and brown, edged with white; underparts buffy white or pinkish buff. Dental formula as in *S. mexicanus*. External measurements average: total length, 468 mm; tail, 210 mm; hind foot, 57 mm. Weight of adults, 600–800 g.

Distribution. Known from the Trans-Pecos and central regions of the state. On the Llano Estacado it is known only from the extreme northwestern part of the plateau in Quay County, New Mexico, just west of the Texas border.

Subspecies. *S. v. buckleyi* in south-central Texas and *S. v. grammurus* to the west.

Habits. Rock squirrels are nearly always found in rocky areas—cliffs, canyon walls, talus slopes, boulder piles, fills along highways, and so forth—where they seek

Rock Squirrel (*Spermophilus variegatus*). Photo courtesy Texas Parks and Wildlife Department.

refuge and have their dens. In the Pecos River Canyon in western Texas, where the walls are a series of alternating, nearly vertical precipices and narrow horizontal shelves, these squirrels are very much at home. They scale the steep, smooth walls with speed and assurance and never hesitate at what appear at a distance to be perfectly smooth surfaces. Closer inspection usually reveals that cracks and fissures in the rocks offer them adequate footing.

Although typical ground squirrels in most respects, they can climb trees nearly as well as tree squirrels. In the Guadalupe Mountains of western Texas, they have been observed 5 or 6 m up in the flowering stalks of agaves feeding on the flowers and buds. They also climb to the tops of junipers to forage on the berries and in mesquites to feed on the buds or beans. Occasionally, they den in tree hollows 5 or 6 m from the ground. The usual den, however, is a burrow dug under a rock; others are in crevices in rock masonry along railroads and highways, cavities in piles of boulders, or small caves and crevices in rocky outcrops. They are diurnal and most active in early morning and late afternoon, but they are rather shy and difficult to observe at close range. Their call is usually a repeated sharp, clear whistle.

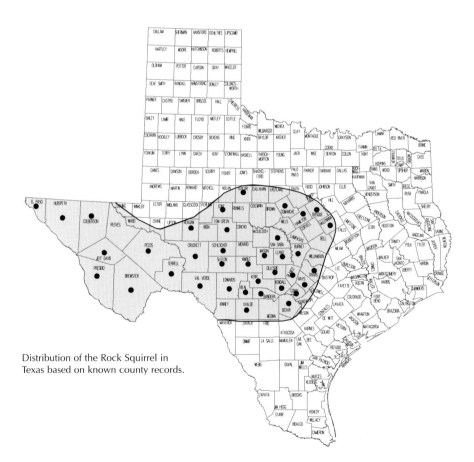

Distribution of the Rock Squirrel in Texas based on known county records.

They feed on a variety of plant materials, depending on availability. Known items include acorns, pine nuts, walnuts, seeds of mesquite, cactus, saltbush, agave, wild gourd, cherries, sumac, spurge, serviceberry, berries of currant and juniper, and all sorts of cultivated fruits and vegetables. Insects are also important in their diet, especially grasshoppers, crickets, and caterpillars. They are fond of flesh and are known to catch and eat small wild turkeys and other birds.

Rock squirrels are facultative hibernators. In central Texas, they hibernate 2–4 months, from November to February or March. Fat is deposited and they store food for winter use. At lower elevations in the Big Bend region of Texas they are active all year.

Populations of rock squirrels tend to be colonial and organized as maternal aggregations. Colonies consist of breeding females and a dominant male, with several subordinate males occupying peripheral areas of the colony. Home ranges are large, and much overlap is found within each colony. Home ranges average 0.4 hectares for dominant males and 0.15 hectares for females. The home ranges of males increase during the breeding season. Females become more territorial during periods of lactation and decrease the size of their home ranges. Many juveniles disperse from the home den in late summer or early fall, and yearlings may disperse from the maternal home range in the spring.

Males enter breeding condition after emerging from hibernation. Males are probably polygamous, and breeding territories are actively defended against intruding males. Breeding season extends for about 6 weeks in March and April in Texas. The gestation period is not known for this species. One litter is produced per year. The young are born in late spring and emerge from burrows from the end of May to mid-August. The number of young in a litter varies from one to seven with an average of four. In years of mild climatic conditions, or in warmer regions, it is possible that a second litter will be produced. Young about quarter-grown have been captured as early as June and as late as 20 September.

Conservation Status. These squirrels are quite common throughout their range and seem to have adapted well to human encroachment.

Black-tailed Prairie Dog
Cynomys ludovicianus (Ord)

Description. A rather large, chunky, ground-dwelling squirrel with upperparts pinkish cinnamon mixed with buff; tail sparsely haired, tipped with black, and about one-fifth of total length; eyes large; ears short and rounded. Dental formula: I 1/1, C 0/0, Pm 2/1, M 3/3 x 2 = 22. External measurements average: total length, 388 mm; tail, 86 mm; hind foot, 62 mm. Weight, 1–2 kg.

Distribution. Occurred in western half of state from north of Rio Grande Plains; easternmost records from Montague and Tarrant counties in north and Bexar County in south; now extirpated over much of its former range.

Subspecies. *C. l. arizonensis* in the Trans-Pecos and *C. l. ludovicianus* elsewhere.

Black-tailed Prairie Dog (*Cynomys ludovicianus*). Photo courtesy U.S. Fish and Wildlife Service.

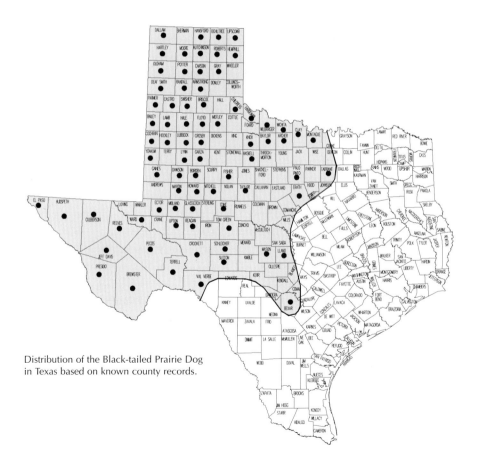

Distribution of the Black-tailed Prairie Dog
in Texas based on known county records.

Habits. Black-tailed prairie dogs typically inhabit short-grass prairies; they usually avoid areas of heavy brush and tall grass, possibly because visibility is considerably reduced. In Trans-Pecos Texas, favored habitat sites are alluvial fans at the mouths of draws, hardpan flats where brush is sparse or absent, and the edges of shallow valleys. Overgrazed or denuded pastureland also provides good habitat for *C. ludovicianus.*

The term "prairie dog" is an unfortunate misnomer because the animal is not even remotely related to a dog. It is a ground squirrel with a superficial resemblance to a small, fat pup. These squirrels are sociable creatures and live in colonies, or towns, that may vary in size from a few individuals to several thousand animals. Vernon Bailey recorded that at the end of the nineteenth century an almost continuous and thickly inhabited dog town extended in a strip approximately 160 km wide and 400 km long on the high plains of Texas. This city had an estimated population of 400 million prairie dogs. Such large concentrations are now a thing of the past, since the extensive use of poisoned grain to kill the animals and the conversion of land for agriculture.

Their homes consist of deep burrows 7–10 cm in diameter. The entrances are funnel-shaped and usually descend at a steep angle for 2–5 m before leveling off. One described burrow dropped nearly vertically for 4.5 m, then turned abruptly and became horizontal for 4 m. From the lower part extended blind side tunnels and nest chambers. The main entrances are made conspicuous by the mounds and parapets constructed around them. These craterlike dikes are often 30 cm or more in height and doubtless serve to keep flash floods from inundating the burrows and also as lookout points for the animals. Those who have hunted prairie dogs know how effective the craters are, both as vantage points and as retreats for the animals.

They are strictly diurnal and are most active in the morning and evening periods. The midday hours are usually spent sleeping below ground. In summer the animals store up reserves of fat to tide them over the winter months. In the northern part of Texas they begin hibernating in November. Hibernation seems to be less complete in prairie dogs than in true ground squirrels.

Their food is chiefly plant materials, particularly low-growing weeds and grasses. In Trans-Pecos Texas burrograss and purple needle grass are especially favored foods. Their year-round diet as determined by one investigator is as follows: grasses (61.55%), goosefoot family (12.73%), mustard family (4.5%), prickly pear (5.98%), other plants (13.94%). Animal matter, chiefly cutworms, accounted for only 1.4% of the total diet. They are voracious eaters. According to C. Hart Merriam, 32 prairie dogs consume as much food per day as one sheep, and 256 eat as much as one cow.

Prairie dogs are highly gregarious. Populations comprise several small coteries, or harems, of two to eight females that are defended by a single dominant male. In turn, coteries are organized into larger population units called wards, which are separated by unoccupied areas of unsuitable habitat or other such barriers.

Activity and breeding are usually conducted within the coteries; however, dispersal between coteries and wards occasionally occurs, usually by young males. This complex social structure is thought to contribute to increased genetic variability between both coteries and wards.

A single litter of young is produced annually in March and April. Litter size is usually 4–5 young, but as many as 10 young have been reported in a litter. At birth the youngsters are blind and hairless and weigh about 15 g. At 13 days fine hair covers the cheeks, nose, and parts of the body; the weight is then about 40 g. At 26 days, the body is well haired and they can crawl awkwardly. Their eyes open at the age of 33–37 days, at which time the young squirrels are able to walk, run, eat green food, and bark. They first appear above ground when about 6 weeks of age and are weaned shortly after that. The family unit remains intact for almost another month, but the ties are gradually broken and the family disperses. Sexual maturity is reached in the second year.

These squirrels have been displaced by livestock and farming interests for the past century. Consequently, their former range and numbers have been considerably reduced. That large concentrations of prairie dogs can damage cultivated crops or compete seriously with livestock cannot be questioned, but the desirability of eliminating them entirely from rangelands has not been satisfactorily demonstrated. Stockmen in certain parts of Texas, for example, claim that removal of prairie dogs has had some direct association with the undesirable spread of brush. This has had detrimental effects on the livestock industry that far outweigh the damage prairie dogs might do.

Conservation Status. The current status of the prairie dog in Texas has been a controversial issue in recent years. It is estimated that 98% of the original prairie dog population in the state has been lost, and that only 300,000 prairie dogs remain. Surviving colonies are fragmented, and most cover less than 50 acres. Prairie dog habitat declined 61% from 1980 to 2000. At this rate of decline and habitat loss, prairie dog eradication could occur during the first half of the twenty-first century. For that reason, the National Wildlife Federation recently petitioned the U.S. Fish and Wildlife Service to list the species as threatened or endangered. The USFWS reviewed the status of the prairie dog and announced its decision in February 2000 that although the status of the species warranted listing as threatened, further action to place it on the list was precluded by actions to address higher-priority species. The black-tailed prairie dog was added to the list of candidates for threatened status, and its status is reviewed annually. Eight western states, including Texas, are working together on a conservation plan for the species.

Eastern Gray Squirrel
Sciurus carolinensis Gmelin

Description. A medium-sized squirrel with upperparts grayish to dark yellowish rusty, especially on head and back; legs, arms, sides of neck, and sides of rump

Eastern Gray Squirrel (*Sciurus carolinensis*). Photo courtesy Texas Parks and Wildlife Department.

with gray-tipped or white-tipped hairs, giving a gray tone to these parts; hairs of tail dull yellow at base, then blackish, and tipped with white; underparts white; ears with conspicuous white spot at base in winter. Dental formula: I 1/1, C 0/0, Pm 2/1, M 3/3 x 2 = 22. External measurements average: total length, 460 mm; tail, 210 mm; hind foot, 61 mm. Weight of adults, 321–590 g.

Distribution. Native distribution includes eastern one-third of state. Introduced at locations to the west of its native range. For example, a thriving population was established in the city of Lubbock in the 1970s, more than 400 miles from the species' normal range.

Subspecies. *S. c. carolinensis.*

Habits. In Texas, gray squirrels live mainly in dense hammocks of live oak and water oak and in the deep swamps of cypress, black gum, and magnolia that border the streams. Phil Goodrum found that they were most abundant in hammocks where the principal vegetation was white oak and water oak mixed with magnolia, linden, sweet gum, and holly. Poorly drained bottomlands with their pin, evergreen and overcup oaks, elms, bitter pecan, black gum, cypress, and ash support much smaller populations. In well-drained bottomlands with post and red oaks, hackberries, gum elastic, and pecan, the populations are still smaller, and upland forests usually are devoid of gray squirrels.

They den in hollow trees when available, but they also utilize outside leaf nests, especially in spring and summer. These serve usually as refuges, resting and

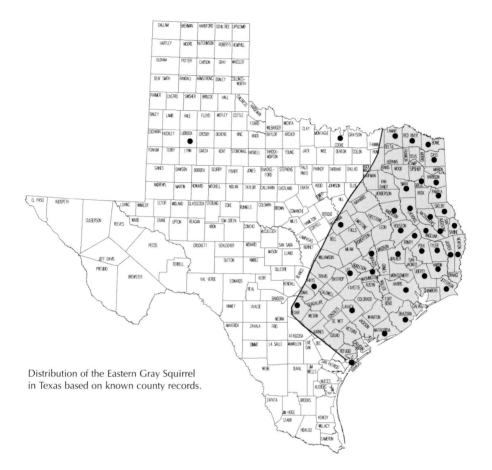

Distribution of the Eastern Gray Squirrel in Texas based on known county records.

feeding stations, and occasionally as nurseries. Placed in trees, they are constructed of twigs, leaves, and so forth on the outside and lined with shredded bark, plant fibers, and grasses. Usually there are two openings.

Gray squirrels feed on a variety of foods, chiefly plant in origin. Goodrum lists buds and mast of oak and pecan trees, grapes, fungi, red haw buds, sedges, grasses, mulberry, larval and adult insects, and amphibians. Their mainstay, however, is mast (acorns etc.). They begin eating acorns in the spring and continue throughout the year if they are available. When mast crops fail in one area, the squirrels usually move en masse to other areas where food is more abundant. This accounts in large measure for the migrations of squirrels that are frequently reported. Normally they feed twice a day (early morning and late afternoon) and are less active at midday.

These squirrels breed throughout the year, but there are two rather distinct peaks, in July, August, and September and again in December, January, and February. Mating is more or less promiscuous; several males usually attempt to mate with each receptive female. After a gestation period of 40–45 days, the two to four naked, blind, and helpless young are born. They remain in the nest for about 6 weeks by which time their eyes are open and their teeth have developed so that they can eat solid foods. By that time they weigh about 200 g. They remain in family groups for a month or so after they begin foraging for themselves. When 6 months old they are nearly adult in size and have left the home territory. They mature sexually in their first year and produce young of their own when about 12 months old.

These squirrels are highly prized as game. They do some damage in pecan orchards, but such depredations are local in nature and can usually be minimized by placing tin shields around the trunks to prevent the squirrels from climbing trees.

Conservation Status. The most serious conservation problems with squirrels in Texas are associated with the gray squirrel. Although still locally common in parts of East Texas, a drastic reduction in suitable habitat occurred throughout the twentieth century as a result of detrimental land-use practices, such as logging of hardwoods, practices of timber stand improvement and establishment of pine plantations, overgrazing by domestic livestock, flooding of bottomland habitats through reservoir impoundments on major streams and rivers, and drainage of lowland bottomlands. Their future will depend on the acreage remaining in hardwood forests, the lengths of timber rotations, the species composition of hardwood stands, and the abundance of mast supplies and dens.

Eastern Fox Squirrel

Sciurus niger Linnaeus

Description. A large tree squirrel with rusty or reddish underparts and brownish or grayish upperparts; tail usually less than half of total length, and cinnamon, mixed with black, in color; feet cinnamon. Dental formula: I 1/1, C 0/0, Pm 1/1, M 3/3 x 2 = 20. External measurements average: total length, 522 mm; tail, 245 mm; hind foot, 72 mm. Weight, 600–1,300 g.

Distribution. Occurs in suitable habitats in eastern three-quarters of state. Range has been expanded westward by introductions. For example, 30 fox squirrels were trapped at Amarillo in about 1987 and released into the city park in Brownfield, Terry County, where they have subsequently spread across the city in tree-lined residential areas.

Subspecies. *S. n. limitis* in most of the western part of the range in the state, *S. n. ludovicianus* in the east, and *S. n. rufiventer* in the Canadian River drainage and adjacent areas of northwestern and extreme north-central Texas.

Habits. Fox squirrels are adaptable to a wide variety of forest habitats, but in most areas open woodlands of mixed trees and bottomland riparian areas along streams and rivers support the heaviest populations. The best habitat is mature oak-hickory woodland broken into small, irregularly shaped tracts of 2–8 ha and connected by strips of woodland that serve as squirrel highways. Intermixture of

Eastern Fox Squirrel (*Sciurus niger*). Photo courtesy Texas Parks and Wildlife Department.

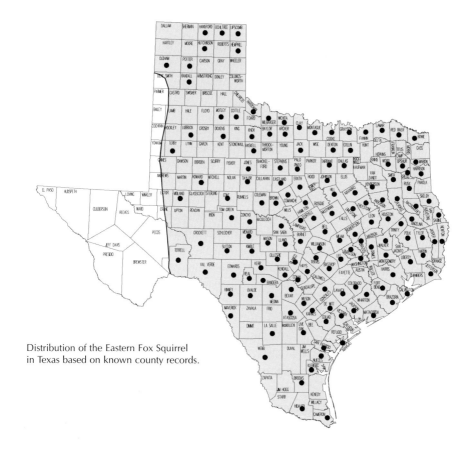

Distribution of the Eastern Fox Squirrel
in Texas based on known county records.

pine, elm, beech, pecan, maple, and other food-producing trees adds to the attractiveness of the habitat. Along the western parts of their range, fox squirrels are restricted more or less to river valleys that support pecans, walnuts, oaks, and other required trees. Mottes of live oak and other tree species in the valleys of the Edwards Plateau are favored habitats.

Where hollow trees are available they are preferred as den sites and nurseries; if they are unavailable, the squirrels build outside leaf nests. These are composed of twigs and leaves, usually cut from the tree in which the nest is placed and fashioned into roughly globular structures 30–50 cm in diameter surrounding an inner cavity 15–20 cm in diameter.

A fox squirrel occupies an area of at least 4 ha in extent in any one season, but during an entire year 16 ha or more may be utilized. Ranges of different fox squirrels overlap, and the animals are somewhat communal in their use of nests and probably also of winter food stores. The average carrying capacity of good, unimproved squirrel habitats is about 1 squirrel to 1 ha.

Acorns are the natural mainstay of fox squirrels, although they are most important in fall and winter. Spring and summer foods consist of leftover mast, insects, green shoots, fruits, and seeds of such trees as elm and maple. Nuts are eaten from the time they start to develop and are buried in the fall in individual caches at the surface of the ground for winter use. The squirrels can relocate them by smell. Buds of many trees and fruits of osage orange add to the winter diet. *S. niger* feeds on a wider variety of items than does the gray squirrel. Water needs are met by consumption of succulent food materials, but during periods of drought an adequate water supply is essential.

Mating occurs principally in two periods, January and February and again in May and June. The first period is most important. Old females usually breed twice a year and yearlings but once. The average female produces only four offspring each year. The gestation period is probably about 6 or 7 weeks, as in the gray squirrel. At birth the young are blind, nearly naked, and helpless. They develop rather slowly; their eyes open in the fifth week. They begin to climb about in the nest tree at the age of 7 or 8 weeks and to venture onto the ground at about 10 weeks. At the age of 3 months they begin to lead a more or less independent existence. Sexual maturity is reached at the age of 10–11 months.

Fox squirrels are important small game animals throughout most of their range, hence they are of decided economic value. Their fondness for green corn, however, often brings them into conflict with farming interests, as does their pilfering in nut orchards.

There is evidence to suggest that fox squirrels may be increasing in abundance at the expense of gray squirrels. The drainage of lowland bottomlands seems to result in a reduction in the number of gray squirrels and an increase in the number of fox squirrels.

Conservation Status. Fox squirrels are common throughout their range in Texas and do not appear to face any serious problems.

Southern Flying Squirrel (*Glaucomys volans*). Photo by E. P. Walker, courtesy Texas Parks and Wildlife Department.

Southern Flying Squirrel

Glaucomys volans (Linnaeus)

Description. A small squirrel with flattened, bushy tail; flying membrane connecting front and hind legs; eyes large; upperparts nearly uniform drab or pinkish cinnamon; underparts creamy white; sides often tinged with buff; toes usually strongly marked with white in winter pelage. Dental formula: I 1/1, C 0/0, Pm 2/1, M 3/3 x 2 = 22. External measurements average: total length, 225 mm; tail, 100 mm; hind feet, 29 mm. Weight, 41–67 g.

Distribution. Known from wooded areas in eastern one-third of state.

Subspecies. *G. v. texensis.*

Habits. These small, nocturnal squirrels inhabit forested areas where suitable trees are present to afford den sites. In the western parts of their range, suitable habitat is restricted largely to areas along rivers and streams. In other parts of their range, they show preference for hammocks where Spanish moss is abundant. In suitable habitat they may be more abundant than most other squirrels. They are sociable and tend to live together in groups.

Holes in stumps are preferred den sites, but the squirrels will utilize almost any cavity that is dry and large enough. Woodpecker nests are ideal, particularly those of the larger species. When such sites are not available, the squirrels construct outside nests. A clump of Spanish moss is ideal.

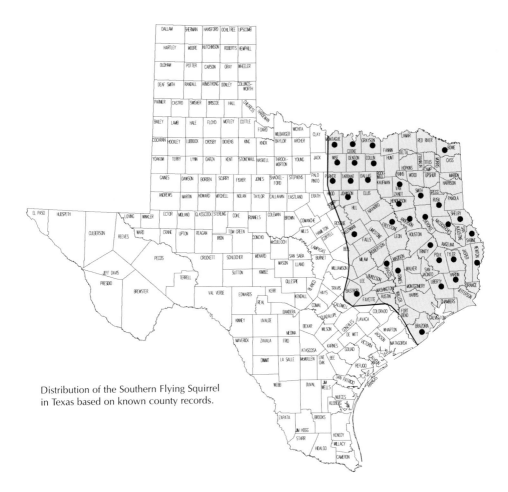

Distribution of the Southern Flying Squirrel
in Texas based on known county records.

They feed on a variety of items, but nuts and acorns are their mainstay. They also eat insect larvae, beetles, young and eggs of birds, persimmon, and cultivated corn. The frequency with which they are caught in traps set for fur animals and baited with meat indicates a decided fondness for flesh. Food is cached in holes in trees or other places for winter use.

There are two breeding seasons, the principal one in late February and March, the other in July. It is not known, however, if an individual female participates in both the spring and fall breeding periods. Captive females mate only once annually. Males are in breeding condition from late January to early September. Mating is probably promiscuous because several males will chase a female in heat. The female alone assumes responsibility for rearing the young. The gestation period is about 40 days. At birth the two or three young are blind, nearly naked, and helpless; they weigh about 3 g each. The membrane between the wrist and ankle is well developed. The eyes open at 26–29 days, and a week later the young begin eating solid foods. At 6 weeks of age they are old enough to fend for themselves. They reach sexual maturity when about a year old.

Flying squirrels do not actually fly but travel by gliding from one tree to another. This is accomplished by stretching the legs to extend a membrane connecting the front and hind legs. Glides are usually only about 6–9 m in length but may extend up to 30 m.

Conservation Status. We know too little about the population abundance of flying squirrels to predict their conservation status in Texas. They occur in the wooded regions of the eastern part of the state and seem to be especially fond of mature forests with lots of tree cavities and hollow trees. Obviously, forestry practices that eliminate that type of habitat would be harmful to its long-term status.

FAMILY GEOMYIDAE (POCKET GOPHERS)

Pocket gophers are named for their fur-lined cheek pouches, or pockets, that they use for food storage and transport. These strictly fossorial rodents dig extensive underground burrow systems and are rarely seen above ground.

The evolutionary history of this family has been difficult to unravel, and systematic mammalogists are continuously working to determine species limits and geographic variation. Thus, the taxonomy of this group is in an almost constant state of flux. At this time, 3 genera and 10 species of pocket gophers are recognized in Texas, and several are unique to the state.

Botta's Pocket Gopher
Thomomys bottae (Eydoux and Gervais)

Description. A medium-sized rodent with external, fur-lined cheek pouches; the outer face of the upper incisors lacks conspicuous grooves; claws on front feet relatively small (less than 10 mm long); upperparts varying from pale gray to russet and blackish; underparts grayish white, white, buffy, or mottled. Dental formula: I 1/1, C 0/0, Pm 1/1, M 3/3 x 2 = 20. External measurements of males average: total length, 267 mm; tail, 81 mm; hind foot, 33 mm; of females, 219-69-28 mm. Weight of males, 160–250 g; of females, 120–200 g.

Distribution. Trans-Pecos Texas and eastward across the Edwards Plateau and immediately adjacent areas to Mason County.

Subspecies. Ten subspecies are recognized in the state. The following eight are all restricted to suitable habitats in the Trans-Pecos region: *T. b. baileyi, T. b. guadalupensis, T. b. lachuguilla, T. b. limpiae, T. b. pervarius, T. b. scotophilus, T. b. spatiosus,* and *T. b. texensis.* Additionally, *T. b. limitaris* occurs in the eastern Trans-Pecos and eastward across the Pecos River onto the western part of the Edwards Plateau, and *T. b. confinalis* occupies parts of the Edwards Plateau to the east.

Botta's Pocket Gopher (*Thomomys bottae*). Photo by John and Gloria Tveten.

Habits. Pocket gophers of this species are extremely adaptable as regards habitat. They occur in soils ranging from loose sands and silts to tight clays and in vegetative zones grading from dry deserts to montane meadows. Perhaps one reason they can tolerate such environmental extremes is that they spend fully 90% of their lives in underground burrows, secure from the elements.

Their burrow systems are often complicated structures consisting of two or more main galleries and several side chambers. A partly excavated burrow extended more than 30 m in length, had four main forks, and averaged 6 cm beneath the surface, although the tunnel leading to the nest descended to a depth of more than 60 cm. Tunnel systems more than 150 m in length are not rare. These ramified travelways probably help the occupants to avoid predators that try to search them out; they are equally important in permitting the gopher to forage over a considerable area without exposing itself unduly to danger. Special side branches serve as storehouses for food, others as repositories for refuse and fecal pellets. In winter, when snow covers the ground, the gophers often extend their burrows into the snow and can then forage above ground in safety.

Although pocket gophers are active year round, they store food to carry them over periods of scarcity, especially periods of drought when food is scarce and burrowing a difficult task. Usually, only one adult animal occupies each burrow system, except for a short time in the breeding period. Associated with this solitary habit is a ferocious and seemingly fearless disposition. When two gophers encounter each other, they either fight or meticulously avoid each other. Desire for companionship seems to be completely lacking in their makeup.

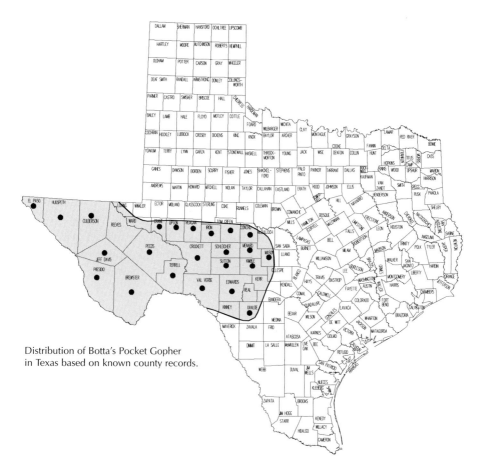

Distribution of Botta's Pocket Gopher
in Texas based on known county records.

They feed on a variety of foods, but fleshy roots and tubers are their main
reliance. Unlike *Geomys bursarius*, Botta's pocket gophers often come to the surface to feed and clip off vegetation around the burrow as far as they can reach in
all directions without losing physical contact with the opening. If molested the animals back into the burrows with amazing speed. At other times, they approach
desirable plants from below and pull the entire upperparts into the burrow, where
they can be cut up and stored or eaten at leisure. The roots of alfalfa are especially prized, but almost any native plant is potential food.

The nest is a compact, hollow ball of dry, shredded vegetation placed in a special chamber off the main gallery, about 30–70 cm beneath the surface of the
ground. Both sexes build nests as sleeping quarters.

This species breeds continuously, with three marked periods of increased
fertility in spring, summer, and early winter. The main breeding season is in
spring, however; summer breeding is mainly by young females, possibly those
born the preceding spring. The winter season is one of slight breeding activity and
often merges with the one in early spring. Old females produce yearly an average

of two litters of five young each; young females are less fecund. The young are blind, naked, unpigmented, and weigh about 4 g at birth. The ears are poorly developed, but the cheek pouches are fully formed, although smaller than in adults. Growth appears to be relatively slow, but details of this phase of their life history are lacking.

In cultivated areas, pocket gophers may be destructive and require control by trapping or poisoning, but on natural lands they are of decided benefit as soil builders. They are the chief natural cultivators of soils, and the maximum thrift of wild vegetation is dependent on their continued activity.

Conservation Status. There is some indication that this species may be losing ground to a competitor, *Cratogeomys castanops,* in western Texas as a result of climate changes involving increased aridity. At least two subspecies, *T. b. baileyi* from Sierra Blanca in Hudspeth County and *T. b. limpiae* from near Fort Davis in Jeff Davis County, are now thought to be extinct in Texas. Populations from the Big Bend not in proximity to *C. castanops* appear to be holding their own.

Desert Pocket Gopher
Geomys arenarius Merriam

Description. A dull, pale brown pocket gopher, with two longitudinal grooves on outer face of each incisor; feet and underparts white. External measurements of

Desert Pocket Gopher (*Geomys arenarius*). Photo by Robert D. Bradley.

males average: total length, 262 mm; tail, 79 mm; hind foot, 33 mm; of females, 243-74-32 mm. Weight of males, 198–254 g; of females, 165–207 g. Dental formula as in *G. bursarius.*

Distribution. Restricted in Texas to the far western Trans-Pecos, where it has been taken at several localities in the cottonwood-willow association along the Rio Grande in El Paso County.

Subspecies. *G. a. arenarius.*

Habits. Near El Paso, these gophers are especially common along irrigation ditches in the sandy river-bottom area. They seemingly cannot tolerate clayey or gravelly soils, a characteristic common to all species of *Geomys.* Their mounds are large and conspicuous, and often one animal will throw up 20 to 30 of them in a relatively short time.

Their underground habits are not well known. Seth Benson reports finding flowers and cut stems of a composite (*Baileya*) in their burrows. Doubtless, these were being eaten. Other than that plant and cultivated alfalfa, their food preferences have not been recorded.

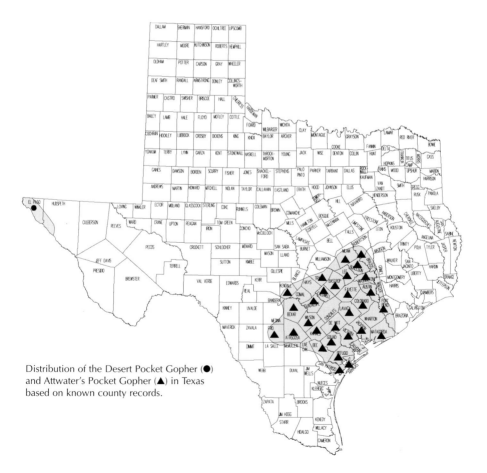

Distribution of the Desert Pocket Gopher (●) and Attwater's Pocket Gopher (▲) in Texas based on known county records.

Raymond Lee captured two gravid females near El Paso on 28 June and one on 8 August. Numbers of embryos were six, four, and four, respectively. Young individuals have been captured in late June, July, and August. These data indicate a prolonged breeding season and suggest that adult females bear more than one litter a year.

Where concentrated in numbers in farming areas, they may do considerable damage. Elsewhere, their burrowing activities are largely beneficial. Frank Blair observed that the bunchgrass *Andropogon* in New Mexico was intimately associated with the mounds of this pocket gopher. The grass appeared to grow more successfully on old gopher mounds than on the valley floor. The excrement of the gophers helped to fertilize the mounds.

Conservation Status. *G. arenarius* remains common in El Paso County as well as several localities where it has been obtained in New Mexico. There are no known threats to its existence, but because of its restricted range in our state periodic monitoring is warranted.

Remarks. Using karyotypic and electrophoretic analyses, David Hafner and Kenneth Geluso found shared genetic characters in *G. arenarius* and *G. knoxjonesi,* then considered a subspecies of *G. bursarius.* The similarities were not sufficient to combine *G. arenarius* with *G. bursarius;* however, Robert Baker and his associates recently elevated *G. knoxjonesi* to full specific status, based on mitochondrial DNA analysis, which indicated that *bursarius* and *knoxjonesi* experienced little gene flow in a zone where the two species narrowly overlap. This left in question the taxonomic relationship between *G. arenarius* and *G. knoxjonesi.* At this time it is uncertain whether Jones's pocket gopher and the desert pocket gopher indeed represent separate species, or if further detailed study of these taxa will show that combining the two as a single species will be warranted. It is distinctly possible that in the future *G. knoxjonesi* will be shown to be an isolated population of the similar *G. arenarius;* however, there are chromosomal differences that suggest that *arenarius* and *knoxjonesi* are distinct genetic units, and therefore, until additional data are available, I recognize both as distinct species.

Attwater's Pocket Gopher
Geomys attwateri Merriam

Description. This pocket gopher closely resembles the plains pocket gopher (*Geomys bursarius*) and Baird's pocket gopher (*G. breviceps*). Morphologically, the three are nearly identical and extremely difficult to distinguish in the field. Of the three, *G. attwateri* is intermediate in size, being larger than *G. breviceps* and smaller than *G. bursarius.* A cranial feature used successfully in separating the species is the length of the jugal bone on the zygomatic arch compared with the width of the rostrum ventral to the infraorbital openings. In *G. bursarius* the dorsal exposure of the jugal is longer than the width of the rostrum, whereas in *G. attwateri* and *G. breviceps* the dorsal exposure of the jugal is shorter than the width of the rostrum.

Attwater's Pocket Gopher (*Geomys attwateri*). Photo by John and Gloria Tveten.

The best distinguishing feature is the karyotype, which in *G. attwateri* has a diploid number of 70 and a fundamental number of either 72 or 74. External measurements average: total length, 216 mm; tail, 62 mm; hind foot, 26 mm. Dental formula as in *G. bursarius*.

Distribution. From the Brazos River in eastern Texas south to southern Texas near the San Antonio River and along the coast from Matagorda to San Patricio counties. This species is unique to Texas—its entire geographic range is restricted to the state. See distribution map in the account for *Geomys arenarius*.

Subspecies. Monotypic species.

Habits. The general habits of *G. attwateri* are similar to *G. bursarius* and *G. breviceps*. Attwater's pocket gopher is also an opportunistic herbivore, consuming a wide range of perennial and annual plant species. On the Welder Wildlife Refuge in south Texas, these gophers consume 41 of the 51 plant species available to them.

In contrast to the burrow systems of the plains pocket gopher, burrows of Attwater's pocket gopher tend to be more circuitous in nature. Their burrows are nonlinear and have few lateral or blind branches. This may be in response to a localized, or clumped, distribution of resources, adaptations to low population densities, or their social structure.

G. attwateri is active at all hours of the day. Peaks in daily activity are not known.

Attwater's pocket gopher breeds from October through June, with peaks in December–January and April–May. Little, if any, breeding occurs during the summer months of July, August, and September. Females produce an average of two or three young per litter and at least two litters per year.

Conservation Status. This species still appears to be locally common, although it is absent from some places where it was previously present. It is possible that fire ants limit the local distribution and abundance of this gopher.

Remarks. A small zone of contact between *G. breviceps* and *G. attwateri* occurs just west of the Brazos River in Burleson County. Of 42 gophers collected in this area, 31% had an apparent karyotype intermediate between the two species, indicating that hybridization may occur in the wild. In general, the range of *G. attwateri* is limited on the north by the Brazos River, although small zones of contact with *G. breviceps* (the range of which is limited on the south by the Brazos River) may occur where the Brazos River has periodically changed course in the past.

Baird's Pocket Gopher
Geomys breviceps Baird

Description. Nearly identical in appearance to *G. bursarius* and *G. attwateri.* Morphologically, this species may be distinguished from *G. bursarius* by cranial characters described in the account for *G. attwateri,* but it is not readily distinguishable from *G. attwateri* without genetic testing.

Baird's Pocket Gopher (*Geomys breviceps*). Photo by John and Gloria Tveten.

The most important feature for identifying this gopher is its karyotype, which has a diploid number of 74 and a fundamental number of 72. *G. breviceps* has 4 more biarmed elements in the autosomal complement than does *G. attwateri.* Compared to *G. bursarius, G. breviceps* has 2 more chromosomes.

G. breviceps is smaller than both *G. attwateri* and *G. bursarius.* External measurements average: total length, 208 mm; tail, 61 mm; hind foot, 26 mm. Dental formula as in *G. bursarius.*

Distribution. This pocket gopher is found in the eastern portion of Texas. The westward limits of its range in the state are from Falls County north to Wise and Cooke counties, and southeastward along the Brazos River to Brazoria County.

Subspecies. *G. b. sagittalis.*

Habits. The habits of *G. breviceps* are essentially the same as those described for *G. bursarius.*

These pocket gophers are polygamous, but breeding is restricted to immediate neighbors. The annual reproductive cycle in eastern Texas shows seven consecutive months of breeding activity, from February until August. A peak in production

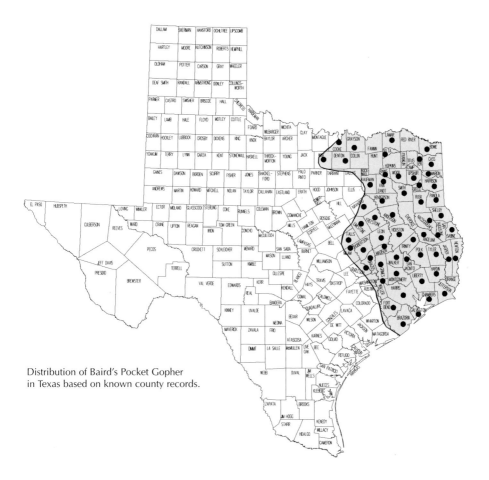

Distribution of Baird's Pocket Gopher
in Texas based on known county records.

occurs in June and July and a lesser peak in April; no young are produced from September through January. Litter size is one to six, with an average of two or three. Females may produce two broods annually. The gestation period is 4–5 weeks and lactation lasts 5–6 weeks, after which the young leave the parental burrow. Young females may reach sexual maturity and produce a litter before the end of the breeding season.

Cellulose-digesting bacteria are known from the cecum and large intestine of *G. breviceps,* which may allow winter feeding on stored, underground rhizomes. Also, these pocket gophers reingest fecal pellets, which apparently increases the efficiency of food utilization.

Conservation Status. This species has declined dramatically in the coastal prairies around the western edge of Galveston Bay. Land clearing and land subsidence have removed many of the low mounds characteristic of the coastal prairie at the turn of the century, and this gopher no longer occurs around Clear Creek and toward Houston. This gopher is common in suitable soil types of the Post Oak Savannah and Pineywoods regions.

Remarks. Recent records for this species from Denton, Grayson, Cooke, and Wise counties extend the distribution westward into the known range of *Geomys bursarius.* This range extension warrants further study as a possible contact zone between the species.

Plains Pocket Gopher

Geomys bursarius (Shaw)

Description. These are medium to small sized, dark brown gophers with large fur-lined cheek pouches. The body is thickset and appears heaviest anteriorly, from which it gradually tapers to the tail, widening a little at the thighs. The eyes are tiny and beadlike, and the ears are very rudimentary, represented only by a thickened ridge of skin at the base. Long curved claws are present on the front feet for digging; the claws on the hind feet are much smaller. All species of *Geomys* in Texas are sexually dimorphic, with females being smaller than males.

Dental formula: I 1/1, C 0/0, Pm 1/1, M 3/3 x 2 = 20. The upper incisors have two grooves. External measurements average: total length, 236 mm; tail, 65 mm; hind foot, 31 mm. Weight of males, 180–200 g; of females, 120–160 g.

Distribution. Northwestern and north-central Texas, south to Midland County in the west and to Grayson, Dallas, and McLennan counties in the east.

Subspecies. *G. b. jugossicularis* in the extreme northwestern part of the Panhandle and *G. b. major* over the remainder of the distribution in Texas.

Habits. This pocket gopher typically inhabits sandy soils where the topsoil is 10 cm or more in depth. Clayey soils are usually avoided. These gophers live most of their solitary lives in underground burrows, coming to the surface only to throw out earth removed in their tunneling and to forage for some items of food. They seldom travel far overland. The average diameter of 40 burrows examined in Texas

Plains Pocket Gopher (*Geomys bursarius*). Photo courtesy U.S. Fish and Wildlife Service.

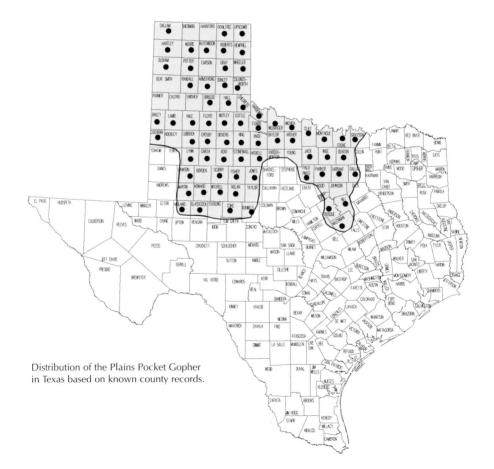

Distribution of the Plains Pocket Gopher
in Texas based on known county records.

was nearly 6 cm; the average depth below the surface, 14 cm, with extremes of 10 cm and 67.5 cm. Much of their burrowing is done in search of food. The underground galleries attain labyrinthine proportions in many instances because the tunnels meander aimlessly through the feeding areas. This is particularly noticeable under oak trees that have dropped a good crop of acorns. Burrows have been examined that extend well over 100 m, excluding the numerous short side branches. Only one adult gopher normally occupies a single burrow system.

The average mound thrown up by these gophers is about 30 by 45 cm, about 8 cm in height, and crescentic in outline. The opening through which the earth is pushed is usually plugged from within. The gopher digs with its front claws and protruding teeth, shoves the loose earth ahead of it with its chin and forefeet, and uses the hind feet for propulsion. The ceaseless energy of these subterranean miners is suggested by the size of the huge winter mounds they make in sites that have poor underground drainage. One was 2 m long, 1.5 m wide, 60 cm high, and weighed an estimated 360 kg. The female that occupied this mound weighed 150 g. A typical winter mound contains numerous galleries, a nest chamber, a toilet, and food storage chambers.

These rodents feed on a variety of plant items, chiefly roots and stems of weeds and grasses. Most plant food is encountered and ingested while the gopher digs, but some grazing of food present along burrow walls probably also occurs. The fur-lined cheek pouches are used to carry food and nesting material but never dirt. Captive gophers have eaten white grubs, small grasshoppers, beetle pupae, and crickets. Earthworms and raw beef were ignored.

Breeding begins in late January or early February and may continue through November. One litter a year, or two in quick succession, appears to be the rule. Litter size varies from one to six young. The young are nearly naked, blind, and helpless at birth. They remain with their mother until nearly full-grown and then are evicted to lead an independent life.

As long as they remain in their burrows, pocket gophers are relatively safe from predators other than those that are specialized for digging, such as badgers and long-tailed weasels. When a gopher leaves its burrow, however, it is highly vulnerable, and most predation losses probably occur on the surface. Known predators, other than those mentioned above, include coyotes, skunks, domestic cats, hawks, owls, and several kinds of snakes. As a result of the protection offered by the burrow, pocket gophers are long-lived relative to many other rodents, insectivores, and lagomorphs, living an average of 1–2 years in the wild.

In farming regions these rodents can be destructive to crops and orchards. The amount of damage is closely associated with the number of animals. The average population density in eastern Texas is about 3.2 gophers per ha. The highest population density of record is 17.6 per ha. These gophers can be controlled on small areas by trapping and on large ones by placing poisoned grain in their burrows.

Conservation Status. This gopher is common in the northern Panhandle of Texas, and there do not appear to be any serious threats to its status.

Remarks. Historically, *Geomys bursarius* has been considered a wide-ranging but morphologically variable species that was distributed over most of the Great Plains and south-central United States, including the Texas Panhandle and eastern Texas. Recent studies by specialists trained in cytological and biochemical taxonomy have revealed that in actuality there are five species of pocket gophers ranging over those regions of Texas (designated *G. bursarius*, *G. attwateri*, *G. breviceps*, *G. knoxjonesi*, and *G. texensis*). They are considered cryptic species, meaning that they cannot be differentiated on the basis of observed morphological characteristics although they are genetically distinct. Karyotypic, electrophoretic, and mitochondrial DNA data are required to distinguish questionable specimens confidently.

Jones's Pocket Gopher

Geomys knoxjonesi Baker and Genoways

Description. This is a cryptic species of the plains pocket gopher, *G. bursarius*. Morphologically, Jones's pocket gopher appears to be slightly smaller, both externally and cranially, than the plains pocket gopher, but careful study of genetic characters is required before the two may be distinguished. Coloration is buff-brown dorsally, somewhat paler on the sides and ventrally, with white feet. Dental formula as in *G. bursarius*.

Distribution. Southwestern plains of Texas and southeastern plains of New Mexico. In Texas, known from Cochran, Yoakum, Terry, Gaines, Dawson, Andrews, Martin,

Jones's Pocket Gopher (*Geomys knoxjonesi*). Photo by Robert D. Bradley.

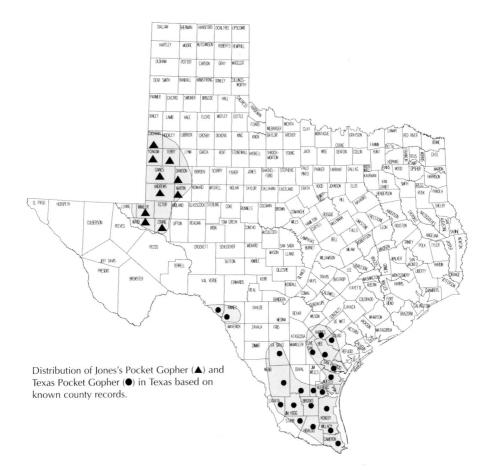

Distribution of Jones's Pocket Gopher (▲) and Texas Pocket Gopher (●) in Texas based on known county records.

Winkler, Ward, and Crane counties at sites of deep sandy soils of aeolian origin. *G. knoxjonesi* has been found in sympatry with *Cratogeomys castanops* near Brownfield in Terry County.

Subspecies. Monotypic species.

Habits. The habits of *G. knoxjonesi* are similar to *G. bursarius*. Pregnant females have been recorded in January from Terry County, March from Cochran and Yoakum counties, and July from Andrews County. Average number of fetuses in seven pregnancies was 2.1 (range 1–3). Although genetic evidence for hybridization with *G. bursarius* has been found, the apparent zone of contact between the two species is extremely narrow, and the resultant hybrid offspring are sterile or have a lower level of fertility, indicating that the two species rarely interact reproductively.

Conservation Status. This gopher appears to be locally common throughout its range.

Remarks. Originally recognized as a new subspecies of *G. bursarius* in 1987, additional genetic analysis of this pocket gopher by Robert Baker and his students has

subsequently shown that Jones's pocket gopher is essentially reproductively isolated from *G. bursarius* and therefore constitutes a separate species. There is still
some question about its distinctness from *G. arenarius*. For a discussion, see the
desert pocket gopher account.

Texas Pocket Gopher
Geomys personatus True

Description. A large, pale drab or grayish drab species with relatively long, scant-
haired tail, the distal half nearly naked; upper incisors with two grooves; underparts marbled white and dusky. External measurements of males average: total
length, 321 mm; tail, 110 mm; hind foot, 41 mm; of females, 303-103-39 mm. Weight,
up to 400 g. Dental formula as in *G. bursarius*.

Distribution. South Texas as far north as Val Verde County on the west and San
Patricio County on the east. See distribution map in the account for *Geomys
knoxjonesi*.

Subspecies. Six currently recognized: *G. p. davisi* in the Rio Grande Valley in western Webb and Zapata counties, *G. p. fallax* from Nueces Bay northward to Karnes
County, *G. p. fuscus* from Kinney and Val Verde counties, *G. p. maritimus* in Kleberg
and Nueces counties, *G. p. megapotamus* from La Salle County southeastward to
the south side of Baffin Bay and to the Rio Grande, and *G. p. personatus* on Mustang
and Padre islands.

Texas Pocket Gopher (*Geomys personatus*). Photo by Robert D. Bradley.

Habits. This species occurs in deep, sandy soils. It is entirely absent from the silt loams of the floodplains of the Rio Grande and also from gravelly, stony, or clayey soils scattered throughout its general range.

Numerous burrows of these gophers occur in the deep drift sands on Mustang and Padre islands where the sand is moist enough to permit packing. Sometimes the tunnels are at the water table and the runways soppy with seepage, but most often they are about halfway between the surface and the water table 50 cm below. Excavated burrows average about 10 cm in horizontal diameter, 12.5 cm in vertical diameter, and 25 cm beneath the surface. In places where the sand is drier, yet still moist enough to maintain a burrow, the tunnels are about 12 by 15 cm in diameter. In the soils near Robstown, Texas, the burrows ranged from 6 to 8 cm in diameter.

One partially excavated burrow system on Padre Island was more than 30 m long. There were numerous short side branches, but no food cache or chamber for fecal pellets (as is usual in burrows of *Geomys*) was found. Another burrow excavated on the mainland contained a food cache of Bermuda grass. The average mounds are large; a typical one might measure 45 by 60 cm in horizontal diameter and 12 cm in height. It could contain almost 6 kg of sand.

These gophers are ferocious isolationists; they resent molestation. When angry they emit a wheezy call at frequent intervals and gnash their teeth.

Their food consists largely of vegetation. Known items include roots of grasses (*Paspalum, Cynodon,* and *Cenchrus*) and the roots, stems, and leaves of a composite (*Helianthus*). Most of their foraging is done underground; the plants often are seized from below and pulled into the burrow. Their feces are capsule-shaped and about 19 mm in length and 7 mm in diameter. Individuals of this species, as well as other *Geomys,* have the interesting habit of ingesting their own fecal pellets. A fecal pellet is taken in the incisors directly from the anus, examined and manipulated with the aid of the forefeet, and then either discarded or thoroughly chewed and swallowed. Usually two to four pellets are produced at a time, with only one or two being eaten, often none. There appears to be no pattern as to which pellet or pellets are eaten. Production of fecal pellets often occurs in the nest, in which case the rejected pellets are simply pushed out into the adjoining tunnel. Pocket gophers may also stop their travels through the burrow system to defecate, again either discarding or eating the pellets after examining each one carefully. Captive individuals have been seen to interrupt a meal of grass, potatoes, or other food to defecate and then consume one or more fecal pellets. This behavior is well documented for many species of rabbits and rodents and may serve to extract maximum sustenance from ingested plant foods.

Their breeding habits are not well known. Pregnant females have been captured in December–March, May, July, October, and November, suggesting that breeding may occur year round. Young gophers about one-fourth grown were trapped in early April. Litter size ranges from one to five, averaging three. Probably no more than two litters are reared yearly.

In southern Texas these gophers have little economic importance except in cultivated fields or where they become established along the highways. Along highways they may undermine the shoulders and initiate erosion.

Conservation Status. One of the subspecies of the Texas pocket gopher bears watching. *G. p. maritimus* is known only from its type locality, at Flour Bluff, near Corpus Christi, and from Kleberg County. Since one of the localities is within the greater Corpus Christi metropolitan area, it obviously could be threatened by urbanization. Other populations of this pocket gopher appear to be in good shape.

Strecker's Pocket Gopher
Geomys streckeri Davis

Description. This is a cryptic species of the Texas pocket gopher, *G. personatus*. Morphologically, Strecker's pocket gopher is significantly smaller, both externally and cranially, than the Texas pocket gopher, but careful study of genetic characteristics and parasites is required to distinguish the two unambiguously. Color similar to that of *G. personatus* but slightly darker; ventral coloration largely plumbeous, with patches of white along the midline.

Distribution. Restricted to Dimmit and Zavala counties in the vicinity of Carrizo Springs and Crystal City in south Texas.

Subspecies. Monotypic species.

Habits. *G. streckeri* appears to occupy the fluvial deposits along the watercourses and the deep Carrizo sands on a western tributary of the Nueces River. It is separated from the nearest populations of *G. personatus* by about 40 km (25 miles) of unsuitable soils along the Nueces River. The habits of *streckeri* are probably similar to those of *personatus*.

Strecker's Pocket Gopher (*Geomys streckeri*). Photo by John and Gloria Tveten.

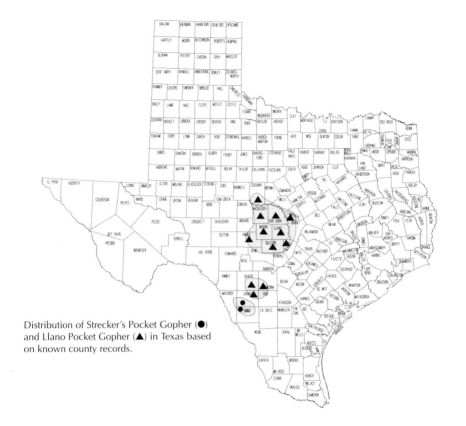

Distribution of Strecker's Pocket Gopher (●) and Llano Pocket Gopher (▲) in Texas based on known county records.

Conservation Status. This pocket gopher is known from only two localities in south Texas. Obviously, there is a need to document its full range and ascertain its population status. Presently it does not appear on any official rare or threatened listing of mammals, but it should be carefully monitored because of its rarity and limited geographic range.

Remarks. Ted Jolley and Rodney Honeycutt of Texas A&M and Robert Bradley of Texas Tech used gene sequencing to verify the specific distinctness of *G. streckeri*. Previously, other geneticists had reported *streckeri* to be the only *personatus*-type gopher in south Texas to have a diploid number of 72. Also, *streckeri* is unique in hosting the louse *Geomydoecus truncatus,* which has not been discovered in populations of *personatus* that host two other species of *Geomydoecus.*

Llano Pocket Gopher

Geomys texensis Merriam

Description. A cryptic species with *G. bursarius* and *G. knoxjonesi.* Morphologically, the Llano pocket gopher is slightly smaller than the plains pocket gopher, but biochemical study is required to separate the two reliably. Dental formula as in *G. bursarius.*

Llano Pocket Gopher (*Geomys texensis*). Photo by Robert D. Bradley.

Distribution.   Occurs only in two apparently isolated areas of the Texas Hill Country. A small area of distribution occurs in Medina, Uvalde, and Zavala counties. In the central Hill Country, recent records from Coleman, Lampasas, Blanco, and Kimble counties have extended the known range north, east, and west. Like *Geomys attwateri,* this species is unique to Texas; it occurs nowhere else in the world. See distribution map in the account for *Geomys streckeri.*

Subspecies.   *G. t. texensis* in the Hill Country; *G. t. bakeri* in south Texas (Medina, Uvalde, and Zavala counties).

Habits.   The natural history of *G. texensis* is undoubtedly similar to that of *G. bursarius.* The Llano pocket gopher is found in deep, brown loamy sands or gravelly sandy loams and is isolated from other species of *Geomys* by intervening shallow, stony to gravelly, clayey soils. *G. texensis* may be found inhabiting valley areas and fluvial soils at the margins of rivers and streams as well as city parks, lawns, and roadside drainage ditches.

Five specimens in the Texas Cooperative Wildlife Collection at Texas A&M University, collected in Llano County in mid-March, were reproductively active when captured. One contained three embryos, one had two embryos, one was inseminated, one was lactating, and the fifth was pregnant with "very small embryos." A sixth specimen from the area contained no embryos and showed no signs of reproductive activity.

Conservation Status.   The subspecies in the Hill Country, *G. t. texensis,* is locally abundant and does not appear to be threatened. Populations from Sycamore Creek and the Rio Grande are now extinct because of the flooding of their habitat when the Amistad Reservoir was created. Populations of *G. t. bakeri,* a recently described subspecies, occur in patchily distributed soils along separate drainages of the Frio River. Given the limited distribution of this species and its subspecies, periodic monitoring is recommended.

Remarks. Scott Block and Earl Zimmerman theorize that increasing warmer and drier periods in Texas climate beginning about 10,000 years ago may have led to the geographic isolation of this pocket gopher. As lengthy drought cycles caused accelerated soil erosion and a decrease in the former mesic vegetation of western Texas, the increasingly xeric conditions may have served to help isolate *G. texensis* in the small range seen today and contributed to its speciation.

Yellow-faced Pocket Gopher
Cratogeomys castanops (Baird)

Description. A moderately large pocket gopher, dull yellowish brown in color, with one deep groove on outer face of each upper incisor; feet blackish (whitish in most other gophers). Dental formula: I 1/1, C 0/0, Pm 1/1, M 3/3 x 2 = 20. External measurements of males average: total length, 295 mm; tail, 95 mm; hind foot, 33 mm; of females, 256-77-33 mm. Weight of males, 216–321 g; of females, 213–330 g.

Distribution. Found in western one-third of state, from Panhandle southward to the extreme northwestern and western portion of the Edwards Plateau and continuing along the Rio Grande into Maverick and Cameron counties.

Yellow-faced Pocket Gopher (*Cratogeomys castanops*). Photo by John and Gloria Tveten.

Subspecies. Seven recognized in Texas: *C. c. angusticeps* known only from the vicinity of Eagle Pass, Maverick County; *C. c. clarkii* in the Big Bend and much of the southern Trans-Pecos area; *C. c. dalquesti* in west-central Texas to the north of the Edwards Plateau but southeast of the Llano Estacado; *C. c. lacrimalis* from the New Mexican border south in the Pecos drainage to Reeves, Ward, and Winkler counties; *C. c. parviceps* in the far western Trans-Pecos; *C. c. perplanus* on the High Plains of northwestern Texas; *C. c. tamaulipensis* known only from Cameron County.

Habits. These large gophers are partial to deep, mellow soils that are relatively free from rocks. Where the three genera (*Cratogeomys, Geomys,* and *Thomomys*) occur in the same general area, as in western Texas, *Thomomys* usually occupies the shallower rocky soils in the mountains, *Geomys* lives in the deep sands along the rivers, and *Cratogeomys* utilizes the areas in between. *Cratogeomys,* however, is likely to occupy the sandy areas where no *Geomys* occur. The three genera are usually mutually exclusive in their distribution.

Their burrows are 75–100 mm in diameter, depending on the texture of the soil. The tunnels and mounds are smaller in clayey than in sandy soils.

Distribution of the Yellow-faced Pocket Gopher in Texas based on known county records.

These gophers are strictly herbivorous, feeding on plant roots, tubers, bulbs, stems, leaves, and even the outer bark of trees. Alfalfa, clover, hay crops, garden vegetables, and lechuguilla are also utilized.

C. castanops is reproductively active throughout the year, with no obvious peaks in activity. Gravid females have been taken during every month. Litters range in size from one to four, with two being the average number of young. In Lubbock County, females have been found to produce as many as three litters per breeding season, extending from January to October, with a peak period in March and April.

It appears that conditions of increasing aridity may favor the distribution of *Cratogeomys* over other gophers, such as *Thomomys*. From early 1969 to April 1970, the Davis Mountains of the Trans-Pecos received little or no rain. As the area became drier, *Thomomys*, which once occurred from near the bed of Limpia Creek to the foot of the rock bluffs lining the canyon, moved closer to the stream and *Cratogeomys* moved into the vacated area. These changes may be linked to a decrease in soil moisture and subsequent increase in xeric-adapted plants, both conditions that would favor *Cratogeomys* over *Thomomys*. The replacement of *Thomomys bottae* populations by *Cratogeomys castanops* in the Southwest has been noted by several authors during the twentieth century. The phenomenon could be considered as strictly natural, one that normally occurs in the evolution and replacement of species over geological time. The problem, however, is complicated by the overgrazing that has taken place in the Davis Mountains since the 1870s; it changes the environment, causing dramatic plant community changes, increased runoff, and, ultimately, more xeric conditions. The xeric conditions, in turn, favor *Cratogeomys* over *Thomomys*.

In situations where *Cratogeomys* and *Geomys* are sympatric in the Texas Panhandle, *Geomys* are restricted to the deep sandy soils, whereas *Cratogeomys* tend to occupy shallower, firmer soils. The yellow-faced pocket gopher does quite well in the deeper soils but is apparently excluded from such sites by the presence of *Geomys*.

Conservation Status. This remains one of the most common pocket gophers throughout its range in Texas, without any apparent serious threats. The two subspecies with highly localized ranges (*C. c. angusticeps* and *C. c. tamaulipensis*) should be monitored periodically to ascertain whether they are under threat.

FAMILY HETEROMYIDAE (POCKET MICE AND KANGAROO RATS)

Heteromyids have external, fur-lined cheek pouches for transporting food. Their diet is dominated by seeds and vegetation but occasionally includes insects and other invertebrates. Many species are extremely well adapted to desert environments and capable of existing with little or no free water intake. All heteromyids are nocturnal. Kangaroo rats are strongly bipedal and have enlarged hindquarters. Texas is home to 13 heteromyid rodents.

Nine-banded Armadillo (*Dasypus novemcinctus*). Photo by John and Gloria Tveten.

Desert Shrew (*Notiosorex crawfordi*). Photo by John and Gloria Tveten.

Eastern Mole (*Scalopus aquaticus*). Photo by John and Gloria Tveten.

Ghost-faced Bat (*Mormoops megalophylla*). Photo by
Merlin D. Tuttle, Bat Conservation International.

Mexican Long-tongued Bat (*Choeronycteris mexicana*). Photo by Merlin D. Tuttle, Bat Conservation International.

Eastern Red Bat (*Lasiurus borealis*). Photo by Merlin D. Tuttle, Bat Conservation International.

Spotted Bat (*Euderma maculatum*). Photo by Merlin D. Tuttle, Bat Conservation International.

Pallid Bat (*Antrozous pallidus*). Photo by Merlin D. Tuttle, Bat Conservation International.

Brazilian Free-tailed Bat (*Tadarida brasiliensis*). Photo by John and Gloria Tveten.

Coyote (*Canis latrans*). Photo by John and Gloria Tveten.

Northern Raccoon (*Procyon lotor*). Photo by John and Gloria Tveten.

American Badger (*Taxidea taxus*). Photo by John and Gloria Tveten.

Northern River Otter (*Lontra canadensis*). Photo by John and Gloria Tveten.

Hog-nosed Skunk (*Conepatus leuconotus*). Photo by John and Gloria Tveten.

Sperm Whale (*Physeter macrocephalus*). Photo by James Mead.

Pygmy Sperm Whale (*Kogia breviceps*). Illustration by Larry Foster.

Bottlenose Dolphin (*Tursiops truncatus*). Photo by Carrie W. Hubard, courtesy NOAA.

Spinner Dolphin (*Stenella longirostris*). Photo by Keith D. Mullin, courtesy NOAA.

Collared Peccary (*Pecari tajacu*). Photo by John and Gloria Tveten.

White-tailed Deer (*Odocoileus virginianus*). Photo by John and Gloria Tveten.

Pronghorn (*Antilocapra americana*). Photo by John and Gloria Tveten.

Southern Flying Squirrel (*Glaucomys volans*). Photo by John and Gloria Tveten.

Plains Pocket Gopher (*Geomys bursarius*). Photo by Rodney Honeycutt.

Plains Pocket Mouse (*Perognathus flavescens*). Photo by John and Gloria Tveten.

Texas Kangaroo Rat (*Dipodomys elator*). Photo courtesy Texas Parks and Wildlife.

American Beaver (*Castor canadensis*). Photo by John and Gloria Tveten.

White-footed Mouse (*Peromyscus leucopus*). Photo by John and Gloria Tveten.

Golden Mouse (*Ochrotomys nuttalli*). Photo by John and Gloria Tveten.

Hispid Cotton Rat (*Sigmodon hispidus*). Photo by John and Gloria Tveten.

Southern Plains Woodrat (*Neotoma micropus*). Photo by John and Gloria Tveten.

Muskrat (*Ondatra zibethicus*). Photo by John and Gloria Tveten.

North American Porcupine (*Erethizon dorsatum*). Photo by John and Gloria Tveten.

Plains Pocket Mouse

Perognathus flavescens Merriam

Description. A small, silky, yellowish buff pocket mouse; upperparts more or less washed with blackish; pelage relatively short. External measurements average: total length, 130 mm; tail, 61 mm; hind foot, 17 mm. Weight of adults, 8–11 g. Dental formula, as in all heteromyids: I 1/1, C 0/0, Pm 1/1, M 3/3 x 2 = 20.

Distribution. A mouse of the Great Plains region. Recorded in Texas from El Paso County and from the High Plains and adjacent areas in northwestern part of state, south to Ward County.

Subspecies. *P. f. copei* in northwestern Texas and *P. f. melanotis* in the western Trans-Pecos.

Habits. This little pocket mouse is partial to sandy soils covered with sparse vegetation. In the sandhills of the Texas Panhandle its burrows are commonly excavated beneath clumps of Spanish bayonet or prickly pear, the entrances usually so distributed as to open from under the plant in all directions. Usually the main entrance is plugged with soil from within during the day, and if it is opened the mouse closes it again. The several inconspicuous openings, hardly large enough to admit the end of one's finger, are seldom plugged and may serve as duckouts.

Their food is almost exclusively the seeds of grasses and weeds. Food items found in their cheek pouches include seeds of needle grass (*Stipa*), bindweed, sandbur grass, a small bean (probably *Astragalus*), and sedge (*Cyperus*). Even those caught in grain fields usually have their pouches filled with weed seeds. Seeds of two species of pigeon grass, a few other grasses, and wild buckwheat have been found in their underground food caches.

Plains Pocket Mouse (*Perognathus flavescens*). Photo by John and Gloria Tveten.

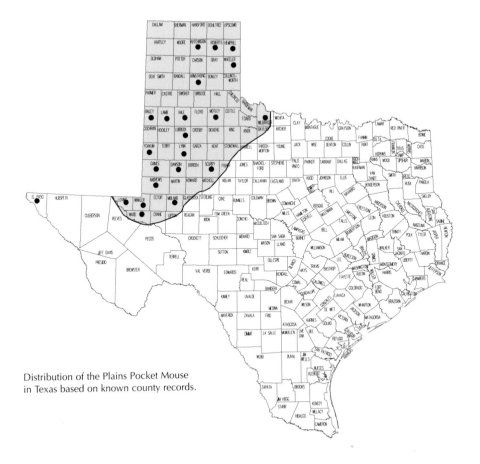

Distribution of the Plains Pocket Mouse
in Texas based on known county records.

Knowledge of their breeding habits is meager. Pregnant females (carrying four to five fetuses) have been trapped in June, July, and August. Specimens in juvenile pelage or molting from juvenile pelage have been recorded in May, June, July, August, and October. No information is available on mating, gestation, birth, growth of the young, and family life. It is possible this pocket mouse enters torpor during the coldest months of the year.

Conservation Status. This pocket mouse remains common throughout its range in the state and does not appear to face any immediate threats.

Silky Pocket Mouse

Perognathus flavus Baird

Description. A small pocket mouse with soft, silky fur, short ears, and short, sparsely haired tail; upperparts pinkish buff, lightly mixed with black; underparts pure white; spot behind ear clear buff and conspicuous; ears light buff on outside, blackish inside; tail pale buffy, slightly darker above. Closely resembles *Perognathus merriami,* from which it differs in the frequency of biochemical genetic markers and in

Silky Pocket Mouse (*Perognathus flavus*). Photo by John and Gloria Tveten.

features of the skull such as larger auditory bullae and a more square interparietal bone. External measurements average: total length, 113 mm; tail, 50 mm; hind foot, 16 mm. Weight, 6–8 g. Dental formula as in *Perognathus flavescens.*

Distribution. Known from the Trans-Pecos and northern Panhandle.

Subspecies. Probably *P. f. flavus,* although some questions remain regarding the taxonomy of this species.

Habits. Silky pocket mice appear to be more tolerant of habitat conditions than some of the other species of small pocket mice. In some areas they are found in rocky situations; in others on hard, stony soils; and in still others on sands. In most localities, however, they occur on mellow soils of valley bottoms where they live among the scattered weeds and shrubs and burrow in the sand.

As with other species of pocket mice the burrows of *P. flavus* are simple in design, usually shallow and barely large enough to admit a man's finger. One excavated near Sierra Blanca, Texas, was in the bank of a dike thrown up to divert water from the highway. The three openings converged to a single burrow that led along the dike for a distance of about 1 m, at no place penetrating more than 10 cm below the surface. Two side branches diverged from the main burrow, one of them sloping upward to near the surface. This branch probably was a duckout, because the occupant escaped from it by breaking through the thin crust of earth at the blind end of the tunnel. No nest or store of food was encountered, although this mouse is known to store food.

P. flavus is nocturnal, but occasionally may be active outside its burrow during the day. At night it forages for seeds, which are collected and cached in its burrow for consumption the following day. *P. flavus* also will feed on green vegetation, juniper berries, and occasionally invertebrates.

Distribution of the Silky Pocket Mouse
in Texas based on known county records.

The breeding season extends from early spring to late fall. Half-grown young have been captured as early as 16 April and as late as 23 September, with other records on 28 May and 3 July; a lactating female was captured in December; and pregnant females have been documented in May, June, August, and October. Probably two or more litters of two to six young are reared each season. Nothing is known of the growth and development of the young and the family relations. An adult female lived in captivity for more than 5 years, but the age attained in the wild is probably not more than 2 or 3 years.

Conservation Status. This pocket mouse remains common throughout its range in the state and does not appear to face any immediate threats.

Merriam's Pocket Mouse

Perognathus merriami Allen

Description. A very small, silky-haired pocket mouse, similar to but slightly smaller than *P. flavescens*; upperparts ochraceous buff mixed with black; sides brighter, less blackish; underparts clear white; spot behind ear clear buff, the one below the ears, white; eye ring light; tail slightly darker above than below; winter pelage

Merriam's Pocket Mouse (*Perognathus merriami*). Photo by R. D. Porter, courtesy Texas Parks and Wildlife Department.

Distribution of Merriam's Pocket Mouse in Texas based on known county records.

brighter than in summer; young grayer, less ochraceous. Dental formula as in *P. flavescens*. External measurements average: total length, 116 mm; tail, 57 mm; hind foot, 16 mm. Weight, 7–9 g.

Distribution. Known from western two-thirds of state, but absent from extreme northern Panhandle and extreme western Trans-Pecos.

Subspecies. Probably *P. m. gilvus* in the western part of the Panhandle, Trans-Pecos, and western Edwards Plateau and *P. m. merriami* in the eastern part of the Panhandle, eastern Edwards Plateau, and south Texas.

Habits. In southern Texas, these tiny mice are most common on sandy soils where vegetation is sparse or at least short. In Trans-Pecos Texas, they are more common on stony and gravelly soils covered with sparse vegetation. On the Edwards Plateau, they are found in rocky habitats with interspersed midgrass species, such as sideoats grama, and in grassland valley habitats. They seem to have difficulty in traveling through heavy vegetation, and if forced into grass several centimeters high, their progress is materially impeded. Near Oiltown, Texas, they were especially common in stands of low Bermuda grass on the shoulders of the highway where they were gathering seeds. These pocket mice are found in soil substrates ranging from sandy, deep soils to clayey, shallow soils.

During cold periods, these small mice become torpid in their burrows, but they do not hibernate. They remain in torpor for only about 24 hours. Seed stores within the burrow are utilized during periods of cold weather, and they also feed on stored seeds before emergence from burrows in the evening hours.

Their tiny burrows are usually dug at the base of a shrub or a clump of cactus. Several were also found in the nearly vertical banks left by road graders at the sides of the highway right-of-way. One den consisted of three tunnels, 30–45 cm in length, which converged under a flat rock to a nest chamber about the size of a man's fist. Burrows were barely large enough to admit a man's index finger. These mice also make use of abandoned burrows of pocket gophers. Silky pocket mice are solitary in habit, save for a female and her offspring.

Their food consists largely of seeds of various grasses and weeds. They also feed on juniper seeds and other fruits if available. Insects make up a minor percentage of the diet. They refuse to drink; in fact, they can live for months without water. Silky pocket mice are rather sedentary in nature and have small home ranges.

The breeding season appears to extend from April to November, and possibly two or more litters of three to six young are reared each season. The gestation period is 26 days or longer in duration. Young in gray juvenile pelage have been captured in June, July, and late November. In the Big Bend region, Richard Porter found that the annual population turnover was 84%; in a study on the Black Gap Area and in the Big Bend, Keith Dixon found the turnover to be 75%. Dixon recorded a maximum life span of 33 and 22 months, respectively, for two mice on the Black Gap.

Conservation Status. This pocket mouse remains common throughout its range in the state and does not appear to face any immediate threats.

Remarks. The taxonomic status of *P. merriami* has had a confusing history. In 1973 Don Wilson presented morphological evidence indicating that *P. merriami* and *P. flavus* represented one species and combined both under the name *P. flavus*. Subsequent study using genetic analyses has shown, however, that two species are indeed represented. Using karyology and starch gel electrophoresis, Tom Lee and Mark Engstrom have shown that although the two taxa are highly similar morphologically, they do not appear to interbreed in areas of sympatry. Thus, in the central Trans-Pecos region and perhaps in the northern Panhandle region, these nearly identical species of pocket mice occur together but are reproductively isolated from each other. Recently, Joel Brant and Tom Lee have demonstrated that the two species can be discriminated using five cranial and three external measurements, but there is still a need for more systematic studies to determine the taxonomic status and exact distribution of these two species in Texas.

Chihuahuan Desert Pocket Mouse
Chaetodipus eremicus (Mearns)

Description. A medium-sized pocket mouse with long, heavily crested, and tufted tail; pelage coarse but lacking spines on rump; sole of hind foot naked to heel; upperparts vinaceous buff finely sprinkled with black, imparting a grayish tone;

Chihuahuan Desert Pocket Mouse (*Chaetodipus eremicus*).
Photo by John and Gloria Tveten.

sides like back; no lateral line; underparts and tail to tuft, white. External measurements average: total length, 205 mm; tail, 109 mm; hind foot, 25 mm. Weight, 15–23 g. Dental formula as in *Perognathus flavescens*.

Distribution. A southwestern pocket mouse that occurs in Texas mainly in the Trans-Pecos eastward to Val Verde and Crockett counties.

Subspecies. Monotypic species.

Habits. This species in general occurs on sandy or soft alluvial soils along stream bottoms, desert washes, and valleys. In the Big Bend of Texas, large numbers of them have been trapped in loose sand along the Rio Grande where the dominant vegetation was *Baccharis* and mesquite and also in a brushy draw where the soil was hard-packed silt. Occasionally they may also occupy desert scrubland and desert grassland habitats, but they are seldom found on gravelly soils or among rocks, a habitat preferred by the externally similar *Chaetodipus intermedius* and *C. nelsoni.* Their burrows, from which the sand has been thrown well out to one side, are usually found near the bases of bushes and are closed in the daytime.

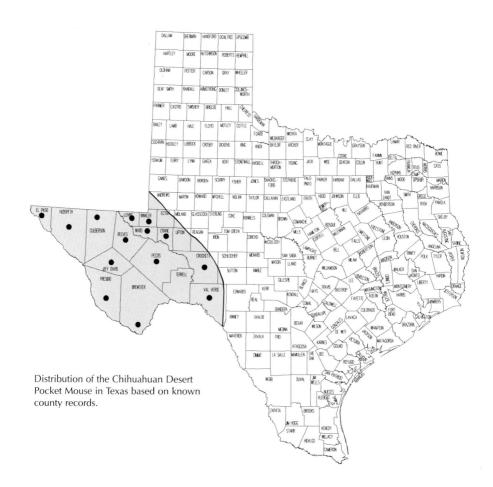

Distribution of the Chihuahuan Desert Pocket Mouse in Texas based on known county records.

Their habits are not well known. Like other pocket mice, they are strictly noc-turnal. They are known to be less active during the winter months and may enter a period of torpor during extremely cold weather. Their food consists of seeds; those of mesquite, creosote bush, and broomweed have been found in their cheek pouches.

Richard Porter found that in the Big Bend area the breeding season of this pocket mouse began in late February, the peak of pregnancies among females was in April, and the peak of juveniles in the population occurred in May. Lesser peaks of pregnancy occurred in June and August. The number of embryos per litter aver-aged 3.6, with extremes of 2 and 6. Many of the young females reached sexual matu-rity early and became pregnant while still in their juvenile pelage.

The annual population turnover in this species is high, nearly 95%, according to Porter's studies. Consequently, only 5% of the individuals present at the sea-son's peak survived 12 months in the wild. Only 2 juveniles of the 89 live-trapped animals he handled survived more than 1 year.

Conservation Status. This species is common throughout its range in Texas and does not appear to face any serious threats at this time.

Remarks. In previous editions this species was referred to as *Chaetodipus penicil-latus.* Recent studies of allozymes, chromosomes, and mitochondrial DNA sequences have shown that *C. penicillatus* should be divided into two species (*C. penicillatus,* a Sonoran Desert form, and *C. eremicus,* a Chihuahuan desert form). Thus, Texas specimens of this species are now classified as *C. eremicus.*

C. eremicus can be confused with two other species of *Chaetodipus, C. nelsoni* and *C. intermedius,* that occur in the Trans-Pecos. All three species have been doc-umented in Big Bend Ranch State Park in southern Presidio County, and Frank Yancey in his study of the mammals of that region documented some useful ways to distinguish them. It is fairly easy to differentiate *C. eremicus* from *C. nelsoni.* The for-mer usually is paler in color, lacks rump spines, and has pale-colored soles on the hind feet. Differentiation between *C. eremicus* and *C. intermedius* poses more of a problem, as the appearance of the dorsal pelage of the two mice is similar. On close examination, weak rump spines can be noticed on *C. intermedius;* they are com-pletely absent from *C. eremicus.* The three species also can be distinguished by pro-fessional mammalogists on the basis of subtle differences in cranial morphology.

Hispid Pocket Mouse

Chaetodipus hispidus Baird

Description. A medium to large pocket mouse with harsh pelage and large hind foot, the sole of which is naked to the heel; tail less than half of total length, dis-tinctly bicolor, sparsely haired, and lacking tuft; upperparts olive buffy, lined with black; lateral line wide and clear buff; underparts white. External measurements average: total length, 198 mm; tail, 93 mm; hind foot, 24 mm. Weight of adults, 30–47 g. Dental formula as in *Perognathus flavescens.*

Hispid Pocket Mouse (*Chaetodipus hispidus*). Photo by John and Gloria Tveten.

Distribution. Statewide except for extreme southeastern portion of the state.

Subspecies. *C. h. hispidus* in the east, *C. h. paradoxus* in the western one-third of the state, and *C. h. spilotis* in a limited area of north-central Texas.

Habits. These large pocket mice prefer a variety of dry, grassland habitats, characterized by areas of sand or other friable soil covered with scattered to moderate stands of herbaceous vegetation. The margins of brush fields and the rank growth in fencerows offer suitable cover along with highway rights-of-way. Dense stands of grasses and brush usually are avoided. These mice are not limited by soil substrate and may be found in sandy, loamy, and shallow rocky soils.

Their burrows are always dug in friable soil. They have been described as resembling 1-inch (25 mm) auger holes bored straight into the ground. Usually all the dirt excavated from the burrow system is piled near one opening, leaving the others inconspicuous and without mounds. The openings usually are plugged in the daytime. A burrow excavated in Brazos County had two openings, neither of which was plugged, connected by a single tunnel that descended to a depth of about 40 cm. A side branch contained food and nest chambers. Another burrow was found opening under a log, which served as a roof for the nest chamber. These mice have been known to inhabit deserted burrows of Mexican ground squirrels in central Texas.

Their nest is composed of shredded dry grasses and weeds. In captivity, the mice pile the nesting material into a loose heap and then mat it down by sleeping on top of the structure. They seem to behave likewise in the wild. They appear to be active through most of the year in the southern part of their range. They are not known to hibernate but may become torpid during periods of food shortage.

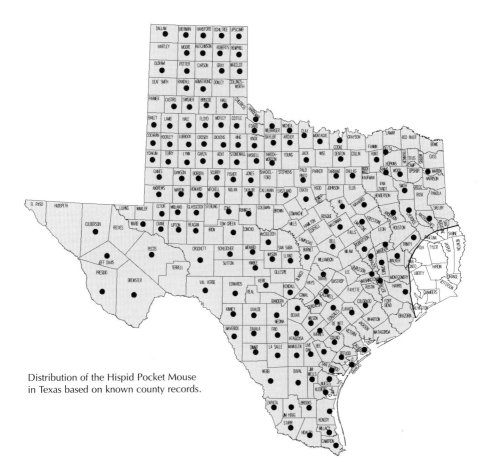

Distribution of the Hispid Pocket Mouse
in Texas based on known county records.

Their food consists almost entirely of vegetation, principally seeds. Seeds most often are collected from the ground, but occasionally this pocket mouse will climb vegetation in an effort to gather food. Frank Blair found the seeds of gaillardia, cactus, evening primrose, and winecup most frequently in their caches; in addition, he lists 23 other species of plants that were utilized. In Texas a cache of about half a liter of *Diodia teres* (poor joe) seeds was found, and in another instance the store was entirely seeds of sandbur grass (*Cenchrus*). Animal matter makes up only a small part of their diet. Blair lists grasshoppers, caterpillars, and beetles.

Some reproduction occurs in Texas throughout the year given favorable conditions. Pregnant females have been taken on the Llano Estacado in May, June, July, August, and November. Young animals out of the nest (about 1 month old) have been captured as early in the year as January and March, and from June through October. Based on embryo counts, the litter varies from two to nine, averaging six. Nothing is known regarding the gestation period or the growth and development of the young.

In sandy-land farming areas these mice can do considerable damage by digging up and carrying away planted seeds of cantaloupe, watermelon, peas, and small grains. In range and pasturelands they perform a service by eating seeds of weeds, sandbur, and other undesirable plants.

Conservation Status. The conservation status of *C. hispidus* seems to be okay at the present time, but this is another species that could be reduced by the continued degradation of grassland habitats in Texas. Thus, its status should be assessed periodically to determine population levels.

Rock Pocket Mouse
Chaetodipus intermedius Merriam

Description. A medium-sized, long-tailed pocket mouse; pelage rather harsh, with weak spines on rump; sole of hind foot naked to heel; tail longer than head and body, crested and distinctly tufted; upperparts drab, with strong admixture of black on back and rump; lateral line pale fawn, narrow; tail dusky above, white below; underparts white. Similar externally to *C. eremicus,* but hind foot usually smaller, upperparts much darker, tail with smaller scales and narrower annulations. External measurements average: total length, 180 mm; tail, 103 mm; hind foot, 23 mm. Weight, 12–18 g. Dental formula as in *Perognathus flavescens.*

Distribution. Common in the western portion of the Trans-Pecos region in El Paso, Hudspeth, Culberson, Jeff Davis, Presidio, Reeves, and Brewster counties. A record from Winkler County was on the map in the 1994 edition and mentioned in the 1974

Rock Pocket Mouse (*Chaetodipus intermedius*). Photo by John and Gloria Tveten.

edition of *The Mammals of Texas;* however, given the overall distribution of this species in Texas, and the ecological conditions in Winkler County, it is doubtful this species occurs there.

Subspecies. *C. i. intermedius.*

Habits. This species inhabits chiefly rocky situations, often where boulders are large and jumbled. At the eastern base of the Guadalupe Mountains in western Texas they have been found inhabiting rocky canyons, and in the Wylie Mountains they lived among huge boulders. Occasionally, they may be found on shrubby desert slopes on pebbly soils, rarely on silt soils. Vernon Bailey reported finding them on sandy soils among rocks. Apparently they rarely occur in areas of loose, alluvial, and windborne sands.

Their burrows are small, inconspicuous, and often closed during the daytime. Tiny trails lead away from them to feeding places among the plants. They choose burrow sites close to or under rocks.

The rock pocket mouse is strictly nocturnal; at night it forages primarily for the seeds of herbaceous plants. Seeds are cached for consumption during periods

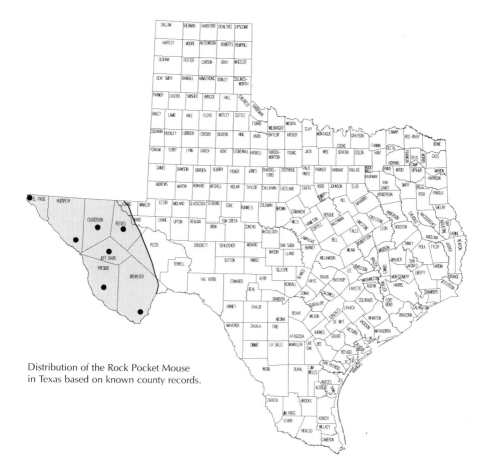

Distribution of the Rock Pocket Mouse
in Texas based on known county records.

of environmental stress. In addition, caching may help this pocket mouse maintain a diverse diet, and the growth of fungi on cached seeds may increase their nutritional value.

Judging from the meager data, breeding begins in February or March and continues for several months. Gravid females have been captured in May, June, and July. The litter varies from three to six. Nearly half-grown young in juvenile pelage have been taken in April, May, June, and August. There is no documentation of this pocket mouse's entering seasonal dormancy, and it probably is active year round. Their general habitat is such that they seldom conflict with human interests.

Conservation Status. This species is common throughout its range in Texas and does not appear to face any serious threats at this time.

Nelson's Pocket Mouse
Chaetodipus nelsoni Merriam

Description. A medium-sized pocket mouse with harsh pelage and numerous black-tipped spines on rump; tail longer than head and body, sparsely haired on basal half, the terminal half crested, penicillate, and indistinctly bicolor, darker above than below; upperparts drab gray, heavily lined with black; underparts pure white; soles of hind feet blackish. External measurements average: total length, 187 mm; tail, 104 mm; hind foot, 22 mm. Weight, 14–17 g. Dental formula as in *Perognathus flavescens.*

Nelson's Pocket Mouse (*Chaetodipus nelsoni*). Photo by John and Gloria Tveten.

Distribution. A Mexican form that commonly occurs in Texas in the southern and central Trans-Pecos region and just east of the Pecos River and the Rio Grande. Its eastern distributional limits are reached on the western Edwards Plateau.

Subspecies. *C. n. canescens.*

Habits. This is a rock-loving species. In Big Bend National Park in southern Brewster County, it occurs most commonly at the base of the Chisos Mountains at altitudes ranging from 700 to 1,450 m. There it is found in rocky areas supporting sparse stands of chino grass, sotol, bear grass (*Nolina*), and candelilla; sandy washes seem to be avoided. At Big Bend Ranch State Park, in southern Presidio County, this pocket mouse has a strong preference for desert scrub and grassland vegetation, although it also was taken in riparian and juniper roughland habitats.

In the Big Bend region, Richard Porter found that the breeding season begins in February, the peak of pregnancy among females is reached in March, and juveniles entered his live traps in April. By inference, therefore, the gestation period is about 1 month, and the young leave the nest when about 4 weeks of age. Pregnant females were captured in each month from March through July. The number of embryos per litter averaged 3.2 with extremes of 2 and 4.

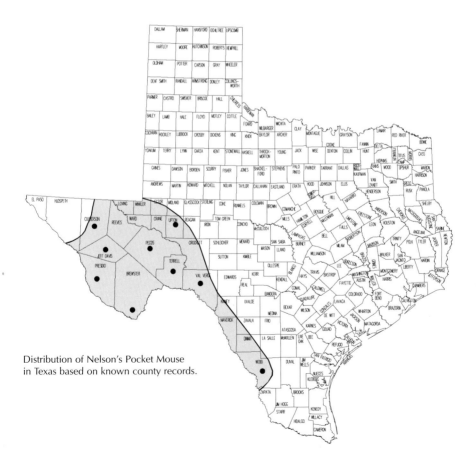

Distribution of Nelson's Pocket Mouse
in Texas based on known county records.

The annual turnover in the population he studied was about 86%; that is, only 14 of each 100 individuals survived from one year to the next. Keith Dixon, working on the Black Gap in the Big Bend, recorded two individuals marked as juveniles that survived for at least 30 months in the wild, one other for 24 months, and two others for about 20 months.

C. nelsoni is strictly nocturnal; at night it forages primarily for seeds, including those of mesquite, creosote bush, and prickly pear. In addition to seeds, it also may consume other plant parts and insects.

Porter reported that *nelsoni* was more active in winter (December) than either of the other two pocket mice (*Perognathus flavus* and *Chaetodipus eremicus*) on his study area. Seemingly, *nelsoni* does not hibernate.

Conservation Status. This species is common throughout its range in Texas and does not appear to face any serious threats at this time.

Gulf Coast Kangaroo Rat

Dipodomys compactus True

Description. A five-toed, medium-sized kangaroo rat; tail relatively short; pelage short and coarse; upperparts range in coloration from grayish to light ochraceous buff intermixed with black; cheeks white, and soles of feet and dorsal and ventral tail stripes brownish. Similar in appearance to *D. ordii* but with shorter tail, shorter and coarser pelage, and less brownish in coloration. *D. compactus* is smaller than *D. ordii* cranially, particularly in length of skull and size of mastoid bullae. External measurements average: total length, 223 mm; tail, 118 mm; hind foot, 36 mm. Weight, 44–60 g. Dental formula as in *Perognathus flavescens.*

Gulf Coast Kangaroo Rat (*Dipodomys compactus*). Photo by John and Gloria Tveten.

Distribution. Known from most of south Texas north to Bexar and Gonzales counties; also known from Mustang and Padre islands.

Subspecies. *D. c. compactus* on the barrier islands and *D. c. sennetti* on the mainland.

Habits. The Gulf Coast kangaroo rat inhabits sandy, sparsely vegetated soils. On Padre Island they dwell among the shifting dunes of the barrier reef and in south Texas are often found on disturbed or overgrazed areas characterized by sparse, open vegetation and deep, loose sand.

Their food consists of the seeds of grasses, annuals, and shrubs. Specific food habits are not known.

Reproductive habits are not well known. A pregnant female containing two embryos was captured on 23 August, and another female taken on 6 July displayed two placental scars.

Conservation Status. This kangaroo rat is common on the mainland and barrier islands of south Texas, but continued development on Mustang and Padre islands could threaten its existence in the future. The status of these populations should be carefully monitored.

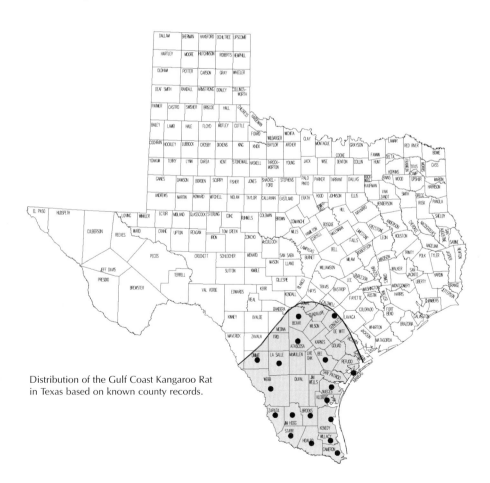

Distribution of the Gulf Coast Kangaroo Rat
in Texas based on known county records.

Texas Kangaroo Rat
Dipodomys elator Merriam

Description. A rather large, four-toed kangaroo rat with conspicuous white banner on tip of tail; tail long, relatively thick, and about 162% of length of head and body; body large (about 121 mm in length); upperparts buffy, washed with blackish; underparts white. This species superficially resembles *Dipodomys spectabilis,* but cranial differences readily separate them, and their distributions are disjunct. External measurements average: total length, 317 mm; tail, 196 mm; hind foot, 46 mm. Dental formula as in *Perognathus flavescens.*

Distribution. Occurs in north-central Texas from Cottle and Motley counties in the west to Montague County in the east.

Subspecies. Monotypic species.

Habits. The Texas kangaroo rat is a rare rodent with habitat preferences unusual for a kangaroo rat. It lives on clay soils supporting sparse, short grasses and small, scattered mesquite bushes. The rats make trails leading to their burrows, which invariably enter the ground at the base of a small mesquite, often in such fashion that one root of the mesquite forms the top or side of the opening. Scratching and dusting places, so characteristic of other species of kangaroo rats, are inconspicuous. The burrow is similar to that of Ord's kangaroo rat, but usually it is shorter and the animal does not plug the entrances during the daytime. Highly nocturnal, these kangaroo rats do not become active until complete darkness and reportedly cease activity on moonlit nights.

Texas Kangaroo Rat (*Dipodomys elator*). Photo courtesy Texas Parks and Wildlife Department.

D. elator feeds on the seeds, stems, and leaves of grasses, forbs, and some perennials. Analysis of material recovered from the cheek pouches of 52 kangaroo rats showed that the seeds of cultivated oats (*Avena*) and Johnsongrass (*Sorghum*) were the most important food items, followed by annual forbs such as stork's bill (*Erodium*), broomweed (*Xanthocephalum*), and bladderpod (*Lesquerella*). Shrubs and insects were not greatly utilized for food. They store food to carry them over periods of scarcity, as do most other kangaroo rats.

D. elator may breed year round. Pregnant females have been collected in February, June, July, and September. The young appear to develop rapidly, as subadult females collected in late summer have also been pregnant. Two peaks in reproductive activity, in early spring and again in late summer, may occur; mature females give birth early in the year, and their rapidly developing young become reproductively active in late summer. Average number of embryos is three.

Conservation Status. Because of its restricted geographic range and because of habitat alteration from time to time for agricultural purposes within that range, Texas Parks and Wildlife lists this species as threatened. U.S. Fish and Wildlife has taken a somewhat more cautious view of its status, all the while seeking additional information. It appears that heavily grazed rangeland and the eroded sites of

Distribution of the Texas Kangaroo Rat
in Texas based on known county records.

well-worn rangeland roadways may provide optimum habitat for this species, in the same manner that overgrazing and trampling by bison may have done in the past.

Merriam's Kangaroo Rat
Dipodomys merriami Mearns

Description. A small, four-toed, usually buff-colored kangaroo rat; tail rather long, usually more than 130% of length of head and body, tip dusky, and dorsal and ventral dusky stripes usually present; length of head and body usually less than 105 mm; dark facial markings rather pale; underparts white; pelage silky. External measurements average: total length, 247 mm; tail, 144 mm; hind foot, 39 mm. Weight, 40–50 g. Dental formula as in *Perognathus flavescens*.

Distribution. A rodent of the Southwest; known in Texas primarily from the Trans-Pecos northeastward to Gaines County in the north, to the extreme western portion of the Edwards Plateau, and to Dimmit County in the south.

Subspecies. *D. m. ambiguus.*

Habits. In its habitat requirements this species is more tolerant than most other species of kangaroo rats. It apparently can succeed equally well on sandy soils, clays, gravels, and even among rocks. Where *merriami* occurs with *Dipodomys ordii* or some other less tolerant and sand-dwelling kangaroo rat, *merriami* usually inhabits the harder, stonier soils. In Trans-Pecos Texas, this is the usual relationship: *D. ordii* is found in areas of loose sands, *D. merriami* in areas of clayey or

Merriam's Kangaroo Rat (*Dipodomys merriami*). Photo by John and Gloria Tveten.

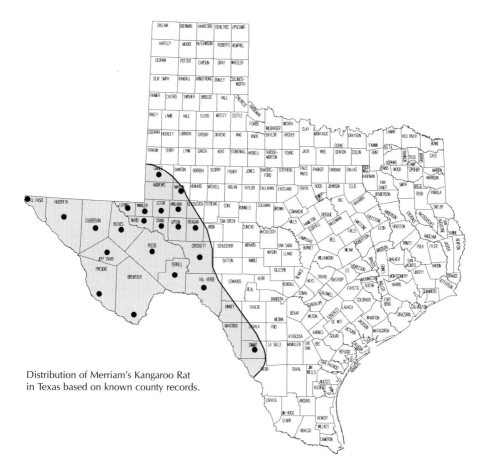

Distribution of Merriam's Kangaroo Rat
in Texas based on known county records.

stony soils that are not suitable habitat for the other species. On the Llano
Estacado *D. merriami* occurs along the southern part of the region where creosote
bush is common.

Their burrows are usually simple in design, shallow and with openings near
the bases of shrubs. In these, the rats live in the daytime and rear their families.
Usually, only one adult occupies each burrow system.

Their food is almost entirely seeds. Seeds of mesquite, creosote bush,
purslane, ocotillo, and grama grass have been found in their cheek pouches, as
well as green vegetation and insects. A study of *D. merriami* in the Guadalupe
Mountains showed that seeds make up 64% of the diet, with seeds of shrubs constituting 23%, those of forbs 24%, those of grasses 4.5%, and those of succulent
plants 12%. The diet varies seasonally, but seeds, green vegetation, and insects are
eaten throughout the year. Green vegetation is most important in midsummer, and
insects are eaten in greatest abundance in winter.

This kangaroo rat breeds throughout the year in the Big Bend region, with
gravid females having been taken in all months save December, January, and

February. The number of young per litter ranges from one to five, averaging about three. The gestation period is 29 days, and sexual maturity of young is usually attained in 60 days.

This species is not important economically. On rangelands, the rats may do some damage by consuming seeds of grasses, but in general, losses attributable to them are negligible.

Conservation Status. This is one of the most common kangaroo rats in the state; it does not appear to face any major threats at the present time.

Ord's Kangaroo Rat
Dipodomys ordii Woodhouse

Description. A five-toed kangaroo rat of medium size; tail relatively long, body actually and relatively short; tail seldom white-tipped; white patches at base of ears and above eyes usually conspicuous; upperparts pale cinnamon buff, intermixed with blackish; dark markings on face conspicuous. Juveniles similar to adults, but pelage duller and darker. External measurements of adults average: total length, 253 mm; tail, 159 mm; hind foot, 41 mm. Weight of adults, 60–70 g. Dental formula as in *Perognathus flavescens*.

Distribution. Known from the western, southwestern, and southern parts of the state.

Subspecies. *D. o. medius* from the central Llano Estacado southward east of the Pecos River to Crane, Crockett, and Upton counties; *D. o. obscurus* in the western, central, and southern parts of the Rio Grande Plains and in the southern Big Bend area; *D. o. ordii* in most of the Trans-Pecos region; and *D. o. richardsoni* from the Panhandle and adjacent areas southward at least to Floyd County and east to Montague County.

Habits. Ord's kangaroo rats, like many others of the genus, are dwellers of wastelands where shifting sands constitute a conspicuous part of the landscape. They are one of the few pioneer mammals that move into shifting dunes and establish themselves with pioneer plants. They rarely occur on hard and gravelly soils. Where they occur in areas with the smaller Merriam's kangaroo rat, Merriam's usually inhabits gravelly or hard soils, and Ord's the sands.

To withstand the extreme climatic conditions in their range, these rats dig deep burrows into the sand; when plugged from the inside, the burrows permit the occupants to spend the daylight hours in comfort and to avoid the hot, desiccating sun or the cold, wintery wind. They become active again at night, leaving their dens after sundown, and go abroad in their quest for food even in the dead of winter when snow is on the ground. They have not developed the convenient ability to hibernate.

Their food consists largely of the seeds of various desert plants, which they gather and place in their cheek pouches for transport to the burrow to be consumed at leisure. Mesquite, sandbur, tumbleweed, Russian thistle, sunflowers, and

Ord's Kangaroo Rat (*Dipodomys ordii*). Photo by John and Gloria Tveten.

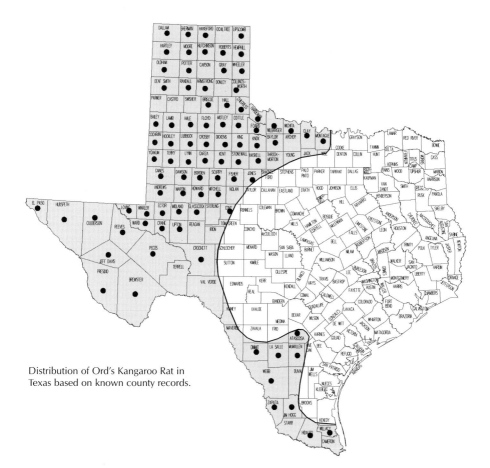

Distribution of Ord's Kangaroo Rat in Texas based on known county records.

countless desert annuals provide them with a wide range of choice. Surface water is not important in their economy. Like many other desert animals, they can produce their needed water physiologically from nearly dry seeds. So averse and unaccustomed to water are they that they have not learned to swim.

In a study of dietary overlap between *D. merriami* and *D. ordii* in the Guadalupe Mountains, Peggy O'Connell found both generally to be opportunistic granivores, with *merriami* eating more insects and green vegetation than *ordii*. Food consumed in fairly large proportions by one species was usually of minor importance in the diet of the other, thus explaining how the two species avoid competition.

In a two-year study conducted in the Texas Panhandle (Hemphill County), Jack Inglis found pregnant females of *D. ordii* in the period from August through February. Young individuals first appeared in his traps in November. Litter size, based on embryo counts, averaged slightly less than three, with extremes of two and four. Rate of reproduction was associated with precipitation, food supply, and population densities of kangaroo rats and other rodents. After a prolonged drought period when the food supply declined, few females became sexually active and few young were born. After a favorable growing season for food plants, most females in the population became pregnant within the first 2 months of the breeding season, and most of them produced two litters; young females born early in the season produced litters themselves before the season ended. The gestation period is about 30 days. The young are born in underground nests and remain there for nearly a month. They appear above ground when they are about three-fourths grown and weigh 40–50 g.

Because of the nature of their habits, they seldom come into serious conflict with humans. In sandy lands near San Antonio, however, they have been reported to gather and consume the seeds of watermelons and other row crops at planting time, but over most of their range they do no harm.

Conservation Status. *D. ordii* is common throughout its range in Texas and does not face any major threats.

Banner-tailed Kangaroo Rat
Dipodomys spectabilis Merriam

Description. A large, four-toed, long-tailed kangaroo rat; tail about 1.5 times as long as head and body, with a distinct white tuft at end; hind foot broad and usually 50 mm or more in length; upperparts dark buff; black facial markings and stripes on tail conspicuous. External measurements average: total length, 350 mm; tail, 210 mm; hind foot, 53 mm. Weight, 115 g. Dental formula as in *Perognathus flavescens*.
Distribution. Occurs in western and central Trans-Pecos region and east to Reagan County and north to Lubbock County.
Subspecies. *D. s. baileyi.*

Habits. This large kangaroo rat appears to be limited in distribution to sparsely brush-covered slopes and low hills at elevations usually between 1,200 and 1,500 m. In the Trans-Pecos it is most abundant on slopes covered with scattered, mixed stands of creosote brush and acacias on hard and moderately gravelly soil. It has never been encountered in loose soils or drift sands.

The large complex mounds of these rats are unmistakable evidence of their presence. On soils that will pack and withstand weathering, the mounds may be over 1 m in diameter and 9–130 cm in height, but on sandy soils they are less pretentious. As many as a dozen openings admit the rat to the complex system of galleries and side branches, and from them lead conspicuous trails across the surrounding sparse vegetation to the feeding areas. In addition, subsidiary burrows or duck-ins are relied on for protection. Usually only one rat occupies each den. In a manner similar to woodrats, *D. spectabilis* creates pathways, often clearly visible for several meters, from the mound to foraging areas. Burrows are occasionally constructed atop buried pipelines where indurated caliche has been loosened and presumably provides easier digging.

These rats are exceedingly fleet and agile, and to catch them at night by running them down is no mean feat. Once in the hand they can inflict painful wounds with their teeth unless handled carefully.

Their food is almost entirely plant materials, with seeds ranking high on the list. Green vegetation is eaten on occasion. Large quantities of food are stored in the dens to carry them over the periods of scarcity. Stores from a fraction of a gram to well over 5 kg have been found. Charles Vorhies and Walter Taylor listed 13

Banner-tailed Kangaroo Rat (*Dipodomys spectabilis*). Photo by John and Gloria Tveten.

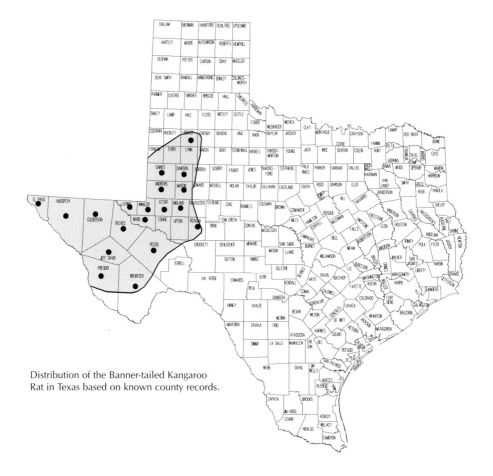

Distribution of the Banner-tailed Kangaroo
Rat in Texas based on known county records.

species of grass and 29 other plants that contribute to their diet. Needle grass, grama grass, mesquite, and a composite weed were the most important foods. They seldom drink, even if water is present.

The breeding season begins in January and continues into August. The young begin to appear in March, sometimes as early as February, and nearly full-grown juveniles are common by April. The gestation period is not known. The young are naked at birth, and the eyes and ears are closed; the number per litter varies from one to three but usually is two. They are born in an underground nest composed of fine vegetation and chaff refuse from the food. Nest chambers vary in size from 15 by 20 cm to 20 by 25 cm.

Their known natural enemies include badger, swift fox, bobcat, and coyote. Other animals also probably prey on them.

Bannertails have little economic impact. In periods of drought they may do some damage to rangelands by gathering and eating grass seeds, but they are not a major problem.

Conservation Status. Banner-tailed kangaroo rats remain common throughout their range in Texas, but further degradation or loss of grassland habitat could severely affect them. This is a species that should be carefully monitored in the future.

Mexican Spiny Pocket Mouse
Liomys irroratus (Gray)

Description. A medium-sized mouse with extremely harsh pelage over entire upperparts (the hairs flattened, sharp-pointed, and grooved); external, fur-lined cheek pouches; and relatively long tail. Similar in general appearance to the spiny-haired pocket mice (*Chaetodipus*), but upper incisors lack the longitudinal groove on the outer face and the pelage is much more spiny and harsh. Tail about as long as head and body, sparsely haired and distinctly bicolor, brownish above, whitish below; upperparts dark gray, grizzled with orange; underparts pure white; sole of proximal half of hind foot hairy, blackish. External measurements average: total length, 237 mm; tail, 122 mm; hind foot, 30 mm. Weight of males, 50–60 g; of females, 35–50 g. Dental formula as in *Perognathus flavescens.*

Distribution. A Mexican form reaching the United States in extreme south Texas, where it has been recorded from seven counties (Cameron, Hidalgo, Jim Hogg, Kenedy, Starr, Willacy, and Zapata) in the lower Rio Grande Valley.

Subspecies. *L. i. texensis.*

Habits. In southern Texas they live in the densest brush on the ridges forming the old banks of the Rio Grande, along oxbows, and in the scattered remnants of the

Mexican Spiny Pocket Mouse (*Liomys irroratus*). Photo by John and Gloria Tveten.

subtropical palm forests of the Rio Grande near Brownsville (Cameron County). They are often closely associated with thickets of prickly pear. In northern Mexico, they may be trapped among dense chaparral, but in the valley of Mexico they occurred around stone fences and among rocks on the sides of mountain slopes. They live in burrows and sometimes throw up small mounds to close the entrances. Usually the openings are covered by vegetation or dead leaves. They are strictly nocturnal.

In southern Texas, they feed on the seeds of hackberry, mesquite, and various other shrubs. In addition, seeds of various weeds may be found in their cheek pouches.

Very little is known about their breeding habits. In Mexico, half-grown young have been found in June and nearly full-grown young in August. None of the females captured in summer was pregnant or lactating. Based on the study of a large number of Mexican records, Theodore Fleming reported immature individuals of *Liomys irroratus* from all months except May; he believed that breeding occurs throughout the year, but most of it is concentrated in the winter period from November to February. Litter size is two to eight, averaging about four.

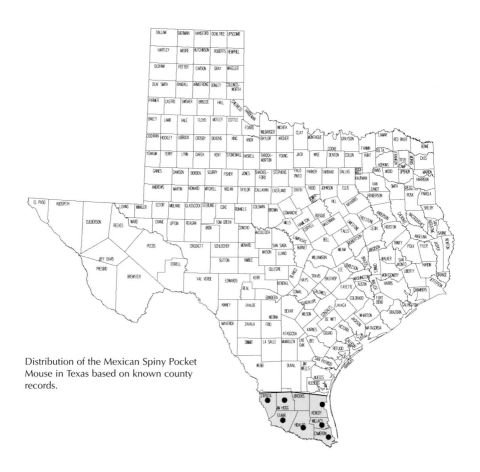

Distribution of the Mexican Spiny Pocket Mouse in Texas based on known county records.

Conservation Status. This species is relatively abundant where it occurs in south Texas, but its restricted range could make it vulnerable to future land clearing and development. It is extremely common throughout most of Mexico, and the species overall is not threatened.

FAMILY CASTORIDAE (BEAVERS)

The Castoridae family contains only two species worldwide. The North American species, *Castor canadensis,* is the largest rodent on the continent and is second in size only to the capybara of South America. Beavers are easily recognized by their distinctive, flattened tails. They are highly adapted for an aquatic existence. The fur of the beaver was so highly prized in the last century that it played a major role in encouraging the exploration of western North America.

American Beaver
Castor canadensis Kuhl

Description. A large, robust, aquatic rodent with a broad, horizontally flattened, scaly tail; hind feet webbed; upperparts in fresh fall pelage dark, rich, chestnut brown that fades by spring; underparts paler, often with silvery sheen. Sexes colored alike. External measurements average: total length, 1,160 mm; tail, 400 mm; hind foot, 178 mm. Weight, averages 18 kg; rarely as much as 27 kg. Dental formula: I 1/1, C 0/0, Pm 1/1, M 3/3 x 2 = 20.

Distribution. Found over most of the state where suitable aquatic habitat prevails. In the western part of its range it occurs in low density and local distribution, and it is absent from the Llano Estacado (except for Randall County) and some adjacent areas and from much of the Trans-Pecos.

Subspecies. *C. c. mexicanus* along the Rio Grande and its immediate tributaries and *C. c. texensis* to the north.

Habits. Beavers are essentially aquatic and require water in the form of a pond, stream, lake, or river for their well-being. Because of their skills in regulating water level and stream flow with dams, beavers are able to convert an otherwise unfavorable area into one that is habitable, but they must be ever alert as water engineers because their ponds tend to fill up with sediment washed off the slopes above and in time become meadows, forcing the beavers to move to new sites. Large rivers and lakes offer suitable habitat in places where natural food and den or house sites are available, but the largest populations are on small bodies of water.

In cold regions, beavers live in houses constructed of sticks and mud and enter and leave them by means of underwater tunnels, or plunge holes; in Texas they may burrow into cut banks of streams or lakes. Burrows examined in the Rio Grande in the Big Bend section of Texas were large enough to admit a man and were 10 m or more in length. Burrows as long as 50 m have been reported. Burrows, or houses, are used for loafing, sleeping, and rearing the young.

American Beaver (*Castor canadensis*). Photo by John and Gloria Tveten.

The average beaver colony consists of 6 or 7 animals, usually including parents and their young of two age classes; rarely is it as large as 12.

Beavers are obligate vegetarians, feeding on the leaves, twigs, and bark of a variety of plants, especially the inner bark of willows and cottonwood trees. In summer a number of herbaceous aquatic plants and sedges are eaten. In central Texas, where willows are absent, beavers in winter utilize as first choice such trees as button willow, juniper, and pecan and rely heavily on Bermuda grass, beard grass, ragweed, and yellow water lily in summer. Along the Rio Grande, beavers seem to prefer willows, although desert willow, mesquite, and tree tobacco also are consumed. Thus, the plants eaten and their order of preference depend in large measure on availability. The digestion of these woody materials is enhanced by a prominent cardiogastric gland in the stomach, glandular digestive areas elsewhere, and a large cecum containing cellulose-degrading microbes.

Breeding begins in January or February, and the young are normally born in May or June after a gestation period of about 107 days. Beavers are usually monogamous, and normally only one litter of three to four kits is produced each year, but some females produce a second litter in August or September.

At birth the kits are fully furred, the eyes are open, and the incisor teeth are visible; they weigh about 450 g. The tail is broad and flat, as in adults. They grow

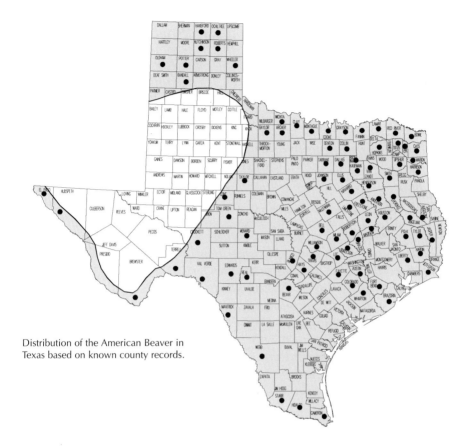

Distribution of the American Beaver in Texas based on known county records.

rather slowly and attain a weight of about 10 kg the first year. They mature sexually the second year. Rarely, yearling females may breed and produce young. The young often stay with the family group through the second year.

Their value as soil and water conservationists is well known and, in most sections of the country, appreciated. They can be destructive to crops, trees, and irrigation systems, however, in which case they can be live-trapped and removed from the area.

Conservation Status. By the 1850s beaver were reduced to very low population numbers over a considerable part of Texas because of excessive annual harvests by trappers. These animals were able to survive, however, on the remote streams of the upper and western Hill Country, along the Devil's River, along the edge of the Panhandle, and around El Paso. By the early 1900s they were found to be increasing in numbers, and shortly thereafter strict harvest regulations were imposed and restocking of depleted populations became common practice. Today, beaver are found over most of the state where suitable aquatic habitat prevails. Possible threats in the future include depletion of natural and man-made surface water and competition with the introduced nutria. Overharvesting is no longer a serious threat.

FAMILY MURIDAE (MICE AND RATS)

The family Muridae includes the mice, rats, hamsters, voles, lemmings, and gerbils. This is the largest family of mammals, with 281 genera and 1,326 species worldwide. Thirty-four species occur in Texas. All murids are relatively small mammals with short life spans and high reproductive rates. All murids have the same dental formula: I 1/1, C 0/0, Pm 0/0, M 3/3 x 2 = 16. They occupy all types of terrestrial habitats, and a few are arboreal or aquatic.

Coues's Rice Rat

Oryzomys couesi (Alston)

Description. Similar to *O. palustris,* but pelage shorter and color ochraceous buffy or ochraceous tawny instead of grayish brown; underparts buffy instead of whitish. External measurements average: total length, 297 mm; tail, 161 mm; hind foot, 34 mm. Weight, 50–86 g, averaging 65.3 g.

Distribution. A Mexican form reaching the United States in the lower Rio Grande Valley in Cameron and Hidalgo counties.

Subspecies. *O. c. aquaticus.*

Habits. Coues's rice rats have been captured in cattail-bulrush marshes and aquatic, grassy zones near resacas (oxbow lakes) in Hidalgo County. Apparently, riparian

Coues's Rice Rat (*Oryzomys couesi*). Photo by John and Gloria Tveten.

woodland and subtropical evergreen woodland near the resacas are avoided, or at least inhabited less commonly. Likewise, brushland habitats near resacas are not frequently used.

They build their nests in cattails and small trees near or above water. Nests are constructed of leaves, twigs, small vines, and cattail, all finely shredded and woven into a globular shape. No information is available on the reproductive biology of these rats, nor are their feeding habits known.

Conservation Status. Texas Parks and Wildlife regards this small rat as threatened in Texas only because it is restricted in occurrence to the grasslands along the southern coast and adjacent inland areas in Cameron and Hidalgo counties. It is a common small mammal from Mexico southward to Panama, where it is in absolutely no danger. Loss of habitat is the primary threat to this species in Texas. The resaca environment is declining in the southern part of Texas, largely because of drainage for irrigated agriculture. Resacas bordered by cattail-bulrush marsh and subtropical woodland are essentially confined to the Cameron-Hidalgo County region.

Marsh Rice Rat
Oryzomys palustris (Harlan)

Description. Ratlike, with long, nearly naked, scaly tail; ears short and hairy; upperparts grizzled grayish brown, heavily lined with black, especially in winter pelage; underparts whitish. External measurements average: total length, 245 mm; tail, 116 mm; hind foot, 29 mm. Weight, 40–68 g, averaging 51 g.

Distribution. Found throughout the eastern part of Texas, west to Denton and Lee counties and then southward at least to Willacy and Cameron counties.

Subspecies. *O. p. texensis.*

Habits. These rats typically inhabit marshy areas, but they may be found in almost any situation where grasses and sedges offer an adequate food supply and protective cover. They are semiaquatic and do not hesitate to swim or dive to escape capture. Near Copano Bay their runways are so situated in salt grasses and sedges that the rats have to travel in shallow water most of the time. In southeastern Texas, the rats are common on dikes and levees thrown up in the coastal marshes. In inland areas they prefer marshes and moist meadows; occasionally they live in forested areas.

Their surface runways resemble those made by cotton rats. They are 5–8 cm in width and lead from shallow burrows or surface nests to feeding areas. The globular nest is composed of grasses, sedges, or weeds and frequently is placed under debris above high water in emergent vegetation. They occasionally take over and remodel for their own use the nests of blackbirds.

The marsh rice rat is omnivorous, with about equal amounts of plant and animal matter making up the diet, although the type of food eaten varies with season

Marsh Rice Rat (*Oryzomys palustris*). Photo by John and Gloria Tveten.

and availability. Plant foods include green vegetation, fungi, and the seeds of sedges, marsh grasses, and rice. Animal foods include insects, fiddler crabs, snails, fish, and the carcasses of small rodents and birds. It is because of their fondness for cultivated rice that they were named rice rats. In most places these rats do no damage, but in rice fields they may become economically important by consuming large quantities of rice.

They are prolific. The breeding season is nearly yearlong, during which time breeding females may bear several litters. A single female may bear five to six litters per year, although suboptimal conditions may restrict reproductive output. Litter size ranges from two to seven (average four) but may be affected by population density, as crowded conditions appear to restrict the number of young produced.

The gestation period is about 25 days. A captive female produced six litters, totaling 20 young, in 1 year, an average of 3.3 young per litter. At birth the young are blind, helpless, nearly naked, and weigh about 3 g each. They grow rather rapidly. Their eyes open on the fifth or sixth day, they are weaned on the eleventh day, and sexual maturity is reached between 40 and 45 days of age. These rats appear to grow continually throughout their lifetime.

Conservation Status. This species is common over most of its range in Texas, but the continued loss of wetlands habitat could place it in jeopardy in the future.

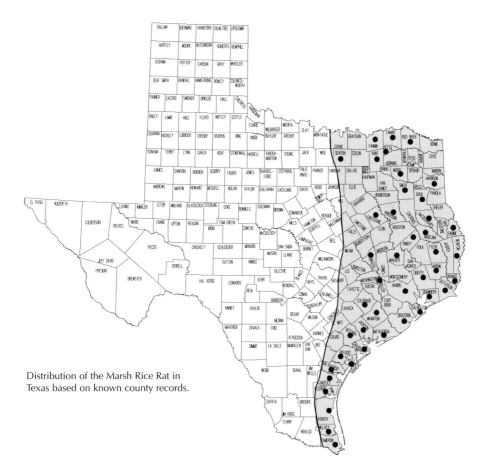

Distribution of the Marsh Rice Rat in
Texas based on known county records.

Fulvous Harvest Mouse

Reithrodontomys fulvescens J. A. Allen

Description. A small mouse with grooved upper incisors, tail much longer than head and body, and inside of ears covered with reddish hairs; differs from the pocket mice (*Perognathus* and *Chaetodipus*), which also have grooved upper incisors and long tail, in the absence of external cheek pouches. Upperparts ochraceous buff, sparingly mixed with blackish brown, sides nearly clear buff; underparts white or pale buff. External measurements average: total length, 165 mm; tail, 93 mm; hind foot, 20 mm. Weight, 14–30 g, averaging about 18 g.

Distribution. Occurs in eastern and central Texas (west to Hemphill, Armstrong, and Floyd counties in the north) and in parts of the Trans-Pecos region. Absent from western Panhandle and Llano Estacado.

Subspecies. *R. f. aurantius* in the eastern part of the state, *R. f. canus* in the eastern and southern Trans-Pecos, *R. f. intermedius* on the Rio Grande Plains and in adjacent areas of southern Texas, and *R. f. laceyi* in the central part of the state.

Habits. These largest of harvest mice occur chiefly in grassy or weedy areas dotted with shrubs or in creek bottoms with their tangles of grasses, vines, and bushes. In Big Bend Ranch State Park in southern Presidio County they showed an affinity for riparian woodlands, although they also occurred in desert scrub dominated by mesquite. In favored habitat they travel from place to place on their own small trails or use those of their animal associates, cotton rats, rice rats, and white-footed mice.

In addition to living in underground burrows, many of them have penthouses in bushes above the ground. These arboreal homes may be converted bird nests or completely of the mouse's own architecture. One found in central Texas was a remodeled cardinal's nest about 1.3 m above the ground in a yaupon bush. When the nest was disturbed, the mouse quickly left it, descended to the ground by jumping from branch to branch, and entered an underground burrow. The mouse's nest, about the size of a baseball, neatly filled the cavity of the bird's nest. It was composed of shredded grass and weed stems and had one opening on the side. Another nest was about 7 cm above the ground, in a clump of bluestem (*Andropogon*).

Their food is nearly all vegetable matter, including seeds and the green blades of grasses and sedges, but may include invertebrates. In coastal areas of Texas, invertebrates predominate in the diet of these mice, but in regions with greater seasonal variation in climate, vegetation dominates the diet in fall and winter and invertebrates are more important in spring and summer. Clearly, their food habits

Fulvous Harvest Mouse (*Reithrodontomys fulvescens*). Photo by John and Gloria Tveten.

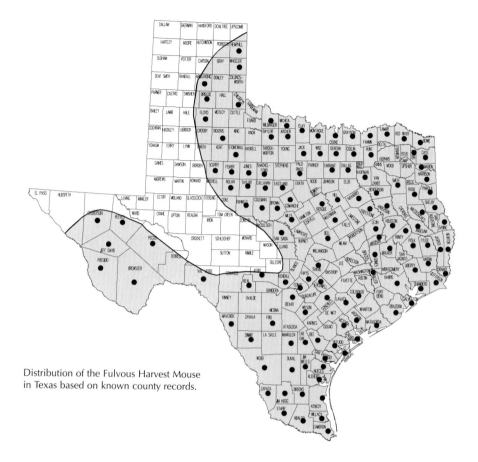

Distribution of the Fulvous Harvest Mouse in Texas based on known county records.

are somewhat opportunistic and based on food availability. They are known to feed on the ground as well as up to 1 meter high in vegetation. They are chiefly nocturnal and are active year round.

In Texas it appears that the breeding season extends from February to October, although peaks in reproductive activity occur in late spring and early autumn. Litter size may range from two to six, averaging three or four. The gestation period probably is about 21 days. At birth, the young are naked, blind, and helpless and weigh about 1 g each. Weaning occurs at 13–16 days when the young weigh 3–3.5 g. By day 11 the young are well furred, and at 9–12 days the eyes open.

These mice seldom conflict with human interests. Their known predators are barn owls, barred owls, and red-tailed hawks, but doubtless, other animals also feed on them.

Conservation Status. This species, throughout its range, prefers weedy or grassy habitats intermixed with shrubs, vines, and bushes. Undoubtedly, it has fared well since the turn of the century as mesquite and other brush have covered many areas of the state that were formerly prairie or grassland. Thus, this species is in no danger in Texas.

Eastern Harvest Mouse

Reithrodontomys humulis (Audubon and Bachman)

Description. A diminutive harvest mouse like *R. montanus,* but upperparts deep brown or gray, heavily mixed with black, especially on the middorsal area; ears blackish all over rather than dark at the base and light at the tip; tail about as long as head and body, the dark dorsal and light ventral stripes about equal in width. External measurements average: total length, 126 mm; tail, 61 mm; hind foot, 16 mm. Weight, 10–15 g.

Distribution. Known in the eastern part of the state, west to Hunt, McLennan, and Fort Bend counties.

Subspecies. *R. h. merriami.*

Habits. The eastern harvest mouse is found mainly in habitats dominated by grasses and other herbaceous plants characteristic of early vegetational succession, including places such as abandoned fields, weed-filled ditches, and brier thickets.

Eastern harvest mice are essentially nocturnal, although at times they may be active during the daylight hours, particularly during cold weather. During periods of cold weather, these mice huddle together in the nest at night to reduce heat loss from their bodies, and they feed in the daytime when it is warmer.

Eastern Harvest Mouse (*Reithrodontomys humulis*). Photo by John and Gloria Tveten.

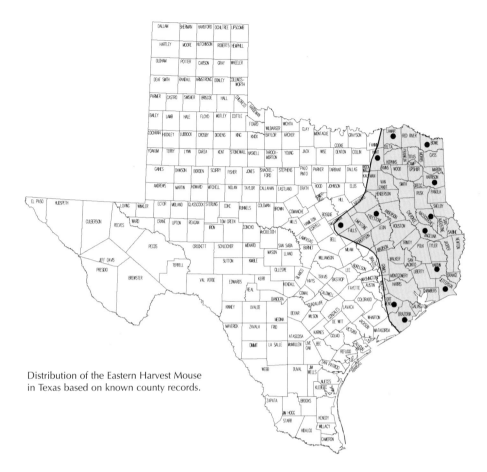

Distribution of the Eastern Harvest Mouse in Texas based on known county records.

R. humulis constructs nests of shredded grass and plant fibers that are placed on the ground in tangled herbage or above the ground in a clump of grass. The nest, which is about the size of a baseball, generally has a single entrance.

Although breeding may occur throughout the year, most births take place between late spring and late fall. Litter sizes range from one to eight (average three to four), and the gestation period is 21–22 days. At birth the young weigh approximately 1.2 g. The eyes do not open until 7–10 days, and weaning takes place between the second and fourth weeks. The young become sexually mature and are capable of breeding at about 11–12 weeks of age.

The food habits of *R. humulis* are not well known. They appear to feed almost wholly on seeds and grain but are known to eat grasshoppers and crickets while in captivity.

Conservation Status. This is the rarest of the harvest mice in Texas, but there is no indication that it faces serious conservation threats at the present time. Continued degradation and fragmentation of grassland habitats in the Blackland Prairies, Post Oak Savannah, and Pineywoods over time would pose a problem.

Western Harvest Mouse
Reithrodontomys megalotis (Baird)

Description. A medium-sized harvest mouse; tail about as long as head and body; the dark dorsal and light ventral stripes about equal in width; ears pale flesh color (or buffy cinnamon); upperparts brownish buff, darkest in middle of back; underparts whitish. Differs from *R. fulvescens* in shorter tail, pale rather than blackish ears basally; from *R. montanus* in larger size and lack of dark color at base of ears. External measurements average: total length, 140 mm; tail, 71 mm; hind foot, 18 mm. Weight, 10–16 g.

Distribution. Western Texas, from the Panhandle, High Plains, and Rolling Plains southward to Trans-Pecos, and barely reaching the northwestern portion of the Edwards Plateau.

Subspecies. *R. m. aztecus* in the northern part of the range and *R. m. megalotis* to the south.

Habits. These mice favor grassy and weedy habitats such as lightly grazed pastures, meadows, fencerows, fallow fields, and edge habitats between agricultural and riparian areas. Meadows, marshes, and weed-covered banks of irrigation ditches seem to offer optimum habitat conditions. The species seldom is found in forested areas. In the Big Bend area it has been taken in grasslands, riparian, and desert scrub situations. On the Llano Estacado it prefers grassy, weedy, brushy fencerows and highway rights-of-way.

Western Harvest Mouse (*Reithrodontomys megalotis*). Photo by John and Gloria Tveten.

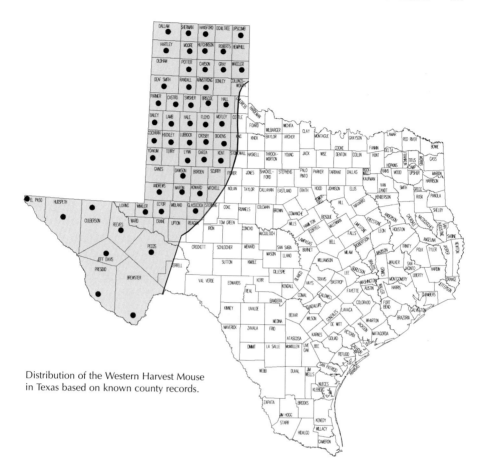

Distribution of the Western Harvest Mouse
in Texas based on known county records.

They utilize the runways and underground burrows of other rodents and frequently take over vacated burrows of pocket gophers. The nest usually is placed
on the ground or slightly above it under some protective cover such as a board, a
clump of lodged grass, or a tangle of weeds. It is a globular structure, about 7 cm
in diameter, composed of plant fibers, and usually has only one opening. These
mice are also known to use the nests of marsh wrens in cattail marshes. They
appear to be strictly nocturnal and active throughout the year. They are almost
entirely vegetarians and feed on the green parts and seeds of plants.

In Texas the breeding season extends through most of the year, with a possible reduction in reproductive activity in midsummer months. On the Llano
Estacado, pregnant females have been taken in all months except January,
February, and June. Several litters a season seem to be the rule. A captive female
produced seven litters, totaling 17 young, in 1 year. Litter size in wild mice, based
on 24 embryo counts, ranged from 1 to 7 and averaged about 4. The gestation period is about 23 days. At birth the young mice are blind, naked, and helpless and
weigh 1–1.5 g. By the end of the first week they are covered with pigmented hair

dorsally; by the eleventh or twelfth day the eyes open, at which time the mice begin to eat solid food. They are weaned by the nineteenth day. Sexual maturity is reached in about 4 months.

These mice seldom are of economic importance. They are utilized as food by a number of flesh eaters, including weasels, foxes, owls, and snakes.

Conservation Status. These mice prefer grassy or weedy areas, especially in the vicinity of water. They appear to be in good shape over most of their range, although they are seldom captured in large numbers by mammalogists.

Remarks. Since the last version of this book, the range of *R. megalotis* has been extended eastward by 13 counties as a result of recent collecting. Frank Yancey and Clyde Jones found that *R. megalotis* and *R. fulvescens* have dispersed back and forth between the High Plains and the Rolling Plains by making extensive use of the grassy habitats associated with a rail trail created when Texas Parks and Wildlife converted about 100 km of former railway into a hiking and horseback trail. This example of using man-made dispersal routes may be representative of the way other small mammals have dispersed across different vegetative regions during this century.

R. megalotis is sometimes confused with *R. montanus* if adults are not compared. In addition to characters listed in the key, the former has a longer tail with a wider, usually less distinct middorsal stripe, and the breadth of its braincase usually is more than 9.8 mm; the braincase width of *R. montanus* is less than 9.5 mm.

Plains Harvest Mouse
Reithrodontomys montanus (Baird)

Description. A small harvest mouse about the size of *R. humulis* and considerably smaller than *R. megalotis* and *R. fulvescens;* tail usually less than half of total length and distinctly bicolor, dark above and light below; upperparts mixed brown and pale yellowish gray; outside of ears and flanks pale yellowish brown; underparts dull whitish. External measurements average: total length, 116 mm; tail, 54 mm; hind foot, 15 mm. Weight, 6–10 g.

Distribution. Found in western and central parts of state, east and southeast to Grayson, Madison, Bexar, and Val Verde counties.

Subspecies. *R. m. griseus* throughout most of the range in Texas and *R. m. montanus* in the Trans-Pecos region.

Habits. These mice appear to prefer climax, or nearly climax, well-drained grassland. They also are known to occupy overgrown highway rights-of-way with mixed grasses and forbs, such as sunflowers. Other suitable habitats include hayfields, moderately grazed pastures, sagebrush habitats, riparian habitats, and abandoned fields. In Brazos County they occur most commonly in blackland prairies where the dominant vegetation is bluestem grass (*Andropogon*). Their nests are composed of fine grass compacted into small balls and are either in bunchgrass or just beneath the ground in their burrows.

Plains Harvest Mouse (*Reithrodontomys montanus*). Photo by John and Gloria Tveten.

Distribution of the Plains Harvest Mouse
in Texas based on known county records.

The plains harvest mouse is herbivorous and insectivorous. Its diet includes mostly grass seeds and some vegetation, but insects are consumed in minor amounts. Seeds are consumed from brome, grama, bluestem, foxtail, and other grasses. The seeds and flower heads of broomweeds, ironweed, and snow-on-the-mountain are known to be eaten.

Available data indicate a yearlong breeding period, at least in Texas. A female captured 13 January near Bryan gave birth to four young in the trap; a gravid female was trapped in October. A captive gave birth to litters in September, October, March, and April. The gestation period is approximately 21 days; the number of young per litter ranges from two to five, averaging three. At birth the young are blind, naked, and weigh about 1 g. They are well haired in 6 days, their eyes open in 8 days, and they are weaned in about 14 days. They are as large as adults in 5 weeks and sexually mature in about 2 months.

Home ranges of *R. montanus* vary from 0.23 ha to 0.84 ha in size in East Texas. Maximum distances moved in an area are small, and roadways may constitute effective barriers to their dispersal. These mice are active throughout the year and do not hibernate.

Conservation Status. This species appears to be in good shape over most of its range, with the possible exception of populations in the Blackland Prairies, although they are seldom captured in large numbers by mammalogists. The continued degradation and loss of grassland habitat constitutes a potential future threat to this harvest mouse.

Texas Mouse
Peromyscus attwateri J. A. Allen

Description. A medium-sized *Peromyscus* with the tail about as long as (or slightly longer than) the head and body, moderately haired, darker above than below (but not sharply bicolor) and usually with a terminal tuft; hind foot large (24–27 mm); ankles usually dark or dusky; dorsal color near sayal brown, darker and mixed with blackish along midline; sides pinkish cinnamon; ventral color pure white, the bases of the hairs plumbeous; length of maxillary tooth row 4 mm or more; each large upper and lower molar has an accessory loph (Fig. 10). External measurements average: total length, 198 mm; tail, 103 mm; hind foot, 25 mm. Weight of adults, 25–35 g.

Distribution. Common in central part of state southward to Uvalde, Medina, and Bexar counties and westward to Randall, Lynn, and Ward counties. It is commonly referred to as the Texas mouse, although its distribution also includes Oklahoma, Kansas, Missouri, and Arkansas.

Subspecies. Monotypic species.

Habits. *P. attwateri* inhabits the cliffs and rocky outcrops of the Edwards Plateau, the west Cross Timbers, the Rolling Plains, and the escarpment of the Llano Estacado in Texas. Vernon Bailey recorded that in the vicinity of Kerrville he

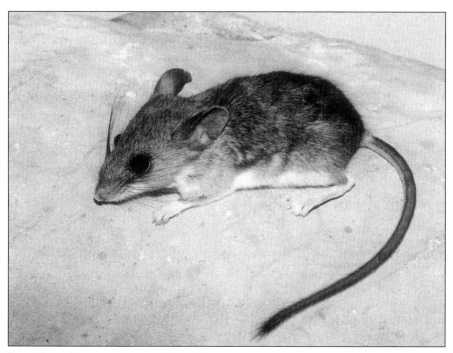

Texas Mouse (*Peromyscus attwateri*). Photo by Robert D. Bradley.

caught many of them in traps set in crevices along the cliffs, under logs in the woods, and under fallen grass and weeds on a creek bank in the bottom of a gulch, as well as under heaps of driftwood. They seem to prefer rocky areas where the dominant vegetation is juniper on the Edwards Plateau. They are adept at climbing. Charles Long recorded that *P. attwateri,* compared with other species of *Peromyscus,* is a superior and more cautious climber, seldom jumps from high places when under stress, and is more capable of finding its way in darkness. Recent studies using tagged *P. attwateri* have shown that this mouse, at least in some areas, is semiarboreal and travels frequently in trees.

Where *P. attwateri* and *P. pectoralis* coexist, *P. pectoralis* specializes in areas of rock ledges and leaf litter, whereas *P. attwateri* is more of a habitat generalist and may be found not only in areas of rock ledges and leaf litter but also more open, grassy areas with only scattered rock cover. Where the two species were sympatric in Tom Green County, *P. attwateri* utilized trees for refuge and escape cover more often than *P. pectoralis.*

The Texas mouse occurs along the escarpment of the Llano Estacado from Armstrong County southward to Martin County, inhabiting rocky, gravelly areas that are vegetated with *Juniperus* spp., *Rhus trilobata, Quercus* spp., and various grasses and forbs. At Palo Duro Canyon, it occurs with *Peromyscus truei,* but there seems to be some microhabitat separation between the two species, with *truei* occupying the more precipitous rocky areas on the escarpment.

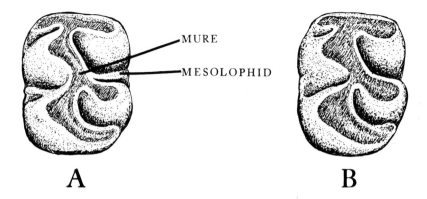

MURE

MESOLOPHID

A

B

Figure 10. Occlusal view of the second lower molar of (A) *Peromyscus attwateri* compared with that of (B) *Peromyscus boylii*. Note that a prominent mesolophid is present in *attwateri* but absent in *boylii*.

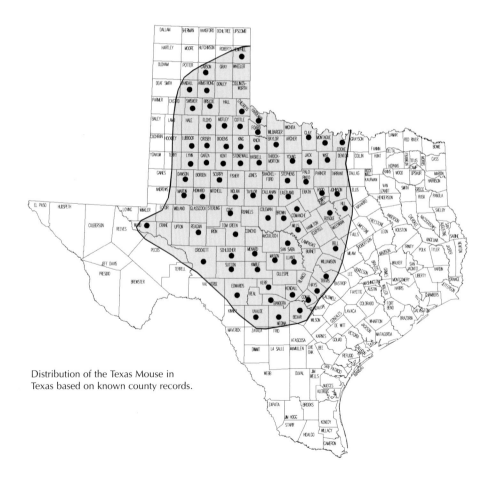

Distribution of the Texas Mouse in Texas based on known county records.

Seeds and insects make up the bulk of its diet. *P. attwateri* readily feeds on grasshoppers, crickets, and other arthropods. Other diet items include juniper berries, green vegetation, acorns, and plant bulbs. This mouse is highly arboreal and may forage for berries and nuts while in trees. It is nocturnal in foraging and activity period.

In an ecological study of this mouse in Lynn County, Herschel Garner found that reproductive activity began in late September and continued throughout the winter. He found no evidence of their breeding during late spring and summer. The number of young per litter varies from one to six and averages about four. Based on data derived from the retrapping of marked animals, Larry Brown estimated the average life span to be 6.8 months, with a maximum of 18 months.

Conservation Status. This species is common throughout its range in Texas and has fared well with the massive expansion of brush species, especially cedar, in the state. There are no immediate threats to its conservation status.

Remarks. *Peromyscus attwateri* was formerly treated as a subspecies of *P. boylii* until I removed *attwateri* and returned it to its original status as a full species. This taxonomic change was based primarily on characteristics of the karyotype (*attwateri* has six large biarmed autosomal chromosomes; *boylii* from west Texas has only two). In addition to chromosomal differences, the most useful morphological features available in the field and to those not trained in cytogenetics are the larger hind foot (24–27 mm in *attwateri* and 20–23 mm in Texas-taken *boylii*) and the structure of the molar teeth. In *attwateri* an accessory loph is present in both the upper and lower molars, but that structure is absent from the lower molars of *boylii* (see Fig. 10).

P. attwateri can be distinguished from *P. truei* by its longer hind foot (23 mm or greater rather than 23 mm or less) and shorter ears (21 mm or less rather than 22 mm or more).

Brush Mouse

Peromyscus boylii (Baird)

Description. A medium-sized, long-tailed, white-footed mouse; tail equal to or longer than head and body, sparsely haired, slightly tufted, and indistinctly bicolor, darker above; ankles dusky, the feet white; ears moderately long (19–22 mm from notch); proximal two-fifths of sole of hind foot hairy; upperparts pale cinnamon or hair brown to sepia; sides with narrow ochraceous buff lateral line; underparts white. External measurements average: total length, 197 mm; tail, 103 mm; hind foot, 22 mm. Weight, 22–36 g. Distinguished from *P. difficilis* chiefly by smaller ears and shorter fur; from *P. pectoralis* by dusky instead of white ankles.

Distribution. Western Trans-Pecos region.

Subspecies. *P. b. rowleyi.*

Habits. These mice are usually associated with brush and trees, but they have been trapped in a number of habitats including stream banks, rock walls, talus slopes, and cabins. In the Guadalupe Mountains of western Texas, they are common in the open pine-fir forest at 2,400 m, where they show a decided preference for areas of down logs and brush piles. Vernon Bailey remarks that they seldom burrow into the ground but rather utilize any natural cavity that offers concealment and protection. The nest is a globular structure of dry plant fibers, mostly grasses.

They are adept at climbing and seem to be at home off the ground. Without doubt they garner much of their food in trees and utilize hollows in them for dens. They are almost entirely nocturnal in habit and are active year round.

They feed on a variety of plant items. In the Guadalupe Mountains they feed extensively on pine nuts and Douglas fir seeds; in the oak belt, acorns are a favorite item. They also feed on hackberries, juniper berries, and cactus fruits.

The breeding season extends through most of the year. Gravid females have been taken from May to December, but the presence of half-grown young in May indicates that breeding begins as early as March or April. Several litters of two to five (average three) young may be reared in a year, but the peak of production is in spring and early summer. The young are blind and hairless and weigh about 2 g at birth.

Usually these mice are of little or no economic importance, except in instances where they occur in numbers around and in cabins and granaries in wooded areas. In such instances they can be removed readily by trapping.

Conservation Status. This species is common throughout its range in Texas and does not appear to face any serious threats.

Brush Mouse (*Peromyscus boylii*). Photo by John and Gloria Tveten.

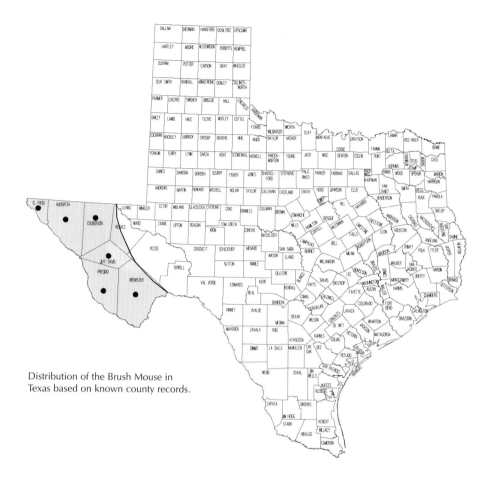

Distribution of the Brush Mouse in Texas based on known county records.

Remarks. The last version of this book listed records of this species from the eastern escarpment of the Llano Estacado and in adjacent parts of the Panhandle. Larry Choate of Texas Tech University, however, has examined all scientific specimens of long-tailed deer mice from this region, and he is convinced they all are *P. attwateri* instead. Thus, *P. boylii* is restricted in distribution to the Trans-Pecos region of the state. On the Llano Estacado, it occurs only on the northwestern part of the escarpment in New Mexico, just to the west of the Texas state line.

Cactus Mouse
Peromyscus eremicus (Baird)

Description. A medium-sized, long-haired mouse; tail longer than head and body, not sharply bicolor, but darker above than below, finely annulated and covered with short hairs; ears large and almost naked; sole of hind foot naked to heel; pelage long, soft and silky; upperparts ochraceous buff, washed with dusky; lateral line pure ochraceous buff; underparts and feet white. Can readily be distinguished from other *Peromyscus* by the combination of long tail, soft pelage, and naked heels. External measurements average: total length, 185 mm; tail, 102 mm; hind foot, 20 mm; ear, 20 mm. Weight, 18–40 g, averaging about 24 g in males and 27 g in females.

Distribution. Trans-Pecos Texas, mainly in lowland desert areas, westward along the Rio Grande to Webb County, and to Val Verde County on the western edge of the Edwards Plateau.

Subspecies. *P. e. eremicus.*

Habits. As the name suggests, these mice are restricted almost entirely to a desert habitat, especially where rocky outcrops or cliffs offer retreats and den sites. In the Trans-Pecos region, they typically occur at the bases of cliffs or in rocky outcrop-pings at elevations below 1,200 m. They are expert at climbing and can scramble up stone walls and cliffs with ease. They have been observed foraging in mesquite trees 1–2 m off the ground, and there is some evidence that they also climb hack-berry trees and gather the seeds. Their population numbers are high in midwinter and very low in midsummer because they are thought to estivate in their burrows during the summer. By employing torpor as a water-conserving device and as a means of prolonging food stores, the mice escape the most rigorous annual period of the desert. By virtue of the ability to estivate, cactus mice are probably able to survive severe desert situations successfully.

Peromyscus eremicus is nocturnal and mostly feeds on the seeds of desert annuals. Other parts of plants, as well as insects, also are consumed. They are also fond of such trap bait as rolled oats, sunflower seeds, and various whole grains. In

Cactus Mouse (*Peromyscus eremicus*). Photo by R. D. Porter, courtesy Texas Parks and Wildlife Department.

captivity they relish water, but in the wild they probably supply this need by feeding on succulent vegetation, since they occur in areas that are waterless except for infrequent rains.

The breeding season extends at least from January to October and possibly throughout the year. The number of young per litter varies from one to four, averaging about three, and two or more litters may be reared each year. A captive female is known to have produced three litters in a year. The cactus mouse has only two pairs of milk glands, so only four young can be nursed at one time. Most white-footed mice (*Peromyscus*) have three pairs. The gestation period is 21 days. At birth the young are blind, pigmented dorsally, and not pink. They weigh about 2.5 g. They develop quite rapidly; the ears unfold in less than 24 hours, and the eyes open in 15–17 days. Because the litters are never produced in quick succession, the young may be nursed for as long as 30–40 days.

Conservation Status. This species is common throughout its range in Texas and does not appear to face any serious threats.

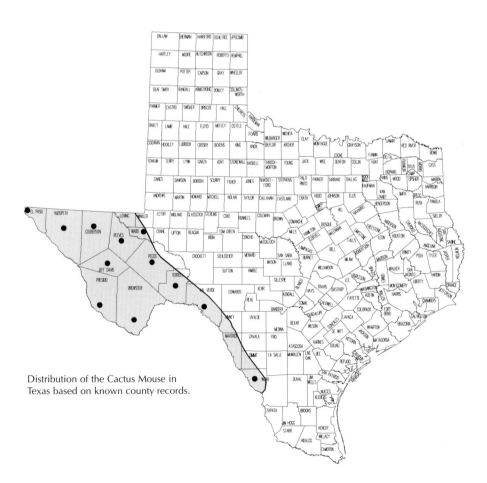

Distribution of the Cactus Mouse in Texas based on known county records.

Remarks. Based on the analysis of mitochondrial DNA in populations of *Peromyscus eremicus* from the Chihuahuan and Sonoran deserts, Deric Walpole and associates at Texas A&M University suggested that the two populations may represent recently diverged cryptic species. More recently, however, Brett Riddle and associates argued against recognizing two distinct species. The taxonomic status of this species remains in question and warrants further investigation.

Cotton Mouse

Peromyscus gossypinus (Le Conte)

Description. A medium-sized, heavy bodied, white-footed mouse; tail much shorter than head and body, between three and four times the length of hind foot and not sharply bicolor, but darker above than below; ears small (16–18 mm from notch); upperparts mummy brown, the middorsal area suffused with black; sides bright russet; underparts creamy white; feet white, but tarsal joint of heel dark like leg. External measurements average: total length, 180 mm; tail, 78 mm; hind foot, 23 mm. Weight, 34–51 g.

This mouse is most easily confused with the white-footed mouse (*Peromyscus leucopus*), from which it can be distinguished by larger size (weight usually over 30 g in adults as opposed to 15–25 g in *leucopus*) and longer skull (27 mm or more in *gossypinus* and less than that in *leucopus*).

Distribution. Found in woodlands in eastern one-fourth of state.

Subspecies. *P. g. megacephalus.*

Cotton Mouse (*Peromyscus gossypinus*). Photo by John and Gloria Tveten.

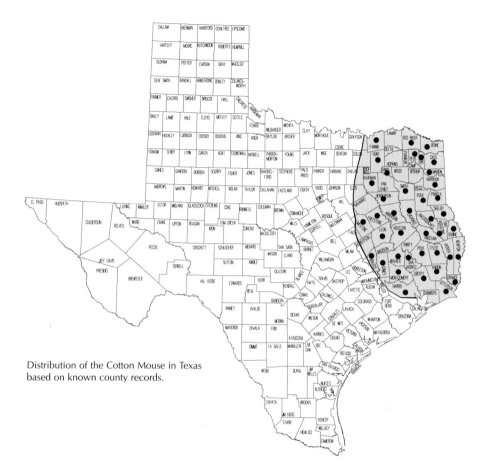

Distribution of the Cotton Mouse in Texas based on known county records.

Habits. Cotton mice are typically woodland dwellers and occur along watercourses where stumps, down logs, and tangles of brush and vines offer suitable retreats; frequently they occur in woodland areas bordering open fields. They have been trapped in eastern Texas in canebrakes, under logs, and around and in old, tumbledown buildings in wooded areas. That they are adept at climbing and may live off the ground in hollows in trees is indicated by the capture of individuals in live traps set on platforms in trees.

Their other habits are not well known. Nothing specific is known of their natural foods, although cotton mice are omnivorous. Over half of their diet may be made up of animal matter, and food availability probably determines the dietary composition. Captive mice seemed to relish rolled oats, wheat, corn, and bread. Green foods were eaten sparingly.

Breeding may occur throughout the year, although there is a decline in reproductive activity during the summer months. In Texas most breeding commences in late August; reaches a peak in November, December, and January; and subsides by early May. The gestation period is about 23 days in nonnursing females and about 30 days in females that are nursing a previous litter. Adult females may produce four or more litters a year. The litter size ranges from one to seven and averages three or four. The young are naked and blind at birth. Their ears open in 5 or 6 days, at which age their incisor teeth erupt. Their eyes open in about 13 days, and shortly after that they begin to eat solid foods. They are completely weaned at an age of 20–25 days. They become sexually mature at about 60–70 days of age.

The name "cotton mouse" was applied to the species by Le Conte, who found that the mice often used cotton for nest construction. Ordinarily, however, they do little or no damage to cotton or foodstuffs.

Conservation Status. The cotton mouse is the most common rodent in the woods of the Big Thicket in southeast Texas. Potential future threats would be excessive logging and conversion to pine plantation habitat, drainage of bottomland wetlands, and habitat fragmentation.

White-footed Mouse
Peromyscus leucopus (Rafinesque)

Description. A medium-sized, short-tailed, white-footed mouse; tail about 43% of total length, sparsely haired, darker above than below but usually not sharply bicolor; upperparts cinnamon rufous mixed with blackish; sides paler, with less admixture of black; underparts and feet white, the ankle slightly brownish. External measurements average: total length, 173 mm; tail, 78 mm; hind foot, 21 mm. Weight, 15–25 g, averaging about 22 g. Most easily confused with *P. gossypinus* and *P. maniculatus. P. leucopus* differs from the former in smaller size, shorter body, lighter weight, and brighter colors; from the latter in less hairy and not sharply bicolor tail, usually shorter pelage, and lack of whitish tufts at base of ears.

Distribution. Statewide except for the northeastern coastal bend.

Subspecies. *P. l. leucopus* in the eastern third of the state, *P. l. texanus* in central Texas westward to Brewster, Terrell, and Val Verde counties, and *P. l. tornillo* in the Panhandle and much of the Trans-Pecos. The subspecies are in need of taxonomic review.

Habits. In the main, these mice are woodland dwellers, a trait best illustrated along the western border of their range, where they are restricted almost entirely to creek and river bottoms. As one progresses eastward, the mice are found in a progressively greater variety of habitats. In east-central Texas they are most abundant in bottomlands, less so in post oak uplands, and almost completely absent from prairie lands. On the Llano Estacado, the white-footed mouse occupies a more catholic variety of habitats, occurring in brushy, weedy fencerows, mesquite grasslands, and near rocks and junipers on the escarpment. They are adept at climbing and often den in hollow trees out of danger from overflow waters. In areas not subject to inundation, they live in dens under logs, in stumps, brush piles, burrows, or buildings.

In much of its range, this mouse is one of the commonest of small mammals. In Brazos County the population of this mouse is exceeded only by that of the

White-footed Mouse (*Peromyscus leucopus*). Photo by John and Gloria Tveten.

cotton rat. In 3,483 trap-nights, 161 cotton rats and 121 white-footed mice were captured, for a ratio, respectively, of 21.6 and 28.7 trap-nights per animal. The maximum home range of adult males is about 0.2 ha, that of adult females about 0.15 ha. The mice seldom travel more than 50 m once they are established in suitable quarters. The dispersal of the population generally is accomplished by movements of the unestablished young mice.

Peromyscus leucopus mostly is nocturnal, and it forages for seeds, mesquite beans, berries, fruits, nuts, and insects at night. In addition, carrion is sometimes consumed. A considerable amount of the foraging activity of the white-footed mouse occurs in brushy vegetation. When food is abundant, they store it in and about their nests for winter use. Caches of several quarts have been reported. Like squirrels, these mice have internal cheek pouches in which they can place food for transport to caches. In spring and summer they feed to some extent on fruits and on insects, snails, and other invertebrates.

Available data suggest that breeding occurs year round during favorable conditions, but that midwinter and midsummer are the least favorable reproductive periods. In east-central Texas, gravid females have been captured in nearly every month of the year, and on the Llano Estacado pregnant females have been recorded for all months except February and July. Litter size varies from 1 to 6, averaging about 4; multiple litters may be produced each year. Captive females have produced as many as 10 litters and 45 offspring in one year. The gestation period is 22–25 days in nonlactating females and 23–37 days in those that are lactating. At birth the young are blind, pink, and weigh about 2 g. They become pigmented dorsally in the first 24 hours, their eyes open in about 13 days, and they are weaned

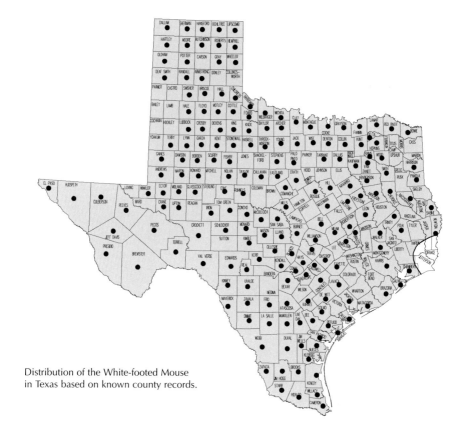

Distribution of the White-footed Mouse
in Texas based on known county records.

at the age of 22 or 23 days if the mother is expecting a new family; otherwise, they may nurse as long as 37 days. Young females mature sexually at the age of 10 or 11 weeks and may bear their first litters at the age of 13 or 14 weeks. Usually, females born in the spring rear one or two litters themselves before winter sets in. They seldom live to be more than 18 months old in the wild.

Where numerous in an area, they can become destructive of stored and shocked grains and consequently need to be controlled, but in most places they are of little or no economic significance if such natural predators as owls, snakes, and weasels are not destroyed.

Conservation Status. The white-footed mouse has a statewide distribution, and it is the most common and widespread of all the species of *Peromyscus* in Texas. There are no immediate threats, although local populations could succumb to land clearing associated with extensive development.

Deer Mouse

Peromyscus maniculatus (Wagner)

Description. A small, white-footed mouse with sharply bicolor tail, white beneath and dark above; ears usually shorter than hind foot, prominent and leaflike;

upperparts bright fulvous or brownish, intermixed with dusky; underparts and feet white. External measurements average: total length, 170 mm; tail, 81 mm; hind foot, 20 mm; ear, 18 (12–20) mm. Weight, 15–32 g.

This species is most easily confused with *Peromyscus leucopus,* from which it differs in (1) sharply bicolor tail, (2) more hairy and often shorter tail, (3) frequently whitish tufts of hair at base of ears, and (4) usually longer pelage.

Distribution. Statewide but uncommon in the eastern, coastal, and southern parts of the state.

Subspecies. *P. m. blandus* in the Trans-Pecos and areas immediately to the east; *P. m. luteus* in the Panhandle, probably south to Winkler County; *P. m. ozarkiarum,* which occurs sympatrically with the following race in Cooke, Denton, and Grayson counties; and *P. m. pallescens* in the eastern part of the range in Texas.

Habits. These mice occupy a variety of habitats, ranging from mixed forests to grasslands to open, sparsely vegetated deserts. In Texas, they usually inhabit grasslands or areas of open brush, especially where weeds and grasses offer concealment and a source of food. Weed-choked fencerows and washes offer almost ideal habitat. Mice of this group seem to be poor climbers and live close to or on the ground. They also are known to live commensally with humans and have probably benefited from human activities and habitat alterations since European settlement of the United States.

They are almost strictly nocturnal. Trapping records indicate that they leave their daytime retreats early in the evening and remain abroad until shortly after sunup. They live in underground burrows, in brush piles, or in crevices among

Deer Mouse (*Peromyscus maniculatus*). Photo by John and Gloria Tveten.

Distribution of the Deer Mouse in Texas
based on known county records.

rocks. The burrow is simple in design and usually consists of two or three short branches converging from as many surface openings to a single tunnel that slopes steeply to the globular nest chamber, which is 7–10 cm in diameter. The nests are hollow balls of dry grass, shredded weed stems, and other available material including rabbit fur and bird feathers.

Deer mice do not hibernate. Their winter activities may include taking up quarters in a pile of logs, from which they venture nightly in search of food. The tracks of one mouse led from the logs to one bush after another in a wandering fashion to the edge of a bare field some 100 m distant and then back to the log pile. The others traveled less than 50 m from their headquarters. Bits of bark, leaves, and seed coats scattered on the snow beneath many of the bushes indicated that they had climbed into them in quest of food. Their food consists of a variety of items, chiefly seeds. In season fruits, bark, roots, and herbage are also consumed and, judging from the behavior of these mice about camps, nearly everything edible is sampled.

Deer mice breed in every month of the year, with peaks in the periods from January through April and from June through November. More than one litter of young may be produced per year. Litters seem to be born in rapid succession. One captive female produced 11 litters with 42 young in a year. The gestation period varies from 22 to 27 days, averaging about 24 days. Litter size ranges from one to nine, averaging about four. At birth the young are blind, pink, and hairless and weigh from 1.1 to 2.3 g. They become pigmented dorsally in about 24 hours, the pinna of the ear unfolds on the third day, the eyes open in 12–17 days, and they are weaned when about 4 weeks old. The longest observed time of suckling is 37 days. Sexual maturity is reached before the young lose their blue juvenile pelage, and females born early in the year may themselves produce young by late summer or early fall.

These mice are often abundant in favorable habitats, and then they may become troublesome, as with other animals that overpopulate an area. Because of their tolerance to a wide variety of habitat conditions and their often large population, they are difficult and expensive to control. Since they are an important source of food for many small carnivores, owls, and snakes, the assistance of those predators should be enlisted in keeping the populations of mice within bounds.

Conservation Status. This species remains common in the Trans-Pecos and northwestern parts of the state, but the loss of native grassland habitat in the central part of Texas represents a major concern for the future of the subspecies, *P. m. pallescens,* from that region. I have attempted without success to collect this subspecies at several localities where it was previously known.

Remarks. The deer mouse has been implicated as the primary reservoir for Sin Nombre virus, a strain of hantavirus responsible for hantavirus pulmonary syndrome. Several people, particularly on the High Plains of Texas, have died from this virus and anyone finding this mouse in their residence should be very careful. This species has a tendency to inhabit old cabins and buildings, and one should watch for these mice, or evidence of their presence, when cleaning such structures.

Northern Rock Mouse

Peromyscus nasutus (J. A. Allen)

Description. A rather large, long-tailed, grayish buff mouse; tail sharply bicolor, brownish to blackish above and white below, slightly tufted, more than 100 mm in length and longer than the combined length of head and body; tops of front and hind feet (including ankles) white; ears about as long as hind feet. External measurements average: total length, 193 mm; tail, 104 mm; hind feet, 22.5 mm. Resembles both *P. boylii* and *P. pectoralis;* differs from *boylii* in having white ankles like *pectoralis,* and differs from *pectoralis* in having a noticeably longer tail and heavier molars (length of maxillary tooth row 4.5 mm as opposed to less than 4 mm). Differs from *P. truei* in grayish buff rather than ochraceous buff upperparts and in smaller ears; differs from *P. attwateri* in shorter hind feet (less than 24 mm) and in white rather than dusky ankles.

Northern Rock Mouse (*Peromyscus nasutus*). Photo by John and Gloria Tveten.

Distribution. Known in Texas only from the Trans-Pecos, where it has been recorded from mountainous regions of Brewster, Culberson, El Paso, Jeff Davis, and Presidio counties. It has been recorded along the northwestern escarpment of the Llano Estacado in Quay and Curry counties in New Mexico, but it has yet to be recorded on the otherwise similar escarpment in Deaf Smith County, Texas, just a few miles to the east.

Subspecies. *P. n. nasutus* from the Guadalupe Mountains in Culberson County, the Davis Mountains in Jeff Davis County, the Chisos Mountains in Brewster County, and the Chinati Mountains in Presidio County; *P. n. penicillatus* in El Paso County.

Habits. This species is found among boulders on rocky mountain slopes and in rock piles in Texas madrone and oak associations where the crevices and cracks are covered with a thick layer of leaves. In the Franklin Mountains (El Paso County), the rock mouse is common in rocky areas and talus slopes. *P. boylii* is absent from rocky areas where *nasutus* is abundant, but *boylii* is abundant in adjacent areas with fewer rocks and more vegetation. It appears that *nasutus* prefers rugged, rocky habitat with sparse vegetation. In the Davis Mountains, where I trapped this species, it showed a decided preference for the cooler and more mesic situations in shaded rocky canyons at the highest elevations of the mountains.

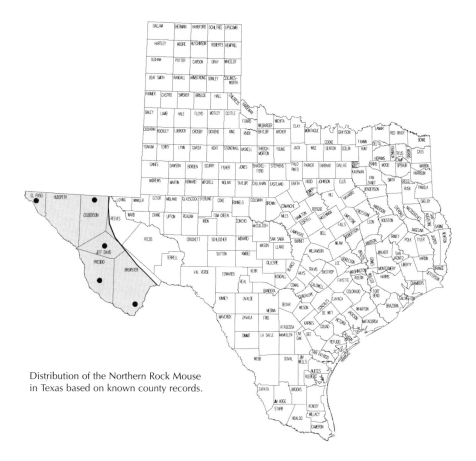

Distribution of the Northern Rock Mouse in Texas based on known county records.

In captivity the rock mouse is docile and easily handled. It is highly gregarious, and a dozen or more individuals of young and adults of both sexes often crowd into one nest without apparent conflict.

Little information is available on its breeding habits. Pregnant females have been taken in June, July, and August. Vernon Bailey reported capture in New Mexico of a female containing four large fetuses in late July and another in late August with six fetuses. Individuals captured alive in the Franklin Mountains readily bred in captivity and produced several litters of two to six young. The gestation period is about 30 days.

Conservation Status. This species has a spotty distribution in the isolated mountains of far western Texas, where it occupies the mesic canyons associated with the forested woodlands of the largest ranges. Nowhere has it been found to be abundant, and its conservation status is unknown. Clearly, it could be threatened by climate change favoring increased aridity, under which conditions it likely would face serious competition from the brush mouse, *P. boylii*. This is a species that warrants careful monitoring in the future.

White-ankled Mouse

Peromyscus pectoralis Osgood

Description. A small-eared, long-tailed, white-footed mouse with tarsal joint of hind foot white; pelage moderately long and lax; tail longer than head and body, scantily haired, not sharply bicolor, but darker above than below, and annulations 20–24 per cm; upperparts grayish to wood brown; underparts and feet white; young, bluish gray. External measurements average: total length, 187 mm; tail, 95 mm; hind foot, 22 mm; ear, 16 mm. Weight, 24–39 g. Most easily confused with *P. eremicus, P. attwateri,* and *P. boylii.* Distinguished from *P. eremicus* by having proximal part of sole of hind foot hairy rather than naked, mammae in three pairs rather than in two. Differs from *P. boylii* and *P. attwateri* in smaller scales on the tail, white rather than dusky tarsal joints, and shorter maxillary tooth row (often less than 4 mm).

Distribution. Recorded from most of Trans-Pecos region and northeastward through the Edwards Plateau in the central part of state to Oklahoma (eastern limits of range along Balcones Escarpment from Bexar County northward to McLennan County).

Subspecies. *P. p. laceianus.*

Habits. This is another rock-dwelling species, and it often is taken in the same habitat occupied by *P. boylii* and *P. attwateri.* The presence of rock, rather than vegetation type, seems to be the primary requirement for suitable habitat. In the Chisos Mountains and in the Delaware Mountains in Trans-Pecos Texas, they have been caught in the oak-juniper belt in traps set among jumbled boulders, near rock walls, in talus slopes, along rocky outcroppings, and in buildings. Near Austin,

White-ankled Mouse (*Peromyscus pectoralis*). Photo by John and Gloria Tveten.

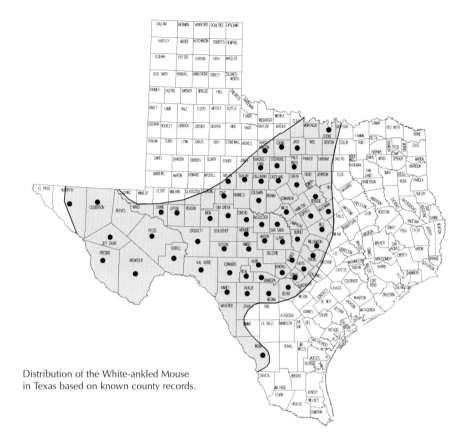

Distribution of the White-ankled Mouse in Texas based on known county records.

white-ankled mice are common in the rocky outcropping where the Colorado River cuts through the Balcones Escarpment; in Kerr County they prefer rocky bluffs along the rivers and creeks. In the Davis Mountains region of the Trans-Pecos, they usually are found in the grama-bluestem association. Elsewhere, in my experience, they are associated with rocks in oak-juniper woodlands, but at Big Bend Ranch State Park they were trapped in riparian woodlands.

They feed on a variety of seeds, including juniper berries, acorns, and hackberries. Although their diet has not been studied in detail, other seeds, cactus fruits, lichen, other fungi, and insects probably are consumed. These mice are active nocturnally and do not hibernate through the winter months.

Their breeding habits are not well known, but it appears that several litters may be reared each year. Pregnant females have been captured from January through March and from July through December on the Edwards Plateau. The average litter size is three, ranging from two to five. The gestation period has not been determined, but it is probably about 23 days as in closely related species. Growth and development of the young is not well known.

These mice are abundant in certain localities and may become troublesome in cabins and ranch buildings. They usually can be controlled easily by the use of traps.

Conservation Status. *P. pectoralis* is one of the most common deer mice in central and west Texas and does not appear to face any serious threats. Indeed, it appears to flourish under conditions of overgrazing and may be increasing in numbers throughout its range.

Pinyon Mouse
Peromyscus truei (Shufeldt)

Description. A moderately sized, large-eared, white-footed mouse; tail as long as, or slightly longer than, head and body and scantily haired; upper parts ochraceous buff mixed with dusky, giving an overall effect of cinnamon or tawny olive in unworn pelage and wood brown in worn pelage; the pronounced lateral line is ochraceous buff; sides of face and nose grayish; ears dusky; feet and underparts white; tail dark above, white below. External measurements average: total length, 204 mm; tail, 100 mm; hind foot, 22.5 mm; ear, 23.5 mm. Weight, 24–39 g.

Distribution. In Texas, known in three distinct populations, one in the Guadalupe Mountains of Culberson County and two others, separated by approximately 120 km of inhospitable habitat, from the northern breaks of the Llano Estacado.

Subspecies. *P. truei comanche,* restricted to Palo Duro and adjacent canyons in Armstrong, Briscoe, and Randall counties, and *P. t. truei,* reaching its eastern distributional limit on the northwestern escarpment of the Llano Estacado in Deaf Smith County. *P. t. truei* also occurs in Guadalupe Mountains National Park in Culberson County of the Trans-Pecos.

Pinyon Mouse (*Peromyscus truei*). Photo by John and Gloria Tveten.

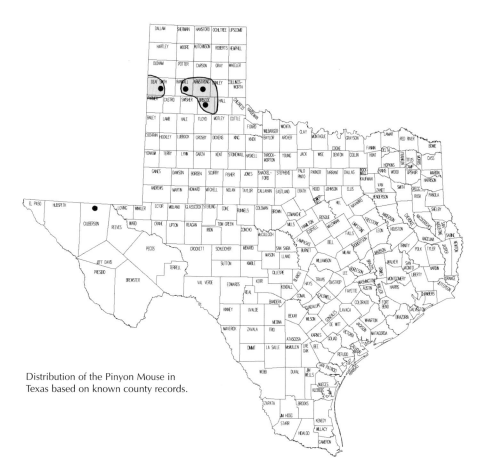

Distribution of the Pinyon Mouse in
Texas based on known county records.

Habits. This species is restricted to rocky situations in cedar forests on canyon
slopes and floors in the Palo Duro Canyon region. Areas in the juniper-mesquite
association that have large, massive boulders seem to support the highest populations. Even so, intensive trapping produces few mice. James Tamsitt reported
that in 1,803 trap-nights he captured only 25 specimens, a success ratio of 72 trap-
nights per mouse caught. In Guadalupe Mountains National Park, the species is
rarely found in the juniper and pinyon woodlands.

The food habits of these mice are not well known. In California, specimens
examined in midsummer had been eating primarily insects and spiders, although
by late summer their diet was predominantly acorn mast. In Colorado the winter
diet is primarily juniper berries.

Breeding habits are likewise poorly known. Frank Yancey studied a population
in Briscoe County and found pregnant females in April, May, and October. An adult
female with four embryos was captured on 24 July in the Guadalupe Mountains of
the Trans-Pecos. These observations compare favorably with a breeding season
from April through September in southwestern Colorado and February through

November in Arizona. Litter size ranges from one to five, average three. At birth, the young are hairless and the eyes and ears are closed. Between 2 and 3 weeks of age the eyes and ears open. The body is haired by 2 weeks of age.

Conservation Status. Both subspecies of the pinyon mouse are relatively rare in Texas and bear watching in the future. Although the pinyon mouse is not currently in direct danger from human activities, it easily could fall victim to a competing southern species in the region, *Peromyscus attwateri,* under a climate-change scenario in which mean annual temperature increased a degree or two. Elsewhere, the pinyon mouse is widespread and common in pinyon and yellow pine forests in western North America.

Remarks. The Palo Duro Canyon population of *P. truei* has had a rather confusing taxonomic history. Frank Blair recognized it as a new species in the *P. truei* group of mice and in 1943 gave it the name *Peromyscus comanche.* Donald Hoffmeister in 1951 placed *comanche* as a subspecies of *Peromyscus nasutus,* and 10 years later he and Luis de la Torre transferred both *nasutus* and *comanche* to the largely Mexican species *Peromyscus difficilis.* In 1972 Raymond Lee and associates examined the karyotypes of *comanche* and found them to be identical with those of *Peromyscus truei* and markedly different from those of *Peromyscus difficilis.* Finally, in 1973 I reviewed its systematic status and arranged *comanche* as a subspecies of *Peromyscus truei.*

Golden Mouse
Ochrotomys nuttalli (Harlan)

Description. A medium-sized, golden-colored (rich ochraceous tawny) white-footed mouse with soft, thick pelage; larger than the fulvous harvest mouse and without grooves on upper incisors; feet white; underparts pale cinnamon buff; tail brownish, darker above than below. External measurements average: total length, 176 mm; tail, 78 mm; hind foot, 19 mm. Weight, 15–25 g.

Distribution. Woodlands of eastern Texas.

Subspecies. *O. n. lisae.*

Habits. These small, arboreal mice are adapted to and occur chiefly in forested areas. Tangles of trees, vines, and brush seem to be a preferred habitat. Specimens have been trapped on dark, wooded slopes where the mice lived in nests in tangles of grapevines; others were taken in an old pasture overgrown with blackberry, wild grape, and a few small trees. Near Bowie, a pair of mice was taken in a hollow, fallen tree in river bottomlands; near Lufkin, one specimen was trapped in a pile of brush in hammock territory near the edge of the Angelina River bottom.

Their nests are constructed of grasses, Spanish moss, or leaves and lined with shredded plant fibers or occasionally feathers. They vary in size from the small brood nest about the size of a baseball to the large communal nests, as big as 20 by 30 cm, that may house half a dozen or more mice. One such nest housed eight mice, all males. Usually the nests are placed in trees or bushes a few centimeters

Golden Mouse (*Ochrotomys nuttalli*). Photo by John and Gloria Tveten.

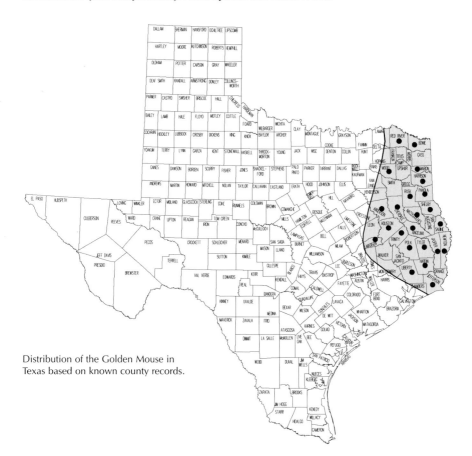

Distribution of the Golden Mouse in
Texas based on known county records.

to 3 m above the ground; occasionally they are on the ground under some protective cover such as a log, a stump, or a pile of brush, or they may be in cavities in standing trees.

Invertebrates make up about 50% of their diet. They also eat a variety of seeds, including sumac, wild cherry, dogwood, greenbrier, poison ivy, and blackberry.

The breeding season begins in September and extends through winter and spring, with little reproductive activity during summer. The peak breeding season is in winter. Adult females may produce up to three litters annually. The young, ranging in number from two to five (average three), are born following a gestation period of 25–30 days.

Newborn golden mice weigh about 2.7 g and are reddish with relatively smooth skin. The eyes and ears are closed at birth but open between 11 and 14 days of age. Weaning is completed at 3 weeks, and adult size is attained between the eighth and tenth weeks. The young mice are sexually mature 1–2 months after birth.

Conservation Status. Few specimens of this mouse have been obtained during the last few decades in eastern Texas, and there is a need to monitor populations and determine their conservation status. When I worked at Big Thicket National Preserve in the late 1970s and early 1980s, I trapped golden mice commonly in the wooded habitats throughout the preserve.

Northern Pygmy Mouse
Baiomys taylori (Thomas)

Description. Smallest of the muroid mice in Texas. (Two harvest mice, *Reithrodontomys humulis* and *R. montanus,* are only slightly larger in size, but both differ in having grooved upper incisors and longer tail.) Upperparts grizzled grayish in adults, blackish in juveniles; underparts smoke gray; tail about three times as long as hind foot, sparsely haired, and decidedly shorter than head and body. They have a strong, musky odor similar to that of house mice, *Mus musculus.* External measurements average: total length, 98 mm; tail, 38 mm; hind foot, 14.5 mm. Weight, 7–10 g, averaging 8 g.

Distribution. Distributed over much of the state; range excludes the Trans-Pecos and the extreme northeastern parts of the state.

Subspecies. *B. t. taylori* over most of the range in Texas and *B. t. subater* in the southeast.

Habits. This is a southern species characteristic of the tropical lowlands of Mexico. Early records indicate that *B. taylori* was restricted to the coastal region of eastern Texas and the mesquite-chaparral regions of southern Texas. Since the early twentieth century, the species has consistently extended its range northward and eastward by invading the oak-hickory association, the Blackland Prairies, the Cross Timbers, the Rolling Plains, and the High Plains.

These mice have a preference for grassy areas, including weedy and overgrown habitats, and they are commonly found in old fields, pastures, and along

Northern Pygmy Mouse (*Baiomys taylori*). Photo by John and Gloria Tveten.

railroad and highway rights-of-way, where they usually live in dense habitat in close association with cotton rats (*Sigmodon hispidus*) and harvest mice (*Reithrodontomys* spp.). If other types of ground cover such as rocks, cactus, and fallen logs are available, the pygmy mouse may be found in areas where grass is relatively sparse. On the Llano Estacado *B. taylori* inhabits thick grassy-weedy habitats along fencerows, highway and railroad rights-of-way, and occasionally upland pastures—mostly places with dense grassy vegetation.

Pygmy mice live in nests placed in burrows in the ground, beneath fallen logs, among cactus pads, or in thick clumps of grass. The nest is typically a ball of finely shredded grass or cactus fibers with a central cavity and one or two openings. A network of runways or beaten paths leads away from the nest sites beneath a thick mat of dead grass.

Their diet is mostly herbivorous and granivorous, but animal matter is consumed if available. Stems and fruits of prickly pear, seeds and leaves of grasses, mesquite beans, insects, terrestrial snails, and small reptiles are included in the diet. They are active year round and do not hibernate; neither do they store food for winter use. Although they are chiefly nocturnal, they have been caught in traps on several occasions in the daytime. Runways are often constructed within

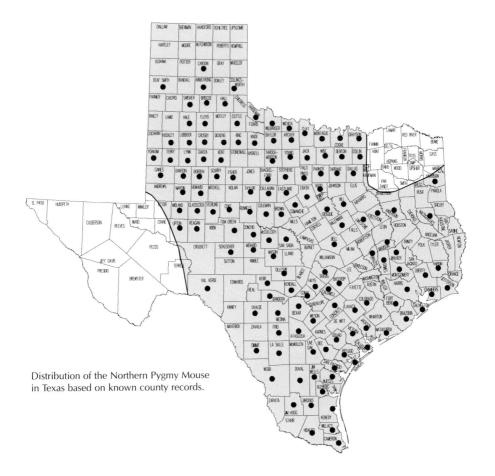

Distribution of the Northern Pygmy Mouse in Texas based on known county records.

an area. These travel routes resemble those made by cotton rats and voles, but are smaller in size. They can swim well when necessary, but water is avoided whenever possible because their short fur is easily water-soaked.

The breeding season is nearly yearlong, with peaks in the late fall and early spring months. On the Llano Estacado reproductive activity is limited to the warmer months. In captivity, one female gave birth to nine litters in 195 days, another to eight litters in 221 days. The gestation period is about 20 days. The litters vary in size from one to five, averaging about three. At birth the young are naked, blind, and helpless and weigh about 1 g each. The eyes open in 12–15 days, the mice are weaned in 18–22 days, and sexual maturity is attained at the age of about 60 days. In captivity, both male and female pygmy mice care for the offspring.

Conservation Status. This little mouse is common and in good shape, having spread over much of Texas during the twentieth century. The development of railroad and highway rights-of-way has facilitated its geographic expansion.

Mearns's Grasshopper Mouse
Onychomys arenicola (Mearns)

Description. A small, fat-tailed mouse with pinkish cinnamon or grayish buff upper-parts and pure white underparts; usually a conspicuous white or grayish tuft at anterior base of ear; nose, cheeks, and sides white; tail sparsely haired, more than 30% of total length, 2–2.5 times as long as hind foot and distinctly bicolor, dark above and white below. Similar to *Onychomys leucogaster* but smaller, with relatively longer tail and smaller teeth. Juveniles similar to adults but upperparts bluish gray. External measurements average: total length, 146 mm; tail, 52 mm; hind foot, 21 mm. Weight of males, 26.5 g (24–30 g); of females, 25 g (22–28 g).

Distribution. Throughout the Trans-Pecos and a few counties east of the Pecos River.

Subspecies. *O. a. arenicola.*

Habits. This mouse chiefly inhabits the low, arid, sandy or gravelly desert areas where desert scrub vegetation in the form of creosote bush, mesquite, yucca, lechuguilla, condalia, and so forth is sparse and scattered. It lives in burrows of its own or in those it usurps from other small rodents. Like the northern grasshopper mouse, it is relatively rare in most localities.

Its behavior and feeding habits are similar to those outlined for *O. leucogaster.*

Mearns's Grasshopper Mouse (*Onychomys arenicola*). Photo courtesy Texas Parks and Wildlife Department.

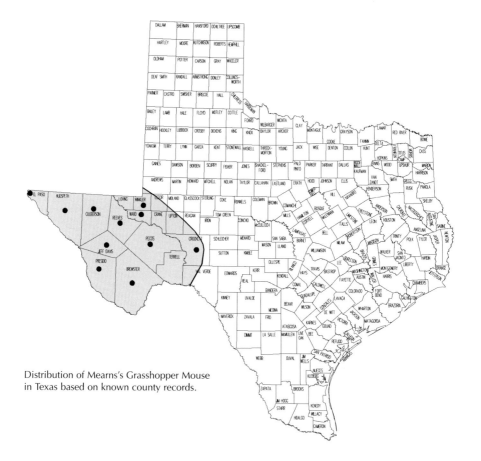

Distribution of Mearns's Grasshopper Mouse
in Texas based on known county records.

Breeding begins in late January or early February and continues into September. Gravid females have been captured as early as 27 February and as late as 5 September. The litters vary in size from 2 to 7, average 4.2. Half-grown young have been captured in April, June, July, and August, suggesting that two or even three litters are produced each year. The young grow rapidly, and females become sexually mature when 7 or 8 weeks of age. A young female can give birth to her first litter at the age of 4 months. The gestation period is 27–30 days.

O. arenicola is active at night, when it forages for insects. Additional food items include other arthropods, especially scorpions, and small mammals. At Big Bend Ranch State Park, Frank Yancey witnessed a grasshopper mouse killing and feeding on a medium-sized kangaroo rat.

These mice are vocal and often emit high-pitched chirps or howls when foraging in an area. They are highly territorial, and their vocalizations may help to identify species territories and reduce antagonistic encounters with conspecifics.

Conservation Status. Although uncommon, this species appears to be in good shape throughout its range in Texas and does not seem to have any serious conservation threats.

Northern Grasshopper Mouse
Onychomys leucogaster (Wied)

Description. A stout-bodied, short-tailed mouse similar to *O. arenicola* but larger, heavier, and shorter-tailed; upperparts drab brown; the nose, sides, cheeks, and underparts white; tuft at anterior base of ear white and conspicuous; tail usually less than 30% of total length and usually 1.5–2 times as long as hind foot. External measurements average: total length, 164 mm; tail, 42 mm; hind foot, 22 mm. Weight, 27–46 g, occasionally as much as 52 g.

Distribution. Throughout most of western Texas (no specimens yet documented from the central part of the Trans-Pecos) and the Rio Grande Plains of south Texas.

Subspecies. *O. l. albescens* in El Paso and Hudspeth counties, *O. l. arcticeps* in the Panhandle and adjacent areas to the east, south to Crockett and Pecos counties, and *O. l. longipes* from Tom Green and Terrell counties southward to the Rio Grande and southeastward to Nueces County.

Habits. These predatory mice occur chiefly in association with sandy or powdery soils in grasslands or open brushlands, but they are never very common as compared with other small mammals.

They are wanderers and do not live long in one place. They are reputed to usurp the burrows of other small mammals rather than take the time to construct their own. This is in keeping with their pugnacious disposition. Vernon Bailey attributes to them many of the habits of the weasel and compares one of their calls to the howl of a wolf, "made with raised nose and open mouth in perfect wolf form." Because of their short legs and chunky body, they are not fleet-footed, but they are expert at dodging, twisting, and turning and in close quarters can easily capture and overpower other mice their own size or even larger.

Northern Grasshopper Mouse (*Onychomys leucogaster*). Photo by John and Gloria Tveten.

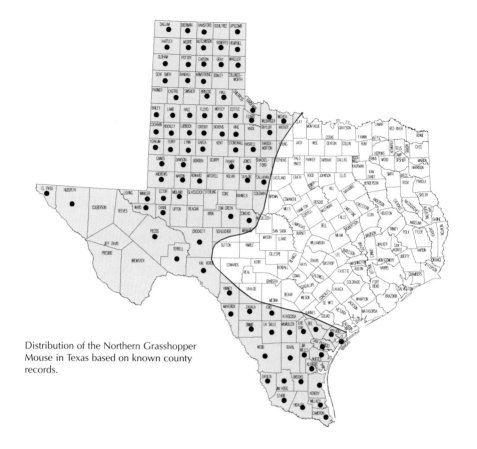

Distribution of the Northern Grasshopper Mouse in Texas based on known county records.

As the name implies, one of their chief food items in season is grasshoppers. In addition, numerous other kinds of insects, scorpions, small mice, and a variety of plants contribute to their diet. Captives are especially fond of raw liver and newborn mice. Vernon Bailey and Charles Sperry report that animal matter makes up nearly 89% of their natural food, plant material only 11%.

The breeding season extends at least from February to October, as judged from pregnancy records, and breeding may occur throughout most of the year in some parts of its range within Texas. Three to six litters of young may be produced annually, but the bulk of the young are born in May and June. The litter size varies from two to six, averaging about four.

The gestation period varies from 32 to 47 days, with the longer periods in lactating females. At birth the young are pink and hairless (except for the prominent vibrissae) and weigh about 2 g each. The eyes and ears are closed, and the tail is characteristically short and thick. Within 3 days the ears unfold, but the eyes remain closed until the nineteenth or twentieth day, at which time the young mice are almost weaned. They are probably evicted from the nest shortly after. Sexual maturity is reached in about 3 months, when the mice are still in the soft, gray juvenile pelage.

Because of their fondness for insects and small mice, their economic status is either neutral or beneficial.

Conservation Status. Although uncommon, this grasshopper mouse appears to be in good shape throughout its range in Texas.

Tawny-bellied Cotton Rat
Sigmodon fulviventer J. A. Allen

Description. A small to medium-sized cotton rat with brownish, buff brown, or fulvous underparts from throat to anus. Dorsal coloration is light brown heavily speckled with dark brown to black, giving a salt-and-pepper or hispid appearance. The tail is uniformly blackish, and the tops of the feet are buff brown.

The tawny-bellied cotton rat is similar in appearance to two other cotton rats that occur in Texas. From the yellow-nosed cotton rat (*S. ochrognathus*), *S. fulviventer* differs in having a rich buffy ventral coloration rather than whitish, a more heavily speckled dorsal coloration, buff-colored tops to the feet rather than grayish, and a uniformly dark-colored tail. Also, *S. fulviventer* lacks the tawny-colored nose of *S. ochrognathus.* The hispid cotton rat (*S. hispidus*) differs from *S. fulviventer* in having gray or whitish underparts, a bicolored tail that is lighter below than above, grayish tops of the feet, and slightly larger ears and hind feet.

External measurements reported for the holotype of *S. f. dalquesti* from Fort Davis were: total length, 242 mm; length of tail, 90 mm; hind foot, 28 mm; ear, 18 mm.

Tawny-bellied Cotton Rat (*Sigmodon fulviventer*). Photo by Robert D. Bradley.

Distribution. In the United States, known from grassland habitats in southeastern Arizona and southwestern New Mexico to middle Rio Grande Valley; in Texas, known only from an isolated population near Fort Davis in Jeff Davis County.

Subspecies. *S. f. dalquesti.*

Habits. The tawny-bellied cotton rat inhabits grassy areas interspersed with shrubby growth that affords cover and allows dense growth of grasses. In Mexico these rats are associated with bunchgrasses in the mesquite-grassland vegetation type. Over their limited range in Arizona and New Mexico, tawny-bellied cotton rats are found in weedy and grassy places in pinyon-juniper–live oak woodland, Mexican oak-pine woodland, and mesquite-yucca-grassland vegetation types, where their runways are hidden in the thick, grassy cover.

Previously unknown in the state, the tawny-bellied cotton rat was first record-ed in Texas in spring 1991 near Fort Davis by Fred Stangl of Midwestern State University. This isolated population represents not only a new species of mammal for Texas but also appears to be a new subspecies, *S. f. dalquesti.* Within a general area described as a "heavily grazed, level valley plain" with "small, scattered mesquite, catclaw, and a fence line" that protected against livestock grazing, tawny-bellied cotton rats were caught in dense grasses along fencerows and in adjacent grassy areas protected by clumps of mesquite and catclaw. Hispid cotton rats were also caught in the areas.

Of 20 Texas specimens captured in late March, 8 were juveniles. Both adult males were in reproductive condition, and of the 10 mature females, 1 was lactat-ing and 4 were pregnant. Embryo counts revealed litter sizes of three, four, four, and four.

Conservation Status. The extent of the tawny-bellied cotton rat's range and relative abundance remain unknown. Given that it is known from only a single location in the Davis Mountains and subsequent attempts to document it at the same place have failed, the suggestion is that the species is extremely rare, worthy of careful monitoring, and probably should be listed as one of the state's rarest and most threatened rodents. Some sort of protective status seems clearly warranted.

Hispid Cotton Rat
Sigmodon hispidus Say and Ord

Description. A moderately large, robust rat with pattern of last two lower molars S-shaped; tail shorter than head and body, sparsely haired, the annulations and scales clearly visible; ears relatively small and blackish or grayish; pelage coarse and grizzled, the black guard hairs rather stiff (hispid); hind foot with six plantar tubercles, three middle toes longer than outer two; upperparts grizzled brown; underparts grayish white or buff. External measurements average: total length, 270 mm; tail, 110 mm; hind foot, 31 mm. Weight, 80–150 g.

Distribution. Statewide.

Subspecies. *S. h. berlandieri* from the Panhandle southward to the Trans-Pecos and the Rio Grande Plains and *S. h. texianus* in the eastern and central parts of the state.

Habits. Normally this rat inhabits tall-grass areas where such grasses as bluestem (*Andropogon*), cordgrass (*Spartina*), or sedges (*Carex*) offer both freedom of movement under a protective canopy and an adequate food supply. In such situations, their runways form a network of interconnecting travelways about 5–8 cm wide. In western Texas, where grassy ground cover is not available, the rats live in dens at the bases of small, low clumps of mesquite in otherwise nearly barren terrain, much after the fashion of white-throated woodrats. Between those two extremes are several types of habitat that may support small populations of cotton rats. Preferred sites are old fields, natural prairie, unmolested rights-of-way for roads and railroads, grassy and weedy valleys, and dense riparian woodland with thick grass.

The rats place their nests either in chambers off underground burrows or above ground in dense clumps of grass, piles of brush, or other situations that offer some concealment and protection. The nests are globular, about 12 cm in diameter, and composed of shredded grasses and weeds. Underground burrows are 3–5 cm in diameter, simple in design, and seldom longer than 8 m. Occasionally, the rats take over and use the discarded burrows of pocket gophers and moles.

S. hispidus primarily is nocturnal but may be active throughout the day. It mostly forages for grasses and seeds but also may feed on insects and eggs of ground-nesting birds. Food gathered during the warmer months is not stored for winter consumption. Rather, fat storage accumulated during spring, summer, and autumn aids in sustaining individuals over winter.

Hispid Cotton Rat (*Sigmodon hispidus*). Photo courtesy Texas Parks and Wildlife Department.

Distribution of the Hispid Cotton Rat
in Texas based on known county records.

Cotton rats are prolific and produce several litters of 2 to 10 young, averaging about 5, a year. Their breeding habits vary in response to levels of precipitation. During wet years, they breed throughout the year; during periods of drought, reproductive activity declines significantly. In the northern part of the state it appears that reproduction is curtailed during the coldest months. Captive females have given birth to as many as nine litters a year; data from wild-caught rats likewise indicate a nearly yearlong breeding season, at least in the warmer parts of their range. The gestation period is approximately 27 days. Females frequently breed again immediately after partus. At birth the young are hairless, for the most part, pink, blind, and weigh about 5 g. They develop rapidly. The eyes open in about 36 hours, the incisors erupt on the fifth or sixth day, and the young rats are usually weaned when 15 or 20 days old. They can be successfully weaned, however, as soon as the teeth have erupted (5–6 days). Sexual maturity is reached in about 40 days, when the animals are still in juvenile pelage; at 6 months young rats are indistinguishable externally from adults.

Cotton rat populations are cyclical and subject to extreme fluctuations in density, and they have the reproductive capacity to increase rapidly under favorable conditions. Incredible densities of cotton rats have been documented following several successive wet, rainy years and mild winters. These outbreaks have caused serious losses (as much as 90% loss in some instances) to farm crops, particularly peas, peanuts, watermelons, and cauliflower. Population explosions have been documented around San Antonio in 1889, statewide in 1919, in McLennan County in 1928, statewide in the late 1930s and 1940s, throughout eastern Texas from 1958 to 1960, and near Wichita Falls in 1961. Extreme outbreaks have not been reported in the past four decades.

Population explosions are not difficult to comprehend when one is aware of the reproductive potential of these rats. Let's repeat some data for emphasis. An adult female may breed throughout the year in Texas when conditions are favorable. She may produce as many as nine litters of 10 young each (normally less). The gestation period is only 4 weeks, and the female breeds again within a few hours after giving birth. Young females are sexually mature in 40 days and can be mothers at the tender age of 68 days and grandmothers at 136 days. Thus, if we assume a new generation of cotton rats every 68 days, a female could be a great-great-great-grandmother at the age of 1 year and be the ancestor of about 15,500 cotton rats. If this same rate of reproduction were extended for only three more generations and all survived, the grand total of offspring from the original female would be more than 3.5 million.

Although this potential is always present in cotton rats, it is seldom realized because of death due to predators, disease, lack of suitable or sufficient food, accidents, smaller litters, fewer litters a year, and so on. When conditions are just right, however, the population explodes, and we are knee-deep in cotton rats before we know it.

Fortunately, every eruption is followed by a crash in the population that is brought on by a combination of factors, principally disease. Predators such as coyotes, bobcats, hawks, owls, and certain snakes take their toll, but the main killer is disease. As the rats increase in numbers, the animals become more and more crowded and provide more contacts for the rapid spread of disease. At the same time, the virulence of the disease increases, until finally the crash occurs and the population is low once again.

Conservation Status. This cotton rat is broadly distributed and probably occurs abundantly in every county of the state. Undoubtedly, it has fared well as a result of the increase throughout the twentieth century of railroad and highway rights-of-way that provide suitable habitat for dispersal.

Yellow-nosed Cotton Rat
Sigmodon ochrognathus Bailey

Description. Similar to *S. hispidus* but paler, and with the snout distinctly orange or rusty; tail hairier and distinctly bicolor, nearly black above, grayish buff below; underparts grayish white. External measurements average: total length, 259 mm; tail, 114 mm; hind foot, 28 mm. Weight, 50–80 g, occasionally as much as 112 g.

Yellow-nosed Cotton Rat (*Sigmodon ochrognathus*). Photo by John and Gloria Tveten.

Distribution.   Generally isolated at higher elevations in the Chisos Mountains, Brewster County; Davis Mountains, Jeff Davis County; and the Sierra Vieja, Presidio County. Recently, this species has been reported from the low country of the Davis Mountains region (Limpia Canyon); Big Bend Ranch State Park, Presidio County; Elephant Mountain Wildlife Management area, Brewster County; and the Guadalupe Mountains, Culberson County (80 miles north of its previously known range).

Subspecies.   Monotypic species.

Habits.   Yellow-nosed cotton rats live primarily in high-elevation grasslands, as well as rocky upland slopes with scattered bunches of grasses in montane riparian habitat. In the Chisos Mountains their runways have been located in lodged needle grass in Laguna Meadow at the foot of Emory Peak. There, the rats occupied an area of about 40 ha. Their runways radiated from underground dens, some of which were under clumps of agaves; others were among the roots of large junipers. A surface nest under a pile of dead blades of agaves was composed of dry grasses and long fibers from the agave plants. It was about 12 cm in outside diameter. Other nests have been found beneath the dead lower leaves of sotol. At Big Bend Ranch State Park, a single individual was obtained in a lowland seasonal streambed near a permanent spring surrounded by willow, false willow, and deergrass.

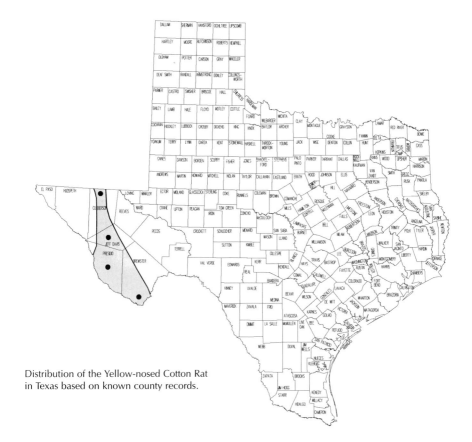

Distribution of the Yellow-nosed Cotton Rat in Texas based on known county records.

These rats can be active in the daytime or at night. They are reported to breed throughout the year. Females give birth to litters of 3 to 5 (average 3.6), possibly several times a year. The gestation period is approximately 35 days.

At birth, young rats weigh 4.5–6.6 g and are haired. They gain about 2 g in weight each day and reach sexual maturity by 45 days. Captive females have produced offspring at 71 days of age.

Conservation Status. Until recently this species was thought to be rare and restricted to montane habitat and possibly in need of listing and special protection. Recent trapping evidence, however, suggests it is becoming more abundant and widespread throughout its range in the Trans-Pecos. Recent collecting shows it to occupy a number of nonmontane habitats. This is another species that may be expanding in association with the increasing aridity in western Texas.

Eastern Woodrat

Neotoma floridana (Ord)

Description. Large rat with long, round, tapering, scantily haired tail, large ears, and bulging black eyes. Upperparts creamy buff to buffy gray, clearest along sides;

Eastern Woodrat (*Neotoma floridana*). Photo by John and Gloria Tveten.

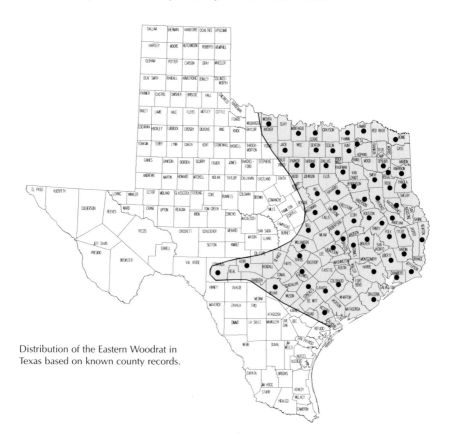

Distribution of the Eastern Woodrat in Texas based on known county records.

underparts and feet white; tail distinctly bicolor, white below and brownish above. External measurements average: total length, 369 mm; tail, 160 mm; hind foot, 40 mm. Weight, 200–350 g.

Distribution. Eastern one-third of Texas west to Wichita, Bell, and Edwards counties; south to Victoria County.

Subspecies. *N. f. attwateri* in the northern and western parts of the range in the state, *N. f. rubida* in the southeast, and *N. f. illinoensis* in extreme northeastern Texas.

Habits. The wide range occupied by the eastern woodrat, encompassing habitats ranging from swamplands along the lower Mississippi River, through forested uplands, to the arid plains of eastern Colorado, is reflected in its geographic variation and in the correlated differences in habits. In the mixed hammock and river bottom associations in eastern Texas, these rats do not construct surface nests but rather live in burrows at the bases of trees. This species is especially abundant in the flatland hardwood, flatland hardwood pine, and lower slope hardwood pine forests in the Big Thicket region of southeast Texas. In the upland post oak association in east-central Texas, they normally use underground burrows but occasionally resort to a combination of surface house and underground burrow or a large surface house built at the base of a tree or against a fallen log with no associated burrow. In central Texas (Edwards Plateau) they frequently live in rocky canyon walls, where they occupy mesic, upland habitats and riparian areas.

In localities where underground dens are the fashion, the rats do not hesitate to take over burrows dug by other and larger animals. In one such den in Brazos County the large nest, located about a meter from the entrance, was composed of dried broom sedge grasses, leaves, and small twigs.

The diet of eastern woodrats consists of varied plants, fruits, and seeds, depending in part on local availability of the food sources. In east-central Texas they feed on acorns, yaupon berries, and the leaves of oaks, yaupon, French mulberry, greenbrier, peppervine, rattan, and hackberry. Many of these items were garnered by the rats well above ground, which indicates that most of their foraging is done in the crowns of trees and shrubs. Gnawed bones have been found associated with their nests, and it is believed they carry bones back to their nests in order to sharpen their teeth and to obtain mineral nutrients.

The breeding season extends from January to September in Texas. Litter size ranges from one to five (average two) and up to three litters may be produced annually. The gestation period is about 33 days. Newborn woodrats are blind, deaf, naked, and weigh only 15 g. The eyes open at about 15 days of age, and weaning takes place around the twentieth day. Woodrats do not reach adult size until they are about 8–9 months of age, and most females do not breed until they are about 1 year old.

The home range is rather limited; the animals usually stay close to the home den. Studies suggest that 85 m is an exceptional distance for them to travel in their foraging activities. Also, they are more or less colonial to the extent that several rats will establish themselves in a relatively restricted locality. In one instance 35 to 50 rats lived in a 180 m distance along a favorable gully.

Since these rats usually inhabit wooded or brushy lands, they seldom come into close contact with humans and conflict but little, if at all, with our economy. They are preyed on by owls, skunks, foxes, and other flesh eaters.

Conservation Status. This species is common throughout its range in Texas and does not appear to face any serious conservation threats.

Remarks. *N. floridana* is often difficult to distinguish from the closely related species *N. micropus* where they co-occur on the Edwards Plateau, and there is some evidence that the two species may hybridize with each other in that area.

Eastern White-throated Woodrat

Neotoma leucodon Merriam

Description. A medium-sized woodrat with large ears, bulging black eyes, and relatively short, distinctly bicolor tail (grayish brown above, white below), densely covered with short hairs; throat, and usually breast and chin, with hairs white to base; upperparts dull pinkish buff, brightest along sides, thinly suffused with blackish; underparts and feet white. External measurements average: total length, 328 mm; tail, 152 mm; hind foot, 34 mm. Weight, 136–294 g.

Eastern White-throated Woodrat (*Neotoma leucodon*). Photo by R. D. Porter, courtesy Texas Parks and Wildlife Department.

Distribution of the Eastern White-throated Woodrat in Texas based on known county records.

Distribution. Found in the Panhandle and broken country south of the Red River throughout the Edwards Plateau to Bexar and Uvalde counties, and westward over most of the southwestern part of state.

Subspecies. *N. l. warreni* in the northern Panhandle and *N. l. robusta* over the remainder of the range.

Habits. This woodrat is known to reside at intermediate elevations primarily in arid lands of the Trans-Pecos, along the rocky slopes of the escarpment surrounding the Llano Estacado, and rocky areas on the Edwards Plateau. It seems to be especially fond of desert scrub vegetation such as prickly pear, cholla cactus, mesquite, sotol, lechuguilla, and creosote bush, and of juniper brakes. Cholla cactus and prickly pear offer preferred homesites because they supply not only protection but also food and water. Occasionally, their houses are built in the open or in sparse vegetation. In rocky situations the associated cracks and crevices afford the usual den site.

The house is a crude cone of sticks, cactus joints, and other rubbish surrounding the nest proper, a compact, cup-shaped structure composed of shredded dry leaves, blades of grass, and weed stems. Access to the house is by means of openings near the base to which well-worn trails lead. Frequently, especially in localities where building materials are scarce, the house is supplemented by a system of underground burrows. Feces are not deposited within the den or house; fecal material is usually deposited in a single area, or midden, in the vicinity of the den.

Although several houses may occupy a small, desirable patch of cacti, the rats are not social creatures. Only one animal or a female and her young occupy each house. Their home ranges or feeding territories overlap considerably, but to each rat his house is a personal affair and thus is not shared.

The menu of these rats consists of a variety of desert plants, but the cactus family led the list of more than 30 items found in the stomachs of 360 rats examined. Mesquite and forbs were next in preference. Grasses constituted less than 5% of their fare, but small quantities were regularly consumed. The amount of animal material consumed (ants, birds, beetles, and grasshoppers) was less than 1% of the total diet. The habit of storing food is not well developed in these rats, but small quantities of food are usually found at each house. Drinking water is not required because of the high water content in their choice of foods.

Breeding may extend throughout the year in parts of Texas, but the primary season is from January to September. At least two and possibly three or more litters of two or three young each may be reared during this period. The period of gestation is approximately 30 days. At birth the young are helpless, weigh about 11 g, and are about twice the size of newborn house rats. As is the case with other woodrats and many related species of mice, the young ones have specially developed front teeth that permit them to grasp the nipples of the mother and to be dragged along behind her, skidding and bouncing along on their backs, when she leaves the nest. They grow rapidly; the ears open on the thirteenth to fifteenth day, the eyes open on the fifteenth to nineteenth day, and they are weaned when 62–72 days old. When about 6 months old they are almost indistinguishable from their elders.

The spiny fortress that surrounds the house, coupled with the nocturnal habits of the rats, makes them relatively safe from most predators. Owls catch a few individuals, as do coyotes, bobcats, ringtails, and weasels, but their chief natural enemies appear to be the large desert gopher snake and the rattlesnake, both of which can enter the houses of the rats with impunity.

Conservation Status. This species appears to be in good shape, with no serious threats throughout its range in Texas.

Remarks. In previous editions this species was referred to as *Neotoma albigula*. Cody Edwards and his associates at Texas Tech, using techniques of molecular genetics, have demonstrated a distinct genetic division between populations of white-throated woodrats located east and west of the Rio Grande in New Mexico. Those populations east of the Rio Grande represent a different species, *Neotoma leucodon*, from those west of the river, *N. albigula*. This is the logic for assigning all Texas populations to the species *N. leucodon*.

Mexican Woodrat
Neotoma mexicana Baird

Description. Medium-sized, about as large as the white-throated woodrat, but white hairs of entire underparts usually buffy basally, not white to roots; first upper molar with deep antero-internal reentrant angle; upperparts grayish buff, moderately darkened over back by blackish hairs; tail brownish above, white below. External measurements average: total length, 300 mm; tail, 125 mm; hind foot, 28 mm. Weight, 140–185 g.

Distribution. Known only from rocky areas at mid to high elevations in Trans-Pecos Texas, where it is common in the mountainous regions of Brewster, Culberson, Hudspeth, Jeff Davis, and Presidio counties.

Subspecies. *N. m. mexicana.*

Habits. These rats frequent rimrocks, canyon walls, and other rocky areas at mid to high elevations, where they establish themselves in cracks and crevices among shrubland or wooded areas. Into these retreats they carry considerable quantities of rubbish with which to build their nests. Preferring to construct their dens among the cracks and crevices of boulders and other rocky situations, these woodrats do not build elaborate, aboveground nests as do other woodrats. Where rocky retreats are not available they construct houses about the roots of trees, in hollow logs, and in piles of logs, or they may take up residence in deserted or little-used cabins. Where they occupy dens among the rocks, their presence is usually evidenced not only by the piles of rubbish at the entrances but also by copious deposits of elongated, capsule-shaped fecal pellets on rocky shelves or in niches in the rocks. Seemingly, they establish regularly used sites for defecation.

Mexican Woodrat (*Neotoma mexicana*). Photo by Robert D. Bradley.

Their food consists of a variety of plants, including green vegetation, nuts, berries, acorns, and fungi. In contrast to *N. leucodon*, *N. mexicana* exhibits a strong distaste for cactus. Also unlike *N. leucodon*, *N. mexicana* regularly stores large quantities of food, presumably for winter consumption. Mexican woodrats typically reside at higher elevations than do white-throated woodrats and thus face longer, colder winters and possible food shortages during that time.

The breeding season of this species extends from early spring through summer in the Trans-Pecos. In Colorado, nearly all adult females produce two litters in quick succession. Litter size for adult females is 2 to 5 (average 3.4); that for young females averages 2.4. The gestation period ranges from 31 to 34 days. At birth the young rats weigh 9–12 g. Growth is rapid, and young females reach sexual maturity in about a month. Females born in April and May often produce litters of their own in June and July while they are still partly or wholly in the gray, juvenile pelage. Young males, however, do not become sexually mature until the following year, when they are 8 or 9 months old.

Since the range of these rats is confined largely to mountainous areas, the rats ordinarily do not conflict seriously with the human economy, but they may rifle mountain cabins and the camps of vacationers.

Conservation Status. Although somewhat isolated in the mid to high elevations of the major mountainous regions in the Trans-Pecos, this species is common throughout its range and does not appear to face any serious threats in our state.

Southern Plains Woodrat
Neotoma micropus Baird

Description. A large, gray-colored rat with large ears and relatively short, heavy, sparsely haired tail. Differs from *Neotoma floridana*, to which it is most closely related and which may occur in the same area, in gray, often bluish gray, dorsal coloration. Upperparts pale drab, mixed with blackish hairs along the back; tail blackish above, grayish below; underparts and feet white. External measurements average: total length, 351 mm; tail, 163 mm; hind foot, 41 mm. Weight of males, 272–310 g; of females, 204–243 g.

Distribution. Found in western two-thirds of state eastward to Johnson County in the north and Calhoun County on the Gulf Coast.

Subspecies. *N. m. canescens* in the western part of the range in the state and *N. m. micropus* in the east.

Habits. This rat is characteristic of the brushlands in the semiarid region between the timberlands and the arid deserts to the west. It occurs primarily in valley pastures and around watercourses on the Edwards Plateau. Unlike other woodrats, it is rarely associated with rocks or cliffs; rather, it is usually found associated with cactus or some of the thorny desert shrubs. It is at home in thickets of cacti, mesquite, or thorn bush, where it constructs a house of sticks, joints of cactus,

Southern Plains Woodrat (*Neotoma micropus*). Photo by John and Gloria Tveten.

Distribution of the Southern Plains Woodrat in Texas based on known county records.

thorns, and other readily available material. Frequently, an underground burrow system is added, particularly in localities where building materials are not abundant. These houses may be a meter or more high with two or more openings near the base to which well-worn trails lead through and over the spiny vegetation. So well protected are these rats by their spiny fortresses that they seldom are molested at home by larger animals.

Their food consists almost entirely of vegetation; the thick blades of the prickly pear and the juicy fruits of many species of cactus are favored items. Specific items include the thick basal parts of the leaves of sotol, blades of agaves, beans and pods of mesquite, and acorns. Their food also supplies the necessary water.

In parts of its range, *N. micropus* is known to breed throughout the year, but on the Llano Estacado pregnant females have been taken from February to May and from July to September. One or two litters may be produced annually. The usual number of young per litter is three but ranges from one to four. The gestation period is about 33 days. At birth the young weigh about 10 g, but growth is rapid. They are weaned when about 30 days old, and at the age of 3 months are nearly full-grown and weigh about 85% as much as adults. At the age of 300 days they are sexually mature.

Under suitable conditions the population density may become high, at which times the rats may compete seriously with livestock and big game animals for forage. Ordinarily, however, they are not serious pests.

Conservation Status. This species is locally abundant over much of its range in Texas, but it appears to be excluded from or its numbers greatly reduced in areas of intensive agricultural activity. Regular plowing, use of defoliants, and the absence of habitat in some areas leave little room for this rodent. There is no reason, however, to place it on any sort of threatened or protected list.

Norway Rat *

Rattus norvegicus (Berkenhout)

Description. Similar to the roof rat but larger and chunkier; tail shorter than length of head and body. External measurements average: total length, 440 mm; tail, 205 mm; hind foot, 46 mm. Weight, 400–500 g.

Distribution. Widespread in Texas but not so common in the southern half of the state as the roof rat.

Habits. The Norway rat (also known as the wharf or brown rat) lives both as a commensal in close association with humans, and in the feral state, chiefly where vegetation is tall and rank and affords adequate protection. For example, the marshy lands on Galveston Island off the coast of Texas offer ideal habitat for them. As a commensal this rat lives principally in basements, on the ground floor, or in burrows under sidewalks or outbuildings. They appear to be most common about feed stores, chicken houses, and garbage dumps. Although more at home on the

Norway Rat (*Rattus norvegicus*). Photo courtesy U.S. Fish and Wildlife Service.

ground, these rats are adept at climbing and have been observed traveling along telephone wires from one building to another. In places they become exceedingly numerous and destructive.

They feed on a variety of items including both plant and animal materials. All sorts of garbage appear to be welcome, but their mainstay is plant material. Grains of various sorts are highly prized. When established around poultry houses, they feed extensively on eggs and young chickens. They even have been known to kill lambs and young pigs.

These rats are prolific breeders. The gestation period varies from 21 to 23 days and the number of young from 2 to 14, averaging 7 or 8. At birth they are blind, naked, and helpless. They grow rapidly; their eyes open in 14–17 days, and they are weaned when 3 or 4 weeks old. There is no delimited breeding season, but there is a tendency for a slowdown in reproduction during fall and winter. The life span is reported to be 2–3 years.

Although these rats are preyed on by a number of animals, including the spotted skunk and the barn owl as well as house cats, such predators often are not able to keep the rat population in check. Considerable destruction of property and foodstuffs can take place where rats are abundant. In addition, they constitute a menace to public health. They are known to be reservoirs of bubonic plague (transmitted to humans by the bite of a flea or other insect), endemic typhus fever, rat-bite fever, and a few other dreaded diseases. Every effort should be made to exterminate them when they are found on your premises, and it is advisable to rat-proof garbage cans and all buildings to prevent their entrance.

Conservation Status. This introduced rat lives in close association with humans and their structures. It is a pest and can have negative effects on native species of rodents.

Roof Rat *
Rattus rattus (Linnaeus)

Description. A blackish (or brownish), medium-sized, slender rat with long, naked, scaly tail; tail usually longer than head and body but not always so; mammae in 5 or 6 pairs. External measurements average: total length, 370 mm; tail, 190 mm; hind foot, 36 mm. Weight, up to 200 g.

Distribution. Common over most of Texas, especially in towns.

Habits. Roof rats are largely commensals and live in close association with humans. They seldom become established as feral animals as do the Norway rats. They inhabit grocery and drug stores, warehouses, feed stores, and poultry houses and can be very common in cotton gins and associated grain warehouses. On farms they live in barns and corncribs. They may live near the ground, but usually they frequent attics, rafters, and crossbeams of buildings. They make typical runways along pipes, beams, or wires, up and down studding, or along horizontal ceiling joists, often leaving a dark-colored layer of grease and dirt to mark their travelways. Like the Norway rat, the roof rat is largely nocturnal, and only where populations are relatively high does one see them frequently in the daytime. There is some indication that the larger and more aggressive Norway rat is supplanting the roof rat in many parts of the United States. In the southern United States, however, the roof rat is by far the more common of the two.

Roof Rat (*Rattus rattus*). Photo by John and Gloria Tveten.

They accept a wide variety of food items, including grains, meats, and almost any item that has nutritive value.

Roof rats breed throughout the year, with two peaks of production, in February and March and again in May and June. The period of least activity is in July and August. The gestation period is approximately 21 days, and the number of young per litter averages almost seven. The young rats at birth are naked, blind, and nearly helpless. They mature rather rapidly, are weaned when about 3 weeks old, and are able to reproduce when approximately 3 months old. In Texas, young females with a head and body length of 125 mm were sexually mature. Like the Norway rat, the roof rat is destructive to property and foodstuffs. Also, it plays an important part in the transmission of such human diseases as endemic typhus, rat-bite fever, and bubonic plague.

Conservation Status. This introduced rat lives in close association with humans and their structures. It is a pest and can have negative effects on native species of rodents.

House Mouse ✳

Mus musculus Linnaeus

Description. A small, scaly-tailed mouse with a distinct notch in the cutting surface of upper incisors (seen best in side view); hair short; ears moderately large and naked; upperparts ochraceous, suffused with black; belly buffy white, or buffy, usually without speckling and with slaty underfur; yellowish flank line usually present; tail brownish with black tip, not distinctly bicolor, but paler on underside; ears

House Mouse (*Mus musculus*). Photo by John and Gloria Tveten.

pale brown, feet drab or buffy, tips of toes white. Mammae in four or five pairs. External measurements average: total length, 169 mm; tail, 93 mm; hind foot, 18 mm. Weight of adults, 17–25 g.

Distribution. Widely distributed over Texas, usually in close association with humans.

Habits. Although not native to North America, the house mouse, since its early accidental introduction at most of our seaport towns, has become widespread throughout the United States and occurs either as a commensal or feral animal in practically all parts of the United States. As commensal animals, house mice live in close association with humans, in our houses, outbuildings, stores, and other structures. Where conditions permit, feral mice may be found in fields, along watercourses, and in other places where vegetation is dense enough to afford concealment. These feral animals make runways through the grass similar to those of *Microtus* or *Baiomys,* or they may utilize runways made by cotton rats and other meadow-inhabiting species. In agricultural regions where irrigation is practiced, house mice often are found in the vegetation along irrigation ditches, sometimes sharing common runways with native mice. Along the Rio Grande in Texas, patches of cane often are honeycombed with the runways of these mice. At one locality along this river several hundred trap-nights yielded only house mice, which suggested that these animals had evicted the native mice from the area.

Although largely nocturnal, house mice are moderately active during the day, chiefly in their quest for food. In the wild they feed on a variety of plant material, including seeds, green stems, and leaves. Alfalfa hay, either in shocks or in stacks, affords an ideal source of food supply, and consequently, it is frequently infested with these mice. As commensals, house mice feed on practically any type of food suitable for the use of man or beast. They are particularly obnoxious around granaries, feed houses, and stores and may do considerable damage in destroying or contaminating food supplies intended for human consumption. In addition they will feed on such animal matter as insects and meat when available.

These mice are exceedingly prolific breeders; as many as 13 litters can be produced in one year. The number of young per litter averages about six. The gestation period is approximately 19 days, varying from 18 to 20. At birth the young mice are nearly naked, with their eyes and ears closed. They develop rapidly; at the age of 3 weeks they are fully weaned, and at 4 weeks some of the young females are ready to assume family duties, although the average age of sexual maturity is about 35 days in females and 60 days in males. With commensals, breeding occurs throughout the year, although it is somewhat curtailed in the colder months. In the wild state breeding appears to be restricted to the period from early June to late fall.

Although these mice are destructive when allowed to run free, they are widely used in laboratories as subjects for biological, genetic, and medical studies. When ranging free, however, they do a considerable amount of damage, although they are not nearly so troublesome as the introduced rat. Mice can be controlled in houses relatively easily with snap traps.

Conservation Status. These introduced, commensal rodents live in close associa-tion with humans and their structures, but they also have become established over much of the state in abandoned fields, fencerows, weedy roadsides, and cul-tivated fields where they may live side by side with various species of native rodents. House mice do compete with and can replace native species, and like other introduced species they can cause serious conservation problems if they get out of control.

Mexican Vole
Microtus mexicanus (Saussure)

Description. A small mouse with short tail, brown color, and only four mammary glands; tail usually less than 35 mm in length, less than twice as long as hind foot; pelage long and fluffy; upperparts dull umber brown, underparts buffy gray, feet and tail brownish gray. External measurements average: total length, 141 mm; tail, 32 mm; hind foot, 21 mm. Weight, 29–48 g.

Distribution. Restricted in Texas to the higher parts of the Guadalupe Mountains in Culberson County.

Subspecies. *M. m. guadalupensis.*

Habits. In the Guadalupe Mountains of western Texas these mice live in colonies in grassy openings of yellow pine forest, especially in the vicinity of old logs that are

Mexican Vole (*Microtus mexicanus*). Photo by John and Gloria Tveten.

partly decayed and well bedded in the soil. Their numerous, well-defined runways meander through the tall grass, radiating chiefly from the logs under which the mice live and rear their families. They also occur on open ridges where their runways wind about among stones, under shinnery oaks, and even into the edge of dry woods.

Their globular nests of dried grasses and herbs are placed in dense clumps of vegetation above ground, in hollowed-out places under logs, or in special underground chambers off their burrows. One located under a log was cup-shaped, rather than globular, about 10 cm in diameter, and contained four small mice.

Trapping records indicate that these mice are more active in the daytime than are most small mammals, especially in places where adequate ground cover offers concealment. More than 90% of a series trapped in the Guadalupe Mountains were caught in the daytime, although the traps were kept set day and night.

Their food is almost entirely vegetation, the green parts of grasses and herbs in summer and the basal portions, roots, bulbs, and bark in winter. There is no evidence that they store food other than the small piles of cut vegetation seen along their trails and at their feeding stations.

Breeding probably continues through most of the year, with an interval of about 30–40 days between litters. Gravid females have been trapped in every month from May to October, inclusive. The size of litters, based on embryo counts, ranges from two to five, averaging three. At birth the young are nearly naked, blind, and helpless. They develop rapidly, as indicated by the records of young females in the black juvenile pelage, weighing slightly more than 20 g, that were sexually mature and gravid. Such mice were probably not more than 6 weeks old.

In Texas these mice are restricted to the high parts of the Guadalupe Mountains and are of no economic importance except as food for furbearers and other flesh eaters. Their remains have been identified in droppings of gray fox, bobcat, badger, coyote, and skunk.

Conservation Status. The species remains in good shape in Texas within the confines of the national park, but it could be threatened by a catastrophic local event such as a massive forest fire within the park.

Prairie Vole
Microtus ochrogaster (Wagner)

Description. A dark (brownish or blackish) mouse with tail less than twice as long as hind foot, ears almost hidden in long, lax fur, and only five plantar tubercles; underparts tinged with buff. External measurements average: total length, 146 mm; tail, 34 mm; hind foot, 20 mm. Weight, 30–50 g.

Distribution. Known in Texas only from Hardin County in southeastern Texas and Hansford and Lipscomb counties in the extreme northern Panhandle.

Subspecies. From Hardin County *M. o. ludovicianus*; in the Panhandle *M. o. taylori*.

Prairie Vole (*Microtus ochrogaster*). Photo by John and Gloria Tveten.

Habits. Prairie voles for the most part inhabit tall-grass prairies. They live in colonies, utilizing underground burrows and surface runways under lodged vegetation for concealment and protection. Their burrows are said to be shallow but complex in their ramifications and to contain large storage chambers. In farming regions they frequently take up winter quarters in shocks of corn and other small grains that offer both food and protection. Their nests are rather large structures, averaging about 20 by 10 by 10 cm in length, width, and height and may be placed either above ground or in underground chambers about 12 cm below the surface. Small hillocks of earth and pieces of grass at the entrances of burrows often indicate the presence of underground nests.

Their food is almost entirely vegetable matter, including green parts of plants, seeds, bulbs, and bark, much of which they store for winter use. They also seem to relish flesh and feed on their own kind caught and killed by traps.

Their breeding habits are not well known. They probably breed throughout the year. Gravid females have been captured in the winter months of November, January, and February. The main season, however, is in spring and summer. Apparently each breeding female produces several litters a year, the size of which varies from two to six and averages about four. At birth the young are blind, nearly naked, and helpless. They mature rather rapidly and are capable of reproducing in their first year.

Conservation Status. The single specimen from Hardin County was taken in 1902 and represents the relictual subspecies *M. o. ludovicianus,* now extinct. It once

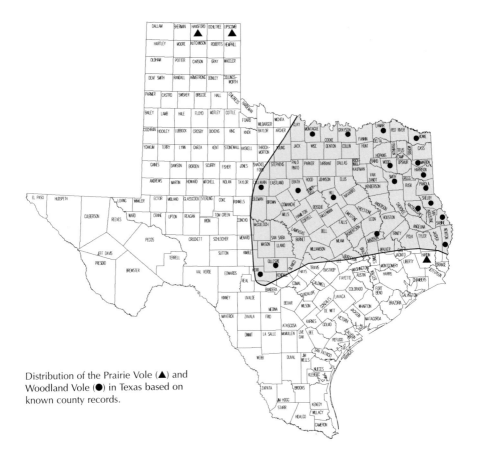

Distribution of the Prairie Vole (▲) and Woodland Vole (●) in Texas based on known county records.

occurred also in adjacent western Louisiana. The Panhandle specimens, nine in all, were collected in the late 1980s, and they represent a totally different subspecies, *M. o. taylori*. With only nine specimens known from but two localities in the Panhandle, it could be argued that this vole ought to be protected somehow, but much more information about where it does or does not occur is needed before any such action should be taken. The status of these populations should be closely monitored in the future.

Woodland Vole

Microtus pinetorum (Le Conte)

Description. A small mouse with short, dense, glossy fur and short tail; five tubercles on sole of hind foot; two pairs of mammary glands, inguinal in position; upperparts dull chestnut tinged with black; underparts tinged with cinnamon; tail slightly darker above than below. Juveniles plumbeous gray, tinged with chestnut. External measurements average: total length, 135 mm; tail, 25 mm; hind foot, 18 mm. Weight, 25–45 g.

Distribution. Found in eastern and central parts of state west to Callahan, Kerr, and Gillespie counties, but nowhere does it appear to be common within its range in Texas. See distribution map in the account for *Microtus ochrogaster.*

Subspecies. *M. p. auricularis* in the southern part of the range in Texas and *M. p. nemoralis* to the north.

Habits. These mice occur largely in woodland areas where ground cover in the form of leaf litter and lodged grasses offers suitable protection. They are rarely, if ever, found westward in the zone of sparse rainfall, which seems to correlate well with their fondness for burrowing just under the surface of the ground, much after the fashion of moles. Although they sometimes use surface runways in grassy areas, they are more inclined to spend their time in underground galleries that they dig for themselves or usurp from moles, short-tailed shrews, or other small mammals. Their burrows are about 4 cm in diameter and seldom more than 7–10 cm beneath the surface of the ground. The normal home range of individuals appears to be about one-tenth of a hectare.

The nest is globular in shape, constructed mainly of dead grasses, leaves, and other vegetation and usually placed in a special chamber in the ground. Occasionally, it is located under a partly buried log or among the roots of a stump. Two or more passages usually lead from it to the surface, thereby providing avenues of escape should the occupants be molested.

The food of these mice is largely roots and tubers. Specific items include peanuts, tuberous roots of violets, berries of red haw, bark from the roots of several kinds of trees, and shrubs and roots of several grasses. In their stores have been found acorns, nuts of various kinds, and tuberous roots of several species of

Woodland Vole (*Microtus pinetorum*). Photo by John and Gloria Tveten.

herbs and grasses. Because of their subterranean habits, these mice rarely sit up to eat. Instead, the food is held pressed against the floor of the burrow and eaten at leisure.

The breeding season extends at least from February to October and may continue through the winter. During the breeding period an adult female may give birth to as many as four litters of two to four young each. At birth the young ones are blind and naked and weigh slightly more than 2 g. In about 1 week they are well furred; the eyes open in 9–12 days; and they are weaned when about 17 days old. They begin to acquire adult pelage at about 4 weeks of age. The gestation period is reported as 24 days.

In orchards these mice may become so abundant as to cause considerable damage by girdling roots and killing trees, but otherwise they are not of much economic importance. Predators include barn owls, hawks, rat snakes, gray foxes, opossums, mink, and weasels.

Conservation Status. This vole has a highly scattered and localized distribution in the eastern and central parts of the state. Nowhere does it appear to be common, and continued degradation of grassland habitats could greatly impair its status in Texas. There are no recent records from the Hill Country or other places where it was once taken and grasslands have been converted to shrubland habitat. This is another vole that bears careful monitoring in the future.

Muskrat (*Ondatra zibethicus*). Photo by John and Gloria Tveten.

Muskrat

Ondatra zibethicus (Linnaeus)

Description. A large, brownish, aquatic, scaly-tailed rodent; feet and toes fringed with short, stiff hairs and toes of hind feet partly webbed; tail about as long as head and body, nearly naked, scaly, and compressed laterally; fur dense; eyes and ears small; upperparts brown to black, sides chestnut to hazel; underparts tawny brown, usually with a white area on chin. External measurements average: total length, 516 mm; tail, 240 mm; hind foot, 74 mm. Weight of males, 923 g; of females, 839 g.

Distribution. Occurs only in suitable aquatic habitats in northern, southeastern, and southwestern parts of the state.

Subspecies. *O. z. cinnamominus* in the north, *O. z. ripensis* along the Rio Grande and Pecos River in the Trans-Pecos region, and *O. z. rivalicius* on the Gulf Coastal Plain as far west as Brazoria County.

Habits. Muskrats are principally marsh inhabitants; creeks, rivers, lakes, drainage ditches, and canals support small populations in places where requisite food and shelter are available. In the interior areas shallow, freshwater marshes with clumps of cattails interspersed among bulrushes, sedges, and other marsh vegetation support the heaviest populations; in coastal areas, the brackish marshes that support good stands of three-square grass (a sedge, *Scirpus*) are most attractive. Such marshes with a stabilized water depth of 15–60 cm seem to offer optimum living conditions.

In marshes, muskrats live in dome-shaped houses or lodges constructed of marsh vegetation. Access to the inner chamber usually is gained by means of two or more underwater openings, the plunge holes of trapper parlance. Such houses are usually 60 cm or more in diameter at water level and project 50–60 cm above the water. They seem to be of two types: those used for feeding only, in which case the floor may be submerged in water, and those used for dens or resting places. Frequently, several animals (usually members of one family) occupy one lodge. Conspicuous travelways radiate from the houses and lead to forage areas. In canals, creeks, rivers, and so forth, where house construction would be out of the question, the muskrats burrow into the banks and live below ground. Entrance to such burrows also is usually by means of underwater openings. Dens that have been excavated were about 10 cm in diameter and 2–3 m in length and usually terminated in an enlarged nest chamber.

The food of muskrats is varied, principally vegetation. Where available the tender basal parts of cattails and rushes are the main reliance. In the brackish marshes of Texas and Louisiana, a sedge is the chief item on their menu. Normally, the animals have well-established feeding stations at the edges of travel lanes or in feeding lodges to which pieces of food are brought to be consumed at leisure. The animals are active throughout the year and store no food for winter use. At that season, when nutritious food is scarce or made unavailable by freezing weather,

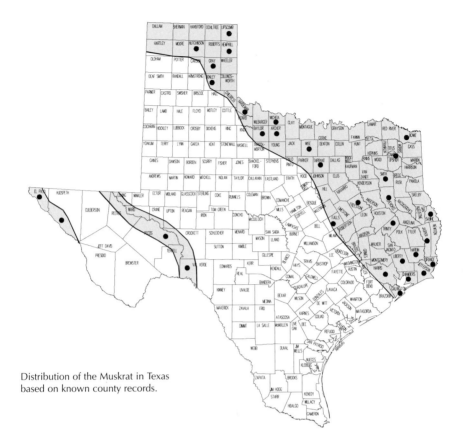

Distribution of the Muskrat in Texas
based on known county records.

the rats will eat almost anything, including parts of their lodges and nests, dead fish, frogs, wood, and so forth, or they may turn cannibalistic and prey on their own kind.

In southeastern Texas the animals breed throughout the year. Breeding females produce two or more litters a year, ranging in size from 1 to 11 and averaging about 6. The gestation period is 22–30 days. At birth the young are blind, almost naked, and helpless and weigh about 21 g. The pelage develops rapidly, and by the end of the first week the young are covered with a good coat of gray-brown fur. Their eyes are open in 14–16 days, at which time they can dive and swim with alacrity. When 4 weeks old they are generally weaned. Sexual maturity is reached in 10–12 months, at which time the rats have attained the size and characteristics of adults.

Muskrats are the victims of many predators. Hawks, large owls, raccoons, foxes, minks, water snakes, and large turtles are known to plague them.

The muskrat was, at one time, the most economically important fur-bearing mammal in eastern Texas, but this is no longer true. In fact, during the 1999–2000 trapping season, fur buyers were not purchasing muskrat pelts.

Conservation Status. In some regions of the state, muskrats appear to have declined or even disappeared, whereas in other regions they have invaded and increased in abundance. Today, they are reasonably common along the upper Texas coast, but they have virtually disappeared from the tributaries of the Canadian River in the Panhandle, as well as from the springs and tributaries associated with the Pecos River and the Rio Grande. The decline of permanent natural surface water, especially the drying up of freshwater springs as a result of irrigation, followed by the reduction of tule marsh habitat, has caused their demise in those regions. This is a species that should be carefully monitored in the future. It could be vulnerable to the rapid expansion and spread of the nutria (*Myocastor coypus*).

FAMILY ERETHIZONTIDAE
(NEW WORLD PORCUPINES)

This family contains 4 genera and 12 species, but only 1 species reaches northward into the United States. Porcupines are heavyset, large rodents characterized by their outer covering of sharp spines, or quills. Porcupines are at home on the ground as well as in trees.

North American Porcupine
Erethizon dorsatum (Linnaeus)

Description. A large rodent with distinct, barbed quills on back, sides, and tail; quills are yellowish white with a tip that varies from brown to black; overall coloration usually appears black or blackish. Dental formula: I 1/1, C 0/0, Pm 1/1, M 3/3 x 2 = 20. External measurements of males average: total length, 808 mm; tail, 235 mm; hind foot, 98 mm; of females, 737-230-81 mm. Weight, 5–11 kg.
Distribution. Known from western half of state, east to Bosque County; an individual was recently recorded from Van Zandt County.
Subspecies. *E. d. epixanthum.*
Habits. The porcupine is adapted to a variety of habitats. It is largely an inhabitant of forested areas in the West and prefers rocky areas, ridges, and slopes. It is less common in flats, valleys, and gulches. On the Llano Estacado, porcupines are associated with rocky escarpment as well as the sand sage–shin oak association and short-grass prairie. On the Edwards Plateau, porcupines have been found most commonly along streams and rivers and in brushy, upland juniper habitats. In recent years, they have expanded their range into southern Texas.

They are expert at climbing trees, although their movements are slow, methodical, and seemingly awkward. They apparently are aware of their limitations, and they take few chances. Porcupines seem to be as much at home in the rocks as on the ground or in trees. The more massive and broken the rocks, the

North American Porcupine (*Erethizon dorsatum*). Photo courtesy U.S. Fish and Wildlife Service.

better they serve the animals, for the numerous crevices and caves can be used as den sites and the large boulders as resting places. Where rocky dens are accessible, they are visited at intervals by many porcupines from the surrounding region and are used from year to year. Where such dens are unavailable, a hollow log, a windfall, or an upturned or loosened tree root system may serve the purpose.

In winter when snow covers the ground, porcupines seldom travel far from their dens, especially in freezing weather. As warm weather approaches, the amount of travel increases.

Herbaceous ground vegetation makes up 85% of the food of both old and young in summer. In fall only 27% of their food is herbaceous; 73% is tree-gathered and includes mistletoe, the inner bark of a variety of trees, and pine needles. In winter the food is wholly from trees, and pine needles and inner bark are consumed at their peak during this season. In spring they again return to herbaceous ground vegetation, which then makes up nearly 40% of their diet. Throughout the year the porcupine is more of a browser than a grazer and subsists in large measure on the inner bark of trees and shrubs; grass is of no importance at any time of the year. Porcupines are especially fond of salt and are easily attracted to it, a trait that is useful in their control.

Breeding takes place in late summer and early fall, with the peak of activity in September and early October. The young, usually one, rarely two, are born about 7 months later in April and May. The gestation period is 209–217 days. At birth the young porcupine weighs about 450 g and is larger than a newborn black bear.

Distribution of the North American Porcupine
in Texas based on known county records.

It is covered with a good coat of blackish hair, the quills are well developed, the
eyes and ears are functional, and the incisors and some of the cheek teeth have
erupted. It is usually suckled for only a short period, begins to feed on vegetation
shortly after birth, and soon becomes entirely dependent on its own resources.
The young porcupines grow slowly compared with most rodents, and females do
not mature sexually until their second fall, when they weigh about 4 kg. Porcupines
have a relatively long life span. One marked female is known to have lived more
than 10 years under natural conditions.

Conservation Status. The porcupine represents another example of a mammal that
has expanded its range in Texas during the twentieth century. Vernon Bailey, when
he and his fellow agents worked in Texas at the end of the nineteenth century,
recorded them only in one county in the Panhandle and in Jeff Davis and Brewster
counties in the western part of the state. None of the early explorers or naturalists,
until the report of Bailey, had documented the porcupine's occurrence in the state.
Today, the species occurs east to Bosque County and appears to be expanding
westward. It does not appear to be under any immediate threat.

FAMILY MYOCASTORIDAE (MYOCASTORIDS)

This family contains only one species, *Myocastor coypus.* The nutria is native to southern Brazil, Bolivia, Paraguay, Uruguay, Argentina, and Chile.

Nutria *
Myocastor coypus (Molina)

Description. A large rodent, nearly as large as a beaver but with long, rounded, scaly, ratlike tail; hind feet webbed; incisors orange-colored; female with mammae along each side of back, not on belly; upperparts reddish brown; the underfur dark slaty; tip of muzzle and chin white. Dental formula: I 1/1, C 0/0, Pm 1/1, M 3/3 x 2 = 20. External measurements of adults average: total length, 800–900 mm; tail, 350–400 mm; hind foot, 130–140 mm. Total length may reach 1.4 m. Weight, normally 8–10 kg.

Distribution. Native to South America; introduced into the southeastern United States in 1938. Now occurs in aquatic habitats in eastern two-thirds of Texas; the range is expanding westward.

Habits. Throughout much of their natural range in South America, nutria prefer a semiaquatic existence in swamps, marshes, and along the shores of rivers and

Nutria (*Myocastor coypus*). Photo by Nancy McKown, courtesy Texas Parks and Wildlife Department.

lakes. In southern Chile and Tierra del Fuego they are found mainly in the channels and bays separating the various islands off the coast. Here, their habitat seems to be mostly in the estuaries of glacier-fed streams, and colonies of nutria are often seen swimming among the floating ice blocks in the vicinity of glaciers. Apparently, the nutria is equally at home in salt and fresh water.

They are docile creatures, much like the beaver in this respect, and can be handled easily in captivity. They are almost entirely nocturnal, consequently their presence in an area usually is revealed only by their trails, feces, and lengths of cut vegetation that have been left in their trails. They are not extensive burrowers. Burrows that have been examined were approximately 20 cm in diameter and extended into the bank for a distance of over 1 m. Often they were open at both ends, with the entrance toward the river usually above water level. Some of the burrows are under roots of trees that are exposed along the banks of the river or stream. Their nests are made of reeds and sedges built up in large piles, somewhat after the fashion of a swan's nest. These are built on land among the marsh vegetation and close to the water's edge.

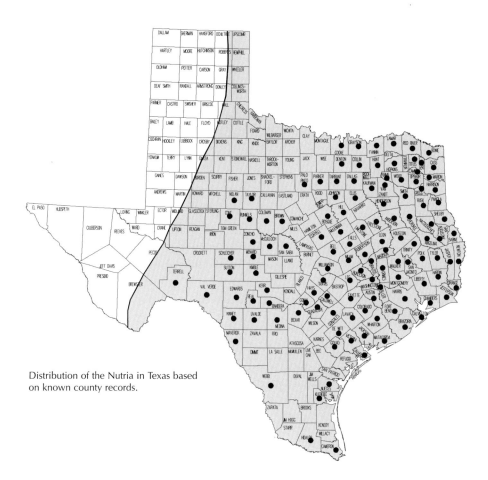

Distribution of the Nutria in Texas based on known county records.

Their natural food consists almost entirely of aquatic and semiaquatic vegetation, but when these animals live along the coast they also feed on shellfish. Cattails, reeds, and sedges appear to be especially prized items of food. When established near gardens, they take cabbage readily; they are also fond of carrots and sweet potatoes.

These animals appear to breed throughout the year. Each adult female produces two or three litters a year. The gestation period is 127–132 days. The number of young per litter ranges from 2 to 11 and averages about 5. At birth the young are fully furred, and their eyes are open; they are able to move about and feed on green vegetation within a few hours. At that time they weigh approximately 200 g. They mature rapidly, increasing at the rate of about 400 g per month during the first year, and reach sexual maturity at the age of 4 or 5 months. Females sometimes give birth to their first litter when they themselves are 8 or 9 months old. The maximum length of life for nutria kept in captivity is 12 years, but the life span in the wild probably is considerably less.

These animals are important fur producers in their native range. They are reared extensively on fur farms in South America, and most of their pelts are sold on the European market. Because of their known competition with muskrats, which are well-established and valuable fur-producing animals in this country, it appears that muskrats may be driven out and replaced by the much less desirable nutria.

Nutria were widely introduced in Texas as a cure-all for ponds choked with vegetation. They do reduce many kinds of aquatic plants, but they will not eat moss (algae) and many submerged plants. The trouble is that once established in a lake, their high reproductive capacity soon results in overpopulation. They become so numerous that the available food supply will not satisfy them, and then trouble begins. The animals move into places where they are not wanted or where they destroy vegetation that is valuable for such wildlife as waterfowl and muskrats.

Conservation Status. The nutria has gradually spread over most of Texas during the latter half of the twentieth century, often to the detriment of the native muskrat, which occupies much the same habitat. In some coastal areas they have become so numerous that they are destroying marsh vegetation and other wetland areas. There is a real need to control this species, which is rapidly becoming a serious pest.

Currently, nutria populations are moderately high and on the increase. The nutria has continued to expand its range and probably will spread throughout the state. Recently, specimens have been reported from Val Verde and Terrell counties and along the Rio Grande in Big Bend National Park, indicating that the species has finally reached the Trans-Pecos.

In Louisiana and Maryland, nutria populations have become so large that they are causing extensive damage to wetlands and marshes. To combat this problem

Congress approved spending $12.5 million over five years to pay hunters and trappers $4 a tail to kill nutria. The program was approved under the Coastal Wetlands Planning Protection and Restoration Act. In another effort to control their population, some of the most renowned, five-star chefs in New Orleans came up with recipes for cooking nutria meat, but nutria fettucine, nutria sausage, and nutria gumbo never caught on. Nutria became such a problem in flood canals around Jefferson Parish in Louisiana a few years back that the sheriff dispatched a team of sharpshooters to take aim at nutria for target practice. That program killed more than 10,500 nutria between 1995 and 2002, but it was still not enough to prevent damage by the prolific pests.

ORDER LAGOMORPHA
Hares and Rabbits

A t least 80 species of lagomorphs are distributed throughout the world. This order includes the hares and rabbits (family Leporidae) and pikas (family Ochotonidae). Mammals assigned to this order superficially resemble rodents, but lagomorphs differ from rodents in several essential features. One is the peculiar tandem arrangement of the front (incisor) teeth, with a large tooth in front on each side and a small peglike tooth directly behind it. Also, the number of premolars is 2/2 or 3/2 (2/1 or 0/0 in rodents), so that the total number of teeth is 26 or 28 and never as few as the 16 to 22 found in rodents.

This group of mammals is largely diurnal or crepuscular in habit; the food is almost entirely vegetable matter—grasses, forbs, bark of trees and shrubs, and so forth. Because of their usually large size and food predilections, lagomorphs frequently come into conflict with grazing, agriculture, and forestry interests. No lagomorphs hibernate.

KEY TO THE HARES AND RABBITS OF TEXAS

1. Interparietal bone indistinct to absent; ears large (greater than 100 mm from notch); tail with black dorsal stripe. *Lepus californicus* (black-tailed jackrabbit), p. 468.

   Interparietal bone distinct; ears shorter (less than 100 mm from notch); tail entirely white or brown in color 2

2. Greatest length of skull in adults 75 mm or more; total length of adults usually near 500 mm; dorsal surface of hind foot brown in color; distinct cinnamon-colored eye ring. *Sylvilagus aquaticus* (swamp rabbit), p. 459.

   Greatest length of skull in adults less than 75 mm; total length of adults usually 450 mm or less; dorsal surface of hind foot white in color; eye ring whitish to buff in color 3

3. Ear 65% to 85% as long as hind foot; hind foot usually less than 90 mm; auditory bullae large and coarse in texture; nuchal patch typically tan in color. *Sylvilagus audubonii* (desert cottontail), p. 461.

   Ear 50% to 60% as long as hind foot; hind foot usually more than 90 mm; auditory bullae small and smooth in texture; nuchal patch typically reddish in color 4

4. Hind foot near 100 mm; ear near 70 mm; premolar enamel patterns highly complex and convoluted. *Sylvilagus robustus* (Davis Mountains cottontail), p. 466.

Hind foot near 90 mm; ear near 55 mm; premolar enamel patterns smooth-walled and simple. *Sylvilagus floridanus* (eastern cottontail), p. 463.

FAMILY LEPORIDAE (HARES AND RABBITS)

There are 15 genera and 54 species of rabbits and hares in the world. Two genera and 5 species occur in Texas. Rabbits are small (relative to hares), solitary to gregarious, and give birth to altricial young. Hares are generally larger, often solitary, and give birth to precocial young. All rabbits and hares are adapted for foraging in open habitats, have large ears, and are capable of instant flight and considerable speed to escape their enemies. They are strictly vegetarian, feeding on a variety of grasses and forbs.

Swamp Rabbit

Sylvilagus aquaticus (Bachman)

Description. Largest of the cottontails within its range; pelage coarse and short for a rabbit; upperparts grayish brown, heavily lined with blackish; rump, upperside of tail, and back of hind legs dull ochraceous brown; sides of head and body paler than back, less suffused with blackish; underparts, including underside of tail, white except for buffy underside of neck; front legs and tops of hind feet cinnamon rufous. External measurements average: total length, 534 mm; tail, 69 mm; hind foot, 106 mm; ear, 70 mm. Weight, 1.5–3 kg.

Swamp Rabbit (*Sylvilagus aquaticus*). Photo by John and Gloria Tveten.

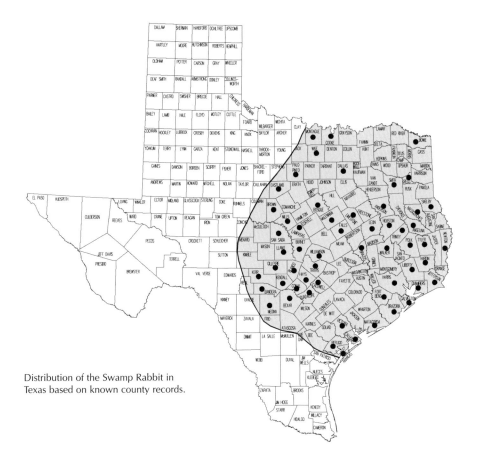

Distribution of the Swamp Rabbit in
Texas based on known county records.

Distribution. Found in eastern half of the state, from Montague and Eastland counties in the Cross Timbers region, south and west to Kerr County in the eastern Edwards Plateau region, and south to Aransas and Refugio counties along the Gulf Coast.

Subspecies. Monotypic species.

Habits. The swamp rabbit, as the name suggests, inhabits poorly drained river bottoms and coastal marshes. Well adapted to a semiaquatic habitat in that its dense fur waterproofs its skin, the animal is at home in the water. In fact, it crosses rivers and streams on its own initiative, a habit usually not found in other rabbits in Texas. It is secretive by day and is seldom seen, except when frightened from its bed in some thicket, but its presence in an area is readily disclosed by the piles of fecal pellets deposited on stumps, down logs, or other elevations. Along the coast it is at home in cane thickets, hence the local name "cane cutter," but in inland areas it is restricted to the floodplains of rivers and streams and their associated tangles of shrubs, trees, and vines.

In southeast Texas, one swamp rabbit per 2.8 ha of poorly drained bottomland is typical. The rabbits frequent a definite local range, which they refuse to leave even when pursued by dogs. Their chief protection is thickets of briers or brush, rather than underground burrows. In this area both eastern cottontails (*S. floridanus*) and swamp rabbits occupy the creek and river bottoms in about equal numbers, but in the uplands only eastern cottontails are found.

Little is known of their food habits, although succulent vegetation, including grasses, forbs, and the new shoots of shrubs, is probably important.

The breeding season extends at least from January to September, but the peak is in February and March when green vegetation is available. Possibly two or more litters of two to three young are reared annually. After a gestation period of 39–40 days, the young are born in, or transferred to, surface nests composed of vegetation and lined with rabbit fur, or nests in holes in logs and stumps. A nest found at the base of a cypress stump was composed of Spanish moss and rabbit fur; it held six small rabbits. Another found under a long, fallen branch of a tree was lined with fur and held two young rabbits. At birth the young are covered with fur, but the eyes and ears are closed. The eyes open and the young rabbit is able to walk in 2 or 3 days.

Among their known natural enemies are the gray fox, great horned owl, and alligator. Doubtless, they are preyed on by many other species. Other than humans, their chief enemy is floods.

Conservation Status. Optimum habitat in much of the swamp rabbit's range is shrinking as wetlands are drained and hardwood forests are cleared, and consequently there is much concern about the future conservation status of this rabbit in Texas. In the Hill Country they are threatened by habitat fragmentation. There is an imperative need to monitor populations in the future.

Desert Cottontail
Sylvilagus audubonii (Baird)

Description. Medium-sized cottontail, with relatively long ears; pelage rather harsh, but not so harsh as in the swamp rabbit; hind feet relatively slender and with relatively short pelage; auditory bullae large, with rough surface; ratio of length of ear to length of hind foot 0.66 or more; upperparts dark buffy brown, heavily lined with black; rump not conspicuously different from back; top of tail like back; nape bright rusty, almost orange rufous; front and outside of forelegs dark ochraceous buff; hind legs brownish cinnamon; underside of neck brownish buff; rest of underparts and underside of tail clear white. External measurements average: total length, 418 mm; tail, 73 mm; hind foot, 86 mm; ear, 60 mm. Weight, 0.5–1.4 kg.

Distribution. Occupies upland habitats in the western half of the state.

Subspecies. *S. a. minor* in the southern Trans-Pecos eastward to Val Verde County, *S. a. neomexicanus* in the northern part of the range in the state (south to Reeves and northern Brewster counties), and *S. a. parvulus* from Llano County southward in south-central Texas to the Rio Grande.

Desert Cottontail (*Sylvilagus audubonii*). Photo by John and Gloria Tveten.

Habits. This species appears to be adapted to a variety of habitats, varying from grassland to creosote brush and cactus deserts. Wherever it may be, it frequents brushy areas or, where the vegetation is short, the underground burrows of prairie dogs, skunks, and so forth. In the Trans-Pecos it is often found in thickets of cat-claw (*Acacia*), mesquite, allthorn, and other desert shrubs and especially in prairie dog towns in short-grass areas. In the plains regions it is so commonly associated with prairie dog towns that it is known locally as prairie-dog rabbit.

Like other cottontails, these are more active in the twilight hours and at night, but they may be active through the day. They are more or less sedentary and seldom range more than 360 m from their preferred thickets, around and in which they feed, sleep, court, and rear their families. Unlike most other cottontails, they are known to climb sloping trees and thick brambles and are not inclined to use beds when resting. Such habits, however, vary from one region to another.

The food is almost entirely vegetation; the kinds eaten vary with availability. In western Texas they eat the leaves and green pods of mesquite, various grasses, forbs, bark and twigs of shrubs, and the juicy pads of prickly pear.

The breeding season is long. In Texas, onset of breeding begins in February, and pregnant females, lactating females, and young in the nest have been found in every month except January, July, and October. There may be two or more litters a year. The number of young per litter varies from one to six, averaging about three. The gestation period is not known, but it is probably about 26–27 days.

As with other cottontails, the young are reared in nests that are made in pear-shaped excavations in the ground, with entrances only about 5 cm in diameter. Below, they are flared out to a width of 15–25 cm; the depth varies from 15 to 25 cm. They are lined with a layer of dried grasses, and the inside is filled entirely with

Distribution of the Desert Cottontail in Texas based on known county records.

rabbit fur, in which the young repose. The female lies or squats over the opening to nurse her young, which are blind and hairless at birth. By 10 days of age the eyes have opened, and within another 4 days the young are able to move outside the nest, although they remain near the nest for about 3 weeks. The life span is 2 years or less.

Golden eagles, northern harriers, Swainson's hawks, great horned owls, barn owls, gray foxes, and gopher snakes are known to prey on desert cottontails. Doubtless, many other animals also feed on them.

Conservation Status. The desert cottontail is abundant throughout its range in the state. There is no reason to be concerned about its status at the present time.

Eastern Cottontail

Sylvilagus floridanus (Allen)

Description. A moderately large, rusty brown cottontail with relatively short ears and large hind feet (ears 50–60% as long as hind feet). Upperparts deep ochraceous buff, heavily lined with blackish, giving a rusty or reddish brown effect; sides paler and grayer; top of tail like back; rump dingy grayish, not conspicuously different

Eastern Cottontail (*Sylvilagus floridanus*). Photo by John and Gloria Tveten.

from back; front and sides of legs deep, rich, rusty reddish; underside of neck buff or ochraceous buff, rest of underparts, including tail, white. Differs from *S. audubonii,* with which its range overlaps, in having small, smoothly rounded bullae (rather than large and rough) and relatively and actually shorter ears. External measurements average: total length, 418 mm; tail, 56 mm; hind foot, 92 mm; ear, 52 mm. Weight, 1–2 kg.

Distribution. Occurs throughout the state.

Subspecies. *S. f. alacer* in eastern Texas; *S. f. chapmani* in the central, southern, and western parts of the state; and *S. f. llanensis* on the Llano Estacado.

Habits. Like other cottontails, this one is a denizen of brushland and marginal areas and seldom ventures far from brushy cover. In central Texas it commonly frequents brush-dotted pastures, the brushy edges of cultivated fields, and well-drained streamsides. Occasionally, it inhabits poorly drained bottomlands with the swamp rabbit. In many places it is common along country roads, especially where the sides are grown up to dense vegetation and adjoining areas are heavily grazed or farmed.

These cottontails are active largely in the twilight hours and at night, when they venture into open pastures, meadows, or lawns to forage. They frequently live on the edges of towns and feed in gardens and flowerbeds. In the daytime they rest in beds in nearby thickets or in underground burrows and small culverts. On the coastal prairies of Texas, a population density of one cottontail to 1.8 ha is not unusual.

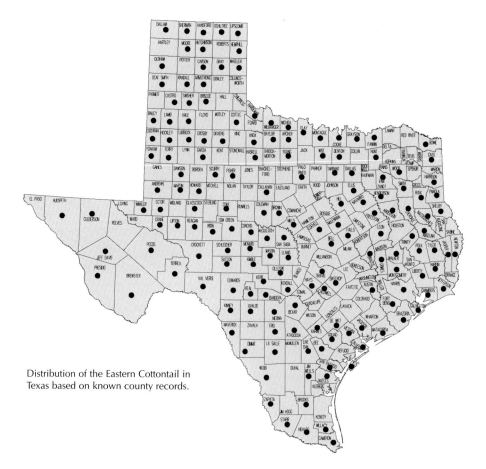

Distribution of the Eastern Cottontail in Texas based on known county records.

The food is variable with the season. They feed on a variety of grasses and forbs, but when such vegetation is scarce, they eat the twigs and bark of shrubs and small trees. These rabbits are not sociable and are seldom seen feeding together.

Eastern cottontails are prolific breeders. In southern Texas the breeding season is yearlong, although the frequency of breeding does fluctuate throughout the year. Breeding activity is stimulated by environmental factors, such as temperature and rainfall, which affect the growth of vegetation. As many as four or five litters of one to eight young (average four) may be reared yearly. The gestation period is 28–29 days. The young are blind and helpless at birth but grow rapidly; when 4–5 months old they are distinguished from adults only with difficulty. Young females born early in the year may mature sexually and produce young in their first summer, but ordinarily they do not breed until their second summer.

These cottontails are known to be preyed on by merlins, barn owls, red-tailed hawks, opossums, coyotes, foxes, and weasels. Doubtless, many others can be added to the list.

Conservation Status. This species is common throughout its range in Texas, and it appears to have no major conservation problems.

Davis Mountains Cottontail

Sylvilagus robustus (V. Bailey)

Description. A large, pale buffy gray species, with rather large ears; upper parts pale, dull buffy, washed with blackish; rump iron gray, contrasting with back; nape rufous; top of tail dull brownish; legs rusty; sides of head and abdomen grayish; shoulders brownish; underside of neck grayish or brownish; rest of underparts, including tail, clear white. External measurements average: total length, 416 mm; tail, 53 mm; hind foot, 98 mm; ear from notch, 71 mm. Weight, 1.3–1.8 kg.

Distribution. In Texas, restricted to the mountains of the central Trans-Pecos (Guadalupe, Davis, and Chisos). Also known from the Guadalupe Mountains in New Mexico and from the Sierra de la Madera of Coahuila, Mexico.

Subspecies. Monotypic species.

Habits. The following account is based on the notes of William B. Davis during his fieldwork in the 1940s in the Chisos Mountains.

In the Chisos Mountains, where he studied them closely, these rabbits prefer thickets of sumac, mountain mahogany, white brush (*Lippia*), and scrub oak as refuge sites. They usually spend the greater part of the day resting in such thickets and emerge late in the evening to feed in the interspersed open areas. On 2 May 1944 Davis flushed five of these rabbits in the Basin of the Chisos Mountains. All were encountered in or near the bottoms of ravines where the brush was fairly dense. Three of them were jumped from forms under the basal rosettes of the large

Davis Mountains Cottontail (*Sylvilagus robustus*). Photo by John and Gloria Tveten.

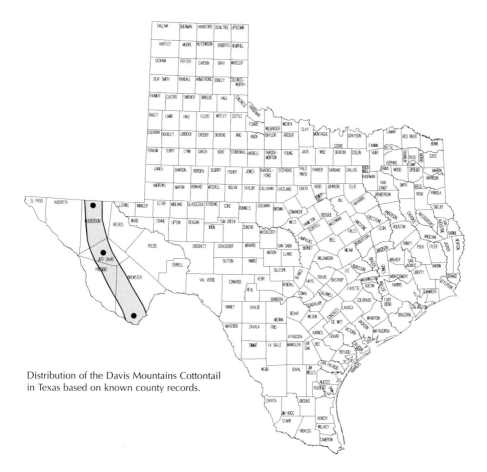

Distribution of the Davis Mountains Cottontail
in Texas based on known county records.

agave (*Agave scabra*). They often disappeared quickly in the dense brush, although
he observed that they rely a good deal on freezing for protection. Their usual tendency is to run a short distance then stop, when they are partly concealed by vegetation, and watch the intruder. They also frequent rocky areas where boulders are
large and utilize the associated crevices and crannies as retreats.

They feed most frequently in the late evening and early morning hours, but
occasionally do so during the hotter part of the day, as evidenced by notebook
records of feeding at 10 A.M. and 2 P.M. in May. Their food consists of grasses (at
least *Muhlenbergia* and *Bouteloua*), leaves of mountain mahogany, white brush, and
numerous herbs.

The breeding season apparently is restricted to spring and early summer. A
female collected in the Chisos Mountains on 6 April was lactating and had given
birth to two young shortly before (determined by uterine scars). Another taken on
16 June was lactating and had borne three young. She was molting extensively on
the back, sides, and breast. Several young of the year about the size of a man's fist
were observed in June.

Nothing is known about the natural enemies of this rabbit, but it is likely that it is preyed on by gray foxes, bobcats, golden eagles, and great horned owls, all of which occur in its restricted range.

Conservation Status. Luis Ruedas has expressed concern that populations of this rabbit have declined dramatically in recent decades. Ruedas has recommended state listing for this species, as well as redbook listing as endangered by the International Union for Conservation of Nature and Natural Resources (IUCN), pending the completion of more detailed studies about the natural history of *S. robustus,* including assessment of population status and life history parameters, long-term ecological studies, and population genetic analyses. The Guadalupe and Chisos mountains populations have been severely reduced, and no specimens have been seen or collected from these areas in the past 30 years. Recently, mammalogists from Texas Tech University obtained several specimens from the Davis Mountains, and it appears that a healthy population remains in the area. Careful monitoring of this species is needed throughout the isolated mountain ranges of the Trans-Pecos and northern Mexico to determine its overall conservation status. Currently, neither Texas Parks and Wildlife nor U.S. Fish and Wildlife lists the species as threatened or endangered.

Remarks. Throughout his many editions of *The Mammals of Texas,* William B. Davis continued to recognize *S. robustus* as a distinct species from *S. floridanus.* In the 1994 edition, authored by Davis and me, however, *S. robustus* was arranged as a subspecies of *S. floridanus* on the basis of nominal cranial differences. In a 1998 article published in the *Journal of Mammalogy,* Luis Ruedas documented distinct differences in size as well as skull and tooth morphology that separated *robustus* from the various subspecies of *floridanus.* On that basis, Ruedas proposed that *S. robustus* is a distinct species.

Clyde Jones and his students at Texas Tech have made an extensive collection of rabbits in the Davis Mountains and have recorded *robustus*-type specimens occurring with *floridanus*-type individuals. On that basis, I have chosen to follow the taxonomic recommendation of Ruedas with regard to *robustus.* A more definitive solution to the question may have to await results of further analyses, including studies of chromosomes and nuclear and mitochondrial DNA.

Black-tailed Jackrabbit

Lepus californicus Gray

Description. A large, long-eared rabbit of the open grasslands and desert scrub of the West; sides differentiated but little, if at all, from the back; ear nearly as long as the hind foot, with black patch at tip; top of tail with black stripe that extends onto rump; underparts clear, ochraceous buff, paler medially; upperparts dark buff, heavily sprinkled with blackish. External measurements average: total length, 604 mm; tail, 95 mm; hind foot, 131 mm; ear, 125 mm. Weight, 1.5–4 kg.

Distribution. Statewide, except for Big Thicket region of extreme southeastern Texas.

Black-tailed Jackrabbit (*Lepus californicus*). Photo
courtesy Texas Parks and Wildlife Department.

Subspecies. *L. c. eremicus* in the El Paso area, *L. c. melanotis* in the north, *L. c. merriami* in the south and southeast, and *L. c. texianus* on the western Edwards Plateau and in the eastern Trans-Pecos. This species is in need of taxonomic review.

Habits. The black-tailed jackrabbit, so familiar to those who know the West, is a common denizen of the hot, dry desert scrubland. It occupies an elevational range from sea level to well over 2,500 m on the southwest slopes of some of the desert mountains but seldom inhabits coniferous forests (pinyon pine and juniper areas excepted), although occasionally it may stray into them.

In summer this rabbit spends the hotter part of the day dozing in a bed scratched out at the base of some shrub or in a clump of tall grass where the shade will protect it from the hot sun. In winter such beds are located in vegetation that offers protection from the chilling winds. It becomes active at twilight and forages well into the night. When molested it depends on speed and its keen senses of hearing and sight to elude its enemies.

The food includes forage crops, cactus, sagebrush, mesquite, and numerous grasses and herbs. Because of a preference for sparsely vegetated areas, this species often concentrates in pastures overgrazed by livestock, further depleting the vegetation. It has been estimated that 128 black-tailed jackrabbits can consume as much range vegetation as one cow or seven sheep. Thus, when these rabbits are concentrated, often as many as 154 per square kilometer, they conflict with

Distribution of the Black-tailed Jackrabbit
in Texas based on known county records.

grazing interests. Such concentrations frequently result from overgrazing, hence
the wise rancher will recognize an overabundance of jackrabbits as an indication
that he has been overstocking his range.

The breeding season extends throughout the year in Texas. Two to six litters
of one to six young may be produced each year. The gestation period is 41–47 days.
The young are precocious and active shortly after birth. They grow rather rapidly
and reach adult size in about 7 or 8 months. Sexual maturity is attained at about
the same time, but young females do not breed until early in the year following
their birth. Usually, the expectant mother provides no nest for her young.

The natural enemies of rabbits include the larger birds of prey and such carnivores as coyotes, foxes, bobcats, badgers, and weasels. Campaigns to eliminate
these predators from rangelands usually are expensive and may lead to an increase
in jackrabbits and many range rodents, which can become serious pests.

Conservation Status. The jackrabbit is very abundant and in good shape across all
of Texas, with the exception of the southeastern part of the state, where populations have declined dramatically this century as a result of declining habitat and
changes in the quality of the coastal prairie.

APPENDIX 1

The measurement system.

I n this edition of *The Mammals of Texas,* all measurements are presented in the metric system, which is the official standard of measurement for scientific communication. For those who are less familiar with the metric system, the following table of metric-to-Roman conversion factors may be helpful.

To Convert	Multiply by
millimeters (mm) to inches	0.039
centimeters (cm) to inches	0.394
meters (m) to feet	3.281
meters to yards	1.094
kilometers (km) to miles	0.621
hectares (ha) to acres	2.471
hectares to square miles	0.004
liters (l) to quarts	1.057
grams (g) to ounces	0.035
kilograms (kg) to pounds	2.205
metric tons to tons	1.102

APPENDIX 2
Observing and collecting mammals.

Whether to satisfy the interest of the casual outdoorsman or to fulfill the needs of scientific research, the observation and collection of mammals are exciting occupations. Practically all that is needed to make interesting and useful observations of mammals is a good pair of binoculars, along with the inclination to rise early and stay late. Unlike birds, most mammals are either crepuscular (twilight active) or nocturnal (night active) in nature, making prolonged observation of behavior, feeding habits, and other aspects of natural history more difficult. Additionally, many species are fossorial (dwell underground) and cannot be directly observed except during the rare and brief moments these animals may appear at their burrow entrances. Finally, many species occur in our bays and oceans and require access to either a boat or airplane to observe, unless they strand on our beaches.

The observation of mammals is often done indirectly, by evaluating the tracks, scats, scrapes, rubs, and other such sign that mammals leave behind as evidence of their activities. Locating sign and drawing accurate deductions of animal activity is an art that for the most part has been lost as people rely less and less on understanding nature to fulfill basic needs. Nevertheless, reading sign is a fascinating occupation, many aspects of which can be learned simply through interest and perseverance. Acquiring one or more of the numerous field guides now available on this subject will speed up the learning process and allow for a more complete understanding of the outdoors.

For scientific purposes, collections of mammals are sometimes made. Collecting and preparing mammals as museum specimens is a complicated process that often requires a great deal of equipment and planning. Numerous techniques and types of traps are available, depending on the animals to be taken, the region studied, and the type of information being sought. For smaller mammals, such as mice, mouse traps of the variety that snap shut on the animal can be purchased in almost every hardware store; however, the larger Museum Special trap is best because the wire that strikes and kills the mouse is far enough from the treadle to keep the head of the mouse from being struck and crushed. For study purposes, broken skulls are less desirable than unbroken ones.

The still larger rat trap is stocked in most hardware stores and is suitable for taking animals the size of woodrats and small ground squirrels. Steel traps in sizes 0 to 4 are used in many areas to secure other animals. McAbee gopher traps are the best yet devised for taking pocket gophers. Several mole traps are on the market; the stabbing variety is preferred by most collectors.

Many specimens are most effectively taken by shooting. For smaller and medium-sized kinds, a shotgun is recommended, but shot of small size should be used to avoid unnecessary mutilation of the animal. Nets of silk or nylon may be useful to the mammal collector, especially in capturing bats. Pitfall traps are often set for shrews by burying a can up to the rim in mammal runways and other likely spots.

In addition to traps that kill the mammal, numerous styles and sizes of live traps are offered for sale by various manufacturers. These include the popular Sherman live trap frequently used for mouse- and rat-sized mammals, up to the equally popular Havahart traps useful for capturing raccoon-sized mammals. Large drive nets, drop nets, and similar traps, often used in conjunction with other equipment such as helicopters and immobilizing drugs, are used by specialists to capture larger mammals for study, such as deer and even elk.

Properly preparing mammals as museum specimens requires skill, patience, and training. The labeling, skinning, and stuffing of mammal skins, as well as the preparation of skeletal material, are demanding, sometimes tedious tasks that require attention to detail and a lot of practice. Several handbooks and guides are available to introduce the mammal enthusiast to this necessary aspect of mammalogy.

For the safe storage of prepared mammal specimens in accessible fashion, a museum cabinet that excludes insects, dust, and light is essential. A visit or a letter of inquiry to the nearest museum known to maintain a collection of study specimens of mammals will yield all needed information about the type of container best suited to the needs of the collector. Advice concerning the preparation of mammals as specimens, including the preparing of skins and cleaning of skeletal material, can be obtained from the same sources.

The trapping of mammals, even for scientific purposes, requires a scientific collecting permit. Every state has its own laws relating to hunting and trapping, and the collector should obtain and read the applicable laws so as to carry on collecting in conformance with the law. In Texas, scientific collecting permits are issued by the Texas Parks and Wildlife Department; advice and clarification on collecting regulations can also be obtained from that department. Collecting on federal lands, such as national parks and monuments, requires a permit from federal authorities. Government personnel at the site to be studied should be contacted for information on obtaining federal collecting permits. Of course, if mammal collecting is to be done on private lands, the permission of the landowner is also required.

Next to conducting mammal collection and observation activities in a lawful and responsible manner, the most important obligation of the mammalogist is to take accurate and complete field notes. Only in this way can new information eventually be provided for the benefit of others. Field notes can usefully be divided into three sections: a catalog of specimens, an itinerary or journal, and accounts of species. For convenience all three sections ordinarily are kept in a single binder, but separate binders may be used. Enter the name of the collector and the year in the upper left-hand corner of every page but far enough from the margin to permit binding of the pages. Each page should be filled before another page is started.

In the catalog, all specimens of vertebrate animals should be given consecutive numbers. Never repeat a number; for instance, do not begin a new series each year. At least one line of each entry should be devoted to the precise locality. Begin this line with the country, if applicable, followed by the state, county, and precise locality description. If possible, use a global positioning system (GPS) to determine the exact UTM coordinates for each specimen collected. If UTM coordinates are not available, include airline distance and direction from some well-established town. Also record the elevation, if applicable. After the locality data, describe each specimen. The description should include the scientific name, sex, and standard measurements of the specimen. Use the vernacular name of the species if you are not sure of the scientific name. If not a conventional specimen, indicate the nature of the preparation type, whether it is, for instance, a skeleton, skull-only, skin-only, or alcoholic. Toward the end of the line it may be desirable to enter, on occasion, the color of iris and soft parts. A typical catalog entry may look like the excerpt shown below.

Given the advent of modern techniques and disciplines such as molecular genetics, toxicology, epidemiology, zoonosis, and archival natural history research, it is crucial to collect tissue or blood samples. The TK (tissues and karyotypes) number assigned to these samples should be recorded in each catalog entry, as shown in the illustration. It is recommended that samples of heart, liver, kidney, spleen, lung, muscle, and blood be obtained from each specimen. These samples should be frozen in the field on either dry ice or liquid nitrogen and stored

160	Texas, La Salle Co.; Chaparral WMA, South Jay Pasture (UTM: 14R 463798E 3139642N) 9 June, 2000
♀	Notiosorex crawfordi TK 75218
	92-27-12-6
161	Texas, La Salle Co.; Chaparral WMA (UTM: 14R 462925E 3131425N) 14 June, 2000
♂	Notiosorex crawfordi TK 75219
	76-27-10-5

long-term, preferably at –80°C. The value of such tissue collections is only now being realized, and it is expected that their value will only increase in the future.

On the first line of the itinerary, enter date and locality. Follow with a concise account of route and travel area and habitats studied, and record number and kinds of traps set, distance between traps, number of vertebrates collected, as well as other pertinent information. For example, record the number of traps set in each type of vegetation and numbers and kinds of animals caught therein.

Accounts of species should be headed with either the scientific or common name, as preferred. The date and locality for the account should be given on the first line. Only one species should be written about on a single page. Information in the account should not be a repetition of material given in the itinerary or journal. Include not only facts but also interpretations and generalizations. The accounts should be written in a style suitable for quoting in any publication. Accounts of species need not be restricted to kinds collected. If the account is about animals collected it is wise to refer to the animals by your field numbers.

Head each and every notebook page with the collector's name and year, page number (if number system is used), locality (in detail the first time used), and date. Write full notes, even at the risk of entering much information of seemingly little value. One cannot anticipate the needs of the future when notes and collections are worked up. The following are suggested topics, but do not restrict yourself to these alone. Be alert for new ideas and new facts. Special data sheets may be helpful.

Describe vegetation (saving plant-press samples of species not positively known), nature of ground, slope, exposure, and drainage in each belt of animal life sampled. Describe the exact location of trap lines, referring to your topographic maps, and also enter a sketch, in profile or surface view or both, to illustrate the location and relations of the different habitats crossed. Properly marked maps for each region worked should ultimately be bound in with the field notes of at least one member of your field party.

Keep a record of closeness of settings of traps, distance covered, and results of each night's trappings; give the number and type of traps put out in each habitat and number of animals of each species captured in each habitat (whether or not preserved). It is advisable to record the sex, age, and breeding condition of each animal. Special data sheets are helpful.

Keep a full record of breeding data, number and approximate size (crown-rump length) of embryos, or of young found in nests. Dig out burrows if practicable; make drawings to scale, plan, and elevation; describe fully.

Record food plants; keep specimens for identification when not known by a definite name; preserve contents of cheek pouches and stomachs. If they are not saved, identify and record the contents.

Note regularly in notebook all pickup, that is, odd skulls or fragments of animals of whatever sort or source, serially numbered along with specimens of the more usual sort. Give full information, as with odd skulls secured from trappers. Label all such specimens adequately, as elsewhere described.

Keep frequent censuses of diurnal mammals, with habitat preferences indicated. These censuses, if short, need not be entered on formal census sheets. When leaving a well-worked locality, enter a summary of species observed, with remarks of a general nature, such as relate to local conditions of terrain, human activities, and other pertinent conditions.

Where feasible interview residents, trappers, state wildlife biologists, and national forest or park rangers at each locality visited. Always record accurately the name, official position, or occupation and address of each person giving information; give also your opinion as to his or her reliability. Note general attitude of person interviewed as to game laws, conservation, and effects of settlement by humans, and record specific comments, complaints, and criticisms.

Ascertain present numbers and distribution of large mammals as compared with former status. As far as possible, get definite statements expressing ratio of abundance now to abundance a definite number of years back. Seek such information when feasible by indirect query; do not risk influencing your informant's statements by leading questions. Record fully all evidence as to human influence on original or natural balance. Record present economic relations of vertebrate animal life (that is, the effect on agriculture and stock raising) with full details. Note opinions of persons interviewed as to whether species should be protected or destroyed. Describe local methods of capture or destruction; give your opinion as to their effectiveness and justification.

Opportunity offering, record detailed observations on the effects on mammals of severe storms; floods; forest, brush, or prairie fires; overgrazing; tree cutting; road-building; or tree-planting.

APPENDIX 3

Selected references on mammals from Texas and adjoining states.

Ad Hoc Committee on Acceptable Field Methods in Mammalogy. 1987. Acceptable field methods in mammalogy: Preliminary guidelines approved by the American Society of Mammalogists. *J. Mamm.* 68 (supplement): 1–18.

Alvarez, T. 1963. The Recent mammals of Tamaulipas, Mexico. *Univ. Kansas Publ., Mus. Nat. Hist.* 14:363–473.

Anderson, S. 1972. Mammals of Chihuahua: Taxonomy and distribution. *Bull. Amer. Mus. Nat. Hist.* 148:151–410.

Bailey, V. 1905. Biological survey of Texas. *North American Fauna* 25:1–222.

Baker, R. H. 1956. Mammals of Coahuila, Mexico. *Univ. Kansas Publ., Mus. Nat. Hist.* 9:125–335.

Bartlett, R. C. 1995. *Saving the best of Texas: A partnership approach to conservation.* Austin: Univ. Texas Press. 221 pp.

Blair, W. F. 1954. Mammals of the Mesquite Plains Biotic District in Texas and Oklahoma, and speciation in the central grasslands. *Tex. J. Sci.* 6:235–264.

Burt, W. H., and R. P. Grossenheider. 1964. *A field guide to the mammals.* 2nd ed. Peterson Field Guide Series No. 5. Boston: Houghton Mifflin Co. 284 pp.

Caire, W., J. D. Tyler, B. P. Glass, and M. A. Mares. 1989. *Mammals of Oklahoma.* Norman: Univ. Oklahoma Press. 567 pp.

Campbell, L. 1995. *Endangered and threatened animals of Texas: Their life history and management.* Austin: Texas Parks and Wildlife Press. 130 pp.

Choate, L. L. 1997. The mammals of the Llano Estacado. *Spec. Publ. Mus. Texas Tech Univ.* 40:1–240.

Dalquest, W. W., and N. V. Horner. 1984. *Mammals of north-central Texas.* Wichita Falls: Midwestern State Univ. Press. 261 pp.

Davis, W. B., and D. J. Schmidly. 1994. *The mammals of Texas.* Austin: Texas Parks and Wildlife Press. 338 pp.

Doughty, R. W. 1983. *Wildlife and man in Texas.* College Station: Texas A&M Univ. Press. 246 pp.

Findley, J. S. 1987. *The natural history of New Mexican mammals.* Albuquerque: Univ. New Mexico Press. 164 pp.

Findley, J. S., A. H. Harris, D. E. Wilson, and C. Jones. 1975. *Mammals of New Mexico.* Albuquerque: Univ. New Mexico Press. 360 pp.

Gehlbach, F. R. 1981. *Mountain islands and desert seas: A natural history of the U.S. Mexican borderlands.* College Station: Texas A&M Univ. Press. 298 pp.

Goetze, J. R. 1998. The mammals of the Edwards Plateau, Texas. *Spec. Publ. Mus. Texas Tech Univ.* 41:1–263.

Hall, E. R. 1962. Collecting and preparing study specimens of vertebrates. *Univ. Kansas Mus. Nat. Hist. Misc. Publ.* 30:1–46.

———. 1981. *The mammals of North America.* 2 vols. New York: John Wiley & Sons. 1,181 pp.

Hice, C. L., and D. J. Schmidly. 1999. The non-volant mammals of the Galveston Bay region, Texas. *Occas. Papers Mus. Texas Tech Univ.* 194:1–23.

———. 2002. The mammals of coastal Texas: A comparison between mainland and barrier island faunas. *Southwestern Nat.* 47:244–256.

Hoffmeister, D. F. 1986. *Mammals of Arizona.* Tucson: Univ. Arizona Press. 602 pp.

Hollander, R. R., J. K. Jones, Jr., R. W. Manning, and C. Jones. 1987. Noteworthy records of mammals from the Texas Panhandle. *Tex. J. Sci.* 39:97–102.

Jones, J. K., Jr. 1993. The concept of threatened and endangered species as applied to Texas mammals. *Tex. J. Sci.* 45:115–128.

Jones, J. K., Jr., and J. A. Homan. 1976. Contributions to a bibliography of Recent Texas mammals, 1961–1970. *Occas. Papers Mus. Texas Tech Univ.* 41:1–21.

Jones, J. K., Jr., and C. Jones. 1992. Revised checklist of Recent land mammals of Texas, with annotations. *Tex. J. Sci.* 44:53–74.

Jones, J. K., Jr., and R. W. Manning. 1992. Illustrated key to skulls of genera of North American land mammals. Lubbock: Texas Tech Univ. Press. 75 pp.

Jones, J. K., Jr., C. Jones, and D. J. Schmidly. 1988. Annotated checklist of Recent land mammals of Texas. *Occas. Papers Mus. Texas Tech Univ.* 119:1–26.

Jones, J. K., Jr., R. W. Manning, C. Jones, and R. R. Hollander. 1988. Mammals of the northern Texas Panhandle. *Occas. Papers Mus. Texas Tech Univ.* 126:1–54.

Jones, J. K., Jr., R. S. Hoffman, D. W. Rice, C. Jones, R. J. Baker, and M. D. Engstrom. 1992. Revised checklist of North American mammals north of Mexico, 1991. *Occas. Papers Mus. Texas Tech Univ.* 146:1–23.

Jones, J. K., Jr., C. J. Young, and D. J. Schmidly. 1985. Contributions to a bibliography of Recent Texas mammals, 1971–1980. *Occas. Papers Mus. Texas Tech Univ.* 95:1–44.

Lowery, G. H., Jr. 1974. *The mammals of Louisiana and its adjacent waters.* Baton Rouge: Louisiana State Univ. Press. 565 pp.

Manning, R. W., and C. Jones. 1998. Annotated checklist of Recent land mammals of Texas. *Occas. Papers Mus. Texas Tech Univ.* 182:1–19.

Martin, R. E., R. H. Pine, and A. F. DeBlase. 2000. *A manual of mammalogy: With keys to families of the world.* 3rd ed. New York: McGraw-Hill. 352 pp.

McCarley, H. 1959. The mammals of eastern Texas. *Tex. J. Sci.* 11:385–426.

Mearns, E. A. 1907. Mammals of the Mexican boundary of the United States. *U.S. Natl. Mus. Bull.* 56. 530 pp.

Mungall, E. C., and W. J. Sheffield. 1994. *Exotics on the open range.* College Station: Texas A&M Univ. Press. 265 pp.

Murie, O. J. 1954. *A field guide to animal tracks.* Peterson Field Guide Series No. 9. Boston: Houghton Mifflin Co. 374 pp.

Principal game birds and mammals of Texas, their distribution and management. 1945. Austin, Tex.: Press of Von Boeckmann-Jones Co. 149 pp.

Raun, G. G. 1962. A bibliography of the Recent mammals of Texas. *Tex. Mem. Mus. Bull.* 3:1–81.

Riley, G., and R. T. McBride. 1972. A survey of the red wolf (*Canis rufus*). *Spec. Sci. Rep.* 162:1–6. U.S. Dept. of Interior, Fish and Wildlife Service.

Sansom, A. 1995. *Texas lost: Vanishing heritage.* Dallas: Parks and Wildlife Foundation of Texas. 135 pp.

Schmidly, D. J. 1977. *The mammals of Trans-Pecos Texas.* College Station: Texas A&M Univ. Press. 225 pp.

———. 1983. *Texas mammals east of the Balcones Fault Zone.* College Station: Texas A&M Univ. Press. 400 pp.

———. 1984. The furbearers of Texas. *Bull. Texas Parks & Wildl.* 111:1–55.

———. 1991. *The bats of Texas.* College Station: Texas A&M Univ. Press. 188 pp.

———. 2002. *Texas natural history: A century of change.* Lubbock: Texas Tech Univ. Press. 576 pp.

Schmidly, D. J., and J. R. Dixon. 1998. William B. "Doc" Davis, 1902–1995. *J. Mamm.* 79:1076–1083.

Sealander, J. A. 1979. *A guide to Arkansas mammals.* Conway: River Road Press. 313 pp.

Swepston, D. A., and B. C. Thompson. 1986. *Texas furbearer bibliography, 1851–1985.* Fed. Aid Proj. W-117R. Austin: Texas Parks and Wildlife Dept. 114 pp.

Vaughan, T. A., J. M. Ryan, and N. J. Czaplewski. 2000. *Mammalogy.* 4th ed. Philadelphia: Saunders College Publishing. 565 pp.

Weniger, D. 1984. The explorers' Texas: The lands and waters. Vol. 1. Austin: Eakin Press. 224 pp.

———. 1997. The explorers' Texas: The animals they found. Vol. 2. Austin: Eakin Press. 200 pp.

Whitaker, J. O., Jr. 1980. *The Audubon Society field guide to North American mammals.* New York: Alfred A. Knopf. 745 pp.

White, R. J. 1986. *Big game ranching in the United States.* Mesilla, N. Mex.: Wild Sheep and Goat International. 355 pp.

Wilson, D. E., and S. Ruff. 1999. *The Smithsonian Book of North American Mammals.* Washington, D.C.: Smithsonian Institution Press. 750 pp.

Würsig, B., T. A. Jefferson, and D. J. Schmidly. 2000. *The marine mammals of the Gulf of Mexico.* College Station: Texas A&M Univ. Press. 232 pp.

Yancey, F. D. II. 1997. The mammals of the Big Bend Ranch State Park, Texas. *Spec. Publ. Mus. Texas Tech Univ.* 39:1–210.

APPENDIX 4
Scientific names.

The scientific name of a mammal as here used consists of two Latinized words followed by the name of a person. The first word designates the genus to which the animal is assigned, the second is the name of the species, and the third the name of the authority for the specific epithet (species name). If the person's name is enclosed in parentheses, it indicates that he or she described the species under a generic name different from that in current use. For example, when Linnaeus described our mole in 1758 and gave it the specific name *aquaticus,* he placed it in the genus *Sorex.* We now reserve the genus *Sorex* for a certain group of shrews and place the Texas moles in the genus *Scalopus.* Consequently, the scientific name of Texas moles is written *Scalopus aquaticus* (Linnaeus). On the other hand, when he described our fox squirrel in 1758 and gave it the specific epithet *niger,* he placed it in the genus *Sciurus.* We currently accept that arrangement, so the scientific name of the fox squirrel appears as *Sciurus niger* Linnaeus—the parentheses are omitted.

APPENDIX 5

Mammalian Species accounts, published by the American Society of Mammalogists, available for the mammals of Texas.

Order and Species	Mammalian Species No.	Year
Order Didelphimorphia		
Didelphis virginiana	40	1974
Order Xenarthra		
Dasypus novemcinctus	162	1982
Order Insectivora		
Blarina carolinensis	673	2001
Blarina hylophaga		
Cryptotis parva	43	1974
Notiosorex crawfordi	17	1972
Scalopus aquaticus	105	1978
Order Chiroptera		
Mormoops megalophylla	448	1993
Leptonycteris nivalis	307	1988
Choeronycteris mexicana	291	1987
Diphylla ecaudata	227	1984
Myotis austroriparius	332	1989
Myotis californicus	428	1993
Myotis ciliolabrum	670	2001
Myotis occultus	142 (as *M. lucifugus*)	1980
Myotis septentrionalis	634	2000
Myotis thysanodes	137	1980
Myotis velifer	149	1981
Myotis volans	224	1984
Myotis yumanensis		
Lasionycteris noctivagans		
Pipistrellus hesperus		
Pipistrellus subflavus	228	1984
Eptesicus fuscus	356	1990
Lasiurus blossevillii		
Lasiurus borealis	183	1982

Lasiurus cinereus	185	1982
Lasiurus ega	515	1995
Lasiurus intermedius	132	1980
Lasiurus seminolus	280	1987
Lasiurus xanthinus		
Nycticeius humeralis	23	1972
Euderma maculatum	77	1977
Corynorhinus rafinesquii	69 (as *Plecotus rafinesquii*)	1977
Corynorhinus townsendii	175 (as *Plecotus townsendii*)	1982
Antrozous pallidus	213	1983
Tadarida brasiliensis	331	1989
Nyctinomops femorosaccus	349	1990
Nyctinomops macrotis	351	1990
Eumops perotis	534	1996

Order Carnivora

Canis latrans	79	1977
Canis lupus	37	1974
Canis rufus	22	1972
Vulpes velox	122, 123	1979
Vulpes vulpes	537	1996
Urocyon cinereoargenteus	189	1982
Ursus americanus	647	2001
Ursus arctos	439	1993
Bassariscus astutus	327	1988
Procyon lotor	119	1979
Nasua narica	487	1995
Mustela frenata	570	1997
Mustela nigripes	126	1980
Mustela vison	608	1999
Taxidea taxus	26	1973
Lontra canadensis	587	1998
Spilogale gracilis	674	2001
Spilogale putorius	511	1995
Mephitis macroura	686	2001
Mephitis mephitis	173	1982
Conepatus leuconotus		
Leopardus pardalis	548	1997
Leopardus wiedii	579	1998
Herpailurus yaguarondi	578	1998
Puma concolor	200 (as *Felis concolor*)	1983
Panthera onca	340	1989

Lynx rufus	563	1997
Monachus tropicalis		

Order Cetacea

Eubalaena glacialis		
Balaenoptera acutorostrata		
Balaenoptera edeni		
Balaenoptera musculus		
Balaenoptera physalus		
Balaenoptera borealis		
Megaptera novaeangliae	604	1999
Physeter macrocephalus		
Kogia breviceps		
Kogia sima	239	1985
Mesoplodon densirostris		
Mesoplodon europaeus	688	2001
Ziphius cavirostris		
Orcinus orca	304	1988
Pseudorca crassidens	456	1994
Feresa attenuata		
Globicephala macrorhynchus		
Peponocephala electra	553	1997
Steno bredanensis		
Grampus griseus		
Tursiops truncatus		
Stenella attenuata	683	2001
Stenella clymene	726	2003
Stenella coeruleoalba	603	1999
Stenella frontalis	702	2002
Stenella longirostris	599	1998
Lagenodelphis hosei	470	1994

Order Sirenia

Trichechus manatus	93	1978

Order Artiodactyla

Sus scrofa		
Pecari tajacu	293 (as *Tayassu pecari*)	1987
Cervus axis		
Cervus dama	317 (as *Dama dama*)	1988
Cervus elaphus		
Cervus nippon	128	1980
Odocoileus hemionus	219	1984

Odocoileus virginianus	388	1991
Antilocapra americana	90	1978
Boselaphus tragocamelus		
Bos bison	266 (as *Bison bison*)	1986
Ovis canadensis	230	1985
Ammotragus lervia	144	1980
Antilope cervicapra		

Order Rodentia

Tamias canipes	411	1992
Ammospermophilus interpres	365	1990
Spermophilus mexicanus	164	1982
Spermophilus spilosoma	101	1978
Spermophilus tridecemlineatus	103	1978
Spermophilus variegatus	272	1987
Cynomys ludovicianus	535	1996
Sciurus carolinensis	480	1994
Sciurus niger	479	1994
Glaucomys volans	78	1977
Thomomys bottae		
Geomys arenarius	36	1974
Geomys attwateri	382	1991
Geomys breviceps	383	1991
Geomys bursarius		
Geomys knoxjonesi	672	2001
Geomys personatus	170	1982
Geomys streckeri		
Geomys texensis	679	2001
Cratogeomys castanops		
Perognathus flavescens	525	1996
Perognathus flavus	471	1994
Perognathus merriami	473	1994
Chaetodipus eremicus		
Chaetodipus hispidus	320	1988
Chaetodipus intermedius		
Chaetodipus nelsoni	484	1994
Dipodomys compactus	369	1991
Dipodomys elator	232	1985
Dipodomys merriami		
Dipodomys ordii	353	1990
Dipodomys spectabilis	311	1988
Liomys irroratus	82	1978
Castor canadensis	120	1979

Oryzomys couesi		
Oryzomys palustris	176	1982
Reithrodontomys fulvescens	174	1982
Reithrodontomys humulis	565	1997
Reithrodontomys megalotis	167	1982
Reithrodontomys montanus	257	1986
Peromyscus attwateri	48	1974
Peromyscus boylii		
Peromyscus eremicus	118	1979
Peromyscus gossypinus	70	1977
Peromyscus leucopus	247	1985
Peromyscus maniculatus		
Peromyscus nasutus		
Peromyscus pectoralis	49	1974
Peromyscus truei	161	1981
Ochrotomys nuttalli	75	1977
Baiomys taylori	285	1987
Onychomys arenicola		
Onychomys leucogaster	87	1978
Sigmodon fulviventer	94	1978
Sigmodon hispidus	158	1981
Sigmodon ochrognathus	97	1978
Neotoma floridana	139	1980
Neotoma leucodon	310 (as *N. albigula*)	1988
Neotoma mexicana	262	1986
Neotoma micropus	330	1989
Rattus norvegicus		
Rattus rattus		
Mus musculus		
Microtus mexicanus		
Microtus ochrogaster	355	1990
Microtus pinetorum	147	1981
Ondatra zibethicus	141	1980
Erethizon dorsatum	29	1973
Myocastor coypus	398	1992

Order Lagomorpha

Sylvilagus aquaticus	151	1981
Sylvilagus audubonii	106	1978
Sylvilagus floridanus	136	1980
Sylvilagus robustus		
Lepus californicus	530	1996

APPENDIX 6
Standard measurements of study specimens.

Each species account in this book includes under the heading "Description" a number of standard measurements that may be helpful in identifying species in the field or specimens in the hand. Measurements are usually recorded in millimeters and weights in grams, although measurements for larger species may be recorded in meters and weights in kilograms.

Explanations of the most common standard measurements for mammals are as follows:

Total length—length from tip of nose pad to tip of fleshy part of tail, excluding hairs that project beyond tip.

Length of tail—with tail held at right angle to body, the length from bend on back to tip of fleshy part of tail, excluding hairs that project beyond tip.

Length of hind foot—distance from tip of longest claw to heel.

Height of ear from notch—distance from notch at front base of ear to distalmost border of fleshy part of ear.

Some mammal descriptions include other measurements appropriate for the species, such as: length of the forearm of bats; length of the metatarsal gland of ungulates; height at shoulder of large mammals such as bears and artiodactyls; length of pectoral fin, height of dorsal fin, and girth of cetaceans.

Measurements of the skull are also useful for identifying specimens, particularly those of small mammals. The figure opposite illustrates some of the more common identifying features of the skull and selected standard measurements.

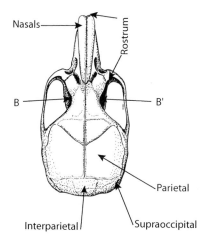

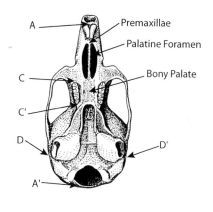

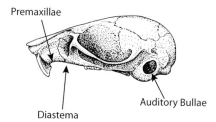

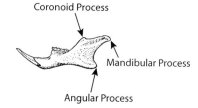

Views of the skull and lower jaw of the white-ankled mouse, *Peromyscus pectoralis,* showing bones and indicating the measurements used in identifying species. Point A to A', condylobasal length; Point B to B', interorbital breadth; Point C to C', length of molar tooth row; Point D to D', mastoidal breadth.

APPENDIX 7
Basis for distribution of species.

E ach species account in this book includes a description of the distribution of the species in Texas, and most accounts include a map of the distribution in Texas based on known county records. The distribution for each species is based on the following types of data:

1. Specimens collected in Texas and held in various museums.
2. Records in published scientific literature.
3. Survey response records of trappers in Texas (furbearers).
4. Texas Department of Health records (bats).
5. Texas Parks and Wildlife Department distribution files and field biologists' reports.
6. Records of the Texas Marine Mammal Stranding Network and the Southeast U.S. Marine Mammal Stranding Database (cetaceans).

GLOSSARY

adult – Generally, a sexually mature and breeding individual in a population.

adult pelage – The type of hair covering characteristic of adults of the species.

agonistic behavior – Fighting or combative behavior.

allopatric – Of populations or species occupying mutually exclusive, but usually adjacent, geographical areas.

allozyme – Variant of an enzyme coded by a different allele.

alluvial – Pertaining to the soil, sand, and gravel deposited by a running watercourse where it issues from a canyon or gorge onto an open plain.

altricial – Pertaining to young born in a very underdeveloped condition, requiring extended development and parental care. Opposite of precocial.

alveolus – A socket in the jaw bone for the root or roots of a tooth.

anal – Located near the anus.

ankle – The joint in the hind limb between the tibia and fibula of the lower leg and the tarsal bones of the foot.

annulation – A circular or ringlike formation, as of the dermal scales on the tail of a mammal where one ring of scales that extends entirely around the tail is succeeded, posteriorly, by other rings.

anterior – Of, or pertaining to, or toward the front end.

antero-internal fold – A fold in the structure of a molar tooth, evident on the occlusal surface and on the anterior and medial side of the tooth.

antitropical – Found in both hemispheres but not in equatorial regions.

antler – A branched bony head ornament found on deer. Covered with skin (velvet) during growth. Shed annually.

aquatic – Inhabiting or frequenting water.

arboreal – Inhabiting or frequenting trees. Contrasted with fossorial, aquatic, or cursorial.

auditory bullae – The bony capsules, one on each side of the skull, enclosing the middle ears.

autosomal – Pertaining to a chromosome other than a sex chromosome.

baculum – A bone in the penises of certain mammals.

baleen – Whalebone; the cornified epithelial plates suspended from the upper jaws of mysticete whales.

beam – The main trunk of an antler.

bicolored – Having two contrasting colors.

bifurcate – To divide or fork into two branches.

biodiversity – The diversity and frequency of organisms in a given area.

biogeography – The study of the distribution of different species around the planet and the factors that influenced their distribution.

biome – A complex biotic community covering a large geographic area and characterized by the distinctive life forms of important climax species.

bipedal – Pertaining to locomotion on only two legs.

blastocyst – An early embryo consisting of 8 to 16 cells.

blowhole – A hole for the escape of air (external nostril) in the top of the head of a whale or other cetacean.

bottomland – Lowlands along streams and rivers, usually on alluvial floodplains, that are periodically flooded.

braincase – That portion of the skull that encloses and protects the brain; the skull posterior to a plane drawn vertically through the anterior margins of the orbits.

breeding season – The time of the year in the reproductive cycle from mating until birth.

brow tine – The first tine above the base of an antler.

browsers – Mammals that feed on tender shoots or twigs of shrubs and trees.

bullae – See *auditory bullae*.

burrow – A tunnel excavated and inhabited by an animal.

cache – The process that a mammal uses to collect, hide, and store food.

calcar – A spur (of cartilage or bone) that projects medially from the ankle in many species of bats and from the wrist of many gliding mammals and that helps support a patagium (membrane or fold of skin between limbs).

canine – Of, pertaining to, or designating the tooth next to the incisors in mammals; fang.

carapace – The bony shell of an armadillo.

carnivore – A mammal that consumes meat as the primary component of its diet; especially any mammal of the Order Carnivora.

carrion – Dead and putrefying flesh that some animals feed upon.

Chagas' disease – An acute and chronic protozoan disease of humans caused by the hemoflagellate *Trypanosoma cruzi*. Also known as trypanosomiasis.

cheek teeth – Collectively, the premolars and molars or any teeth posterior to the position of the canines.

chromosome – A deeply staining DNA-containing threadlike structure in the nucleus of a cell that carries the linearly arranged genetic units.

classification – The assignment of groups to taxa.

claw – The most common form of digital keratinization found in mammals; usually long, curved, and sharply pointed.

colonial – Pertaining to a group of organisms of the same kind living in close association, e.g., colonial bats living in a cave.

condyloid process – Point of articulation with the mandibular fossa of the temporal bone.

conspecific – A condition where populations or specimens are not sufficiently distinct to be considered separate species.

copulation – Coitus; the union of male and female reproductive organs to facilitate reception of sperm by the female.

coronoid process – The projection of the posterior portion of the dentary that is dorsal to the mandibular condyle.

coterie – A family group consisting of a male, several females, and their young.

crepuscular – Active during the twilight periods of dusk and dawn.

crown – The portion of a tooth extending above the gum line.

crown-rump length – The measurement of the total length of an embryo from tip of snout to end of body.

Conservation Reserve Program – A voluntary government program established in 1985 that offers financial assistance to farmers to establish approved cover on highly erodible cropland or pastureland.

cusp – A point, projection, or bump on the crown of a tooth, usually distinguished by a particular name, such as "hypocone."

delayed fertilization – An adaptation of certain species of hibernating bats in which mating occurs in late summer but fertilization does not occur until the following spring.

delayed implantation – Phenomenon found in most temperate species of the Mustelidae and several other kinds of mammals in which implantation of the embryo, along with subsequent growth, is delayed for several months.

den – A cave, hollow log, burrow, or other cavity used by a mammal for shelter.

dental formula – A brief method for expressing the number and kind of teeth of mammals. The abbreviations I (incisor), C (canine), P or Pm (premolar), and M (molar) indicate the kinds in the permanent dentition. The numbers of teeth in each jaw are written in pairs, like a fraction, with the figure in front of the diagonal line showing the number in the upper jaw and that after the line showing the number in the lower jaw. The dental formula of an adult coyote is I 3/3, C 1/1, Pm 4/4, M 2/3 x 2 = 42.

dentary – One of the two bones that form the mandible (lower jaw) of mammals.

dentition – The teeth, considered collectively, of an animal.

description – A statement of characters and supplementary information that accompanies the naming of a new taxon.

digit – Any finger or toe.

dimorphism – Occurrence of two distinct morphological types in a single population.

diploid – Having a double set of chromosomes (2N); the normal chromosome number of cells (except for mature germ cells) in any individual derived from a fertilized egg.

disjunct population – A population of a species that is separated geographically from the main range of the species.

dispersal – The permanent emigration of individuals from a population.

diurnal – Active by day, as opposed to nocturnal.

dorsal – Pertaining to the back or upper surface.

dorsal fin – In mammals, a middorsal projection of fibrous connective tissue found only in certain cetaceans.

echolocation – Sonar; the process of locating objects by emitting sound pulses and receiving and identifying the echoes of those sounds reflected by the objects; used by most bats and cetaceans.

Edwards Plateau – A region of west-central Texas known as the Hill Country, bordered on the east and south by the Balcones Escarpment and on the west by the Pecos River.

elbow – The joint in the forelimb between the humerus and the radius and ulna.

electrophoresis – A process by which enzymes are separated based on differences in electrical charge. Observed differences between or within species indicate mutation and genetic divergence over long periods of time, thus elucidating the genetic distinctness of organisms.

emigration – The process whereby individuals move away from a population.

enamel – Extremely hard outer layer on the crown of a tooth, consisting of calcareous compounds and a small amount of organic matrix. Usually white but sometimes brown, red, or yellow in rodents and some other mammals.

Endangered Species Act – U.S. law, passed in 1973 and subsequently amended, that regulates the capture, possession, and sale of threatened and endangered species of wildlife.

endemic – Pertaining to a mammal that is peculiar to a certain region.

estivate – To pass the summer or dry season in a dormant condition.

estrus – A period of time when female mammals may accept males and mating occurs, specifically, when ovulation occurs. At this time, the pituitary output is predominantly luteinizing hormone and the newly formed corpus luteum is producing large quantities of progesterone. In vaginal smears, the cells are cornified.

estuary – A river mouth where tidal action brings about a mixing of salt and fresh water.

eurythermic – Tolerating a wide variation in temperature.

exotic – An animal introduced from a foreign country; nonnative.

extirpate – To destroy, make extinct, or exterminate.

femur – The single bone of the upper (proximal) portion of each pelvic limb.

feral – Pertaining to formerly domesticated animals now living in a wild state.

fetus – The unborn offspring of viviparous mammals in the latter stages of development.

flippers – Feet fully adapted for an aquatic life; digits elongate and fully webbed.

flukes – Lateral projections of a whale's tail, supported entirely by fibrous connective tissue (no skeletal support).

foraging – The process of wandering in search of food.

forbs – Herbaceous plants other than grasses or sedges.

fossorial – Pertaining to life under the surface of the ground; adapted for digging.

fragmentation – Division of a large piece of habitat into a number of smaller, isolated patches.

fulvous – Tawny or dull yellow.

fundamental number *(FN)* – The total number of chromosome arms, exclusive of the sex chromosomes, in a diploid cell.

fur – Dense underhair with definitive growth; serves primarily for insulation.

furbearer – A category of mammals harvested for direct commercial use and sale of hides and pelts; includes most small and large carnivores.

GAP – The acronym used to refer to the Gap Analysis Program of the U.S. Geological Survey. Gap analysis is a proactive approach to protecting biodiversity; it seeks to identify gaps between land areas that are rich in biodiversity and areas that are managed for conservation.

generalist – A species with broad preferences of food, habitat, or other factors.

genus – A category within a taxonomic family, consisting of one or more generally similar species. The name of a genus is called the generic name.

gestation period – The length of time from fertilization until birth of a fetus; the period of pregnancy.

global warming *(or climate change)* – An increase in the average temperature of the earth's atmosphere, especially a sustained increase sufficient to cause climatic change.

GPS *(global positioning system)* – An instrument for determining precise latitude and longitude of places on the earth's surface.

granivorous – Feeding on grains or seeds.

gravid – Pregnant.

grazers – Mammals that feed on grass and other herbage by cropping and nibbling.

gregarious – Pertaining to social animals that live in groups or herds.

guard hairs – Outer coat of coarse, protective hairs found on most mammals.

habitat – The kind of environment in which a species or organism is normally found.

herbaceous – Resembling or pertaining to an herb, which is a seed plant that lacks a persistent, woody stem above ground and dies at the end of the season.

herbivore – An animal that consumes plant material as the primary component of its diet.

hibernacula – Winter shelters where animals pass the winter in an inactive (torpid or dormant) state.

hibernation – Of an animal, torpidity, especially in winter; the body temperature approximates that of the surroundings; the rate of respiration and the heart beat ordinarily are much slower than in an active mammal.

hispid – Rough with bristles, stiff hairs, or minute spines.

home range – The area that a mammal occupies during the course of its life, exclusive of migration, emigration, or unusual erratic wanderings.

hoof – The digital keratinization in ungulate mammals, a horny sheath completely encasing the tip of a phalanx and usually providing the animal's only point of contact with the substrate.

horn – Structure projecting from the head of a mammal and generally used for offense, defense, or social interaction. Cattle, sheep, Old World antelopes, and other members of the family Bovidae have horns formed by permanent, hollow, keratin sheaths growing over bone cores.

host – The animal parasitized by a parasite.

hybrid – The offspring resulting from a cross between individuals of two species.

hybridization – The mating of individuals from different species or subspecies.

immigration – The process whereby individuals move into a population.

implantation – The attachment of the embryo to the uterine wall of the female mammal.

incisor – The front or cutting teeth between the canines.

infraorbital opening – An opening in the skull through the zygomatic process of the maxilla (in front of the orbit to the side of the rostrum).

inguinal – Pertaining to or in the region of the groin.

insectivorous – Eating insects; preying or feeding on insects.

interfemoral membrane – In a bat, the fold of skin stretching from hind legs to tail.

interorbital breadth – A measurement of the skull taken at the least diameter of the frontal bones between the orbital openings (also *interorbital constriction*).

interparietal – An unpaired bone on the dorsal part of the braincase between the parietals and just anterior to the supraoccipital; absent in some mammals.

isolated population – A population that is separated by some sort of barrier from the main body of the species.

jugal – The bone that forms the central section of the zygomatic arch and is located between the zygomatic process of the maxilla and the squamosal.

juvenile – An individual that is physiologically immature or undeveloped. In mammals, juveniles often have distinctive pelage coloration and texture.

juvenile pelage – The type of pelage characteristic of a juvenile of a species.

karyotype – An arrangement of chromosomes of a cell according to shape, centromere position, and number; used to aid in identification of species and subspecies within a species.

knee – The joint in the pelvic limb between the femur and the tibia and fibula.

known age – Age established for individual based on observation of birth or other equally reliable criteria.

labial shelf – A thin, narrow, horizontally flattened projection of enamel extending along the side of a tooth closest to the lips.

lactating female – A female mammal that is producing milk (nursing young).

lactation – Production of milk by the mammary glands.

litter – The set of young born of a female mammal following a pregnancy.

litter size – The number of young delivered by a female from one pregnancy.

loph – A transverse ridge of enamel across the occlusal (crushing) surface of a tooth.

mammary gland *(pl. mammae)* – Milk-producing gland unique to mammals. Its growth and activity are governed by hormones of the ovary, uterus and pituitary.

mandible – The lower jaw; in mammals, composed of a single pair of bones, the dentaries.

mandibular symphysis – The suture between the paired bones of the lower jaw.

mast – Collectively, nuts that serve as food for hogs, squirrels, and other mammals.

mastoid breadth – A measurement of the greatest width across the skull between the two mastoid processes.

maxilla *(maxillary bone)* – One of a pair of bones that forms part of the rostrum, palate, and zygomatic process and bears all upper teeth except the incisors.

maxillary tooth row – A measurement of the alveolar distance from the anterior border of the anterior molar to the posterior border of the posterior molar.

mesic – Characterized by a moderate amount of moisture.

metabolic rate – The rate at which an animal's body consumes oxygen.

metabolic water – The water produced as a by-product of metabolism.

metacarpal – Any bone of the hand between the wrist and fingers.

metapopulation – A regional population consisting of semi-isolated local populations; literally, a "population of populations."

metatarsal gland – A gland located on the lower outside portion of the hind leg of some mammals, especially artiodactyls. The function of the gland may be to produce an alarm pheromone or to help in regulating the animal's body temperature.

midden – An accumulation of refuse about a dwelling place.

migration – A movement of animals involving a journey to a definite area and a return journey to the area from which the movement arose, often in response to seasonal patterns of resource availability.

milk tooth – Any tooth in the deciduous set of teeth of mammals with diphyodont dentition; replaced by the permanent teeth.

mist net – A net of fine mesh used to capture birds and bats.

mitochondrial DNA – The DNA contained in the mitochondria of a cell; because offspring typically inherit only their mother's mitochondria, mitochondrial DNA is useful in tracing maternal lineages.

molar – Any cheek tooth situated posterior to the premolars and having no deciduous precursor. One of the four kinds of teeth in mammals.

molt – In a mammal, the act or process of shedding or casting off the hair or horns; most mammals shed the hair once, twice, or three times annually.

monestrous – Pertaining to species that have only one period of estrus or heat per year.

monogamous – Consorting with only one mate; opposite of polygamous.

monotypic – Consisting of only one type, e.g., a monotypic species has no subspecies.

montane – Pertaining to a biogeographic zone of the mountains.

morphology – A branch of biology that deals with structure and form of an organism at any stage of its life history.

musk – Scent secretion from any one of a variety of special scent glands in many kinds of animals.

muzzle – The projecting part of the head of certain animals, such as dogs, including the mouth, nose, and jaws; the snout.

nail – Flat, keratinized, epidermal, translucent growth protecting the upper portion of the tip of a digit; a nail is a modified claw.

nasals – The pair of bones on the rostrum that form a roof over the nasal passages. Usually situated between the dorsal margins of the premaxillae and maxillae.

nasal leaf *(also nose leaf)* – A structure on the noses of some bats; ranges from a small, simple flap to a highly complex structure of numerous projections and chambers; believed to aid in echolocation.

nest – A structure (of grass, leaves, or some other material) built by a mammal for shelter or insulation.

nestling – An individual, generally recently born, that is still confined to a nest.

nocturnal – Active by night, as opposed to diurnal.

ochraceous – Reddish yellow.

omnivorous – Pertaining to those animals that eat quantities of both animal and vegetable food.

opposable – Capable of being placed opposite something else; said of the first toe of the hind foot in an opossum in the sense that it can be placed opposite each of the other toes on that same foot.

orbit – The socket in the skull in which the eyeball is situated.

ovulation – The release of an egg (by the ovary) into the oviduct.

ovum – The haploid reproductive cell (gamete) produced by a female of a species; egg.

palate – The bony roof of the mouth.

palmate antler – Antlers in which the distal portions are broad, flat, and lobed.

pantropical – Distributed throughout the tropics.

parturition – Birth.

pectoral – Pertaining to the chest.

pedalfer soil – A soil of humid regions that is rich in aluminum oxide and iron and deficient in carbonates.

pedocal soil – A soil of semiarid and arid regions that is rich in calcium carbonate and lime.

pelage – Collectively, all the hairs on a mammal.

penis – The intromittent organ that the male mammal inserts into the vagina of the female for the purpose of insemination.

permanent teeth – Teeth in the second of the two sets of dentition in diphyodont mammals, succeeding the milk or deciduous teeth.

pest – A destructive or obnoxious animal that annoys or causes harm or damage to some man-made or human-supported object or activity.

phalanx *(pl. phalanges)* – Any one of the distal two or three bones in each manual and pedal digit.

phylogenetic analysis – An analysis of the evolutionary history of an organism or groups of related organisms.

pinna *(pl. pinnae)* – External ear, the flap located around the external auditory meatus. It gathers sound vibrations and channels them toward the tympanum. Absent in many aquatic and fossorial mammals.

placenta – An apposition or fusion of the fetal membranes to the uterine mucosa for physiological exchange.

placental scar – The scar that remains on the uterine wall after a deciduate placenta detaches at parturition.

polyembryony – A reproductive mechanism in which several young are produced from a single egg fertilized by a single sperm.

polygamous – Having more than one mate at a time.

population density – A measure of the number of individuals that occupy a given area.

postauricular – Behind the ear.

postnatal – Development that occurs subsequent to birth.

postocular – Situated behind the socket of the eye (syn. postorbital).

postpalatal process – A projection along the posterior margin of the palate.

postpartus – The period shortly after giving birth.

postorbital breadth – Distance across the top of the skull posterior to the postorbital process.

precocial – Pertaining to young at birth that are capable of moving about and feeding with little parental assistance; opposite of altricial.

predator – A mammal that lives by killing and consuming other animals or mammals.

premaxillae – The paired bones at the anterior end of the rostrum that hold the incisor teeth.

premolar – Pertaining to one of the teeth (a maximum of 4 on each side of upper jaw and lower jaw of placental mammals, or 16 in all) in front of the true molars. When canine teeth are present, premolars are behind them; premolars are preceded by deciduous teeth, and in the upper jaw are confined to the maxillary bone.

prey – An animal that is pursued by a predator.

protrusible – In reference to an anatomical part of a mammal that can be thrust out or projected, such as the tongue of an anteater or nectar-feeding bat.

rabies – An acute, encephalitic viral infection transmitted to humans by the bite of a rabid animal.

rack – The pair of antlers on a cervid.

ramus *(pl. rami)* – A bony process extending like a branch from a larger bone, especially the ascending part of the lower jaw that makes a joint at the temple.

reentrant angle – Inward-pointing angle along the margin of a cheek tooth.

reproductive isolation – The mechanisms that isolate one species reproductively from others.

riparian – Associated with the bank of a natural watercourse, such as a river or stream.

roosting site – A perch or a resting place where a mammal will light, sit, or rest during the day or evening. Often used in reference to bats perching in a cave, building, or tree.

root – The portion of a tooth below the gum line that fits into the socket (alveolus).

rostrum – The facial region of the skull anterior to a plane drawn through the anterior margins of the orbits.

rumen – The first compartment of the stomach of a ruminant; here food is collected and returned to the mouth as cud for chewing.

russet – Yellowish brown, light brown, or reddish brown.

rutting season *(or rut)* – Season when mating occurs; particularly applied to deer and other artiodactyls.

salivary – Pertaining to the secretion of saliva.

savannah – A grassland containing scattered trees and drought-resistant undergrowth.

scat – Mammal feces or droppings.

scent glands – Sweat, sebaceous, or a combination of these two gland types modified for the production of odoriferous secretions.

scent marking – The behavioral process by which a mammal intentionally leaves an olfactory indication of its presence in its environment, normally accomplished by deposition of glandular, odoriferous secretions.

scent post – A place or object where a mammal intentionally leaves an indication of its presence in an environment, as described in "scent marking."

sedentary – Pertaining to animals that move about very little.

semiaquatic – Pertaining to mammals that are partially, but not fully, adapted to life in water, for example, otters, beavers.

sexual dimorphism – The condition that exists when there is an externally apparent difference other than external genitalia between the males and females of a particular species.

sign – Any indication of an animal's presence, such as footprints, scats, burrows, runways.

species – Groups of actually (or potentially) interbreeding natural populations that are reproductively isolated from other such groups. Reproductive isolation implies that interbreeding between individuals of two species normally is prevented by intrinsic factors.

sperm storage – The situation in some species of mammals in which females do not ovulate until long after they have been inseminated, but are able to store viable sperm in the uterus for several months.

stenothermic – Able to tolerate only small variations in temperature.

steppe – Vast tract of land that is generally level and without forests.

subadult – An individual, generally smaller than an adult, that may be a young of the year and may or may not be in breeding condition.

submaxillary gland – A large salivary gland located below the mandible on each side of the jaw.

subspecies – Geographically defined aggregate of local populations that differs taxonomically from other such subdivisions of the species.

supraoccipital – The dorsal element of the occipital bone located above the foramen magnum and the occipital condyles.

sympatric – Pertaining to two or more populations that occupy overlapping geographical areas.

symphysis – A growing together of bones originally separate, as of the two pubic bones or the two halves of the lower jawbone. Also, a line or junction thus formed.

tarsal joint – Series of bones in the ankle. They are distal to the fibula and tibia and proximal to the metatarsals.

taxonomy – The science of classifying organisms.

temporal ridge – One of a pair of ridges on the top of the braincase of many mammals.

terrestrial – Referring to mammals that live on land as opposed to living in the water.

territory – An area defended by an individual or group. Behavior associated with the defense of a territory is referred to as territoriality.

testis *(pl. testes)* – Gonad of the male. The organ of sperm formation.

tibia – More medial (and usually larger) of the two bones between the knee and ankle in the lower hind limb. The shin bone.

tine – A spike or prong on an antler.

torpid – Without most of the power of exertion; dormant. A ground squirrel is torpid when it is hibernating.

tragus – The fleshy projection located in the lower portion of the ear of most bats.

trail – A pathway created by repeated use by animals.

trap line – A line of traps placed at regular or irregular intervals to secure specimens for identification, study skins, or autopsy purposes.

trap-night – One trap set for one night.

tricolored – Having three colors; said of hair on the back of a mammal when the hair has three bands, each of a different color.

tularemia – A bacterial infection of wild mammals (particularly rodents and lagomorphs) caused by *Pasteurella tularensis,* which may be transmitted to humans and some domesticated animals.

tympanic bullae – See *auditory bullae*.

type locality – The place where the type specimen (holotype) of a species or subspecies was collected.

ultrasonic – Pertaining to vibrations and sound waves with frequencies above the range audible to the human ear (generally greater than 20,000 hertz).

underfur – The short hair of a mammal; in temperate and boreal climates the underfur ordinarily is denser (made up of more hairs) than the longer and coarser overhair.

underpart – The underneath (ventral) side of a mammal (not the back or sides), as of a wood mouse with white underparts.

ungulate – A mammal having hooves, not claws.

unicuspid – Having a single cusp.

upperpart – The top (dorsal) surface and all of the sides (not belly, chest, or throat), as of a wood mouse with reddish brown upperparts.

uropatagium – The interfemoral membrane of a bat; the fold of skin that stretches from the hind legs to the tail.

uterus – In female mammals a muscular expansion of the reproductive tract in which the embryo and fetus develop; opens externally by way of the vagina.

vagina – That portion of the female reproductive tract that receives the male's penis during copulation and through which the fetus passes at parturition.

vaginal plug – A plug of coagulated semen found in the vagina after copulation; found only in certain mammalian species.

vegetative canopy – The total mass of plant life that occupies a given area, such as a canopy of trees covering a streambed.

velvet – The skin covering a growing antler.

vibrissae – Long, stiff hairs that serve primarily as tactile receptors.

volant – Flying or capable of flying.

volplane – To glide.

webbed – Having a membrane or fold of skin between digits.

wetland – Areas inundated or saturated by surface or ground water at a frequency and duration sufficient to support a prevalence of vegetation typically adapted for life in saturated soil conditions.

wildlife (big game) ranching – The intentional raising of wildlife, especially ungulates, for any purpose, including hunting. Domestic livestock may be raised simultaneously with game on a big game ranch.

wing – A forelimb modified for sustained flight; among mammals, found only in bats.

wool – Hair or underhair with angora growth; serves primarily for insulation.

wrist – The joint between the manus, or hand, and the rest of the forelimb.

xeric – Characterized by a dry, desertlike climate.

young of the year – General age description for an animal that was born in the most recent breeding season and is less than a year old. Frequently used when it is difficult to assign individuals to more precise age categories or when a collective term is needed for this group of young animals.

zygomatic arch – An arch of bone in the skull that encloses the orbit and temporal fossa laterally and is formed by the jugal bone and processes of the maxilla and squamosal.

zygomatic breadth – A measurement of the skull representing the greatest breadth across the zygomatic arches.